T0138663

ARTIFICIAL INTELLIGENCE

CRITICAL CONCEPTS

ARTIFICIAL INTELLIGENCE

Critical Concepts

Edited by Ronald Chrisley
Editorial Assistant: Sander Begeer

Volume III

London and New York

First published 2000
by Routledge
11 New Fetter Lane, London EC4P 4EE

Simultaneously published in the USA and Canada
by Routledge
29 West 35th Street, New York, NY 10001

Routledge is an imprint of the Taylor & Francis Group

Editorial matter and selection © 2000 Ronald Chrisley, individual
owners retain copyright in their own material

Typeset in Times by RefineCatch Limited, Bungay, Suffolk
Printed and bound in Great Britain by
TJ International Ltd, Padstow, Cornwall

All rights reserved. No part of this book may be reprinted or
reproduced or utilised in any form or by any electronic,
mechanical, or other means, now known or hereafter
invented, including photocopying and recording, or in any
information storage or retrieval system, without permission in
writing from the publishers.

British Library Cataloguing in Publication Data
A catalogue record for this book is available from the British Library

Library of Congress Cataloging in Publication Data
Artificial intelligence: critical concepts/edited by Ronald Chrisley with Sander Begeer.
p. cm.
Includes bibliographical references.
ISBN 0–415–19331–1 (set)—ISBN 0–415–19332–X (v. 1)—ISBN 0–415–19333–8 (v. 2)
—ISBN 0–415–19334–6 (v. 3)—ISBN 0–415–19335–4 (v. 4)
1. Artificial intelligence. I. Chrisley, Ronald. II. Begeer, Sander.
Q335.5.A7825 2000
006.3—dc21   00–062568

ISBN 0–415–19331–1 (set)
ISBN 0–415–19334–6 (volume 3)

The publishers have made every effort to contact authors/copyright
holders of works reprinted in *Artificial Intelligence: Critical Concepts*.
This has not been possible in every case, however, and we would
welcome correspondence from those individuals/companies whom we
have been unable to trace.

References within each chapter are as they appeared in the original complete work.

CONTENTS

CONTENTS

CONTENTS

Part I

APPROACHES: SITUATED, DYNAMIC AND EVOLUTIONARY ARTIFICIAL INTELLIGENCE

INTRODUCTION

Intelligence as a Way of Life

Ronald Chrisley

The most recent challenge to symbolic artificial intelligence is from a loose coalition of positions that has much in common with the field of artificial life. Although much of their critiques can be understood without adopting a biological perspective, the intellectual trend which these independent movements constitute is best grasped when acknowledging a common emphasis on studying the intelligence of living systems. This goes beyond the subsymbolism of neural networks to address the ecological, temporal and phylogenetic aspects of cognition.

An early instance of work in this vein is Dennett's call to build entire functioning systems, organisms rather than competences. But not only is organismal unity just one aspect of the artificial life approach to artificial intelligence; Dennett's proposal is only for a methodological change, whereas the artificial life development in artificial intelligence involves conceptual changes as well.

A more comprehensive account, then, is given by Steels. Artificial life approaches constitute a conceptual change in artificial intelligence since they adopt a more biological notion of intelligence: a behaviour is intelligent to the extent that it maximises the chances for self-preservation. Steels points out the advantages of this definition, including the fact that it permits quantifiable measurement in a way that is superior to the subjectivity of the Turing Test. However problems with Steels' definition also quickly present themselves. By identifying intelligence with survival, one might think that it has been broadened beyond recognition, since any living system, even viruses and societies, will come out as intelligent on this account (*pace* Steel's *ad hoc* exclusion of everything not on the scale of animals). The definition is too promiscuous in another sense: it classifies as intelligent behaviour which only assists survival by chance. For example, if I walk into a rubbish bin and the noise causes a workman to avoid whacking me with the plank he is carrying, then my clumsy behaviour comes out as intelligent on Steels' account. But not only does his definition include too much; it includes too little as well, by excluding behaviour that we would intuitively count as intelligent. For example, intelligent altruistic behaviour would be deemed conceptually impossible on Steels' view. And we, unlike Steels, can make sense of a behaviour being intelligent even if, because of some fluke, or even incomplete or inaccurate information on the organism's part, it actually decreases the chances of the organism's survival. Furthermore, Steels' definition can be criticised as being too exclusive because it is not biological *enough*; a true biological notion of intelligence, some might argue, would be expressed in terms of reproduction, not survival. An organism is only being intelligent in so far as it is maximising the chances for spreading its genes – living as a hermit might maximise your survival chances, but it is not biologically "intelligent".

As in subsymbolism, the emphasis of this approach to artificial intelligence is on emergence. But the methodology is to exploit the emergence that can come about from dynamic coupling with the environment, something not incompatible with connectionism but in fact absent from most of that work. This kind of non-conceptual coupling with the environment requires the intelligent artefact to have a body, so it should be no surprise that robotics plays a central role for the artificial life approach. However, as Steels points out, exploiting the environment renders a behavioural system dependent on that environment, so many environment-specific structures are required to achieve the kind of generality indicative of what one might intuitively consider a single, human-level intelligent capacity.

1 Situated artificial intelligence

Although Bateson's text is not an early one from the cybernetic point of view, and is intended for a purpose quite different than the use to which it is being put here, it is nonetheless a clear statement of some of the cybernetic ideas that serve as an intellectual background to situated artificial intelligence. "Situated" is a tricky term; of course, all robots are "situated" some way or another. But the methodology of cybernetics, and situated artificial intelligence after it, explicitly acknowledges the centrality of this relationship for intelligent action, and reflects this awareness in design. Bateson expresses this in a point which he seems to label "epistemological", but which is, in fact, ontological: *"the mental characteristics of the system are immanent, not in some part, but in the system as a whole"*. This does not just mean that for some mental faculties, there is no one part of the brain where it is located; it means that it may not be localisable within the brain, or even the body, at all. The "system as a whole", in which mind resides, may involve aspects on both sides of the traditional agent/environment boundary: brain plus body, or human plus environment. Of most relevance to our concerns is Bateson's explicit application to the case of artefacts:

The computer is only an arc of a larger circuit which always includes a man and an environment from which information is received and upon which efferent messages from the computer have effect. This total system, or ensemble, may legitimately be said to show mental characteristics.

Since contemporary philosophy of mind has only recently started catching on to this idea (cf. Tuomela 1989, Clark and Chalmers 1998), we have here a notable (but by no means unique) inversion of the usual direction of intellectual influence; instead of philosophy driving artificial intelligence, artificial intelligence is informing philosophy of mind. Or rather, *Western* philosophy of mind: Bateson sees the mistake of locating the mind (and therefore intelligence) in the organism/computer as a particularly Occidental phenomenon not common in Oriental thinking.

Bateson's reasons for redrawing the mind/world boundary have to do with that most fundamental of cybernetic concepts: feedback. Since the actions of the computer/robot typically affect the environment in a way which in turn affects the computer/robot, one will not be able to design capacities for intelligent behaviour if one considers the computer/robot in isolation, *a fortiori* the computer on its own. Bateson illustrates this notion of circular causation with the Watt steam engine governor, a favourite example of the cyberneticists, and one that would take centre-stage in arguments for a dynamical approach to understanding the human mind (van Gelder 1995), the cognitive science counterpart to dynamical artificial intelligence.

Finally, Bateson's text contains the oft-quoted (but rarely cited) line: "A bit of information is a difference that makes a difference".

Smith's paper is a response to the CYC paper by Lenat and Feigenbaum in Volume II, article 36. The title merits discussion (apparently Smith wanted to counter their "On the Thresholds of Knowledge" with "Beyond Belief", but Dennett had already used that title). Smith's analysis is that CYC could be little more than an electric encyclopaedia. It could not have an original semantics; it could only have one derived from us. But true intelligence requires the original semantics and, Smith claims, that requires situatedness and embodiment. Thus, an artificial agent which could truly think about an owl would resemble an owl itself more than an encyclopaedia entry about owls. Also, in invoking Lear's "The Owl and the Pussycat" the title reflects what Smith takes to be the fanciful nature of the CYC proposal.

Central to Smith's argument is the idea that from a broad perspective CYC has more commonalties with than differences from the logicist approach which Lenat and Feigenbaum criticise. He shows this by exposing the agreement of the two approaches on most of twelve crucial questions concerning artificial intelligence methodology. By contrast, Smith's own assessment of "the minimum an AI system will require in order to achieve anything like genuine intelligence", which he dubs the "embedded computation" approach, offers distinct answers to most of these questions. The embedded computation approach to artificial intelligence is to employ representations that are often inexplicit, situated, and of various forms and schemes. It is to insist on a notion of meaning in the artefact that is use-based (cf. Wittgenstein), not derived, and that may differ from the theorist's (see the discussion of Minsky's Japan lecture in Volume II, the Introduction to Part I). It is also to acknowledge that representation is not the only key to intelligence: embodiment, participation and action are also crucial.

There is much in Smith's paper that expresses intellectual developments in the concept of intelligence and how it might be constructed. For example, he counters the traditional link between intelligence and objectivity as a "view from nowhere" (cf. Nagel 1986) with "intelligence should prepare you for being anywhere, not for being nowhere". He is similarly critical of most of the conceptual foundations of artificial intelligence, likening our position to the Dark Ages, and saying "the intellectual tools of the last 100 years . . . will be about as much preparation for AI as a good wheel-barrow would be for a 24-hour dash across Europe".

Brooks, unlike Smith, is a practising robotocist, and it is the practicalities of trying to get robots to behave intelligently in the real world that leads him to similar, if less conciliatory, conclusions. More than a third of his paper is a historical analysis of artificial intelligence since the Second World War, with (roughly) the Dartmouth crew the bad guys and the cyberneticists the good guys. He laments the degree to which digital computer technology has shaped our view of what intelligence is. Although the paper is packed with conceptual and methodological alternatives to the symbolic approach to artificial intelligence, three points can be singled out as central: intelligence is often a matter of reactive routines rather than problem-solving or planning (cf. Agre and Chapman 1987); intelligence is an instrumental phenomenon, in that intentional descriptions can be true of an agent even though there are no structures inside the agent that can be mapped to each component of the intentional description (cf. Dennett 1987); and intelligent artefacts need to be developed and tested in the real world. Brooks offers a range of arguments and evidence for the situated and embodied approach, although his appeals to biology (specifically neurophysiology and psychology) are not as persuasive as the considerations he marshals from his practical experience with robot building.

Kirsh's critique of situated artificial intelligence is aimed squarely at Brooks. Given that Brooks admits that representations are required for intelligence, Kirsh interprets the difference between Brooks' approach and symbolic artificial intelligence to lie in the role of concepts (the ability to predicate properties of reidentifiable objects in a systematic manner) in intelligent behaviour. Kirsh takes Brooks to be claiming that most intelligence does not involve concepts, and disagrees, arguing that much intelligence necessarily involves the application of concepts, although he admits these need not be realised in a language-like symbol system. The strength of Kirsh's paper is increased by the fact that he does not try to establish the centrality of concepts by looking at domains that are the traditional favourites of the symbolist, such as chess playing and theorem proving. Rather, he seeks a victory on Brooks' home turf, by arguing that concepts are required for intelligent performance in action, perception, learning and control.

However, the sophistication of the positions of both Kirsh and Brooks makes a clear verdict difficult, and perhaps unnecessary. For example, Kirsh establishes that memory is required for intelligent action. Brooks has softened some of the situatedness rhetoric and agreed that memory and representation are indeed required. But he can deny that these require concepts – prediction of properties to objects – if this is understood as requiring language-like, centralised representations. But Kirsh has softened the conceptualist position as well, allowing that the representational manifestation of concepts may not need to be linguiform: "In principle, there could be computational architectures which implement the cognitive capacities we suppose concept-using creatures to have, but which do not pass notational elements around". But at this point it seems that there is little left about concepts for Brooks to object to. His concern is mainly about the nature of the vehicle of intelligent capacities – he is adamant they are not language-like. So he can concede what Kirsh wants – that concepts are required for intelligence – because of the possibility that these concepts are realised in situated, non-symbolic vehicles. Kirsh does not convincingly show that this is impossible; in fact, his broadening of concepts to include non-linguistic representations encourages this development of Brooks' position.

2 Dynamical artificial intelligence

Ashby's paper is a departure from what had gone before in two respects. First, he considers the possibility of artificial intelligence as a kind of prosthesis, rather than an autonomous intellect. He starts with a metaphor: just as machines such as pulleys and levers can amplify the strength of a person, so also can we build intelligence amplifiers that will enable us to solve currently insoluble problems. He makes the analogy more precise by viewing intelligence as a form of selection. Even the dust motes in one cubic centimetre of air blink out theorems of trigonometry in Morse code 100,000 times per second!; the trick is to select the results that are meaningful. We apply energy in stoking a fire, but then the energy of what we stoked, which is independent of the energy we expended, takes over (compare von Neumann's discussion of switches in Volume I article 22). So also can selection be divided into these two phases: we select a machine and some criteria for a solution, and the machine then selects over a different set of variables in order to find a solution.

Ashby's second departure from what had gone before in artificial intelligence is revealed in his proposal for how to build such selection machines. The basic design is that of selection by equilibrium. We set up a dynamic system S (which includes both machine and world) in such a way that it only halts when some condition which we want to be true (such as the condition that some problem is solved) is met. By definition, when S stops running, a solution has been found. This extremely simplistic viewpoint is not meant to provide any particular answers so much as an alternative intellectual framework for understanding the task of artificial intelligence. The view of intelligence here is an entirely causal, as opposed to rational, one: the idea is to set up a correspondence between problem states and physical states, such that the natural laws which govern physical states will lead, inexorably, to the physical state that corresponds to a solution. This view that any dynamical system can, potentially, be harnessed to do computational work is often referred to by mentioning the idea of a "soap-bubble computer"; it is a precursor to the ideas behind neural networks, particularly of the non-connectionist and non-"parallel distributed processing" variety (such as Hopfield 1982).

Ashby anticipates the objection that the variation in S's variables come from the designer, so no amplification of the designer's intelligence has been achieved. But Ashby points out that this is not so: the variation in S can be random, and the same result is achieved. A stronger objection is a famous one from Eddington (1929:72):

> If I let my fingers wander idly over the keys of a typewriter it *might* happen that my screed made an intelligible sentence. If an army of monkeys were strumming on typewriters they *might* write all the books in the British Museum. The chance of their doing so is decidedly more favourable than the chance of the molecules returning to one half of the vessel.

That is, relying on a chance solution to the problem seems overly optimistic – the monkeys might possibly finish off the works of Shakespeare before Ashby's amplifier converges on a solution. The second half of Ashby's paper is spent rebutting this kind of objection. True, the upper bound on the amount of time taken is the exponential product of all the variables searched over. But Ashby gives a few reasons to believe that the actual time taken will often be much lower than this upper bound. For one thing, models of the environment can often be used, reducing search time. Also, the variables may not be independent, or their range may be restricted. More particularly, often the function of the variables is continuous, which strongly constrains the search space. Evolution would have been much slower if not for the continuity between some genotypes and some phenotypes. Prior knowledge can reduce search time significantly, but the most dramatic reduction is possible when the variables can be optimised one by one. In a dynamic systems context, we can see dramatic reductions if the system is partly reducible, even if not completely reducible. Ashby points out that partly reducible dynamical systems are ubiquitous in the physical world. However, that (again) might be like the proverbial drunk looking for his keys where the light is best: it may be that such systems seem more common because we have more traffic with them and are more interested in them, which in turn is because the very fact of their partial reducibility means that we can solve them, constrain the world to be describable in terms of them, etc. In any event, Ashby takes this ubiquity to be a reason to believe that reducible systems are common in social and economic systems, which is his intended area of application for an intelligence amplifier. He tries to bolster this view by giving examples of switching functions which look complex, but turn out to be reducible. As part of his response to the "typing monkeys" objection, he estimates the lower bound on the search time, and finds it to be reassuringly low.

Although the foregoing discussion talks freely of "search", it is important to remember, if one wishes correctly to assess Ashby's distinctive contribution, that this search is not through a space of conceptual, propositional hypotheses, but in a non-conceptual physical configuration space.

The dynamical approach lends itself to situatedness, as Beer's paper, following Ashby, makes clear. Once intelligence is seen in dynamical terms, it becomes natural to analyse intelligent behaviour as the upshot of the interaction of two coupled dynamical systems, corresponding to the agent and the world, respectively. Beer explains this by pointing out that coupled dynamical systems can generate a richer range of behaviour than the component systems can on their own. The tacit assumption is that natural selection would favour agents which exploit this advantage, so we should not be surprised that evolved intelligence is essentially dynamically situated.

Since on this approach intelligence is re-construed in terms of biological fitness, Beer formulates fitness in dynamical terms: fitness is the maintenance, in the face of environmental perturbations, of one's dynamical trajectory within the volume of state space meeting some constraint C. In the case of biological systems, C corresponds to the integrity and survival of the organism; in (current) artificial systems, C corresponds to the task we have in mind for the artefact. Thus, homeostasis, the maintenance of variables within certain ranges in the face of change, is an important aspect of intelligence, natural or artificial. However, it is natural to wonder if artificial intelligence will be fundamentally limited until C is generalised from any particular set of tasks to full, unrestricted survival. Perhaps it is only at such a point that true autonomy and thus capacities recognisably akin to human (or even animal) intelligence are achieved.

In any case, this theoretical analysis transforms the methodology of artificial intelligence into the task of solving the synthesis problem:

> Given an environment dynamics E, find an agent dynamics A and
> sensory and motor maps S and M such that a given constraint C on
> the coupled agent-environment dynamics is satisfied.

Beer describes his synthesis of walking in a simulated (*pace* Brooks) insect-like robot as a way of illustrating this methodology. The heart of his way of solving the synthesis problem in this case is the use of a genetic algorithm to find the parameters for the robot's dynamical system which, when coupled with the environment, will give rise to walking.

To his credit, Beer does not rely on genetic algorithms alone, but acknowledges that, in general, synthesis of intelligent artefacts requires the analysis of previous attempts. Thus he adds to the synthesis problem the analysis problem: "Given an environment dynamics E, and agent dynamics A, and sensory and motor maps S and M, explain how the observed behaviour $M(x_{st})$ of the agent is generated."

This problem, well-known in connectionist circles, is one which all non-symbolic approaches share. While there may be advantages to designing artefacts which do not operate according to our everyday conceptual analysis of their domains, the disadvantage is that it is by the same token difficult for us to understand how such artefacts work.

Beer proceeds, then, to provide a careful dynamical analysis of the evolved leg controllers in a way which explains how walking behaviour emerges from their activity. He closes with a theoretical discussion of, among other things, how the scaling issues raised by Kirsh can be addressed, and to what extent the use of internal state to produce intentional behaviour is *ipso facto* a use of internal representations.

3 Evolutionary artificial intelligence

Perhaps the first serious proposal to evolve an intelligent artefact rather than constructing it directly or having it learn from experience was made by Fogel, Owens and Walsh. The notion of intelligence they were working with was not particularly biological, but, in a line of reasoning that closely presages much later thinking in this area, they came to the conclusion that artificial evolution might overcome three particular problems of artificial intelligence. First, there is the problem of the complexity of the brain, which seems to stymie a direct-design approach, and necessitates some kind of adaptivity, perhaps learning. But the second and third problems have to do with learning: the learning systems with which the authors were familiar had two limitations. They used a fixed input "alphabet", so "conditional dependencies which lie beyond the alphabet of the input symbols cannot be recognised". Also, such systems require a teacher, and thus do not allow for true intelligence, since "*artificial intelligence is realised only if an inanimate machine can solve problems that have, thus far, resisted solution by man; not because of the machine's sheer speed and accuracy, but because it can discover for itself new techniques for solving the problem at hand".* Thus, Fogel, Owens and Walsh fall squarely into the camp of pursuing artificial intelligence as a way to transcend human intelligence. It is notable that they retain the assumption that the machine they are striving to produce would still be non-living, even though it would be produced by means of an evolutionary process. The authors anticipate the findings of chaos theory when they note that it is unlikely that artificial evolution could recapitulate the evolutionary history of, say, humans. They retreat to engineering, and retain interest in science only from a normative perspective, describing "what *ought to be* rather than what *is.*"

Detail concerning the evolutionary approach is provided by Husbands, Harvey, Cliff and Miller. They develop the complexity issue mentioned by Fogel, Owens and Walsh (whom, oddly, they do not cite) into a central motivation for the evolutionary approach: intelligent control systems seem to require emergent interactions, and humans are poor at designing such systems. They hold out the possibility that evolved systems may be analysable, but like Fogel et al. they ultimately retreat to the position that artificial intelligence is about building, not understanding. Husbands et al. also agree that one of the advantages of evolutionary approaches is the possibility of evolving the agent's morphology (e.g. the "input alphabet"), and later work by their team has incorporated this. Potential difficulties for the approach, which they discuss, include the slowness of blind processes such as natural selection, and the difficulty of designing evaluation functions for these processes. This last point highlights a similarity between learning and evolutionary approaches: both seem to require human intervention, but for both there are ways to eliminate this. In the case of learning, the "teacher" can be eliminated by using reinforcement learning, or by using "self-supervised" learning schemes in which the environment provides the training signal. For the evolutionary approach, the human can be taken out of the loop by embracing Steels' vision of robots that are embedded in a real ecology, and for whom the only objective is to survive and reproduce.

The similarities between learning and evolution do not stop there; in fact, it seems that at this point there is no substantive distinction between learning approaches and evolutionary ones. Most evolutionary schemes at the present can be reconceptualised as one individual learning via a special kind of breadth-first search. Thus, there can be at this point no in-principle advantage, with respect to the three problems that Fogel et al. mention, on the part of evolutionary approaches. A substantial distinction between learning and evolution approaches to artificial intelligence will appear only when there are aspects of the artificial evolutionary process that cannot be reconceptualised as elements of a learning algorithm. For example, if the conspecifics within a generation are allowed to interact (co-operate or compete) with each other, then the adaptive process that results cannot be reconceptualised as that of a single learner. Once evolutionary approaches become this embodied they will present a significant alternative to learning-based adaptivity.

References

Agre, P. and Chapman, D. (1987) "Pengi: An Implementation of a Theory of Activity", *AAAI-87*, Seattle, WA: AAAI Press, pp 168–272.

Clark, A. and Chalmers, D. (1998) "The Extended Mind", *Analysis* 58: 1.

Dennett, D. (1987) *The Intentional Stance*, Cambridge: MIT Press.

Eddington, A. S. (1929) *The Nature of the Physical World: The Gifford Lectures, 1927*, New York: Macmillan.

van Gelder, T. (1995) "What might Cognition be, if not Computation?" *Journal of Philosophy* 91: 345–81.

Hopfield, J. (1982) "Neural Networks and Physical Systems with Emergent Collective Computational Abilities", *Proceedings of the National Academy of Sciences of the U.S.A.* 79: 2554–8.

Nagel, T. (1986) *The View From Nowhere*, Oxford: Oxford University Press.

Tuomela, R. (1989) "Methodological Solipsism and Explanation in Psychology", *Philosophy of Science* 56: 23–47.

46

WHY NOT THE WHOLE IGUANA?

Daniel C. Dennett

Source: *Behavioral and Brain Sciences* 1, 1978: 103–4.

I have no disagreements worth mentioning with Pylyshyn's paper, but would like to explore two comments of his.

"There have been grand theoreticians in psychology in the past (e.g., Fraud, James, Hull) who have sought . . . general principles with very limited success," Pylyshyn suggests, because they tacked "a powerful technical tool to discipline and extend the power of the imagination." And now for the first time we have the tool that might permit us to express and test at least *sketches* of unified cognitive theories of whole creatures, the sort of theories to which Freud et al. aspired. Moreover, as Pylyshyn observes, the users of that tool have come to a consensus of sorts that theories of the whole creature are what is needed:

"The recurrence of major problems of organization and representation of knowledge, and the organization and distribution of responsibility or control . . . have produced the growing conviction among cognitive scientists that intelligence is not to be had by putting together language abilities, sensory abilities, visual abilities, memory, motivation, and reasoning (as the chapters of typical psychology textbooks suggest) but by bringing a large base of knowledge to bear in a disciplined way in all cognitive tasks."

Very true, but then why have cognitive scientists persisted in attempting to model sub-subsystems with artificially walled-off boundaries (not just language understanders, but nursery-story-only understanders, for instance)? Why are they not trying to model whole cognitive creatures? Because a model of a whole human being would be too big to handle; people know too much about too many topics, have too many interests, capacities, modalities of perception and action. One has to restrict oneself to a "toy" problem in a particular domain in order to keep the model "small" enough to be designed and tested at a reasonable cost in time and money. But faced with the conclusions quoted above, why not obtain one's simplicity and scaling down by attempting to model a whole cognitive creature of much less sophistication than a human being? Why not try to do a whole starfish, for instance? It has no eyes or ears, only rudimentary pattern-discrimination capacities, few modes of action, few needs or intellectual accomplishments. That could be a warm-up exercise for something a bit more challenging: a turtle, perhaps, or a mole. A turtle must organize its world knowledge, such as it is, so that it can keep life and limb together by making real time decisions based on that knowledge, so while a turtle-simulation would not need a natural language parser, for instance, it would need just the sorts of efficient organization and flexibility of control distribution you have to provide in the representation of world knowledge behind a natural language parsing system of a simulated human agent such as SHRDLU.

Perhaps there are good reasons for not pursuing such projects. I suspect that one of the *real* reasons such projects are not pursued is that in order to design a computer simulation of a turtle you would have to learn all about turtles, and who wants to go to all that trouble, when you already know enough about yourself and your friends (you think) to have all the performance data you need for the human mini-task of your choice? Moreover, only people who also knew a great deal about turtles would be knowledgeable enough to be impressed by your results.

Considering the abstractness of the problems properly addressed in A.I. (Dennett, 1978), one can put this attitude in a better light: one does not want to get bogged down with technical problems in modeling the cognitive eccentricities of turtles if the point of the exercise is to uncover very general, very abstract principles that will apply as well to the cognitive organization of the most sophisticated human beings. So why not then make up a whole cognitive creature, a Martian three-wheeled iguana, say, and an environmental niche for it to cope with? I think such a project could teach us a great deal about the deep principles of human cognitive psychology, but if it could not, I am quite sure that most of the current A.I. modeling of familiar human mini-tasks could not either.

References

Dennett, D.C. Artificial Intelligence as Philosophy and as Psychology. In: M. Ringle (ed.), *Philosophical Perspectives in Artificial Intelligence*. New York, The Humanities Press, 1978.

THE ARTIFICIAL LIFE ROOTS OF ARTIFICIAL INTELLIGENCE

Luc Steels

Source: C. G. Langton, *Artificial Life, An Overview*, Massachusetts Institute of Technology Centre for Advanced Engineering, 1996, pp. 75–110.

Abstract Behavior-oriented Artificial Intelligence (AI) is a scientific discipline that studies how behavior of agents emerges and becomes intelligent and adaptive. Success of the field is defined in terms of success in building physical agents that are capable of maximizing their own self-preservation in interaction with a dynamically changing environment. The paper addresses this Artificial Life route toward AI and reviews some of the results obtained so far.

Keywords autonomous robots, artificial intelligence, adaptive behavior

1 Introduction

For several decades, the field of Artificial Intelligence (AI) has been pursuing the study of intelligent behavior using the methodology of the artificial [104]. But the focus of this field and, hence, the successes have mostly been on higher-order cognitive activities such as expert problem solving. The inspiration for AI theories has mostly come from logic and the cognitive sciences, particularly cognitive psychology and linguistics. Recently, a subgroup within the AI community has started to stress embodied intelligence and made strong alliances with biology and research on artificial life [59]. This is opening up an "artificial life route to artificial intelligence" [112], which has been characterized as Bottom-Up AI [19], the Animat approach [133], Behavior-based AI [108], or Animal Robotics [75]. These terms identify a loose network of engineers and biologists who share the common goal of understanding intelligent behavior through the construction of artificial systems. The researchers also share a growing number of assumptions and hypotheses about the nature of intelligence. In view of the strong links with biology and complex systems theory, the research has so far received more attention in the Artificial Life (AL) community than in the AI field itself.

The aim of this paper is to review this approach and identify some major unresolved issues. Given that substantial engineering efforts and nontrivial experimentation is required, the first solid experimental and technical results have only recently begun to appear. Good sources for tracking the field are the conferences on the simulation of adaptive behavior [79,80] and the associated journal [102], the conferences on AL [30,59,60,124], and the associated journal [4]. There are also occasional contributions to international conferences on AI (such as International Joint Conference on Artificial Intelligence [IJCAI], American Association for Artificial Intelligence [AAAI], or European Conference on Artificial Intelligence [ECAI]), neural networks (Neural Information Processing Society Conference [NIPS]), or robotics (Institute of Electronic and Electrical Engineers Conference [IEEE]). Reports of some milestone workshops have been published [65,112,113,123].

Section 2 of the paper delineates the AL approach to AI. Section 3 identifies the fundamental units of this approach, which are behavior systems. Section 4 and 5 focus on contributions toward a central theme of AL research, which is the origin of complexity through emergent functionality. A short review of some other issues concludes the paper.

2 Delineating the field

2.1 The subject matter is intelligent behavior

The phenomena of interest are those traditionally covered by ethology and ecology (in the case of animals) or psychology and sociology (in the case of humans). The behavior by an individual or a group of individuals is studied, focusing on what makes behavior intelligent and adaptive and how it may emerge. Behavior is defined as a regularity observed in the interaction dynamics between the characteristics and processes of a system and the characteristics and processes of an environment [106]. Behavior is intelligent if it maximizes preservation of the system in its environment. The main emphasis is not on the physical basis of behavior, as in the case of neural network research, but on the principles that can be formulated at the behavioral level itself. An example of a theory at the behavioral level is one that explains the formation of paths in an ant society in terms of a set of behavioral rules without reference to how they are neurophysiologically implemented [91]. Another example is a study of how certain behavioral strategies (such as retreat when attacked) and their associated morphological characteristics are evolutionary stable [72].

Given this emphasis on behavior, the term *behavior-oriented* seems appropriate to distinguish the field, particularly from the more knowledge-oriented approach of classical AI. It will be used in the rest of the paper.

2.2 The methodology is based on building artificial systems

Scientists traditionally construct models in terms of a set of equations that relate various observational variables and hypothesized theoretical variables. Technological advances in the second half of this century have resulted in two additional types of models:

- *Computational models:* These consist of a process-oriented description in terms of a set of data structures and algorithms. When this description is executed, that is, the algorithm is carried out causing the contents of the data structures to be modified over time, phenomena can be observed in the form of regularities in the contents of the data structures. If these synthetic phenomena show a strong correspondence with the natural phenomena, they are called simulations, and the process descriptions constitute a theory of the natural phenomena.
- *Artificial models:* One can also construct a physical device (an artifact) whose physical behavior gives rise to phenomena comparable to the natural phenomena in similar circumstances. The device will have components with a particular structure and functioning that have been put together in a particular way. The design and implementation of these components and their mode of combination constitutes another possible way to theorize about the phenomena.

Computational models and artificial models, or what Pattee [92] calls simulations and realizations, must be clearly distinguished. For example, it is possible to build a computational model of how a bird flies, which amounts to a simulation of the environment around the bird, a simulation of the aerodynamics of the body and the wings, a simulation of the pressure differences caused by movement of the wings, etc. Such a model is highly valuable but would, however, not be able to fly. It is forever locked in the data structures and algorithms implemented on the computer. It flies only in a virtual world. In contrast, one could make an artifact in terms of physical components (a physical body, wings, etc.). Such an artifact would only be viewed as satisfactory if it is able to perform real flying. This is a much stronger requirement. Very often, results from simulation only partially carry over to artificial systems. When constructing a simulation, one selects certain aspects of the real world that are carried over into the virtual world. But this selection may ignore or overlook essential characteristics that play a role unknown to the researcher. An artificial system cannot escape the confrontation with the full and infinite complexity of the real world and is, therefore, much more difficult to construct.

The term *artificial* in "artificial life" (and also in "artificial intelligence") suggests a scientific approach based on constructing artificial models. The methodological steps are as follows: A phenomenon is identified (e.g., obstacle avoidance behavior), an artificial system is constructed that has this as competence, the artificial system is made to operate in the environment, the resulting phenomena are recorded, and these recordings are compared with the original phenomena. Potential misfits feed back into a redesign or reengineering of the artificial system.

Although AI is sometimes equated with the simulation of intelligent behavior, this is too narrow an interpretation. The goal is to build artifacts that are "really" intelligent, that is, intelligent in the physical world, not just intelligent in a virtual world. This makes unavoidable the construction of robotic agents that must sense the environment and can physically act upon the environment, particularly if sensorimotor competences are studied. This is why behavior-oriented AI researchers insist so strongly on the construction of physical agents [21,130]. Performing simulations of agents (as in Beer [15]) is, of course, an extremely valuable aid in exploring and testing out certain mechanisms, the way simulation is heavily used in the design of airplanes. But a simulation of an airplane should not be confused with the airplane itself.

2.3 Behavior-oriented AI is strongly influenced by biology

We have already identified two key ingredients of the behavior-oriented approach: the study of intelligent behavior, and the methodology of constructing artificial systems. The third ingredient is a strong biological orientation. Intelligence is seen as a biological characteristic, and the "core of intelligence and cognitive abilities is [assumed to be] the same as the capacity of the living" ([124], backcover).

The biological orientation clearly shows up in the way intelligence is defined. The "classical" AI approach defines intelligence in terms of knowledge: A system is intelligent if it maximally applies the knowledge that it has (cf. Newell's principle of rationality [87]). The behavior-oriented approach defines intelligence in terms of observed behavior and self-preservation (or autonomy) (see, e.g., [76,124]). It is based on the idea that the essence of biological systems is their capacity to continuously preserve and adapt themselves [71]: *The behavior of a system is intelligent to the extent that it maximizes the chances for self-preservation of that system in a particular environment.*

The drive toward self-preservation applies to all levels of complexity: genes, cells, multicellular structures, plants, animals, groups of animals, societies, species. Behavior-oriented AI focuses upon the behavior of organisms of the complexity of animals. Systems of this complexity are called agents. When several of them cooperate or compete, we talk about multiagent systems.

In order to explain how a system preserves itself even if the environment changes, adaptivity and learning are corollary conditions of viable intelligent agents: *A system is capable of adapting and learning if it changes its behavior so as to continue maximizing its intelligence, even if the environment changes.*

The biological orientation also shows up in a focus on the problem of how complexity can emerge. The origin of order and complexity is a central theme in biology [53] and is usually studied within the context of self-organization [95] or natural selection [16]. Behavior-oriented AI research is focusing on the concepts of emergent behavior and emergent functionality as a possible explanation for the emergence of functional complexity in agents. These concepts will be discussed in more detail later. A preliminary definition is as follows: *A behavior is emergent if it can only be defined using descriptive categories that are not necessary to describe the behavior of the constituent components. An emergent behavior leads to emergent functionality if the behavior contributes to the system's self-preservation and if the system can build further upon it.*

Behavior-oriented AI studies the origin of complexity at different levels: from components and complete agents to multiagent systems. Systems at each level maximize their self-preservation by adapting their behavior so that it comes closer to the optimal. Coadaptation ensures that different elements at one level contribute to the optimality of the whole. At every level there is cooperation and competition: Different agents cooperate and compete inside a multiagent system. Different behavior systems cooperate and compete inside the agent. Different components cooperate and compete to form coherent behavior systems. So the ingredients of cooperation, competition, selection, hierarchy, and reinforcement, which have been identified as crucial for the emergence of complexity in other areas of biology [59], are found at the behavioral level, making it possible to carry over results from other biological disciplines to behavior-oriented AI and vice versa.

All of the elements of the previous definitions for intelligence, adaptivity, and emergence can be quantitatively and objectively established. We can quantify the aspects of the environment that act as pressures on the system considered, the success in self-preservation, the optimality of particular behaviors with respect to their contribution to self-preservation, and the success of adaptation and learning to improve this optimality. All this is illustrated in McFarland and Boesser [76]. We can also quantitatively identify the onset of emergence once a suitable mathematical framework exists for defining the notion of a minimal description. An example of such a framework can be found in Chaitin's work on algorithmic complexity. (See the discussion in Nicolis and Prigogine [89].) The objective nature of these definitions makes them preferable to those relying on the subjective assignment of knowledge or on subjective criteria of similarity to human intelligence as in the Turing Test.

19

2.4 Behavior-oriented AI is complementary to other approaches to AI

The behavior-oriented approach is complementary to the currently dominating trend in AI (also known as the classical approach), which is almost exclusively concentrated on the problems of identifying, formalizing, and representing knowledge [38]. The emphasis on knowledge leads almost automatically to a focus on disembodied intelligence. Classical AI systems, therefore, do not include a physical body, sensing, or acting. If intelligent robots have been considered (as in Nilsson [90]), sensing and action has been delegated to subsystems that are assumed to deliver symbolic descriptions to the central planning and decision-making modules. Moreover, knowledge-oriented theories do not include environmental pressures on the self-preservation of the agent, and the role of adaptivity and emergence is taken over by the programmer. However, the claim (made, e.g., in Maes [66]) that the classical, knowledge-oriented approach works only for "simulated toy problems" and makes too many simplifying assumptions (e.g., static environments, single tasks, etc.) is simply not true. Objective results achieved in knowledge engineering for large-scale, extremely challenging real-world problems (like the assignment of train engines and personnel to routes taking into account a large number of possibly conflicting constraints, or the diagnosis of printed circuit boards assembled in digital telephone switch boards) cannot and should not be dismissed.

The behavior-oriented approach is also complementary to the artificial neural network approach, which is based on an even more radical bottom-up attitude because it focuses on the physical basis of behavior and hopes that this is sufficient to explain or synthesize intelligence [56], that is, that no separate behavioral level is necessary. The distinction between the two fields is of course a matter of degree. Behavior-oriented researchers heavily make use of neural network techniques to implement certain aspects of an overall design, and some neural network researchers are beginning to consider the problem of building complete agents (cf. Edelman's NOMAD [34]).

There are obviously strong ties between behavior-oriented AI and robotics, because the construction of physical agents is seen as a condition sine qua non for applying the method of the artificial properly. But the two fields should not be equated. The goal of robotics is to identify, design, and engineer the most reliable and most cost-effective solution for a sensorimotor task in a particular, usually fixed and known, environment [17]. Behavior-oriented AI uses the tools of roboticists to study biological issues, but very different criteria for success apply.

2.5 The rest of the paper focuses on emergence

A review of the field can be organized along several lines. One way would be to look at the progress toward the achievement of specific competences, for example, the different approaches for "navigation towards a target": using potential fields [7], cognitive maps with landmarks [70], phonotaxis [129], global reference frames [86], pheromone trails or agent chains [41], and so on. Another approach would be to review the large amount of work on building technical hardware and software platforms that now make it possible to execute experiments easily and at low cost [31,35,50]. This technical work is in some way a revival of earlier cybernetics work by Walter [128] and Braitenberg [18] but now with better hardware and more advanced software. Yet another way is to look at progress on the theoretical questions outlined earlier, for example, the definition and use of optimality criteria [76] or the development of quantitative behavioral descriptions using techniques from complex systems theory [89].

These overviews would all be valuable but require much more space than available here. Instead, we will focus on how behavior-oriented AI may contribute to the field of AL as a whole, and more specifically to its central research theme, which is the origin of complexity. The focus on the interaction between physical agents and the world through sensing and effecting introduces a special perspective that is not found in other AL work. The emergence of complexity must come through the dynamics of interacting with an infinitely complex, dynamically changing, real world and not only through the internal dynamics as in the case of cellular automata, for example.

In order to limit further the scope of the paper, we will only focus on how the behavior of a single agent is established. There is a lot of fascinating work on multiagent systems, and often it is not even possible to study single agents without taking other agents into account. Nevertheless, a review of work on multiagent systems would have doubled the size of the present paper.

3 Behavior systems

When one is studying multiagent systems (like ant societies), the units of investigation are clearly visible. But the units causing the behavior of a single agent are not directly observable. Sensors, neurons, networks of neurons, propagation processes, and actuators are the obvious building blocks. But many of these must work together and interact with structures and processes in the environment in order to establish a particular behavior, and the same components may dynamically be involved in many different behaviors. This is the reason why it is so difficult to bridge the gap between neurology and psychology.

There is a growing consensus in behavior-oriented AI research that behavior systems be considered as the basic units [19]. Other terms for the basic behavioral unit are task-achieving module [68] or schema [5].

To define the notion of a behavior system, we have to make a distinction between a functionality, a behavior, a mechanism, and a component:

- *Functionalities:* A functionality is something that the agent needs to achieve, for example, locomotion, recharging, avoiding obstacles, finding the charging station, performing a measurement, signaling another agent. Other terms used for functionality are task, goal, and competence. Functionalities belong to the descriptive vocabulary of the observer.
- *Behaviors:* A behavior is a regularity in the interaction dynamics between an agent and its environment, for example, maintaining a bounded distance from the wall, or having a continuous location change in a particular direction. One or more behaviors contribute to the realization of a particular functionality. Behaviors belong also to the descriptive vocabulary of the observer. By looking at the same agent in the same environment, it is possible to categorize the behavior in different ways. This does not mean that behavior characterization is subjective. It can be defined and measured fully objectively.
- *Mechanisms:* A mechanism is a principle or technique for establishing a particular behavior, for example, a particular coupling between sensing and acting, the use of a map, an associative learning mechanism.
- *Components:* A component is a physical structure or process that is used to implement a mechanism. Examples of components are body parts, sensors, actuators, data structures, programs, communication hardware, and software.

A *behavior system* is the set of all mechanisms that play a role in establishing a particular behavior. The structures of a behavior system that can undergo a change due to learning are usually called behavior programs. Observed behavior will, of course, depend almost as much on the state of the environment as on the mechanisms and components of the agent. Often the name of the behavior system indicates the functionality to which it contributes. But strictly speaking, we should be more careful. For example, there could be a "homing in" functionality achieved by a "zigzag behavior" toward a goal location that is the result of a "phototaxis mechanism." Phototaxis means that the goal location has a light source acting as beacon and that the robot uses light sensors to minimize the distance between itself and the beacon. The reason why we need to be careful in mixing functional and behavior terminology is because the same behavior system may contribute to different functionalities.

Behavior systems may be very simple, implementing direct reflexes between sensing and action (as in Brooks [19]). They may also be more complex, building up and using cognitive world maps (as in Mataric [70]). When enough complexity is reached, a large collection of interacting behavior systems may resemble a society of interacting agents [84]. Each behavior system is most adapted to a particular class of environments. This environment can be characterized in terms of a set of constraints [48] or cost functions [75].

Note that a behavior system is a theoretical unit. There is not a simple one-to-one relation between a functionality, a behavior, and a set of mechanisms achieving the behavior. The only thing that has physical existence are the components. This is obvious if emergent functionality comes into play (see sections 4 and 5). On the other hand, behavior systems form a real unit in the same way that a society forms a real unit. The interaction between the different mechanisms and the success in the behavior to achieve tasks that contribute to the agent's self-preservation give a positive enforcement to all the elements forming part of a behavior system.

3.1 Behavior systems should be viewed as living systems

In view of the biological orientation discussed earlier, it is not surprising that many behavior-oriented AI researchers view behavior systems very much like living systems. This means that behavior systems are viewed as units that try to preserve themselves. An analogy with cells that are the smallest biological autonomous units helps to make this concrete (Table 1). A cell consists of a group of biochemical structures and processes. The processes are guided by genes, which are themselves represented as molecular structures inside the cell. The processes take place in interaction with material outside the cell that is passing through the cell membrane in both directions. Cells may change their internal structure and functioning, to a certain limit, and adapt to the surrounding environment [97].

A behavior system consists also of a set of dynamic and static structures. The structures include physical components like sensors and body parts, as well as networks, temporary states, and electrical signals propagating in these networks. The internal processes combine and transform signals. These transformation processes are guided by a behavior program that is itself a

Table 1 Comparison Between Cells and Behavior Systems.

Cell	Behavior System
Biochemical processes	Transformation processes
Biochemical structures	Electrical signals and states
Genes	Behavior programs
Incoming material	Energy transduced by sensors
Outgoing material	Energy transduced by actuators
Adaptation to cell environment	Adaptation to external environment

(distributed) physical structure and can be subjected to processes that change it. The transformation processes are partially caused by energy coming from the outside through sensors that convert this to internal energy, and they produce signals impacting the actuators that convert internal energy to mechanical energy so that there is a continuous inflow and outflow of energy to the environment. Behavior systems that change their internal structure and functioning are better adapted to the environment and may better work together with other behavior systems. The main criterion for survival of a behavior system is its utility for the complete agent.

This comparison between cells and behavior systems illustrates several points. (a) It emphasizes in the first place that the components of behavior systems are physical systems and that behavior is a physical phenomenon. There are extreme functionalist tendencies in AI (and also in AL) that equate intelligence or living with disembodied abstractions, but this is not intended here. (b) The behavior programs and the transformation processes can be interpreted in information-processing terms, but that is not necessary and may occasionally be harmful [107]. (c) The transformation processes can be implemented as computational processes but then only if we remind ourselves that computational processes are physical processes, which happen to be instantiated in a physical system of a certain organization that we call a computer.

The comparison also emphasizes the dynamical aspects. Like a cell, a behavior system is continuously active and subjected to inflow and outflow of energy. Like a cell, a behavior system adapts continuously to changes in the environment. Moreover, comparing behavior programs with genes immediately suggests the use of selectionist principles as a way to arrive at new behavior systems without prior design (see section 5).

A concrete example for obstacle avoidance in an artificial agent may be helpful to clarify the discussion (Figure 1). Obstacle avoidance can be achieved by a behavior system that maintains a certain distance from obstacles. The components of this behavior system include a left and right infrared sensor, which emit infrared light and capture the reflection coming from obstacles; a translational and rotational motor, which are connected with the wheels and can steer the robot left or right; and a behavior program that causes processes to transform the changes in detected infrared reflection into changes in the motor speeds. As already suggested in Braitenberg [18], obstacle avoidance can be achieved by a direct coupling between infrared reflection and rotational motor speed. If the amount of reflection increases on one side, then the rotational motor speed going in the same direction increases. In a real-world environment, adaptation is necessary because infrared reflection depends on changing environmental circumstances (e.g., amount of background infrared in the environment or battery level). Adaptation can here be achieved by incorporating structures that act as "weights" on the effect of increased reflection. When the weights become higher, less reflection will

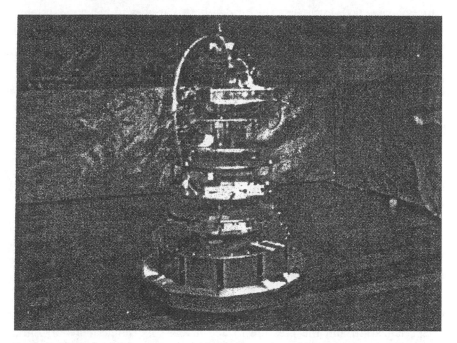

Figure 1 Typical robotic agent used in behavior-oriented AI experiments. The robot has a ring of infrared sensors and a ring of bumper sensors. It has additional light sensors and microphones. There is a translational motor for forward/backward movement and a rotational motor for turning left or right. The agent has a central PC-like processor and dedicated hardware for signal processing and interdevice communication.

have a greater impact. The weights can be subject to change depending on environmental conditions using Hebbian learning mechanisms (see section 5).

3.2 Some guidelines are known for designing behavior systems

At the moment, the design of behavior systems for artificial agents is very much an art, and the complexity reached so far is still limited. But there are some strong tendencies among practitioners suggesting a set of design guidelines. Following are some examples of these guidelines:

Guideline 1: Make behavior systems as specific as possible. One of the important lessons from classical AI research is the specificity-generality trade-off. More specific knowledge, that is, knowledge more strongly tailored to the task and the domain, is more effective than generic mechanisms, such as general problem solvers or universal representation schemes. Success in expert systems has depended almost entirely on the encoding of situation-specific knowledge. This trade-off also applies to behavior systems. Rather than trying to build a general-purpose vision module for example, it is much more effective to tailor the sensing and actuating to a particular task, a particular domain, and a particular environment. Of course, such a solution will not work outside its "niche." But it will perform well and in a very cost-effective way, as long as the conditions are appropriate. A good illustration of this design guideline is a visual navigation system developed by Horswill [49], who has shown that by making a set of strong assumptions about the environment, the complexity of visual interpretation can be reduced drastically. One example is the detection of the vanishing point, which in theory can be done by identifying edges, grouping them into line segments, intersecting the segments, and clustering on the pairwise intersections. Horswill shows that each of these activities can be highly optimized. For example, although in general edge detection is complex and computationally intensive, a simple algorithm based on a gradient threshold will do, if the edges are strong and straight. This work goes in the direction of the theory of visual routines [122], which has abandoned the idea that there is a general purpose vision system and proposes instead a large collection of special purpose mechanisms that can be exploited in particular behavior systems.

Specialization and the pressure to act in real time suggests a horizontal organization, as opposed to a vertical or hierarchical organization, typical for more classical approaches [21]. In a vertical organization, the different modules perform specific functions like vision, learning, world representation, communication, or planning. This leads to a sense-think-act cycle that does not guarantee real-time response when needed. In a horizontal organization, every module combines all these functions but specialized and optimized with respect to a particular behavior in a particular environment. The relation between task and behavior thus becomes much more indirect. This is reminiscent of horizontal organizations now becoming more common in corporations [93].

Guideline 2: Exploit the physics. Surprisingly, it is sometimes easier to achieve a particular behavior when the physics of the world, the morphology of the body, and the physics of the sensors and the actuators of the agent are properly exploited [21]. This is already the case for obstacle avoidance. A robot may be equipped with bumpers that cause a (sudden) slowdown and an immediate retraction in a random direction. This may get the robot out of situations that appear to be dead-end situations in simulations. Another good illustration of this design principle can be found in Webb [129], who has developed a model in the form of an artificial system for navigation based on the phonotaxis behavior of crickets. Webb points out that the determination of the direction in crickets is not based on intensity or phase differences, which would require complex neural processing, but on an extra tracheal tube that transfers vibration from one ear to the other. The length and characteristics of this tube are such that the indirectly arriving sound and the directly arriving sound interfere to give the final intensity, which varies strongly with the direction of the sound. This is an example where "sensory mechanisms exploit the specificity of the task and the physics of their environment so as to greatly simplify the processing required to produce the right behavior" [129, p. 1093]. Many more biological examples of how physics may "solve" problems, so that additional processing can be minimized, can be found in Alexander [3] and Vogel [127].

Guideline 3: Do not think of sensing and acting in terms of symbol processing. The classical AI approach has been criticized because the symbols and symbol structures on which planning and decision making are based are not grounded in the real world [43]. The problem is that unequivocally decoding sensory data into a symbol and turning a command without error into its intended action may be unsolvable – not in principle but in practice. Behavior-oriented AI cannot escape the grounding problem. But a novel solution is proposed. Rather than trying hard to establish a better correspondence between symbols (like distance or turn with a given angle) and the physical properties of the robot in the environment, it is also possible to dispense altogether with the idea that a symbolic interpretation is necessary [107]. For example, rather than having a rule of the sort "if the distance is greater than *n*, then turn away at a certain angle *a*," a dynamical coupling between infrared reflection and path deflection, implemented, for example, as differences between left and right motor speed, can be set up. This coupling is designed without reference to concepts like "distance" and "turn away." Therefore, it is truly subsymbolic.

Guideline 4. Simple mechanisms may give rise to complex behavior. Another strong tendency in the field is to make the mechanisms underlying a behavior system as simple as possible and to rely strongly on the interactions between different mechanisms and the environment to get the required behavior. This theme underlies other work in AL as well and is related to the topic of emergence that is discussed more extensively in sections 4 and 5. This tendency to search for simple mechanisms is particularly strong in the dislike of complex "objective" world models [22]. The de-emphasis of complex representations is shared by researchers criticizing cognitivism [125] and is related to the trend for situated cognition [115], which hypothesizes that intelligence is the result of simple situation-specific agent/environment mechanisms that are strongly adapted to moment-to-moment decision making. Some biologists have called this the TODO principle: Do whatever there is to do at a particular moment, instead of making complex representations and following elaborated plans [47].

It can be expected that many more design guidelines will become explicated as experience in building robotic agents continues. Some more extensive overviews can be found in Malcolm, Smithers, and Hallam [69]; Brooks [22]; Pfeifer and Verschure [94]; and Maes [66].

3.3 Different approaches are explored for designing the behavior programs

Although there seems to be a consensus in the field that behavior systems are appropriate units, different avenues are explored regarding the best way to design the underlying behavior programs. They fall roughly in four groups: neural network approaches, algorithmic approaches, circuit approaches, and dynamics approaches.

3.3.1 Neural networks approaches

Several researchers use artificial neural networks, in order to stay close to plausible biological structures [5,27,94]. This approach is strongly related to biological cybernetics and neuroethology [15]. A neural network consists of a set of nodes linked together in a network. Each node receives input from a set of nodes and sends activation as output to another set of nodes. Some inputs could come immediately from sensors. Some outputs are linked with actuators. The links between nodes are weighted. When the sum of the weighted inputs to a node exceeds a threshold, activation propagates to the output nodes. There are many variants of neural networks, depending on the type of propagation and the adaptation mechanism that is used for changing the weights [56]. Usually a single neural network (even with multiple layers) is not enough to build a complete robotick agent. More structure is needed in which different neural networks can be hierarchically combined. Several architectures and associated programming languages have been proposed. One of the best worked-out examples is reported by Lyons and Arbib [62]. It centers around the schema concept [7].

An advantage of neural network approaches is that they immediately incorporate a mechanism for learning. A disadvantage is that the global search space for an agent is too big to start from zero with neural network techniques. Much more initial structure must typically be encoded, which is sometimes difficult to express in network terms.

3.3.2 Algorithmic approaches

Other researchers have stayed closer to the methods traditionally used in computer programming so that powerful abstraction mechanisms can be used to cope with the complexity of programming complete robotic agents. One of the best known examples is the subsumption architecture [19], which makes two fundamental assumptions: (a) behavior programs are defined algorithmically, and (b) there is a hierarchical but distributed control between different behavior systems based on subsumption relations.

The algorithmic descriptions in the subsumption architecture use a Turing-compatible formalism in the form of an augmented finite-state

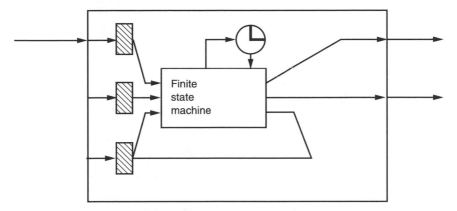

Figure 2 The augmented finite-state automata have a set of internal registers, inputs and outputs, and a clock. The automaton cycles through a set of states.

machine (Figure 2). An augmented finite-state machine has a set of registers that can hold discrete values. On a robot, some of the registers hold the most recent value obtained from sensors. Others contain action parameters to be sent as fast as possible to the actuators. An augmented finite-state machine also has a set of states in which the automaton can be. Operations consist of changing the contents of a register or moving to a new state. These operations can be controlled by first checking whether a condition on the state of the registers is true. An important feature of the finite-state machines used by Brooks is access to a clock. This introduces an additional kind of operation: wait for a certain period of time and resume operation after that. It gives a handle on the difficult problems in fine-tuning the temporal aspects of behavior.

In a single agent, there will be a collection of behavior systems whose behavior programs are defined in terms of augmented finite-state machines. The term subsumption refers to the way different behavior systems are made to operate together. It is assumed that in principle, each behavior system is self-controlled, that is, it is always active and moving through its different states conditioned by the incoming sensory signals. However, one behavior system may inhibit that inputs arrive at the automaton or that outputs have their effect. Inhibition is done by an explicit subsumption link that is under the control of the behavior system (Figure 3).

In a concrete agent, the number and complexity of the finite-state automata quickly grows to hundreds of states and registers. A higher-level language, known as the behavior language [20], has been designed to make the definition of large collections of behavior systems possible. Many of the low-level details of programming finite-state automata are removed, and consequently more complex applications can be tackled. The behavior language

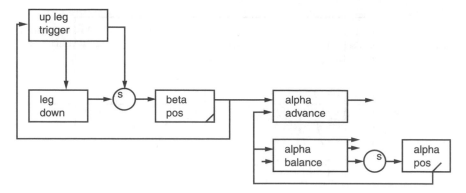

Figure 3 Partial network of finite-state automata for the locomotion of a six-legged
robot. The boxes are state variables. Boxes with a line in the bottom right
corner are finite-state automata. Alpha balance is another network. Nodes
marked "s" establish a subsumption relation. For example, activation of "up
leg trigger" inhibits the inflow of "leg down" to the "beta pos" automaton.
Adapted from Brooks [19].

and the subsumption architecture have been implemented on various
computational platforms (mostly of the 68000 family) in different robotic
hardware structures.

The recognized advantages of the subsumption architecture are as follows:
(a) A universal computational formalism is used that gives a high degree of
freedom and expressability to the developer, and (b) subsumption allows the
modular buildup of new competences by layering one behavior system on
top of another.

Some of the disadvantages are (a) algorithmic descriptions are more difficult to acquire or adapt (although see the work on genetic programming by
Koza [58] discussed in section 5); (b) an algorithmic specification makes it
more difficult to get smooth behavior because conditions are expressed in
terms of discrete thresholds; and (c) the subsumption relation works well for
basic sensorimotor competence, like six-legged locomotion, but it seems
weak to regulate the interaction of more complex behavior systems that
cannot be fined-tuned in advance.

3.3.3 Circuit approaches

A third approach stays closer to electrical engineering by assuming that
behavior programs, in order to be as efficient as possible, should take the
form of combinatorial circuits [2,100]. This approach potentially leads to
direct hardware implementation using Very Large Scale Integration (VLSI).
A combinatorial circuit consists of a set of components that perform a transformation from inputs to outputs. The outputs of one component may be
inputs to one or more other components, thus forming a network. Each

component is very simple, performing Boolean operations, equality tests, etc. On an autonomous robot, the inputs would be connected to sensory signals and the outputs to action parameters. Signals propagate through the network, thus relating sensing to action. A language (called REX) has been developed to describe circuits. Compilers and interpreters exist that allow REX-defined circuits to run on physical robots.

To make programming circuits more tractable, Rosenschein and Kaelbling [100] have developed a higher-level language that is based on a logical formalism known as situated automata. A translator has also been developed that transforms expressions expressed in this logical formalism into circuits.

A circuit approach has a number of advantages from an engineering point of view. For example, performance can be predicted in terms of propagation steps needed. However, the circuit is completely fixed at run-time, and it is less clear how continuous adaptation or the creation of new circuits can take place on-line.

3.3.4 Dynamics approaches

Yet another approach is based on the hypothesis that behavior systems should be viewed as continuous dynamical systems instead of discrete computational systems as in the algorithmic approach. This dynamics approach has been put forward by a number of researchers (see, e.g., [107,114]). It is more in line with standard control theory, which is also based on dynamical systems [42]. Artificial neural networks are a special case of dynamical systems and can be incorporated easily in this paradigm.

An example of a worked-out dynamics architecture is described in Steels [114]. It supports the formulation of processes and their combination in the design of complete behavior systems. Each process establishes a continuous relationship between a set of quantities. The quantities are either sensory signals, action parameters, or internal states. A process is always active. A collection of processes can be described in terms of a set of differential equations. Because of the implementation on digital computers, the differential equations are turned into difference equations that can be directly implemented, similar to the way cellular automata are discreted versions of continuous systems [120]. Each process partially determines the change to a quantity enacted at the next time step, as a function of current values of the same or other quantities. At each computation cycle, all the changes are summed, and the values of all the quantities take on their new values. The cycle time depends on the speed of the processor and the number of processes. There is no addressable global clock, as in the subsumption architecture. The complexity of the agent will be bound by its computational power. When the cycle time becomes too slow, reactivity is no longer guaranteed.

A programming language, PDL, has been developed to make the

implementation of behavior systems using this dynamics architecture more productive (Figure 4). The PDL compiler links with the necessary low-level software modules to handle sensory input and action parameter output. It maintains the different internal quantities and performs the basic cycle of determining all changes (by running the processes) and then summing and enacting the changes. PDL has been implemented on different PC-like hardware platforms for quite different robotic hardware structures.

A dynamics architecture approaches the problem of combining and coordinating different behavior systems differently from the subsumption architecture. Control is also distributed, but one behavior system can no longer influence another one through a subsumption link. Instead, each behavior system is active at all times, and the combined effect is added at the level of actions. For example, if one behavior system influences the motors strongly to go left and the other one weakly to go right, then there will be a left tendency. The unsupervised combination of different behavior systems poses no special problems when they are orthogonal. It also poses no problem when temporal relations are implicitly present. For example, an infrared-based obstacle avoidance behavior system will necessarily become active before a touch-based obstacle avoidance behavior system because the infrared sensors will "see" the obstacle earlier. Therefore, no explicit control relations are needed. When behavior systems are not orthogonal or are not temporally ordered by the interaction dynamics, (partial) control of the actuators must take into account the fact that other behavior systems will have an impact at the same time. In these cases, the interaction must be regulated by structural coupling [71] or coadaptation: Behavior systems develop in the context of other behavior systems, and, hence, their internal structure and functioning reflects this context. More complex control situations require the introduction of motivational variables that causally influence behavior systems and have a dynamics on their own.

The advantages of a dynamics architecture follow: (a) The dynamical systems paradigm is closer to descriptions used in physics, biology, and control theory. This is an advantage because it makes it easier to carry over results from these fields (e.g., on adaptive processes). (b) Dynamic control leads in general to smoother behavior because it is not subject to sudden state changes due to discrete conditions. (c) Additive control does not enforce a layering. All behavior systems are at the same level. In many cases, it is easier to add behavioral competence than with a subsumption architecture. In some cases, it is more difficult because a structural coupling must be established.

Some of the disadvantages of a dynamics architecture follow: (a) Thinking in terms of dynamical systems instead of algorithms requires quite a shift from the viewpoint of developers who are used to algorithmic programming. Higher-level abstractions still need to be developed. (b) The developer can-

```
void down_to_default_speed (void)

{
        if (value(forward_speed) > 10)

        add_value(forward_speed, –1):
}

void up_to_default_speed (void)

{
        if (value(forward_speed) < 10)

        add_value(forward_speed, 1);
}
```

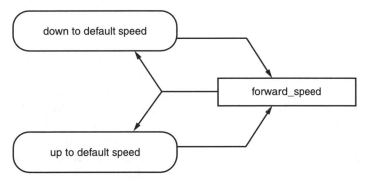

Figure 4 Process descriptions in PDL implementing a process network that will maintain the default forward speed at 10 by increasing or decreasing the speed in increments of 1.

not explicitly control the timing of actions. This is an advantage because it removes one aspect of complexity. It is also a disadvantage because the problem of timing must be handled in different ways, for example, by restructuring the behavior systems so that there is as little cascading as possible, or by decomposing behavioral competences in other ways.

There is still quite some work needed on additive control structures, particularly for hierarchical behavior systems, that is, behavior systems that control a set of other behavior systems that are possibly internally temporally ordered. Work by Rosenblatt and Payton [99] and Tyrrell [121] shows the direction in which this is being explored.

These four different approaches to the design and implementation of behavior programs (neural networks, algorithms, circuits, dynamical systems) will undoubtedly be explored further in the near future, and new approaches may come up. In any case, all approaches need more high level abstractions to hide complexity and allow reuse of large chunks from one experiment to another.

4 Emergent behavior

Agents can become more complex in two ways. First, a designer (or more generally a designing agency) can identify a functionality that the agent needs to achieve, then investigate possible behaviors that could realize the functionality, and then introduce various mechanisms that sometimes give rise to the behavior. Second, existing behavior systems in interaction with each other and the environment can show side effects, in other words, emergent behavior. This behavior may sometimes yield new useful capabilities for the agent, in which case we talk about *emergent functionality*. In engineering, increased complexity through side effects is usually regarded as negative and avoided, particularly in computer programming. But it seems that in nature, this form of complexity buildup is preferred. Emergent functionality has disadvantages from an engineering point of view because it is less predictable and appears less certain to a designer. Moreover, the side effects are not always beneficial. But for an agent operating independently in the world, it has advantages because less intervention from a designing agency is needed. In fact, it seems the only way in which an agent can autonomously increase its capability. This is why emergent functionality has become one of the primary research themes in behavior-oriented AI. It is also the research theme that has the most connections to other areas of AL.

4.1 Emergence can be defined in terms of the need for new descriptive categories

Many researchers in the AL community have attempted to define emergence (see, e.g., [8,24,36,59,111]). For the present purposes, we will define emergence from two viewpoints: that of the observer and that of the components of the system.

From the viewpoint of an observer, we call a sequence of events a behavior if a certain regularity becomes apparent. This regularity is expressed in certain observational categories, for example, speed, distance to walls, changes in energy level. A behavior is emergent if new categories are needed to describe this underlying regularity that are not needed to describe the behaviors (i.e., the regularities) generated by the underlying behavior systems on their own. This definition is compatible with the one used in chemistry and physics (see, e.g., [88]). Thus, the regularities observed in the collective behavior of many molecules requires new categories like temperature and pressure over and above those needed to describe the motion of individual molecules. Whether a behavior is emergent or not does not change according to this definition, with respect to who acts as observer, nor is it related to an element of unpredictability or surprise. Moreover, it is not necessary that the two descriptions (the emergent behavior and the behavior of the individual components) are at different levels, although that is not excluded.

Emergence can also be defined from the viewpoint of the components implicated in the emergent behavior [111]. We can make a distinction between controlled and uncontrolled variables. A controlled variable can be directly influenced by a system, for example, a robot can directly control its forward speed, although maybe not with full accuracy. An uncontrolled variable changes due to actions of the system, but the system cannot directly impact it, only through a side effect of its actions. For example, a robot cannot directly impact its distance to the wall; it can only change its direction of movement, which will then indirectly change the distance.

We can also make a distinction between a visible variable and an invisible variable. A visible variable is a characteristic of the environment that, through a sensor, has a causal impact on the internal structures and processes and, thus, on behavior. For example, a robot may have a sensor that measures distance directly. Distance would then be a visible variable for this robot. An invisible variable is a characteristic of the environment, which we as observers can measure, but the system has no way to sense it, nor does it play a role in the components implicated in the emergent behavior. For example, the robot could just as well not have a sensor to measure distance.

For a behavior to be emergent, we expect at least that the regularity involves an uncontrolled variable. A stricter requirement is that the behavior (i.e., the regularity) involves only invisible variables. So, when a behavior is emergent, we should find that none of the components is directly sensitive to the regularities exhibited by the behavior and that no component is able to control its appearance directly.

A further distinction can be made between emergent behavior upon which the system does not build further, and semantic emergence [24] or second-order emergence [9], in which the system is able to detect, amplify, and build upon emergent behavior. The latter can only happen by operating on the behavior programs that causally influence behavior, similar to the way genetic evolution operates on the genes. The remainder of this section discusses first-order emergence. Section 5 looks at semantic emergence.

4.2 The most basic form of emergent behavior is based on side effects

The first type of first-order emergence occurs as a side effect when behavior systems are made to operate together in a particular environment (Figure 5).

Consider the task of wall following. The behavioral regularity needed for this task is to have a bounded distance between the agent and the wall. This regularity can be achieved in a directly controlled, nonemergent way, by measuring the distance and using feedback control to steer away or toward the wall. Note that in this case, the distance is required to describe the behavior causing wall following and that distance is a visible variable.

Maintaining a distance from the wall can be achieved in an emergent way by the simultaneous operation of two behavior systems (as demonstrated by Nehmzow, Smithers, & McGonigle [85] and in our laboratory). The first one achieves regular obstacle avoidance, for example, in terms of a dynamic coupling between infrared reflection and deflection of the path as described earlier. The second behavior system exhibits wall seeking. This behavior system maintains an internal variable c, which reflects "the motivation of making contact with the left wall." The variable c decreases to 0 when contact is made with the left wall (sensed by infrared reflection) and moves up otherwise. It influences the deflection of the forward motion path toward the wall. The higher is c, the stronger the deflection. The two behavior systems together implement an attraction and repulsion behavior that added up and in the presence of a (left) wall gives the desired (left) wall-following behavior.

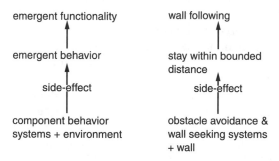

Figure 5 Left: Emergent behavior occurs as a side effect of the interaction between behaviors and the environment. New descriptive categories are needed to describe it. Right: example for wall following resulting from the operation of the obstacle- and wall-seeking behaviors.

An analogous behavior system is needed for making contact with a right wall.

Wall following is emergent in this case because the category "equidistance to the (left/right) wall" is not explicitly sensed by the robot or causally used in one of the controlling behavior systems.

Emergent behavior has two advantages compared to directly programmed behavior: (a) No additional structure is needed inside the agent to get additional capabilities. Therefore, we do not need any special explanations how the behavior may come about. (b) Emergent behavior tends to be more robust because it is less dependent on accurate sensing or action and because it makes less environmental assumptions. For example, the wall-following mechanism described previously continues to work even if the robot is momentarily pushed aside, if the wall is interrupted, or if the wall has a strong curvature. Emergent behavior usually has also disadvantages, for example, it is typically less efficient.

Here is a second example of emergent behavior. Suppose we want an agent that is able to position itself accurately between two poles that are part of a charging station. The charging station has an associated light source, and the agent has two light sensitive sensors. The agent starts with two behavior systems: one based on phototaxis resulting in a zigzag behavior toward the light source (and, therefore, the charging station) and one achieving obstacle avoidance by retracting and turning away when sensing an obstacle.

Because the agent may approach the charging station from any direction, it might seem that an additional positioning behavior is required, which makes sure that the agent enters the charging station between the two poles. However, a positioning behavior system is not necessary. The obstacle avoidance behavior causes retraction and turning away when the poles are hit. Because the robot is still attracted by the light source, it will again approach the charging station but now from a new angle. After a few trials, the robot enters the charging station as desired. The positioning behavior is emergent because position relative to the poles of the charging station is irrelevant to describe the behavior of the implicated behavior systems (obstacle avoidance and phototaxis). There is no separate structure in the agent that is measuring position with respect to the poles and causally influences motion based on this measurement. Nevertheless, the positioning behavior occurs reliably without any additional structure in the agent.

4.3 A second form of emergent behavior is based on spatiotemporal structures

A second case of (first-order) emergence is based on temporary spatiotemporal structures (Figure 6). These structures themselves emerge as a side effect of interactions between certain actions of the agent and the environment. Local properties of the temporary structure in turn causally influence the

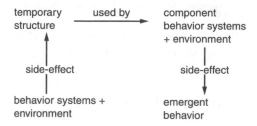

Figure 6 A second type of emergence is based on the formation of an emergent temporary structure that is then exploited by other behavior systems to establish the new emergent behavior.

observed behavior. The temporary structure is also emergent in the same sense as before, that is, new descriptive categories are needed to identify the structure. These categories are neither needed to describe the behavior of the underlying behavior systems that are causing the structure to appear nor are they sensitive to the structure as a whole. Also the behavior that results from making use of the structure is emergent because new descriptive categories are required that play no causal role in the underlying behavior systems.

This phenomenon is most easily observed in multiagent systems but can also be used for establishing behaviors of a single agent. The classical example for multiagent systems is the formation of paths. It has been well studied empirically not only in ant societies [91] but also in many other biological multielement systems [10]. It is also well understood theoretically in terms of the more general theory of self-organization [89]. The phenomenon has been shown in simulation studies [29,32,108] and recently on physical robots [14].

The temporary structure in the case of path formation in ant societies is a chemical pheromone gradient deposited in the environment. Ants are attracted to the pheromone and, therefore, have a tendency to aggregate along the path. Ants deposit the pheromone as they are carrying food back to the nest and are responsible for the pheromone gradient in the first place. The pheromone dissipates so that it will disappear gradually when the food source is depleted. This emergent temporary structure is the basis of a derived emergent behavior, namely the formation of a path, defined as a regular spatial relation among the ants (Figure 7). The path, as a global structure, is emergent because it is not needed to describe the behavior of the individual agents, and none of the agents recognize the fact that there is a path. The agents operate uniquely on local information of the pheromone gradient. Only the observer sees the global path. The efficient transport of food benefits the multiagent system as a whole and, thus, contributes to its self-preservation.

A difference with the examples discussed in the previous paragraph is that the emergent temporary structure sustains itself: As more ants are

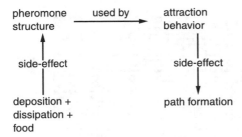

Figure 7 Path formation in ant societies is a classical example of emergent behavior due to the formation of a temporary structure. The structure in this case is a chemical pheromone gradient to which the ants are attracted.

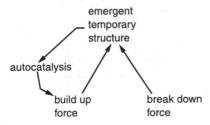

Figure 8 Emergent phenomena usually involve a force that builds up the phenomenon, a force that breaks it down, and an autocatalytic process so that the temporary structure builds upon itself.

attracted to the pheromone concentration, there is a higher chance that they will carry back food and deposit more pheromone. This increases the concentration of pheromone, which will attract even more ants, and so on. So there are three forces in the system: buildup of the path (by depositing pheromone), breakdown (by dissipation), and autocatalysis (through the chance of increased build-up) (Figure 8). These forces are recognized as the essential ingredients for emergent temporary structures in general [59,111].

Emergent temporary structures have also been used in individual agents. For example, several researchers have explored the creation of gradient fields over analogical representations of the environment. The best known example are potential fields [6,7]. A potential field is a dynamical temporary structure created over an analogical representation of the environment by various repulsion and attraction forces. The attraction force may come from the location of the desired goal toward which the agent wants to move. Repulsion may be generated by processes that are linked to the sensing of obstacles. Locomotion is influenced by the combined impact of attraction and repulsion forces (Figure 12 from Arkin [7]. p. 99).

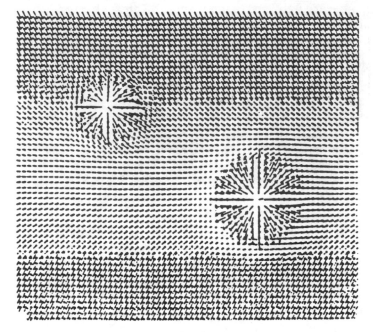

Figure 9 A potential field is a temporary structure created over an analogical representation of the world. The structure consists of vector fields that can either attract or repel robot movement. The sum of all the fields generates a path that the robot can follow. The example shows repulsion from two obstacles and a left and right wall. Adapted from Arkin [7]. p. 99.

Other types of dynamics have been explored to generate and maintain emergent temporary structures to aid in navigation, for example, fluid mechanics so that a fluid flow between the agent's location in an analogical map and the goal location emerges [28], or reaction-diffusion dynamics to generate concentration gradients that can be exploited in navigation or movement control [109].

The creation of temporary structures through a self-organizing mechanism that combines buildup, breakdown, and feedback giving rise to autocatalysis has been used also for other aspects of intelligent behavior. For example, Maes [64] describes an action selection system (which perhaps should be better called a motivational system) in which the strength of a motivation is subject to positive enforcement (e.g., when the conditions for its satisfaction are sensed to hold) or negative enforcement (e.g., if contradicting motivations are active). These two processes generate a temporal ordering of the strength of motivations and consequently between the strength with which an action should get priority in execution. There is also a feedback mechanism: As motivation builds up, it will be able to inhibit competitors more effectively and gain additional strength. The temporary strength differences can be used by a decision module to determine which action will be selected next.

A particularly fascinating application of this mechanism for modeling spinal reflex behaviors of the frog is reported in Giszter [39]. The behaviors include limb withdrawal, aversive turns, and wiping away of nociceptive stimuli. The latter requires, for example, different simpler component behaviors: optional flexion, then place motion, and then whisk motion. Each of these has certain conditions that need to be satisfied, and each will make certain conditions true. If one behavior needs to be executed (e.g., "place motion"), it will pass activation along its predecessor link to "optional flexion," thus raising its level of activation. When flexion executes, it will establish conditions that make "place motion" executable, and so on.

Another example of the creation of temporary emergent structures for a frame recognition system is reported in Steels [110]. Each frame has a particular strength that corresponds to the applicability of the frame in a particular situation. There is an activation/inhibition dynamics and autocatalytic processes that create a temporal ordering on the frames so that the most appropriate frame for the given situation progressively gets the highest strength.

5 Emergent functionality

The examples in the previous section showed that complexity may arise as a side effect of the operation of simpler mechanisms, but they do not indicate how there could be a progressive buildup of more complexity. The only way this can happen is by the formation of new behavior systems. There is so far very little progress in this area, and new ideas are needed. Lack of progress comes partly from the practical difficulties in working with real physical agents, but these difficulties will progressively be alleviated as the technology matures. The real challenge is to find mechanisms that do not strain the limited resources of the agent and let the agent remain viable in the environment as it builds up more complexity.

5.1 There are severe difficulties in using existing artificial neural network techniques or evolutionary methods

At first sight, it may seem that mechanisms developed in artificial neural network research or genetic algorithms can be applied in a straightforward manner to the development of new functionality in autonomous agents. However, this is not the case.

Let us first look at supervised learning, that is, learning with the aid of examples or counterexamples. One of the best known supervised learning algorithms is back propagation [101]. Behavior programs could be represented as artificial neural networks associating sensory signals to actuator outputs. Changes in behavior programs could then be based on the error between the desired outcome and the outcome derived from using the association. For example, if X is a sensory signal, Y an action, and w the weight with which X influences the action, then an error would be the difference between the expected action and the action produced by $Y = wX$. There exist methods for adapting the weights w, which will lead to convergence [98]. Convergence means that, given a consistent set of sense-act pairs, the learning method will settle on a stable set of weights that "correctly" relates X with Y. It can be shown that certain functions (such as the XOR function) require a multilayered network [83]. The weights in multilayered networks can still be learned if the error is back-propagated through nodes at successive layers based on the relative contribution of each node to the derived outcome [101]. See Kosko ([56], chapter 5) for a review of these and other supervised learning methods.

Although supervised learning methods have been demonstrated to be successful in simulation experiments, their application to autonomous agents runs into several problems. The first difficulty is that the methods require an adequate computation of the error and, therefore, a good enough prediction of what the actual outcome should be. A robot that is crashing into the wall gets feedback that there was a control error but cannot necessarily compute what would have been the right control actions to avoid the crash. Supervised learning methods require a teacher that is more intelligent than the agent. But this is in contradiction with the objective of understanding how complexity might have arisen in the first place. A second difficulty is that the dynamics of weight adaptation requires a large amount of resources. The learning time grows very rapidly with the complexity of the network, and an unrealistically high number of presentations of the correct sense-act pattern is typically required [131, p. 87]. A third difficulty is that not all networks will learn. If the network is too complex (too many layers or too many nodes) or too simple, it will not be able to generalize. Too many presentations may degrade performance. Moreover, the input and output representation must be carefully chosen, increasing the role of the designing agency [131, p. 87]. These difficulties explain why no one has as yet been able to convincingly use supervised learning methods on autonomous physical robots.

Another major neural network mechanism is known as reinforcement learning [118]. Reinforcement learning methods increase (and decrease) the probability that a particular association between sensing and acting will be used, based on a reward or reinforcement signal. The reinforcement signal is produced as a direct or indirect consequence of the use of the association. Many different associations may play a role in a particular behavior, and there may be a delay between a behavior and its (positive or negative) consequences. This introduces a credit assignment problem [82]. Early proposals ranked the possible situation-action associations, selected the best one (possibly with some variation to avoid local minima), and increased or decreased the probability of future choice depending on the effect of the chosen action [12, 132]. More recent mechanisms go in the direction of having the agent develop a more sophisticated representation of the result of an action. For example, a prediction of reward is introduced, or a prediction of (long-term) cumulative reward, that is, return [118]. A technique useful for learning temporal chains is to hand out reinforcement to the last action and from there back to previous associations that played a role. This technique is known as the bucket brigade algorithm and originally due to Holland [46].

Reinforcement learning methods have been shown to be capable of impressive learning behavior in simulations or engineering contexts [81], but there are again serious difficulties in the application to physical autonomous agents. The first major difficulty lies in the determination of the reinforcement signal. It is unrealistic to assume that the agent gets a clear scalar reinforcement signal after each action or series of actions. The second difficulty is that reinforcement learning assumes a trial-and-error search to find a viable association. Unless the agent is already close to the desired behavior, it may take quite a while before such an association is discovered [52]. The third difficulty is the credit assignment problem. Proposed solutions all go in the direction of new complexity (in the form of models of return, or in more recent cases world models predicting return [61, 118]). Often, many simplifying assumptions are made about the nature of sensory interpretations or actions. For example, most methods assume that it is possible to select each time the "best" action. But agents always execute several actions at the same time, and in many cases actions (like turn left) are abstractions from the viewpoint of the designer that do not correspond to explicit commands in the robot, particularly not in dynamics architectures. Despite these difficulties, there are some preliminary experiments on physical mobile robots [52, 67]. The general conclusion seems to be that "current reinforcement-learning algorithms can be made to work robustly on simple problems, but there are a variety of dimensions in which they must be improved before it will be possible to construct artificial agents that adapt to complex domains" [52, p. 46].

Supervised learning or reinforcement learning are both constructivist techniques: They modify weights based on minimizing the error or on reinforcement. The alternative is known as selectionism: A complete behavior system is generated, for example, by mutation or recombination based on existing behavior systems and then tested as a whole. This mechanism is similar to evolution by natural selection as operating on the genes.

Evolutionary development has been shown in other areas of AL to be an extremely powerful source for generating more complexity (see, e.g., [96]). It has also been proposed by some neurobiologists to be the major mechanism underlying the formation of new structure (and, therefore, functionality) in the brain [25,33]. Evolutionary algorithms have been worked out in great detail and studied from a mathematical point of view (see review in Baeck & Schwefel [11]). The major variants are genetic algorithms [40] usually operating on classifier systems [45] and evolution strategies [103]. Applications have focused mostly on parameter optimization [63]. More recently, higher-level descriptions as opposed to bit strings have been used for the representation of the algorithm that needs to be derived, and, as a result, more complex algorithms have been generated [58].

Evolutionary techniques start from a population of individuals (which in the present case would be equal to behavior systems) that each derive a different solution in the space of possible solutions. The population is initialized in an arbitrary fashion. There is a fitness function that is defined over the space of all individuals. Individuals with higher fitness reproduce more often, and, thus, the distribution of individuals of a certain type in the population changes. Reproduction means that copies are made, possibly after mutation (which introduces a random change), or recombination (which combines parts of two algorithms). Because mutation and recombination may potentially result in a better algorithm, and because this algorithm will then be further reinforced by the selection step, the overall process evolves toward better and better regions of the search space.

Although this technique has resulted in very impressive results in an engineering context, the application to the development of autonomous agents poses some serious difficulties. The first problem is that genetic evolution requires quite a number of computational resources. The different individuals in the population need to be represented in memory, and a large number of cycles are required to arrive at working, let alone optimal, solutions. This is a problem for a robot that has to remain viable and maintain real-time responses within limited resource constraints. Consequently, most researchers so far follow an off-line approach [26, 57]. The genetic algorithm runs on a computer external to the robot. When a valid solution is found, it is loaded and integrated in the other behavior systems. Thus, Koza [57] has shown how to derive the behavior programs for wall following and obstacle avoidance that were earlier demonstrated to function on a real robot programmed in the subsumption architecture [70]. The primitive building blocks of the behavior programs are in this case the sensory inputs and action parameter outputs, Boolean connectives, conditionals, and the subsumption primitives. However, Brooks [23] has criticized these results, mostly because the primitive building blocks were well chosen (based on an analysis of a known solution), and simplifying assumptions were made concerning the Boolean nature of certain conditionals.

Off-line evolution creates a new problem, which is the gap between the virtual world of the simulator and the real world. Koza [57] uses a very simple virtual world. Cliff, Husbands, and Harvey [26] use a much more sophisticated simulation to test out the fitness of a solution. But, as Brooks [23] points out, the gap between simulated and real world will always remain quite large. One possible way out is to use the real robot as soon as reasonable solutions have been discovered. An example application of this technique is discussed in Shibata and Fukuda [105]. The application concerns the optimization of path planning. Each robot is assumed to have a (static) map of the world that contains the obstacles and the goal toward which the robot needs to navigate. The genetic algorithm is used to search for a path toward the goal. The path is then executed and its quality evaluated with respect to effective use. Based on this new evaluation and additional information derived from the execution of the path, a new path is derived again using genetic techniques. The obvious problem with this approach is that only few solutions can be tried, which diminishes the chances that a good solution is found in a genetic way.

There is another yet more fundamental problem with current evolutionary techniques, which is the definition of the fitness function. The search toward a solution critically depends on the prior definition of this fitness function. But this introduces an important role for the designer. In the context of emergent functionality, we expect that the fitness function should be subject to evolution and should be local to the organism that evolves (as is indeed the case in Ray [96]). Cariani [24] calls this pragmatic emergence.

5.2 A selectionist approach may be the key for generating emergent functionality

Although convincing examples of emergent functionality on physical robots operating in the real world do not exist, we are beginning to see the glimpses of it, and breakthroughs can be expected soon. These examples build further on the techniques discussed in the previous paragraphs but combine them in a novel way.

When we study synthetic examples of emerging complexity, like that of Ray [96], we see that they are based on selectionist mechanisms and that they have in addition two crucial features:

1. There is enough initial complexity to make a viable organism, and there are many diverse organisms. The buildup of complexity is as much due to the competitive interaction between organisms as to their interactions with the world.
2. The ecological pressures on organisms are real and come partly from other organisms. In other words, there are no predefined or static fitness functions or rewards, as assumed in genetic algorithms and reinforcement learning. There is no teacher around as assumed in supervised learning.

To make selectionism work for robots, it seems appropriate to draw a parallel between organisms and behavior systems. This means that we should not concentrate on the acquisition of a single behavior system (e.g., for locomotion or obstacle avoidance), but that there should be many diverse behavior systems that are complementary but still in competition. Paradoxically, it might be easier to develop many behavior systems at once than to concentrate on one behavior system in isolation.

Each behavior system, except for the basic reflexes, should remain adaptive, just as each individual organism remains adaptive (within the bounds of the genotype). New behavior systems begin their life by accessing the same or other visible variables and the same or other controlled variables. The new behavior system monitors the situation and adapts itself so as to have a similar impact on the controlled variables as the base line behavior systems, but using other sensory modalities. The important point here is that the generation of the new behavior system does not take place by trial and error.

Most of the time, behavior systems will have a different functionality. If there are behavior systems with the same functionality (e.g., obstacle avoidance), the diversity should not lie in variants of the same approach to a solution, as in the case of genetic algorithms, but in fundamental differences in how the functionality is approached (e.g., obstacle avoidance using touch-based reactive reflexes vs. obstacle avoidance using infrared-based classification).

We should also introduce real environmental pressures, such as limited internal energy availability, and real-time or memory constraints, in addition to real environmental pressures such as limited external energy availability, avoiding of self-damage, etc. These pressures should feedback on the formation or adaptation of behavior systems. A behavior system is less competitive if the sensory patterns to which the behavior system responds do not occur (e.g., its thresholds are too high), if the time to make a decision on how to influence actuation is too long so that the conditions for activation are no longer satisfied, if other behavior systems always override the influence on actuation, if many memory resources are needed, etc. There may also be behavior systems that specialize in monitoring internal and external environmental conditions and act as a "reaper" [96], weakening or eliminating other behavior systems. An example of this is already shown in Nehmzow and McGonigle [86].

Large-scale experiments incorporating this approach do not exist yet. But reason for the optimism that emergent functionality may be demonstrated soon comes from some initial experiments that show how new behavior systems may bootstrap themselves in the context of other behavior systems. Let us look at one concrete example in the context of obstacle avoidance. This example was first suggested and tested in simulation by Pfeifer and Verschure [94]. We have since done similar experiments on a real robot and with different sensory modalities in Brussels.

The baseline behavior systems are:

- maintain a default speed in a forward direction.
- maintain a forward direction.

- reverse speed if touching an obstacle in the front.
- turn away left if touched on the right side.
- turn away right if touched on the left side.

Following a dynamics viewpoint, each of these behavior systems establishes a continuous relationship between sensory signals and action parameters. For example, a positive default speed is maintained by increasing it, if it is below the default, or decreasing it, if it is above. Reversing the speed is done by a sudden decrease of the speed if a touch sensor is active. The positive default speed is then automatically restored by the "maintain a positive default speed" system.

The two emergent behavior systems (one that will do obstacle avoidance for obstacles on the left and another one that will do the same for obstacles on the right) are sensitive to the infrared sensors, and they impact the rotational motor. They use associative or Hebbian learning. In Hebbian learning, an association between two elements (e.g., sensors and actuators) is made stronger based on co-occurrence [44]. It is also made weaker, for example, due to a constant forgetting rate. Associative learning has been extensively studied in the artificial neural network field (reviewed in Kosko [56], chapter 4). In the present case, there will be a progressively stronger association between particular states of the infrared sensors (determined by the environment) and particular action parameters of the rotational motor (determined by the turn away left and turn away right behavior systems). Thus, we see a form of classical conditioning with the touch sensors as the unconditioned stimulus and the infrared as the conditioned stimulus.

To get emergent functionality, an additional step is needed. The new behavior systems so far perform the same activity as the baseline behavior systems and are not yet competitive. A behavior system becomes competitive if it causes a qualitatively different action that has an additional advantage for the agent. This can happen in many ways. For example, the new behavior systems could involve only some of the controlled variables so that some actions no longer take place, giving an overall qualitatively different behavior, or a behavior system may sense more quickly the upcoming situation and influence the action before the already existing behavior systems.

In the present case, the infrared-based obstacle avoidance system can become more competitive because the infrared sensors have a further range than the touch sensors. Therefore, they can react more quickly to the presence of obstacles. Due to the progressive strengthening of the association, there will be a particular point in time in which the infrared-based behavior systems react earlier than the touch-based ones. This is the point where the newly emergent functionality becomes visible. Without infrared-based obstacle avoidance, a reversing of speed took place so that the robot is backing up while turning away. This reversal of speed is no longer present when infrared-based obstacle avoidance is strong enough because the agent no longer touches the obstacles. Instead, we observe a deviation away from obstacles. This deviation is from the viewpoint of energy usage more beneficial to the agent.

The associative learning mechanism has an autocatalytic element because the triggering due to infrared itself also enforces the association. Thus, the association strengths in the new behavior systems feed on themselves and become progressively stronger (Figure 10).

This is indeed an example of emergence, according to the earlier definitions. Different sensory modalities are used compared to the original behavior systems, and there is also a qualitatively different behavior, which is more beneficial to the agent. The example illustrates that emergent functionality is not due to one single mechanism but to a variety of factors, some of them related to internal structures in the agent, some of them related to the properties of certain sensors and actuators, and some of them related to the interaction dynamics with the environment.

Because the formation of the new behavior system here happens in the context of other behavior systems, the agent always remains viable. For example, if the new infrared-based obstacle avoidance behavior systems fail, the touch-based solution is still there and will immediately become active. Because the formation is guided by existing behavior systems, it evolves quickly without trial and error or search. All the time the agent remains viable.

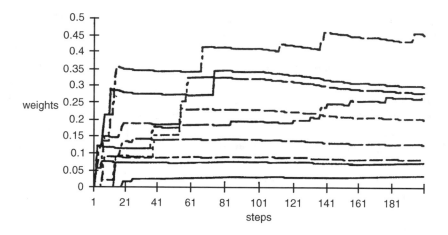

Figure 10 Evolution of the weights based on Hebbian learning. The weights determine the impact of the infrared sensors on the rotational motor. The increase feeds on itself. The decrease due to constant forgetting is also clearly visible.

It is obvious that more work is needed to achieve emergent functionality in physical autonomous robots, but current work exploring neural network techniques and evolutionary algorithms gives a good starting point. Their integration into an overall selectionist approach where diverse behavior systems compete and coadapt give reasons for optimism.

6 Conclusions

Behavior-oriented AI research has opened up an "artificial life route to artificial intelligence." It has three aspects: First, the problem of intelligence is framed within the general context of biology. Intelligent behavior is defined as maximizing the agent's chances for self-preservation. Successful adaptation and learning are defined as changes in the internal structure of the agent that maximize intelligence. Second, the tasks being explored by behavior-oriented AI researchers are very different from those considered in classical AI. They center around sensorimotor competence and the ability to operate autonomously in a dynamically changing environment. Third, the models take inspiration from the way intelligent behavior appears to be established in natural systems. It is hypothesized that the principles that underlie the living are also the ones that give rise to intelligent behavior. Many researchers hope to contribute to biology by testing out in artificial models whether certain biological hypotheses are plausible.

Behavior-oriented AI research made a slow start around the mid-1980s but is currently exploding. Many research laboratories have now acquired the competence to build their own robots and to perform experiments. Rapid experimental progress can be expected in the coming 5 years, if only by further pursuit of the research lines that have been briefly summarized in this paper. What is particularly needed are larger-scale efforts: agents with many different behavioral competences operating in ecosystems with a multitude of challenges, multiagent systems with a sufficient number and diversity of the agents, learning methods applied over sufficiently long periods of time to get nontrivial buildup of complexity, and so on. At the same time, the experimental rigor needs to be increased so that quantitative performance measures can be applied.

Given the current state of the art and the rapid evolution in mechanical engineering and computer technology, we can also expect rapid technological progress, leading toward the first real-world applications, possibly in the area of environmental monitoring, space exploration, or microsystems. In general, it takes about 10 years before a technology becomes sufficiently accepted for serious real-world applications. Major hurdles are not only technical. In this respect, the state of the art of behavior-oriented AI can be compared to that of knowledge engineering in the late 1960s, when the shift toward situation-specific knowledge and rule-based formalisms was taking place. It took several decades to turn these results into a solid engineering methodology and develop a number of well-established industrial achievements, like XCON for configuring computer installations [74].

Some open issues

There are also many open problems beyond increasing the complexity of current systems. One of them, which has hardly been addressed, concerns the relation between the mechanisms used in behavior-oriented AI and those used in knowledge-oriented AI. Some researchers (on both sides) suggest that the other approach is irrelevant to reach human-level intelligence. They then have to prove that their methods will work all the way. Other researchers believe that the symbolic level exists as an independent level, which is causally influenced by and causally influences the dynamics level. No concrete proposals operational on physical autonomous robots exist today to allow a technical discussion of the subject, but one day the problem will have to be tackled.

Another question concerns adequate formalization and theory formation. There is already a wide body of literature with formal results for the mechanisms discussed earlier (error-driven learning, genetic evolution, etc.), but application to integrated physical agents operating in real-world environments will require more work. Several researchers have proposed a state-space approach for defining the dynamics of the observed behavior and the internal operation of the agent (e.g., [37,54,77,119]). Once a state-space description is available, the concepts of dynamical systems theory (attractors, transients, recurrent trajectories, etc.) (1) can be used to characterize qualitatively and quantitatively behaviors and internal structures like perceptions, representations, and actions. Within this framework, concepts like emergent functionality can be formalized and the results of emergent functionality better understood. At the same time, work must proceed on developing formal theories to characterize the challenges in ecosystems; the optimality of behavior; and, thus, the chances of self-preservation of the agent [76].

The field of behavior-oriented AI research shows enormous signs of vitality. This paper focused only on a few aspects, ignoring other topics such as multiagent systems, communication and cooperation, the formation of new sensory modalities, and so on. There is no doubt that major contributions can be expected in the coming decade, particularly as the technical tools mature and more researchers get involved.

Acknowledgment

The writing of this paper was partly sponsored by the ESPRIT basic research project SUBSYM and the IUAP Action of the Belgian Science Ministry. Comments from Chris Langton, David McFarland, Walter Van de

Velde, and Anne Sjostrom have improved the paper. Continuous discussions with members of the VUB autonomous agents group and with Rodney Brooks, David McFarland, Rolf Pfeifer, and Tim Smithers have helped to shape the viewpoints expressed in this paper. I am strongly indebted to the hospitality of the Aamodt family; the writing of this paper started in the peaceful surroundings of their Norwegian home.

References

1. Abraham, R. H., & Shaw, C. D. (1992). *Dynamics. The geometry of behavior* (2nd ed.). Reading, MA: Addison-Wesley.
2. Agre, P., & Chapman, D. (1987). Pengi: an implementation of a theory of activity. In *Proceedings of the Sixth National Conference on Artificial Intelligence* (pp. 268–272). San Mateo, CA: Morgan Kaufmann.
3. Alexander, R. M. (1968). *Animal mechanics*. London: Sidgewick and Jackson.
4. Alife. (1994). *Journal of Artificial Life*. Cambridge, MA: The MIT Press.
5. Arbib, M. A., & Hanson, D. H. (1987). *Vision, brain, and cooperative computation*. Cambridge, MA: The MIT Press/Bradford Books.
6. Arbib, M. A., & House, D. H. (1987). Depth and detours: an essay on visually guided behavior. In M. A. Arbib & A. R. Hanson (Eds.), *Vision, brain, and cooperative computation* (pp. 129–163). Cambridge, MA: The MIT Press/ Bradford Books.
7. Arkin, R. (1989). Motor schema based mobile robot navigation. *International Journal of Robotics Research, 8*(4), 92–112.
8. Assad, A., & Packard, N. (1991). Emergent colonization in an artificial ecology. In F.J. Varela & P. Bourgine (Eds.), *Toward a practice of autonomous systems. Proceedings of the First European Conference on Artificial Life* (pp. 143–152). Cambridge, MA: The MIT Press/Bradford Books.
9. Baas, N. (1993). *Second order emergence*. Oral communication at the second European Conference on Artificial Life, ULB Brussels.
10. Babloyantz, A. (1986). *Molecules, dynamics, and life. An introduction to the self-organisation of matter*. New York: Wiley.
11. Baeck, T., & Schwefel, H.-P. (1993). An overview of evolutionary algorithms for parameter optimization. *Evolutionary Computation, 1*(1), 1–23.
12. Barto, A. G., & Sutton, R. S. (1991). Landmark learning: An illustration of associative search. *Biological Cybernetics, 42*, 1–8.
13. Barto, A. G. (1990). Connectionist learning for control. In T. W. Miller, R. S. Sutton, & P. J. Werbos (Eds.), *Neural networks for control* (pp. 5–58). Cambridge, MA: The MIT Press/Bradford Books.
14. Beckers, R. (1993). Demonstration at the Alife Meeting, Technical University of Delft.
15. Beer, R. D. (1990). *Intelligence as adaptive behavior: An experiment in computational neuroethology*. Cambridge, MA: Academic Press.
16. Bonner, J. T. (1988). *The evolution of complexity by means of natural selection*. Princeton, NJ: Princeton University Press.
17. Brady, J. M., & Paul, R. (1984). *Robotics research: The First International Symposium*. Cambridge, MA: The MIT Press.

18. Braitenberg, V. (1984). *Vehicles: Experiments in synthetic psychology.* Cambridge, MA: The MIT Press.
19. Brooks, R. (1986). A robust layered control system for a mobile robot. *IEEE Journal of Robotics and Automation, 2*(1), 14–23.
20. Brooks, R. (1990). *The behavior language; user's guide* (Memo 1127). Cambridge, MA: MIT AI Lab.
21. Brooks, R. (1991). Intelligence without reason. In *Proceedings of IJCAI-91* (pp. 569–595). San Mateo, CA: Morgan Kaufmann.
22. Brooks, R. (1991b). Challenges for complete creature architectures. In J.-A. Meyer & S. W. Wilson (Eds.), *From animals to animals. Proceedings of the First International Conference on Simulation of Adaptive Behavior* (pp. 434–443). Cambridge, MA: The MIT Press/Bradford Books.
23. Brooks, R. (1992). Artificial life and real robots. In F. J. Varela & P. Bourgine (Eds.), *Toward a practice of autonomous systems. Proceedings of the First European Conference on Artificial Life* (pp. 3–10). Cambridge, MA: The MIT Press/Bradford Books.
24. Cariani, P. (1991). Emergence and artificial life. In C. G. Langton, C. Taylor, J. D. Farmer, & S. Rasmussen (Eds.), *Artificial life II. Proceedings of the Workshop on Artificial Life* (pp. 775–797). Reading, MA: Addison-Wesley.
25. Changeux, J.-P. (1986). *Neuronal man: The biology of mind.* Oxford, UK: Oxford University Press.
26. Cliff, D., Husbands, P., & Harvey, I. (1993). Evolving visually guided robots. In J.-A. Meyer, H. L. Roitblatt, & S. W. Wilson (Eds.), *From animals to animats 2. Proceedings of the Second International Conference on Simulation of Adaptive Behavior* (pp. 374–383). Cambridge, MA: The MIT Press/Bradford Books.
27. Cruse, H., Muller-Wilm, U., & Dean, J. (1993). Artificial neural nets for controlling a 6-legged walking system. In J.-A. Meyer, H. L. Roitblatt, & S. W. Wilson (Eds.), *From animals to animats 2. Proceedings of the Second International Conference on Simulation of Adaptive Behavior* (pp. 52–60). Cambridge, MA: The MIT Press/Bradford Books.
28. Decuyper, J., & Keymeulen, D. (1991). A reactive robot navigation system based on a fluid dynamics metaphor. In F. J. Varela & P. Bourgine (Eds.), *Toward a practice of autonomous systems. Proceedings of the First European Conference on Artificial Life* (pp. 348–355). Cambridge, MA: The MIT Press/Bradford Books.
29. Deneubourg, J.-L., & Goss, S. (1990). Collective patterns and decision making. *Ecology, Ethology and Evolution, 1*, 295–311.
30. Deneubourg, J.-L., et al. (1993). Self-organisation and life: from simple rules to global complexity. In *Proceedings of the Second European Conference on Artificial Life* ULB, Brussels.
31. Donnett, J., & Smithers, T. (1990). Lego vehicles: a technology for studying intelligent systems. In J.-A. Meyer, H. L. Roitblatt, & S. W. Wilson (Eds.), *From animals to animats 2. Proceedings of the Second International Conference on Simulation of Adaptive Behavior* (pp. 540–569). Cambridge, MA: The MIT Press/Bradford Books.
32. Drogoul, A., & Ferber, J. (1993). From Tom Thumb to the Dockers: some experiments with foraging robots. In J.-A. Meyer, H. L. Roitblatt, & S. W. Wilson (Eds.), *From animals to animats 2. Proceedings of the Second International*

Conference on Simulation of Adaptive Behavior (pp. 451–459). Cambridge, MA: The MIT Press/Bradford Books.

33. Edelman, G. (1987). *Neural Darwinism: The theory of neuronal group selection.* New York: Basic Books.

34. Edelman, G. (1992). *Bright air, brilliant fire. On the matter of the mind.* New York: Basic Books.

35. Flynn, A., & Brooks, R. (1989). Building robots: expectations and experiences. In *IEEE Workshop on Intelligent Robots and Systems* (pp. 236–243). IROS '89. Tuskuba, Japan.

36. Forrest, S. (1989). *Emergent computation: self-organizing, collective, and cooperative phenomena in natural and artificial computing networks.* Amsterdam: North-Holland Pub. Co.

37. Gallagher, J., & Beer, R. (1993). A qualitative dynamical analysis of evolved locomotion controllers. In J.-A. Meyer, H. L. Roitblatt, & S. W. Wilson (Eds.), *From animals to animats 2. Proceedings of the Second International Conference on Simulation of Adaptive Behavior* (pp. 71–80). Cambridge, MA: The MIT Press/Bradford Books.

38. Genesereth, M., & Nilsson, N. (1987). *Logical foundations of artificial intelligence.* Los Altos, CA: Morgan Kaufmann.

39. Giszter, S. (1993). Behavior networks and force fields for simulating spinal reflex behaviors of the frog. In J.-A. Meyer, H. L. Roitblatt, & S. W. Wilson (Eds.), *From animals to animats 2. Proceedings of the Second International Conference on Simulation of Adaptive Behavior* (pp. 172–181). Cambridge, MA: The MIT Press/Bradford Books.

40. Goldberg, D. E. (1989). *Genetic algorithms in search, optimization and machine learning.* Reading, MA: Addison-Wesley.

41. Goss, S., & Deneubourg, J.-L. (1992). Harvesting by a group of robots. In F. J. Varela & P. Bourgine (Eds.), *Toward a practice of autonomous systems. Proceedings of the First European Conference on Artificial Life* (pp. 195–204). Cambridge, MA: The MIT Press/Bradford Books.

42. Hallam, J. (1993). Playing with toy cars. In L. Steels & R. Brooks (Eds.), *The "artificial life" route to "artificial intelligence." Building situated embodied agents.* Hillsdale, NJ: Lawrence Erlbaum.

43. Hamad, S. (1990). The symbol grounding problem. *Physica D, 42*(1–3), 335–346.

44. Hebb, D. O. (1949). *The organization of behaviour.* New York: Wiley.

45. Holland, J. H. (1975). *Adaptation in natural and artificial systems.* Ann Arbor, MI: The University of Michigan Press.

46. Holland, J. H. (1985). Properties of the bucket brigade algorithm. In J. J. Grefenstette (Ed.), *Proceedings of the First International Conference on Genetic Algorithms and Their Applications* (pp. 1–7). Pittsburgh.

47. Hoogeweg, P. (1989). Mirror beyond mirror: Puddles of life. In C. G. Langton (Ed.), *Artificial life. Santa Fe Institute studies in the sciences of complexity* (Vol. VI, pp. 297–316). Reading, MA: Addison-Wesley.

48. Horswill, I. (1992). Characterizing adaptation by constraint. In F. J. Varela & P. Bourgine (Eds.), *Toward a practice of autonomous systems. Proceedings of the First European Conference on Artificial Life* (pp. 58–63). Cambridge, MA: The MIT Press/Bradford Books.

49. Horswill, I. (1993). A simple, cheap, and robust visual navigation system. In J.-A.

Meyer, H. L. Roitblatt, & S. W. Wilson (Eds.), *From animals to animals 2. Proceedings of the Second International Conference on Simulation of Adaptive Behavior* (pp. 129–136). Cambridge, MA: The MIT Press/Bradford Books.

50. Jones, J. L., & Flynn, A. M. (1993). *Mobile robots. Inspiration to implementation.* Wellesley, MA: A. K. Peters.

51. Kaelbling, L., & Rosenschein, S. (1990). Action and planning in embedded agents. *Journal of Robotics and Autonomous Systems, 6*, 35–48.

52. Kaelbling, L. (1992). An adaptable mobile robot. In F. J. Varela & P. Bourgine (Eds.), *Toward a practice of autonomous systems. Proceedings of the First European Conference on Artificial Life* (pp. 41–47). Cambridge, MA: The MIT Press/ Bradford Books.

53. Kauffman, S. A. (1993). *The origins of order: Self organization and selection in evolution.* Oxford, UK: Oxford University Press.

54. Kiss, G. (1991). Autonomous agents, AI and chaos theory. In J. A. Meyer & S. W. Wilson (Eds.), *From animals to animats. Proceedings of the First International Conference on Simulation of Adaptive Behavior* (pp. 518–524). Cambridge, MA: The MIT Press/Bradford Books.

55. No entry.

56. Kosko, B. (1992). *Neural networks and fuzzy systems. A dynamical systems approach to machine intelligence.* Englewood Cliffs, NJ: Prentice-Hall.

57. Koza, J. (1991). Evolving emergent wall following robotic behavior sing the Genetic Programming Paradigm. In F. J. Varela & P. Bourgine (Eds.), *Toward a practice of autonomous systems. Proceedings of the First European Conference on Artificial Life* (pp. 110–119). Cambridge, MA: The MIT Press/Bradford Books.

58. Koza, J. (1992). *Genetic programming.* Cambridge, MA: The MIT Press.

59. Langton, C. G. (1989). *Artificial life. Santa Fe Institute studies in the sciences of complexity* (Proc. Vol. VI). Reading, MA: Addison–Wesley.

60. Langton, C. G., Taylor, C., Farmer, J. D., & Rasmussen, S. (1992). Artificial life II. In *Proceedings of the Workshop on Artificial Life.* Reading, MA: Addison–Wesley.

61. Lin, L.-J., & Mitchell, T. M. (1993). Reinforcement learning with hidden states. In J.-A. Meyer, H. L. Roitblatt, & S. W. Wilson (Eds.), *From animals to animats 2. Proceedings of the Second International Conference on Simulation of Adaptive Behavior* (pp. 271–280). Cambridge, MA: The MIT Press/Bradford Books.

62. Lyons, D. M., & Arbib, M. A. (1989). A formal model of computation for sensory-based robotics. *IEEE Transactions on Robotics and Automation, 5,* 280–293.

63. Maenner, R., & Manderick, B. (1992). *Parallel problem solving from nature* (Vol. 2). Amsterdam: North–Holland Pub. Co.

64. Maes, P. (1989). The dynamics of action selection. In *Proceedings of the 11th International Joint Conference on AI (IJCAI 89)* (pp. 991–997). Los Altos, CA: Morgan Kaufmann.

65. Maes, P. (1990). *Designing autonomous agents: theory and practice from biology to engineering and back.* Cambridge, MA: The MIT Press/Bradford Books.

66. Maes, P. (1993). Behavior-based artificial intelligence. In J.-A. Meyer, H. L. Roitblatt, & S. W. Wilson (Eds.), *From animals to animats 2. Proceedings of the Second International Conference on Simulation of Adaptive Behavior* (pp. 2–10). Cambridge, MA: The MIT Press/Bradford Books.

67. Maes, P., & Brooks, R. (1990). Learning to coordinate behaviors. In *Proceedings*

of the Eighth National Conference on Artificial Intelligence (pp. 796–802). San Mateo, CA: Morgan Kaufmann.

68. Malcolm, C., & Smithers, T. (1988). Programming assembly robots in terms of task achieving behavioural modules: first experimental results. In *Proceedings International Advanced Robotics Programme* (pp. 15.1–15.6). Manchester, UK.

69. Malcolm, C. A., Smithers, T., & Hallam, J. (1989). An emerging paradigm in robot architecture. In T. Kanade, F. Groen, & L. Herzberger (Eds.), *Intelligent autonomous systems 2* (pp. 546–564). Amsterdam.

70. Mataric, M. (1990). Environment learning using a distributed representation. In *Proceedings of 1990 IEEE International Conference on Robotics and Automation* (pp. 402–406).

71. Maturana, H. R., & Varela, F. J. (1987). *The tree of knowledge: the biological roots of human understanding*. Boston: Shamhala Press.

72. Maynard-Smith, J. (1982). *Evolution and the theory of games*. Cambridge, UK: Cambridge University Press.

73. No entry.

74. McDermott, J. (1982). RI: a rule-based configurator of computer systems. *Artificial Intelligence Journal, 19*(1), 39–88.

75. McFarland, D. (1992). Animals as cost-based robots. *International Studies in the Philosophy of Science, 6*(2), 133–153.

76. McFarland, D., & Boesser, T. (1994). *Intelligent behavior in animals and robots*. Cambridge, MA: The MIT Press/Bradford Books.

77. McFarland, D., & Houston, A. (1981). *Quantitative ethology: the state-space approach*. London: Pitman Books.

78. Meyer, J.-A., & Guillot, A. (1991). Simulation of adaptive behavior in animats: review and prospect. In J.-A. Meyer & S. W. Wilson (Eds.), *From animals to animats. Proceedings of the First International Conference on Simulation of Adaptive Behavior* (pp. 2–14). Cambridge, MA: The MIT Press/Bradford Books.

79. Meyer, J.-A., Roitblatt, H. L., & Wilson, S. W. (1993). *From animals to animats 2. Proceedings of the Second International Conference on Simulation of Adaptive Behavior*. Cambridge, MA: The MIT Press/Bradford Books.

80. Meyer, J.-A., & Wilson, S. W. (1991). *From animals to animats. Proceedings of the First International Conference on Simulation of Adaptive Behavior*. Cambridge, MA: The MIT Press/Bradford Books.

81. Miller, W. T., Sutton, R. S., & Werbos, P. J. (Eds.), *Neural networks for control*. Cambridge, MA: The MIT Press/Bradford Books.

82. Minsky, M. (1961). Steps towards artificial intelligence. In E. Feigenbaum & J. Feldman (Eds.), *Computers and thought* (pp. 406–450). New York: McGraw-Hill.

83. Minsky, M., & Papert, S. (1988). *Perceptrons*. Cambridge, MA: The MIT Press.

84. Minsky, M. (1985). *The society of mind*. New York: Simon and Schuster.

85. Nehmzow, U., Smithers, T., & McGonigle, B. (1993). Increasing behavioural repertoire in a mobile robot. In J.-A. Meyer, H. L. Roitblatt, & S. W. Wilson (Eds.), *From animals to animats 2. Proceedings of the Second International Conference on Simulation of Adaptive Behavior* (pp. 291–297). Cambridge, MA: The MIT Press/Bradford Books.

86. Nehmzow, U., & McGonigle, B. (1993). Robot navigation by light. In J.-L. Deneubourg et al. (Eds.), *Self-Organisation and Life: From Simple Rules to Global*

Complexity. Proceedings of the Second European Conference on Artificial Life (pp. 835–844). ULB, Brussels.

87. Newell, A. (1982). The knowledge level. *Artificial Intelligence Journal, 18*, 87–127.

88. Nicolis, G. (1989). Physics of far-from-equilibrium systems and self-organisation. In P. Davis (Ed.), *The new physics* (pp. 316–347). Cambridge, UK: Cambridge University Press.

89. Nicolis, G., & Prigogine, I. (1985). *Exploring complexity*. Munchen: Piper.

90. Nilsson, N. (Ed.) (1984). *Shakey the robot*. SRI AI center. Technical Note 323.

91. Pasteels, J. M., & Deneubourg, J.-L. (1987). *From individual to collective behaviour in social insects*. Basel: Birkhauser.

92. Pattee, H. (1989). Simulations, realizations, and theories of life. In C. Langton (Ed.), *Artificial life* (pp. 63–77). Redwood City, CA: Addison-Wesley.

93. Peters, T. (1990). *Liberation management. Necessary disorganization for the nano-second nineties*. London: MacMillan.

94. Pfeifer, R., & Verschure, P. (1992). Distributed adaptive control: a paradigm for designing autonomous agents. In F. J. Varela & P. Bourgine (Eds.), *Toward a practice of autonomous systems. Proceedings of the First European Conference on Artificial Life* (pp. 21–30). Cambridge, MA: The MIT Press/Bradford Books.

95. Prigogine, L., & Stengers, I. (1984). *Order out of chaos*. New York: Bantam Books.

96. Ray, T. (1992). An approach to the synthesis of life. In C. G. Langton, C. Taylor, J. D. Farmer, & S. Rasmussen (Eds.), *Artificial life II. Proceedings of the Workshop on Artificial Life* (pp. 325–371).

97. Rose, S., & Bullock, S. (1991). *The chemistry of life* (3rd ed.). London: Penguin Books.

98. Rosenblatt, F. (1962). *Principles of neurodynamics*. New York: Spartan Books.

99. Rosenblatt, K. J., & Payton, D. (1989). A fine-grained alternative to the subsumption architecture for mobile robot control. In *Proceedings of the IEEE/INNS International Joint Conference on Neural Networks*.

100. Rosenschein, S., & Kaelbling, L. (1986). The synthesis of digital machines with provable epistemic properties. In J. Halpern (Ed.), *Theoretical aspects of reasoning about knowledge* (pp. 83–98). San Mateo, CA: Morgan Kaufmann.

101. Rumelhart, J., McClelland, J., & the PDP Research Group. (1986). *Parallel distributed processing*. Cambridge, MA: The MIT Press.

102. *Adaptive Behavior*. Cambridge, MA: The MIT Press.

103. Schwefel, H.-P. (1981). *Numerical optimization of computer models*. Chichester, UK: Wiley.

104. Shapiro, S. C. (1992). *Encyclopedia of artificial intelligence* (2nd ed.). New York: Wiley.

105. Shibata, T., & Fukuda, T. (1993). Coordinative balancing in evolutionary multi-agent robot systems. In F. J. Varela & P. Bourgine (Eds.), *Toward a practice of autonomous systems. Proceedings of the First European Conference on Artificial Life* (pp. 990–1003). Cambridge, MA: The MIT Press/Bradford Books.

106. Smithers, T. (1992). Taking eliminative materialism seriously: a methodology for autonomous systems research. In F. J. Varela & P. Bourgine (Eds.), *Toward a practice of autonomous systems. Proceedings of the First European Conference on Artificial Life* (pp. 31–40). Cambridge, MA: The MIT Press/Bradford Books.

107. Smithers, T. (1993). Are autonomous agents information processing systems? In L. Steels & R. Brooks (Eds.), *The "artificial life" route to "artificial intelligence." Building situated embodied agents*. Hillsdale, NJ: Lawrence Erlbaum.

108. Steels, L. (1990a). Cooperation between distributed agents through self-organisation. In Y. Demazeau & J.-P. Muller (Ed.), *Decentralized AI* (pp. 175–196). Amsterdam: North-Holland.

109. Steels, L. (1990b). Exploiting analogical representations. In P. Maes (Ed.), *Designing autonomous agents: theory and practice from biology to engineering and back* (pp. 71–88). Cambridge, MA: The MIT Press/Bradford Books.

110. Steels, L. (1991a). Emergent frame recognition and its use in artificial creatures. In *Proceedings of the 10th IJCAI*. San Mateo, CA: Morgan Kaufmann.

111. Steels, L. (1991b). Towards a theory of emergent functionality. In J.-A. Meyer & S. W. Wilson (Eds.), *From animals to animats. Proceedings of the First International Conference on Simulation of Adaptive Behavior* (pp. 451–461). Cambridge, MA: The MIT Press/Bradford Books.

112. Steels, L., & Brooks, R. (Eds.) (1993). *The "artificial life" route to "artificial intelligence." Building situated embodied agents*. Hillsdale, NJ: Lawrence Erlbaum.

113. Steels, L. (Ed.) (1993a). *The biology and technology of intelligent autonomous agents*. NATO ASI Series. Berlin: Springer Verlag.

114. Steels, L. (1993b). Building agents with autonomous behavior systems. In L. Steels & R. Brooks (Eds.), *The "artificial life" route to "artificial intelligence." Building situated embodied agents*. Hillsdale, NJ: Lawrence Erlbaum.

115. Suchman, L. (1987). *Plans and situated action. The problem of human machine interaction*. Cambridge, UK: Cambridge University Press.

116. No entry.

117. No entry.

118. Sutton, R. S. (1992). Special issue on reinforcement learning. *Machine Learning*, 8, 3–4.

119. Toffoli, T., & Margolus, N. (1977). *Cellular automata machines*. Cambridge, MA: The MIT Press.

120. Todd, P. M., & Wilson, S. (1993). Environment structure and adaptive behavior from the ground up. In J.-A. Meyer, H. L. Roitblatt, & S. W. Wilson (Eds.), *From animals to animats 2. Proceedings of the Second International Conference on Simulation of Adaptive Behavior* (pp. 11–20). Cambridge, MA: The MIT Press/Bradford Books.

121. Tyrell, T. (1993). The use of hierarchies for action selection. In J.-A. Meyer, H. L. Roitblatt, & S. W. Wilson (Eds.), *From animals to animats 2. Proceedings of the Second International Conference on Simulation of Adaptive Behavior* (pp. 138–147). Cambridge, MA: The MIT Press/Bradford Books.

122. Ullman, S. (1984). Visual routines. *Cognition, 18*, 97–159.

123. Van de Velde, W. (1992). *Learning robots*. Cambridge, MA: The MIT Press/Bradford Books.

124. Varela, F. J., & Bourgine, P. (Eds.), *Toward a practice of autonomous systems. Proceedings of the First European Conference on Artificial Life*. Cambridge, MA: The MIT Press/Bradford Books.

125. Varela, F. J., Thompson, E. & Rosch, E. (1992). *Embodied mind*. Cambridge, MA: The MIT Press.

126. No entry.
127. Vogel, F. (1989). *How life learned to live*. Cambridge, MA: The MIT Press.
128. Walter, W. G. (1950). An imitation of life. *Scientific American, 185*(2), 42–45.
129. Webb, B. (1993). Modeling biological behaviour or "dumb animals and stupid robots." In J.-L. Deneubourg et al. (Eds.), *Self-organisation and life: from simple rules to global complexity. Proceedings of the Second European Conference on Artificial Life* (pp. 1090–1103). ULB, Brussels.
130. Webb, B., & Smithers, T. (1992). The connection between AI and biology in the study of behaviour. In F. J. Varela & P. Bourgine (Eds.), *Toward a practice of autonomous systems. Proceedings of the First European Conference on Artificial Life* (pp. 421–428). Cambridge, MA: The MIT Press/Bradford Books.
131. No entry.
132. Widrow, B., Gupta, N., & Maitra, S. (1973). Punish/reward: learning with a critic in adaptive threshold systems. *IEEE Transactions on Systems, Man, and Cybernetics, 5*, 455–465.
133. Wilson, S. W. (1991). The animat path to AI. In J.-A. Meyer & S. W. Wilson (Eds.), *From animals to animats. Proceedings of the First International Conference on Simulation of Adaptive Behavior* (pp. 15–22). Cambridge, MA: The MIT Press/Bradford Books.

Section 1.1: Situated Artificial Intelligence

48

EPISTEMOLOGY AND ONTOLOGY

Excerpt from "The Cybernetics of 'Self': A Theory of Alcoholism"

Gregory Bateson

Source: *Psychiatry* 34(1), 1971: 1–18.

Philosophers have recognized and separated two sorts of problem. There are first the problems of how things are, what is a person, and what sort of a world this is. These are the problems of ontology. Second, there are the problems of how we know anything, or more specifically, how we know what sort of a world it is and what sort of creatures we are that can know something (or perhaps nothing) of this matter. These are the problems of epistemology. To these questions, both ontological and epistemological, philosophers try to find true answers.

But the naturalist, observing human behavior, will ask rather different questions. If he be a cultural relativist, he may agree with those philosophers who hold that a "true" ontology is conceivable, but he will not ask whether the ontology of the people he observes is "true." He will expect their epistemology to be culturally determined or even idiosyncratic, and he will expect the culture as a whole to make sense in terms of their particular epistemology and ontology.

If, on the other hand, it is clear that the local epistemology is *wrong*, then the naturalist should be alert to the possibility that the culture as a whole will never really make "sense," or will make sense only under restricted circumstances, which contact with other cultures and new technologies might disrupt.

In the natural history of the living human being, ontology and epistemology cannot be separated. His (commonly unconscious) beliefs about what sort of world it is will determine how he sees it and acts within it, and his ways of perceiving and acting will determine his beliefs about its nature. The living man is thus bound within a net of epistemological and ontological premises which—regardless of ultimate truth or falsity—become partially self-validating for him.[1]

It is awkward to refer constantly to both epistemology and ontology and incorrect to suggest that they are separable in human natural history. There seems to be no convenient word to cover the combination of these two concepts. The nearest approximations are "cognitive structure" or "character structure," but these terms fail to suggest that what is important is a body of habitual assumptions or premises implicit in the relationship between man and environment, and that these premises may be true or false. I shall therefore use the single term "epistemology" in this essay to cover both aspects of the net of premises which govern adaptation (or maladaptation) to the human and physical environment. In George Kelly's vocabulary, these are the rules by which an individual "construes" his experience.

I am concerned especially with that group of premises upon which Occidental concepts of the "self" are built, and conversely, with premises which are corrective to some of the more gross Occidental errors associated with that concept.

The epistemology of cybernetics

What is new and surprising is that we now have partial answers to some of these questions. In the last twenty-five years extraordinary advances have been made in our knowledge of what sort of thing the environment is, what sort of thing an organism is, and, especially, what sort of thing a *mind* is. These advances have come out of cybernetics, systems theory, information theory, and related sciences.

We now know, with considerable certainty, that the ancient problem of whether the mind is immanent or transcendent can be answered in favor of immanence, and that this answer is more economical of explanatory entities than any transcendent answer: it has at least the negative support of Occam's Razor.

On the positive side, we can assert that *any* ongoing ensemble of events and objects which has the appropriate complexity of causal circuits and the appropriate energy relations will surely show mental characteristics. It will *compare*, that is, be responsive to *difference* (in addition to being affected by the ordinary physical "causes" such as impact or force). It will "process information" and will inevitably be self-corrective either toward homeostatic optima or toward the maximization of certain variables.

A "bit" of information is definable as a difference which makes a difference. Such a difference, as it travels and undergoes successive transformation in a circuit, is an elementary idea.

But, most relevant in the present context, we know that no part of such an internally interactive system can have unilateral control over the remainder or over any other part. The mental characteristics are inherent or immanent in the ensemble as a *whole*.

Even in very simple self-corrective systems, this holistic character is evident. In the steam engine with a "governor," the very word "governor" is a misnomer if it be taken to mean that this part of the system has unilateral control. The governor is, essentially, a sense organ or transducer which receives a transform of the *difference* between the actual running speed of the engine and some ideal or preferred speed. This sense organ transforms these differences into differences in some efferent message, for example, to fuel supply or to a brake. The behavior of the governor is determined, in other words, by the behavior of the other parts of the system, and indirectly by its own behavior at a previous time.

The holistic and mental character of the system is most clearly demonstrated by this last fact, that the behavior of the governor (and, indeed, of every part of the causal circuit) is partially determined by its own previous behavior. Message material (*i.e.*, successive transforms of difference) must pass around the total circuit, and the *time* required for the message material to return to the place from which it started is a basic characteristic of the total system. The behavior of the governor (or any other part of the circuit) is thus in some degree determined not only by its immediate past, but by what it did at a time which precedes the present by the interval necessary for the message to complete the circuit. There is thus a sort of determinative *memory* in even the simplest cybernetic circuit.

The stability of the system (*i.e.*, whether it will act self-correctively or oscillate or go into runaway) depends upon the relation between the operational product of all the transformations of difference around the circuit and upon this characteristic time. The "governor" has no control over these factors. Even a human governor in a social system is bound by the same limitations. He is controlled by information from the system and must adapt his own actions to its time characteristics and to the effects of his own past action.

Thus, in no system which shows mental characteristics can any part have unilateral control over the whole. In other words, *the mental characteristics of the system are immanent, not in some part, but in the system as a whole.*

The significance of this conclusion appears when we ask, "Can a computer think?" or, "Is the mind in the brain?" And the answer to both questions will be negative unless the question is focused upon one of the few mental characteristics which are contained within the computer or the brain. A computer is self-corrective in regard to some of its internal variables. It may, for example, include thermometers or other sense organs which are affected by differences in its working temperature, and the response of the sense organ to these differences may affect the action of a fan which in turn corrects the temperature. We may therefore say that the system shows mental characteristics in regard to its internal temperature. But it would be incorrect to say that the main business of the computer—the transformation of input differences into output differences—is "a mental process." The computer is only an arc of a larger circuit which always includes a man and an environment from which information is received and upon which efferent messages from the computer have effect. This total system, or ensemble, may legitimately be said to show mental characteristics. It operates by trial and error and has creative character.

Similarly, we may say that "mind" is immanent in those circuits of the brain which are complete within the brain. Or that mind is immanent in circuits which are complete within the system, brain *plus* body. Or, finally, that mind is immanent in the larger system—man *plus* environment.

In principle, if we desire to explain or understand the mental aspect of any biological event, we must take into account the system—that is, the network of *closed* circuits, within which that biological event is determined. But when we seek to explain the behavior of a man or any other organism, this "system" will usually *not* have the same limits as the "self"—as this term is commonly (and variously) understood.

Consider a man felling a tree with an axe. Each stroke of the axe is modified or corrected, according to the shape of the cut face of the tree left by the previous stroke. This self-corrective (*i.e.*, mental) process is brought about by a total system, tree-eyes-brain-muscles-axe-stroke-tree; and it is this total system that has the characteristics of immanent mind.

More correctly, we should spell the matter out as: (differences in tree)—(differences in retina)—(differences in brain)—(differences in muscles)—(differences in movement of axe)—(differences in tree), etc. What is transmitted around the circuit is transforms of differences. And, as noted above, a difference which makes a difference is an *idea* or unit of information.

But this is *not* how the average Occidental sees the event sequence of tree felling. He says, "*I* cut down the tree" and he even believes that there is a delimited agent, the "self," which performed a delimited "purposive" action upon a delimited object.

It is all very well to say that "Billiard ball A hit billiard ball B and sent it into the pocket"; and it would perhaps be all right (if we could do it) to give a complete hard-science account of the events all around the circuit containing the man and the tree. But popular parlance includes *mind* in its utterance by invoking the personal pronoun, and then achieves a mixture of mentalism and physicalism by restricting mind within the man and reifying the tree. Finally the mind itself becomes reified by the notion that, since the "self" acted upon the axe which acted upon the tree, the "self" must also be a "thing." The parallelism of syntax between "*I* hit the billiard ball" and "The ball hit another ball" is totally misleading.

If you ask anybody about the localization and boundaries of the self, these confusions are immediately displayed. Or consider a blind man with a stick. Where does the blind man's self begin? At the tip of the stick? At the handle of the stick? Or at some point halfway up the stick? These questions are nonsense, because the stick is a pathway along which differences are transmitted under transformation, so that to draw a delimiting line *across* this pathway is to cut off a part of the systemic circuit which determines the blind man's locomotion.

Similarly, his sense organs are transducers or pathways for information, as also are his axons, etc. From a systems-theoretic point of view, it is a misleading metaphor to say that what travels in an axon is an "impulse." It would be more correct to say that what travels is a difference, or a transform of a difference. The metaphor of "impulse" suggests a hard-science line of thought which will ramify only too easily into nonsense about "psychic energy," and those who talk this kind of nonsense will disregard the information content of *quiescence*. The quiescence of an axon *differs* as much from activity as its activity does from quiescence. Therefore quiescence and activity have equal informational relevance. The message of activity can only be accepted as valid if the message of quiescence can also be trusted.

It is even incorrect to speak of the "message of activity" and the "message of quiescence." Always the fact that information is a transform of difference should be remembered, and we might better call the one message "activity—not quiescence" and the other "quiescence—not activity."

Similar considerations apply to the repentant alcoholic. He cannot simply elect "sobriety." At best he could only elect "sobriety—not drunkenness," and his universe remains polarized, carrying always both alternatives.

The total self-corrective unit which processes information, or, as I say, "thinks" and "acts" and "decides," is a *system* whose boundaries do not at all coincide with the boundaries either of the body or of what is popularly called the "self" or "consciousness"; and it is important to notice that there are *multiple* differences between the thinking system and the "self" as popularly conceived:

(1) The system is not a transcendent entity as the "self" is commonly supposed to be.

(2) The ideas are immanent in a network of causal pathways along which transforms of difference are conducted. The "ideas" of the system are in all cases at least binary in structure. They are not "impulses" but "information."

(3) This network of pathways is not bounded with consciousness but extends to include the pathways of all unconscious mentation—both autonomic and repressed, neural and hormonal.

(4) The network is not bounded by the skin but includes all external pathways along which information can travel. It also includes those effective differences which are immanent in the "objects" of such information. It includes the pathways of sound and light along which travel transforms of differences originally immanent in things and other people—and especially *in our own actions*.

It is important to note that the basic—and I believe erroneous—tenets of popular epistemology are mutually reinforcing. If, for example, the popular premise of transcendence is discarded, the immediate substitute is a premise of immanence in the body. But this alternative will be unacceptable because large parts of the thinking network are located outside the body. The so-called "Body-Mind" problem is wrongly posed in terms which force the argument toward paradox: if mind be supposed immanent in the body, then it must be transcendent. If transcendent, it must be immanent. And so on.[2]

Similarly, if we exclude the unconscious processes from the "self" and call them "ego-alien," then these processes take on the subjective coloring of "urges" and "forces"; and this pseudodynamic quality is then extended to the conscious "self" which attempts to "resist" the "forces" of the unconscious. The "self" thereby becomes itself an organization of seeming "forces." The popular notion which would equate "self" with consciousness thus leads into the notion that ideas are "forces"; and this fallacy is in turn supported by saying that the axon carries "impulses." To find a way out of this mess is by no means easy.

Note

1   J. Ruesch and G. Bateson, *Communications: The Social Matrix of Psychiatry*, New York, Norton, 1951.
2   R. G. Collingwood, *The Idea of Nature*, Oxford, Oxford University Press, 1945.

Developments

49

THE OWL AND THE ELECTRIC
ENCYCLOPEDIA

Brian Cantwell Smith

Source: *Artificial Intelligence* 47, 1991: 251–88.

Abstract

Smith, B.C., The owl and the electric encyclopedia, Artificial
Intelligence 47 (1991) 251–288.

A review of "On the thresholds of knowledge", by D.B. Lenat
and E.A. Feigenbaum.

1 Introduction

At the 1978 meeting of the Society for Philosophy and Psychology,[1] somewhat to the audience's alarm, Zenon Pylyshyn introduced Terry Winograd
by claiming that his pioneering work on natural language processing had
represented a "breakthrough in enthusiasm". Since those heady days, AI's
hubris has largely passed. Winograd himself has radically scaled back his
estimate of the field's potential (see, in particular [70, 72]), and most other
practitioners are at least more sober in their expectations. But not to worry.
Unbridled enthusiasm is alive and well, living in points South and West.[2]

Enthusiasm takes many forms, even in AI. Most common is the belief that
a simple mechanism can accomplish extraordinary feats, if only given
enough of some resource (time, information, experience, computing power).
Connectionist networks are a current favourite, but the tradition is time-
honoured. Feedback circuits, theorem provers, production systems, procedural representations, meta-level architectures—all have had their day. In
their present paper, Lenat and Feigenbaum take up the enthusiast's cause,
defending a new flavour of "great expectation". They suggest that just a
million frames, massaged by already-understood control structures, could
intelligently manifest the sum total of human knowledge.

The paper exhibits another kind of zeal as well—more general than

67

precipitate faith in mechanism, and ultimately more damaging. This time the fervour is methodological: an assumption that you can move directly from broad intuition to detailed proposal, with essentially no need for intermediate conceptual results. Let's look at this one first.

General insights, even profound ones, often have the superficial air of the obvious. Suppose Newton, in an attempt to strike up a conversation at a seventeenth century Cambridge pub, opened with the line that he had made an astonishing discovery: that it takes energy to do work. It is hard to believe the remark would have won him an extra pint. Newton is famous not for enunciating glib doctrines, but for elaborating a comprehensive system of details reaching from those encompassing insights all the way through to precise differential equations. It is this intermediating conceptual structure that rescues his original insight from fatuity.

Lenat and Feigenbaum (L&F) announce their own impressive generalizations: the Knowledge Principle, the Breadth Hypothesis, the Empirical Inquiry Hypothesis, etc. Each, in its own way, makes sense: that competence in a domain arises because of specific knowledge of the constitutive subject matter; that "intelligent performance often requires the problem solver to fall back on increasingly general knowledge, and/or to analogize to specific knowledge from far-flung domains"; etc. I agree; I expect most readers would agree—and so, I'd wager, would Newton's drinking partners. The problem is that L&F, with only the briefest of intervening discussion, then arrive at radically concrete claims, such as that three decades will suffice to carry out the following sweeping three-stage research program: (i) the slow hand-coding of a frame-based knowledge base, approximating "the full breadth of human knowledge" ($50 million, due to be completed by 1994), sufficient to bring the system to a point (ii) where it will be able to read and assimilate the remaining material on its own (approximately the turn of the century), followed by a stage (iii) where it is forced to carry out its own program of research and discovery, since it will have advanced "beyond the frontier of human knowledge".

One is reminded of tunnel diodes. For a moment the argument is on the plane of common sense, and then—presto!—it is suddenly at an extreme level of specificity, without ever having been anywhere in between. From the generality of human knowledge to the intricacies of slot inheritance; from the full flowering of intelligence to particular kinds of controlled search—leaps like these are taken without warning, often mid-sentence. The problem is not simply that the reader may disagree with the conclusions, but that there is no hint of the complex intellectual issues and decades of debate that lie in the middle, i.e., whereas tunneling electrons—or so we're told—genuinely switch from one place to another without ever being half-way in between, arguments don't have this luxury. Truth and reason are classical, so far as we know, constrained to follow continuous trajectories. That's why the middle ground of conceptual analysis and carefully laid-out details is the stuff and substance of AI.

So: After giving a better sense (in the next section) of the sort of argument that's missing, I will take it as the task of this review to map out at least some of the intermediate conceptual territory. The immediate goal will be to figure out what view of its structure could have led L&F to tunnel through in the way they did. As for their conclusions, I've already suggested I find them implausible, but others will want to judge for themselves. My larger aim is to convince the reader that any serious assessment of L&F's paper (or indeed of any analogous proposal) must be made against the backdrop of that hidden middle realm.

2 Conceptual tunneling

L&F start with the Knowledge Principle, cited above: that you have to know specific things about a domain to be competent at it. This insight is then used to discriminate a set of levels of expertise: rudimentary, middle-level prac-titioner, and expert. These levels are introduced with tautological generaliza-tion: to get started, you need to know something; the more you know, the less you need to search; once you know enough, additional knowledge will only infrequently (though still occasionally) be useful. Little more is said, unfortunately. And if the text is read closely, it shifts from the banal to the false.

Take the middle "practitioner" level. Without comment, L&F claim that "today's expert systems . . . include enough knowledge to reach the level of a typical practitioner performing the task." This claim may be true in a few limited, carefully chosen domains. In the sweeping context of the paper, on the other hand, the remark implies something different: that moderate expertise is achievable in arbitrary (if still specific) arenas. The latter claim simply isn't true; we don't yet have expert system personnel managers, nurses, or private detectives, and there are many, including some of the tech-nology's protagonists (see, e.g., [16]), who suspect we never will. So the reader ends up caught between the plausibility of the narrow reading and the presumption of the broad one.

Similarly, consider L&F's comments about getting started. They claim that to solve a problem you need a minimum amount of knowledge in order to "state [it] in a well-formed fashion". This is a major assumption, again debatable. As students of AI are increasingly realizing (see [1, 2, 13, 21, 24, 39, 44, 48, 57–59, 67, 72] for a variety of such views), there's no reason to believe that people formulate anything like all the problems they solve, even internally.[3] Children happily charge around the world long before they acquire any conceptual apparatus (such as the notions of "route" and "des-tination") with which to formulate navigational problems. So too with lan-guage: fluent discourse is regularly conducted in complete absence of a single linguistic concept—including "word" or "sentence", let alone Bosworth's "prose" or the logician's "substitution *salve veritate*". Similarly, when you reach around and retrieve your coffee cup from the side table, there is no reason—especially no a priori reason—to believe that you formulate much of anything at all. Problems stated in words have to be formulated, yes: but only because to "formulate" means to state in words.

Here we see the beginning of the tunnel. If (i), in order to sidestep issues of explicit formulation, and to avoid foundering in simplistic cases, the minimalist threshold were generalized to "the solution of any complex task requires some minimum amount of knowledge"; and (ii) the notion of "knowledge", which L&F never really explain, were generalized to include perception, motor coordination, tacit expertise, explicit conceptual powers, and all the rest—then, well, yes, we would have a more tenable reading. The problem is, we would also have a vacuous reading: no one could rationally imagine anything else. On the other hand, if instead we try to put some meat on the skeletal insights, and prohibit wanton generalization, it becomes unclear how to hang on to the original intuition without running counter to fact.[4]

Such worries don't deflect these authors, however. Without breaking stride, they claim that the Knowledge Principle is "a mandate for humanity to concretize the knowledge used in solving hard problems in various fields." Three lines later this has turned into a mandate to "spend the resources necessary to construct one immense knowledge base spanning human consensus reality". But why? Even the untenably "formulated" readings of these putative principles aren't in themselves mandates to *do* anything at all. The underlying (tunneled) argument must include something like the following presumptions: we know how to write "knowledge" down (i.e., the knowledge representation problem will imminently be solved); there won't be any interaction effects; we can ride rough-shod over all ontological problems about how people conceptualize the world;[5] and so on and so forth.

What of the other principles? At the level of grand generality, the Breadth Principle is again something that no one could plausibly deny. It recommends the use of generalization and analogy when more specific things fail. Consider just analogy. Is it important? Undoubtedly. Understood? It's unlikely that its full-time students would say so.[6] Does L&F's paper illuminate its subtleties? Very little. All that is presented are a few paragraphs barely hinting at the issues involved. Take for example the postulated Analogical Method: "If *A* and *B* appear to have some unexplained similarities, then it's worth your time to hunt for additional shared properties." But it is well known that there are just too many properties, too many similarities, to be relevant. Thomas Jefferson and John Adams both died (within an hour of each other) on July 4, 1826—50 years to the day after the signing of the Declaration of Independence they co-authored. It's rumoured that the price of bananas and the suicide rate in France tracked each other almost perfectly for years. The words "abstemious" and "facetious" exhibit all five vowels in alphabetic order. Do we have an explanation for these facts? No. So, should we look for additional similarities? Probably not. A proper treatment of analogy requires a notion of *relevant* similarity. Nor can their suggestion of entering "specialized versions" of analogical reasoning in an *n*-dimensional matrix (according to "task domains, . . . user-modes . . . analogues with various epistemological statuses", etc.) be more than a data structural encoding of hope.

Furthermore, nothing in the paper clues the reader into the fact that these issues have been investigated for years. All we get are statements like this: "we already understand deduction, induction, analogy, specialization, generalization, etc., etc., well enough to have knowledge be our bottleneck, not control strategies." Breathtaking, but simplistic. And in a disingenuous sleight of hand, the passage continues: "On the other hand, all such strategies and methods are themselves just pieces of knowledge", with the implication that it should be straightforward to have them selected and applied at the meta-level. But this is simply not a serious argument. To start with, you can't have it both ways; either we do know enough about control structure, or we don't. And if we don't, then we're probably not ready to write it down, either. Furthermore, relying on universal meta-levels is like defending Von Neumann machines as cognitive models because they would exhibit intelligent behaviour, if only they were given the right programs. It isn't false, but it isn't useful, either.[7]

There's more. We are told that:

> . . . In a sense, natural language researchers have cracked the language understanding problem. But to produce a general Turing-testable system, they would have to provide more and more semantic information, and the program's semantic component would more and more resemble the immense [knowledge base] mandated by the Breadth Hypothesis.

This time we're given neither supporting details nor motivating intuition. On the unwarranted assumption that parsing is solved, and if by "semantic information" one includes *everything* else—pragmatic assumption, concept formation, inference, induction over experience, formations of judgment, theory change, discourse understanding, etc., coupled with everything that anyone could ever need to know or be in order to be a competent participant in a dialogue, including what L&F call "consensus reality"—then, well, yes, that's all we need to do.

The authors take that "consensus reality" seriously: it is intended to include the entire fabric of assumptions and common sense underlying all of human knowledge. One of the paper's most spectacular assertions is the claim that all people know can be captured in a million frames—a statement reinforced by citing three independent estimates, two based on sheer guesses of how many frames are needed to understand an article or word (guesses because we as yet have no real assurance that any computer has ever really understood a single word, let alone a sentence or longer text), another on an estimate of four entries into long-term memory per hour. No room is made for such commonplace phenomena as the recognition, many years later, of a face once glimpsed for just a few seconds—an ability still well beyond computational emulation. Or the empathetic stance necessary in order to understand allusions and insinuations in any piece of serious writing. Or even simple acts of speculation. Imagine, for example, a toboggan careening down an ice-clad winter hill, increasingly out of control, with the initial look of terrified glee steadily draining out of the face of the 13-year old at the helm, being replaced by an anguished expression of sheer panic. Now quick: how many "pieces" of knowledge did you just use in picturing this scene?

And so it goes. The paper accuses others of premature formalization, without even entertaining the thought that setting out to code up human knowledge in a million frames might be an instance of the very phenomenon. Empirical inquiry is endorsed, but seems only to involve the investigation of computer programs, not the phenomena they are being used to model (and even that seems confused: L&F claim we should use computers "as a tool", the way astronomers use telescopes, an injunction that I would have thought applied to physics but exactly not to AI[8]). The issues are so complex it is hard to tell what they think; at best they seem to have in mind what would normally be called *hypothesis testing*, not *empirical inquiry*. There's no admission that there are external data and practices to be studied—that ours isn't an entirely internalist, constructed game (they do say that "intelligence is still so poorly understood that Nature still holds most of the important surprises", but shortly thereafter dismiss all of deduction, induction, and so on as essentially solved). In a similar vein, it's striking that genuine semantics isn't even mentioned—not the question of "semantic representation" (i.e., how concepts and meanings and the like are stored in the head), but the tougher question of how symbols and representations relate to the world.

Alas, it looks as if what discouraged Winograd hasn't even been imagined by the present authors.

3 The structure of the middle realm

Perhaps someone will object. L&F march to the pragmatist's drum, after all. So is it unfair to hold them to clear theoretical standards? I think not. For one thing, in a volume on the foundations of AI, explicating premises should be the order of the day. Second, there is the matter of scale. This is a large project they propose—all of consensus reality, 50 million dollars for the first stage, etc. Untutored pragmatism loses force in the face of a task of this magnitude (you can bridge a creek without a theory, but you won't put a satellite into orbit around Neptune). Furthermore, citing the modesty of human accomplishment ("people aren't perfect at these things") won't let L&F off the hook, especially when what is particularly modest is people's understanding of their own intellectual prowess. Fortunately, we humans don't have to know much about reasoning to be good at it—cf. the discussion of formulation, above. But L&F can't piggy-back off our native competence, in creating a computational version. Given that they're both starting from scratch, and committed to an explicit-representation stance, they must understand what they're doing.

So we're brought right back to where we started: with that hidden middle realm. Let's dig deeper, therefore, and uncover some of its inner structure. I'll do this by locating L&F's position with respect to twelve foundational questions—questions that could be asked of any proposed reasoning or inference system. Given that we lack a general theory of representation (not only those of us in AI, but the wider intellectual community as well—a sobering fact, since our systems rest on it so fundamentally), posing such questions is as good an analytic strategy as any. Furthermore, these twelve will help reveal L&F's representational assumptions.

The answers are summarized in Table 1. To convey a better sense of the structure of the territory, I've flanked L&F's position with two other replies. On the left is the position of traditional formal logic (the system studied by philosophers and logicians, not "logic-based" theorem provers or logic programming languages—both too ill-defined to be of much help here). On the right is my own assessment of the minimum an AI system will require in

Table 1 A dozen foundational questions (Boxes indicate agreement).

	Logic	L&F	EC
1. Primary focus on explicit representation?	yes	yes	no
2. Contextual (situated) content?	no	no	yes
3. Meaning dependent on use?	no	no	yes
4. Consistency mandated?	yes	no	no
5. Single representational scheme?	yes	yes	no
6. Entirely discrete (no continuity, images. . . .)?	yes	yes	no
7. Representation captures all that matters?	yes	yes	no
8. Reasoning and inference central?	yes	yes	yes
9. Participation and action crucial?	no	no	yes
10. Physical embodiment important?	no	no	yes
11. Support for "original" semantics?	no	no	yes
12. Distinguish theorist's and agent's conceptual schemes?	no	no	yes

order to achieve anything like genuine intelligence. For discussion, I'll call it a notion of "embedded computation" (EC).

One point needs emphasizing, before turning to specifics. Embedded computation is still an emerging perspective, not yet a technical proposal. That doesn't make it sheer speculation, however, nor is it purely idiosyncratic. A growing number of researchers are rallying around similar views—so many, in fact, that one wonders whether something like it won't be the next AI stage, beyond the "explicit knowledge" phase that L&F represent.[9] Nonetheless, I would be the first to admit that details remain to be worked out. But that's exactly my point. I'm contrasting it with L&F's position exactly in order to highlight how far I believe we are from achieving their stated goals. For purposes of the present argument, in other words, any claim that we don't yet understand some aspect of the speculative EC view—what nondiscrete computation would be like, say—counts *for* my position, and *against* L&F.[10] All that matters is that there is some reason to believe that the issue or phenomenon in question is at least partially constitutive of intelligence. L&F are the ones with the short-term timetable, after all, not I.

Question 1. Does the system focus primarily on explicit representation?

	Logic	L&F	EC
	yes	yes	no

In the current design of computer systems, there is probably no more time-worn a technique than that of "explicit representation". And there is no difficulty in discerning L&F's views on the subject, either. They line up directly with tradition. In fact that representation be explicit is the only specific coding requirement they lay down (it is mandated in their "Explicit Knowledge Principle"). Similarly, the CYC project takes explicit representation as its fundamental goal.

Unfortunately, however, it is unclear what L&F (or anyone else, for that matter) mean by this term—what, that is, the implicit/explicit distinction comes to (see [42] for a recent paper on the notion). This is not to say that the notion doesn't matter. Many programmers (and I count myself as one of them) would stubbornly insist that choices about explicit representation impinge on effectiveness, control flow, and overall system architecture. The question is what that insistence is about.

When pressed for examples of explicit representation, people typically point to such cases as the grammarian's "$S \rightarrow NP\ VP$", logical formulae such as "$P(a) \supset Q(b)$", frames in such systems as KRL, or nodes in semantic nets. The examples are almost always taken from language-like representational schemes, suggesting that some combination is required of conceptual categorization, recursive method of combination, and relative autonomy of representational element[11] (images and continuous representations are rarely, though not never, cited as paradigmatically explicit). Explicitness is also relational, holding between something (a representation) and something else (what it represents). This provides some freedom: a given structure can be implicit, explicit, neither (if, like a bread-basket, it doesn't represent anything), or both (if it represents severally). Logical axioms, for example, are often viewed as explicit representations of their own particular contents, but (in ways that Levesque [45], Halpern [26], and others have tried to make precise) as implicit representations of what they imply.

So what does explicitness come to? Though it's currently impossible to say, it seems to require a roughly determinate object (sentence, frame, whatever), of a readily discriminable type, that simultaneously plays two rather direct roles: straightforwardly representing some content or other (John's having brown hair, say), and, again quite directly, playing a causal role in the course of the system's life that constitutes that system's knowing or believing the corresponding content (or would at least lead an observer to say that the system knows or believes it).[12] I.e., explicitness seems to require (a) a degree of modularity or autonomy, (b) a coincidence of semantic and causal role, and (c) a relative directness or immediacy of the latter.

In contrast, people would label as *implicit* the representation of the letter "A" in a run-length encoded bitmap representation of a page of text, or the representation of the approach velocity of an oncoming car in the frequency difference between the outgoing and incoming radar signals in a police speed trap, or (as suggested above) the representation of a fact by the explicit representation of a different set of facts, when the first is a distant entailment of the latter set. In each case the representational element is either itself relationally encoded, or else one of its two "consequent" relations, instead of being direct, is in turn complex and relational; between the structure and its content, or between the structure and the inferential role relevant to that content.

Assuming this reconstruction points in even roughly the right direction, let's go back to L&F. To start with, it makes sense of why L&F contrast explicit with "compiled" representations (since compilation often removes the structural autonomy of distinct source elements), and of their assumption that facts can be represented in relative independence: simple content and simple causal consequence, neither depending much on what else is represented, or how anything else is used. As will become clearer in a moment, this theme of modularity, directness, and relative independence characterizes L&F's proposal at a variety of levels. (I'm prepared to argue that L&F's proposal won't work, but I'm not claiming it doesn't have a degree of integrity.)

What about the flanking views? At the level of whole systems, formal logic is paradigmatically explicit (in spite of the "implicit" treatment of entailment mentioned above—what matters is that the explicit representations are the ones that are theoretically analyzed). If forced at theoretical gun-point to produce an "explicit representation" of the structure of Abelian groups, for example, it's hard to imagine a better place to start than with first-order axiomatization. And yet, in part as indicated by their repeated desire for a relatively minimal role for deduction and complex reasoning (see Question 8, below), L&F are even more committed to explicit representation than adherents of logic. That is to endorse a very serious amount of explicitness indeed.

The embedded view? It would be hard to argue that explicit representation isn't powerful, but, as discussions of the next questions will suggest, it carries a price of potentially unwarranted definiteness, premature categorization, and resistance to some sorts of recognition. My main dispute, however, isn't over its utility. Rather, I question whether, if explicit representation is indeed an identifiable subspecies (the only construal on which it could matter at all), it is the only sort that's required. That is something I wouldn't want to admit without a lot more evidence. In particular, I worry that a system comprised only of explicit representations would be fatally disconnected from the world its representations are about.[13]

Question 2. Is representational content	Logic	L&F	EC
contextual (situated)	no	no	yes

Under the general rubric of the term "situated" ("situated language" [8], "situated action" [67], "situated automata" [58]) a variety of people have recently argued that adequate theory cannot ignore the crucial role that context plays in determining the reference and semantic import of virtually all linguistic and other intentional phenomena. Context is obviously important in interpreting "now", "tomorrow", and "it's raining"; and in determining the temporal implications of tense. In its full glory, however, the situated claim goes much deeper: that you can't ultimately understand anything except as located in the circumstances in which it occurs. Linguistic evidence is impressive. In spite of the assumption that is sometimes made that proper names function essentially as logical constants, it's common sense that "Tom", "Dick" and "Harry" in fact refer to *whatever people in the appropriate context have those names*. Even "1989" isn't absolute; when it appears in the *New York Times*, it usually refers to the Gregorian calendar, not the Julian or Islamic one.

But language has no patent on contextual dependence. Computational examples are equally common. When you button "QUIT" on the Macintosh file menu, for example, the process that quits is *the one that is running*. The simple e-mail address "JOHN", without an appended "@HOST" suffix, identifies the account of whoever has that username *on the machine from which the original message is sent*. If I set the alarm to ring at 5:00 p.m., it will ring at 5:00 p.m. *today*. The machine language instruction "RETURN" returns control from the *current stack frame*. If you button "EJECT", it ejects the floppy *that is currently in the drive*.

Some quick comments on what contextual dependence isn't. First, none of the cited examples should be read as implying that terms like "now", proper names (or their internal analogues), machine instructions, and the like are ambiguous. There's no reason (other than a stubborn retention of prior theory) to treat the contextual dependence of reference as a matter of ambiguity. Second, though related, the present issue of contextuality cross-cuts the explicit/implicit distinction of question 1 ("here" and "now" are explicit representations of contextually determined states, for example, whereas QUIT and RETURN represent their contextually determined arguments implicitly, if at all). Third, as with many semantical phenomena, representations typically have (contextually dependent) contents; it's a category error to assume that those contents have to be computed. Fourth—and even more important— contents not only don't have to be, but typically can't be, determined solely by inspecting the surrounding *representational* context. In the "QUIT" case, for example, the process to be killed is instantiated on the machine, but that doesn't imply that it is represented. Similarly, in the e-mail case, the host machine plays a role in determining the relevant addressee, but the ego- centricity obtains in virtue of the machine's existence, not in virtue of any self-reference. And in the use of Gregorian dates, or in the fact that "1:27 p.m." (on my word processor, today) refers to 1:27 p.m. Pacific Standard Time, not only is the relevant context not *represented* by the machine, *it is not a fact within the machine at all*, having instead to do with where and when the machine is located in the world.[14]

Here's a way to say it: the sum total of facts relevant to the semantical valuation of a system's representational structures (i.e., the relevant context) will always outstrip the sum total of facts that that system represents (i.e., its content).

What, then, of the three proposals under review? Traditional logic, again paradigmatically, ignores context.[15] The logical viewpoint, to use a phrase of Nagel's [50], embodies the historical imagination's closest approximation yet to a "view from nowhere". Contextual influence isn't completely gone, of course—it still plays a role in assigning properties and relations to predicates, for example, in selecting the "intended interpretation". But as far as possible logical theories ignore that ineliminable residue.

L&F are like the logicians: they ignore context too. *And they have to.* Context isn't a simple thing—something they don't happen to talk about much, but could add in, using their touted mechanism for coping with representational inadequacy: namely, adding another slot. On the contrary, their insistence that their "knowledge base" project can proceed without concern as to time, place, or even kind of use, is essentially an endorsement of a-contextual representation.

For my part (i.e., from the embedded perspective). I think the situated school is on to something. Something important. Even at its most objective, intelligence should be viewed as a "view from somewhere" [65]. Take an almost limiting case: suppose you were to ask L&F's system how many years it would be before the world's population reached 7 billion people? Without a contextual grounding for the present tense, it would have no way to answer, because it wouldn't know what time it was.[16]

Question 3. Does meaning depend on use?

$$\left(\begin{array}{ccc} \text{Logic} & \text{L\&F} & \text{EC} \\ \boxed{\text{no} \qquad \text{no}} & & \text{yes} \end{array} \right)$$

This question gets at a much more radical claim than the last. The idea is not only that content or final interpretation of a representational structure (sentence, frame, whatever) depends on the situation in which it is used, but that what the structure means can't be separated from the whole complex of inferential, conversational, social, and other purposes to which it is put.[17]

It's one thing to say that the word "now", for example, or the state of an internal clock, refers to the time of its use; that doesn't bring purpose or function into the picture. But if you go on to say that the question of whether such a use refers to a particular recent event can't be determined except in light of the whole social pattern of activity in which it plays a role (which, as I'll admit in a moment, I believe), then, from the point of view of developing a (middle-realm) theory, you are taking on a much larger task.

To see, this, consider a series of examples. First, assume that the term "bank" is ambiguous, as between financial institutions and edges of rivers. Although neither L&F nor I have talked about ambiguity, that shouldn't be read as implying that it is trivial. Still, let's assume it can somehow be handled. Second, the word "today", as noted above, is also referentially plural—in the sense of being usable to refer to many different things, depending (typically) on the time of utterance. But "today" is indexical, not ambiguous (here's a discriminating rule of thumb: ambiguity, but not indexicality, leads to different dictionary entries[18]). As a consequence, its referential plurality (unlike that of a truly ambiguous term) can't be resolved at the parsing or internalization stage—so the indexicality will be inherited by the corresponding internal data structure. Third, and different from both, is Winograd's example of "water" [72, pp. 55–56], as used for example in the question "Is there any water in the refrigerator?". It is this last kind of example I mean to describe as having *use-dependent meaning*. In particular, depending on a whole variety of things, the word in context could mean any of a million things: Is there literally any H_2O present in the metal-contained volume (such as in the cells of the eggplant)? Is there any potable liquid? Has any condensation formed on the walls? . . . The point is that there is no reason to suppose these variations in meaning could (or should) be systematically catalogued as properties of the *word* (as was suggested for the referent of "today"). Instead, Winograd suggests (and I agree) something more like this: the meaning of "water" is as much determined by the meaning of the discourse as the meaning of the discourse is determined by the meaning of "water".

Nothing in this view is incoherent, or even (at least necessarily) repellent to systematic analysis: imagine that semantical interpretation (including the non-effective semantical relations to the world) works in the cycle of a relaxation algorithm, influenced by a variety of forces, including the actual participatory involvement of the agent in the subject matter. Still, use-dependent meaning does pose problems for a theorist. Take just two examples. First, it undermines the very coherence of the notion of sound (or complete) inference: those concepts make sense only if the semantic values of representational formulae are conceptually independent of their role in reasoning. The problem isn't just that there is no obvious model-theoretic analysis, since it is unclear what model-theoretic structure would be assigned to the term "water". Or even, setting model theory aside, that it is unclear what a well-defined semantical value for such a term could be. More seriously, soundness is fundamentally a claim that the use of a term or predicate has respected its independently given semantical value. Making interpretation dependent on use, at least at first blush, therefore gives one every reason to suppose that the notion of soundness is rendered circular, hence vacuous.[19]

Second, it is a likely consequence of this view that the meaning or significance of a complex representational structure won't be able to be derived, systematically, from the "bottom up", but will instead have to be arrived at in some more holistic way. It challenges, in other words, the traditional view that semantics can be "compositionally" defined on top of a base set of atomic values.[20] I.e., the point isn't just that the interpretation of a sentence (its propositional value) is sometimes determined by mutually interlocking constraints established by various sentential constituents (as suggested in indexical cases, such as for the pronoun structure in "though Jim didn't like her, Mary was perfectly happy with him"), say by some sort of relaxation method. Rather, a deeper claim is being made; that the very meaning of the parts of a discourse can depend on the interpretation of the whole. For example, suppose the clouds clear, and you make a comment about the relentless sun. It is easy to imagine that I understand the meaning of "relentless"[21] in virtue of knowing what you're talking about, rather than the other way around. And if it is whole sentences that connect with situations, this may have to be done not bottom-up in terms of the representational constituents, but if anything top-down.

None of this suggests that representation, or interpretation, is impossible. What it does bring into question are the assumptions on which such a system should be built, including for example the inferential viability of a system without any access to the interpretation of its representational structures—without, that is to say, *participating* in the subject matters about which it *reasons* (one way in which to resolve the obvious difficulty raised by the statement just made: that an agent knows what is being said other than through the vehicle of the saying). But I'll leave some of these speculations until a later question.

For the time being, note merely that logic avoids this "meaning-depends-on-use" possibility like the plague. In fact the "use = representation + inference" aphorism reflects exactly the opposite theoretical bias: that representation (hence meaning) is an independent module in the intentional whole.

Once again, L&F's position is similar: nothing in their paper suggests they are prepared to make this radical a move. At one point they do acknowledge a tremendous richness in lexical significance, but after claiming this is all metaphor (which typically implies there is a firm "base case"), they go on to assert, without argument, that "these layers of analogy and metaphor eventually 'bottom out' at physical—somatic—primitives: up, down, forward, back, pain, cold, inside, seeing, sleeping, tasting, growing, containing, moving, making noise, hearing, birth, death, strain, exhaustion, . . . " It's not a list I would want to have responsibility for completing.

More seriously, the integrity of L&F's project *depends* on avoiding use-dependent meaning, for the simple reason that they don't intend to consider use (their words: "you can never be sure in advance how the knowledge already in the system is going to be used, or added to, in the future", which they take as leading directly to the claim that it must be represented explicitly). If we were to take the meaning-depends-on-use stance seriously, we would be forced to conclude that *nothing in their knowledge base means anything*, since no one has yet developed a theory of its use.

I.e., L&F *can't* say yes to this one; it would pull the rug out from under their entire project.

In contrast (and as expected), the embedded view embraces the possibility. Perhaps the best way to describe the tension is in terms of method. A liberal logicist might admit that, in natural language, meaning is sometimes use-dependent in the ways described, but he or she would go on to claim that proper scientific method requires idealizing away from such recalcitrant messiness. My response? That such idealization throws the baby out with the bathwater. Scientific idealization is worth nothing if in the process it obliterates the essential texture of what one hopes to understand. And it is simply my experience that much of the structure of argument and discourse—even, the *raison d'être* of rationality—involves negotiating in an international space where meanings are left fluid by our linguistic and conceptual schemes, ready to be grounded in experience.

	Logic	L&F	EC
Question 4. Is consistency mandated?	yes	no	no

L&F are quite explicit in rejecting an absolute dependence on consistency, to which traditional logical systems are so famously vulnerable. As indicated in the table, this is the first of the dozen questions where they and the embedded view align. That much said, however, it's not clear how deep the similarity goes. In particular, I'm unsure how much solace can be found in their recommendation that one carve the "knowledge base" into separate "buttes", and require each to be locally consistent, with neighbouring buttes maximally coherent. At least it's not clear, once again, without a much better intermediate theory.[22]

Fundamentally, the problem is that consistency is a relational property—the consistency of a set of sentences stands or falls on the set as a whole, not on an individual basis. This means that some relations between or among sentences (or frames) will have to be used as a basis for the partition (and to tie the resulting "buttes" together). Call these the system's *organizational principles*. Without them (on any remotely reasonable assumptions of error rates, dependence, etc.) the number of possible different configurations meeting their structural requirements would be intractably immense.

Furthermore, the organizational principles can't themselves be defined in terms of consistency; organizing a database *by* internal consistency would be crazy. Rather, I take it that what L&F really want is to be able to demonstrate (local) consistency for a database organized according to some other metric. What other metric? Surely only one makes sense: according to similarity or integrity of subject matter. *X* should be stored next to *Y*, in other words, because of the presence of (semantic) compatibility, not just the absence of (syntactic) incompatibility. Otherwise, descriptions of national politics might nestle up to lists of lemon meringue pie ingredients, but be kept separated from other statements about Washington policy making—so that things ended up together not because they agreed, but because they didn't have anything to do with one another.

So adequate organization will need to be defined in terms of a notion of subject matter. But where are we to find a theory of that? The problem is similar to that of representation in general: no one has one. The issue comes up in natural language attempts to identify topic, focus, etc. in theories of discourse (see. e.g., [30]), and in some of the semantical work in situation theory [3, 5]. But these are at best a start. Logic famously ducks the question. And informal attempts aren't promising: if my experience with the KRL project can be taken as illustrative [10], the dominant result of any such attempt is to be impressed with how seamlessly everything seems to relate to everything else.

When all is said and done, in other words, it is unclear how L&F plan to group, relate, and index their frames. They don't say, of course, and (in this case) no implicit principles can be inferred. But the answer is going to matter a lot—and not just in order to avoid inconsistency, but for a host of other reasons as well, including search, control strategy, and driving their "analogy" mechanism. Conclusion? That viable indexing (a daunting problem for any project remotely like L & F's), though different from consistency, is every bit as much in need as anything else of "middle-realm" analysis.

And as for consistency itself, we can summarize things as follows. Logic depends on it. L & F retain it locally, but reject it globally, without proposing a workable basis for their "partitioning" proposal. As for the embedded view (as mentioned in footnote 22) the standard notion of consistency doesn't survive its answer to question 3 (about use-dependent meaning). That doesn't mean, however, that I won't have to replace it with something analogous. In particular, I have no doubt that *some* notion of semantic viability, integrity, respect for the fact that the world (not the representation) holds the weight—something like that will be required for any palatable intentional system. Important as contextual setting may be, no amount of "use", reasoning processes, or consensual agreement can rescue a speaker from the potential of being wrong. More seriously, I believe that what is required are global *coordination conditions*—conditions that relate thinking, action, perception, the passing of the world, etc., in something of an indissoluble whole. To say more now, however—especially to assume that logic's notion can be incrementally extended, for example by being locally proscribed—would be to engage in tunneling of my own (but see [65]).

	Logic	L&F	EC
Question 5. Does the system use a single representational scheme?	yes	yes	no

Tucked into a short paragraph of L&F's Section 9 is their response to the charge that one might encounter representational difficulties in trying to capture all of human knowledge. Their strategy is simple: "when something proves awkward to represent, add new kinds of slots to make it compactly representable". In fact they apparently now have over 5000 kinds. If only representation were so simple.

Several issues are involved. To start with, there is the question of the expressive adequacy of their chosen representational system—frames, slots, and values. Especially in advance, I see no reason to believe (nor argument to convince me) that mass nouns, plurals, or images should succumb to this scheme in any straightforward way—or, to turn it upside down, to suppose that, if an adequate solution were worked out within a frame-and-slot framework, that the framework would contribute much to the essence of the solution. Frames aren't rendered adequate, after all, by encoding other representational schemes within them.[23]

Furthermore, one wonders whether any single representational framework—roughly, a representation system with a single structural grammar and interpretation scheme—will prove sufficient for all the different kinds of representation an intelligent agent will need. Issues range from the tie-in to motor and perceptual processing (early vision doesn't seem to be frame-like, for example; is late vision?) to the seeming conflict between verbal, imagistic, and other flavours of memory and imagination. You might view the difficulties of describing familiar faces in words, or of drawing pictures of plots or reduction arguments, as problems of externalizing a single, coherent, mentalese, but I suspect they really indicate that genuine intelligence depends on multiple representations, in spite of the obvious difficulties of cross-representational translation.

Certainly our experience with external representations supports this conclusion. Consider architecture: it is simply impossible not to be impressed with the maze of blueprints, written specifications, diagrams, topological maps, pictures, icons, annotations, etc., vital to any large construction project. And the prospect of reducing them all to any single representational scheme (take your choice) is daunting to the point of impossibility. Furthermore, there are reasons for the range of type: information easily captured in one (the shape of topological contours, relevant to the determination of building site, e.g.) would be horrendously inefficient if rendered in another (say, English).[24]

The same holds true of computation. It is virtually constitutive of competent programming practice to be able to select (from a wide range of possibilities) a particular representational scheme that best supports an efficient and consistent implementation of desired behaviour. Imagine how restrictive it would be if, instead of simply enumerating them in a list, a system had to record N user names in an unordered conjunction of N^2 first-order claims:

$$(\exists\, x_1 \mid \text{user}(x_1)) \wedge (\exists\, x_2 \mid \text{user}(x_2)) \wedge \cdots \wedge (\exists x_n \mid \text{user}(x_n))$$

$$\wedge\, ((x_1 \neq x_2) \wedge (x_1 \neq x_3) \wedge \cdots \wedge (x_1 \neq (x_n))$$

$$\wedge\, ((x_2 \neq x_3) \wedge \cdots) \wedge \cdots \wedge ((x_{n-1} \neq x_n))$$

Or how equally untenable it would be to prohibit a reasoning system from using existentials, or to limit it to domains where uniqueness of names could always be assumed. Yet one or other options would be forced by commitment to a "single scheme". Similarly, it's as unthinkable to prohibit display hardware from using bitmaps, in favour of frame-and-slot representations of each illuminated spot, as to force all representation into a bit-per-pixel mold.

Against all such considerations, however, logic and L&F are once again similar in pledging allegiance to a single representational scheme. As representative of the embedded view, I'll vote for variety.

Question 6. Are there only discrete propositions (no continuous representation, images, . . .)?	Logic	L&F	EC
	yes	yes	no

If pressed to represent continuous phenomena, L&F would presumably entertain real numbers as slot values, but that barely scratches the surface of the differences between discrete representations like formulae in a formal language, and various easily imagined forms of continuity, vagueness, indeterminacy, analogues, etc. And it is not just that we can imagine them; anything like real intelligence will have to deal with phenomena like this. We have the whole messy world to capture, not just the distilled, crystalline structure of Platonic mathematics.

In assessing the typology of representation, the distinction between discrete (digital) and continuous (analogue[25]) representations is sometimes given pride of place, as if that were the ultimate division, with all other possibilities subcategorized below it. But other just as fundamental divisions cross-cut this admittedly important one. For example, there is a question of whether a representation rests on a conception or set of formulated categories, or is in some way pre- or non-conceptual (terminology from [15]). The natural tendency, probably because of the prevalence of written language, is to assume that discrete goes with conceptual, continuous with non-conceptual, but this isn't true. The use of ocean buoys to demarcate treacherous water, for example, is presumably discrete but non-conceptual: intonation patterns to adjust the meanings of words ("what an *extraordinary* outfit") are at least plausibly both continuous and conceptual. Or consider another distinction: whether the base or "ur-elements" on which a representation is founded have determinate edges or boundaries. Both discrete and continuous objects of the sort studied in mathematics (the integers, the real line, and even Gaussian distributions and probability densities) are determinate, in the sense that questions about them have determinate answers. It's unclear, however, in questions about when tea-time ends, or about what adolescence is, or about exactly how many clouds there were when you poked your head out of your tent and said, with complete confidence, "there are lots of clouds today"—it's unclear in such cases whether there are determinate answers at all. The problem isn't an epistemic one, about incomplete knowledge, or a linguistic one, about the exact meanings of the words. The point is that the metaphysical facts just aren't there—nor is there any reason to suppose they should be there—to support a clean, black-and-white distinction. The competent use of the English plural, that is to say, doesn't require the existence of a denumerable base set of discrete elements. I am convinced that this distinction between phenomena that have sharp boundaries (support determinate answers) and those that don't is more profound and more consequential for AI than the distinction between discrete and continuous instances of each variety.

Modern logic, needless to say, doesn't deal with foundational indeterminacy. Nor are we given any reason to suppose that L&F want to take it on. One wonders, however, whether our lack of understanding of how relative certainty can arise on top of a foundationally vague base (no one would deny that there were lots of clouds outside that tent, after all) may not be the most important obstacle to the development of systems that aren't brittle in the way that even L&F admit we're limited to today.

Question 7. Do the representations capture all that matters?

	Logic	L&F	EC
	yes	yes	no

The situated view of representation cited earlier rests on the tenet that language, information, and representation "bridge the gap", in Perry's terms,[26] between the state of the user(s) of the representation, and the state of the world being referred to. It's a position that accords with a familiar view of language as dynamic action, rather than simply as static description. And it has among its more extreme consequences the realization that not all of what matters about a situation need be captured, at least in the traditional sense, in the meanings of its constituent representations.

For example, if someone simply yells "fire!", then some of what matters, including your understanding of what fire is, may be contributed by the surrounding situation, possibly even including the impinging thermal radiation. Call this totality of what matters—i.e., everything relevant to an assessment of whether the communication worked properly—its *full significance*. The claim, then, is that *the full significance of an intentional action can outstrip its content*. Facts of embodiment, of being there, of action, of experience, can, along with the content, influence the net or intended result.

To understand what this means, consider three things that it doesn't. First, it isn't merely a repetition of the claim made in discussing question 2: that conceptual content isn't uniquely determined by the type of representation used, but is partially determined by the context of its use. Nor, second, is it a replay of the stronger claim made in discussing question 3: that even the meanings—not just contents! (see footnote 17)—of words or internal structures may depend on their actual use. Although both of these involve use and context in a variety of ways, they remain claims about the relation between a representation and its semantic value. The current claim is stronger: that the full significance of an intentional act will outstrip even the situated semantic value of the representational ingredients constitutive of it, no matter how indexical, use-dependent, or situated a notion of content you care to come up with.

Even this last way of putting it, however, isn't strong enough, because it allows room for a third possible stance, stronger than the previous two (i.e., stronger than the embedded responses to questions 2 and 3), but still weaker than I have in mind here. In particular, someone might agree that an intentional action's full significance lies outside the content of the particular act itself, but go on to look for that additional contribution in the content of other representational structures. Thus, in determining the significance of "fire", you might look to other representations already present in the agent's head, or to conclusions that could be (quickly) drawn from things already represented. For example, you might expect to find the escape heuristic (that if someone shouts "fire!" it's good to get out of the way) represented in a previously stored internal frame.

I don't disagree that this can happen; in fact I take it as almost obvious (what else is inference for, after all?). However, I intend with this seventh question to get at a stronger position yet: that the full significance of an intentional action (not just a communicative one) can crucially involve *non-representational* phenomena, as well as representational ones. I.e., it is a claim that the millennial story about intelligence won't consist solely of a story about representation, but will inevitably weave that story together with analyses of other, non-representational aspects of an intentional agent. Some of these other ingredient stories will describe salient facts of embodiment (possibly even including adrenaline levels), but they will talk about other things as well, including genuine *participation* in represented subject matters,[27] and the internal *manifestation* (rather than *representation*) of intentionally important properties. Some modern roboticists, for example, argue that action results primarily from the dynamical properties of the body; the representational burden to be shouldered by the "mind", as it were, may consist only of adjustments or tunings to those non-representational capacities (see, e.g., [55, 56]). Rhythm may similarly as much be exhibited as encoded in the intelligent response to music. Or even take a distilled example from LISP: when a system responds with the numeral "3" to the query "(LENGTH '(A B C))", it does so by interacting with non-representational facts, since (if implemented in the ordinary way) the list '(A B C) will *have* a cardinality, but not one that is *represented*.

Distinguishing representational from non-representational in any careful way will require a better theory of representation than any we yet have.[28] Given such a story, it will become possible to inquire about the extent to which intelligence requires access to these non-formulated (non-formulable?) aspects of the subject matter. Although it's premature to take a definite stand, my initial sense is that there is every reason to suppose (at least in the human case) that it does. Introspection, common sense, and even considerations of efficient evolutionary design would all suggest that inferential mechanisms should avail themselves of any relevant available resources, whether those have arisen through representational channels, or otherwise. If this is true, then it follows that a system lacking any of those other channels—a system without the right kind of embodiment, for example— won't be able to reason in the same way we do. And so much the worse, I'd be willing to bet, for it.

How do our three players stand on this issue? I take it as obvious that L&F require what logic assumes: that representation has to capture all that matters, for the simple reason that there isn't anything else around. For L&F, in other words, facts that can't be described might as well not be true, whether about fire, sleep, internal thrashing, or the trials of committee work. They are forced to operate under a maxim of "inexpressible → irrelevant".

In contrast, as I've already indicated, I take seriously the fact that we are beaten up by the world—and not only in intentional ways. I see no reason to assume that the net result of our structural coupling to our environment— even that part of that coupling salient to intelligent deliberation—is exhausted by its representational record. And if that is so, then it seems overwhelmingly likely that the full structure of intelligence will rely on that residue of maturation and embodiment. So I'll claim no less for an embedded computer.

Here's a way to put it. L&F believe that intelligence can rest entirely on the meaning of *representations*, without any need for correlated, *non-representational experience*. On the other hand, L&F also imagine their system starting to read and distill things on its own. What will happen, however, if the writers tacitly rely on non-representational actions on the part of the reader? The imagined system wouldn't be able to understand what it was reading. For example, there is no way in which L&F's system would ever be able to understand the difference between right and left.[29]

Question 8. Are reasoning and inference central?

	Logic	L&F	EC
	yes	yes	yes

When logicians develop axiomatic accounts of set theory, criteria of elegance and parsimony push towards a minimal number of axioms—typically on the order of a dozen—from which an infinite number of truths follow. It's a general truth: economy of statement is often a hallmark of penetrating insight.

No one, however, expects distilled scientific theories alone to sustain complete, workaday, general-purpose reasoning. It is obvious that any reasonable problem solver (like any imaginable person), rather than deriving all its conclusions from first principles, will depend on a rich stock of facts and heuristics, derived results and rules of thumb—to say nothing of a mass of a-theoretic but relevant particulars (such as who it's talking to). So we should expect general intelligence to rest on a relatively high ratio of relevant truths to foundational axioms, especially in the face of resource-bounded processing, complex or just plain messy subject matters, and other departures from theoretical purity.

Nonetheless, you can't literally know everything. No matter how knowledgeable, an agent will still have to think in order to deal with the world *specifically*—to conclude that if today is Tuesday then tomorrow must be Wednesday, for example (derived from the general fact that Wednesdays follow Tuesdays), or to figure out whether your friend can walk from Boston to Cambridge, not otherwise having heard of your friend. Universal instantiation and modus ponens may not be all there is to thought, but without some such faculty a system would be certifiably CPU-dead.[30] And instantiating universals is only the beginning. "Inference" includes not only deduction, but induction, abduction, inference to the best explanation, concept formation, hypothesis testing—even sheer speculation and creative flights of fancy. It can hardly be argued that some such semantically coordinated processing[31] is essential to intelligence.

It shouldn't be surprising, then, that inference is the one issue on which all three positions coincide—logic, L&F, and EC. But superficial agreement doesn't imply deep uniformity. There are questions, in each case, as to what that commitment means.

To see this, note that any inference regimen must answer to at least two demands. The first is famous: though mechanically defined on the form or structure of the representational ingredients,[32] inference must make semantic sense (that's what makes it *inference*, rather than ad hoc symbol mongering). There simply must be some semantic justification, that is to say—some way to see how the "formal" symbol manipulation coordinates with semantic value or interpretation. Second, there is a question of finitude. One cannot forget, when adverting to inference as the mechanism whereby a finite stock of representations can generate an indefinite array of behaviour, that the inference mechanism itself must be compact (and hence productive). The deep insight, that is to say, is not that reasoning allows a limited stock of information to generate an unlimited supply of answers, but that a synchronously finite system can manifest diachronically indefinite semantic behaviour.

Logic, of course, supplies a clear answer to the first demand (in its notion of soundness), but responds only partially to the second (hence the dashed lines around its positive answer). A collection of inferential schemata are provided—each demonstrably truth-preserving (the first requirement), and each applicable to an indefinite set of sentences (the second). But, as AI knows so well, something is still missing: the higher-level strategies and organizational principles necessary to knit these atomic steps together into an appropriate rational pattern.[33] Being able to reason, that is to say, isn't just the ability to take the right atomic steps; it means knowing how to think in the large—how to argue, how to figure things out, how to think creatively about the world. Traditional logic, of course, doesn't address these questions. Nor—and this is the important point—is there any a priori reason to believe that that larger inferential demand can be fully met within the confines of logic's peculiar formal and semantic conventions.

On the other hand—and this takes us to the embedded view—once one moves beyond logic's familiar representational assumptions (explicit, a-contextual representation, and so forth), no one has yet presented an inferential model that meets the first demand. To accept the embedded answers to questions 1–7 is thus to take on a substantial piece of homework: developing, from the ground up, a semantically coordinated and rationally justifiable notion of inference itself. This is just one of the reasons why the embedded perspective is still emerging.

Nonetheless, important steps are being taken in this direction. The development of a contextually sensitive model of inference (based on a semantic notion of information, rather than symbolic form) is constitutive of Barwise and Etchemendy's work on situation theory, for example [6, 7]. Similarly, in the situated automata work of Rosenschein, a similarly non-syntactic notion of inference is analyzed in terms of a machine's carrying information relative to the structure of its embedding environment.[34] In a somewhat different vein, I have argued that an embedded notion of inference will ultimately be as relevant to clocks and other transducers as to sentential transformation [64]. It is also becoming clear that even more traditional (i.e., linguistic) forms of inference will as much involve the preservation of reference across a change in context, as the more familiar preservation of truth across a change in subject matter.[35] Important as these new thrusts are, however, they are still just early steps.

What about L&F? They have two options. To the extent that they agree with the present characterization of their position, vis-à-vis questions 1–7, they would probably want to avail themselves of logic's notion of inference. For reasons discussed earlier, however, this isn't enough: they would still have to take a stand on the relationship between truth-preserving logical entailment and the appropriate structure of rational belief revision, for example (see footnote 33), to say nothing of providing a finite account of an appropriate set of high-level control strategies, in order to provide a complete answer to the second demand. On the other hand, to the extent that they feel confined by logic's stringent representational restrictions (as they admit they do, for example, at least with respect to its insistence on full consistency—see question 4), and want to embrace something more like the embedded view, then they too must answer to the much larger demand: of not simply presenting their inferential mechanism (let alone claiming to have embraced 20 different ones), but of explaining what their very notion of inference is.

Question 9. Are participation and action crucial?

Logic	L&F	EC
no	no	yes

Reasoning is a form of action. Earlier I commented on L&F's relegation of reasoning to a secondary status by their treatment of it as search, their suggestion that the "control" problem is largely solved, and their claim that with enough "knowledge" deep reasoning will be largely unnecessary.

But reasoning isn't the only kind of action that (at least in humans) has to be coordinated with representation. If you wander around Kyoto for the first time, poking your head into small shops, stopping for tea on the Philosopher's Walk, and gradually making your way back to the ryokan by something like dead reckoning, then your emergent conceptual understanding of the layout of the city must be constantly coordinated with your on-going but non-conceptual bodily movements. For example, if you remember that the hotel is somewhere off to your right, and then turn in that direction, you need to know that it is now roughly in front of you. In a similar way, we all need to know that tomorrow today will be "yesterday". Representations that lead to action often have to be revised in light of that very action's being taken.

Coordination management, as I will call this indissoluble blend of adjust-ment, feedback, action, belief revision, perception, dance, etc., arises in many corners of AI, ranging from planning and robotics to systems dealing with their own internal state (reflection and meta-level reasoning). Nor is AI the first discipline to recognize its importance: philosophers of science, and theorists of so-called "practical reasoning", have always realized the importance—and difficulty—of connecting thinking and doing. Students of perception, too, and of robotics, wrestle with their own versions of the coordination problem.

Curiously enough, even L&F, although they don't embrace a participatory stance, won't entirely be able to avoid it. Though their system will clearly shun the external world as much as possible,[36] it will still have to grapple with internal participation, if they go ahead with their proposal to encode (at the meta-level) such control knowledge as turns out genuinely to be needed. For example, suppose someone adds the following rule: that if the system uses any search strategy for more than 10 seconds without making definite pro-gress, it should abandon that approach and try an alternative. Obeying this injunction requires various kinds of participation: recognizing that you have wasted 10 seconds (perception); stopping doing so (action); registering what it was that you were doing (perception); selecting a plausible alternative (inference); setting that new goal in motion (action); "letting go" of the meta-level deliberations (action on inference). Introspection and reflection might be better described as varieties of self-*involvement* than of self-*reference* (in spite of my "Varieties of Self-Reference" [63]; see also [65]).[37]

So we end this one with a curious tally. In virtue of its utterly disconnected stance, and of *not being a computational system*, logic is singularly able to ignore action and subject matter participation. On the embedded side, I take participatory connections with the world as not just important, but as essen-tial. In fact the embedded view could almost be summed up in the following claim:

> *Participation in the subject matter is partially constitutive of intelligence.*

When all is said and done, in other words, I believe the term "intelligent" should be predicated of an integrated way of being that includes both thought and action, not simply an abstract species of disconnected symbol manipulation. This may contravene current theoretical assumptions, but I suspect it is consonant with ordinary common sense. Frankly, I don't see how you could believe a system could comprehend all of consensus reality without being able to understand "See you tomorrow!".[38]

Between these two, L&F occupy a somewhat unstable middle ground. I have listed them with logic, since that's where their claims go; there is no hint that they envisage tackling issues of coordination. On the other hand, they will have to confront coordination management merely in order to get their system to turn over, quite apart from whether it manifests any thing I would call intelligence.

Question 10. Is physical embodiment important?	Logic	L&F	EC
	no	no	yes

The authors of the mathematical theory of computability claimed as a great victory their elevation of the subject of computation from messy details of physical implementation and fallible mechanism onto a pure and abstract plane. And the prime results of recursive function theory, including the famous proofs of undecidability, genuinely didn't seem to rely on any such implementational details. Modern programmers don't typically traffic in recursive function theory in any very conscious way, but they still accept the legacy of a computational level of analysis separate from (and possibly not even theoretically reducible to[39]) the physical level at which one understands the underlying physical substrate.

More recently, however, especially with the increasing realization that relative computability is as important as (if not more important than) the absolute computability of the 1930s, the story is growing murkier. Though it treats its subject matter abstractly, complexity theory still deals with something called time and space; it's not entirely clear what relation those rather abstract notions bear to the space and time of everyday experience (or even to those of physics). At least with regard to time, though, real (non-abstract) temporal properties of computation are obviously important. Whether differences among algorithms are measured in minutes, milliseconds, or abstract "unit operations", the time they take when they run is the same stuff that I spend over lunch. And the true spatial arrangement of integrated circuits—not just an abstracted notion of space—plays an increasing role in determining architectures.

Although it isn't clear where this will all lead, it does allow the question to be framed of whether considerations of physical embodiment impinge on the analysis of a given computational system. For traditional logic, of course, the answer is *no*; it is as pure an exemplar as anything of the abstract view of computation and representation. And once again L&F's stance is similar: nothing suggests that they, along with most of the formal tradition, won't ignore such issues.

Again the embedded view is different. I am prepared to argue that physical constraints enter computational thinking in a variety of familiar places. For one thing, I have come to believe that what (in a positive vein[40]) we call the "formality" of computation—the claim, for example, that proof procedures rely solely on the formal properties of the expressions they manipulate— amounts in the end to neither more nor less than "whatever can be physically realized in a causally efficacious manner".[41] But this is not the only place where physical realization casts its shadow. Consider one other example: the notion of locality that separates doubly-linked lists from more common singly-linked ones, or that distinguishes object-oriented from function-based programming languages. Locality, fundamentally, is a physical notion, having to do with genuine metric proximity. The question is whether the computational use is just a metaphor, or whether the "local access" that a pointer can provide into an array is metaphysically dependent on the locality of the underlying physics. As won't surprise anyone, the embedded viewpoint endorses the latter possibility.

Question 11. Does the system support "original" semantics?	Logic	L&F	EC
	no	no	yes

It has often been pointed out that books and encyclopedias derive their semantics or connection to what they're about from the people that use them. The analogous question can be asked about computers: whether the interpretations of the symbol structures they use are in any sense "authentic" or "original" to the computers themselves, or whether computational states have their significance only through human attribution (see, e.g., [17; 31, pp. 32ff; 60].

The question is widely accepted, but no one has proposed a really good theory of what is required for semantical originality, so not a whole lot more can be said. Still, some of the themes working their way through this whole set of questions suggest that this issue of originality may be relevant not only for philosophical reasons but also for purposes of adequate inference and reasoning. In particular, if the only full-blooded connection to subject matter is through external users, then it follows that a system won't be able to avail itself of that connection in carrying out its processes of symbol manipulation, reasoning, or inference. If, on the other hand, the semantic connection is autonomous (as one can at least imagine it is, for example, for a network mail system that not only represents facts about network traffic, but also sends and receives real mail), then the chances of legitimate inference may go up.[42]

So the question should be read as one of whether the way of looking at the system, in each case, points towards a future in which systems begin to "own" their semantic interpretations—if still in a clunky and limited way, then at least with a kind of proto-originality.

Even that vague a formulation is sufficient to corral the votes—and to produce another instance of what is emerging as the recurring pattern. Like logic, L&F neither address nor imagine their system possessing anything like the wherewithal to give its frames and slots autonomous referential connection with the world. In fact something quite else suggests itself. Given the paucity of inference they imagine, the heavy demands on indexing schemes, and the apparent restriction of interaction to console events, L&F's system is liable to resemble nothing so much as an electric encyclopedia. No wonder its semantics will be derivative.

Now it's possible, of course, that we might actually want an electric encyclopedia. In fact it might be a project worth pursuing—though it would require a major and revealing revision of both goals and procedure. Note that L&F, on the current design, retain only the formal data structures they generate, discarding the natural language articles, digests, etc., used in its preparation. Suppose, instead, they were to retain all those English entries, thick with connotation and ineffable significance, *and use their data structures and inference engines as an active indexing scheme*. Forget intelligence completely, in other words; take the project as one of constructing the world's largest hypertext system, with CYC functioning as a radically improved (and active) counterpart for the Dewey decimal system. Such a system might facilitate what numerous projects are struggling to implement: reliable, content-based searching and indexing schemes for massive textual databases. CYC's inference schemes would facilitate the retrieval of articles on related topics, or on the target subject matter using different vocabulary. And note, too, that it would exploit many current AI techniques, especially those of the "explicit representation" school.

But L&F wouldn't be satisfied; they want their system itself to know what those articles mean, not simply to aid us humans. And it is against that original intention that the embedded view stands out in such stark contrast. With respect to owls, for example, an embedded system is more likely to resemble the creatures themselves than the *Britannica* article describing them. And this, I submit, to return to the question we started with, is the direction in which semantical originality lies.

Question 12. Is room made for a divergence between the representational capacities of theorist and agent?

	Logic	L&F	EC
	no	no	yes

The final question has to do with the relation between the representational capacities of a system under investigation, and the typically much more sophisticated capacities of its designer or theorist. I'll get at this somewhat indirectly, through what I'll call the *aspectual* nature of representation.

It is generally true that if X represents Y, then there is a question of *how* it represents it—or, to put it another way, of how it represents it *as being*. The two phrases "The Big Apple" and "the hub of the universe" can both be used to represent New York, but the latter represents it as something that the former does not. Similarly, "the MX missile" and Reagan's "the Peacemaker".

The "represent *as*" idiom is telling. If we hear that someone knew her brother was a scoundrel, but in public *represented him as* a model citizen, then it is safe for us to assume that she possessed the representational capacity to represent him in at least these two ways. More seriously—this is where things can get tricky—we, *qua* theorists, who characterize her, *qua* subject, know what it is to say "as a scoundrel", or "as a citizen". We know because we too can represent things as scoundrels, as citizens, and as a myriad other things as well. And we assume, in this example, that our conceptual scheme and her conceptual scheme overlap, so that we can get at the world in the way that she does. So long as they overlap, trouble won't arise.[43]

Computers, however, generally don't possess anything remotely like our discriminatory capacities,[44] and as a result, it is a very substantial question for us to know how (from their point of view) they are representing the world as being. For example (and this partly explains McDermott's [49] worries about the wishful use of names), the fact that we use English words to name a computer system's representational structures doesn't imply that the resulting structure represents the world for the computer in the same way as that name represents it for us. Even if you could argue that a KRYPTON node labeled $DETENTE genuinely represented detente, it doesn't follow that it represents it as what we would call detente. It is hard to know how it does represent it as being (for the computer), of course, especially without knowing more about the rest of its representational structures.[45] But one thing seems likely: $DETENTE will mean less for the computer than "detente" means for us.

I suspect that the lure of L&F's project depends in part on their ignoring "as" questions, and failing to distinguish theorists' and agents' conceptual schemes. Or at least this can be said: that they are explicitly committed to not making a distinction between the two. In fact quite the opposite is presumably their aim: what they want, of the system they propose to build, is something that we can interact with, in our own language (English), in order to learn or shore up or extend our own understanding of the world. In order for such interaction to work—and it is entirely representational interaction, of course—the two conceptual schemes will have to be commensurable, on pain of foundering on miscommunication.

Here, though, is the problem. I assume (and would be prepared to argue) that an agent (human or machine) can only carry on an intelligent conversation using words that represent the world in ways that are part of that agent's representational prowess. For an example, consider the plight of a spy. No matter how carefully you try to train such a person to use a term of high-energy physics, or the language of international diplomacy, subsequent conversations with genuine experts are almost sure to be awkward and "unintelligent" (and the spy therefore caught!) unless the spy can genuinely come to register the world in the way that competent users of that word represent the world as being.

It follows, then, that L&F's project depends for its success on the consonance of its and our conceptual schemes. Given that, the natural question to ask is whether the sketch they present of its construction will give it that capacity. Personally, I doubt it, because, like Evans [25], I am convinced that most common words take their aspectual nature not only from their "hook-up" to other words, but from their direct experiential grounding in what they are about. And, as many of the earlier questions have indicated, L&F quite clearly don't intend to give their system that kind of anchoring.

So once again we end up with the standard pattern. Neither traditional logic nor L&F take up such issues, presuming instead on what may be an unwarranted belief of similarity. It is characteristic of the embedded view to take the opposite tack; I don't think we'll ever escape from surprises and charges of brittleness until we take seriously the fact that our systems represent the world differently from us.

4 The logical point of view

No twelve questions, briefly discussed, can exhaust the representational terrain. Still, the general drift is clear. The repeated overlap between L&F and traditional logic betrays L&F's conception of what it is to be an "intelligent system". They must have in mind something similar to the prototypical logic-based theorem prover or question and answer system: the user types in a question and the system types back the answer, or the user types in a statement and the system types T or F, depending on its truth—that kind of thing. The system is conceived of entirely abstractly; it would have to be physically embodied, of course, in order to be typed at, but the level at which it was analyzed (syntax of frames, values of slots, etc.) would abstract away from all such physical considerations. Such a system would not only be analyzed as disembodied, and be entirely disconnected from any of the subject domains that it "knew" about, it would thereby achieve what humans so rarely do: the ability to look out on the world from a completely objective, detached, a-contextual, universal ("from nowhere") vantage point.

As the reader will have guessed, I don't for a minute think such an achievement is possible, for man or machine (or even desirable; at its best intelligence should prepare you for being anywhere, not for being nowhere). But that's not really my point. Here, in the end, is what is most impressive about their paper. When all is said and done, L&F's vision of an intelligent system is remarkably similar to the traditional logical one: a complete axiomatization of the world manipulated by a general purpose inference engine. *The "logicists", after all, never assumed that theorem proving was any substitute for competent axiomatization*; exactly the opposite is argued by McCarthy, Hayes, Hobbs, and others [34–37, 47]. L&F, however, have the distinction of using a much less expressive language (at least as far as we can tell, given that no semantic account seems to be in the cards), and of assuming no definite control regimen. Plus one more thing: unlike any modern logicist writer, they claim they can do the whole thing.

5 Conclusion

To take representing the world seriously (it's world representation, after all, not knowledge representation, that matters for AI) is to embrace a vast space of possibilities. You quickly realize that the intellectual tools developed over the last 100 years (primarily in aid of setting logic and meta-mathematics on a firm foundation) will be about as much preparation as a good wheel-barrow would be for a 24-hour dash across Europe. The barrow shouldn't be knocked; there are good ideas there—such as using a wheel. It's just that a little more is required.

So there you have it. L&F claim that constructed intelligence is "within our grasp". I think it's far away. They view representation as explicit—as a matter of just writing things down. I take it as an inexorably tacit, con-textual, embodied faculty, that enables a participatory system to stand in relation to what is distal, in a way that it must constantly coordinate with its underlying physical actions. L&F think you can tunnel directly from generic insight to system specification. I feel we're like medieval astrologers, groping towards our (collective?) Newton, in a stumbling attempt to flesh out the theoretical middle realm. There is, though, one thing on which we do agree: we're both enthusiastic. It's just that I'm enthusiastic about the work that lies ahead; L&F seem enthusiastic that it won't be needed.

Why?—why this difference? Of many reasons, one goes deep. From my point of view, knowledge and intelligence require participation in the world. Lenat and Feigenbaum, apparently, think not. I can only conclude that they would not agree with Yeats, who I think said it well:

> I have found what I wanted—to put it all in a phrase, I say, "Man can embody the truth, but cannot know it."[46]

Notes

1 Tufts University, Medford, MA.
2 Or at least it is alive. The original version of Lenat and Feigenbaum's paper (the one presented at the Foundations of AI conference, in response to which this review was initially written) was considerably more optimistic than the revision published here some four years later. For one thing, their estimate of the project's scale has grown; whereas in 1987 they suggested the number of things we know to be "many hundreds of thousands—perhaps a few million", that estimate has now increased to "many millions (perhaps a few hundred million)". In addition, whereas their original paper suggested that inference was essentially a non-problem (a sentiment still discernible in their "Knowledge Is All There Is Hypothesis", p. 192), the project is now claimed to incorporate at least "two dozen separate inference engines", with more on the way. Again, not only has the sophis-tication of their representation scheme increased, but (as predicted here in Section 3) their representational conventions have developed from those of a simple frame system towards something much more like full predicate calculus, complete with propositions, constraints, set-theoretic models, etc. (Their words: "the need for

more formality, for a more principled representation language" was one of the "surprises that actually trying to build this immense KB has engendered".) All these signs of increased sobriety are reassuring, of course, although, given their ambition and eclecticism, one wonders whether the resulting complexity will be manageable.

More seriously, a conceptual shift has overtaken the project—more ramifying than these relatively simpler issues of scale. At the 1988 CYC review meeting (in Palo Alto), Lenat claimed that whereas he and Feigenbaum had initially taken their project as one of coding up everything in the encyclopedia (hence the name "CYC"), they were now convinced that the real task was to write down the *complement* of the encyclopedia: everything we know, but have never needed to say. This is an astounding reversal. Dreyfus should feel vindicated [22], since this shift in focus certainly strengthens any doubts about the ultimate adequacy of an allegiance to explicit representation.

For all that, their optimism remains intact. They still believe that by 1994 they will approach the crossover point where a system will pass the point of needing any further design or hands-on implementation, and will from then on improve simply by reading and asking questions (implying, I suppose, that AI's theoretical preliminaries will be concluded). Furthermore, they suggest that this second "language-based learning" stage will in turn end by about the end of the decade, at which point we will have a system "with human-level breadth and depth of knowledge". They claim these things, furthermore, in spite of such telling admissions as the following, written in 1989: "much of the 1984–89 work on CYC has been to get an adequate global ontology; i.e., has been worrying about ways to represent knowledge; most of the 1990–94 work will be actually representing knowledge, entering it into CYC."

3 Suchman [67], for example, argues that conceptualizing action is often a retrospective practice—useful for a variety of purposes (such as explanation), but not implicated in engendering the action in the first place, especially in routine or everyday cases.

4 For example, consider one possible defense: (a) that L&F are implicitly assuming intellectual competence can be separated into two categories—one relatively tacit, perceptually or experientially grounded, less dependent on explicit formulation: the other, a kind of higher-level, fully conceptual, "expertise", relying on careful articulation: and (b) that a system manifesting the second can be constructed without any roots in the first. If this is their position, it is very, very strong— needing not just admission but defense. At a minimum, they would have to argue at least two things (in opposition to Dreyfus [21], Suchman [67], Winograd [70, 72], and others): (a) that the following three distinctions align (or at least coincide on the right): amateur versus expert, tacit versus articulated, and perceptual versus cognitive: and (b) that common sense, by their own admission a necessary ingredient in expert reasoning, *can be captured solely in "knowledge" of the second kind.* But of course no such argument is forthcoming.

5 See, e.g., Bobrow [9], Hayes [34, 35], Hobbs and Moore [36], Hobbs et al. [37], and Levy et al. [46]. It's not so much that L&F think that ontology is *already* solved, as that they propose, in a relatively modest time-period, to accomplish what others spend lives on.

6 See for example Gentner and Gentner [29], and—to the extent that analogy ties in with metaphor—the papers in Ortony [52].

7 Actually, it might be false. Encoding control directions at the meta-level is another instance of L&F's unswerving allegiance to explicit formulation. Unfortunately, however, as has been clear at least since the days of Lewis Carroll, not *everything*

can be represented explicitly: at some point a system must ground out on a non-represented control regimen. Now L&F are presumably relying on the computational conceit that any control structure whatsoever can be *implemented* explicitly, by representing it in a program to be run by another, non-represented, underlying control regimen. Proofs of such possibility, however, ignore resource bounds, real-time response, and the like. It is not clear that we should blithely assume that our conceit will still hold under these more restrictive constraints, especially in as pragmatic a setting as L&F imagine.

8 For astronomers, telescopes are *tools*, not *subject matters*: the theoretical notions in terms of which we understand telescopes aren't the constitutive notions in terms of which we understand *what is seen through telescopes*. AI, in contrast, is different: we exactly *do* claim that computational notions, such as formal symbol manipulation, *are* applicable to the emergent intelligence we computationally model.

Note in passing that although this is reminiscent of Searle's [60] notions of *strong* and *weak* AI, there is a crucial difference. In making such distinctions, Searle is distinguishing the *relation* between a computational system and the mind: whether only their *surface behaviours* are claimed similar (weak), or whether the way in which the computational process works is claimed to be the way in which the mind works (strong). L&F, on the other hand, at least in this proposal, are making no psychological claims: hence Searle's terms, strictly speaking, don't apply (although L&F, if pressed, would presumably opt for the weak option). In contrast—and in complete independence of psychology—they propose to build a *computer system*, and computer systems *necessarily* work in computational ways, i.e., they have to be "strong" about their own project: otherwise they would be in the odd position of having no idea how to go about developing it. And it is clear, in this sense, that they are "strong"; why else would they be discussing slots, frames, and meta-rules?

So what of empiricism? As L&F suggest (this is their primary brief), the computational models they recommend building should of course be *tested*. But as I suggest in the text, to claim that isn't to claim that computers are the paradigmatic object of *study*. On the contrary, I would have thought an appropriate "empirical" stance for computational AI would go something as follows: one would (a) study intelligent behaviour, independent of form (biological, artifactual, whatever), but known in advance (i.e., pre-theoretically) to be intelligent behaviour; (b) construct (strong) computational models that manifest the essential principles that are presumed or hypothesized to underlie that intelligence; and then (c) conduct experiments to determine those models' adequacy. The point is that it is the first stage, not the third, that would normally be called "empirical".

9 In part, but not solely, because of its potential compatibility with connectionism. For specific discussion and results see, e.g., [1, 2, 12–15, 39, 48, 51, 55, 57–59, 66, 67, 72].

10 In fact, as it happens, it doesn't even matter whether you think the EC view *is computational at all*. What's at stake here are the requisite underpinnings for *intelligence*; it is a secondary issue as to whether those underpinnings can be computationally realized. As it happens, I believe that the (real) notion of computation is so much wider than L&F's construal that I don't take the discrepancy between genuine intelligence and their proposal as arguing against the very possibility of a computational reconstruction. But that's a secondary point.

11 "Explicit" fragments of a representational scheme are usually the sort of thing one can imagine removing—surgically, as it were—without disturbing the structural integrity or representational content of the remainder.

12 See the discussion of the "Knowledge Representation Hypothesis" in [62].

13 Some of the reasons will emerge in discussions of later questions, and are argued in [65]. For analogous views, again see the exploratory systems of Rosenschein and Kaelbling [58], Brooks [12], and Chapman and Agre [13], and the writings of Suchman [67], Cussins [15], Dreyfus [21], and Smolensky [66].

L&F may of course reply that they do embrace implicit representation, in the form of compiled code, neural nets, unparsed images. But this isn't strictly fair. By "the L&F position" I don't mean the CYC system *per se*, in inevitably idiosyncratic detail, but rather the general organizing principles they propose, the foundational position they occupy, the theoretical contributions they make, i.e., it isn't sufficient to claim that the actual CYC software does involve this or that embedded aspect, as, in many cases. I believe it *must*, in order to work at all—see, e.g., footnotes 16 and 29. Rather, my plaint is with overarching intellectual stance.

14 I am intentionally ignoring scads of important distinctions—for example, between the indexicality of representational content (of which "here" and "now" are paradigmatic exemplars), and the even more complex relation between what's in fact the case and how it's represented as being (the latter is more Suchman's [67] concern). Sorting any of these things out would take us far afield, but I hope just this much will show how rich a territory isn't explored by L&F's proposal.

15 Except the limiting case of intrasentential linguistic context necessary to determine by which quantifier a variable is bound.

16 L&F might reply by claiming they could easily add the "current date" to their system, and tie in arithmetic procedures to accommodate "within 10 years". My responses are three: (i) that to treat the particular case in this ad hoc way won't generalize: (ii) that this repair practice falls outside the very foundational assumptions on which the integrity of the rest of their representational project is founded: and (iii) that the problem it attempts to solve absolutely permeates the entire scope of human knowledge and intelligence.

17 Careful distinctions between meaning and content aren't particularly common in AI and I don't mean to use the terms technically here, but the situation-theoretic use is instructive: the *content* of a term or sentence is taken to be what a use of it refers to or is about (and may differ from use to use), whereas the *meaning* is taken, at least approximately, to be a function from context to content, and (therefore) to remain relatively constant. So the content of "I", if you use it, would be you: whereas it's meaning would (roughly) be A SPEAKER SPEAKER. (This is approximate in part because no assumption is made in situation theory that the relationship is *functional*. See [5].)

18 Imagine the dictionary entry if "today" were taken to be ambiguous: ... today ....: June 24, 1887: today. . . .: June 25, 1887: today. . . .: June 26, 1887: . . .!

19 See the discussion of *coordination conditions* in [65] for one suggestion as to how to retain the integrity of intentional analysis (better: integrity to the notion of intentionality) in the face of this radical a theoretical revision.

20 To make this precise, you have to rule out cheats of encoding or implementation, of the following sort: Suppose there is some holistic regularity $\mathcal{H}$, a function of all kinds of contextual aspects $\mathcal{C}$, whereby complete intentional situations take on a meaning or significance $\mathcal{M}$, and suppose that $\mathcal{H}$ is in some way parameterized on the constituent words w_1, w_2, etc. (which of course it will be—on even the most situated account it still matters what words you use). By a kind of invested currying process, this can be turned into a "bottom-up" analysis, based on a meaning of the form $\lambda \mathcal{C}_1 \mathcal{C}_2 \ldots f_k(\mathcal{H})$ for each word w_k, so that when it is all put together $\mathcal{M}$ results, rather in the way in which control irregularities in programming languages (like QUIT, THROW, and ERROR) are handled in denotational semantics of

programming languages by treating the continuation as a component of the context. The problem with such deviousness is that it essentially reduces compositionality to mean no more than that there exists *some* systematic overall story.

21 Or, again, the meaning of the internal data structure or mental representation to which the word "relentless" corresponds. Nothing I am saying here (or anywhere else in this review) hinges on *external* properties of language. It's just simpler, pedagogically, to use familiar examples from natural language than to construct what must inevitably be hypothetical internal cases. As pointed out a few paragraphs back, of all the sorts of referential indefiniteness under review, only genuine ambiguity can be resolved during the parsing phase.

22 There's one problem we can set aside. As it happens, the very notion of consistency is vulnerable to the comments made in discussing question 3 (about use-dependent meaning). Like soundness and completeness, consistency, at least as normally formulated, is founded on some notion of semantic value *independent* of use, which an embedded view may not support (at least not in all cases). This should at least render suspicious any claims of *similarity* between the two positions. Still, since they stay well within the requisite conceptual limits, it's kosher to use consistency to assess L&F on their own (not that that will resolve them of all their troubles).

23 As indicated in their current comments, L&F have apparently expanded their representational repertoire in recent years. Instead of relying solely on frames and slots, they now embrace, among other things: blocks of compiled code, "unparsed" digitized images, and statistical neural networks. But the remarks made in this section still largely hold, primarily because no mention is made of how these different varieties are integrated into a coherent whole. The challenge—still unmet, in my opinion—is to show how the "contents" contained in a diverse set of representational schemes are semantically commensurable, in such a way as to support a generalized, multi-modal notion of inference, perception, judgment, action. For some initial work in this direction see [6] for a general introduction, and [7] for technical details.

24 Different representational types also differ in their informational prerequisites. Pictures and graphs, for example, *can't* depict as little information as can English text—imagine trying to draw a picture of "either two adults or half a dozen children".

25 Calling continuous representations "analogue" is both unfortunate and distracting. "Analogue" should presumably be a predicate on a representation whose structure corresponds to that of which it represents: continuous representations would be analogue if they represented continuous phenomena, discrete representations analogue if they represented discrete phenomena. That continuous representations should historically have come to be called analogue presumably betrays the recognition that, at the levels at which it matters to us, the world is more foundationally continuous than it is discrete.

26 The phrase is from various of John Perry's lectures given at CSLI during 1986–88.

27 The foundational notion underlying the view of embedded computation, in particular, is one of *partially disconnected participation*; see [65].

28 Though some requirements can be laid down: such as that any such theory have enough teeth so that not *everything* is representational. That would be vacuous.

29 All the remarks made in footnote 16 apply here: it won't do to reply that L&F could build a model of right and left inside the system, or even attach a camera, since that would fall outside their stated program from representing the world. I too (i.e., on the embedded view) would attach a camera, but I want a *theory* of what it is to attach a camera, and of some other things as well—such as how to

integrate the resulting images with conceptual representations, and how envision-
ment works, and how this all relates to the existence of "internal" sensors and
effectors, and how it ties to action, and so on and so forth—until I get a theory
that, as opposed to slots-and-frames, really does do justice to full-scale participation in the world. Cameras, in short, are just the tip of a very large iceberg.

30 To imagine the converse, furthermore, would be approximately equivalent to the
proposal that programming languages do away with procedures and procedure
calls, in favour of the advance storage of the sum total of all potentially relevant stack frames, so that any desired answer could merely be "read off", without having to do any work. This is no more plausible a route to intelligence
than to satisfactory computation more generally. And it would raise daunting
issues of indexing and retrieval—a subject for which, as discussed under question 4 (on consistency), there is no reason to suppose that L&F have any unique
solution.

31 By "semantically coordinated" I mean only to capture what deduction, induction,
reasoning, contemplation, etc., have in common; roughly, some kind of coordination between what is done to (or happens because of, or whatever) a representation and its semantic value or content. Soundness, completeness, and consistency
are particularly disconnected species: I suspect much more complicated versions
will ultimately be required.

32 Or so, at least, it is traditionally argued. This is not a view I am ultimately prepared to accept.

33 For simplicity, I'm assuming that rational belief revision will consist of a pattern
of sound inference steps—almost certainly not true. See e.g. [38].

34 Where information is approximately taken as counterfactual supporting correlation, in the spirit of Dretske [19] and Barwise and Perry [8]. See also Rosenschein
[57].

35 For the application of some of these ideas to the design of an embedded
programming language, see [18].

36 One thing it won't be able to shun, presumably, will be its users. See footnote 37.

37 This paragraph makes explicit something I have otherwise tried, in this article, to
sidestep: the fact that (at least on my analysis) L&F's theoretical framework is not
only inadequate for understanding *intelligence*, but is also inadequate for understanding *their own system* (which, I am claiming, won't be *intelligent*, but will still
exist). Driving a wedge between what computation is actually like and how we
think of it is a primary brief of [65]; for the moment, simply assume that L&F, if
they proceed with their project, will have to resort to a-theoretical programming
techniques to handle this and other such issues. Control structure is only one
example; another is user interaction. To the extent computers carry on conversations, after all, they actually *carry them on*, rather than merely representing them
as being carried on (though they may do that as well).

38 Again, as I said in footnote 16, it won't do to reply that they could simply add a
counter to mark the passage of time. For one thing (or at least so I claim) this
example, although simple, is symptomatic of a deep problem; it's not a surface
nuisance to be programmed around. Furthermore, even if it were simply disposed
of, for L&F to treat it in an ad hoc, procedural way would be to part company with
their own analysis.

39 *Reducibility*, as the term is normally used in the philosophy of science, is a relation
between *theories*; one theory is reducible to another if, very roughly, its predicates
and claims can be translated into those of another. In contrast, the term *supervenience* is used to relate phenomena themselves; thus the strength of a beam would be
said to supervene on the chemical bonds in the constitutive wood. The two

relations are distinguished because people have realized that, somewhat contrary to untutored intuition, supervenience doesn't necessarily imply reducibility (see [27, 33, 40, 41]).

40 As opposed to the "negative" reading: namely, that a formal computational process proceed independently of the semantics. That the two readings are *conceptually* distinct is obvious: that they get at different things is argued in [65].

41 I am not asking the reader to agree with this statement, without more explanation—just to admit that it is conceptually coherent.

42 I am not suggesting that physical involvement with the subject matter is sufficient for original intentionality; that's obviously not true. And I don't mean, either, to imply the strict converse: that anything like simple physical connection is *necessary*, since we can obviously genuinely refer to things from which we are physically disconnected in a variety of ways—by distance, from other galaxies; by fact, from Santa Claus; by possibility, from a round square; by type, from the number 2. Still, I am hardly alone in thinking that *some kind of causal counectivity* is at least a constituent part of the proper referential story. See e.g. Kripke [43], Dretske [19], and Fodor [28].

43 In logic, this required overlap of registration scheme turns up in the famous mandate that a metalanguage used to express a truth theory must *contain* the predicate of the (object) language under investigation (Tarski's convention T). Overlap of registration scheme, however, is at least potentially a much more complex issue than one of simple language subsumption.

44 Obviously they are simpler, but the differences are probably more interesting than that. The individuation criteria for computational processes are wildly different from those for people, and, even if AI were to succeed up to if not beyond its wildest dreams, notions like "death" will probably mean something rather different to machines than to us. Murder, for example, might only be a misdemeanor in a society with reliable daily backups.

45 It would also be hard (impossible, in fact) for us to say, exactly, what representing something as detente would mean for *us*—but for a very different reason. At least on a view such as that of Cussins [15], with which I am sympathetic, our *understanding* of the concept "detente" is not itself a conceptual thing, and therefore can't necessarily be captured in words (i.e., concepts aren't conceptually constituted). Cf. the discussion of formulation in Section 2.

46 Taken from a letter Yeats wrote to a friend shortly before his death. Dreyfus cites the passage at the conclusion of the introduction to the revised edition of his *What Computers Can't Do* [21. p. 66]; it has also been popularized on a poster available from Cody's Books in Berkeley.

References

[1] P.E. Agre, Routines, AI Memo 828, MIT, Cambridge, MA (1985).

[2] P.E. Agre, The dynamic structure of everyday life, Ph.D. Thesis, Tech. Rept., MIT, Cambridge, MA (1989).

[3] J. Barwise, The situation in logic II: conditionals and conditional information, in: E.C. Traugott, C.A. Ferguson and J.S. Reilly. eds., *On Conditionals* (Cambridge University Press, Cambridge, 1986): also: Rept. No. CLSI-85–21, Stanford, CA (1985): reprinted in: J. Barwise, *The Situation of Logic*, CLSI Lecture Notes **17** (University of Chicago Press, Chicago, IL, 1989) Chapter 5.

[4] J. Barwise, *The Situation of Logic*, CLSI Lecture Notes **17** (University of Chicago Press, Chicago, IL, 1989).

[5] J. Barwise and J. Etchemendy, Model-theoretic semantics, in: M. Posner, ed., *Foundations of Cognitive Science* (MIT Press, Cambridge, MA, 1989).

[6] J. Barwise and J. Etchemendy, Visual information and valid reasoning, in: W. Zimmermann, ed., *Visualization in Mathematics* (Mathematical Association of America, to appear).

[7] J. Barwise and J. Etchemendy, Information, infons, and inference, in: R. Cooper, K. Mukai and J. Perry, eds., *Situation Theory and Its Applications* I, CLSI Lecture Notes (University of Chicago Press, Chicago, IL, 1990) 33–78.

[8] J. Barwise and J. Perry, *Situations and Attitudes* (MIT Press, Cambridge, MA, 1983).

[9] D. G. Bobrow, ed., *Qualitative Reasoning about Physical Systems* (North-Holland, Amsterdam, 1984).

[10] D.G. Bobrow, T. Winograd et al., Experience with KRL-0: one cycle of a knowledge representation language, in: *Proceedings IJCAI-77*, Cambridge, MA (1977) 213–222.

[11] R. Boyd, Metaphor and theory change: what is "metaphor" a metaphor for?, in: A. Ortony, ed., *Metaphor and Thought* (Cambridge University Press, Cambridge, 1979).

[12] R.A. Brooks. A robust layered control system for a mobile robot, *IEEE J. Rob. Autom.* **2** (1986) 14–23.

[13] D. Chapman and P.E. Agre, Abstract reasoning as emergent from concrete activity, in: M.P. Georgeff and A.L. Lansky, eds., *Reasoning about Action and Plans: Proceedings of the 1986 Workshop* (Morgan Kaufmann, Los Altos, CA, 1987) 411–424.

[14] W.J. Clancey, The frame of reference problem in the design of intelligent machines, in: K. VanLehn, ed., *Architectures for Intelligence* (Erlbaum, Hillsdale, NJ, to appear).

[15] A. Cussins, The connectionist construction of concepts, in: M. Boden. ed., *The Philosophy of Artificial Intelligence*, Oxford Readings in Philosophy Series (Oxford University Press, Oxford, 1990) 368–440.

[16] R. Davis, ed., *Expert Systems: How Far Can They Go? AI Mag.* **10** (1–2) (1989).

[17] D.C. Dennett, *The Intentional Stance* (MIT Press, Cambridge, MA, 1987).

[18] M.A. Dixon, Open semantics and programming language design (working title), Doctoral Dissertation, Computer Science Department, Stanford University, Stanford, CA (to appear).

[19] F. Dretske, *Knowledge and the Flow of Information* (MIT Press, Cambridge, MA, 1981).

[20] F. Dretske, *Explaining Behavior: Reasons in a World of Causes* (MIT Press/ Bradford Books, Cambridge, MA, 1988).

[21] H.L. Dreyfus, *What Computers Can't Do: The Limits of Artificial Intelligence* (Harper Row, New York, rev. ed., 1979).

[22] H.L. Dreyfus, From micro-worlds to knowledge representation: AI at an impasse, in: J. Haugeland, ed., *Mind Design: Philosophys, Psychology, Artificial Intelligence* (MIT Press, Cambridge, MA, 1981) 161–205.

[23] H.L. Dreyfus, ed., *Husserl, Intentionality, and Cognitive Science* (MIT Press, Cambridge, MA, 1982).

[24] H.L. Dreyfus and S.E. Dreyfus, *Mind over Machine: The Power of Human*

Intuition and Expertise in the Era of the Computer (Macmillan/Free Press, New York, 1985).

[25] G. Evans, *The Varieties of Reference* (Oxford University Press, Oxford, 1982).

[26] R. Fagin and J.Y. Halpern, Belief, awareness, and limited reasoning, in: *Proceedings IJCAI-85*, Los Angeles, CA (1985) 491–501.

[27] J.A. Fodor, Special sciences (or: the disunity of science as a working hypothesis), *Synthese* **28** (1974) 97–115; reprinted in: N. Block, ed., *Readings in the Philosophy of Psychology* (Harvard University Press, Cambridge, MA, 1980) 120–133.

[28] J.A. Fodor, *Psychosemantics* (MIT Press/Bradford Books, Cambridge, MA, 1987).

[29] D. Gentner and D. Gentner, Flowing waters or teeming crowds: Mental models of electricity, in: D. Gentner and A. Stevens, eds., *Mental Models* (Erlbaum, Hillsdale, NJ, 1983).

[30] B.J. Grosz and C.L. Sidner, Attention, intentions, and the structure of discourse, *Comput. Linguistics* **12** (3) (1986) 175–204.

[31] J. Haugeland, Semantic engines: introduction to mind design, in: J. Haugeland, ed., *Mind Design: Philosophy, Psychology, Artificial Intelligence* (MIT Press, Cambridge, MA, 1981) 1–34.

[32] J. Haugeland, ed., *Mind Design: Philosophy, Psychology, Artificial Intelligence* (MIT Press, Cambridge, MA, 1981).

[33] J. Haugeland, Weak supervenience, *Am. Philos. Q.* **19** (1) (1982) 93–103.

[34] P.J. Hayes, The second naive physics manifesto, in: J.R. Hobbs and R.C. Moore, eds., *Formal Theories of the Commonsense World* (Ablex, Norwood, NJ, 1985) 1–36.

[35] P.J. Hayes, Naive physics I: ontology for liquids, in: J.R. Hobbs and R.C. Moore, eds., *Formal Theories of the Commonsense World* (Ablex, Norwood, NJ, 1985) 71–107.

[36] J.R. Hobbs and R.C. Moore, eds., *Formal Theories of the Commonsense World* (Ablex, Norwood, NJ, 1985).

[37] J.R. Hobbs et al., Commonsense summer: final report, Tech. Rept. CSLI-85–35. Stanford University, Stanford, CA (1985).

[38] D.J. Israel, What's wrong with non-monotonic logic?, in: *Proceedings AAAI–80*, Stanford, CA (1980).

[39] L. Kaelbling, An architecture for intelligent reactive systems, in: M.P. Georgeff and A.L. Lansky, eds., *Reasoning about Action and Plans: Proceedings of the 1986 Workshop* (Morgan Kaufmann, San Mateo, CA, 1987) 395–410.

[40] J. Kim, Supervenience and nomological incommensurables, *Am. Philos. Q.* **15** (1978) 149–156.

[41] J. Kim, Causality, identity, and supervenience in the mind-body problem, *Midwest Stud. Philos.* **4** (1979) 31–49.

[42] D. Kirsh, When is information explicitly represented?, in: P. Hanson, ed., *Information, Language, and Cognition*, Vancouver Studies in Cognitive Science **1** (University of British Columbia Press, Vancouver, BC, 1990) 340–365.

[43] S.A. Kripke, *Naming and Necessity* (Harvard University Press, Cambridge, MA, 1980).

[44] J. Lave, *Cognition in Practice: Mind, Mathematics, and Culture in Everyday Life* (Cambridge University Press, Cambridge, 1988).

[45] H.J. Levesque, A logic of implicit and explicit belief, in: *Proceedings AAAI-84*, Austin, TX (1984) 198–202.

[46] D.M. Levy, D.C. Brotsky and K.R. Otson, Formalizing the figural, in: *Proceedings ACM Conference on Document Processing Systems*, Santa Fe, NM (1988) 145–151.

[47] J. McCarthy and P.J. Hayes, Some philosophical problems from the standpoint of artificial intelligence, in: B. Meltzer and D. Michie, eds., *Machine Intelligence* 4 (American Elsevier, New York, 1969) 463–502.

[48] J.L. McClelland, D.E. Rumelhart and the PDP Research Group, eds., *Parallel Distributed Processing: Explorations in the Microstructure of Cognition* 2: *Psychological and Biological Models* (MIT Press/Bradford Books, Cambridge, MA, 1986).

[49] D.V. McDermott, Artificial intelligence meets natural stupidity, in: J. Haugeland, ed., *Mind Design: Philosophy, Psychology, Artificial Intelligence* (MIT Press, Cambridge, MA, 1981) 143–160.

[50] T. Nagel, *The View from Nowhere* (Oxford University Press, Oxford, 1986).

[51] D.A. Norman, *The Psychology of Everyday Things* (Basic Books, New York, 1988).

[52] A. Ortony, ed., *Metaphor and Thought* (Cambridge University Press, Cambridge, 1979).

[53] J. Perry, The problem of the essential indexical, *NOUS* 13 (1979) 3–21.

[54] J. Perry and D. Israel, What is information?, in: P. Hanson, ed., *Information, Language, and Cognition*, Vancouver Studies in Cognitive Science 1 (University of British Columbia Press, Vancouver, BC, 1990) 1–19.

[55] M.H. Raibert, Legged robots, *Commun. ACM* 29 (6) (1986) 499–514.

[56] M.H. Raibert and I.E. Sutherland, Machines that walk. *Sci. Am.* 248 (1) (1983) 44–53.

[57] S. Rosenschein, Formal theories of knowledge in AI and robotics, *New Generation Comput.* 3 (4) (1985).

[58] S. Rosenschein and L. Kaelbling, The synthesis of digital machines with provable epistemic properties, in: *Proceedings Workshop on Theoretical Aspects of Reasoning about Knowledge* (Morgan Kaufmann, Los Altos, CA, 1986): also: Tech. Rept. CSLI-87-83, Stanford University, Stanford, CA (1987).

[59] D.E. Rumelhart, J.L. McClelland and the PDP Research Group, eds., *Parallel Distributed Processing: Explorations in the Microstructure of Cognition* 1: Foundations (MIT Press/Bradford Books, Cambridge, MA, 1986).

[60] J.R. Searle, Minds, brains, and programs, *Behav. Brain Sci.* 3 (1980) 417–424; reprinted in: J. Haugeland, ed., *Mind Design: Philosophy, Psychology, Artificial Intelligence* (MIT Press, Cambridge, MA, 1981) 282–306.

[61] J.R. Searle, *Minds, Brains, and Science* (Harvard University Press, Cambridge, MA, 1984).

[62] B.C. Smith, Prologue to "Reflection and semantics in a procedural language", in: R.J. Brachman and H.J. Levesque, eds., *Readings in Knowledge Representation* (Morgan Kaufmann, Los Altos, CA, 1985) 31–39.

[63] B.C. Smith, Varieties of self-reference, in: J.Y. Halpern, ed., *Theoretical Aspects of Reasoning about Knowledge: Proceedings of the 1986 Conference* (Morgan Kaufmann, Los Altos, CA, 1986).

[64] B.C. Smith, The semantics of clocks, in: J. Fetzer, ed., *Aspects of Artificial Intelligence* (Kluwer Academic Publishers, Boston, MA, 1988) 3–31.

[65] B.C. Smith, *A View from Somewhere: An Essay on the Foundations of Computation and Intentionality* (MIT Press/Bradford Books, Cambridge, MA, to appear).

[66] P. Smolensky, On the proper treatment of connectionism, *Behav. Brain Sci.* **11** (1988) 1–74.

[67] L.A. Suchman, *Plans and Situated Actions* (Cambridge University Press, Cambridge, 1986).

[68] A. Tarski, The concept of truth in formalized languages, in: A. Tarski, ed., *Logic, Semantics, Metamathematics* (Clarendon Press, Oxford, 1956) 152–197.

[69] T. Winograd, Moving the semantic fulcrum, Tech. Rept. CSLI-84–77, Stanford University, Stanford, CA (1984).

[70] T. Winograd, Thinking machines: Can there be? Are we? Tech. Rept. CSLI-87–100, Stanford University, Stanford, CA (1987).

[71] T. Winograd, Three responses to situation theory, Tech. Rept. CSLI-87–106, Stanford University, Stanford, CA (1987).

[72] T. Winograd and F. Flores, *Understanding Computers and Cognition: A New Foundation for Design* (Ablex, Norwood, NJ, 1986).

50

INTELLIGENCE WITHOUT REASON

Rodney A. Brooks

Source: MIT AI Lab Memo 1293, April 1991, Reprinted in *Proceedings of 12th International Joint Conference on Artificial Intelligence*, Sydney, Australia, August 1991, pp. 1–27.

Abstract *Computers* and *Thought* are the two categories that together define Artificial Intelligence as a discipline. It is generally accepted that work in Artificial Intelligence over the last thirty years has had a strong influence on aspects of computer architectures. In this paper we also make the converse claim; that the state of computer architecture has been a strong influence on our models of thought. The Von Neumann model of computation has led Artificial Intelligence in particular directions. Intelligence in biological systems is completely different. Recent work in behavior-based Artificial Intelligence has produced new models of intelligence that are much closer in spirit to biological systems. The non-Von Neumann computational models they use share many characteristics with biological computation.

1 Introduction

Artificial Intelligence as a formal discipline has been around for a little over thirty years. The goals of individual practitioners vary and change over time. A reasonable characterization of the general field is that it is intended to make computers do things, that when done by people, are described as having indicated intelligence. Winston [**Winston 84**] characterizes the goals of Artificial Intelligence as both the construction of useful intelligent systems and the understanding of human intelligence.

There is a temptation (often succumbed to) to then go ahead and define *intelligence*, but that does not immediately give a clearly grounded meaning to the field. In fact there is danger of deep philosophical regress with no recovery. Therefore I prefer to stay with a more informal notion of intelligence being the sort of stuff that humans do, pretty much all the time.

1.1 Approaches

Traditional Artificial Intelligence has tried to tackle the problem of building artificially intelligent systems from the top down. It tackled intelligence through the notions of *thought* and *reason*. These are things we only know about through introspection. The field has adopted a certain *modus operandi* over the years, which includes a particular set of conventions on how the inputs and outputs to thought and reasoning are to be handled (e.g., the subfield of knowledge representation), and the sorts of things that thought and reasoning do (e.g., planning, problem solving, etc.). I will argue that these conventions cannot account for large aspects of what goes into intelligence. Furthermore, without those aspects the validity of the traditional Artificial Intelligence approaches comes into question. I will also argue that much of the landmark work on thought has been influenced by the technological constraints of the available computers, and thereafter these consequences have often mistakenly become enshrined as principles, long after the original impetus has disappeared.

From an evolutionary stance, human level intelligence did not suddenly leap onto the scene. There were precursors and foundations throughout the lineage to humans. Much of this substrate is present in other animals today. The study of that substrate may well provide constraints on how higher level *thought* in humans could be organized.

Recently there has been a movement to study intelligence from the bottom up, concentrating on physical systems (e.g., mobile robots), situated in the world, autonomously carrying out tasks of various sorts. Some of this work is based on engineering from first principles, other parts of the work are firmly based on biological inspirations. The flavor of this work is quite different from that of traditional Artificial Intelligence. In fact it suggests that despite our best introspections, traditional Artificial Intelligence offers solutions to intelligence which bear almost no resemblance at all to how biological systems work.

There are of course dangers in studying biological systems too closely. Their design was not highly optimized from a global systems point of view. Rather they were patched together and adapted from previously working systems, in ways which most expeditiously met the latest environmental pressures. Perhaps the solutions found for much of intelligence are terribly suboptimal. Certainly there are many vestigial structures surviving within humans' and other animals' digestive, skeletal, and muscular systems. One should suppose then that there are many vestigial neurological structures, interactions, and side effects. Their emulation may be a distraction.

1.2 Outline

The body of this paper is formed by five main sections: 2 *Robots*, 3 *Computers*, 4 *Biology*, 5 *Ideas* and 6 *Thought*. The theme of the paper is how computers and thought have been intimately intertwined in the development of Artificial Intelligence, how those connections may have led the field astray, how biological examples of intelligence are quite different from the models used by Artificial Intelligence, and how recent new approaches point to another path for both computers and thought.

The new approaches that have been developed recently for Artificial Intelligence arose out of work with mobile robots. Section 2 (Robots) briefly outlines the context within which this work arose, and discusses some key realizations made by the researchers involved.

Section 3 (Computers) traces the development of the foundational ideas for Artificial Intelligence, and how they were intimately linked to the technology available for computation. Neither situatedness nor embodiment were easy to include on the original agenda, although their importance was recognized by many early researchers. The early framework with its emphasis on search has remained dominant, and has led to solutions that seem important within the closed world of Artificial Intelligence, but which perhaps are not very relevant to practical applications. The field of Cybernetics with a heritage of very different tools from the early digital computer, provides an interesting counterpoint, confirming the hypothesis that models of thought are intimately tied to the available models of computation.

Section 4 (Biology) is a brief overview of recent developments in the understanding of biological intelligence. It covers material from ethology, psychology, and neuroscience. Of necessity it is not comprehensive, but it is sufficient to demonstrate that the intelligence of biological systems is organized in ways quite different from traditional views of Artificial Intelligence.

Section 5 (Ideas) introduces the two cornerstones to the new approach to Artificial Intelligence, *situatedness* and *embodiment*, and discusses both intelligence and emergence in these contexts.

The last major section, 6 (Thought), outlines some details of the approach of my group at MIT to building complete situated, embodied, artificially intelligent robots. This approach shares much more heritage with biological systems than with what is usually called Artificial Intelligence.

2 Robots

There has been a scattering of work with mobile robots within the Artificial Intelligence community over the years. Shakey from the late sixties at SRI (see [**Nilsson 84**] for a collection of original reports) is perhaps the best known, but other significant efforts include the CART ([**Moravec 82**]) at Stanford and Hilare ([**Giralt, Chatila and Vaisset 84**]) in Toulouse.

All these systems used offboard computers (and thus they could be the largest most powerful computers available at the time and place), and all operated in mostly[1] static environments. All of these robots operated in environments that at least to some degree had been specially engineered for them. They all sensed the world and tried to build two or three dimensional world models of it. Then, in each case, a planner could ignore the actual world, and operate in the model to produce a plan of action for the robot to achieve whatever goal it had been given. In all three of these robots, the generated plans included at least a nominal path through the world model along which it was intended that the robot should move.

Despite the simplifications (static, engineered environments, and the most powerful available computers) all these robots operated excruciatingly slowly. Much of the processing time was consumed in the perceptual end of the systems and in building the world models. Relatively little computation was used in planning and acting.

An important effect of this work was to provide a framework within which other researchers could operate without testing their ideas on real robots, and even without having any access to real robot data. We will call this framework, the *sense-model-plan-act* framework, or *SMPA* for short. See section 3.6 for more details of how the SMPA framework influenced the manner in which robots were built over the following years, and how those robots in turn imposed restrictions on the ways in which intelligent control programs could be built for them.

There was at least an implicit assumption in this early work with mobile robots, that once the simpler case of operating in a static environment had been solved, then the more difficult case of an actively dynamic environment could be tackled. None of these early SMPA systems were ever extended in this way.

Around 1984, a number of people started to worry about the more general problem of organizing intelligence. There was a requirement that intelligence be reactive to dynamic aspects of the environment, that a mobile robot operate on time scales similar to those of animals and humans, and that intelligence be able to generate robust behavior in the face of uncertain sensors, an unpredicted environment, and a changing world. Some of the key realizations about the organization of intelligence were as follows:

- Most of what people do in their day to day lives is not problem-solving or planning, but rather it is routine activity in a relatively benign, but certainly dynamic, world. Furthermore the representations an agent uses of objects in the world need not rely on a semantic correspondence with symbols that the agent possesses, but rather can be defined through interactions of the agent with the world. Agents based on these ideas have achieved interesting performance levels and were built from combinatorial circuits plus a little timing circuitry (**[Agre and Chapman 87]**, **[Agre and Chapman 90]**).

- An observer can legitimately talk about an agent's beliefs and goals, even though the agent need not manipulate symbolic data structures at run time. A formal grounding in semantics used for the agent's design can be compiled away. Agents based on these ideas have achieved interesting performance levels and were built from combinatorial circuits plus a little timing circuitry (**[Rosenschein and Kaelbling 86]**, **[Kaelbling and Rosenschein 90]**).

- In order to really test ideas of intelligence it is important to build complete agents which operate in dynamic environments using real sensors. Internal world models which are complete representations of the external environment, besides being impossible to obtain, are not at all necessary for agents to act in a competent manner. Many of the actions of an agent are quite separable—coherent intelligence can emerge from subcomponents interacting in the world. Agents based on these ideas have achieved interesting performance levels and were built from combinatorial circuits plus a little timing circuitry (**[Brooks 86]**, **[Brooks 90b]**, **[Brooks 91a]**).

A large number of others have also contributed to this approach to organizing intelligence. **[Maes 90a]** is the most representative collection.

There is no generally accepted term to describe this style of work. It has sometimes been characterized by the oxymoron *reactive planning*. I have variously used *Robot Beings* **[Brooks and Flynn 89]** and *Artificial Creatures* **[Brooks 90b]**. Related work on non-mobile, but nevertheless active, systems has been called *active vision*, or *animate vision* **[Ballard 89]**. Some workers refer to their beings, or creatures, as *agents*; unfortunately that term is also used by others to refer to somewhat independent components of intelligence within a single physical creature (e.g., the agencies of **[Minsky 86]**). Sometimes the approach is called *behavior-based* as the computational components tend to be direct behavior producing modules[2]. For the remainder of this paper, we will simply call the entities of discussion "robots" or "behavior-based robots".

There are a number of key aspects characterizing this style of work.

- **[Situatedness]** The robots are situated in the world—they do not deal with abstract descriptions, but with the here and now of the world directly influencing the behavior of the system.
- **[Embodiment]** The robots have bodies and experience the world directly—their actions are part of a dynamic with the world and have immediate feedback on their own sensations.
- **[Intelligence]** They are observed to be intelligent—but the source of intelligence is not limited to just the computational engine. It also comes

from the situation in the world, the signal transformations within the sensors, and the physical coupling of the robot with the world.

- **[Emergence]** The intelligence of the system emerges from the system's interactions with the world and from sometimes indirect interactions between its components—it is sometimes hard to point to one event or place within the system and say that is why some external action was manifested.

Recently there has been a trend to try to integrate traditional symbolic reasoning, on top of a purely reactive system, both with real robots (e.g., **[Arkin 90]**, **[Mitchell 90]**) and in simulation (e.g., **[Firby 89]**). The idea is that the reactive system handles the realtime issues of being embedded in the world, while the deliberative system does the "hard" stuff traditionally imagined to be handled by an Artificial Intelligence system. I think that these approaches are suffering from the well known "horizon effect"—they have brought a little better performance in their overall system with the reactive component, but they have simply pushed the limitations of the reasoning system a bit further into the future. I will not be concerned with such systems for the remainder of this paper.

Before examining this work in greater detail, we will turn to the reasons why traditional Artificial Intelligence adopted such a different approach.

3 Computers

In evolution there is a theory **[Gould and Eldredge 77]** of punctuated equilibria, where most of the time there is little change within a species, but at intervals a subpopulation branches off with a short burst of greatly accelerated changes. Likewise, I believe that in Artificial Intelligence research over the last forty or so years, there have been long periods of incremental work within established guidelines, and occasionally a shift in orientation and assumptions causing a new subfield to branch off. The older work usually continues, sometimes remaining strong, and sometimes dying off gradually. This description of the field also fits more general models of science, such as **[Kuhn 70]**.

The point of this section is that all those steady-state bodies of work rely, sometimes implicitly, on certain philosophical and *technological* assumptions. The founders of the bodies of work are quite aware of these assumptions, but over time as new people come into the fields, these assumptions get lost, forgotten, or buried, and the work takes on a life of its own for its own sake.

In this section I am particularly concerned with how the architecture of our computers influences our choice of problems on which to work, our models of thought, and our algorithms, and how the problems on which we work, our models of thought, and our algorithm choice puts pressure on the development of architectures of our computers.

Biological systems run on massively parallel, low speed computation, within an essentially fixed topology network with bounded depth. Almost all Artificial Intelligence research, and indeed almost all modern computation, runs on essentially Von Neumann architectures, with a large, inactive memory which can respond at very high speed over an extremely narrow channel, to a very high speed central processing unit which contains very little state. When connections to sensors and actuators are also considered, the gap between biological systems and our artificial systems widens.

Besides putting architectural constraints on our programs, even our mathematical tools are strongly influenced by our computational architectures. Most algorithmic analysis is based on the RAM model of computation (essentially a Von Neumann model, shown to be polynomially equivalent to a Turing machine, e.g., [Hartmanis 71]). Only in recent years have more general models gained prominence, but they have been in the direction of oracles, and other improbable devices for our robot beings.

Are we doomed to work forever within the current architectural constraints?

Over the past few centuries computation technology has progressed from making marks on various surfaces (chiselling, writing, etc.), through a long evolutionary chain of purely mechanical systems, then electromechanical relay based systems, through vacuum tube based devices, followed by an evolutionary chain of silicon-based devices to the current state of the art.

It would be the height of arrogance and foolishness to assume that we are now using the ultimate technology for computation, namely silicon based integrated circuits, just as it would have been foolish (at least in retrospect) to assume in the 16th century that Napier's Bones were the ultimate computing technology [Williams 83]. Indeed the end of the exponential increase in computation speed for uni-processors is in sight, forcing somewhat the large amount of research into parallel approaches to more computation for the dollar, and per second. But there are other more radical possibilities for changes in computation infrastructure[3]. These include computation based on optical switching ([Gibbs 85], [Brady 90]), protein folding, gene expression, non-organic atomic switching.

3.1 Prehistory

During the early 1940's even while the second world war was being waged, and the first electronic computers were being built for cryptanalysis and trajectory calculations, the idea of using computers to carry out intelligent activities was already on people's minds.

Alan Turing, already famous for his work on computability [Turing 37] had discussions with Donald Michie, as early as 1943, and others less known to the modern Artificial Intelligence world as early as 1941, about using a computer to play chess. He and others developed the idea of minimaxing a tree of moves, and of static evaluation, and carried out elaborate hand simulations against human opponents. Later (during the period from 1945 to 1950 at least) he and Claude Shannon communicated about these ideas[4]. Although there was already an established field of mathematics concerning a theory of games, pioneered by Von Neumann [Von Neumann and Morgenstern 44], chess had such a large space of legal positions, that even though everything about it is deterministic, the theories were not particularly applicable. Only heuristic and operational programs seemed plausible means of attack.

In a paper titled *Intelligent Machinery*, written in 1948[5], but not published until long after his death [Turing 70], Turing outlined a more general view of making computers intelligent. In this rather short insightful paper he foresaw many modern developments and techniques. He argued (somewhat whimsically, to the annoyance of his employers [Hodges 83]) for at least some fields of intelligence, and his particular example is the learning of languages, that the machine would have to be embodied, and claimed success "seems however to depend rather too much on sense organs and locomotion to be feasible".

Turing argued that it must be possible to build a thinking machine since it was possible to build imitations of "any small part of a man". He made the distinction between producing accurate electrical models of nerves, and replacing them computationally with the available technology of vacuum tube circuits (this follows directly from his earlier paper [Turing 37]), and the assumption that the nervous system can be modeled as a computational system. For other parts of the body he suggests that "television cameras, microphones, loudspeakers", etc., could be used to model the rest of the system. "This would be a tremendous undertaking of course." Even so, Turing notes that the so constructed machine "would still have no contact with food, sex, sport and many other things of interest to the human being". Turing concludes that the best domains in which to explore the mechanization of thought are various games, and cryptanalysis, "in that they require little contact with the outside world"[6].

Turing thus carefully considered the question of embodiment, and for technical reasons chose to pursue aspects of intelligence which could be viewed, at least in his opinion, as purely symbolic. Minimax search, augmented with the idea of pursuing chains of capture to quiescence, and clever static evaluation functions (the *Turochamp* system of David Champernowne and Alan Turing[7], [Shannon 50]) soon became the dominant approach to the problem. [Newell, Shaw and Simon 58] compared all four known implemented chess playing programs of 1958 (with a total combined experience of six games played), including Turochamp, and they all followed this approach.

The basic approach of minimax with a good static evaluation function has not changed to this day. Programs of this ilk compete well with International

Grand Masters. The best of them, *Deep Thought* **[Hsu, Anantharaman, Campbell and Nowatzyk 90]**, uses special purpose chips for massive search capabilities, along with a skillful evaluation scheme and selective deepening to direct that search better than in previous programs.

Although Turing had conceived of using chess as a vehicle for studying human thought processes, this notion has largely gotten lost along the way (there are of course exceptions, e.g., **[Wilkins 79]** describes a system which substitutes chess knowledge for search in the middle game—usually there are very few static evaluations, and tree search is mainly to confirm or deny the existence of a mate). Instead the driving force has always been performance, and the most successful program of the day has usually relied on technological advances. Brute force tree search has been the dominant method, itself dominated by the amount of bruteness available. This in turn has been a product of clever harnessing of the latest technology available. Over the years, the current "champion" program has capitalized on the available hardware. *MacHack-6* **[Greenblatt, Eastlake and Crocker 67]** made use of the largest available fast memory (256K 36 bits words—about a megabyte or so, or $45 by today's standards) and a new comprehensive architecture (the PDP-6) largely influenced by Minsky and McCarthy's requirements for Lisp and symbolic programming. *Chess 4.0* and its descendants **[Slate and Atkin 84]** relied on the running on the world's fastest available computer. *Belle* **[Condon and Thompson 84]** used a smaller central computer, but had a custom move generator, built from LSI circuits. Deep Thought, mentioned above as the most recent champion, relies on custom VLSI circuits to handle its move generation and tree search. It is clear that the success and progress in chess playing programs has been driven by technology enabling large tree searches. Few would argue that today's chess programs/hardware systems are very good models for general human thought processes.

There were some misgivings along the way, however. In an early paper **[Selfridge 56]** argues that better static evaluation is the key to playing chess, so that look-ahead can be limited to a single move except in situations close to mate (and one assumes he would include situations where there is capture, and perhaps exchanges, involved). But, he claims that humans come to chess with a significant advantage over computers (the thrust of the paper is on learning, and in this instance on learning to play chess) as they have concepts such as "value", "double threat", the "centre" etc., already formed. Chess to Selfridge is not a disembodied exercise, but one where successful play is built upon a richness of experience in other, perhaps simpler, situations.

There is an interesting counterpoint to the history of computer chess; the game of Go. The search tree for Go is much much larger than for chess, and a good static evaluation function is much harder to define. Go has never worked out well as a vehicle for research in computer game playing—any reasonable crack at it is much more likely to require techniques much closer to those of human thought—mere computer technology advances are not going to bring the minimax approach close to success in this domain (see **[Campbell 83]** for a brief overview).

Before leaving Turing entirely there is one other rather significant contribution he made to the field which in a sense he predated. In **[Turing 50]** poses the question "Can machines think?". To tease out an acceptable meaning for this question he presented what has come to be known as the *Turing test*, where a person communicates in English over a teletype with either another person or a computer. The goal is to guess whether it is a person or a computer at the other end. Over time this test has come to be an informal goal of Artificial Intelligence[8]. Notice that it is a totally disembodied view of intelligence, although it is somewhat situated in that the machine has to respond in a timely fashion to its interrogator. Turing suggests that the machine should try to simulate a person by taking extra time and making mistakes with arithmetic problems. This is the version of the Turing test that is bandied around by current day Artificial Intelligence researchers[9].

Turing advances a number of strawman arguments against the case that a digital computer might one day be able to pass this test, but he does not consider the need that the machine be fully embodied. In principle, of course, he is right. But how a machine might be then programmed is a question. Turing provides an argument that programming the machine by hand would be impractical, so he suggests having it learn. At this point he brings up the need to embody the machine in some way. He rejects giving it limbs, but suspects that eyes would be good, although not entirely necessary. At the end of the paper he proposes two possible paths towards his goal of a "thinking" machine. The unembodied path is to concentrate on programming intellectual activities like chess, while the embodied approach is to equip a digital computer "with the best sense organs that money can buy, and then teach it to understand and speak English". Artificial Intelligence followed the former path, and has all but ignored the latter approach[10].

3.2 Establishment

The establishment of Artificial Intelligence as a discipline that is clearly the foundation of today's discipline by that name occurred during the period from the famous "Dartmouth Conference" of 1956 through the publication of the book "Computers and Thought" in 1963 (**[Feigenbaum and Feldman 63]**).

Named and mostly organized by John McCarthy as "The Dartmouth Summer Research Project on Artificial Intelligence" the six-week long workshop brought together those who would establish and lead the major Artificial Intelligence research centers in North America for the next twenty years. McCarthy jointly established the MIT Artificial Intelligence Laboratory with Marvin Minsky, and then went on to found the Stanford Artificial Intelligence Laboratory. Allen Newell and Herbert Simon shaped and led the group that turned into the Computer Science department at Carnegie-Mellon University. Even today a large portion of the researchers in Artificial Intelligence in North America had one of these four people on their doctoral committee, or were advised by someone who did. The ideas expressed at the Dartmouth meeting have thus had a signal impact upon the field first named there.

As can be seen from interviews of the participants published in [McCorduck 79] there is still some disagreement over the intellectual property that was brought to the conference and its relative significance. The key outcome was the acceptance and rise of search as the pre-eminent tool of Artificial Intelligence. There was a general acceptance of the use of search to solve problems, and with this there was an essential abandonment of any notion of situatedness.

Minsky's earlier work had been involved with neural modeling. His Ph.D. thesis at Princeton was concerned with a model for the brain [Minsky 54]. Later, while at Harvard he was strongly influenced by McCulloch and Pitts (see [McCulloch and Pitts 43]), but by the time of the Dartmouth meeting he had become more involved with symbolic search-based systems. In his collection [Minsky 68] of versions of his students' Ph.D. theses, all were concerned to some degree with defining and controlling an appropriate search space.

Simon and Newell presented their recent work on the *Logic Theorist* [Newell, Shaw and Simon 57], a program that proved logic theorems by searching a tree of subgoals. The program made extensive use of heuristics to prune its search space. With this success, the idea of heuristic search soon became dominant within the still tiny Artificial Intelligence community.

McCarthy was not so affected by the conference that he had organized, and continues to this day to concentrate on epistemological issues rather than performance programs. However he was soon to invent the Lisp programming language [McCarthy 1960] which became the standard model of computation for Artificial Intelligence. It had great influence on the models of thought that were popular however, as it made certain things such as search, and representations based on individuals, much easier to program.

At the time, most programs were written in assembly language. It was a tedious job to write search procedures, especially recursive procedures in the machine languages of the day, although some people such as [Samuel 59] (another Dartmouth participant) were spectacularly successful. Newell and Simon owed much of their success in developing the Logic Theorist and their later General Problem Solver [Newell, Shaw and Simon 59], to their use of an interpreted language (IPL-V—see [Newell, Shaw and Simon 61]) which supported complex list structures and recursion. Many of their students' projects reported in [Feigenbaum and Feldman 63] also used this language.

McCarthy's Lisp was much cleaner and simpler. It made processing lists of information and recursive tree searches trivial to program—often a dozen lines of code could replace many hundreds of lines of assembler code. Search procedures now became even easier and more convenient to include in Artificial Intelligence programs. Lisp also had an influence on the classes of representational systems used, as is described in section 3.5.

In **[Minsky 61]**, Artificial Intelligence was broken into five key topics: search, pattern recognition, learning, planning and induction. The second through fourth of these were characterized as ways of controlling search (respectively by better selection of tree expansion operators, by directing search through previous experience, and by replacing a given search with a smaller and more appropriate exploration). Again, most of the serious work in Artificial Intelligence according to this breakdown was concerned with search.

Eventually, after much experimentation **[Michie and Ross 70]**, search methods became well understood, formalized, and analyzed **[Knuth and Moore 75]**, and became celebrated as the primary method of Artificial Intelligence **[Nilsson 71]**.

At the end of the era of establishment, in 1963, Minsky generated an exhaustive annotated bibliography (**[Minsky 63]**) of literature "directly concerned with construction of artificial problem-solving systems"[11]. It contains 925 citations, 890 of which are to scientific papers and books, and 35 of which are to collections of such papers. There are two main points of interest here. First, although the title of the bibliography, "A Selected Descriptor-Indexed Bibliography to the Literature on Artificial Intelligence", refers to Artificial Intelligence, in his introduction he refers to the area of concern as "artificial problem-solving systems". Second, and somewhat paradoxically, the scope of the bibliography is much broader than one would expect from an Artificial Intelligence bibliography today. It includes many items on cybernetics, neuroscience, bionics, information and communication theory, and first generation connectionism.

These two contrasting aspects of the bibliography highlight a trend in Artificial Intelligence that continued for the next 25 years. Out of a soup of ideas on how to build intelligent machines the disembodied and non-situated approach of problem-solving search systems emerged as dominant, at least within the community that referred to its own work as Artificial Intelligence.

With hindsight we can step back and look at what happened. Originally search was introduced as a mechanism for solving problems that arguably humans used some search in solving. Chess and logic theorem proving are two examples we have already discussed. In these domains one does not expect instantaneous responses from humans doing the same tasks. They are not tasks that are situated in the world.

One can debate whether even in these tasks it is wise to rely so heavily on search, as bigger problems will have exponentially bad effects on search time—in fact **[Newell, Shaw and Simon 58]** argue just this, but produced a markedly slower chess program because of the complexity of static evaluation and search control. Some, such as **[Samuel 59]** with his checker's

118

playing program, did worry about keeping things on a human timescale. **[Slagle 63]** in his symbolic integration program, was worried about being economically competitive with humans, but as he points out in the last two paragraphs of his paper, the explosive increase in price/performance ratio for computing was able to keep his programs ahead. In general, performance increases in computers were able to feed researchers with a steadily larger search space, enabling them to feel that they were making progress as the years went by. For any given technology level, a long-term freeze would soon show that programs relying on search had very serious problems, especially if there was any desire to situate them in a dynamic world.

In the last paragraph of **[Minsky 61]** he does bring up the possibility of a situated agent, acting as a "thinking aid" to a person. But again he relies on a performance increase in standard computing methods (this time through the introduction of time sharing) to supply the necessary time relevant computations.

In the early days of the formal discipline of Artificial Intelligence, search was adopted as a basic technology. It was easy to program on digital computers. It led to reasoning systems which are not easy to shoe-horn into situated agents.

3.3 Cybernetics

There was, especially in the forties and fifties, another discipline which could be viewed as having the same goals as we have identified for Artificial Intelligence—the construction of useful intelligent systems and the understanding of human intelligence. This work, known as *Cybernetics*, had a fundamentally different flavor from today's traditional Artificial Intelligence.

Cybernetics co-evolved with control theory and statistical information theory—e.g., see **[Wiener 48, 61]**. It is the study of the mathematics of machines, not in terms of the functional components of a machine and how they are connected, and not in terms of what an individual machine can do here and now, but rather in terms of *all* the possible behaviors that an individual machine can produce. There was a strong emphasis on characterizing a machine in terms of its inputs and outputs, and treating it as a *black box* as far as its internal workings were unobservable. The tools of analysis were often differential or integral equations, and these tools inherently limited cybernetics to situations where the boundary conditions were not changing rapidly. In contrast, they often do so in a system situated in a dynamically changing world—that complexity needs to go somewhere; either into discontinuous models or changed boundary conditions.

Cybernetics arose in the context of regulation of machinery and electronic circuits—it is often characterized by the subtitle of Wiener's book as the study of "control and communication in the animal and the machine". The model of computation at the time of its original development was analog. The inputs to and outputs from the machine to be analyzed were usually thought of as almost everywhere continuous functions with reasonable derivatives, and the mechanisms for automated analysis and modeling were usually things that today would be characterized as analog components. As such there was no notion of symbolic search—any search was couched in terms of minimization of a function. There was also much less of a notion of representation as an abstract manipulable entity than was found in the Artificial Intelligence approaches.

Much of the work in Cybernetics really was aimed at understanding animals and intelligence. Animals were modeled as machines, and from those models, it was hoped to glean how the animals changed their behavior through learning, and how that led to better adaptation to the environment for the whole organism. It was recognized rather early (e.g., **[Ashby 52]** for an explicit statement) that an organism and its environment must be modeled together in order to understand the behavior produced by the organism— this is clearly an expression of situatedness. The tools of feedback analysis were used (**[Ashby 56]**) to concentrate on such issues as stability of the system as the environment was perturbed, and in particular a system's *homeostasis* or ability to keep certain parameters within prescribed ranges, no matter what the uncontrolled variations within the environment.

With regards to embodiment there were some experiments along these lines. Many cybernetic models of organisms were rather abstract demonstrations of homeostasis, but some were concerned with physical robots. **[Walter 50, 51, 53]**[12] describes robots built on cybernetic principles which demonstrated goal-seeking behavior, homeostasis, and learning abilities.

The complexity and abilities of Walter's physically embodied machines rank with the purely imaginary ones in the first half dozen chapters of **[Braitenberg 84]** three decades later.

The limiting factors in these experiments were twofold; (1) the technology of building small self contained robots when the computational elements were miniature (a relative term) vacuum tubes, and (2) the lack of mechanisms for abstractly describing behavior at a level below the complete behavior, so that an implementation could reflect those simpler components. Thus in the first instance the models of thought were limited by technological barriers to implementing those models, and in the second instance, the lack of certain critical components of a model (organization into submodules) restricted the ability to build better technological implementations.

Let us return to Wiener and analyze the ways in which the mechanisms of cybernetics, and the mechanisms of computation were intimately interrelated in deep and self limiting ways.

Wiener was certainly aware of digital machines[13] even in his earlier edition of **[Wiener 48]**. He compared them to analog machines such as the Bush differential analyzer, and declares that the digital (or *numerical*, as he called them) machines are superior for accurate numerical calculations. But in some deep sense Wiener did not see the flexibility of these machines. In an added chapter in **[Wiener 61]** he discussed the problem of building a self repro-ducing machine, and in the Cybernetic tradition, reduced the problem to modeling the input/output characteristics of a black box, in particular a non-linear transducer. He related methods for approximating observations of this function with a linear combination of basis non-linear transducers, and then showed that the whole problem could be done by summing and multiplying potentials and averaging over time. Rather than turn to a digital computer to do this he stated that there were some interesting possibilities for multiplica-tion devices using piezo-electric effects. We see then the intimate tying together between models of computation, i.e., analog computation, and models of the essentials of self-reproduction. It is impossible to tease apart cause and effect from this vantage point. The critical point is the way in which the mathematical proposal is tied to a technological implementation as a certification of the validity of the approach[14].

By the mid sixties it was clear that the study of intelligence, even a study arising from the principles of cybernetics, if it was to succeed needed to be more broad-based in its levels of abstraction and tools of analysis. A good example is **[Arbib 64]**[15]. Even so, he still harbors hope that cybernetic methods may turn out to give an understanding of the "overall coordinating and integrating principles" which interrelate the component subsystems of the human nervous system.

3.4 Abstraction

The years immediately following the Dartmouth conference shaped the field of Artificial Intelligence in a way which has not significantly changed. The next few years, in the main, amplified the abstraction away from situatedness, or connectedness to the world[16]. There were a number of demonstrations along the way which seemed to legitimize this abstraction. In this section I review some of those events, and argue that there were fundamental flaws in the conclusions generally drawn.

At MIT **[Roberts 63]** demonstrated a vision program that could match pre-stored models to visual images of blocks and wedges. This program was the forerunner of all modern vision programs, and it was many years before its performance could be matched by others. It took a grey level image of the world, and extracted a cartoonlike line drawing. It was this line drawing that was then fitted, via an inverse perspective transform to the pre-stored models. To those who saw its results this looked like a straightforward and natural way to process images and to build models (based on the pre-stored library) of the objective reality in front of the camera.

The unfortunate truth however, is that it is extraordinarily difficult to extract reliable line drawings in any sort of realistic cases of images. In

Roberts' case the lighting was carefully controlled, the blocks were well painted, and the background was chosen with care. The images of his blocks produced rather complete line drawings with very little clutter where there should, by human observer standards, be no line elements. Today, after almost thirty years of research on bottom-up, top-down, and middle-out line finders, there is still no line finder that gets such clean results on a single natural image. Real world images are not at all the clean things that our personal introspection tells us they are. It is hard to appreciate this without working on an image yourself[17].

The fallout of Roberts' program working on a very controlled set of images was that people thought that the line detection problem was doable and solved. E.g., [Evans 68] cites Roberts in his discussion of how input could be obtained for his analogy program which compared sets of line drawings of 2-D geometric figures.

During the late sixties and early seventies the Shakey project [Nilsson 84] at SRI reaffirmed the premises of abstract Artificial Intelligence. Shakey, mentioned in section 2, was a mobile robot that inhabited a set of specially prepared rooms. It navigated from room to room, trying to satisfy a goal given to it on a teletype. It would, depending on the goal and circumstances, navigate around obstacles consisting of large painted blocks and wedges, push them out of the way, or push them to some desired location.

Shakey had an onboard black and white television camera as its primary sensor. An offboard computer analyzed the images, and merged descriptions of what was seen into an existing first order predicate calculus model of the world. A planning program, STRIPS, operated on those symbolic descriptions of the world to generate a sequence of actions for Shakey. These plans were translated through a series of refinements into calls to atomic actions in fairly tight feedback loops with atomic sensing operations using Shakey's other sensors such as a bump bar and odometry.

Shakey was considered a great success at the time, demonstrating an integrated system involving mobility, perception, representation, planning, execution, and error recovery.

Shakey's success thus reaffirmed the idea of relying completely on internal models of an external objective reality. That is precisely the methodology it followed, and it appeared successful. However, it only worked because of very careful engineering of the environment. Twenty years later, no mobile robot has been demonstrated matching all aspects of Shakey's performance in a more general environment, such as an office environment.

The rooms in which Shakey operated were bare except for the large colored blocks and wedges. This made the class of objects that had to be represented very simple. The walls were of a uniform color, and carefully lighted, with dark rubber baseboards, making clear boundaries with the lighter colored floor. This meant that very simple and robust vision of trihedral corners between two walls and the floor, could be used for relocalizing the robot in order to correct for drift in the robot's odometric measurements. The blocks and wedges were painted different colors on different planar surfaces. This ensured that it was relatively easy, especially in the good lighting provided, to find edges in the images separating the surfaces, and thus making it easy to identify the shape of the polyhedron. Blocks and wedges were relatively rare in the environment, eliminating problems due to partial obscurations. The objective reality of the environment was thus quite simple, and the mapping to an internal model of that reality was also quite plausible.

Around the same time at MIT a major demonstration was mounted of a robot which could view a scene consisting of stacked blocks, then build a copy of the scene using a robot arm (see **[Winston 72]**—the program was known as the *copy-demo*). The programs to do this were very specific to the blocks world, and would not have worked in the presence of simple curved objects, rough texture on the blocks, or without carefully controlled lighting. Nevertheless it reinforced the idea that a complete three dimensional description of the world could be extracted from a visual image. It legitimized the work of others, such as **[Winograd 72]**, whose programs worked in a make-believe world of blocks—if one program could be built which understood such a world completely and could also manipulate that world, then it was assumed that programs which assumed that abstraction could in fact be connected to the real world without great difficulty. The problem remained of slowness of the programs due to the large search spaces, but as before, faster computers were always just around the corner.

The key problem that I see with all this work (apart from the use of search) is that it relied on the assumption that a complete world model could be built internally and then manipulated. The examples from Roberts, through Shakey and the copy-demo all relied on very simple worlds, and controlled situations. The programs were able to largely ignore unpleasant issues like sensor uncertainty, and were never really stressed because of the carefully controlled perceptual conditions. No computer vision systems can produce world models of this fidelity for anything nearing the complexity of realistic world scenes even object recognition is an active and difficult research area. There are two responses to this: (1) eventually computer vision will catch up and provide such world models—I don't believe this based on the biological evidence presented below, or (2) complete objective models of reality are unrealistic—and hence the methods of Artificial Intelligence that rely on such models are unrealistic.

With the rise in abstraction it is interesting to note that it was still quite technologically difficult to connect to the real world for most Artificial Intelligence researchers[18]. For instance, **[Barrow and Salter 70]** describe efforts at Edinburgh, a major Artificial Intelligence center, to connect sensing to action, and the results are extraordinarily primitive by today's standards—both MIT and SRI had major engineering efforts in support of their successful activities. **[Moravec 81]** relates a sad tale of frustration from the early seventies of efforts at the Stanford Artificial Intelligence Laboratory to build a simple mobile robot with visual input.

Around the late sixties and early seventies there was a dramatic increase in the availability of computer processing power available to researchers at reasonably well equipped laboratories. Not only was there a large increase in processing speed and physical memory, but time sharing systems became well established. An individual researcher was now able to work continuously and conveniently on a disembodied program designed to exhibit intelligence. However, connections to the real world were not only difficult and overly expensive, but the physical constraints of using them made development of the "intelligent" parts of the system slower by at least an order of magnitude, and probably two orders, as compared to the new found power of timesharing. The computers clearly had a potential to influence the models of thought used—and certainly that hypothesis is not contradicted by the sort of micro-world work that actually went on.

3.5 Knowledge

By this point in the history of Artificial Intelligence, the trends, assumptions, and approaches had become well established. The last fifteen years have seen the discipline thundering along on inertia more than anything else. Apart from a renewed flirtation with neural models (see section 3.8 below) there has been very little change in the underlying assumptions about the models of thought. This coincides with an era of very little technical innovation in our underlying models of computation.

For the remainder of section 3, I rather briefly review the progress made over the last fifteen years, and show how it relates to the fundamental issues of situatedness and embodiment brought up earlier.

One problem with micro-worlds is that they are somewhat uninteresting. The blocks world was the most popular micro-world and there is very little that can be done in it other than make stacks of blocks. After a flurry of early work where particularly difficult "problems" or "puzzles" were discovered and then solved (e.g., [Sussman 75]) it became more and more difficult to do something new within that domain.

There were three classes of responses to this impoverished problem space:

- Move to other domains with equally simple semantics, but with more interesting print names than *block-a* etc. It was usually not the intent of the researchers to do this, but many in fact did fall into this trap. [Winograd and Flores 86] expose and criticize a number of such dressings up in the chapter on "Understanding Language".
- Build a more complex semantics into the blocks world and work on the new problems which arise. A rather heroic example of this is [Fahlman 74] who included balance, multi-shaped blocks, friction, and the like. The

problem with this approach is that the solutions to the "puzzles" become so domain specific that it is hard to see how they might generalize to other domains.

- Move to the wider world. In particular, represent knowledge about the everyday world, and then build problem solvers, learning systems, etc., that operate in this semantically richer world.

The last of these approaches has spawned possibly the largest recognizable subfield of Artificial Intelligence, known as Knowledge Representation. It has its own conferences. It has theoretical and practical camps. Yet, it is totally ungrounded. It concentrates much of its energies on anomalies within formal systems which are never used for any practical tasks.

[Brachman and Levesque 85] is a collection of papers in the area. The knowledge representation systems described receive their input either in symbolic form or as the output of natural language systems. The goal of the papers seems to be to represent "knowledge" about the world. However it is totally ungrounded. There is very little attempt to use the knowledge (save in the naive physics **[Hayes 85]**, or qualitative physics **[de Kleer and Brown 84]** areas—but note that these areas too are ungrounded). There is an implicit assumption that someday the inputs and outputs will be connected to something which will make use of them (see **[Brooks 91a]** for an earlier criticism of this approach).

In the meantime the work proceeds with very little to steer it, and much of it concerns problems produced by rather simple-minded attempts at representing complex concepts. To take but one example, there have been many pages written on the problem of penguins being birds, even though they cannot fly. The reason that this is a problem is that the knowledge representation systems are built on top of a computational technology that makes convenient the use of very simple individuals (Lisp atoms) and placing links between them. As pointed out in **[Brooks 90b]**, and much earlier in **[Brooks 91a]**, such a simple approach does not work when the system is to be physically grounded through embodiment. It seems pointless to try to patch up a system which in the long run cannot possibly work. **[Dreyfus 81]**[19] provides a useful criticism of this style of work.

Perhaps the pinnacle of the knowledge-is-everything approach can be found in **[Lenat and Feigenbaum 91]** where they discuss the foundations of a 10-year project to encode knowledge having the scope of a simple encyclopedia. It is a totally unsituated, and totally disembodied approach. Everything the system is to know is through hand-entered units of "knowledge", although there is some hope expressed that later it will be able to learn itself by reading. **[Smith 91]** provides a commentary on this approach, and points out how the early years of the project have been devoted to finding a more primitive level of knowledge than was previously envisioned for grounding the higher levels of knowledge. It is my opinion, and also Smith's, that there is a fundamental problem still and one can expect continued regress until the system has some form of embodiment.

3.6 Robotics

Section 2 outlined the early history of mobile robots. There have been some interesting developments over the last ten years as attempts have been made to embody some theories from Artificial Intelligence in mobile robots. In this section I briefly review some of the results.

In the early eighties the Defense Advanced Research Projects Agency (DARPA) in the US, sponsored a major thrust in building an Autonomous Land Vehicle. The initial task for the vehicle was to run along a paved road in daylight using vision as the primary perceptual sense. The first attempts at this problem (e.g., **[Waxman, Le Moigne and Srinivasan 85]**) followed the SMPA methodology. The idea was to build a three-dimensional world model of the road ahead, then plan a path along it, including steering and velocity control annotations. These approaches failed as it was not possible to recover accurate three-dimensional road models from the visual images. Even under fairly strong assumptions about the class of roads being followed the programs would produce ludicrously wrong results.

With the pressure of getting actual demonstrations of the vehicle running on roads, and of having all the processing onboard, radical changes had to be made in the approaches taken. Two separate teams came up with similar approaches, **[Turk, Morgenthaler, Gremban, and Marra 88]** at Martin Marietta, the integrating contractor, and **[Thorpe, Hebert, Kanade, and Shafer 88]** at CMU, the main academic participant in the project, both producing vision-based navigation systems. Both systems operated in picture coordinates rather than world coordinates, and both successfully drove vehicles along the roads. Neither system generated three dimensional world models. Rather, both identified road regions in the images and servo-ed the vehicle to stay on the road. The systems can be characterized as reactive, situated and embodied. **[Horswill and Brooks 88]** describe a system of similar vintage which operates an indoor mobile robot under visual navigation. The shift in approach taken on the outdoor vehicle was necessitated by the realities of the technology available, and the need to get things operational.

Despite these lessons there is still a strong bias to following the traditional Artificial Intelligence SMPA approach as can be seen in the work at CMU on the Ambler project. The same team that adopted a reactive approach to the road following problem have reverted to a cumbersome, complex, and slow complete world modeling approach **[Simmons and Krotkov 91]**.

126

3.7 Vision

Inspired by the work of **[Roberts 63]** and that on Shakey **[Nilsson 84]**, the vision community has been content to work on scene description problems for many years. The implicit intent has been that when the reasoning systems of Artificial Intelligence were ready, the vision systems would be ready to deliver world models as required, and the two could be hooked together to get a situated, or embodied system.

There are numerous problems with this approach, and too little room to treat them adequately within the space constraints of this paper. The fundamental issue is that Artificial Intelligence and Computer Vision have made an assumption that the purpose of vision is to reconstruct the static external world (for dynamic worlds it is just supposed to do it often and quickly) as a three dimensional world model. I do not believe that this is possible with the generality that is usually assumed. Furthermore I do not think it is necessary, nor do I think that it is what human vision does. Section 4 discusses some of these issues a little more.

3.8 Parallelism

Parallel computers are potentially quite different from Von Neumann machines. One might expect then that parallel models of computation would lead to fundamentally different models of thought. The story about parallelism, and the influence of parallel machines on models of thought, and the influence of models of thought on parallel machines has two and a half pieces. The first piece arose around the time of the early cybernetics work, the second piece exploded in the mid-eighties and we have still to see all the casualties. The last half piece has been pressured by the current models of thought to change the model of parallelism.

There was a large flurry of work in the late fifties and sixties involving linear threshold devices, commonly known as perceptions. The extremes in this work are represented by **[Rosenblatt 62]** and **[Minsky and Papert 69]**. These devices were used in rough analogy to neurons and were to be wired into networks that learned to do some task, rather than having to be programmed. Adjusting the weights on the inputs of these devices was roughly equivalent in the model to adjusting the synaptic weights where axons connect to dendrites in real neurons—this is currently considered as the likely site of most learning within the brain.

The idea was that the network had specially distinguished inputs and outputs. Members of classes of partners would be presented to the inputs and the outputs would be given a correct classification. The difference between the correct response and the actual response of the network would then be used to update weights on the inputs of individual devices. The key driving force behind the blossoming of this field was the perception convergence theorem that showed that a simple parameter adjustment technique would always let a single perceptron learn a discrimination if there existed a set of weights capable of making that discrimination.

To make things more manageable the networks were often structured as layers of devices with connections only between adjacent layers. The directions of the connections were strictly controlled, so that there were no feedback loops in the network and that there was a natural progression from one single layer that would then be the input layer, and one layer would be the output layer. The problem with multi-layer networks was that there was no obvious way to assign the credit or blame over the layers for a correct or incorrect pattern classification.

In the formal analyses that were carried out (e.g., **[Nilsson 65]** and **[Minsky and Papert 69]**) only a single layer of devices which could learn, or be adjusted, were ever considered. **[Nilsson 65]** in the later chapters did consider multi-layer machines, but in each case, all but one layer consisted of static unmodifiable devices. There was very little work on analyzing machines with feedback.

None of these machines was particularly situated, or embodied. They were usually tested on problems set up by the researcher. There were many abuses of the scientific method in these tests—the results were not always as the researchers interpreted them.

After the publication of **[Minsky and Papert 69]**, which contained many negative results on the capabilities of single layer machines, the field seemed to die out for about fifteen years.

Recently there has been a resurgence in the field starting with the publication of **[Rumelhart and McClelland 86]**.

The new approaches were inspired by a new learning algorithm known as *back propagation* (**[Rumelhart, Hinton and Williams 86]**). This algorithm gives a method for assigning credit and blame in fully connected multi-layer machines without feedback loops. The individual devices, within the layers have linearly weighted inputs and a differentiable output function, a sigmoid, which closely matches a step function, or threshold function. Thus they are only slight generalizations of the earlier perceptrons, but their continuous and differentiable outputs enable hill climbing to be performed which lets the networks converge eventually to be able to classify inputs appropriately as trained.

Back propagation has a number of problems; it is slow to learn in general, and there is a learning rate which needs to be tuned by hand in most cases. The effect of a low learning rate is that the network might often get stuck in local minima. The effect of a higher learning rate is that the network may never really converge as it will be able to jump out of the correct minimum as well as it can jump out of an incorrect minimum. These problems combine to make back propagation, which is the cornerstone of modern neural network research, inconvenient for use in embodied or situated systems.

In fact, most of the examples in the new wave of neural networks have not been situated or embodied. There are a few counterexamples (e.g., **[Sejnowksi and Rosenberg 87]**, **[Atkeson 89]** and **[Viola 90]**) but in the main they are not based on back propagation. The most successful recent learning techniques for situated, embodied, mobile robots, have not been based on parallel algorithms at all—rather they use a reinforcement learning algorithm such as Q-learning (**[Watkins 89]**) as for example, **[Kaelbling 90]** and **[Mahadevan and Connell 90]**.

One problem for neural networks becoming situated or embodied is that they do not have a simple translation into time varying perception or action pattern systems. They need extensive front and back ends to equip them to interact with the world—all the cited examples above had such features added to them.

Both waves of neural network research have been heralded by predictions of the demise of all other forms of computation. It has not happened in either case. Both times there has been a bandwagon effect where many people have tried to use the mechanisms that have become available to solve many classes of problems, often without regard to whether the problems could even be solved in principle by the methods used. In both cases the enthusiasm for the approach has been largely stimulated by a single piece of technology, first the perceptron training rule, and then the back propagation algorithm.

And now for the last half-piece of the parallel computation story. The primary hope for parallel computation helping Artificial Intelligence has been the Connection Machine developed by **[Hillis 85]**. This is a SIMD machine, and as such might be thought to have limited applicability for general intelligent activities. Hillis, however, made a convincing case that it could be used for many algorithms having to do with knowledge representation, and that it would speed them up, often to be constant time algorithms. The book describing the approach is exciting, and in fact on pages 4 and 5 of **[Hillis 85]** the author promises to break the Von Neumann bottleneck by making all the silicon in a machine actively compute all the time. The argument is presented that most of the silicon in a Von Neumann machine is devoted to memory, and most of that is inactive most of the time. This was a brave new approach, but it has not survived the market place. New models of the connection machine have large local memories (in the order of 64K bits) associated with each one bit processor (there can be up to 64K processors in a single Connection Machine). Once again, most of the silicon is inactive most of the time. Connection machines are used within Artificial Intelligence laboratories mostly for computer vision where there is an obvious mapping from processors and their NEWS network to pixels of standard digital images. Traditional Artificial Intelligence approaches are so tied to their traditional machine architectures that they have been hard to map to this new sort of architecture.

4 Biology

We have our own introspection to tell us how our minds work, and our own observations to tell us how the behavior of other people and of animals works. We have our own partial theories and methods of explanation[20]. Sometimes, when an observation, internal or external, does not fit our pre-conceptions, we are rather ready to dismiss it as something we do not understand, and do not need to understand.

In this section I will skim over a scattering of recent work from ethology, psychology, and neuroscience, in an effort to indicate how deficient our everyday understanding of behavior really is. This is important to realize because traditional Artificial Intelligence has relied at the very least implicitly, and sometimes quite explicitly, on these folk understandings of human and animal behavior. The most common example is the story about getting from Boston to California (or vice-versa), which sets up an analogy between what a person does mentally in order to *Plan* the trip, and the means-ends method of planning. See **[Agre 91]** for a more detailed analysis of the phenomenon.

4.1 Ethology

Ethology, the study of animal behavior, tries to explain the causation, development, survival value, and evolution of behavior patterns within animals. See **[McFarland 85]** for an easy introduction to modern ethology.

Perhaps the most famous ethologist was Niko Tinbergen (closely followed by his co-Nobel winners Konrad Lorenz and Karl von Frisch). His hierarchical view of intelligence, described in **[Tinbergen 51]**, is often quoted by Artificial Intelligence researchers in support of their own hierarchical theories. However, this approach was meant to be a neurobiologically plausible theory, but it was described in the absence of any evidence. Tinbergen's model has largely been replaced in modern ethology by theories of motivational competition, disinhibition, and dominant and sub-dominant behaviors.

There is no completely worked out theory of exactly how the decision is made as to which behavioral pattern (e.g., drinking or eating) should be active in an animal. A large number of experiments give evidence of complex internal and external feedback loops in determining an appropriate behavior. **[McFarland 88]** presents a number of such experiments and demonstrates the challenges for the theories. The experimental data has ruled out the earlier hierarchical models of behavior selection, and current theories share many common properties with the behavior-based approach advocated in this paper.

4.2 Psychology

The way in which our brains work is quite hidden from us. We have some introspection, we believe, to some aspects of our thought processes, but there are certainly perceptual and motor areas that we are quite confident we have no access to[21]. To tease out the mechanisms at work we can do at least two sorts of experiments: we can test the brain at limits of its operational envelop to see how it breaks down, and we can study damaged brains and get a glimpse at the operation of previously integrated components. In fact, some of these observations call into question the reliability of any of our own introspections.

There have been many psychophysical experiments to test the limits of human visual perception. We are all aware of so-called *optical illusions* where our visual apparatus seems to break down. The journal *Perception* regularly carries papers which show that what we perceive is not what we see (e.g., **[Ramachandran and Anstis 85]**). For instance in visual images of a jumping leopard whose spots are made to artificially move about, we perceive them all as individually following the leopard. The straightforward model of human perception proposed by **[Marr 82]**, and almost universally accepted by Artificial Intelligence vision researchers, does not account for such results. Likewise it is now clear that the color pathway is separate from the intensity pathway in the human visual system, and our color vision is something of an illusion[22]. We are unaware of these deficiencies—most people are not aware that they have a blind spot in each eye the size of the image of the moon— they are totally inaccessible to our consciousness. Even more surprising, our very notion of consciousness is full of inconsistencies—psychophysical experiments show that our experience of the flow of time as we observe things in the world is an illusion, as we can often consciously perceive things in a temporal order inconsistent with the world as constructed by an experimenter (see **[Dennett and Kinsbourne 90]** for an overview).

We turn now to damaged brains to get a glimpse at how things might be organized. This work can better be termed *neuropsychology*. There is a large body of literature on this subject from which we merely pick out just a few instances here. The purpose is to highlight the fact that the approaches taken in traditional Artificial Intelligence are vastly different from the way the human brain is organized.

The common view in Artificial Intelligence, and particularly in the knowledge representation community, is that there is a central storage system which links together the information about concepts, individuals, categories, goals, intentions, desires, and whatever else might be needed by the system. In particular there is a tendency to believe that the knowledge is stored in a way that is independent from the way or circumstances in which it was acquired.

[McCarthy and Warrington 88] (and a series of earlier papers by them and their colleagues) give cause to doubt this seemingly logical organization. They report on a particular individual (identified as TOB), who at an advanced age developed a semantic deficit in knowledge of living things, but retained a reasonable knowledge of inanimate things. By itself, this sounds perfectly plausible—the semantic knowledge might just be stored in a category specific way, and the animate part of the storage has been damaged. But, it happens that TOB is able to access the knowledge when, for example he was shown a picture of a dolphin—he was able to form sentences using the word "dolphin" and talk about its habitat, its ability to be trained, and its role in the US military. When verbally asked what a dolphin is, however, he thought it was either a fish or a bird. He has no such conflict in knowledge when the subject is a wheelbarrow, say. The authors argue that since the deficit is not complete but shows degradation, the hypothesis that there is a deficit in a particular type of sensory modality access to a particular category subclass in a single database is not valid. Through a series of further observations they argue that they have shown evidence of modality-specific organization of meaning, besides a category specific organization. Thus knowledge may be duplicated in many places, and may by no means be uniformly accessible. There are examples of where the knowledge is shown to be inconsistent. Our normal introspection does not reveal this organization, and would seem to be at odds with these explanations. Below, we call into question our normal introspection.

[Newcombe and Ratcliff 89] present a long discussion of visuospatial disorders in brain damaged patients. Many of these severely tax the model of a person as an integrated rational agent. One simple example they report is finger agnosia, where a patient may be quite impaired in the way he can carry out conscious simple tasks using their fingers, but could still do things such as thread a needle, or play the piano well. This suggests the existence of multiple parallel channels of control, rather than some centralized finger control box, for instance.

[Teitelbaum, Pellis and Pellis 90] summarize work which shows that rat locomotion involves a number of reflexes. Drugs can be used to shut off many reflexes so that a rat will appear to be unable to move. Almost all stimuli have no effect—the rat simply remains with its limbs in whatever configuration the experimenter has arranged them. However certain very specific stimuli can trigger a whole chain of complex motor interactions— e.g., tilting the surface on which the rats feet are resting to the point where the rat starts to slide will cause the rat to leap. There has also been a recent popularization of the work of [Sacks 74] which shows similar symptoms, in somewhat less understood detail, for humans. Again, it is hard to explain these results in terms of a centralized will—rather an interpretation of multiple almost independent agencies such as hypothesized by [Minsky 86] seems a better explanation.

Perhaps the most remarkable sets of results are from split brain patients. It has become common knowledge that we all possess a left brain and a right brain, but in patients whose *corpus callosum* has been severed they really do become separate operational brains in their own rights **[Gazzaniga and LeDoux 77]**.

Through careful experimentation it is possible to independently communicate with the two brains, visually with both, and verbally with the left. By setting up experiments where one side does not have access to the information possessed by the other side, it is possible to push hard on the introspection mechanisms. It turns out that the ignorant half prefers to fabricate explanations for what is going on, rather than admit ignorance. These are normal people (except their brains are cut in half), and it seems that they sincerely believe the lies they are telling, as a result of confabulations generated during introspection. One must question then the ordinary introspection that goes on when our brains are intact.

What is the point of all this? The traditional Artificial Intelligence model of representation and organization along centralized lines is not how people are built. Traditional Artificial Intelligence methods are certainly not necessary for intelligence then, and so far they have not really been demonstrated to be sufficient in situated, embodied systems. The organization of humans is by definition sufficient—it is not known at all whether it will turn out to be necessary. The point is that we cannot make assumptions of necessity under either approach. The best we can expect to do for a while at least, is to show that some approach is sufficient to produce interesting intelligence.

4.3 Neuroscience

The working understanding of the brain among Artificial Intelligence researchers seems to be that it is an electrical machine with electrical inputs and outputs to the sensors and actuators of the body. One can see this assumption made explicit, for example, in the fiction and speculative writing of professional Artificial Intelligence researchers such as **[Dennett 81]** and **[Moravec 88]**. This view, and further reduction, leads to the very simple models of brain used in connectionism (**[Rumelhart and McCelland 86]**).

In fact, however, the brain is embodied with a much more serious coupling. The brain is situated in a soup of hormones, that influences it in the strongest possible ways. It receives messages encoded hormonally, and sends messages so encoded throughout the body. Our electrocentrism, based on our electronic models of computation, has led us to ignore these aspects in our informal models of neuroscience, but hormones play a strong, almost dominating, role in determination of behavior in both simple (**[Kravitz 88]**) and higher animals (**[Bloom 76]**)[23].

Real biological systems are not rational agents that take inputs, compute logically, and produce outputs. They are a mess of many mechanisms working in various ways, out of which emerges the behavior that we observe and rationalize. We can see this in more detail by looking both at the individual computational level, and at the organizational level of the brain.

We do not really know how computation is done at the lowest levels in the brain. There is debate over whether the neuron is the functional unit of the nervous system, or whether a single neuron can act as many independent smaller units ([Cohen and Wu 90]). However, we do know that signals are propagated along axons and dendrites at very low speeds compared to electronic computers, and that there are significant delays crossing synapses. The usual estimates for the computational speed of neuronal systems are no more than about 1 KiloHertz. This implies that the computations that go on in humans to effect actions in the subsecond range must go through only a very limited number of processing steps—the network cannot be very deep in order to get meaningful results out on the timescales that routinely occur for much of human thought. On the other hand, the networks seem incredibly richly connected, compared to the connection width of either our electronic systems, or our connectionist models. For simple creatures some motor neurons are connected to tens of percent of the other neurons in the animal. For mammals motor neurons are typically connected to 5,000 and some neurons in humans are connected to as many as 90,000 other neurons ([Churchland 86]).

For one very simple animal *Caenorhabditis elegans*, a nematode, we have a complete wiring diagram of its nervous system, including its development stages ([Wood 88]). In the hermaphrodite there are 302 neurons and 56 support cells out of the animal's total of 959 cells. In the male there are 381 neurons and 92 support cells out of a total of 1031 cells. Even though the anatomy and behavior of this creature are well studied, and the neuronal activity is well probed, the way in which the circuits control the animal's behavior is not understood very well at all.

Given that even a simple animal is not yet understood one cannot expect to gain complete insight into building Artificial Intelligence by looking at the nervous systems of complex animals. We can, however, get insight into aspects of intelligent behavior, and some clues about sensory systems and motor systems.

[Wehner 87] for instance, gives great insight into the way in which evolution has selected for sensor-neurological couplings with the environment which can be very specialized. By choosing the right sensors, animals can often get by with very little neurological processing, in order to extract just the right information about the here and now around them, for the task at hand. Complex world model building is not possible given the sensors' limitations, and not needed when the creature is appropriately situated.

[Cruse 90] and [Götz and Wenking 73] give insight into how simple animals work, based on an understanding at a primitive level of their neurological circuits. These sorts of clues can help us as we try to build walking robots—

for examples of such computational neuroethology see **[Brooks 89]** and **[Beer 90]**.

These clues can help us build better artificial systems, but by themselves they do not provide us with a full theory.

5 Ideas

Earlier we identified situatedness, embodiment, intelligence, and emergence, with a set of key ideas that have led to a new style of Artificial Intelligence research which we are calling behavior-based robots. In this section I expound on these four topics in more detail.

5.1 Situatedness

Traditional Artificial Intelligence has adopted a style of research where the agents that are built to test theories in intelligence are essentially problem solvers that work in a symbolic abstracted domain. The symbols may have referents in the minds of the builders of the systems, but there is nothing to ground those referents in any real world. Furthermore, the agents are not situated in a world at all. Rather they are given a problem, and they solve it. Then, they are given another problem and they solve it. They are not participating in a world as would agents in the usual sense.

In these systems there is no external world per se, with continuity, surprises, or ongoing history. The programs deal only with a model world, with its own built-in physics. There is a blurring between the knowledge of the agent and the world it is supposed to be operating in—indeed in many Artificial Intelligence systems there is no distinction between the two—the agent has access to direct and perfect perception, and direct and perfect action. When consideration is given to porting such agents or systems to operate in the world, the question arises of what sort of representation they need of the real world. Over the years within traditional Artificial Intelligence, it has become accepted that they will need an objective model of the world with individuated entities, tracked and identified over time—the models of knowledge representation that have been developed expect and require such a one-to-one correspondence between the world and the agent's representation of it.

The early robots such as Shakey and the Cart certainly followed this approach. They built models of the world, planned paths around obstacles, and updated their estimate of where objects were relative to themselves as they moved. We developed a different approach **[Brooks 86]** where a mobile robot used the world as its own model—continuously referring to its sensors rather than to an internal world model. The problems of object class and identity disappeared. The perceptual processing became much simpler. And the performance of the robot was better in comparable tasks than that of the

Cart[24], and with much less computation, even allowing for the different sensing modalities.

[Agre 88] and [Chapman 90] formalized these ideas in their arguments for *deictic* (or *indexical-functional* in an earlier incarnation) representations. Instead of having representations of individual entities in the world, the system has representations in terms of the relationship of the entities to the robot. These relationships are both spatial and functional. For instance in Pengi [Agre and Chapman 87], rather than refer to *Bee-27* the system refers to *the-bee-that-is-chasing-me-now*. The latter may or may not be the same bee that was chasing the robot two minutes previously—it doesn't matter for the particular tasks in which the robot is engaged.

When this style of representation is used it is possible to build computational systems which trade off computational depth for computational width. The idea is that the computation can be represented by a network of gates, timers, and state elements. The network does not need long paths from inputs (sensors) to outputs (actuators). Any computation that is capable of being done is done in a very short time span. There have been other approaches which address a similar time-bounded computation issue, namely the *bounded rationality* approach [Russell 89]. Those approaches try to squeeze a traditional Artificial Intelligence system into a bounded amount of computation. With the new approach we tend to come from the other direction, we start with very little computation and build up the amount, while staying away from the boundary of computation that takes too long. As more computation needs to be added there is a tendency to add it in breadth (thinking of the computation as being represented by a circuit whose depth is the longest path length in gates from input to output) rather than depth.

A situated agent must respond in a timely fashion to its inputs. Modeling the world completely under these conditions can be computationally challenging. But a world in which it is situated also provides some continuity to the agent. That continuity can be relied upon, so that the agent can use its perception of the world instead of an objective world model. The representational primitives that are useful then change quite dramatically from those in traditional Artificial Intelligence.

The key idea from situatedness is:

The world is its own best model.

5.2 Embodiment

There are two reasons that embodiment of intelligent systems is critical. First, only an embodied intelligent agent is fully validated as one that can deal with the real world. Second, only through a physical grounding can any internal symbolic or other system find a place to bottom out, and give "meaning" to the processing going on within the system.

136

The physical grounding of a robot in the world forces its designer to deal with all the issues. If the intelligent agent has a body, has sensors, and has actuators, then all the details and issues of being in the world must be faced. It is no longer possible to argue in conference papers, that the simulated perceptual system is realistic, or that problems of uncertainty in action will not be significant. Instead, physical experiments can be done simply and repeatedly. There is no room for cheating[25]. When this is done it is usual to find that many of the problems that seemed significant are not so in the physical system (typically "puzzle" like situations where symbolic reasoning seemed necessary tend not to arise in embodied systems), and many that seemed non-problems become major hurdles (typically these concern aspects of perception and action)[26].

A deeper problem is "can there be disembodied mind?". Many believe that what is human about us is very directly related to our physical experiences. For instance [Johnson 87] argues that a large amount of our language is actually metaphorically related to our physical connections to the world. Our mental "concepts" are based on physically experienced exemplars [Smith 91] suggests that without physical grounding there can be no halt to the regress within a knowledge based system as it tries to reason about real world knowledge such as that contained in an encyclopedia (e.g., [Lenat and Feigenbaum 91]).

Without an ongoing participation and perception of the world there is no meaning for an agent. Everything is random symbols. Arguments might be made that at some level of abstraction even the human mind operates in this solipsist position. However, biological evidence (see section 4) suggests that the human mind's connection to the world is so strong, and many faceted, that these philosophical abstractions may not be correct.

The key idea from embodiment is:

The world grounds regress.

5.3 *Intelligence*

[Brooks 91a] argues that the sorts of activities we usually think of as demonstrating intelligence in humans have been taking place for only a very small fraction of our evolutionary lineage. Further, I argue that the "simple" things to do with perception and mobility in a dynamic environment took evolution much longer to perfect, and that all those capabilities are a necessary basis for "higher-level" intellect.

Therefore, I proposed looking at simpler animals as a bottom-up model for building intelligence. It is soon apparent, when "reasoning" is stripped away as the prime component of a robot's intellect, that the dynamics of the interaction of the robot and its environment are primary determinants of the structure of its intelligence.

Earlier, [Simon 69] had discussed a similar point in terms of an ant walking along the beach. He pointed out that the complexity of the behavior of the ant is more a reflection of the complexity of its environment than its own internal complexity. He speculated that the same may be true of humans, but within two pages of text had reduced studying human behavior to the domain of crypto-arithmetic problems.

It is hard to draw the line at what is intelligence, and what is environmental interaction. In a sense it does not really matter which is which, as all intelligent systems must be situated in some world or other if they are to be useful entities.

The key idea from intelligence is:

> *Intelligence is determined by the dynamics of interaction with the world.*

5.4 Emergence

In discussing where intelligence resides in an Artificial Intelligence program [Minsky 61] points out that "there is never any 'heart' in a program" and "we find senseless loops and sequences of trivial operations". It is hard to point at a single component as the seat of intelligence. There is no homunculus. Rather, intelligence emerges from the interaction of the components of the system. The way in which it emerges, however, is quite different for traditional and behavior-based Artificial Intelligence systems.

In traditional Artificial Intelligence the modules that are defined are information processing, or functional. Typically these modules might be a perception module, a planner, a world modeler, a learner, etc. The components directly participate in functions such as perceiving, planning, modeling, learning, etc. Intelligent behavior of the system, such as avoiding obstacles, standing up, controlling gaze, etc., emerges from the interaction of the components.

In behavior-based Artificial Intelligence the modules that are defined are behavior producing. Typically these modules might be an obstacle avoidance behavior, a standing up behavior, a gaze control behavior, etc. The components directly participate in producing behaviors such as avoiding obstacles, standing up, controlling gaze, etc. Intelligent functionality of the system, such as perception, planning, modeling, learning, etc., emerges from the interaction of the components.

Although this dualism between traditional and behavior-based systems looks pretty it is not completely accurate. Traditional systems have hardly ever been really connected to the world, and so the emergence of intelligent behavior is something more of an expectation in most cases, rather than an established phenomenon. Conversely, because of the many behaviors present in a behavior-based system, and their individual dynamics of interaction with the world, it is often hard to say that a particular series of actions was produced by a particular behavior. Sometimes many behaviors are operating simultaneously, or are switching rapidly **[Horswill and Brooks 88]**.

Over the years there has been a lot of work on emergence based on the theme of self-organization (e.g., **[Nicolis and Prigogine 77]**). Within behavior-based robots there is beginning to be work at better characterizing emergent functionality, but it is still in its early stages, e.g., **[Steels 90a]**. He defines it as meaning that a function is achieved "indirectly by the interaction of more primitive components among themselves and with the world".

It is hard to identify the seat of intelligence within any system, as intelligence is produced by the interactions of many components. Intelligence can only be determined by the total behavior of the system and how that behavior appears in relation to the environment.

The key idea from emergence is:

Intelligence is in the eye of the observer.

6 Thought

Since late 1984 I have been building autonomous mobile robots in the "Mobot Lab" at the MIT Artificial Intelligence Laboratory; **[Brooks 86]** gives the original ideas, and **[Brooks 90b]** contains a recent summary of the capabilities of the robots developed in my laboratory over the years.

My work fits within the framework described above in terms of situatedness, embodiment, intelligence and emergence. In particular I have advocated situatedness, embodiment, and highly reactive architectures with no reasoning systems, no manipulable representations, no symbols, and totally decentralized computation. This different model of computation has led to radically different models of thought.

I have been accused of overstating the case that the new approach is all that is necessary to build truly intelligent systems. It has even been suggested that as an evangelist I have deliberately overstated my case to pull people towards the correct level of belief, and that really all along, I have known that a hybrid approach is necessary.

That is not what I believe. I think that the new approach can be extended to cover the whole story, both with regards to building intelligent systems and to understanding human intelligence—the two principal goals identified for Artificial Intelligence at the beginning of the paper.

Whether I am right or not is an empirical question. Multiple approaches to Artificial Intelligence will continue to be pursued. At some point we will be able to evaluate which approach has been more successful.

In this section I want to outline the philosophical underpinnings of my work, and discuss why I believe the approach is the one that in the end will prove dominant.

6.1 Principles

All research goes on within the constraints of certain principles. Sometimes these are explicit, and sometimes they are implicit. In the following paragraphs I outline as explicitly as I can the principles followed.

The first set of principles defines the domain for the work.

- The goal is to study complete integrated intelligent autonomous agents.
- The agents should be embodied as mobile robots, situated in unmodified worlds found around our laboratory[27]. This confronts the embodiment issue. The environments chosen are for convenience, although we strongly resist the temptation to change the environments in any way for the robots.
- The robots should operate equally well when visitors, or cleaners, walk through their workspace, when furniture is rearranged, when lighting or other environmental conditions change, and when their sensors and actuators drift in calibration. This confronts the situatedness issue.
- The robots should operate on timescales commensurate with the time scales used by humans. This too confronts the situatedness issue.

The specific model of computation used was not originally based on biological models. It was one arrived at by continuously refining attempts to program a robot to reactively avoid collisions in a people-populated environment, [Brooks 86]. Now, however, in stating the principles used in the model of computation, it is clear that it shares certain properties with models of how neurological systems are arranged. It is important to emphasize that it only shares certain properties. Our model of computation is not intended as a realistic model of how neurological systems work. We call our computation model the *subsumption architecture* and its purpose is to program intelligent, situated, embodied agents.

Our principles of computation are:

- Computation is organized as an asynchronous network of active computational elements (they are *augmented finite state machines*—see [Brooks 89] for details[28]), with a fixed topology network of unidirectional connections.
- Messages sent over connections have no implicit semantics—they are small numbers (typically 8 or 16 bits, but on some robots just 1 bit) and their meanings are dependent on the dynamics designed into both the sender and receiver.
- Sensors and actuators are connected to this network, usually through asynchronous two-sided buffers.

These principles lead to certain consequences. In particular:

- The system can certainly have state—it is not at all constrained to be purely reactive.
- Pointers and manipulable data structures are very hard to implement (since the model is Turing equivalent it is of course possible, but hardly within the spirit).
- Any search space must be quite bounded in size, as search nodes cannot be dynamically created and destroyed during the search process.
- There is no implicit separation of data and computation, they are both distributed over the same network of elements.

In considering the biological observations outlined in section 4, certain properties seemed worth incorporating into the way in which robots are programmed within the given model of computation. In all the robots built in the mobot lab, the following principles of organization of intelligence have been observed:

- There is no central model maintained of the world. All data is distributed over many computational elements.
- There is no central locus of control.
- There is no separation into perceptual system, central system, and actuation system. Pieces of the network may perform more than one of these functions. More importantly, there is intimate intertwining of aspects of all three of them.
- The behavioral competence of the system is improved by adding more behavior-specific network to the existing network. We call this process *layering*. This is a simplistic and crude analogy to evolutionary development. As with evolution, at every stage of the development the systems are tested—unlike evolution there is a gentle debugging process available. Each of the layers is a behavior-producing piece of network in its own right, although it may implicitly rely on presence of earlier pieces of network.
- There is no hierarchical arrangement—i.e., there is no notion of one process calling on another as a subroutine. Rather the networks are designed so that needed computations will simply be available on the appropriate input line when needed. There is no explicit synchronization between a producer and a consumer of messages. Message reception buffers can be overwritten by new messages before the consumer has looked at the old one. It is not atypical for a message producer to send 10 messages for every one that is examined by the receiver.
- The layers, or behaviors, all run in parallel. There may need to be a conflict resolution mechanism when different behaviors try to give different actuator commands.
- The world is often a good communication medium for processes, or behaviors, within a single robot.

It should be clear that these principles are quite different to the ones we have become accustomed to using as we program Von Neumann machines. It necessarily forces the programmer to use a different style of organization for their programs for intelligence.

There are also always influences on approaches to building thinking machines that lie outside the realm of purely logical or scientific thought. The following, perhaps arbitrary, principles have also had an influence on the organization of intelligence that has been used in Mobot Lab robots:

- A decision was made early on that all computation should be done onboard the robots. This was so that the robots could run tether-free and without any communication link. The idea is to download programs over cables (although in the case of some of our earlier robots the technique was to plug in a newly written erasable ROM) into non-volatile storage on the robots, then switch them on to interact with and be situated in the environment.
- In order to maintain a long term goal of being able to eventually produce very tiny robots (**[Flynn 87]**) the computational model has been restricted so that any specification within that model could be rather easily complied into a silicon circuit. This has put an additional constraint on designers of agent software, in that they cannot use non-linear numbers of connections between collections of computational elements, as that would lead to severe silicon compilation problems. Note that the general model of computation outlined above is such that a goal of silicon compilation is in general quite realistic.

The point of section 3 was to show how the technology of available computation had a major impact on the shape of the developing field of Artificial Intelligence. Likewise there have been a number of influences on my own work that are technological in nature. These include:

- Given the smallness in overall size of the robots there is a very real limitation on the amount of onboard computation that can be carried, and by an earlier principle all computation must be done onboard. The limiting factor on the amount of portable computation is not weight of the computers directly, but the electrical power that is available to run them. Empirically we have observed that the amount of electrical power available is proportional to the weight of the robot[29].
- Since there are many single chip microprocessors available including EEPROM and RAM, it is becoming more possible to include large numbers of sensors which require interrupt servicing, local calibration, and data massaging. The microprocessors can significantly reduce the overall wiring complexity by servicing a local group of sensors (e.g., all those on a single leg of a robot) *in situ*, and packaging up the data

to run over a communication network to the behavior-producing network.

These principles have been used in the programming of a number of behavior-based robots. Below we point out the importance of some of these robot demonstrations in indicating how the subsumption architecture (or one like it in spirit) can be expected to scale up to very intelligent applications. In what follows individual references are given to the most relevant piece of the literature. For a condensed description of what each of the robots is and how they are programmed, the reader should see **[Brooks 90b]**; it also includes a number of robots not mentioned here.

6.2 Reactivity

The earliest demonstration of the subsumption architecture was on the robot *Allen* (**[Brooks 86]**). It was almost entirely reactive, using sonar readings to keep away from people and other moving obstacles, while not colliding with static obstacles. It also had a non-reactive higher level layer that would select a goal to head towards, and then proceed to that location while the lower level reactive layer took care of avoiding obstacles.

The very first subsumption robot thus combined non-reactive capabilities with reactive ones. But the important point is that it used exactly the same sorts of computational mechanism to do both. In looking at the network of the combined layers there was no obvious partition into lower and higher level components based on the type of information flowing on the connections, or the state machines that were the computational elements. To be sure, there was a difference in function between the two layers, but there was no need to introduce any centralization or explicit representations to achieve a higher level, or later, process having useful and effective influence over a lower level.

The second robot, *Herbert* (**[Connell 89]**), pushed on the reactive approach. It used a laser scanner to find soda can-like objects visually, infrared proximity sensors to navigate by following walls and going through door-ways, a magnetic compass to maintain a global sense of orientation, and a host of sensors on an arm which were sufficient to reliably pick up soda cans. The task for Herbert was to wander around looking for soda cans, pick one up, and bring it back to where Herbert had started from. It was demonstrated reliably finding soda cans in rooms using its laser range finder (some tens of trials), picking up soda cans many times (over 100 instances), reliably navigating (many hours of runs), and in one finale doing all the tasks together to navigate, locate, pickup and return with a soda can[30].

In programming Herbert it was decided that it should maintain no state longer than three seconds, and that there would be no internal communication between behavior generating modules. Each one was connected to sensors on the input side, and a fixed priority arbitration network on the output side. The arbitration network drove the actuators.

In order to carry out its tasks, Herbert, in many instances, had to use the world as its own best model and as a communication medium. E.g., the laser-based soda can object finder drove the robot so that its arm was lined up in front of the soda can. But it did not tell the arm controller that there was now a soda can ready to be picked up. Rather, the arm behaviors monitored the shaft encoders on the wheels, and when they noticed that there was no body motion, initiated motions of the arm, which in turn triggered other behaviors, so that eventually the robot would pick up the soda can.

The advantage of this approach was that there was no need to set up internal expectations for what was going to happen next; that meant that the control system could both (1) be naturally opportunistic if fortuitous circumstances presented themselves, and (2) it could easily respond to changed circumstances, such as some other object approaching it on a collision course.

As one example of how the arm behaviors cascaded upon one another, consider actually grasping a soda can. The hand had a grasp reflex that operated whenever something broke an infrared beam between the fingers. When the arm located a soda can with its local sensors, it simply drove the hand so that the two fingers lined up on either side of the can. The hand then independently grasped the can. Given this arrangement, it was possible for a human to hand a soda can to the robot. As soon as it was grasped, the arm retracted—it did not matter whether it was a soda can that was intentionally grasped, or one that magically appeared. The same opportunism among behaviors let the arm adapt automatically to a wide variety of cluttered desktops, and still successfully find the soda can.

In order to return to where it came from after picking up a soda can, Herbert used a trick. The navigation routines could carry implement rules such as: *when passing through a door southbound, turn left.* These rules were conditionalized on the separation of the fingers on the hand. When the robot was outbound with no can in its hand, it effectively executed one set of rules. After picking up a can, it would execute a different set. By carefully designing the rules, Herbert was guaranteed, with reasonable reliability, to retrace its path.

The point of Herbert is two-fold.

- It demonstrates complex, apparently goal directed and intentional, behavior in a system which has no long term internal state and no internal communication.
- It is very easy for an observer of a system to attribute more complex internal structure than really exists. Herbert appeared to be doing things like path planning and map building, even though it was not.

6.3 Representation

My earlier paper **[Brooks 91a]** is often criticized for advocating absolutely no representation of the world within a behavior-based robot. This criticism is invalid. I make it clear in the paper that I reject traditional Artificial Intelligence representation schemes (see section 5). I also made it clear that I reject explicit representations of goals within the machine.

There can, however, be representations which are partial models of the world—in fact I mentioned that "individual layers extract only those *aspects* of the world which they find relevant—projections of a representation into a simple subspace" **[Brooks 91a]**. The form these representations take, within the context of the computational model we are using, will depend on the particular task those representations are to be used for. For more general navigation than that demonstrated by Connell it may sometimes[31] need to build and maintain a map.

[Mataric 90, 91] introduced *active-constructive representations* to subsumption in a sonar-based robot, *Toto*, which wandered around office environments building a map based on landmarks, and then used that map to get from one location to another. Her representations were totally decentralized and non-manipulable, and there is certainly no central control which build, maintains, or uses the maps. Rather, the map itself is an active structure which does the computations necessary for any path planning the robot needs to do.

Primitive layers of control let Toto wander around following boundaries (such as walls and furniture clutter) in an indoor environment. A layer which detects landmarks, such as flat clear walls, corridors, etc., runs in parallel. It informs the map layer as its detection certainty exceeds a fixed threshold. The map is represented as a graph internally. The nodes of the graph are computational elements (they are identical little subnetworks of distinct augmented finite state machines). Free nodes arbitrate and allocate themselves, in a purely local fashion, to represent a new landmark, and set up topological links to physically neighboring nodes (using a limited capacity switching network to keep the total virtual "wire length" between finite state machines to be linear in the map capacity). These nodes keep track of where the robot is physically, by observing changes in the output of the landmark detector, and comparing that to predictions they have made by local message passing, and by referring to other more primitive (magnetic compass based) coarse position estimation schemes.

When a higher layer wants the robot to go to some known landmark, it merely "excites", in some particular way the particular place in the map that it wants to go. The excitation (this is an abstraction programmed into the particular finite state machines used here—it is not a primitive—as such there could be many different types of excitation co-existing in the map, if other types of planning are required) is spread through the map following topological links, estimating total path link, and arriving at the *landmark-that-I'm-at-now* node (a deictic representation) with a recommendation of the direction to travel right now to follow the shortest path. As the robot moves so too does its representation of where it is, and at that new node the arriving excitation tells it where to go next. The map thus bears a similarity to the *internalized plans* of **[Payton 90]**, but it is represented by the same computational elements that use it—there is no distinction between data and process. Furthermore Mataric's scheme can have multiple simultaneously active goals—the robot will simply head towards the nearest one.

This work demonstrates the following aspects of behavior-based or subsumption systems:

- Such systems can make predictions about what will happen in the world, and have expectations.
- Such systems can make plans—but they are not the same as traditional Artificial Intelligence plans—see **[Agre and Chapman 90]** for an analysis of this issue.
- Such systems can have goals—see **[Maes 90b]** for another way to implement goals within the approach.
- All these things can be done without resorting to central representations.
- All these things can be done without resorting to manipulable representations.
- All these things can be done without resorting to symbolic representations.

6.4 Complexity

Can subsumption-like approaches scale to arbitrarily complex systems? This is a question that cannot be answered affirmatively right now—just as it is totally unfounded to answer the same question affirmatively in the case of traditional symbolic Artificial Intelligence methods. The best one can do is point to precedents and trends.

There are a number of dimensions along which the scaling question can be asked. E.g.,

- Can the approach work well as the environment becomes more complex?
- Can the approach handle larger numbers of sensors and actuators?
- Can the approach work smoothly as more and more layers or behaviors are added?

We answer each of these in turn in the following paragraphs.

The approach taken at the Mobot Lab has been that from day one always test the robot in the most complex environment for which it is ultimately destined. This forces even the simplest levels to handle the most complex environment expected. So for a given robot and intended environment the scaling question is handled by the methodology chosen for implementation. But there is also the question of how complex are the environments that are targeted for with the current generation of robots. Almost all of our robots have been tested and operated in indoor environments with people unrelated to the research wandering through their work area at will. Thus we have a certain degree of confidence that the same basic approach will work in out-door environments (the sensory processing will have to change for some sensors) with other forms of dynamic action taking place.

The number of sensors and actuators possessed by today's robots are piti-ful when compared to the numbers in even simple organisms such as insects. Our first robots had only a handful of identical sonar sensors and two motors. Later a six legged walking robot was built [Angle 89]. It had 12 actuators and 20 sensors, and was successfully programmed in subsumption ([Brooks 89]) to walk adaptively over rough terrain. The key was to find the right factoring into sensor and actuator subsystems so that interactions between the subsystems could be minimized. A new six legged robot, recently completed ([Brooks and Angle 90], is much more challenging, but still nowhere near the complexity of insects. It has 23 actuators and over 150 sensors. With this level of sensing it is possible to start to develop some of the "senses" that animals and humans have, such as a kinesthetic sense—this comes from the contributions of many sensor readings. Rather, than feed into a geometric model the sensors feed into an estimate of bodily motion. There is also the question of the types of sensors used. [Horswill and Brooks 88] generalized the subsumption architecture so that some of the connec-tions between processing elements could be a *retina bus*, a cable that transmitted partially processed images from one site to another within the system. The robot so programmed was able to follow corridors and follow moving objects in real time.

As we add more layers we find that the interactions can become more complex. [Maes 89] introduced the notion of switching whole pieces of the network on and off, using an *activation* scheme for behaviors. That idea is now incorporated into the subsumption methodology [Brooks 90c], and pro-vides a way of implementing both competition and cooperation between behaviors. At a lower level a hormone-like system has been introduced ([Brooks 91b]) which models the hormone system of the lobster [Kravitz 88] ([Arkin 88] had implemented a system with similar inspiration). With these additional control mechanisms we have certainly brought ourselves breathing room to increase the performance of our systems markedly. The key point about these control systems is that they fit exactly into the existing structures, and are totally distributed and local in their operations.

6.5 Learning

Evolution has decided that there is a tradeoff between what we know through our genes and what we must find out for ourselves as we develop. We can expect to see a similar tradeoff for our behavior-based robots.

There are at least four classes of things that can be learned:

1. representations of the world that help in some task
2. aspects of instances of sensors and actuators (this is sometimes called calibration)
3. the ways in which individual behaviors should interact
4. new behavioral modules

The robots in the Mobot Lab have been programmed to demonstrate the first three of these types of learning. The last one has not yet been successfully tackled[32].

Learning representations of the world was already discussed above concerning the work of **[Mataric 90, 91]**. The next step will be to generalize active-constructive representations to more classes of use.

[Viola 90] demonstrated calibration of a complex head-eye system modeling the primate vestibulo-ocular system. In this system there is one fast channel between a gyroscope and a high performance pan-tilt head holding the camera, and a slower channel using vision which produces correction signals for the gyroscope channel. The same system was used to learn how to accurately saccade to moving stimuli.

Lastly, **[Maes and Brooks 90]** programmed an early six legged robot to learn to walk using the subsumption architecture along with the behavior activation schemes of **[Maes 89]**. Independent behaviors on each leg monitored the activity of other behaviors and correlated that, their own activity state, and the results from a belly switch which provided negative feedback, as input to a local learning rule which learned under which conditions it was to operate the behavior. After about 20 trials per leg, spread over a total of a minute or two, the robot reliably learns the alternating tripod gait—it slowly seems to emerge out of initially chaotic flailing of the legs.

Learning within subsumption is in its early stages but it has been demonstrated in a number of different critical modes of development.

6.6 Vistas

The behavior-based approach has been demonstrated on situated embodied systems doing things that traditional Artificial Intelligence would have tackled in quite different ways. What are the key research areas that need to be addressed in order to push behavior-based robots towards more and more sophisticated capabilities?

In this section we outline research challenges in three categories or levels[33]:

- Understanding the dynamics of how an individual behavior couples with the environment via the robot's sensors and actuators. The primary concerns here are what forms of perception are necessary, and what relationships exist between perception, internal state, and action (i.e., how behavior is specified or described).
- Understanding how many behaviors can be integrated into a single robot. The primary concerns here are how independent various perceptions and behaviors can be, how much they must rely on, and interfere with each other, how a competent complete robot can be built in such a way as to accommodate all the required individual behaviors, and to what extent apparently complex behaviors can emerge from simple reflexes.
- Understanding how multiple robots (either a homogeneous, or a heterogeneous group) can interact as they go about their business. The primary concerns here are the relationships between individuals' behaviors, the amount and type of communication between robots, the way the environment reacts to multiple individuals, and the resulting patterns of behavior and their impacts upon the environment (which night not occur in the case of isolated individuals).

Just as research in Artificial Intelligence is broken into subfields, these categories provide subfields of behavior-based robots within which it is possible to concentrate a particular research project. Some of these topics are theoretical in nature, contributing to a science of behavior-based systems. Others are engineering in nature, providing tools and mechanisms for successfully building and programming behavior-based robots. Some of these topics have already been touched upon by researchers in behavior-based approaches, but none of them are yet solved or completely understood.

At the individual behavior level some of the important issues are as follows:

Convergence

Demonstrate or prove that a specified behavior is such that the robot will indeed carry out the desired task successfully. For instance, we may want to give some set of initial conditions for a robot, and some limitations on possible worlds in which it is placed, and show that under those conditions, the robot is guaranteed to follow a particular wall, rather than diverge and get lost.

Synthesis

Given a particular task, automatically derive a behavior specification for the creature so that it carries out that task in a way which has clearly demonstrable convergence. I do not expect progress in this topic in the near future.

Complexity

Deal with the complexity of real world environments, and sift out the relevant aspects of received sensations rather than being overwhelmed with a multitude of data.

Learning

Develop methods for the automatic acquisition of new behaviors, and the modification and tuning of existing behaviors.

As multiple behaviors are built into a single robot the following issues need to be addressed:

Coherence

Even though many behaviors may be active at once, or are being actively switched on or off, the robot should still appear to an observer to have coherence of action and goals. It should not be rapidly switching between inconsistent behaviors, nor should two behaviors be active simultaneously, if they interfere with each other to the point that neither operates successfully.

Relevance

The behaviors that are active should be relevant to the situation the robot finds itself in—e.g., it should recharge itself when the batteries are low, not when they are full.

Adequacy

The behavior selection mechanism must operate in such a way that the long term goals that the robot designer has for the robot are met—e.g., a floor cleaning robot should successfully clean the floor in normal circumstances, besides doing all the ancillary tasks that are necessary for it to be successful at that.

Representation

Multiple behaviors might want to share partial representations of the world—in fact the representations of world aspects might generate multiple behaviors when activated appropriately.

Learning

The performance of a robot might be improved by adapting the ways in which behaviors interact, or are activated, as a result of experience.

When many behavior-based robots start to interact there are a whole new host of issues which arise. Many of these same issues would arise if the robots were built using traditional Artificial Intelligence methods, but there has been very little published in these areas.

Emergence

Given a set of behaviors programmed into a set of robots, we would like to be able to predict what the global behavior of the system will be, and as a consequence determine the differential effects of small changes to the individual robots on the global behavior.

Synthesis

As at single behavior level, given a particular task, automatically derive a program for the set of robots so that they carry out the task.

Communication

Performance may be increased by increasing the amount of explicit communication between robots, but the relationship between the amount of communication increase and performance increase needs to be understood.

Cooperation

In some circumstances robots should be able to achieve more by cooperating—the form and specification of such possible cooperations need to be understood.

Interference

Robots may interfere with one another. Protocols for avoiding this when it is undesirable must be included in the design of the creatures' instructions.

Density dependence

The global behavior of the system may be dependent on the density of the creatures and the resources they consume within the world. A characterization of this dependence is desirable. At the two ends of the spectrum it may be the case that (a) a single robot given n units of time performs identically to n robots each given 1 unit of time, and (2) the global task might not be achieved at all if there are fewer than, say, m robots.

Individuality

Robustness can be achieved if all robots are interchangeable. A fixed number of classes of robots, where all robots within a class are identical, is also robust, but somewhat less so. The issue then is to, given a task, decide how many classes of creatures are necessary

Learning

The performance of the robots may increase in two ways through learning. At one level, when one robot learns some skill it might be able to transfer it to another. At another level, the robots might learn cooperative strategies.

These are a first cut at topics of interest within behavior-based approaches. As we explore more we will find more topics, and some that seem interesting now will turn out to be irrelevant.

6.7 Thinking

Can this approach lead to thought? How could it? It seems the antithesis of thought. But we must ask first, what is thought? Like intelligence this is a very slippery concept.

We only know that thought exists in biological systems through our own introspection. At one level we identify thought with the product of our consciousness, but that too is a contentious subject, and one which has had little attention from Artificial Intelligence.

My feeling is that thought and consciousness are epiphenomena of the process of being in the world. As the complexity of the world increases, and the complexity of processing to deal with that world rises, we will see the same evidence of thought and consciousness in our systems as we see in people other than ourselves now. Thought and consciousness will not need to be programmed in. They will emerge.

7 Conclusion

The title of this paper is intentionally ambiguous. The following interpretations all encapsulate important points.

- An earlier paper [**Brooks 91a**][34] was titled *Intelligence without Representation*. The thesis of that paper was that intelligent behavior could be generated without having explicit manipulable internal representations. *Intelligence without Reason* is thus complementary, stating that intelligent behavior can be generated without having explicit reasoning systems present.
- *Intelligence without Reason* can be read as a statement that intelligence is an emergent property of certain complex systems—it sometimes arises without an easily identifiable reason for arising.
- *Intelligence without Reason* can be viewed as a commentary on the bandwagon effect in research in general, and in particular in the case of Artificial Intelligence research. Many lines of research have become goals of pursuit in their own right, with little recall of the reasons for pursuing those lines. A little grounding occasionally can go a long way towards helping keep things on track.
- *Intelligence without Reason* is also a commentary on the way evolution built intelligence—rather than reason about how to build intelligent systems, it used a generate and test strategy. This is in stark contrast to the way all human endeavors to build intelligent systems must inevitably proceed. Furthermore we must be careful in emulating the results of evolution—there may be many structures and observable properties which are suboptimal or vestigial.

We are a long way from creating Artificial Intelligences that measure up to the standards of early ambitions for the field. It is a complex endeavor and we sometimes need to step back and question why we are proceeding in the direction we are going, and look around for other promising directions.

This report describes research done at the Artificial Intelligence Laboratory of the Massachusetts Institute of Technology. Support for this research was provided in part by the University Research Initiative under Office of Naval Research contract N00014–86-K-0685, in part by the Advanced Research Projects Agency under Office of Naval Research contract N00014–85-K-0124, in part by the Hughes Artificial Intelligence Center, in part by Siemens Corporation, and in part by Mazda Corporation.

Acknowledgements

Maja Mataric reviewed numerous drafts of this paper and gave helpful criticism at every stage of the process. Lynne Parker, Anita Flynn, Ian Horswill and Pattie Maes gave me much constructive feedback on later drafts.

Notes

1 In the case of Shakey, experiments included the existence of a gremlin who would secretly come and alter the environment by moving a block to a different location. However, this would usually happen only once, say, in a many hour run, and the robot would not perceive the dynamic act, but rather might later notice a changed world if the change was directly relevant to the particular subtask it was executing. In the case of the CART, the only dynamic aspect of the world was the change in sun angle over long time periods, and this in fact caused the robot to fail as its position estimation scheme was confused by the moving shadows.

2 Unfortunately this clashes a little with the meaning of behavior as used by ethologists as an observed interaction with the world, rather than as something explicitly generated.

3 Equally radical changes have occurred in the past, but admittedly they happened well before the current high levels of installed base of silicon-based computers.

4 Norbert Wiener also outlines the idea of minimax in the final note of the original edition of **[Wiener 48]**. However he restricts the idea to a depth of two or three plays—one assumes for practical reasons, as he does express the general notion for *n* plays. See Section 3.3 for more details on the ways in which cybernetic models of thought were restricted by the computational models at hand.

5 Different sources cite 1947 and 1948 as the time of writing.

6 Interestingly, Turing did not completely abstract even a chess playing machine away from embodiment, commenting that "its only organs need be 'eyes' capable of distinguishing the various positions on a specially made board, and means for announcing its own moves".

7 See *Personal Computing* January 1980, pages 80–81, for a description of this hand simulation of a chess machine.

8 Turing expresses his own belief that it will be possible for a machine with 109 bits of store to pass a five minute version of the test with 70% probability by about the year 2000.

9 In fact there is a yearly competition with a $100,000 prize for a machine that can pass this version of the Turing test.

10 An excerpt from Turing's paper is reprinted in **[Hofstadter and Dennett 81]**. They leave out the whole section on learning and embodiment.

11 It also acted as the combined bibliography for the papers in **[Feigenbaum and Feldman 63]**.

12 Much of the book **[Walter 53]** is concerned with early work on electroencephalography and hopes for its role in revealing the workings of the brain—forty years later these hopes do not seem to have been born out.

13 In the introduction to **[Wiener 48]** he talks about embodying such machines with photoelectric cells, thermometers, strain gauges and motors in the service of mechanical labor. But, in the text of the book he does not make such a connection with models of organisms. Rather he notes that they are intended for many successive runs, with the memory being cleared out between runs and states that "the brain, under normal circumstances, is not the complete analogue of the computing machine but rather the analogue of a single run on such a machine". His

models of digital computation and models of thought are too dis-similar to make the connection that we would today.

14 With hindsight, an even wilder speculation is presented at the end of the later edition. Wiener suggests that the capital substances of genes and viruses may self reproduce through such a spectral analysis of infra-red emissions from the model molecules that then induce self organization into the undifferentiated magma of amino and nucleic acids available to form the new biological material.

15 Arbib includes an elegant warning against being too committed to models, even mathematical models, which may turn out to be wrong. His statement that the "mere use of formulas gives no magical powers to a theory" is just as timely today as it was then.

16 One exception was a computer controlled hand built at MIT, [Ernst 61], and connected to the TX-0 computer. The hand was very much situated and embodied, and relied heavily on the external world as a model, rather than using internal representations. This piece of work seems to have gotten lost, for reasons that are not clear to me.

17 Try it! You'll be amazed at how bad it is.

18 It is still fairly difficult even today. There are very few turnkey systems available for purchase which connect sensors to reasonable computers, and reasonable computers to actuators. The situation does seem to be rapidly improving however—we may well be just about to step over a significant threshold.

19 Endorsement of some of Dreyfus' views should not be taken as whole hearted embrace of all his arguments.

20 See [Churchland 86] for a discussion of folk psychology.

21 This contrasts with a popular fad in Artificial Intelligence where all reasoning of a system is supposed to be available to a meta-reasoning system, or even introspectively to the system itself.

22 See the techniques used in the current trend of "colonization" of black and white movie classics for a commercial capitalization on our visual deficiencies.

23 See [Bergland 85] for a history of theories of the brain, and how they were influenced by the current technologies available to provide explanatory power. Unfortunately this book is marred by the author's own lack of understanding of computation which leads him to dismiss electrical activity of the brain as largely irrelevant to the process of thought.

24 The tasks carried out by this first robot, *Allen*, were of a different class than those attempted by Shakey. Shakey could certainly not have carried out the tasks that Allen did.

25 I mean this in the sense of causing self-delusion, not in the sense of wrong doing with intent.

26 In fact, there is some room for cheating as the physical environment can be specially simplified for the robot—and in fact it may be very hard in some cases to identify such self delusions. In some research projects it may be necessary to test a particular class of robot activities, and therefore it may be necessary to build a test environment for the robot. There is a fine and difficult to define line to be drawn here.

27 This constraint has slipped a little recently as we are working on building prototype small legged planetary rovers ([Angle and Brooks 90]). We have built a special purpose environment for the robots—a physically simulated lunar surface.

28 For programming convenience we use a higher level abstraction known as the *Behaviour Language*, documented in [Brooks 90c]. It complies down to a network of machines as described above.

29 Jon Connell, a former member of the Mobot Lab, plotted data from a large

number of mobile robots and noted the empirical fact that there is roughly one watt of electrical power available for onboard computation for every pound of overall weight of the robot. We call this *Connell's Law*.

30 The limiting factor on Herbert was the mechanical seating of its chips—its mean time between chip seating failure was no more than 15 minutes.

31 Note that we are saying only *sometimes*, not *must*—there are many navigation tasks doable by mobile robots which appear intelligent, but which do not require map information at all.

32 We did have a failed attempt at this through simulated evolution—this is the approach taken by many in the Artificial Life movement.

33 The reader is referred to **[Brooks 90a]** for a more complete discussion of these issues.

34 Despite the publication date it was written in 1986 and 1987, and was complete in its published form in 1987.

References

[Agre 88] "The Dynamic Structure of Everyday Life", Philip E. Agre, *MIT AI TR-1085*, Oct., 1988.

[Agre 91] "The Dynamic Structure of Everyday Life", Philip E. Agre, *Cambridge University Press*, Cambridge, UK, 1991.

[Agre and Chapman 87] "Pengi: An Implementation of a Theory of Activity", Philip E. Agre and David Chapman, *AAAI-87*, Seattle, WA, 1987, 268–272.

[Agre and Chapman 90] "What Are Plans for?" Philip E. Agre and David Chapman, *in* **[Maes 90a]**, 1990, 17–34.

[Angle 89] "Genghis, a Six Legged Autonomous Walking Robot", Colin M. Angle, *MIT SB Thesis*, March, 1989.

[Angle and Brooks 90] "Small Planetary Rovers", Colin M. Angle and Rodney A. Brooks, *IEEE/RSJ International Workshop on Intelligent Robots and Systems*, Ikabara, Japan, 1990, 383–388.

[Arbib 64] "Brains, Machines and Mathematics", Michael A. Arbib, *McGraw-Hill*, New York, NY, 1964.

[Arkin 89] "Homeostatic Control for a Mobile Robot: Dynamic Replanning in Hazardous Environments", Ronald C. Arkin, *SPIE Proceedings 1007, Mobile Robots III, William J. Wolfe* (ed), 1989, 407–413.

[Arkin 90] "Integrating Behavioral, Perceptual and World Knowledge in Reactive Navigation", Ronald C. Arkin, *in* **[Maes 90a]**, 1990, 105–122.

[Ashby 52] "Design for a Brain", W. Ross Ashby, *Chapman and Hall*, London, 1952.

[Ashby 56] "An Introduction to Cybernetics", W. Ross Ashby, *Chapman and Hall*, London, 1956.

[Atkeson 89] "Using Local Models to Control Movement", Christopher G. Atkeson, *in Neural Information Processing 2, David S. Touretzky* (ed), *Morgan Kaufmann*, Los Altos, CA, 1989, 316–324.

[Ballard 89] "Reference Frames for Active Vision", Dana H. Ballard, *Proceedings IJCAI-89*, Detroit, MI, 1989, 1635–1641.

[Barrow and Salter 70] "Design of Low-Cost Equipment for Cognitive Robot Research", H. G. Barrow and S. H. Salter, *Machine Intelligence 5, Bernard Meltzer and Donald Michie* (eds), *American Elsevier Publishing*, New York, NY, 1970, 555–566.

[Beer 90] "Intelligence as Adaptive Behavior", Randall D. Beer, *Academic Press*, San Diego, CA, 1990.

[Bergland 85] "The Fabric of Mind", Richard Bergland, *Viking*, New York, NY, 1985.

[Bloom 76] "Endorphins: Profound Behavioral Effects", F. E. Bloom, *Science 194*, 1976, 630–634.

[Braitenberg 84] "Vehicles: Experiments in Synthetic Psychology", Valentino Braitenberg, *MIT Press*, Cambridge, MA, 1984.

[Brachman and Levesque 85] "Readings in Knowledge Representation", Ronald J. Brachman and Hector J. Levesque, *Morgan Kaufmann*, Los Altos, CA, 1985.

[Brady 90] "Switching Arrays Make Light Work in a Simple Processor", David Brady, *Nature 344*, 1990, 486–487.

[Brooks 86] "A Robust Layered Control System for a Mobile Robot", Rodney A. Brooks, *IEEE Journal of Robotics and Automation, RA-2*, April, 1986, 14–23.

[Brooks 89] "A Robot that Walks: Emergent Behavior from a Carefully Evolved Network", Rodney A. Brooks, *Neural Computation 1:2*, 1989, 253–262.

[Brooks 90a] "Challenges for Complete Creature Architectures", Rodney A. Brooks, *Proc. First Int. Conf. on Simulation of Adaptive Behavior, MIT Press*, Cambridge, MA, 1990, 434–443.

[Brooks 90b] "Elephants Don't Play Chess", Rodney A. Brooks, *in* [Maes 90a], 1990, 3–15.

[Brooks 90c] "The Behavior Language; User's Guide", Rodney A. Brooks, *MIT A.I. Lab Memo* 1227, 1990.

[Brooks 91a] "Intelligence Without Representation", Rodney A. Brooks, *Artificial Intelligence, 47*, 1991, 139–160.

[Brooks 91b] "Integrated Systems Based on Behaviors", Rodney A. Brooks, *special issue of SIGART on Integrated Intelligent Systems*, July, 1991.

[Brooks and Flynn 89] "Robot Beings", Rodney A. Brooks and Anita M. Flynn, *IEEE/RSJ International Workshop on Intelligent Robots and Systems*, Tsukuba, Japan, 1989, 2–10.

[Campbell 83] "Go", J. A. Campbell, *in Computer Game-Playing: Theory and Practice, M. A. Bramer* (ed), *Ellis Horwood*, Chichester, UK, 1983.

[Chapman 90] "Vision, Instruction and Action", David Chapman, *MIT AI TR-1085*, June, 1990.

[Churchland 86] "Neurophilosophy", Patricia Smith Churchland, *MIT Press*, Cambridge, MA, 1986.

[Cohen and Wu 90] "One Neuron, Many Units?" Larry Cohen and Jain-young Wu, *Nature 346*, 1990, 108–109.

[Condon and Thompson 84] "Belle", J. H. Condon and Ken Thompson, *in Chess Skill in Man and Machine, P. W. Frey* (ed), *Springer-Verlag*, 1984.

[Connell 89] "A Colony Architecture for an Artificial Creature", Jonathan H. Connell, *MIT AI TR-1151*, June, 1989.

[Cruse 90] "What Mechanisms Coordinate Leg Movement in Walking Arthropods?", Holk Cruse, *Trends in Neurosciences 13:1*, 1990, 15–21.

[de Kleer and Brown 84] "A Qualitative Physics Based on Confluences", Johann de Kleer and John Seely Brown, *Artificial Intelligence 24*, 1984, 7–83.

[Dennett 78] "Where Am I?", Daniel C. Dennett, *in* [Hofstadter and Dennett 81], 1981.

[Dennett and Kinsbourne 90] "Time and the Observer: the Where and When of

Consciousness in the Brain", Daniel Dennett and Marcel Kinsbourne, *Technical Report, Center for Cognitive Studies, Tufts University*, 1990.

[Dreyfus 81] "From Micro-Worlds to Knowledge Representation: AI at an Impasse", Hubert L. Dreyfus, *in Mind Design, John Haugeland* (ed), *MIT Press*, Cambridge, MA, 1981, 161–204.

[Ernst 61] "MH-1. A Computer-Operated Mechanical Hand", Heinrich A. Ernst, *MIT Ph.D. Thesis*, Dec, 1961.

[Evans 68] "A Program for the Solution of Geometric-Analogy Intelligence Test Questions", Thomas G. Evans, *in* [Minsky 68], 1968, 271–353.

[Fahlman 74] "A Planning System for Robot Construction Tasks", Scott E. Fahlman, *Artificial Intelligence 5*, 1974, 1–50.

[Feigenbaum and Feldman 63] "Computers and Thought", Edward A. Feigenbaum and Julian Feldman, *McGraw-Hill*, New York, NY, 1963.

[Firby 89] "Adaptive Execution in Dynamic Domains", R. James Firby, *Ph.D. Thesis*, Yale, 1989.

[Flynn 87] "Gnat Robots (And How They Will Change Robotics)", Anita M. Flynn, *IEEE Micro Robots and Teleoperators Workshop*, Hyannis, MA, Nov., 1989.

[Gazzaniga and LeDoux 77] "The Integrated Mind", Michael S. Gazzaniga and Joseph E. LeDoux, *Plenum*, New York, NY, 1977.

[Gibbs 85] "Optical Bistability: Controlling Light with Light", H. M. Gibbs, *Academic Press*, New York, NY, 1985.

[Giralt, Chatila and Vaisset 84] "An Integrated Navigation and Motion Control System for Multisensory Robots", Georges Giralt, Raja Chatila, and Marc Vaisset, *Robotics Research 1, Brady and Paul* (eds), *MIT Press*, Cambridge, MA, 191–214.

[Götz and Wenking 73] "Visual Control of Locomotion in the Walking Fruitfly *Drosophilia*", Karl Georg Götz and Hans Wenking, *Journal of Computational Physiology 85*, 1973, 235–266.

[Gould and Eldredge 77] "Punctuated Equilibria: The Tempo and Mode of Evolution Reconsidered", S. J. Gould and N. Eldredge, *Paleobiology 3*, 1977, 115–151.

[Greenblatt, Eastlake and Crocker 67] "The Greenblatt Chess Program", R. D. Greenblatt, D. E. Eastlake and S. D. Crocker, *Am. Fed. Inf. Proc. Soc. Conference Proceedings, 31*, 1967, 801–810.

[Hartmanis 71] "Computational Complexity of Random Access Stored Program Machines", Juris Hartmanis, *Mathematical Systems Theory 5:3*, 1971, 232–245.

[Hayes 85] "The Second Naive Physics Manifesto", Patrick J. Hayes, *in Formal Theories of the Commonsense World, Jerry R. Hobbs and Robert C. Moore* (eds), *Ablex*, Norwood, NJ, 1985, 1–36.

[Hillis 85] "The Connection Machine", W. Daniel Hillis, *MIT Press*, Cambridge, MA, 1985.

[Hodges 83] "Alan Turing: The Enigma", Andrew Hodges, *Simon and Schuster*, New York, NY, 1983.

[Hofstadter and Dennett 81] "The Mind's I", Douglas R. Hofstadter and Daniel C. Dennett, *Bantam Books*, New York, NY, 1981.

[Horswill and Brooks 88] "Situated Vision in a Dynamic World: Chasing Objects", Ian D. Horswill and Rodney A. Brooks, *AAAI-88*, St Paul, MN, 1988, 796–800.

[Hsu, Anantharaman, Campbell and Nowatzyk 90] "A Grandmaster Chess Machine", Feng-hsiung Hsu, Thomas Anantharaman, Murray Campbell and Andreas Nowatzyk, *Scientific American, 263(4)*, Oct. 1990, 44–50.

[Johnson 87] "The Body in the Mind", Mark Johnson, *University of Chicago Press*, Chicago, IL, 1987.

[Kaelbling 90] "Learning in Embedded Systems", Leslie Pack Kaelbling, *Ph.D. Thesis*, Stanford, 1990.

[Kaelbling and Rosenschein 90] "Action and Planning in Embedded Agents", Leslie Pack Kaelbling and Stanley J. Rosenschein, *in* **[Maes 90a]**, 1990, 35–48.

[Knuth and Moore 75] "An Analysis of Alpha-Beta Pruning", Donald E. Knuth and Ronald E. Moore, *Artificial Intelligence 6*, 1975, 293–326.

[Kravitz 88] "Hormonal Control of Behavior: Amines and the Biasing of Behavioral Output in Lobsters", Edward A. Kravitz, *Science 241*, Sep. 30, 1988, 1775–1781.

[Kuhn 70] "The Structure of Scientific Revolutions", Thomas S. Kuhn, *Second Edition, Enlarged, University of Chicago Press*, Chicago, IL, 1970.

[Lenat and Feigenbaum 91] "On the Thresholds of Knowledge", Douglas B. Lenat and Edward A. Feigenbaum, *Artificial Intelligence, 47*, 1991, 185–250.

[Maes 89] "The Dynamics of Action Selection", Pattie Maes, *IJCAI-89*, Detroit, MI, 1989, 991–997.

[Maes 90a] "Designing Autonomous Agents: Theory and Practice from Biology to Engineering and Back", Pattie Maes *(ed), MIT Press*, Cambridge, MA, 1990.

[Maes 90b] "Situated Agents Can Have Goals", Pattie Maes, *in* **[Maes 90a]**, 1990, 49–70.

[Maes and Brooks 90] "Learning to Coordinate Behaviors", Pattie Maes and Rodney A. Brooks, *AAAI-90*, Boston, MA, 1990, 796–802.

[Mahadevan and Connell 90] "Automatic Programming of Behavior-based Robots using Reinforcement Learning", Sridhar Mahadevan and Jonathan Connell, *IBM T.J. Watson Research Report*, Dec., 1990.

[Marr 82] "Vision", David Marr, *Freeman*, San Francisco, CA, 1982.

[Mataric 90] "Navigation with a Rat Brain: A Neurobiologically-Inspired Model for Robot Spatial Representation", Maja J Mataric, *Proc. First Int. Conf. on Simulation of Adaptive Behavior, MIT Press*, Cambridge, MA, 1990, 169–175.

[Mataric 91] "Behavioral Synergy Without Explicit Integration", Maja J. Mataric, *special issue of SIGART on Integrated Intelligent Systems*, July, 1991.

[McCarthy 60] "Recursive Functions of Symbolic Expressions", John McCarthy, *CACM 3*, 1960, 184–195.

[McCarthy and Warrington 88] "Evidence for Modality-Specific Systems in the Brain", Rosaleen A. McCarthy and Elizabeth. K. Warrington, *Nature 334*, 1988, 428–430.

[McCorduck 79] "Machines Who Think", Pamela McCorduck, *Freeman*, New York, NY, 1979.

[McCulloch and Pitts 43] "A Logical Calculus of the Ideas Immanent in Nervous Activity", W. S. McCulloch and W. Pitts, *Bull. of Math. Biophysics 5*, 1943, 115–137.

[McFarland 85] "Animal Behavior", David McFarland, *Benjamin/Cummings*, Menlo Park, CA, 1985.

[McFarland 88] "Problems of Animal Behavior", David McFarland, *Longman*, Harlow, UK, 1988.

[Michie and Ross 70] "Experiments with the Adaptive Graph Traverser", Donald Michie and Robert Ross, *Machine Intelligence 5, Bernard Meltzer and Donald Michie* (eds), *American Elsevier Publishing*, New York, NY, 1970, 301–318.

[Minsky 54] "Neural Nets and the Brain Model Problem", Marvin Minsky, *unpublished Ph.D. dissertation, Princeton University*, 1954, available from University Microfilms, Ann Arbor, MI.

[Minsky 61] "Steps Toward Artificial Intelligence", Marvin Minsky, *Proc. IRE 49*, Jan. 1961, 8–30, also in **[Feigenbaum and Feldman 63]**, 1963, 453–523.

[Minsky 63] "A Selected Descriptor-Indexed Bibliography to the Literature on Artificial Intelligence", Marvin Minsky, *in* **[Feigenbaum and Feldman 63]**, 1963, 453–523.

[Minsky 68] "Semantic Information Processing", Marvin Minsky *(ed), MIT Press*, Cambridge, MA, 1968.

[Minsky 86] "The Society of Mind", Marvin Minsky, *Simon and Schuster*, New York, NY, 1986.

[Minsky and Papert 69] "Perceptrons", Marvin Minsky and Seymour Papert, *MIT Press*, Cambridge, MA, 1969.

[Mitchell 90] "Becoming Increasingly Reactive", Tom M. Mitchell, *AAAI-90*, Boston, MA, 1990, 1051–1058.

[Moravec 81] "Robot Rover Visual Navigation", Hans P. Moravec, *UMI Research Press*, Ann Arbor, MI, 1981.

[Moravec 82] "The Stanford Cart and the CMU Rover", Hans P. Moravec, *Proceedings of the IEEE, 71(7)*, 1982, 872–884.

[Moravec 88] "Mind Children", Hans P. Moravec, *Harvard University Press*, Cambridge, MA, 1988.

[Newcombe and Ratcliff 89] "Freda Newcombe and Graham Ratcliff", Disorders of Visuospatial Analysis, *in Handbook of Neuropsychology, Vol 2, Elsevier*, New York, NY, 1989.

[Newell, Shaw and Simon 57] "Empirical Explorations with the Logic Theory Machine", Allen Newell, J. C. Shaw, Herbert Simon, *Proc. Western Joint Computer Conference 15*, 1957, 218–329, also in **[Feigenbaum and Feldman 63]**.

[Newell, Shaw and Simon 58] "Chess Playing Programs and the Problem of Complexity", Allen Newell, J. C. Shaw, Herbert Simon, *IBM Journal of Research and Development 2*, Oct. 1958, 320–335, also in **[Feigenbaum and Feldman 63]**.

[Newell, Shaw and Simon 59] "A General Problem-Solving Program for a Computer", Allen Newell, J. C. Shaw, Herbert Simon, *Computers and Automation 8(7)*, 1959, 10–16.

[Newell, Shaw and Simon 61] "Information Processing Language V Manual", Allen Newell, J. C. Shaw, Herbert Simon, *Prentice-Hall*, Edgewood Cliffs, NJ, 1961.

[Nicolis and Prigogine 77] "Self-Organization in Nonequilibrium Systems", G. Nicolis and I. Prigogine, *Wiley*, New York, NY, 1977.

[Nilsson 65] "Learning Machines", Nils J. Nilsson, *McGraw-Hill*, New York, NY, 1965.

[Nilsson 71] "Problem-Solving Methods in Artificial Intelligence", Nils J. Nilsson, *McGraw-Hill*, New York, NY, 1971.

[Nilsson 84] "Shakey the Robot", Nils J. Nilsson *(ed), SRI A.I. Center Technical Note 323*, April, 1984.

[Payton 90] "Internalized Plans: A Representation for Action Resources", David W. Payton, *in* **[Maes 90a]**, 1990, 89–103.

[Ramachandran and Anstis 85] "Perceptual Organization in Multistable Apparent

Motion", Vilayanur S. Ramachandran and Stuart M. Anstis, *Perception 14*, 1985, 135–143.

[Roberts 63] "Machine Perception of Three-Dimensional Solids", Larry G. Roberts, *MIT Lincoln Laboratory, Technical Report No. 315*, May, 1963.

[Rosenblatt 62] "Principles of Neurodynamics", Frank Rosenblatt, *Spartan*, New York, NY, 1962.

[Rosenschein and Kaelbling 86] "The Synthesis of Machines with Provable Epistemic Properties", Stanley J. Rosenschein and Leslie Pack Kaelbling, *Proc. Conf. on Theoretical Aspects of Reasoning about Knowledge, Joseph Halpern* (ed), *Morgan Kaufmann*, Los Altos, CA, 1986, 83–98.

[Rumelhart, Hinton and Williams 86] "Learning Internal Representations by Error Propagation", D. E. Rumelhart, G. E. Hinton, and R. J. Williams, *in* **[Rumelhart and McClelland 86]**, 1986, 318–364.

[Rumelhart and McClelland 86] "Parallel Distributed Processing", David E. Rumelhart and James L. McClelland, *MIT Press*, Cambridge, MA, 1986.

[Russell 89] "Execution Architectures and Compilation", Stuart J. Russell, *Proceedings IJCAI-89*, Detroit, MI, 1989, 15–20.

[Sacks 74] "Awakenings", Oliver W. Sacks, *Doubleday*, New York, NY, 1974.

[Samuel 59] "Some Studies in Machine Learning Using the Game of Checkers", Arthur L. Samuel, *IBM Journal of Research and Development 3*, July 1959, 211–229, also in **[Feigenbaum and Feldman 63]**.

[Sejnowski and Rosenberg 87] "Parallel Networks that Learn to Pronounce English Text", T. J. Sejnowski and C. R. Rosenberg, *Complex Systems 1*, 145–168.

[Selfridge 56] "Pattern Recognition and Learning", Oliver G. Selfridge, *Proc. Third London Symp. on Information Theory, Colin Cherry* (ed), *Academic Press*, New York, NY, 1956, 345–353.

[Shannon 50] "A Chess-Playing Machine", Claude E. Shannon, *Scientific American 182(2)*, February, 1950.

[Simon 69] "The Sciences of the Artificial", Herbert A. Simon, *MIT Press*, Cambridge, MA, 1969.

[Simmons and Krotkov 91] "An Integrated Walking System for the Ambler Planetary Rover", Reid Simmons and Eric Krotkov, *Proc. IEEE Robotics and Automation*, Sacramento, CA, 1991, 2086–2091.

[Slagle 63] "A Heuristic Program that Solves Symbolic Integration Problems in Freshman Calculus", James R. Slagle, *in* **[Feigenbaum and Feldman 63]**, 1963, 191–206 (from a 1961 MIT mathematics Ph.D. thesis).

[Slate and Atkin 84] "Chess 4.5–The Northwestern University Chess Program", David J. Slate and Lawrence R. Atkin, *in Chess Skill in Man and Machine, P. W. Frey* (ed), *Springer-Verlag*, 1984.

[Smith 91] "The Owl and the Electric Encyclopedia", Brian Cantwell Smith, *Artificial Intelligence, 47*, 1991, 251–288.

[Steels 90a] "Towards a Theory of Emergent Functionality", Luc Steels, *Proc. First Int. Conf. on Simulation of Adaptive Behavior, MIT Press*, Cambridge, MA, 1990, 451–461.

[Steels 90b] "Exploiting Analogical Representations", Luc Steels, *in* **[Maes 90a]**, 1990, 71–88.

[Sussman 75] "A Computer Model of Skill Acquisition", Gerald J. Sussman, *Elsevier*, New York, NY, 1975.

[Teitelbaum, Pellis and Pellis 90] "Can Allied Reflexes Promote the Integration of a Robot's Behavior", Philip Teitelbaum, Vivien C. Pellis and Sergio M. Pellis, *Proc. First Int. Conf. on Simulation of Adaptive Behavior, MIT Press*, Cambridge, MA, 1990, 97–104.

[Thorpe, Hebert, Kanade, and Shafer 88] "Vision and Navigation for the Carnegie-Mellon Navlab" Charles Thorpe, Martial Hebert, Takeo Kanade, and Steven A. Shafer, *IEEE Trans. PAMI, 10(3)*, May 1988, 362–373.

[Tinbergen 51] "The Study of Instinct", Niko Tinbergen, *Oxford University Press*, Oxford, UK, 1951.

[Turing 37] "On Computable Numbers with an Application to the Entscheidungs-problem", Alan M. Turing, *Proc. London Math. Soc. 42*, 1937, 230–65.

[Turing 50] "Computing Machinery and Intelligence", Alan M. Turing, *Mind 59*, Oct. 1950, 433–460, also in **[Feigenbaum and Feldman 63]**.

[Turing 70] "Intelligent Machinery", Alan M. Turing, *Machine Intelligence 5, Bernard Meltzer and Donald Michie* (eds), *American Elsevier Publishing*, New York, NY, 1970, 3–23.

[Turk, Morgenthaler, Gremban, and Marra 88] "VITS-A Vision System for Autonomous Land Vehicle Navigation", Matthew A. Turk, David G. Morgenthaler, Keith D. Gremban, and Martin Marra, *IEEE Trans. PAMI, 10(3)*, May 1988, 342–361.

[Viola 90] "Adaptive Gaze Control", Paul A. Viola, *MIT SM Thesis*, 1990.

[Von Neumann and Morgenstern 44] "Theory of Games and Economic Behavior", J. von Neumann and O. Morgenstern, *John Wiley and Sons*, New York, NY, 1944.

[Walter 50] "An Imitation of Life", W. Grey Walter, *Scientific American, 182(5)*, May 1950, 42–45.

[Walter 51] "A Machine That Learns", W. Grey Walter, *Scientific American, 185(2)*, August 1951, 60–63.

[Walter 53] "The Living Brain", W. Grey Walter, *Duckworth*, London, 1953, republished by *Penguin*, Harmondsworth, UK, 1961.

[Watkins 89] "Learning from Delayed Rewards", Christopher Watkins, *Ph.D. Thesis*, King's College, Cambridge, 1989.

[Waxman, Le Moigne and Srinivasan 85] "Visual Navigation of Roadways", Allen M. Waxman, Jacqueline Le Moigne and Babu Srinivasan, *Proc. IEEE Robotics and Automation*, St Louis, MO, 1985, 862–867.

[Wehner 87] "'Matched Filters'—Neural Models of the External World", Rüdiger Wehner, *J. comp. Physiol. A 161*, 1987, 511–531.

[Wiener 48] "Cybernetics", Norbert Wiener, *John Wiley and Sons*, New York, NY, 1948.

[Wiener 61] "Cybernetics", Norbert Wiener, *Second Edition, MIT Press*, Cambridge, MA, 1961.

[Wilkins 79] "Using Patterns and Plans to Solve Problems and Control Search", David E. Wilkins, *Stanford AI Memo 329*, July, 1979.

[Williams 83] "From Napier to Lucas", Michael R. Williams, *Annals of the History of Computing*, (5)3, 1983, 279–96.

[Winograd 72] "Understanding Natural Language", Terry Winograd, *Academic Press*, New York, NY, 1972.

[Winograd and Flores 86] "Understanding Computers and Cognition", Terry Winograd and Fernando Flores, *Addison-Wesley*, Reading, MA, 1986.

[Winston 72] "The MIT Robot", Patrick H. Winston, *Machine Intelligence 7, Bernard Meltzer and Donald Michie* (eds), *John Wiley and Sons*, New York, NY, 1972, 431–463.

[Winston 84] "Artificial Intelligence", Patrick Henry Winston, *Second Edition, Addison-Wesley*, Reading, MA, 1984.

[Wood 88] "The Nematode *Caenorhabditis Elegans*", William B. Wood, *Cold Spring Harbor Laboratory*, Cold Spring Harbor, NY, 1988.

51

TODAY THE EARWIG,
TOMORROW MAN?

David Kirsh

Source: *Artificial Intelligence* 47, 1991: 161–84.

Abstract

Kirsh, D., Today the earwig, tomorrow man?, Artificial Intelligence 47 (1991) 161–184.

A startling amount of intelligent activity can be controlled without reasoning or thought. By tuning the perceptual system to task relevant properties a creature can cope with relatively sophisticated environments without concepts. There is a limit, however, to how far a creature without concepts can go. Rod Brooks, like many ecologically oriented scientists, argues that the vast majority of intelligent behaviour is concept-free. To evaluate this position I consider what special benefits accrue to concept-using creatures. Concepts are either necessary for certain types of perception, learning, and control, or they make those processes computationally simpler. Once a creature has concepts its capacities are vastly multiplied.

Introduction

Is 97% of human activity concept-free, driven by control mechanisms we share not only with our simian forbears but with insects? This is the challenge proposed by Rod Brooks and fellow moboticists to mainstream AI. It is not superficial. Human activities fall along a continuum. At one extreme are highly reactive, *situationally determined* activities: walking, running, avoiding collisions, juggling, tying shoelaces. At the other extreme are highly *cerebral* activities: chess, bridge playing, mathematical problem solving, replying to non-obvious questions, and most discursive activities found in university research laboratories. It is an open question just where to draw the line between situationally determined activity—activity that can be initiated and regulated by smart perception-action systems—and activity that requires thought, language-like conceptualization, and internal search.

Brooks' position is that if we consider precisely what sensing is required to intelligently control behaviour in specific tasks, we make the startling discovery that in most cases there is no need, or next to no need, for symbolic representation. Reasoning in the familiar sense of retrieving cases, drawing inferences, and running through possibilities ahead of time is costly and unnecessary. In fact representations often *get in the way* of behaviour control. Accordingly, efficiency and parsimony dictate using action control systems that are representation free.

Moreover, unless we *first* understand the 97% of behaviour that is non-representational, Brooks argues, we will never correctly understand the remainder. The trouble with AI so far is that it makes false abstractions. Theorists don't study the genuine requirements of intelligent behaviour. Instead of finding out exactly what vision and the rest of our sensors should deliver to permit the intelligent control of behaviour, AI researchers have cavalierly defined nicely formal models of the world—the alleged true output of the senses—and have simply assumed that somehow sensory systems can build these up. Within these false castles AI theorists have tried to solve their own versions of the planning problem, the learning problem and so on. But, of course, the assumptions of these models are false—so false, in fact, that no step by step relaxation of assumptions can bring them closer to reality. The models are false and so are the problems: cognitive phlogiston.

In what follows I will question these claims. I am not yet convinced that success in duplicating insect behaviours such as wandering, avoiding obstacles, and following corridors proves that the mobotics approach is the royal path to higher-level behaviours. Insect ethologists are not cognitive scientists. There is a need for the study of representations. Nor do I think that existing research in reasoning is foundationless. Whatever the shape of robotics in the future it will have to accommodate theories of reasoning roughly as we know them. Abstractions are necessary.

My primary focus will be the claim that the majority of intelligent activity is *concept-free*. I use the term concept-free rather than representation-free, as Brooks prefers, because it seems to me that the deepest issues posed by the mobotics approach really concern the place of conceptualization in intelligent activity, rather than representation per se.

The concept of representation remains a sore spot in foundational studies of mind. No one is quite sure exactly what the analysis of "state X represents the information that p is H" should be. A glance at Brooks' mobots shows that they are riddled with wires that carry messages which covary with equivalence classes of earlier signals (e.g. an edge covaries with an equivalence class of pixel configurations) and which often covary with properties in the environment (e.g. real edges, hand manipulations). If covariation is sufficient for representation then Brooks too accepts the need for representations.

It is clear that by representation, however, he means symbolic, probably conceptual representation. Let us define a symbolic representation as one which can be combined and manipulated. This condition adds the notion of *syntax* to representation. To get systematic generation of representations it is necessary to have a notation that is sufficiently modular that individual elements of the notation can be combined to make molecular expressions. In this way, ever more complex structures can be constructed and used by a finite system. Semantic discipline is maintained on these symbol structures by enforcing Frege's requirement that however complex the symbol, its meaning is a function of the meaning of its parts and their syntactic arrangement.

If an agent has symbolic representations in the sense just defined, we may assume it has concepts.[1] But too little is understood about the nature of computation to require that all concept-imbued creatures operate with language-like internal notational elements. In principle, there could be computational architectures which implement the cognitive capacities we suppose concept-using creatures to have, but which do not pass notational elements around. These systems have the capacity for systematic representation in that they can systematically predicate property referring states—that is *predicates*—with states that refer to individual subjects—that is, *names*. But they do not have local notational structures which we can readily identify with symbols.

This capacity to predicate is absolutely central to concept-using creatures. It means that the creature is able to identify the common property which two or more objects share and to entertain the possibility that other objects also possess that property. That is, to have a concept is, among other things, to have a capacity to find an invariance across a range of contexts, and to reify that invariance so that it can be combined with other appropriate invariances. Moreover, combinations can be considered counterfactually. Thus if an agent has the concept red then, at a minimum, the agent is able to grasp that apples can be red, paint can be red, and so on.[2] The agent knows the satisfaction conditions of the predicate. Similarly, if an agent has the capacity to make a judgement about an individual—a person, number, or an object in the visual field, for example—then the agent must be able to make other judgements about that individual too. For instance, that 5 is prime, that it comes after 4, that it is a natural number.

In the same spirit, it is because we have concepts that we can make judgements of identity, as when we decide that the person we see in the mirror is the same person we see over there. Or again, because of concepts we can reidentify an individual, recognizing that the object or person in front of us now is the same one we met on other occasions.

Animals which have such capacities clearly have extra talents, though just what these extra talents are, is not entirely understood. Human newborns are largely devoid of them, but soon acquire them; dogs may have elements of them; chimps certainly do, and praying mantises certainly do not. Possession of concepts in a full-blooded form appears only some way up the evolutionary ladder.

The problem which I see Brooks posing is this: At what point in a theory of action must we advert to concepts? Which activities presuppose intelligent manipulation of concepts, and which do not? Accordingly, this is not simply a question of the role of model-based planning in intelligent activity. It is a question of the role of *thought* in action.

There are many ways of thinking that do not presuppose use of an articulated world model, in any interesting sense, but which clearly rely on concepts. Recall of cases, analogical reasoning, taking advice, posting reminders, thoughtful preparation, mental simulation, imagination, and second guessing are a few. I do not think that those mental activities are scarce, or confined to a fraction of our lives.

Nor do I think they are slow. When a person composes a sentence, he is making a subliminal choice among dozens of words in hundreds of milliseconds. There can be no doubt that conceptual representations of some sort are involved, although how this is done remains a total mystery. As an existence proof, however, it establishes that conceptual reasoning can be deployed quickly. Yet if in language, why not elsewhere?

Brooks' own position is extreme: at what point must we advert to concepts?—almost never. Most activity is thought-free, concept-less. It is this view I shall be questioning.

My paper has two parts. In the first I spell out what I take to be the strongest reasons for extending the domain of concept-free action beyond its usual boundaries. There is in Brooks' work, the outline of an alternative theory of action well worth understanding. It has clear kinship lines with associationism, ethology, the theory of J.J. Gibson, and the Society of Mind theory of Minsky. But it departs from these in interesting ways.

In the second part I consider what conceptualization buys us. More particularly, I explore the motives for postulating conceptual representations in (1) a theory of action; (2) a theory of perception; (3) a theory of learning; and (4) a theory of control.

1 Action and conceptualization

From a philosophical point of view the idea that concepts might not play an essential role in a theory of human action is unthinkable. According to received wisdom, what differentiates an *action* from a mere movement such as twitching or wincing is that the agent knows what he or she is doing at the time of action. The action falls under a description, understood by the agent, and partly constituting its identity. Thus the qualitative movement of raising an arm might at one moment be a communicative act such as gesturing goodbye, while at another moment be an act of stretching. Just which act is being performed is a function of at least two factors: the agent's intention, and the social context.

For an agent to have an intention, and hence to know the action performed, it is not necessary that he or she be aware of the action's description or that he or she consciously think before acting. Few agents are aware of putting their words together in sentences before they speak, or even of mapping between words in different languages when they fluently translate. This absence of conscious thought does not prevent them from saying what they mean and from translating aptly. Yet, any reasonable account of their practice must refer to their concepts, ideas, presuppositions, beliefs, etc. Introspection is misleading, then, as an indicator of when concepts and beliefs are causally involved in action.

Philosophy has bequeathed to AI this legacy of unconscious beliefs, desires and rational explanation. AI's signal contribution to action theory, so far, has been its computational revamping. In practical terms, this has meant that an agent acts only after planning, and that in order to plan, the agent must call on vast fields of largely unconscious beliefs about its current situation, the effects of actions, their desirability, and so forth.

Brooks' rebellion, not surprisingly, stems from a dissatisfaction with this approach in dealing with real world complexities and uncertainties. Surely children do not have to develop well-formed beliefs about liquids, however naively theoretical, in order to drink or go swimming. Even if we do require such implicit theories of children we cannot require them of gerbils or sea lions. The two forms of knowledge—theoretical and practical—can be divorced. But if we do not need an account of theoretical knowledge to explain the majority of animal skills and abilities, why invoke concepts, models, propositional reasoning—declarative representations more generally—to explain the majority of human action?

There are really three issues here which it is wise to distinguish. First, there is the question of what someone who wishes to explain a system—say, the designer of an intelligent system—must know in order to have proper understanding of its behaviour. Must he have an explicit theory of liquid behaviour in order to understand and design competent systems? If I am right in my interpretation of the doctrine of mobotics, pursuit of such theories is fine as an intellectual pastime but unnecessary for the business of making mobots. It is not evident what *practical* value formal theories of naive physical, social, geometrical, mechanical knowledge can possibly have for experienced mobot makers.

Second, there is the question of whether declarative representations, even if these are not truly concept-based declaratives, are required for intelligent control of activity.[3] Not all declarative representations that appear in the course of a computation are conceptual. When a vision system creates intermediate representations, such as edges, texture fields, depth gradients, we need not suppose that it has concepts of these entities in the full-blooded manner in which I defined conceptual representation earlier, that is, as being subjects or objects of predication. Information is certainly being represented explicitly, but it is not the sort of information that can be used in thought; its significance is internal to the specific phase of visual processing taking place at that moment. Thus it cannot be shunted off to a long-term memory system because the representation is in the language of early vision. It fails to qualify as a predicate, since it is not predicable of anything outside its current context. The agent does not know its satisfaction conditions.

Brooks' stand on the need for these intermediate representations in a theory of intelligent action is less clear. One difficulty is that he does not explicitly distinguish representations that are *non-conceptual* declaratives from those that are *conceptual* declaratives. Consequently, much of the rhetoric that, in my opinion, is properly directed against conceptual declaratives is phrased in a manner that makes it apply to declarative representation more universally. Thus he deems it good design philosophy to avoid at all costs extracting higher visual properties such as depth maps, 3D sketches, and most particularly, scene parsings. Mobots are constructed by linking small state FSM's that sample busses with tiny probes, e.g. 10 or 20 bits. The assumption is that this approach will scale up—that a mobot can gain robustness in performance by overlaying more and more specialized mechanisms, without ever having to design fairly general vision systems that might extract edges or higher visual properties. Accordingly, although some intermediate representations are inevitable—the readings of tiny probes—more general intermediate representations are outlawed even if some of these are non-conceptual.

Finally, there is the question of names and predicates. On these representations Brooks' position is unambiguous: declarative representations of individuals and properties is positively pernicious for efficient robotics. Flexible activity is possible without much (any) processing that involves drawing inferences, retrieving similar cases from memory, matching and comparing representations and so on. In virtually all cases these computations are complex, frail, prone to bottlenecks and they make false assumptions about the sparseness of real world attributes.

I will have something to say about all these forms of representation. It seems to me that there is no escaping the fact that intelligent systems often frame or pose problems to themselves in a certain way, that they search through some explicit hypothesis space at times, and that they have a memory that contains encoded propositions or frames or some other structured symbol, and that part of intelligence consists in knowing how to find the structures in memory that might be helpful in a task and putting those structures to use. Usually these processes make sense only if we assume that the creature has conceptual representations; but occasionally we can view them as involving intermediate representations alone. I believe, moreover, that there are clearly times when as designers we need an adequate domain theory to construct robots in a principled fashion. Accordingly, I will argue that all three forms of representation are necessary for an adequate science of robotics. But equally I think we should appreciate how far we can get *without* such representations. This is the virtue of Brooks' alternative theory of action.

2 An alternative theory of action

We may usefully itemize the core ideas underlying this alternative theory of action as follows:

(1) Behaviour can be partitioned into task-oriented activities or skills, such as walking, running, navigating, collecting cans, vacuuming, chopping vegetables, each of which has its own sensing and control requirements which can be run in parallel with others.[4]

(2) There is a partial ordering of the complexity of activities such that an entire creature, even one of substantial complexity, can be built incrementally by first building reliable lower-level behavioural skills and then adding more complex skills on top in a gradual manner.[5]

(3) There is more information available in the world for regulating task-oriented activities than previously appreciated; hence virtually no behavioural skill require maintaining a world model.[6] If you treat the world as external memory you can retrieve the information you require through perception.

(4) Only a fraction of the world must be sampled to detect this task-relevant information. Smart perception can index into the world cleverly, extracting exactly what is needed for task control without solving the general vision problem.[7]

(5) The hardest problems of intelligent action are related to the control issues involved in coordinating the various behavioural abilities so that the world itself and a predetermined dominance or preference ordering will be sufficient to decide which activity layer has its moment in the sun.

In short, the theme of this alternative theory is that representation can be exchanged for control. If a creature knows where to look and when to look, and knows what activities to activate and deactivate, then it can approximate arbitrarily rational agents.

To take a rather simple example consider an insect which feeds off of sugar, and lives in an environment of wily but slow predators. Such a creature must be able to sense sugars or the probability of sugars at a small distance. "Feed" on those sugars when possible, "Move" in a specified direction, "Run Away" when it gets too close to certain objects—particularly predators, "Stop Short" if it is about to hit an object directly in front of it, and be able to perform compounds of these low level abilities such as

"Wander" so that it might improve its probability of finding food, "Avoid Obstacles" and "Follow Freeways" so that it may move through irregular terrain or flee predators without stumbling. Each of these activities is tuned to certain environmental conditions, such that the activity is turned on or off, amplified or diminished according to locally detectable conditions in conjunction with the internal switching circuitry. If all works well, the net effect is that as the world changes, either because the robot itself is moving through it, or because of external events, the robot will behave as if it is choosing between many goals. Sometimes it runs, sometimes it wanders, sometimes it feeds.

Obviously, the trick in making a mobot behave in a way that looks like it is choosing between many goals without it explicitly predicting the effects which the various behaviours would have on the world, is to design the right pattern of control into the circuitry. Certain pathways will carry messages which dominate the normal input to a module or which suppress the normal output. Accordingly, one goal of research is to find a way of minimizing the amount of this control. Each FSM should be tuned to the *right* stimuli so as to let the world force choice whenever possible.

Thus, for example, when the senses register a looming stimulus, the Stop Short module, takes command. Stop Short was primed; it was in a state which acts on a looming stimulus and is hooked up to output so that its signal overrides any others that may also be transmitted. Similarly, if a system were on a coke can collecting mission, the Move Hand module might take over as soon as the system sensed a halt in optical flow and a streak of red. A complex cooperative behaviour might emerge, therefore, simply because each component activity becomes primed for particular changes in the state of the world that matter to it. Hence, coordination is achieved automatically without posting requests on some central blackboard or relying on some active arbitrator to pass control to slave activities because the preference relations among activities have been built into the switching network of the system.

Let us call behaviour that is controlled by the situation in this way, *situation-determined behaviour*. Situation-determined behaviour can be considerably more complex than the stimulus driven behaviour found in behaviourist theory. For instance, humans, when putting together jig saw puzzles, may be said to be situationally determined if there is enough joint constraint in the tiles and assembled layout to ensure that they can complete the puzzle without wasted placements. No behaviourist theory can explain jig saw performance, however, because there is no readily definable set of structural properties—i.e. stimulus conditions—that are the causes of jig saw placements—i.e. responses. The agent is too active in perceptually questioning the world. On two confrontations with the same world the same agent might perceive different situations as present because it asked a different set of perceptual questions. These questions are a function of the state of the agent and its most recent interactions with the world.

We can say that jig saw puzzles are perceptually hard but intellectually simple. The actions are intentional but under perceptual rather than conceptual guidance. Thus it is the eye, not the thinking center, which must be trained to look for the salient corners that differentiate tiles and signal proper fit. It is a problem of perceptual search.

Viewing situation-determined behaviour to be a solution to a perceptual problem points out several worthwhile aspects of situationally determined tasks.

First, there is enough local constraint in the world to "determine" successful placement despite there being several tiles that can be successfully played at any moment. In a sense each move is underdetermined, hence no deterministic behaviourist theory can explain placement behaviour. Nonetheless, given a tile and an existing layout, the situation wholly determines whether or not the tile can be correctly placed at that time and where. There is no need to check downstream effects. In the jig saw game, successful placements are additive. Good moves do not interact hostilely with other good moves. There are no traps, dead ends, or loops that may stymie a player. The situation contains enough information to pre-empt the need for lookahead. This is the main point of assumption three.

Second, the perceptual problem is tractible in the sense that only a fraction of the visible world state must be canvassed to determine where to move. The point of sensing is to provide enough information to permit a creature to choose between the actions it can perform next. In the case of jig saw it is conceivable that to solve the puzzle one must identify the overall shape of all the pieces first. If this were true, a jig saw puzzle would be a tedious game indeed, for either it would require collosal visual processing each move, or it would require tremendous visual memory of shapes. How much easier if complete shape identification is unnecessary.

Is this possible? Is it possible to decide which tile to place next by using a strategy of visually questioning the board that does not require computing the overall shape of each tile? The question is important because if perceptual questioning can be confined to simple features there will be no need for higher level intermediate representations.

Imagine a case where a player cannot decide which of five tiles to play in a particular opening. Each tile seems like it might be a proper fit, but it is hard to tell. An obvious aid to the problem is to have the player try to fit one of the tiles in the opening to let the world highlight the crucial feature that differentiates the proper tile from the near misses. The function of this test move is to focus the player's attention on the situationally *salient* features of the tiles. It is to identify the crucial differentiating features. Now a true expert of the game might not need this help; his perceptual system may be so tuned to the task that he can home right in on the relevant differentiating features. If so, this possibility affirms the point of assumption four: that if one knows what to look for, there is a fairly local feature which correlates with correct moves. Not only does the situation contain enough local constraint to determine good moves, these constraints are highly specific to the task and learnable.

It is worth dwelling on this issue for it emphasizes the truth of assumption five: that control is the hard problem, and the methodological importance of assumption one: that behaviour can be partitioned into task oriented activities. These, I take it, are the backbone of this alternative approach to action.

It is standard in decision theory to treat perception as a bounded resource that must be guided in order to be used to its fullest. The problem which decision-theoretic accounts encounter, however, is that to know what question it is best to ask next, or which test it is best to perform next, the agent must know all the sources of information available now and in the future, all the decisions that might be taken now and in the future, their consequences, utilities, etc. To achieve optimality is clearly impossible in practice, for it requires knowing where you are most likely to get the information you want before you know exactly which decisions you must make. If one restricts the horizon of one's decisions to specific task-oriented activities the problem is simpler. Must I halt now? Can I proceed in that direction? Is there a predator nearby? For each of these questions there may be a straightforward test which is decisive, or nearly decisive, or indicative of what to test next. Once again the question is whether the test (or perceptual query) is computationally cheap.

In a situationally determined context such questions are necessarily cheap. The environment can be factored into a set of partial states or *indicators* which correlate well with the presence or absence of the larger environmental factors which affect task performance. Thus for a robot whose environment contains doors with right angles it may be possible to discover an invariant *microfeature* of doors which under normal conditions can be seen from all angles. Relative to door entering activity, this invariant may be all that need be sought. Moreover, it may be simple—a top right and bottom left corner in suitable opposition for example. This fraction of doorness is sufficient for door recognition in this environment, as long as the robot remains upright, as long as no new doors are introduced, and so forth. It correlates with all and only doors. Consequently, one of the hardest problems for mobot designers is to discover these indicators, and the perceptual queries that best identify them. For each activity the designer must determine which possible indicators correlate well with the likelihood of success or failure of the activity given the current state of the world. This is a hard problem for most activities. But the key point is that without the assumption that behaviour can be partitioned into task-oriented activities, it would be impossible to discover these indicators at all.

This introduces the third and final respect situationally determined tasks are illustrative of the alternative theory of action: what is most salient in the environment is usually discernable and economically detectable from the *agent's perspective*. Most task indicators are egocentrically definable. This is a crucial factor in deciding how much of activity can be intelligently controlled without concepts because concepts are often held to be non-egocentric, public or quasi-public entities.

Developmental psychologists draw a distinction between the *egocentric space* of an agent and the *public space*, which as observers we see the agent performing in. The distinction is intuitive. In egocentric space, the agent is always at the spatio-temporal origin of its world. It sees the environment from its own perspective. Indexical terms such as beside-me, to my right, in front, on top, nearby, occluded-right-now, are all well defined, and depend essentially on the agent's location. They shift as it moves about.

In public space, by contrast, the world is understood almost as if viewed from nowhere. If the agent is included in the world at all it is included objectively as another entity in relation with objects in the world. This is done to facilitate useful generalization. Two people can see the same ball; a ball remains the same ball despite its currently being outside the agent's visual field; and it remains beside a companion ball whether partly occluded or not. Because we can count on the permanence of objects and on a consensual understanding of space-time we can usefully organize our experience of the world by appeal to public objects, public space, and public time. We can describe actions and strategies in a manner which allows people in different circumstances to use them; and we can talk about consequences of actions as if we were not there to see them. Thus, in describing the action of lifting a box five feet in the air it is usually irrelevant whether the agent approaches the box from the right or left. Where the agent was positioned in the situation is less important than what it did to make the box go up. This can be stated in terms of the lawful changes which the objects in the environment undergo.

In the classical theory of action, the beliefs that were thought causally important in determining action were stated in the language of public objects and properties. Actions were defined as situation-action rules— transformations between pre and postconditions, and were understood as transformations over public states.

The practice of enumerating the troubles of situation action rules based on public concepts is by now a familiar pastime in discussions of AI planning. It is therefore regarded a virtue of the situationally determined account that the indicators which matter to situationally determined task performance are definable from an egocentric perspective.

J.J. Gibson, for example, argued at length that the genuine environment of action is not a world of objects and objective relations but a world of surfaces and textural flows as seen by the agent. Gibson, in his ecological approach to perception, emphasized that action and perception are not distinct processes. Animals and people do not passively perceive the world. They move about in it actively, picking up the information needed to guide their movement. This information is always available in an egocentric form, because as a result of the interlocking between perception and action, certain egocentric invariants emerge. Flies can find landing sites by detecting wiping of texture in the optic flow [17, pp. 215–218], chicks and babies can avoid precipices by detecting motion parallax and texture gradients [17, pp. 234–235]. These invariants can be picked up early. They do not require the level of visual processing involved in creating a full 3-D representation. The same it seems holds for most situationally determined tasks: the indicators which matter can be gleaned by relatively early attention to egocentric invariants, or properties.

The upshot is that for situationally determined activity, perception, particularly egocentric perception, rather than conceptual reasoning is the determining factor of success. This holds because there is a reliable correlation between egocentrically noticeable properties of the environment and actions that are effective.[8]

Now, from both a scientific and engineering standpoint nothing but good can come from exploring in silicon and metal how much of intelligent activity can be duplicated following the principles of this alternative theory of action. Until we construct creatures which can have hundreds of procedures turned on and waiting, we cannot know how effective the world might possibly be in deciding the sequence of the procedures to use. There may be far more indicators in the world that are able to bias performance than we would have dreamed possible prior to designing creatures to run in the real world.

Nevertheless, as with most nascent areas of AI, it is easy to see early results as compelling evidence for strong conclusions. In Brooks' case, the success of this design strategy for simple insect-like creatures is meant to justify a host of methodological directives and criticisms for design strategies of far more complex creatures and behaviours.

Accordingly, let us consider some of the limits of situationally determined actions, and the attendant reasons higher-level creatures are likely to use concepts and representations in action, perception, and control.

3 The limits of situationally determined action

Situationally determined activity has a real chance of success only if there are enough egocentrically perceptible cues available. There must be sufficient local constraint in the environment to determine actions that have no irreversibly bad downstream effects. Only then will it be *un*necessary for the creature to represent alternative courses of actions to determine which ones lead to dead ends, traps, loops, or idle wandering.

From this it follows that if a task requires knowledge about the world that must be obtained by reasoning or by recall, rather than by perception, it cannot be classified as situation determined. Principle candidates for such tasks are:

- Activities which involve other agents, since these often will require making *predictions* of their behaviour.
- Activities which require response to events and actions beyond the creature's current sensory limits, such as taking precautions now for the future, avoiding future dangers, contingencies, idle wandering—the standard motive for internal lookahead.
- Activities which require understanding a situation from an objective perspective such as when a new recipe is followed, advice is assimilated, a strategy from one context is generalized or adapted to the current situation. All these require some measure of conceptualization.
- Activities which require some amount of problem solving, such as when we wrap a package and have to determine how many sheets of paper to use, or when we rearrange items in a refrigerator to make room for a new pot.
- Activities which are creative and hence stimulus free, such as much of language use, musical performance, mime, self-amusement.

These activities are not isolated episodes in a normal human life. Admittedly, they are all based on an underlying set of reliable control systems; but these control systems are not sufficient themselves to organize the *global* structure of the activity.

Thus, to prepare tea requires coordinating both global and local constraints. At the global level, teamakers must be sensitive to the number of people they are serving, ensuring there is enough water, tea, cups, saucers and biscuits. Once these items are laid out more mobot-like control systems may take over, pouring the water, stirring etc. But the initial resource allocation problems are hard to solve. Animals are notoriously ineffective at them. Moreover, can we expect mobots to intelligently arrange plates on the tray? Arrangement or bin packing requires attention to a number of non-local factors, such as how many items remain to be placed, how well they can be expected to stack, and how stable the overall configuration must be, given the path to the parlour. Anticipation of the future is required. Hence, whenever global considerations enter the control of action, the creature must either be pre-tuned to the future, or it must be able to call on memories, reason about contingencies, ask for advice, and so forth.

In short, the world of human action regularly falls short of total situation determinedness. Most of our life is spent managing locally constrained choice.[9] It is at this management level that we can best appreciate the virtue of concepts and representations.

4 The virtues of concepts and representations

Concepts are involved in the management of action because they serve at least three organizing functions in cognitive economies. At the *perceptual* level, concepts unify perceptions into equivalence classes. An agent possessing the concept of a dog, for instance, should be able to recognize dogs from different points of view. A dog is an invariant across images. It is also an object for the visual system in the sense that the visual field will be segmented into dog images and non-dog images, offering whatever attentional mechanisms reside in the perceptual system to be directed at specifics of dog images. Accordingly, one aspect of saying that a creature has a concept of dog is to say that he or she can identify dogs perceptually. This means that a vast array of perceptual circumstances can be simplified and reasoned about economically, and that a host of perceptual mechanisms are coordinated around the perceptual object dog.

At a more *conceptual* level, concepts license inferences. A dog is *not* identical with the set of its possible appearances. It is a spatially extended temporally enduring entity that can enter into causal relations with other objects. It is a possible subject of predication. Hence much of what is true of other objects—other possible subjects of predication—will be true of dogs. Many of these *inheritable* truths constitute the *presuppositions* which a creature able to have beliefs and thoughts about dogs will hold. In thinking about dogs, then, the creature will have in mind an entity that is alive, breathes, normally has four legs, and so on. This information is readily accessible, but of course need not be conscious. It enables the creature, however, to intelligently respond to invisible properties of dogs [18]. Thus, a child may resist striking a dog because it knows it would hurt the dog, despite the fact that the property of being open to hurt is not a perceptually present property of dogs.[10]

At a *linguistic* level, a concept is the meaning of a term. To know the meaning of "dog" in English is to have the concept of dog, and to know that the English word signifies that concept. The concept dog is a semantic value; in the Fregean system, when coupled with another appropriate semantic value it constitutes a proposition, or truth bearer.

Now, when an agent has a concept it can do things and think thoughts it could not otherwise. As developmentalists have pointed out, once a child has the concept of an object, it can know that the same object can present different appearances. It can decide that what looks like a dog is not really a dog, but a misleading image of a bear. It can infer that your image of this dog is different than mine, but that we both know it is the same dog [14]. And it can infer that dogs feel pain because they are alive. Concept users understand a great deal about their environment when they conceptualize it.

There can be no doubt that the skills we identify with possession of concepts are of great value for certain forms of intelligent behaviour. But how widespread is this behaviour? Can we approximate most intelligent behaviour without concepts? This is Brooks' challenge.

One of the most important uses of concepts is to organize memory. Whether or not a system has limited memory, it has a need to index memories in a manner that facilitates recall. In action management, an effective creature will benefit from its performances in the past. It will remember dangers, failures, helpful tricks, useful sub-goals. It may recall unexpected consequences of its previous performances. These memory accesses need not be conscious. Nor need they be complete. Someone describing a particular pet dog may not have accessed all the related information he or she knows about the animal. Some information lies untouched. But this information is *primed* in the sense that retrieving that related information in the near future takes less time than had the topic never been discussed [10].

In general, if memory is deemed useful for an action it is less plausible to call that action situation determined. The strong empirical claim Brooks makes, then, is that to access organized memories takes too long for most actions. Given the pressing exigencies of the real world, there is no time to retrieve and reason with conceptualized information.

Short of knowing the actual time a particular creature takes for accessing memory it is impossible to argue for or against Brooks' thesis. But we can have intuitions. For instance, in tasks where the time to react is very short, recall will be costly; some recall may be possible but it must be directly applicable to tasks without much reasoning.

Yet how much of life is reactive? In driving home, for instance, I am often on autopilot, but I do come to genuine choice points, where I must decide whether to take, for example, Torrey Pines Blvd. or the highway [9]. In assessing my options I have conceptualized the possibilities. My preferences are over world states, conceived sometimes as my possible future experiences, sometimes as objective states of the world. My response is not reactive, it is thoughtful. My decision depends on how I think of the future.

The point, here, is that if I wish to accommodate my present action to events, objects or actions that are distant in time and space, I shall have to anticipate them now. A perception-driven creature can only anticipate the future if there is evidence of the future in its present. With memory, however, it can remember that Y follows X, and so coordinate its actions to a broader environment than that perceptually given.

If the future is a simple function—possibly Markovian—of the perceptually present, a system of linked FSMs might cope with simple futures. FSMs have state and so can encode information about the future. But the future they encode cannot be complicated or complexly branching. When the future is complex simple FSMs will be unreliable. For it is inevitable that one set of future states which correlates with the present will recommend action in one direction, while others, also correlating with the present, will recommend action in other directions. How is choice to be made? Prudent decision-making in such situations requires an all things considered approach. It requires balancing the recommendations, and setting a course of action which may involve the future coordination of a complex network of acts. It is hard to see how this could be done without the simplifications of the world which conceptualization gives us.

This capacity to accommodate the future ties in with a second ability that comes naturally to systems with concepts: to *take advice*, and to learn by imitation [11]. It is characteristic of humans that if they are in the middle of a task that has several parts they can make use of hints or suggestions. These need not be linguistic clues because often it is enough if someone shows us manually what to do, or shows us a technique or move that is similar to the one we must perform. New ideas can bias performance. This implies that whatever means we have for controlling our behaviour it must be *permeable* to new information.

What makes this permeability hard to capture in models built on the alternative theory of action is that hints and advice are often offered from a non-egocentric point of view. Hence there is no reason why a hint or a suggestion should be meaningful input to the home system. This is not to say that concept using agents have no trouble assimilating advice. Advice can be more or less ready for use. Hints phrased from an objective, perspectiveless orientation may be hard to put into practice by agents wholly immersed in their own perspective. But some form of this translation problem is solved every time we understand that other agents see the world differently.

Advice taking also has a sensory side. Suppose I am told that a friend has been in a car accident and broken his legs. I now expect to see a person on crutches. Hence I can recognize him at a distance, and not be deceived by appearances.

This adaptation of future expectations is impossible to explain without concepts. There must be some device in an agent which functions like an indexed long-term memory of objects which keeps track of changes and which allows it to update expectations about the behaviour and appearance of objects in a controlled manner. Somehow it must be able to systematically change the attributes that an object may be assumed to inherit or possess by default.

This same idea applies to behaviour in strategic environments where the effectiveness of an action often depends on the interpretation which other agents impose on it. To take advantage of these dependencies requires knowing the interpretations of others. It presupposes that the agent can understand its opponents or colleagues as systems whose behaviour is a partial function of its current and future behaviour. It is hard to see how the effects of this recursive interpretation can be achieved without conceptual representations. First, it will require understanding other agents as agents in a common world playing in a common field, hence operating in a public domain rather than an egocentric one. Second, it will require understanding them counterfactually, in terms of how they might interpret the agent if it were to do *X* instead of *Y*.

5 The need for representation in a theory of perception

I have been describing the importance of representation, particularly conceptual representation, for a theory of action: there are limits to how subtly a system can act if it is entirely situation determined. The ability to frame and test hypotheses about the future and about other agents' behaviour is essential for survival in human style environments. But there are equally strong reasons to suppose that representation is important for a theory of perception.

The field of computational vision has done much to explode the myth that vision is strongly under the influence of expectations, memory and inference *at early stages of processing*. But there are few who believe that extraction and identification of shapes can occur without at least some models of shape in memory.

Shape models are not the same as concepts. They constitute equivalence classes of perceptions, but they carry no implications of objecthood. Accordingly, it is not until *scene parsing*, where items are identified in the visual scene and conceptualized as organized, that we are justified in claiming that a system imposes concepts.

Brooks' position on this is, I believe, much like Gibson's. Organisms detect without inference or reconstruction those properties of things which they need to achieve their goals. In general, this will not require visual processing to the point of 3-D shape recognition, and certainly never to the point of scene recognition. Brooks believes it will never require more processing than that required for a viewer-centered representation of objects; and most often the information needs of action can be fulfilled by special purpose detectors.[11]

The trouble with this view, however, is that it doesn't make clear how some of the interesting visual properties that need detecting can actually be accomplished.

For instance, how can an object seen from one orientation be recognized as the same object when viewed from another orientation. This is necessary for backtracking in the world.

A key assumption of the alternative theory of action is that the world is benign: ineffective moves can be tolerated because seldom is it the case that they lead to irrecoverable states. If an ineffective move is made, the creature can either just continue from its new position, or backtrack in the world—provided, of course, the creature could remember its path. But this is the problem: how can the creature recognize where it's been if it cannot recognize the same object from both front and back?

To cope with the memory demands of search in the world humans trailblaze—they leave markers of where they've been. They can then reuse pre-existing procedures, such as, go to the first visible landmark that you haven't already visited. But there are obviously environments where trailblazing is impractical. In such cases, a snapshot of the relevant portion of the world state is required. This is akin to episodic memory. But the episode is not recorded as a simple snapshot. For if the creature is to use the snapshot, it must record the scene in a perspective neutral way. Otherwise the image will be the wrong orientation to resemble what the agent sees as it backtracks. Records more abstract than agent-oriented images are required.

As a rule animals do not rely on such sophisticated perception and perceptual recall. I do not know whether they do much controlled search in the world but they can easily determine whether they have visited a spot by scent. They are locally driven machines. Such is not always the case with humans. Early in our evolution we traded olfactory prowess for visual intelligence, with the attendant advantage that we now can determine whether we have visited a spot without sniffing it at close range.

In the same way our abilities to handle complex objects without practice also feed off of our advanced visual intelligence. Funny shapes require funny grasps. Unevenly distributed masses require prudent grips, and heavy objects require appropriate force. We don't approach a weighty textbook the way we do a paper container.

How do we determine our approach to these objects without performing enough computation to determine (1) the center of mass of the object, (2) a set of points or regions of opposition, and (3) the texture of the surface so that we can make a good guess about the object's material and hence its weight? One possibility is that we use a vast table look up which associates shapes with grasps. Yet grasps vary with hardness, smoothness and weight too. These too will have to be built into a table. The net effect would be a table of enormous complexity, Accordingly, the obvious alternative is to invoke intermediate representations and compute solutions on-line. These intermediate representations are not conceptual; they represent properties that are relevant for grasping. But they do emphasise that perception must solve big problems, and frequently in a way that is general. At the very least, the complexity of vision argues for the need to analyse the problem at a general level, if only to construct the look up table.

6 The need for representations in a theory of learning

Skill generalization is a further area that may pose problems for the mobotics approach. One reason we currently believe that representations—of both the conceptual and non-conceptual variety—are vital to learning is that we know of no other way of *simplifying* situations so that what is similar between situations is easy to note. Obviously we want systems that can apply existing knowledge to new tasks, systems that can *transfer* expertise. Unless mobots can generalize stimuli they will have to be reprogrammed to perform what are essentially the same tasks on slightly different objects. If a mobot can pick up a coke can it should be able to pick up a coffee cup.

The trouble with coordinated FSMs is that they are each carefully tuned to the particular properties of specific tasks. If a hand-control system that regulates coke can grasping focusses on specific coke can properties—a red streak, a shiny "circular" surface—then it is not easy to see how that control system can be used for grasping coffee cups. The issue is not whether some of the constituent modules of the coke grasping reflex can be used; it is, rather, that one or several FSMs depend on specific perceptual microfeatures of coke cans.

Now sometimes this task specificness is justified. Perhaps the ability to pick up cans is different than the ability to pick up cups with handles, or to pick up flyswatters. But how are we to know this? The mobot engineering philosophy is to test out designs to see what is common across tasks. If coke can grasping does not work on coffee cups then add extra control layers. This same process will continue until someone decides that the grasping system is too complex. At that moment, a redesigned system will be constructed that simplifies the system on the basis of what has been learned.

There is nothing objectionable in this familiar engineering approach. But it is based on two rather strong assumptions. First, that it is imprudent to pursue prior analysis because one cannot know what are the natural groupings of grasping until one knows how a grasper relying on microfeatures might work. Second, generalization of the grasping system can be achieved without extracting higher-order structural properties.

The virtue of representations, both intermediate and conceptual, is that they let us see similarity in superficial disparity. Two objects may differ in almost all their microfeatures, but be deemed relevantly similar at a more abstract level. Thus the generalization problem: is X relevantly similar to Y, is easy to solve if we have characterized X and Y in a relatively sparse feature space, but hard in a dense lower level space. The questions: "What are the task-relevant properties common across objects?", "What properties of objects must be made explicit to simplify control?" are what the study of representation is all about. Only in a rhetorical sense, then, can moboticists contend that they abjure representations.

7 The need for representations in a theory of control

Any system that is to forever substitute control for representation must be able to:

(1) cope with increasingly *complex desire systems*; and
(2) resourcefully recover from failure.

If we are ever to build the much awaited household robot, it will have to be designed with both these abilities. I think designers, however, will have an impossibly difficult time building in such abilities without using conceptual representations. Consider desire systems first.

Any household robot worth its salt must be able to make us a midnight snack. Before I rely on such a device, though, I will want it to be able to operate with complex goal systems. I want it to be able to balance competing desiderata when it reaches the fridge. The trouble is that mobots, as we envisage them today, operate with an impoverished goal system and so are limited in their performance.

Basically, a mobot-inspired creature would work on what might be called the *refrigerator model of desire*. Open up the refrigerator, look in, and let the contents and some simple capacitor notion of wants decide what to select. This has the nice property that the creature doesn't have to have a fixed idea of what to select in advance, it can let the possibilities decide for it. Thus the choice problem is solved in the simplest way possible: thirst is valued more than appearance and less than gut hunger. If hunger has been largely satisfied so that the *capacitor* measuring hunger is low, then thirst prevails, and so forth.

The problem with this approach is that if the creature is to cope with many desires it is not at all clear how a ranking can be provided in so simple a fashion. Given a choice between filboid sludge for breakfast and taking a chit for a five course lunch at Panache, I'll choose the chit. My top level goal may be the allayment of hunger but how I subgoal may be complex and sensitive to many desiderata, such as taste, appearance, comfort, diet, to name a few. Desires do not just compete in a simple winner take all fashion, because in complex desires system it is not possible to rank desires according to a small number of lexicographically ordered dimensions. There are real limits to the capacitor concept of desire.

What this means is that when desire systems get large there must be some type of desire management, such as deliberation, weighing competing benefits and costs, and so on. This applies whether the mobot is out there in the field doing my bidding or it is an autonomous creature with its own set of desires. Without representation, desires lack the *modularity* to be reasoned about, or even flexibly assembled. If the representations are not conceptual they will not be about enduring states of the world that can be entertained and reasoned over. Conceptual representation is necessary for desire management. Without desire management, mobots will be little more than insects or lower animals.

Now consider the value of belief systems for flexible control.

One of the lessons learned from first generation expert systems is that unless an agent has some understanding of why certain if-then rules work it will be unable to respond flexibly when it finds that it has no rule that will apply in its current context or when it discovers that one of its rules fails to have the desired outcome. Models of underlying relations are important.

To take a simple example, if a radio repairman is unable to fix a broken set by standard tweaks, he will try to discover by reasoning the cause of the system's observed behaviour. The customary imputation is that experts have levels of understanding: for standard cases they operate with an abstracted representation of a device or possibly a set of precompiled procedures. But when necessary they can reflect on the rationale of those procedures, on why they work in certain cases and why they may fail in others; they may even reason from first principles.

Now in a typical mobotic system there can be no more than a small number of fixes one could try in problematic situations. In some cases this strategy will work. It achieves a type of robustness: a system that announces it doesn't know what to do is more resilient than a system which is determined to try something, no matter how ham fisted.

The problem is that if one wants to do better than giving up, the fix has to be appropriate to the case. The lesson of second generation expert systems is that such fixes require being selective about choosing what additional information to seek. This is a hard problem and requires a fairly deep understanding of the situation. But it is unclear that Rod's robots can have this kind of understanding without having the equivalent of models of the domain. How can a system whose response to failure is to try a simpler behaviour achieve this innovative resilience?

The reason this is a hard problem is that the response the system has to make varies across situations. The same behavioural failure can require different fixes. That means that at a superficial level there is not enough information to determine an action. The system must conjecture and test. Since the range of conjecture is vast, the state space of FSM's would have to be correspondingly vast. But once again this vast space would not be systematically generated, except, of course, by the designer who used concepts and compiled his answer to hide the systematicity.

8 Conclusion

I have been arguing that although AI can substantially benefit from greater attention to the richness of perceptual information, this richness will never replace the need for internal representations. Any plausible household robot, even one that does not have the full improvisational skills of a human, will have to rely on symbolic representations at least sometimes.

This is especially obvious if we consider how language use can accelerate evolution. No one understands how closely language is tied to vision, or how closely it is tied to reasoning. But it is widely recognized that once language is acquired certain forms of learning and reasoning become possible and certain other forms are accelerated.

For instance, with linguistic communication comes the possibility of identifying and storing very precise information. Without language it is hard to draw someone's attention to a particular perceptual fact; for it is difficult to specify *which* condition of the situation is the salient condition. The problem becomes exponentially more difficult if the condition is abstract. Imagine trying to draw someone's attention to the *bluntness* of a particular pin.

Similarly, once arbitrary amounts of knowledge can be stored and passed on from generation to generation, we can accelerate the rate at which our abilities grow by learning from the lessons of others. Cultural transmission of information is much faster than genetic transmission of information. This might explain the shockingly brief time it took for man to develop his higher mental skills when compared with the great length of time evolution took to develop sophisticated motor skills.

Thus, is 97% of life concept-free? The answer depends on how you count abilities. If an ability is defined relative to an environment, then the richness of the human environment suggests that there are wildly more tasks that can be done in the human world, than in environments characteristic of less language, norm-ridden creatures. Once language-like communication emerged the rate at which we could acquire new abilities rose dramatically because we could identify, create, and teach new abilities.

The magic that made this take-off possible was the ability to remember facts, rules, norms, strategies and the like. With specific cases in mind we could avoid pitfalls, with norms and rules we could cleave to the conservative but safe path; with strategies and plans we could find our way where random search would be disastrous. And of course with the ability to communicate— which these higher order abilities presuppose—we could also take advice.

These goods seem to flow from the ability to internally represent facts and to reason explicitly. Any theory that asserts that we can get by without conceptual representation will have to *explain away* these goods by showing that they are not necessary for intelligent activity.

Acknowledgement

In writing this paper I have benefited considerably from insightful discussions with Peter Cudhea, Pattie Maes, Jean Mandler, Eric Saund and Bob Stalnaker.

Notes

1 I am fully aware that identifying syntactic symbol manipulation with possession of concepts begs the question of symbol grounding and the philosophical problems of reference. For the purposes of assessing Brooks' position, however, the identification is fair since one of his targets is clearly declarative representations.
2 Providing of course that it has the other relevant concepts, apples, paint . . .
3 A declarative is not an easy entity to define. For my purposes I will assume that if information is encoded in a state, structure or process in a form that can be interpreted in a model-theoretic semantics, then it is declarative. Declaratives release their information upon being *read*, whereas procedures release their information upon being *run*. But clearly, there is no straightforward way of defining the

difference between declaratives and procedures since in certain programming languages both can serve as first class objects. For related discussions see [7].

4 Many ethologists regard compiling an *ethogram* to be the first step in the description of a species. An ethogram is a behavioural vocabulary of a species which lists all the basic types of behaviours an organism can perform. These behaviours are unit-like in that they can be performed in sequences. Brooks' notion, it seems to me, departs from this more classical notion in being more task oriented. Thus, an activity may be a controlled collection of simpler activities, grouped together by their common purpose of, say, grasping coke cans. Ethologists too look for the function of activities and cluster more basic behavioural units together, but their definition of function is strongly tied to the concept of evolutionary adaption. See [13].

5 Cf. [3]. Brooks diverges from Gallistel in treating the interaction of activities to be often more complex than that found in simple hierarchies.

6 This idea I take to be Gibson's principle contribution to the study of sensory systems. Cf. [4,5]. Where Brooks departs from Gibson on this point is in viewing the process as akin to information retrieval. Gibson supposes that the information is directly picked up.

7 Again compare [4,5]. In Gibson's view the senses are not passive receptors of information; they are active seeking mechanisms, searching out the information—often minimal information—required for effective action and avoidance of physical harm.

8 The conception of situation determinedness I offer is stipulative. Others can be proposed. For instance, one could propose that a context situationally determines an action for an agent if the situation in conjunction with the inner state of the agent determines what he will do next. But to stretch the definition in that direction is to give up the distinction between situation determinedness and determinedness simplicitur. Agents are usually determined by the union of mental state and local environment. The noteworthy condition of true situation determinedness is that reasoning is not required for action.

9 For an outline of the virtues and problems with local choice, see [6].

10 Gibson argues that sentience and the like are perceivable properties of an animal. But in his system, there is almost no action-relevant property that is not perceivable. Thus, post boxes have the perceivable property of affording letter posting. Just how many non-obvious properties can be perceived or registered is a deep question which the alternative theory of action raises. But I think we may safely say that the line must be drawn short of *all* action-relevant properties. Default reasoning will be valuable for these.

11 The justification for this claim, it seems to me, is the Gibsonian theory that perception involves active exploration by an organism. Instead of asking how an organism infers the structure of its environment from the pattern of activations on its receptive field, we ask how the organism picks up what it needs to know by moving through the "ambient optical array" containing the information. By dynamically sampling this optical array the creature is supposed to be able to get whatever information it needs about objects and layouts to fulfill its objectives.

References

[1] R.A. Brooks, Intelligence without representation, *Artif. Intell.* **47** (1991) 139–159, this volume.

[2] R.A. Brooks, A robust layered control system for a mobile robot, *IEEE. J. Rob. Autom.* **2** (1986) 14–23.

[3] C.R. Gallistel, *The Organization of Action* (Erlbaum, Hillsdale, NJ, 1980).

[4] J.J. Gibson, *The Senses Considered as Perceptual Systems* (Houghton Mifflin, Boston, MA, 1966).

[5] J.J. Gibson, *The Ecological Approach to Visual Perception* (Houghton Mifflin, Boston, MA, 1979).

[6] D. Kirsh, Managing local choice, in: *Proceedings AAAI Workshop on AI and Rational Choice* (1989).

[7] D. Kirsh, When is information explicitly represented?, in: P. Hanson, ed., *Information, Content and Meaning* (UBC Press, Vancouver, BC, 1990).

[8] N.J. Mackintosh, *Conditioning and Associative Learning* (Oxford University Press, Oxford, 1983).

[9] G. Mandler, *Cognitive Psychology* (Erlbaum, Hillsdale, NJ, 1985).

[10] G. Mandler, Memory: Conscious and unconscious, in: P.R. Solomon, G.R. Goethals, C.M. Kelley and B.R. Stephens, eds., *Memory: Interdisciplinary Approaches* (Springer, New York, 1989).

[11] J. Mandler, How to build a baby: on the development of an accessible representational system, *Cogn. Dev.* **3** (1988) 113–136.

[12] M. Minsky, *The Society of Mind* (Simon and Schuster, New York, 1986).

[13] V. Reynolds, The origins of a behavioural vocabulary: The case of the rhesus monkey, *J. Theor. Social Behav.* **6** (1976) 105–142.

[14] M. Siegel, *Knowing Children: Experiments in Conversation and Cognition* (Erlbaum, Hillsdale, NJ, 1990).

[15] E.S. Spelke, Where perceiving ends and thinking begins: the apprehension of objects in infancy, in: A. Yonas, ed., *Perceptual Development in Infancy* (Erlbaum, Hillsdale, NJ, 1988).

[16] R. Sternberg, ed., *Advances in the Psychology of Intelligence* **4** (Erlbaum, Hillsdale, NJ, 1988).

[17] B. Vicki, and P. Green, *Visual Perception, Physiology, Psychology and Ecology* (Erlbaum, Hillsdale, NJ, 1985).

[18] H.M. Wellman and S.A. Gelman, Children's understanding of the nonobvious, in: R. Sternberg, ed., *Advances in the Psychology of Intelligence* **4** (Erlbaum, Hillsdale, NJ, 1988).

Section 1.2: Dynamical Artificial Intelligence

52

DESIGN FOR AN INTELLIGENCE-AMPLIFIER

W. Ross Ashby

Source: C. E. Shannon and J. McCarthy (eds), *Automata Studies*, Princeton University Press, 1956, pp. 215–33.

Section I

1 Introduction

For over a century Man has been able to use, for his own advantage, physical powers that far transcend those produced by his own muscles. Is it impossible that he should develop machines with "synthetic" intellectual powers that will equally surpass those of his own brain? I hope to show that recent developments have made such machines possible – possible in the sense that their building can start today. Let us then consider the question of building a mechanistic system for the solution of problems that are beyond the human intellect. I hope to show that such a construction is by no means impossible, even though the constructors are themselves quite averagely human.

There is certainly no lack of difficult problems awaiting solution. Mathematics provides plenty, and so does almost every branch of science. It is perhaps in the social and economic world that such problems occur most noticeably, both in regard to their complexity and to the great issues that depend on them. Success in solving these problems is a matter of some urgency. We have built a civilisation beyond our understanding and we are finding that it is getting out of hand. Faced with such problems, what are we to do?

Our first instinctive action is to look for someone with corresponding intellectual powers: we think of a Napoleon or an Archimedes. But detailed study of the distribution of Man's intelligence shows that this method can give

191

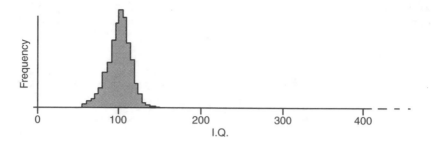

Figure 1 Distribution of the adult human Intelligence Quotient (after Wechsler, 1).

little. Figure 1, for instance, shows the distribution of the Intelligence Quotient in the normal adult population, as found by Wechsler [1]. What is important for us now is not the shape on the left but the absolute emptiness on the right. A variety of tests by other workers have always yielded about the same result: a scarcity of people with I.Q.s over 150, and a total absence of I.Q.s over 200. Let us admit frankly that Man's intellectual powers are as bounded as are those of his muscles. What then are we to do?

We can see something of how to proceed by comparing our position today in respect of intellectual problems with the position of the Romans in respect of physical problems. The Romans were doubtless often confronted by engineering and mechanical problems that demanded extreme physical strength. Doubtless the exceptionally strong slave was most useful, and doubtless the Romans sometimes considered the possibility of breeding slaves of even greater strength. Nevertheless, such plans were misdirected only when men turned from their own powers to the powers latent in Nature was the revolution inaugurated by Watt possible. Today, a workman comes to his task with a thousand horsepower available, though his own muscles will provide only about one-tenth. He gets this extra power by using a "power-amplifier". Had the present day brain-worker an "intelligence-amplifier" of the same ratio, he would be able to bring to his problems an I.Q. of a million.

If intellectual power is to be so developed, we must, somehow, construct amplifiers for intelligence – devices that, supplied with a little intelligence, will emit a lot. To see how this is to be done, let us look more closely at what is implied.

2 *The criterion of intelligence*

Let us first be clear about what we want. There is no intention here to enquire into the "real" nature of intelligence (whatever that may mean). The position is simple: we have problems and we want answers. We proceed then to ask, where are the answers to be found?

It has often been remarked that any random sequence, if long enough, will contain *all* the answers. Nothing prevents a child from doodling

$$\cos^2 x + \sin^2 x = 1,$$

or a dancing mote in the sunlight from emitting the same message in Morse or a similar code. Let us be more definite. If each of the above thirteen symbols might have been any one of fifty letters and elementary signs, then as 50^{13} is approximately 2^{73}, the equation can be given in coded form by 73 binary symbols. Now consider a cubic centimeter of air as a turmoil of colliding molecules. A particular molecule's turnings after collision, some-times to the left and sometimes to the right, will provide a series of binary symbols, each 73 of which, on some given code, either will or will not repre-sent the equation. A simple calculation from the known facts shows that the molecules in every cubic centimeter of air are emitting this sequence *correctly* over a hundred thousand times a second. The objection that "such things don't happen" cannot stand.

Doodling, then, or any other random activity, is capable of producing all that is required. What spoils the child's claim to be a mathematician is that he will doodle, with equal readiness, such forms as

$$\cos^2 x + \sin^2 x = 2 \quad \text{or} \quad ci)xsi = nx1$$

or any other variation. After the child has had some mathematical experience he will stop producing these other variations. He becomes not more but less productive: he becomes selective.

The close, indeed essential, relation between intelligence and selection is shown clearly if we examine the tests specially devised for its objective meas-urement. Take, for instance, those of the Terman and Merrill [2] series for Year IV. In the first Test the child is shown a picture of a common object and is asked to give its name. Out of all the words he knows he is asked to select one. In the second Test, three model objects – motor-car, dog, shoe – are placed in a row and seen by the child; then all are hidden from him and a cover is placed over the dog; he is then shown motor-car, cover, shoe, and asked what is under the cover. Again his response is correct if, out of all possible words, he can select the appropriate one. Similarly the other Tests, for all ages, evoke a response that is judged "correct" or "incorrect" simply by the subject's power of appropriate selection.

The same fact, that getting a solution implies selection, is shown with special clarity in the biological world. There the problems are all ultimately of how to achieve survival, and survival implies that the essential variables – the supply of food, water, etc. – are to be kept within physiological limits. The solutions to these problems are thus all selections from the totality of possibilities.

The same is true of the most important social and economic problems. What is wanted is often simple enough in aim – a way of ensuring food for all with an increasing population, or a way of keeping international frictions small in spite of provocations. In most of these problems the aim is the keeping of certain variables within assigned limits; and the problem is to find, amid the possibilities, some set of dynamic linkages that will keep the system both stable, and stable within those limits. Thus, finding the answer is again equivalent to achieving an appropriate selection.

The fact is that in admiring the *productivity* of genius our admiration has been misplaced. Nothing is easier than the generation of new ideas: with some suitable interpretation, a kaleidoscope, the entrails of a sheep, or a noisy vacuum tube will generate them in profusion. What is remarkable in the genius is the discrimination with which the possibilities are winnowed.

A possible method, then, is to use some random source for the generation of all the possibilities and to pass its output through some device that will select the answer. But before we proceed to make the device we must dispose of the critic who puts forward this well known argument: as the device will be made by some designer, it can select only what he has made it to select, so it can do no more than he can. Since this argument is clearly plausible, we must examine it with some care.

To see it in perspective, let us remember that the engineers of the middle ages, familiar with the principles of the lever and cog and pulley, must often have said that as no machine, worked by a man, could put out more work than he put in, therefore no machine could ever amplify a man's power. Yet today we see one man keeping all the wheels in a factory turning by shovelling coal into a furnace. It is instructive to notice just how it is that today's stoker defeats the mediaeval engineer's dictum, while being still subject to the law of the conservation of energy. A little thought shows that the process occurs in two stages. In Stage One the stoker lifts the coal into the furnace; and over this stage energy is conserved strictly. The arrival of the coal in the furnace is then the beginning of Stage Two, in which again energy is conserved, as the burning of the coal leads to the generation of steam and ultimately to the turning of the factory's wheels. By making the whole process, from stoker's muscles to factory wheel, take place in two stages, involving two lots of energy whose sizes can vary with some independence, the modern engineer can obtain an overall amplification. Can we copy this method in principle so as to get an amplification in selection?

3 The selection-amplifier

The essence of the stoker's method is that he uses his (small) power to bring into action that which will provide the main power. The designer, therefore, should use his (small) selectivity to bring into action that which is going to do the main selecting. Examples of this happening are common-place once one knows what to look for. Thus a garden sieve selects stones from soil; so if a gardener has sieves of different mesh, his act of selecting a sieve means that he is selecting, not the stones from the soil, but that which will do the selecting. The end result is that the stones are selected from the soil, and this has occurred as a consequence of his primary act; but he has achieved the selection mediately, in two stages. Again, when the directors of a large firm appoint a Manager of Personnel, who will attend to the selection of the staff generally, they are selecting that which will do the main selecting. When the whole process of selection is thus broken into two stages the details need only a little care for there to occur an amplification in the degree of selection exerted.

In this connexion it must be appreciated that the *degree* of selection exerted is not defined by what is selected: it depends also on what the object is selected from. Thus, suppose I want to telephone for a plumber, and hesitate for a moment between calling Brown or Green, who are the only two I know. If I decide to ring up Green's number I have made a one-bit selection. My secretary, who will get the number for me, is waiting with directory in hand; she also will select Green's number, but she will select it from 50,000 other numbers, a 15.6-bit selection. (Since a 1-bit selection has directly determined a 15.6-bit selection, some amplification has occurred.) Thus two different selectors can select the same thing and yet exert quite different degrees of selection.

The same distinction will occur in the machine we are going to build. Thus, suppose we are tackling a difficult social and economic problem; we first select what we want, which might be:

An organisation that will be stable at the conditions:
Unemployed   <   100,000 persons
Crimes of violence   <   10 per week
Minimal income per family   >   £500 per annum

This is *our* selection, and its degree depends on what other conditions we might have named but did not. The solving-machine now has to make *its* selection, finding this organisation among the multitudinous other possibilities in the society. We and the solving-machine are selecting the same entity, but we are selecting it from quite different sets, or contexts, and the degrees of selection exerted can vary with some independence. (The similarity of this relation with those occurring in information theory is unmistakable; for in the latter the information-content of a message depends not only on what is in the message but on what population of messages it came from [3, 4].)

The building of a true selection-amplifier – one that selects over a greater range than that covered when it was designed – is thus possible. We can now proceed to build the system whose selectivity, and therefore whose intelligence, exceeds that of its designer.

(From now on we shall have to distinguish carefully between *two* problems: our problem, which is to design and build the solving-machine, and the solving-machine's problem – the one we want it to solve.)

4 Basic design

Let us suppose for definiteness that the social and economic problem of the previous article is to be the solver's problem. How can we design a solver for it? The construction would in practice be a formidable task, but here we are concerned only with the principles. First, how is the selection to be achieved automatically?

SELECTION BY EQUILIBRIUM. We can take advantage of the fact that if any two determinate dynamic systems (X and S in Figure 2) are coupled through channels G and U so that each affects the other, then any resting state of the whole, (that is, any state at which it can stay permanently,) must be a resting state in each of the two parts individually, each being in the conditions provided by the other. To put it more picturesquely, each part has a power of veto over resting states proposed by the other. (The formulation can be made perfectly precise in the terms used in Article 6.)

It is only a change of words to say that each part acts selectively towards the resting states of the other. So if S has been specially built to have resting states only on the occurrence of some condition ζ in S, then S's power of veto ensures that a resting state of the whole will always imply ζ in S. Suppose next that the linkage G is such that G will allow ζ to occur in S if and only if the condition η occurs in X. S's power of veto now ensures that any resting state of the whole must have condition η in X. So the selection of S and G to have these properties ensures that the only states in X that can be permanent are those that have the condition η.

It must be noticed that the selection of η, in the sense of its retention in X, has been done in two stages. The first occurred when the designer specified S and G and ζ. The second occurred when S, acting without further reference

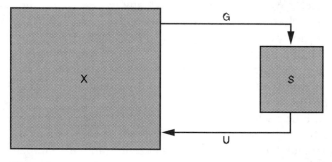

Figure 2

to the designer, rejected state after state of X, accepting finally one that gave the condition η in X. The designer has, in a sense, selected η, as an ultimate consequence of his actions, but his actions have worked through two stages, so the selectivity achieved in the second stage may be larger, perhaps much larger, than that used in the first.

The application of this method to the solving of the economic problem is, in principle, simple. We identify the real economic world with X and the conditions that we want to achieve in it with η. The selection of η in X is beyond our power, so we build, and couple to it, a system S, so built that it has a resting state if and only if its information through G is that η has occurred in a resting state in X. As time progresses, the limit of the whole system, X and S, is the permanent retention of η in X. The designer has to design and build S and G, and to couple it to X; after that the process occurs, so far as he is concerned, automatically.

5 *The Homeostat*

To see the process actually at work, we can turn briefly to the Homeostat. Though it has been described fully elsewhere [5], a description of how its action appears in the terms used here may be helpful in illustration. (Figure 3 is intended to show its principle, not its actual appearance.)

It consists of four boxes (F) of components, freely supplied with energy, that act on one another in a complex pattern of feedbacks, providing initially a somewhat chaotic system, showing properties not unlike those sometimes seen in our own society. In this machine, S has been built, and G arranged, so

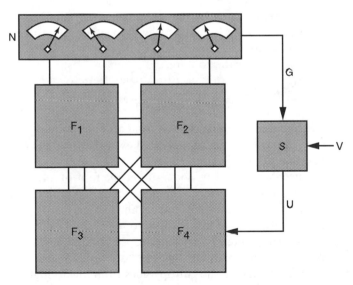

Figure 3

that S has a resting state when and only when four needles N are stable at the central positions. These are the conditions η. N and the F's correspond to X in Figure 2. S affects the F's through the channel U, whose activity causes changes in the conditions within the boxes.

Suppose now that the conditions within the boxes, or in the connexions between them, are set in some random way, say as a by-stander pleases; then if the conditions so set do not satisfy η, S goes into activity and enforces changes till η is restored. Since η may refer to certain properties of the stability within F, the system has been called "ultrastable", for it can regulate the conditions of its own stability within F. What is important in principle is that the combinations in F that restore η were not foreseen by the designer and programmed in detail; he provided only a random collection of about 300,000 combinations (from a table of random numbers), leaving it to S to make the detailed selection.

One possible objection on a matter of principle is that all the variation going to the trials in X seems, in Figure 2, to be coming from S and therefore from the designer, who has provided S. The objection can easily be met, however, and the alteration introduces an important technical improvement. To make the objection invalid, all the designer has to do is to couple S, as shown in Figure 3, to some convenient source of random variation V – a noisy vacuum tube say – so that the SV combination

(i) sends disturbance of inexhaustible variety along U if ζ is not occurring in S, and

(ii) keeps U constant, i.e., blocks the way from V to U, if ζ *is* occurring.

In the Homeostat, V is represented by the table of random numbers which determined what entered F along U. In this way the whole system, X and S, has available the inexhaustible random variation that was suggested in Article 2 as a suitable source for the solutions.

6 Abstract formulation

It is now instructive to view the whole process from another point of view, so as to bring out more clearly the deep analogy that exists between the amplification of power and that of intelligence.

Consider the engineer who has, say, some ore at the foot of a mine-shaft and who wants it brought to the surface. The power required is more than he can supply personally. What he does is to take some system that is going to change, by the laws of nature, from low entropy to high, and he couples this system to his ore, perhaps through pistons and ropes, so that "low entropy" is coupled to "ore down" and "high entropy" to "ore up". He then lets the whole system go, confident that as the entropy goes from low to high so will it change the ore's position from down to up.

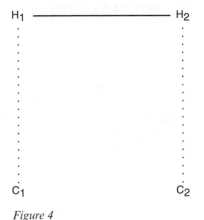

Figure 4

Abstractly (Figure 4) he has a process that is going, by the laws of nature, to pass from state H_1 to state H_2. He wants C_1 to change to C_2. So he couples H_1 to C_1 and H_2 to C_2. Then the system, in changing from H_1 to H_2, will change C_1 to C_2, which is what he wants. The arrangement is clearly both necessary and sufficient.

The method of getting the problem-solver to solve the set problem can now be seen to be of essentially the same form. The job to be done is the bringing of X, in Figure 2, to a certain condition or "solution" η. What the intelligence engineer does first is build a system, X and S, that has the tendency, by the laws of nature, to go to a state of equilibrium. He arranges the coupling between them so that "not at equilibrium" is coupled to not-η, and "at equilibrium" to η. He then lets the system go, confident that as the passage of time takes the whole to an equilibrium, so will the conditions in X have to change from not-η to η. He does not make the conditions in X change by his own efforts, but allows the basic drive of nature to do the work.

This is the fundamental principle of our intelligence-amplifier. Its driving power is the tendency for entropy to increase, where "entropy" is used, not as understood in heat-engines but as understood in stochastic processes.

AXIOMATIC STATEMENT. Since we are considering systems of extreme generality, the best representation of them is given in terms of the theory of sets. I use the concepts and terminology of Bourbaki [6].

From this point of view a machine, or any system that behaves in a determinate way, can be at any one of a set of states at a given moment. Let M be the set of states and μ some one of them. Time is assumed to be discrete, changing by unit intervals. The internal nature of the machine, whose details are irrelevant in this context, causes a transformation to occur in each interval of time, the state μ passing over determinately to some state μ′ (not necessarily different from μ), thereby defining a mapping t of M in M:

$$t: \mu \rightarrow \mu' = t(\mu).$$

If the machine has an input, there will be a set I of input states ι, to each of which will correspond a mapping t_ι. The states ι may, of course, be those of some other machine, or may be determined by it; in this way machine may be coupled to machine. Thus if machine N with states v has a set K of inputs κ and transformations u_κ, then machines M and N can be coupled by defining a mapping λ of M in K, $\kappa = \lambda (\mu)$, and a mapping m of N in I, $\iota = m(v)$, giving a system whose states are the couples (μ, v) and whose changes with time are defined by the mapping of M × N in M × N:

$$(\mu, v) \rightarrow (t_{m(v)}(\mu), u_{\lambda(\mu)}(v)).$$

The abstract specification of the principle of ultrastability is as follows, Figure 5 corresponding to Figure 2:

GIVEN:
(1) A set Γ consisting of two elements γ_1 and γ_2;
(2) A set Ξ of elements ξ;
(3) A mapping g of Ξ in Γ;
(4) A set Σ of elements σ;
(5) A family of mappings χ_σ of Ξ in Ξ;
(6) A random variable v, inexhaustible in variety;
(7) A double family of mappings $s_{\gamma v}$ of Σ in Σ, with the property that, for all $\sigma \ \varepsilon\Sigma$ and all values of v,

$$s_{\gamma_1 v}(\sigma) \neq \sigma \quad \text{and} \quad s_{\gamma_2 v}(\sigma) \neq \sigma;$$

(8) Time, advancing by discrete intervals, induces the operations χ_σ and $s_{\gamma v}$ and the successive values of v simultaneously, once in each interval.

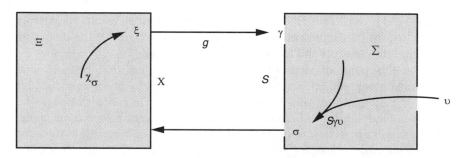

Figure 5

THEOREM: If the series of states of Ξ, induced by time, has a limit ξ^*, then $\xi^* \in g^{-1}(\gamma_2)$.

PROOF. The state of the whole system, apart from υ, is given by the couple (ξ, σ), an element in $\Xi \times \Sigma$. The passage of one interval of time induces the mapping $(\xi, \sigma) \rightarrow (\chi_\sigma(\xi), s_{g(\xi)}, {}_\upsilon(\sigma))$. If the series is at a limit-state (ξ^*, σ^*), then $s_{g(\xi^*)}, {}_\upsilon(\sigma^*) = \sigma^*$ for all values of υ. Therefore $g(\xi^*) = \gamma_2$, and $\xi^* \in g^{-1}(\gamma_2)$.

Section II

With this theorem our problem is solved, at least in principle. Systems so built can find solutions, and are not bounded by the powers of their designers. Nevertheless, there is still a long way to go before a man-made intelligence-amplifier will be actually in operation. Space prohibits any discussion of the many subsidiary problems that arise, but there is one objection that will probably be raised, suggesting that the method can never be of use, that can be dealt with here. It is of the greatest importance in the subject, so the remainder of the paper will be devoted to its consideration.

7 *Duration of trials*

What we have discussed so far has related essentially to a process that, it is claimed, has "solution" as its limit. The question we are now coming to is, how fast is the convergence? how much time will elapse before the limit is reached?

A first estimate is readily made. Many of the problems require that the answer is an n-tuple, the solver being required to specify the value of each of n components. Thus the answer to an economic problem might require answers to each of the questions:

(1) What is the optimal production-ratio of coal to oil?
(2) What amount should be invested annually in heavy industry?
(3) What should be the differential between the wages of skilled and unskilled workers?

except that in a real system n would be far larger than three.

A first estimate of the number of states to be searched can be made by finding the number of states in each component, assuming independence, and then finding the product so as to give the number of combinations. The time, with a state by state search, will then be proportional to this product. Thus, suppose that there are on a chessboard ten White and ten Black men; each can move to one of six squares; how many possibilities will have to be searched if I am to find the best next two moves, taking White's two moves and Black's two into account? – With each man having about six moves (when captures are allowed for), the possible moves at each step are approximately 6^{10}; and the total possibilities are about 6^{40}. To find the best of them, even if some machine ran through them at a million a second, would take nearly a billion billion years – a prohibitively long time. The reason is that the time taken increases, in this estimate, exponentially with the number of components; and the exponential rate of increase is extremely fast. The calculation is not encouraging, but it is very crude; may it be seriously in error?

It is certainly in error to some extent, for it is not strictly an estimate but an upper bound. It will therefore always err by overestimation. This however is not the chief reason for thinking that our method may yet prove practical. The reasons for thinking this will be given in the next three articles.

8 The method of models

The first factor that can be used to reduce the time of search is of interest because it is almost synonymous with the method of science itself. It is, to conduct the search, not in the real physical thing itself but in a model of it, the model being chosen so that the search can proceed in it very much more rapidly. Thus Leverrier and Adams, searching for a planet to explain the aberrations of Uranus, used pencil, paper and mathematics rather than the more obvious telescope; in that way they found Neptune in a few months where a telescopic search might have taken a lifetime.

The essence of the method is worth noticing explicitly. There is a set R, containing the solutions r, a subset of R; the task is to find a member of r. The method of models can be used if we can find some other set R' whose elements can be put into correspondence with those of R in such a way that the elements (a set r') in R' that correspond to those in r can be recognised. The search is then conducted in R' for one of r'; when successful, the correspondence, used inversely, identifies a solution in R. For the method to be worth using, the search in R' must be so much faster than that in R that the time taken in the three operations

  (i) change from R to R',
 (ii) search in R',
(iii) change back from r' to r

is less than that taken in the single operation of searching in R.

Such models are common and are used widely. Pilot plants are used for trials rather than a complete workshop. Trials are conducted in the drawing-office rather than at the bench. The analogue computer is, of course, a model in this sense, and so, in a more subtle way, is the digital computer. Mathematics itself provides a vast range of models which can be handled on paper, or made to "behave", far faster than the systems to which they refer.

The use of models with the word extended to mean any structure isomorphic with that of the primary system, can thus often reduce the time taken to a fraction of what might at first seem necessary.

9 Constraints

A second reason why the time tends to fall below that of the exponential upper bound is that often the components are *not* independent, and the effect of this is always to reduce the range of possibilities. It will therefore, other things being equal, reduce the time of search. The lack of independence may occur for several reasons.

CONSTRAINT BY RELATION. Suppose we are looking for a solution in the n-tuple $(a_1, \ldots, a_n)$, where a_1 is an element in a set A_1, etc. The solution is then one of a subset of the product set $A_1 \times A_2 \times \ldots \times A_n$. A relation between the a's, $\varphi(a_1, \ldots, a_n)$, always defines a subset of the product space [6], so if the relation holds over the a's, the solution will be found in the subset of the product-space defined by φ. An obvious example occurs when there exist invariants over the a's. k invariants can be used to eliminate k of the a's, which shows that the original range of variation was over $n - k$, not over n, dimensions. More generally, every law, whether parliamentary, or natural, or algebraic [7] is a constraint, and acts to narrow the range of variation and, with it, the time of search.

Similarly, every "entity" that can be recognised in the range of variation holds its individuality only if its parts do *not* vary over the full range conceivable. Thus, a "chair" is recognisable as a thing partly because its four legs do not move in space with all the degrees of freedom possible to four independent objects. The fact that their actual degrees of freedom are 6 instead of 24 is a measure of their cohesion. Conversely, their cohesion implies that any reckoning of possibilities must count 6 dimensions in the product or phase space, not 24.

It will be seen therefore that *every relation that holds between the components of an n-tuple lessens the region of search.*

CONSTRAINT BY CONTINUITY. Another common constraint on the possibilities occurs where there are functional relations within the system such that the function is continuous. Continuity is a restriction, for if $y = f(z)$ and f is continuous and a series of arguments $z, z', z'', \ldots$ has the limit $z*$, then the corresponding series $y, y', y'', \ldots$ must have the limit $f(z*)$. Thus f is not free to relate y and z, y' and z', y'' and z'', $\ldots$ arbitrarily, as it could do if it were unrestricted. This fact can also be expressed by saying that as adjacent values of z make the values of f(z) adjacent, these values of f(z) tend to be highly correlated, so that the values of f(z) can be adequately explored by a mere sampling of the possibilities in z: the values of y do not have to be tested individually.

A rigorous discussion of the subject would lead into the technicalities of topology; here it is sufficient to notice that the continuity of f puts restrictions on the range of possibilities that will have to be searched for a solution.

Continuity helps particularly to make the search easy when the problem is to find what values of a, b, c, . . . will make some function $\lambda(a, b, c, . . .)$ a maximum. Wherever λ is discontinuous and arbitrary there is no way of finding the maximum, or optimum, except by trying every combination of the arguments individually; but where λ is continuous a maximum can often be preceded to directly. The thesis is well illustrated in the art of aircraft design, which involves knowing the conditions that will make the strength, lightness, etc., an optimum. In those aspects of design in which the behaviour of the aircraft is a continuous function of the variables of design, the finding of an optimum is comparatively direct and rapid; where however the relations are discontinuous, as happens at the critical values of the Reynolds' and Mach numbers, then the finding of an optimum is more laborious.

Chess, in fact, is a difficult game largely because of the degree to which it is discontinuous, in the sense that the "value" of a position, to White say, is by no means a continuous function of the positions of the component pieces. If a rook, for instance, is moved square by square up a column, the successive values of the positions vary, sometimes more or less continuously, but often with marked discontinuity. The high degree of discontinuity occurring throughout a game of chess makes it very unlike the more "natural" systems, in which continuity is common. With this goes the corollary that the test so often proposed for a mechanical brain – that it should play chess – may be misleading, in that it is by no means representative of the class of problem that a real mechanical brain will one day have to deal with.

The commonness of continuity in the world around us has undoubtedly played an important part in Darwinian evolution in that progress in evolution would have been far slower had not continuity been common. In this paper I have tended to stress the analogy of the solving process with that of the amplification of physical power; I could equally have stressed its deep analogy with the processes of evolution, for there is the closest formal similarity between the process by which adaptation is produced automatically by Darwinian selection and the process by which a solution is produced automatically by mechanical selection of the type considered in Article 4. Be that as it may, every stock-breeder knows that selection for good strains can procede much more rapidly when the relation between genotype and phenotype is continuous [8]. The time taken for a given degree of improvement to be achieved is, of course, correspondingly reduced.

To sum up: Continuity being common in the natural world, the time taken in the solution of problems coming from it may be substantially below that given by the exponential bound.

CONSTRAINT BY PRIOR KNOWLEDGE. It is also only realistic to consider, in this connexion, the effect on solving of knowledge accumulated in the past. Few problems are wholly new, and it is merely common sense that we, and the problem-solver, should make use of whatever knowledge has already been won.

The effect of such knowledge is again to put a constraint on the possibilities, lessening the regions that have to be searched, for past experience will act essentially by warning us that a solution is unlikely to lie in certain regions. The constraint is most marked when the problem is one of a class, of which several have already been solved. Having such knowledge about other members of the same class is equivalent to starting the solving process at some point that is already partly advanced towards the goal. Such knowledge can naturally be used to shorten the search.

"Solving a problem" can in fact be given a perfectly general representation. The phase- or sample-space of possibilities contains many points, most of them corresponding to "no solution" but a few of them corresponding to an acceptable "solution". Finding a solution then becomes a matter of starting somewhere in this unknown distribution of states and trying to find one of the acceptable states.

If the acceptable states are distributed wholly at random, i.e., with no recognisable pattern, then we are considering the case of the problem about which nothing, absolutely nothing, is known. After two hundred years of scientific activity, such problems today are rare; usually some knowledge is available from past experience, and this knowledge can be used to constrain the region of search, making it smaller and the search more rapid. Thus suppose, as a simple example, that there are 144 states to be examined and that 40 of them are acceptable, i.e., correspond to solutions. If they are really scattered at random, as are the black squares in I of Figure 6, then the searcher has no better resource than to start somewhere and to wander at random. With this method, in this particular example, he will usually require about 3.6 trials to find a black square. If, however, past experience has shown that the black squares are distributed as in II, advantage can be taken to shorten the search; for wherever the search may start, the occurrence of two white squares in succession shows the searcher that he is in an all-white quadrant. A move of four squares will take him to a checkered quadrant where he will find a dark square either at once or on the next move. In this case his average number of trials need not exceed about 2.4 (if we ignore the complications at the boundaries).

Information theory and the strategy of games are both clearly involved here, and an advanced knowledge of such theories will undoubtedly be part of the technical equipment of those who will have to handle the problem-

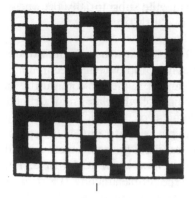
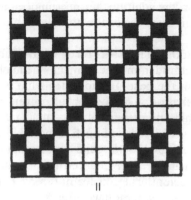

I   II

Figure 6

solvers of the future. Meanwhile we can sum up this Article by saying that it has shown several factors that tend to make the time of search less than that given by the exponential bound.

10 Selection by components

We now come to what is perhaps the most potent factor of all for reducing the time taken. Let us assume, as before, that the solver is searching for an element in a set and that the elements are n-tuples. The solver searches, then, for the n values of the n components.

In the most "awkward" problems there is no means of selection available other than the testing of every element. Thus, if each of the n components can take any one of k values, the number of states to be searched is k^n, and the time taken will be proportional, as we saw in Article 7, to the exponential bound. This case, however, is the worst possible.

Next let us consider the other extreme. In this case the selection can be conducted component by component, each component being identified independently of the others. When this occurs, a very great reduction occurs in the time taken, for now the number of states to be searched is kn.

This second number may be very much smaller than the first. To get some idea of the degree of change implied, let us take a simple example. Suppose there are a thousand components, each of which has a hundred possibilities. If the search has to be over every *combination* separately, the number of states to be searched is the exponential bound, 100^{1000}. If the states could be examined at one a second it would take about 10^{1993} years, a duration almost beyond thinking. If we tried to get through the same selection by the method of models, using some device that could test, say, a million in each microsecond, the time would drop to 10^{1981} years, which is practically no change at all. If however the components could be selected individually and

206

independently, then the number of selections would drop to 100,000; and at one per second the problem could be solved in a little over a day.

This illustration will suffice to illustrate the general rule that selection by components is so much faster than selection by elements that a search that is utterly impractical by the one may be quite easy by the other.

The next question is to what extent problems are susceptible of this faster method. About *all* problems one can say nothing, for the class is not defined; but about the problems of social and economic type, to which this paper is specially directed, it is possible to form some estimate of what is to be expected. The social and economic system is highly dynamic, active by its own energies, and controllable only through a number of parameters. The solver thus looks for suitable values in the n-tuple of parameters. (Its number of components will not usually be the same as those of the variables mentioned in the next paragraph.)

Now a dynamic system may be "reducible"; this happens when the system that seems to be single really consists of two or more adjacent, but functionally independent, parts. If the parts, P and Q say, are quite independent, the whole is "completely" reducible; if part P affects part Q, but Q has no effect on P, then the whole is simply "reducible". In the equations of such a system, which can be given in the canonical form [5]

$$\frac{dx_1}{dt} = f_1(x_1, \ldots, x_n)$$

$$\cdots\cdots\cdots$$

$$\frac{dx_n}{dt} = f_n(x_1, \ldots, x_n)$$

reducibility is shown by the Jacobian of the n functions f_i with respect to the n variables x_j having, when partitioned into the variables that belong to P and those that belong to Q, one or more all-zero quadrants, being like I when reducible and like II when completely reducible:

$$\begin{bmatrix} J_1 & o \\ K & J_2 \end{bmatrix} \qquad \begin{bmatrix} J_1 & o \\ o & J_2 \end{bmatrix}$$
$$\quad\;\text{I} \qquad\qquad\qquad\quad \text{II}$$

Such reducibility corresponds, in a real dynamic system, with the possibility of searching to some extent by components, the components being the projections [6] of the abstract space on those variables, or "coordinates", that occur together in one part (P, or Q) of the reducible system. The more a system is reducible, the more does it offer the possibility of the search being made by the quick method of finding the components separately.

Though the question has not yet been adequately explored, there is reason to believe that part-functions, i.e., variables whose f_i (above) are zero for many values of their arguments, are common in social and economic systems. They are ubiquitous in the physical world, as I have described elsewhere [5]. Whenever they occur, they introduce zeros into the Jacobian of the system (for if x_j is constant, over some interval of time, f_i must be zero and therefore so will be $\partial f_i/\partial x_j$); they therefore tend to introduce temporary reducibilities. This means that the problem may be broken up into a series of conditional and transient sub-problems, each of which has a solution that can be found more or less easily. The whole search thus has something of the method of search by components.

In this connexion it is instructive to consider an observation of Shannon's [9] on the practicability of using relays as devices for switching, for it involves a property closely related to that of reducibility. One of the problems he solved was to find how many elements each relay would have to operate if the network was to be capable of realising all possible functions on n variables. The calculation gave a number that was, apparently, ridiculously high for, did one not know, it would suggest that relays were unsuitable for practical use in switching. The apparent discrepancy proved to be due to the fact that the functions commonly required in switching are not as complicated as the class that can be considered in theory. The more they *look* complicated the more they tend to have hidden simplicities. These simplicities are of the form in which the function is "separable", that is to say, the variables go in sets, much as the variables in a reducible system go in sets. Separability thus makes what seems to be an impractical number of elements become practical. It is not unlikely that reducibility will act similarly towards the time of search.

11 The lower bound

It can now be seen that problem-solving, as a process of selection, is related to the process of message-receiving as treated in information theory [3, 10]. The connexion can be seen most readily by imagining that the selection of one object from N is to be made by an agent A who acts according to instructions received from B. As the successive elements appear, B will issue signals: "..., reject, reject, ..., accept" thereby giving information in calculable quantity to A. Usually the number of binary signals so given is likely to be greater than the number necessary, for the probabilities of the two signals, "reject" and "accept", are by no means equal. The most efficient method of selection is that which makes the two signals equally likely. This will happen if the whole set of N can be dichotomised at each act of selection. In this way we can find a *lower bound* to the time taken by the process, which will be proportional to log N. This time is none other than the least time in which, using binary notation, the solution can be written down, that is, identified from its alternatives.

We see therefore that, though the upper (exponential) bound is forbiddingly high, the lower bound is reassuringly low. What time will actually be taken in some particular problem can only be estimated after a direct study of the particular problem and of the resources available. I hope, however, that I have said enough to show that the mere mention of the exponential bound is not enough to discredit the method proposed here. The possibility that the method will work is still open.

Summary

The question is considered whether it is possible for human constructors to build a machine that can solve problems of more than human difficulty. If physical power can be amplified, why not intellectual?
Consideration shows that:

Getting an answer to a problem is essentially a matter of selection.

Selection can be amplified.

A system with a selection-amplifier can be more selective than the man who built it.

Such a system is, in principle, capable of solving problems, perhaps in the social and economic world, beyond the intellectual powers of its designer.

A first estimate of the time it will take to solve a difficult problem suggests that the time will be excessively long: closer examination shows that the estimate is biassed, being an upper bound.

The lower bound, achievable in some cases, is the time necessary for the answer to be written down in binary notation.

It is not impossible that the method may be successful in those social and economic problems to which the paper is specially addressed.

53

A DYNAMICAL SYSTEMS PERSPECTIVE ON AGENT-ENVIRONMENT INTERACTION

Randall D. Beer

Source: *Artificial Intelligence* 72(1–2), 1995: 173–215.

Abstract Using the language of dynamical systems theory, a general theoretical framework for the synthesis and analysis of autonomous agents is sketched. In this framework, an agent and its environment are modeled as two coupled dynamical systems whose mutual interaction is in general jointly responsible for the agent's behavior. In addition, the adaptive fit between an agent and its environment is characterized in terms of the satisfaction of a given constraint on the trajectories of the coupled agent-environment system. The utility of this framework is demonstrated by using it to first synthesize and then analyze a walking behavior for a legged agent.

1 Introduction

This paper is concerned with properly characterizing the interaction between an autonomous agent and its environment. By *autonomous agent*, I mean any embodied system designed to satisfy internal or external goals by its own actions while in continuous long-term interaction with the environment in which it is situated. The class of autonomous agents is thus a fairly broad one, encompassing at the very least all animals and autonomous robots. An animal, for example, may simply be trying to survive, while a robot might be designed to carry out specific tasks, such as keeping some designated area clean or exploring the surface of another planet. The task is thus to abstract over particular details of implementation and embodiment (e.g., nerve cells vs. finite state machines or muscles vs. motors) in order to understand the essential character of this class of systems. However short of this ambitious goal the present paper may fall, the long-term aim is nothing less than a general theoretical framework for the explanation and design of autonomous agents.

The central problem for any autonomous agent, and thus the primary concern in this paper, is the generation of the appropriate behavior at the appropriate time as both its internal state and external situation continuously change. For an embodied agent, action must always take precedence over any other activity. Abstract reasoning, when it can be afforded at all, is profitable only insofar as it is ultimately reflected in improved behavior. This does not necessarily imply that an embodied agent must be purely reactive, reflexively responding only to its immediate situation. Rather, it means an autonomous agent must be able to flexibly combine its immediate circumstances with its long-term goals so as to continuously adjust its behavior in ways appropriate to both. An animal moving throughout its environment, for example, needs to adopt many different modes of behavior as it becomes hungry or tired and encounters potential food, predators and mates, all the while adjusting its posture and leg movements to the constantly changing terrain which it is traversing.

Traditionally, such "low level" concerns of embodiment have not played a major role in AI research. Instead, work in AI has tended to emphasize "high level" intellectual skills, such as language, problem solving and abstract reasoning. Embodied agents, when they have been considered at all, have been viewed as merely symbolic reasoning engines with sensors and effectors attached. Accordingly, the problems of embodied agents have usually been formulated as special cases of the problems of disembodied intelligent systems. Of course, it has long been realized that embodiment raises certain additional technical issues. Sensors, for example, introduce the problem of constructing, and maintaining the consistency of, internal representations of the environment from physical signals, while effectors introduce the problem of translating representations of action into actual motor commands. Furthermore, physical embodiment introduces real-time constraints on an agent's action that limit the amount of time that can be spent reasoning. However, these technical problems are usually seen as merely complicating, rather than invalidating, the classical picture.

In recent years, however, a growing number of AI researchers have begun to appreciate the fundamental importance of embodiment. There are a number of reasons for this change in perspective. Designing agents that can interact with the real world with the versatility and robustness of even simple animals has turned out to be considerably more subtle and difficult than originally realized, and approaches developed for disembodied agents have not in general translated well to the noisy, unpredictable, open-ended and dynamic nature of the real world. Furthermore, many problems that seemed intractable for disembodied systems have turned out to be considerably simplified by active participation in an environment. Work on animate vision, for example, has demonstrated that a number of visual problems are drastically simplified if the agent is given the ability to control its own gaze direction [8]. Likewise, work on situated agents has shown that the potentially brittle and combinatorially explosive nature of general planning can be significantly alleviated by using the immediate situation to guide behavior [3, 20]. Indeed, there is a growing realization that, far from being a mere complication for a disembodied intellect, embodiment may in fact be the more fundamental issue. Certainly, from an evolutionary perspective, the human capacity for language and abstract thought is a relatively recent elaboration of a much more basic capacity for situated action that is universal among animals.

This reassessment of the importance of embodiment has led to an explosion of recent work on autonomous agents. Brooks, working in the area of mobile robotics, was one of the first AI researchers to point out the limitations of classical AI techniques in the face of real-world complexity and the need for a renewed emphasis on embodiment and situated action [18, 20]. Agre and Chapman's work on routine activity grew out of a similar frustration with the limitations of classical planning in realistic environments and led to similar conclusions [2, 3, 22]. Building on Rosenschein's situated automata theory [56], Rosenschein and Kaelbling developed methods for deriving finite state machine controllers for an agent from a formal specification of its knowledge and goals [42]. My own work [11, 14] and that of Cliff [24] has demonstrated the significant potential for interaction between autonomous agent research and work on the neural basis of animal behavior. Biological design principles have also been stressed by Arbib and Liaw [5]. Surveys of recent work in autonomous agents can be found in the collections edited by Maes [45] and Meyer and Wilson[49].

This body of work is loosely characterized by a number of shared ideas. It emphasizes the primacy of actually taking action in the world over the abstract descriptions that we sometimes make of it. It focuses on the development of complete agents capable of carrying out open-ended tasks in unconstrained environments rather than isolated cognitive skills in restricted task domains. It emphasizes behavior and the fundamental importance that the immediate situation plays in guiding an agent's behavior, ideas historically associated with behaviorism, over reasoning and symbolic models of the world. Another common theme of this work has been that a significant fraction of behavior must be seen as emerging from the ongoing interaction between an agent and its environment, an idea often associated with cybernetics. This work has also begun to question the central role that internal representation has been assumed to play in intelligent behavior by most work in cognitive science.

In this paper, I will attempt to show that these and other ideas that are emerging from recent work on autonomous agents, as well as work on the neural basis of animal behavior, can be naturally cast into the language of dynamical systems theory. Furthermore, I will argue that this language can form the basis for a powerful theoretical framework for the explanation and design of autonomous agents in general. Section 2 reviews some of the basic concepts of dynamical systems theory that are required to present this framework. In Section 3, I sketch the theoretical framework itself and draw out some of its conceptual consequences. Section 4 demonstrates the utility of this framework by illustrating in some detail its application to the synthesis and analysis of a walking behavior for a simulated legged agent. Finally, Section 5 discusses the assumptions of the proposed framework, considers its broader implications, and suggests some directions for future work.

2 Dynamical systems

This section will briefly review the essential concepts and terminology of the qualitative theory of dynamical systems that will be required for the theoretical framework to be presented in Section 3. The presentation is necessarily informal and incomplete. The reader interested in a more thorough treatment should refer to one of the many available texts on dynamical systems including, in order of increasing mathematical sophistication, the books by Abraham and Shaw [1], Hale and Koçak [33] and Wiggins [66].

Consider the following three mathematical systems:

$$x_{n+1} = \mu x_n (1 - x_n) \tag{1}$$

$$ml \frac{d^2\theta}{dt^2} + \gamma \frac{d\theta}{dt} + mg \sin \theta = A \cos(\omega t) \tag{2}$$

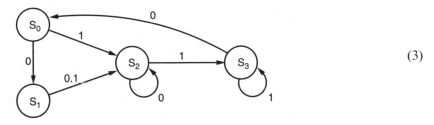

$$(3)$$

At first glance, these three systems may appear to have very little in common. The first equation is an example of an iterated map. The second system is a second-order differential equation describing the motion of a damped, sinusoidally-driven pendulum. The third system is a finite state machine with input. However, all of these systems are also instances of *dynamical systems* and the underlying similarity of many of the questions one might ask about each of these systems only becomes apparent in this formalism.

For our purposes here, a dynamical system is characterized by a set of *state variables* x and a *dynamical law* $\mathcal{F}$ that governs how the values of those state variables change with time. The set of all possible values of the state variables constitutes the system's *state space*. For simplicity, I will assume here that the state space is continuous (i.e., the state variables are real-valued), though most of the concepts that I will be introducing hold in some form for any metric space. Often the geometry of the state space is assumed to be simply Euclidean. Sometimes, however, other spaces arise. Perhaps the most common examples are cylindrical and toroidal state spaces, which occur naturally when some of the state variables are periodic (e.g., θ in Eq. (2)).

If the dynamical law depends only upon the values of the state variables and the values of some set of fixed *parameters u*, then the system is said to be autonomous.[1] In a continuous-time dynamical system, the dynamical law is given in terms of a set of differential equations: $\dot{x} = \mathcal{F}(x;u)$. In this case, the dynamical law defines a *vector field* on the state space. In a discrete-time dynamical system, the dynamical law is simply a map from current state to next state: $x_{n+1} = \mathcal{F}(x_n; u)$. A dynamical system is said to be *linear* or *non-linear* according to the linearity or nonlinearity of $\mathcal{F}$ in the state variables.

As a concrete example, consider the following system of equations, which describe the behavior of a fully-interconnected network of two simple model neurons:

$$\dot{y}_1 = -y_1 + w_{11}\sigma(y_1 - \theta_1) + w_{21}\sigma(y_2 - \theta_2),$$
$$\dot{y}_2 = -y_2 + w_{12}\sigma(y_1 - \theta_1) + w_{22}\sigma(y_2 - \theta_2), \tag{4}$$

where y_i is the state of the ith neuron, $\sigma(\xi) = (1 + e^{-\xi})^{-1}$ is the standard sigmoidal (S-shaped) activation function, θ_i controls the offset or threshold of the activation function and w_{ij} is the weight of the connection from the ith to the jth neuron. This system is a simplification of a common neural network model that will be employed in Section 4. Note that this is a nonlinear system due to the nonlinearity of the activation function σ.

Starting from some *initial state* x_0, the sequence of states generated by the action of the dynamical law is called a *trajectory* of the system and is often denoted $\varphi_1(x_0)$. A trajectory has the property that its tangent at each point is equal to the value of the vector field at that point. Some representative trajectories of the two-node network (4) are shown in Fig. 1. The set of all such trajectories through every point in the state space is called the *flow*, denoted φ_i. In the classical theory of differential equations, one is typically interested only in individual solutions, which correspond to individual trajectories of the dynamical system. In contrast, in the qualitative theory of dynamical systems, one is usually more interested in the geometrical or topological structure of the entire flow.

Of particular interest is the possible long-term behavior of a dynamical system. The state of some systems will simply diverge to infinity (e.g., the

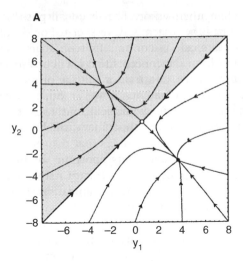

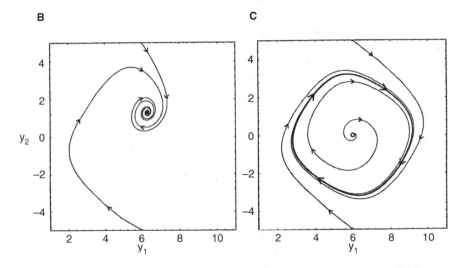

Figure 1 Phase portraits for the two-neuron system (Eq. (4)) for several parameter settings. All of these systems are structurally stable, that is, the qualitative structures of their phase portraits persist for small variations in the parameters. (A) Here the system exhibits two stable equilibrium points near $(-3, 4)$ and $(4, -3)$ with basins of attraction shown in gray and white respectively. The open point near $(0, 0)$ is a repellor and the inset of this repellor (dark diagonal line) forms the separatrix between the two basins of attraction. The parameter values are $w_{11} = w_{22} = 4$, $w_{12} = w_{21} = -3$, $\theta_1 = \theta_2 = 0$. (B) Here the system exhibits a single equilibrium point attractor. The parameter values are $w_{11} = 2.75$, $w_{12} = -6$, $w_{22} = w_{21} = 6$, $\theta_1 = 6$, $\theta_2 = 0$. (C) Here the system exhibits a limit cycle (dark oval) and a repellor (open point near $(6, 0)$). This phase portrait was derived from the one shown in B by increasing the single parameter w_{11} from 2.75 to 6.

system $\dot{y} = y$), while others will eventually converge to *limit sets*. A limit set is a set of points that is invariant with respect to the dynamical law, so that if the state of a dynamical system ever falls on a limit set, the action of the dynamical law will keep it there indefinitely. The *stable* limit sets or *attractors* are especially important. An attractor has the property that the trajectories passing through all nearby states converge to the attractor. This means that if the state of the system is perturbed a sufficiently small distance away from an attractor, the action of the dynamical law will bring the state back to the attractor. The open set of initial states that converge to a given attractor is termed its *basin of attraction*. Those portions of the trajectories through such points which do not lie on the attractor itself are called *transients*. The solid point near (− 3, 4) in Fig. 1(A) is an example of an attractor, and its basin of attraction is shown in gray.

Repellors are limit sets that are *unstable*. Repellors have the property that at least some nearby trajectories diverge from them. Despite the fact that the repellor itself is invariant, if the state of the system is perturbed even an infinitesimal distance from the repellor, the action of the dynamical law will serve to carry it away. The open point near (0, 0) in Fig. 1(A) is an example of a repellor. Attractors are important because they govern the long-term behavior of any physical system. Regardless of the initial state, a physically embodied dynamical system will always be found near an attractor after transients have passed. Due to their instability, repellors can only be observed by starting a dynamical system on a repellor and then never perturbing it. Since any physical system has some noise, it could never stay on a repellor indefinitely.

Four major classes of attractors are usually distinguished. *Equilibrium point* attractors are stable limit sets which consist of single points, such as the solid point near (4, − 3) in Fig. 1(A). An equilibrium point x^* represents a constant solution to the system: $\varphi_t(x^*) = x^*$. *Periodic* attractors or *limit cycles* are stable limit sets which are closed trajectories in the state space. These correspond to periodic or oscillatory solutions, with the property that $\varphi_t(x^*) = \varphi_{t+T}(x^*)$ for some minimum period $T > 0$ and any point x^* lying on the attractor. An example of a limit cycle is shown in Fig. 1(C).

The remaining two classes of limit sets, *quasiperiodic* attractors and *chaotic* attractors, are much more complicated than either equilibrium points or limit cycles. Chaotic attractors, for example, possess a fractal structure and they exhibit a sensitive dependence on initial conditions. No matter how closely two unequal initial states are chosen, their resulting trajectories can diverge exponentially even while remaining bounded on the attractor until they become completely uncorrelated. For this reason, despite the underlying determinism of its dynamical law, the behavior of a chaotic attractor is in many ways indistinguishable from a random process. While I will not discuss quasiperiodic or chaotic attractors further in this paper, it is important to realize that such complicated behavior is quite common in higher dimensional nonlinear dynamical systems.

In general, the state space of a dynamical system will contain multiple attractors, each surrounded by its own basin of attraction. These basins are separated by unstable manifolds called *separatrices*. The dark diagonal line separating the white and gray basins of attraction of the two equilibrium point attractors in Fig. 1(A) is an example of a separatrix. Thus one can visualize these separatrices as dividing the flow of a dynamical system into a number of "cells" each containing an attractor of some type. A global characterization of this cellular structure is called the *phase portrait* of the system (Fig. 1).

We have been holding the parameters u of the dynamical law $\mathcal{F}$ constant and considering the global structure of the resulting flow. What happens when these parameters are changed? Since $\mathcal{F}$ is a function of u, the vector field that it determines, and hence the resulting flow φ, that this vector field induces on the state space, will most certainly change as these parameters are varied. Thus a parameterized dynamical law actually defines a family of dynamical systems, with any particular flow corresponding to a single setting of the parameters.

Just as we were previously interested in the structure of any given flow in state space, we can now inquire into the structure of a family of flows in parameter space. Most dynamical systems are *structurally stable*, that is, for most parameter settings, small changes in the parameter values will produce small changes in the flow. Limit sets and basins of attraction may deform and move around a bit, but the new flow will be qualitatively similar (i.e., topologically equivalent, or *homeomorphic*) to the old one. However, at certain parameter values, dynamical systems can become *structurally unstable*, so that even infinitesimal changes in parameter values can cause drastic changes in the flow, producing phase portraits that are qualitatively different from the original. These qualitative changes in the types of limit sets are called *bifurcations*.

For example, as the parameter w_{11} in our example system (4) is increased from 2.75 to 6, the equilibrium point attractor shown in Fig. 1(B) loses its stability and bifurcates into the repelling point and limit cycle shown in Fig. 1(C) (the actual bifurcation, and therefore the structurally unstable flow that separates these two structurally stable flows, occurs around a w_{11} value of 3.25). Much more complicated bifurcations can occur. Thus, just as we can visualize separatrices as dividing the state space of any given dynamical system into basins of attraction of different attractors, we can think of the sets of bifurcation points corresponding to structurally unstable flows as dividing the parameter space of a family of dynamical systems into different structurally stable flows.

Up to this point, we have only considered autonomous dynamical systems, that is, systems in which the parameters have been held fixed for the duration of any particular trajectory. What happens when these parameters are allowed to vary in time as the trajectory evolves? A *nonautonomous* dynamical system is one in which one or more parameters are allowed to vary in time: $\dot{x} = \mathcal{F}(x;u(t))$. We can think of such parameters as *inputs* to the system. Because, as described above, the flow is a function of the parameters, in a nonautonomous dynamical system the system state is governed by a flow which is changing in time (perhaps drastically if the parameter values cross bifurcation points in parameter space). Nonautonomous systems are much more difficult to characterize than autonomous ones unless the input has a particularly simple (e.g., periodic) structure. In the nonautonomous case, most of the concepts that we have described above (e.g., attractors, basins of attraction, etc.) apply only on timescales small relative to the timescale of the parameter variations. However, one can sometimes piece together a qualitative understanding of the behavior of a nonautonomous system from an understanding of its autonomous dynamics at constant inputs and the way in which its input varies in time.

3 A theoretical framework

The qualitative theory of dynamical systems allows one to build up a global understanding of both the possible behaviors of a dynamical system and the dependence of those behaviors on external parameters even when the solutions have no closed-form expression in terms of elementary mathematical functions. In this section, I will use this formalism to sketch a theoretical framework for characterizing the interaction between autonomous agents and their environments. Only the basic framework will be described here. Some sample applications of the framework will be presented in Section 4, and Section 5 discusses the assumptions of the proposed framework and considers some of its broader implications and directions for future work. This framework owes a great debt to the perspective that the cybernetic tradition has long taken on many of these same questions. I have been particularly influenced by the work of Ashby [6] and Maturana and Varela [47, 48].

3.1 Agents and their environments

Following Ashby [6], I will model an agent and its environment as two dynamical systems $\mathcal{A}$ and $\mathcal{E}$, respectively. I will assume that $\mathcal{A}$ and $\mathcal{E}$ are continuous-time dynamical systems: $\dot{x}_{\mathcal{A}} = \mathcal{A}(x_{\mathcal{A}};u_{\mathcal{A}})$ and $\dot{x}_{\mathcal{E}} = \mathcal{E}(x_{\mathcal{E}};\ u_{\mathcal{E}})$. In addition, I will assume that both $\mathcal{A}$ and $\mathcal{E}$ have convergent dynamics, that is, the values of their state variables do not diverge to infinity, but instead eventually converge to some limit set. Note that the division between an agent and its environment is somewhat arbitrary (e.g., is an artificial limb or a tool part of the agent or part of the environment?) and therefore our theoretical framework should not depend overly much on the exact nature of this

218

division. Our first act as scientific observers is to partition the world into individual components whose interactions we seek to understand, and there are many different ways to do this. For example, it will sometimes be convenient to view an agent's body as part of $\mathcal{A}$ and sometimes as part of $\mathcal{E}$.

An agent and its environment are in constant interaction. Formally, this means that $\mathcal{A}$ and $\mathcal{E}$ are coupled nonautonomous dynamical systems. In order to couple two dynamical systems, we can make some of the parameters of each system functions of some of the state variables of the other. I will represent this coupling with a sensory function S from environmental state variables to agent parameters and a motor function M from agent state variables to environmental parameters. $S(x_{\mathcal{E}})$ corresponds to an agent's sensory inputs, while $M(x_{\mathcal{A}})$ corresponds to its motor outputs. Thus, we have the following (Fig. 2):

$$\dot{x}_{\mathcal{A}} = \mathcal{A}(x_{\mathcal{A}};S(x_{\mathcal{E}});u'_{\mathcal{A}}),$$
$$\dot{x}_{\mathcal{E}} = \mathcal{E}(x_{\mathcal{E}};M(x_{\mathcal{A}});u'_{\mathcal{E}}), \tag{5}$$

where $u'_{\mathcal{A}}$ and $u'_{\mathcal{E}}$ represent any remaining parameters of $\mathcal{A}$ and $\mathcal{E}$ respectively that do not participate in the coupling. I will assume that this coupled agent-environment system also exhibits only convergent dynamics.

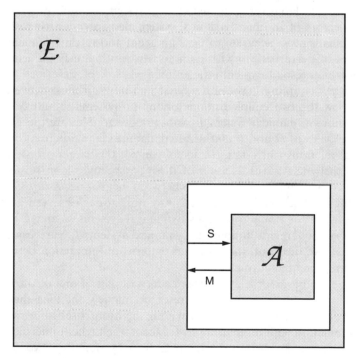

Figure 2 An agent and its environment as coupled dynamical systems.

Note that I am using the terms "sensory input" and "motor output" in a fairly broad sense here. S, for example, is intended to represent *all* effects that $\mathcal{E}$ has on $\mathcal{A}$, whether or not this influence occurs through what is normally thought of as a sensor. This breadth of usage is justified by the observation that any such effect can influence the subsequent trajectory of $\mathcal{A}$. Likewise, M is intended to represent all effects that $\mathcal{A}$ has on $\mathcal{E}$, whether or not they occur through what is normally thought of as an effector.

I cannot overemphasize the fundamental role that feedback plays in this relationship. Any action that an agent takes affects its environment in some way through M, which in turn affects the agent itself through the feedback it receives from its environment via S. Likewise, the environment's effects on an agent through S are fed back through M to in turn affect the environment itself. Thus, each of these two dynamical systems is continuously deforming the flow of the other (perhaps drastically if any coupling parameters cross bifurcation points in the receiving system's parameter space), and therefore influencing its subsequent trajectory. Note that one dynamical system cannot in general completely specify the trajectory of another dynamical system to which it is coupled. Rather, a dynamical system follows a trajectory specified by its own current state and dynamical laws. By varying some of the parameters of these laws, a second dynamical system can certainly bias the intrinsic "tendencies" of the first (or even cause qualitative changes in behavior if bifurcations occur). However, one dynamical system cannot in general "steer" the trajectory of another dynamical system along any desired path. It is therefore perhaps most accurate to view an agent and its environment as mutual sources of perturbation, with each system continuously influencing the other's potential for subsequent interaction.

Given this tight coupling between an agent and its environment, we can equally well view the two coupled nonautonomous systems $\mathcal{A}$ and $\mathcal{E}$ as a single autonomous dynamical system $\mathcal{U}$ whose state variables are the union of the state variables of $\mathcal{A}$ and $\mathcal{E}$ and whose dynamical laws are given by all of the internal relations (including S and M) among this larger set of state variables and their derivatives. Neither of these perspectives is intrinsically better than the other, and one could switch between them as necessary. Given everything that has been said in Section 2, any trajectories observed in the interaction between the nonautonomous dynamical systems $\mathcal{A}$ and $\mathcal{E}$ must be trajectories of the larger autonomous dynamical system $\mathcal{U}$. Furthermore, after transients have died out, the observed patterns of interaction between $\mathcal{A}$ and $\mathcal{E}$ must represent an attractor of $\mathcal{U}$.

We thus have the basis for a dynamical understanding of one of the central themes of recent autonomous agent research, namely the idea that an agent's behavior arises not simply from within the agent itself, but rather through its interaction with its environment. Due to the higher dimensionality of its state space, a dynamical system formed by coupling two other systems can generate a richer range of dynamical behavior than either system could individually, and properties of the coupled system can therefore not generally be attributed to either subsystem alone. Therefore, an agent's behavior properly resides only in the dynamics of the coupled system $\mathcal{U}$ and not in the individual dynamics of either $\mathcal{A}$ or $\mathcal{E}$ alone. This suggests that we must learn to think of an agent as containing only a latent potential to engage in appropriate patterns of interaction. It is only when coupled with a suitable environment that this potential is actually realized through the agent's behavior in that environment.

3.2 Adaptive fit

What constitutes an "appropriate" pattern of interaction between an agent and its environment? It is often said that the behavior of animals is amazingly well adapted to the environments in which they must live. While, strictly speaking, evolution directly selects only for reproductive success, it is only animals whose behavior "fits" the dynamical and statistical structure of their environments that survive long enough to reproduce. We would like the behavior of the autonomous agents that we design to be similarly well-adapted to the environments in which they must function. Thus, the notion of adaptive fit is crucial to understanding the relationship between an agent and its environment. But what does it mean for an agent to be adapted to its environment?

Let us focus for the moment on animals, whose adaptive fitness is related to their survival. Then we can temporarily reformulate the question What does it mean for an agent to be adaptively fit to an environment? to the question What does it mean for an animal to survive? In order to answer this question, it will be useful to begin with a simple analogy to autonomous dynamical systems. As we have seen in Section 2, a dynamical law induces change on the state variables of a dynamical system. However, not all states are treated equally. While most states will be changed into other states through the action of the dynamical law, some states will persist indefinitely because they are invariant with respect to the changes caused by the dynamical law (i.e., an equilibrium point attractor of the system). Invariant states "survive" in the same way that rocks do, by resisting change.

Unlike rocks, animals actively engage their environments in order to stably maintain their existence. Similarly, we expect the agents that we design to accomplish particular tasks in their environments, not to sit immobile and ignore the world around them. In order to capture this more dynamic notion of survival, we can extend our analogy to periodic trajectories, which persist in a far more interesting way than do equilibrium points. In the case of a limit cycle, no single state is invariant with respect to the dynamical law. Rather, all of the states along a limit cycle have the property that the action of the dynamical law carries them to other states along the limit cycle, forming a closed curve which is itself invariant. Thus, the persistence of a limit

221

cycle is achieved only by coordinating the effects of the dynamical law on all of the state variables of the system in such a way that a closed trajectory is formed.

Even such a dynamically maintained invariant as a limit cycle does not quite capture the notion of survival that we are after. It falls short in two ways. First, as explained in Section 3.1, an animal is not an autonomous dynamical system, but rather a nonautonomous one which is constantly perturbed by its environment. Second, an animal does not really have to maintain any *particular* trajectory in order to survive, as suggested by the limit cycle metaphor. Rather, in order to survive, any living organism must maintain the integrity of the network of biochemical processes that keep it alive. Maturana and Varela [47, 48] have termed this network of processes an *autopoietic* system.[2] If an animal's autopoiesis is sufficiently disrupted, either as a result of its own internal dynamics or as a result of environmental perturbations that it cannot properly compensate for, then the animal will cease to exist. Thus, an animal's autopoiesis serves as a crucial constraint on its behavioral dynamics. We can visualize this constraint as a (perhaps very complex and time-varying) volume in an animal's state space (Fig. 3; [6]). An animal is adaptively fit to an environment only so long as it maintains its trajectory within this constraint volume despite the perturbations that it receives from its environment.

In order to elaborate this basic account of adaptive fit, the nature of the constraint volume would need to be more completely characterized. For any real animal, this volume must obviously be very complicated, varying in time with its internal state. Indeed, the separation between the animal's behavioral dynamics and its constraint volume is fundamentally somewhat artificial, because any given animal's behavioral dynamics is clearly related to the particular way in which its autopoiesis is realized and this itself changes through evolution [47, 48]. However, for our purposes here, I take the existence of an agent (living or otherwise) for granted and focus instead on the behavioral dynamics required to maintain that existence. This focus justifies the separation of behavioral dynamics from autopoietic constraints, and allows me to assume that the constraint volume is given *a priori*.

The adaptive fit of natural animals to their environments results from an evolutionary process involving reproduction with heritable variation and natural selection. When animals reproduce, mutations and sexual recombination of their genetic material lead to variations in their design. Because the genetic material of those animals which do not survive long enough to reproduce is not passed on to descendants, inappropriate designs are pruned away, while successful designs proliferate. In terms of our framework, we can think of evolution as trying out many different agent dynamics and retaining only those that, on average, are capable of satisfying their autopoietic constraints long enough to reproduce.

How might this notion of an autopoietic constraint apply to artificial

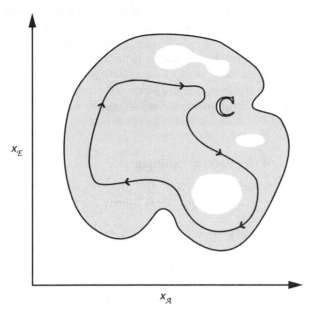

Figure 3 An illustration of adaptive fit. This simple example assumes that both the agent and its environment are one-dimensional dynamical systems. As the state of the environment x_E moves up and down, the state of the agent x_A must move back and forth accordingly so that the trajectory of the coupled system always remains within the constraint volume $\mathbb{C}$. Here the two-dimensional coupled agent-environment system exhibits a limit cycle that satisfies the given constraint, but this is only one of an infinite number of possible agent-environment trajectories that satisfy $\mathbb{C}$.

agents? Homeostatic processes may be involved even for a robot. For example, an autonomous robot may need to regularly replenish its energy and avoid any potentially damaging situations. However, since the agents that we design are not living organisms, their existence does not strictly depend upon autopoiesis. Instead, the success of an artificial agent is typic-ally measured in terms of its ability to accomplish some desired task in a given environment. For our purposes here, however, this external criterion plays the same role as autopoiesis in living animals, that is, it serves as a constraint on the admissible trajectories of the agent-environment dynamics. The only real difference is that, while autopoiesis is largely an intrinsic con-straint on an animal's own state, it is usually an artificial agent's effects on its environment that are constrained by an external designer.

Thus, we can immediately generalize the above notion of adaptive fit to an arbitrary constraint $\mathbb{C}$ on the dynamics of a coupled agent-environment sys-tem (Fig. 3). I will say that an adaptive fit exists between an agent and its environment as long as the trajectory of the agent-environment dynamics satisfies this constraint, that is, as long as their interaction results in an adequate performance of the task for which the agent was designed. As a somewhat fanciful example, we might consider a robot vacuum cleaner to be adaptively fit to its environment as long as its interactions with its environment are such that the floor remains clean, despite the complicating factors found in a typical home (e.g., children, pets, rearrangement of furniture, and so on).

4 A concrete example

The basic theoretical framework sketched in the previous section is rather abstract in nature. In order to make the general framework that I have proposed more concrete, this section will show how it can be applied to examples of each of the two major problems in autonomous agents research, namely the *synthesis* problem and the *analysis* problem. Loosely speaking, the synthesis problem is the problem of constructing an agent that does what we want in a given environment, while the analysis problem is the problem of understanding how a given agent does what it does in a given environment. I will show how a walking behavior for a simulated legged agent can be synthesized and analyzed from the dynamical systems perspective of this framework. Along the way, I will point out some of the distinct advantages of this approach.

4.1 Synthesis of a walking agent

A major concern of much of the work on situated agents has been how to design agents that engage in some desired interaction with their environments. In terms of our framework, we can state this synthesis problem somewhat more formally as follows:

The Synthesis Problem. Given an environment dynamics $\mathscr{E}$, find an agent dynamics $\mathscr{A}$ and sensory and motor maps S and M such that a given constraint $\mathbb{C}$ on the coupled agent-environment dynamics is satisfied.

In order to illustrate the advantage of a dynamical systems perspective on the synthesis of autonomous agents, let us consider the problem of designing a dynamical neural network that will make a simulated insect-like agent walk (Fig. 4; [11]). In terms of our framework, the dynamics of the agent's body is $\mathscr{E}$ and the dynamics of the neural network that controls it is $\mathscr{A}$. $M(x_{\mathscr{A}})$ gives the transformation from neural activity to body effectors, while the transformation from body sensors to neural inputs is given by $S(x_{\mathscr{E}})$. Here $\mathbb{C}$ is a constraint on $\mathscr{E}$ only, namely that the average velocity of the body be greater than zero (where positive velocities correspond to forward motion and

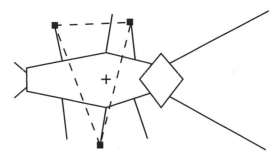

Figure 4 The body model of the simulated insect. The legs can swing about their single joint with the body. A supporting foot is denoted by a black square. The body can only move when it is statically stable, i.e., when the polygon formed by the supporting feet (dashed line) contains the center of mass (cross) of the body.

negative velocities correspond to backward motion). We will assume that S and M are given *a priori* in this example and the problem is to design a neural network controller whose dynamics are such that, when coupled to the agent's body, they cause it to walk. Note that the design of locomotion controllers for hexapod robots is currently a problem of some practical interest [15, 19, 26]. For a complete description of this work, as well as additional examples, see [13].

The body operates as follows. There are six legs, each with a foot that may be either up or down. When its foot is down, a leg provides support to the body and any forces that it generates contribute to the body's translation under Newtonian dynamics (the stance phase). When its foot is up, any forces generated by the leg cause it to swing (the swing phase). Each leg is controlled by three effectors: one governs the state of the foot and the other two determine the clockwise and counterclockwise torques about the leg's single joint. Each leg also possesses a single sensor that measures its angle relative to the body. The body can only move when it is stably supported, that is, when the polygon formed by the supporting feet contains the body's center of mass.

The agent is controlled by a continuous-time recurrent neural network. Such networks were briefly introduced in Section 2. In their most general form, an interconnected network of N such neurons is described by the following system of equations:

$$\tau_i \dot{y}_i = -y_i + \sum_{j=1}^{N} w_{ji}\sigma(y_j - \theta_j) + I_i(t) = 1, 2, \ldots, N \tag{6}$$

where y is sometimes interpreted as the mean membrane potential of the neuron, $\sigma(\xi) = (1 + e^{-\xi})^{-1}$ is a sigmoidal (S-shaped) function which can be

225

interpreted as its short-term average firing frequency, θ_j is a bias term associated with the cell's firing threshold, τ is a time constant related to the passive properties of the cell membrane, w_{ji} represents the strength of the connection from the jth to the ith neuron, and $I(t)$ represents a time-varying external input to the network (such as from a sensor). By restricting the matrix of connection weights to be zero-diagonal symmetric, Hopfield [38] demonstrated that such networks could be used as associative memories, with each pattern stored as a different equilibrium point attractor of the network dynamics. When no such restriction is placed on the connection weights, these networks are capable of exhibiting a much wider range of dynamical behavior. This is the form in which they will be used here. Note that no claim is being made about the general applicability of this particular neural model. It was merely selected to illustrate the framework due to its simplicity and widespread use.

Each leg of the agent was controlled by a 5-neuron fully-interconnected network (Fig. 5(A)). Three of these neurons are motor neurons whose outputs drive the three effectors of the leg, while the other two neurons are interneurons whose role is unspecified. All five neurons received a weighted input from the leg's angle sensor. Six copies of the single leg controller were combined in an architecture loosely based upon the organization of the neural circuitry underlying insect locomotion [11] to form a full locomotion controller with 30 neurons (Fig. 5(B)). Symmetry considerations were used to reduce the number of free parameters in this circuit to 50 (5 thresholds, 5 time constants, 25 leg controller weights, 5 sensor weights, 5 crossbody connection weights and 5 intersegmental connection weights). We wish to find settings of these 50 parameters such that the dynamics of the network causes the agent to walk when coupled to the body shown in Fig. 4.

Regardless of the particular control mechanism used, the majority of current work on situated agents relies on a human designer to manually construct a controller that will cause the agent to engage in some desired interaction with its environment. However, a number of researchers have begun to realize that manual design may not be the best approach. What is difficult about the synthesis problem is that the constraint to be satisfied may be very complex and its specification may be very far removed from the actual agent dynamics required to satisfy it. For example, the constraint that the average velocity of the body be greater than zero does not immediately specify what signals need to be sent to the body's eighteen effectors in order to satisfy this constraint. In addition, natural environments are rather complicated and somewhat unpredictable. Manual design often fails because designers, in trying to anticipate the possible opportunities and contingencies that might arise, build too many unwarranted assumptions into their designs. For these reasons, a number of researchers have begun to explore automated techniques for autonomous agent design, such as reinforcement and other forms of learning (e.g., [9, 10, 23, 41, 46]) or genetic algorithms (e.g., [17, 40,

A

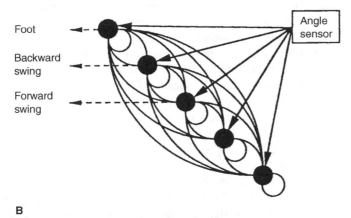

Foot

Backward
swing

Forward
swing

Angle
sensor

B

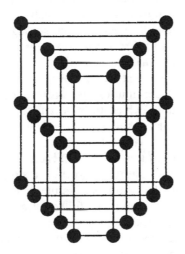

Figure 5 Network architecture of the locomotion controller. (A) A leg
controller. (B) Coupling between adjacent leg controllers.

65, 67]). We used a genetic algorithm to search the space of network parameters for networks whose dynamics make the body shown in Fig. 4 walk.[3]

A genetic algorithm (GA) is a search technique whose operation is loosely
based on natural evolution [31,37]. The basic cycle of a genetic algorithm
operates as follows. The space to be searched (in our case, the 50
network parameters) is usually encoded as a binary string. An initially

random population of such strings is maintained. At each iteration, the performance of each individual is evaluated. A new generation of individuals is then produced by applying a set of genetic operators to selected individuals from the previous generation. Individuals are selected for reproduction with a probability proportional to their fitness. The standard genetic operators are mutation (in which bits are randomly flipped) and crossover (in which portions of the genetic strings of two individuals are exchanged). By iterating the processes of selection, recombination and mutation, the population accumulates information about the distribution of fitness in the search space. This information focuses subsequent search into fruitful subspaces.

In order to guide its search, a genetic algorithm requires a real-valued measure of performance rather than a rigid constraint to be satisfied. In this case, the constraint C can be thought of as some minimum acceptable level of performance. We used the total forward distance traveled by the agent in a fixed amount of time as the performance measure to be optimized.[4] Note that, by optimizing distance traveled in a fixed amount of time, we are not only demanding that the insect walk, but that it walk as quickly as possible. Because the insect can only make forward progress when it is statically stable, the GA must find a network dynamics that not only appropriately generates the three control signals required to operate each leg, but also properly coordinates the independent movements of the six legs so that stability is continuously maintained in order to satisfy the constraint that the average velocity of the body be greater than 0.

There are two different ways that we can think about these experiments. Abstractly, we can think of continuous-time recurrent neural networks as simply a basis dynamics out of which to build whatever agent dynamics is required and we can think of GAs as simply a technique for searching the family of flows defined by the parameterized network architecture for one whose dynamics cause the agent to walk when it is coupled to the body. More concretely, we can think of our neural network as a simple model of a nervous system and the genetic algorithm as a simple model of evolution. This second perspective can actually be quite useful because it allows comparisons to be made between the model and biology.

However, we must be careful not to lose sight of the many simplifications involved in this latter perspective. Both nervous systems and evolution are considerably more complicated than these simple models would suggest. To take just one example, while we have externally imposed a notion of fitness on the GA, no such external fitness measure exists in natural evolution. Indeed, because an animal's environment includes many other animals that are simultaneously evolving, the relationship of a given behavior to reproductive success may change significantly over time. Fitness is something intrinsic to natural environments rather than being externally specified. The significance of this difference between extrinsic and intrinsic fitness is that, by favoring particular behaviors over others in a fixed, *a priori* fashion, extrinsic fitness functions limit the range of behaviors that can possibly evolve in a way that intrinsic fitness does not.

We evolved eleven different locomotion controllers in all. Though the specific parameter values found by the GA were quite different in these eleven networks, the dynamics of all of them have the property that, when coupled to the insect-like body shown in Fig. 4, they cause it to walk in such a way that stability is continuously maintained. The behavior of a typical controller is shown in Fig. 6(A). All of these controllers generate a pattern of leg movements known as the *tripod gait*, in which the front and back legs on each side of the body swing in unison with the middle leg on the opposite side. The tripod gait is ubiquitous among fast-walking insects [32].

As the networks evolved, they passed through several more or less distinct stages. Very early on, agents appeared that put down all six feet and pushed until they fell. These agents thus exhibit roughly the proper phasing of the three signals controlling each leg, but lack the ability to recover a leg after a stance phase as well as the ability to coordinate the motions of the different legs. In the next stage, agents evolved the ability to rhythmically swing their legs in an uncoordinated fashion. Such agents made forward progress, but

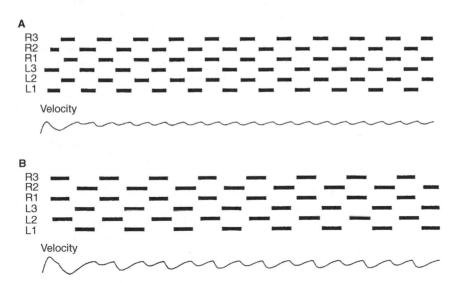

Figure 6 Behavior of a typical mixed locomotion controller with (A) and without (B) its sensors. Black bars represent the swing phase of a leg and the space between bars represents a stance phase. The legs are labeled L for the left and R for right and numbered from 1 to 3 starting at the front of the agent. Note that the stepping frequency is higher, the swings of the three legs in each tripod are more tightly coordinated and the velocity varies less when the sensors are intact (A). However, this controller can generate a reasonably good tripod gait even in the complete absence of any sensory feedback from the body (B).

they fell quite often. Finally, agents utilizing statically stable gaits began to appear, but their coordination was still suboptimal. Subsequently, the efficiency of locomotion slowly improved.

During these experiments, we discovered that the nature of the environment in which the locomotion controllers were evolved had a major impact on their functional organization. In particular, the relative contributions of $\mathcal{A}$ and $\mathcal{E}$ to the generation of a walking pattern varied according to the dependability of sensory feedback during evolution. Three different classes of locomotion controllers were found:

(1) If sensors were enabled during the GA search, then *reflexive patterns generators* always evolved (5 trials). A reflexive controller is one which depends upon sensory feedback for its operation. If the sensors are later removed, reflexive controllers exhibit inappropriate phasing of motor outputs, and some cannot even oscillate in isolation. A reflexive controller is therefore not robust to sensor loss. Reflexive controllers take advantage of the fact that there is no point putting into the agent any dynamics that already appear to be in the environment. All that matters is that the coupled agent-environment system satisfy the given constraint.

(2) If the sensors were disabled during the GA search, then no access is provided to $\mathcal{E}$. In this case, so-called *central pattern generators* (CPGs; [25]) always evolved (4 trials). Even though the individual neurons are not oscillatory, a CPG is capable of generating the rhythmic control signals required for walking. The drawback of a CPG is that its output is stereotyped. It can make no use of sensory feedback to fine-tune its operation.

(3) Finally, if the presence of sensors was unreliable during the GA search (i.e., sensors were sometimes available and sometimes not), then *mixed pattern generators* evolved (2 trials). A mixed locomotion controller is one that works better with its sensors intact, but is quite capable of generating the basic motor pattern required for walking even without its sensors (Fig. 6). Though mixed controllers are robust to sensory damage, they are capable of using sensory feedback to improve their performance when it is available. Such mixed organizations are the most typical among biological pattern generators.

In this section, I formulated the problem of designing a walking agent as a search through a space of dynamical systems for those that, when coupled to a given body, maximize the forward distance that the body travels in a fixed amount of time. This same general approach has also been used to evolve a variety of chemotactic agents that were capable of using chemical signals to find their way to a patch of food [13]. The most notable result from these chemotaxis experiments were agents that utilized a bifurcation in their network dynamics to switch between distinct strategies depending upon the intensity of the chemical signal (which in turn depended upon the agent's distance from the food patch). Furthermore, I have demonstrated how manipulating characteristics of the environment (i.e., sensor dependability) puts selective pressure on the development of controllers with very different functional organizations. This ability to automatically tailor agent dynamics to fit the dynamical and statistical structure of a given environment is a significant advantage of automated agent design techniques.

4.2 Analysis of a walking agent

Given that some agent already exists, we might like to explain its behavior in a given environment. This is in fact the major problem faced by Neuro-ethologists, who seek to explain an animal's observed behavior in terms of its nervous system, its body and its environment. In terms of our framework, we can state this analysis problem somewhat more formally as follows:

The Analysis Problem. Given an environment dynamics $\mathcal{E}$, an agent dynamics $\mathcal{A}$, and sensory and motor maps S and M, explain how the observed behavior $M(x_{\mathcal{A}})$ of the agent is generated.

In order to illustrate the utility of a dynamical systems perspective on the analysis of autonomous agents, we would like to understand the operation of the evolved locomotion controllers described in the previous section. Unfortunately, a dynamical analysis of these 30 neuron networks would be far too complicated for our illustrative purposes here. However, in a set of closely related experiments, we also evolved five-neuron controllers for single-legged insects [13]. Note that, for the purposes of evolving single leg controllers, we had to modify the stability criteria so that a single-legged insect could move whenever its single foot was down. Except for the lack of an interleg coordination problem to be solved, these experiments were in every way analogous to those described in the previous section. These leg controllers passed through similar evolutionary stages and we also found reflexive, central and mixed pattern generators depending upon the conditions under which they were evolved. Fig. 7 shows the activity of a mixed leg controller with and without its sensors. Because these five-neuron networks are much more amenable to a dynamical analysis, we will focus on them here. For additional information on this analysis, see [12, 29].

4.2.1 Analysis of a central pattern generator

Because they have no sensory input, central pattern generators are autonomous dynamical systems. For this reason, CPGs are in some sense the simplest leg controllers to understand. In the case of a CPG, the dynamics of the neural network simply exhibits a limit cycle whose motor space projection

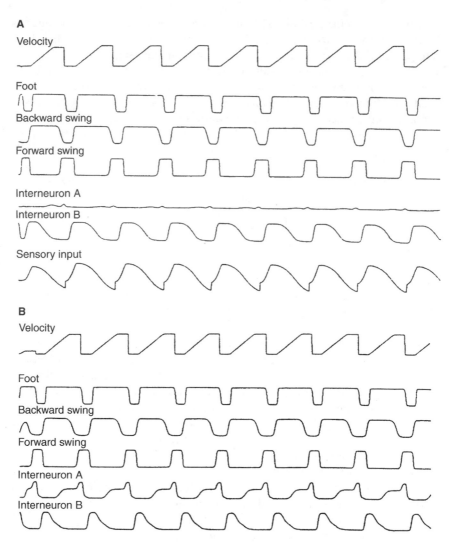

Figure 7 Activity of a typical mixed leg controller with (A) and without (B) its sensor. Each group of plots shows the forward velocity of the body, the output of the foot, backward swing and forward swing motor neurons and the output of the two interneurons. The velocity ramps up to a maximum value during each stance phase and then drops to zero when the insect lifts its single leg each swing phase and falls. The top plot also shows the output of the leg angle sensor. In both groups of plots, the leg was initialized at 95% of its full backward position (i.e., near the point where a swing phase should begin). Note that, with its sensor intact (A), this controller almost immediately begins a swing phase. However, without its sensor, this controller inappropriately attempts to generate a stance phase, effectively wasting a step, because it has no access to the leg's angular position. Note also that Interneuron A appears to play a much larger role in the walking pattern when the sensor is absent (B) than when it is present (A).

232

$M(x_{sd})$ causes the insect's single leg to rhythmically stance and swing in a fashion appropriate to walking. The three-dimensional motor space projection of the five-dimensional limit cycle exhibited by one CPG is shown in Fig. 8. This limit cycle repeatedly takes the state of the system through the regions in motor space associated with stance phase (upper left-hand corner) and swing phase (lower right-hand corner). Since a limit cycle is a primitive concept in dynamical systems theory, there is really nothing more to be said at this level of discussion about the operation of a CPG (though there is of course much more that might be said about the way in which this limit cycle is realized in this particular circuit).

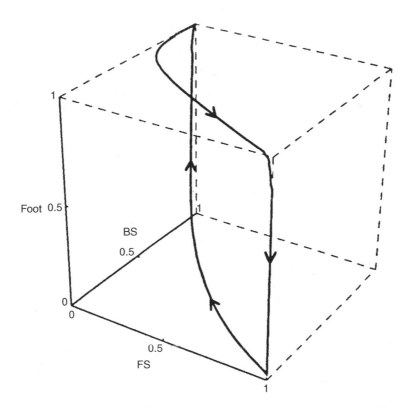

Figure 8 A motor space projection of the five-dimensional limit cycle generated by a typical central pattern generator. The output of the foot, backward swing (BS) and forward swing (FS) motor neurons are plotted. Note that the foot is considered to be down when the output of the foot motor neuron is above 0.5 and up otherwise. A stance phase (foot and backward swing motor neurons active, forward swing motor neuron inactive) corresponds to a region near the back, upper left-hand corner of the state space, while a swing phase (forward swing motor neuron active, foot and backward swing motor neurons inactive) corresponds to a region near the front, lower right-hand corner of the state space.

4.2.2 Analysis of a reflexive pattern generator

Due to the presence of a sensory feedback signal, reflexive leg controllers are nonautonomous dynamical systems. When coupled to the body, the motor space projection of the dynamics of a reflexive controller also exhibits a suitable limit cycle (Fig. 9). However, we already know that reflexive controllers do not produce appropriate rhythmic output when their sensory input is removed. Unlike a CPG, the limit cycle of a reflexive leg controller arises only when it is coupled to the body. Technically, this limit cycle is a three-dimensional projection of a higher dimensional trajectory of the coupled agent-environment system $\mathcal{U}$. How does the interaction between a reflexive controller's autonomous dynamics and the sensory feedback that it receives from the body produce the observed limit cycle?

One way to approach this question is to think of a reflexive controller as an autonomous dynamical system whose flow is parameterized by the sensory input that it receives from the leg's angle sensor. At any given point in time, the network's state is flowing toward the attractor in whose basin it finds itself. However, because the angle of the leg is constantly changing, the structure of the network's flow is changing also, perhaps even undergoing bifurcations. We can visualize the instantaneous phase portrait of the autonomous network dynamics corresponding to any given leg angle. We can also visualize the network's state and the trajectory that it is instantaneously following at any point in the limit cycle. Of course, the system state generally never completely traverses these instantaneous trajectories because the phase portrait continuously changes as the leg moves. However, by piecing together these instantaneous pictures at many different points in time, we can build up a picture of the dynamics underlying the limit cycle observed when a reflexive controller is coupled to the body. Note that the leg actually passes through any given angle twice; once in swing phase and once in stance phase. While the phase portrait is the same in each case (since it depends only on the leg angle), the system's state, and hence the trajectory that it is following, will in general be different.

Such an analysis of one reflexive controller is presented in Fig. 9. The visualization of this particular controller is simplified by the fact that once transients have passed, the outputs of its two interneurons become constant. In other words, once the limit cycle is established, the dynamics of this network are essentially three-dimensional. The limit cycle that this reflexive controller exhibits when it is coupled to the body is shown at the center of Fig. 9. Surrounding this central plot are smaller plots showing the instantaneous autonomous dynamics of the network at different points in the swing/stance cycle. At (1), the foot has just been put down and a stance phase begun. At this point, the network's state is flowing toward the equilibrium point attractor in the upper left-hand corner of the state space. The position of this attractor corresponds to a situation in which the foot and backward

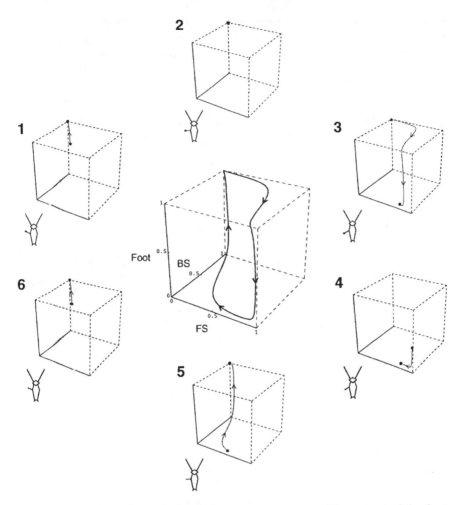

Figure 9 Operation of a typical reflexive pattern generator. The output of the foot, backward swing (BS) and forward swing (FS) motor neurons are plotted. The limit cycle generated when this controller is coupled to the body is shown at the center. Surrounding this central plot are plots of the instantaneous autonomous dynamics of the network at different points in the step cycle. In each case, the solid point denotes an equilibrium point attractor, the gray point denotes the instantaneous system state, and the gray line shows the trajectory that the system would follow if the leg angle were to remain at its present angle. The top three plots roughly correspond to the beginning (1), middle (2) and end (3) of a stance phase, while the bottom three plots roughly correspond to the beginning (4), middle (5) and end (6) of a swing phase. Vertical columns of plots (i.e., (1) and (6), (2) and (5), and (3) and (4)) correspond to approximately the same leg angle and therefore the same phase portrait, though the system state and therefore the trajectory it is following differs between the upper and lower plots of each column.

swing motor neurons are active and the forward swing motor neuron is inactive (i.e., a stance phase). Due to the dynamics of the body, this pattern of motor neuron activity means that the foot is down and the leg is applying a force to the body that causes it to move forward, changing the leg angle and thus the output of the leg angle sensor. As the leg continues to stance at (2), the system state has essentially reached the equilibrium point. As the leg passes from (2) to (3), however, this equilibrium point suddenly disappears and is replaced by another equilibrium point near the lower right-hand corner of the state space that now begins to attract the system state. The position of this attractor corresponds to a state in which the foot and backward swing motor neurons are inactive and the forward swing motor neuron is active (i.e., a swing phase).

The system state now begins to flow toward this new attractor (3). Between (3) and (4), the output of the foot motor neuron falls below the activation threshold of the foot (0.5) and the foot is lifted, actually beginning a swing phase. As the leg passes from (4) to (5), the equilibrium point attractor in the lower right-hand corner of the state space disappears and the earlier equilibrium point attractor in the upper left-hand corner reappears. The network state now moves toward this attractor through (6) until the output of the foot motor neuron goes above the activation threshold for the foot at (1) and the foot is once again put down, beginning a new stance phase. Thus we can see how the limit cycle observed in the coupled network/body system arises as the network's state is alternately attracted by the two equilibrium points.

We can now explain the reason that this controller is a reflexive pattern generator by observing that, when its sensor is removed, the autonomous dynamics of this controller is governed by an equilibrium point. By convention, a leg that is perpendicular to the long axis of the body is assigned a leg angle of 0. Since we modeled the removal of a sensor by setting its output to 0, the autonomous dynamics exhibited when the sensor is removed is identical to that exhibited when the leg is fixed in a horizontal position (i.e., plots (2) and (5) in Fig. 9). Thus, if the sensor is removed, the system state will flow toward the equilibrium point attractor in the upper left-hand corner of the state space and remain there, causing the leg to go into a permanent stance phase.

The switch between equilibrium points that occurs between (2) and (3) in Fig. 9, and again between (4) and (5), appears to be essential for the operation of this reflexive controller. How is this switch actually accomplished? This question is answered in Fig. 10, which shows a sequence of bifurcations that occur in the autonomous dynamics of this network as the leg moves from an angle of about 23 degrees past horizontal to 16 degrees past horizontal during swing phase (between plots (4) and (5) in Fig. 9). The sequence begins with a single equilibrium point attractor at the bottom of the state space (1). At (2), a second equilibrium point attractor appears at the top. Note that, during swing phase, the system state is still in the basin of

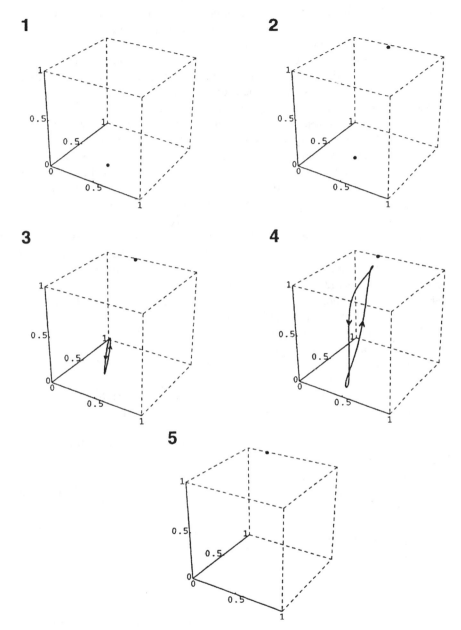

Figure 10 A sequence of bifurcations underlying the operation of the reflexive pattern generator shown in Fig. 9. Only attractors are shown. During swing phase (between plots (4) and (5) in Fig. 9), the autonomous dynamics of the network undergoes the sequence of bifurcations shown here. During stance phase (between plots (2) and (3) in Fig. 9), this sequence of bifurcations is reversed.

attraction of the lower attractor at this point. At (3), the lower equilibrium point bifurcates into a limit cycle, which then begins to expand (4). Eventually, this limit cycle disappears, leaving behind only a single equilibrium point at (5). Now the system state is attracted by this upper equilibrium point. This sequence of bifurcations is reversed during stance phase. A complete bifurcation diagram for this network can be found in [12].

Because these bifurcations take place in such a narrow range of leg angles (approximately 7 degrees), the system state never really "sees" the intermediate attractors. For example, the limit cycle that briefly appears plays no functional role whatsoever in the network's dynamics because the system state never has a chance to get near it, let alone go around it. During the normal operation of this controller, this bifurcation sequence occurs in about 10 integration steps, during which the system state moves only an average Euclidean distance of 0.025 in the state space. However, the net effect of this sequence of bifurcations is to alternately switch the network's phase portrait between the two equilibrium points that are crucial to its operation. This particular sequence of bifurcations is unique to this controller, and was not observed in any of the other controllers that were analyzed.

From this dynamical analysis we can summarize the nature of the interaction between $\mathcal{A}$ and $\mathcal{E}$ that underlies the operation of this reflexive controller. The autonomous dynamics of $\mathcal{A}$, and its parametrization by S, is such that $\mathcal{E}$ can deform it, via a series of intermediate bifurcations, into essentially two kinds of flows. In one of these flows, there is a single fixed-point attractor near the upper left-hand corner of the state space, while in the other there is a single fixed-point attractor near the lower right-hand corner. The nature of $\mathcal{E}$, and its parameterization by M, is such that, when the network state is in the neighborhood of the upper left-hand attractor, the state of the body is changing in such a way that S will cause the lower right-hand attractor to appear in $\mathcal{A}$. Likewise, when the network state is in the neighborhood of the lower right-hand attractor, the state of the body is changing in such a way that S will cause the upper left-hand attractor to appear in $\mathcal{A}$. This reciprocal relationship between $\mathcal{A}$ and $\mathcal{E}$ is what gives rise to the observed rhythmic walking pattern. Therefore, both $\mathcal{A}$ and $\mathcal{E}$ play absolutely essential and deeply intertwined roles in the operation of this reflexive controller.

4.2.3 Analysis of a mixed pattern generator

As shown in Fig. 11, we can approach the analysis of a mixed leg controller in a fashion similar to our analysis of the reflexive controller. However, because the dynamics of this circuit is fundamentally five-dimensional, we only plot the three-dimensional motor space projection of this system's trajectories. The limit cycle that this controller exhibits when it is coupled to the body is shown in the center. While the shape of this limit cycle is somewhat different from the one generated by the reflexive controller discussed above, they both exhibit the proper phasing of motor outputs necessary to make the leg walk. Surrounding this central plot are smaller plots that show the instantaneous autonomous dynamics at various points along this limit cycle. As for the reflexive controller, we can understand the dynamics of the coupled network/body system by piecing together these instantaneous snapshots. However, unlike the reflexive controller, the autonomous dynamics of this mixed controller exhibits limit cycles rather than equilibrium points through most of the cycle. When the mixed controller is coupled to the body, this limit cycle is continuously deformed as shown in Fig. 11 as the leg angle

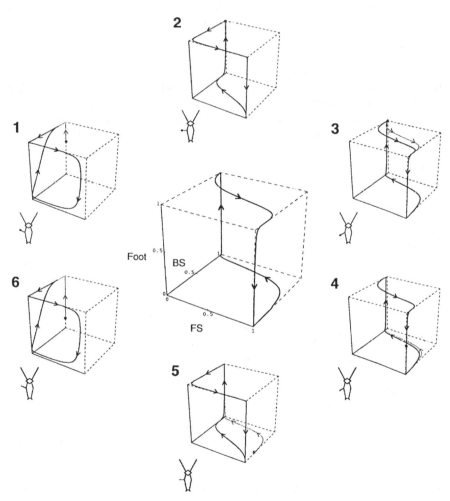

Figure 11 Motor space projection of the operation of a typical mixed pattern generator. The layout of this figure is the same as for Fig. 9.

changes, and the system state is constantly attracted by this deforming limit cycle. The reason that this mixed controller can tolerate the loss of its sensor is because the autonomous limit cycle that it generates when the sensory input is set to 0 (see plots (2) and (5) in Fig. 11) is appropriate to make the leg walk. In the absence of any sensory input, the system state would follow this limit cycle rather than the limit cycle shown in the center of Fig. 11.

Since a mixed controller is capable of autonomously generating an appropriate limit cycle, what role if any is the sensory feedback it receives from the body actually playing in its operation? In order to explore this question, we examined how the controller responds when it is artificially driven with sinusoidal sensory input whose frequency is higher or lower than normal. Under these conditions, we found that the motor output pattern that the controller generates speeds up or slows down accordingly (Fig. 12). The sensory signal is thus capable of entraining the intrinsic oscillation produced by the controller itself. Despite the fact that the activity pattern of the interneurons changes considerably throughout this range of operating frequencies, the amplitude, shape and phasing of the motor outputs remains appropriate for walking. Within a significant range about its normal operating frequency, the motor pattern remains 1:1 phase-locked with the sensory signal. We have observed other ratios of phase-locking at higher or lower driving frequencies. Entrainment by sensory feedback is a common feature of biological pattern generators. For example, the pattern generator underlying locust flight can be entrained by rhythmic stimulation of wing stretch receptors [64].

This entrainment has an interesting functional consequence. Suppose that the legs of the agent were to grow during its "life". For a given amount of applied torque, longer stancing legs will take more time to swing through a given angle than shorter legs. Thus, the sensory feedback signal from a longer leg will be spread out in time relative to that of a normal length leg. Since the mixed controller is entrained by the sensory feedback that it receives from the body, the sensory feedback from a longer leg will cause the leg controller to slow down its motor output pattern accordingly. Adapting their output to a changing periphery is a general problem that pattern generators have to deal with, for example in development or following peripheral damage. Note, however, that this adaptation does not come about through any structural change to the neural network itself, nor does it require a separate learning algorithm to modify the network parameters. Rather, it arises as a natural consequence of the dynamics of the mixed controller and its coupling with the body. This is a kind of functional plasticity which is quite different from what is normally thought of as learning. However, there are many examples of such plasticity in biology (for instance, the ability of an insect to immediately adjust its gait following the loss of a leg [32]).

The dynamical sophistication of this mixed leg controller is truly remarkable. With only *five neurons* (three of which are motor neurons), this

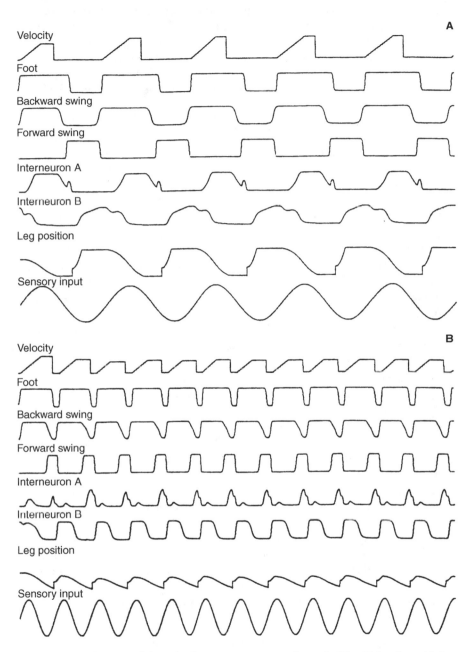

Figure 12 Entrainment of the mixed pattern generator shown in Fig. 11 by sinusoidal sensory input. When the driving frequency is lower (A) or higher (B) than normal, the motor pattern slows down or speeds up accordingly.

controller can (1) generate the basic swing/stance leg movements necessary for walking; (2) take advantage of sensory feedback if it is available but can tolerate its absence with only a slight degradation in performance; and (3) adapt its operation to morphological changes in the body without requiring a separate learning mechanism. The likelihood of anyone designing such a flexible and compact leg controller by hand is probably rather low.

4.2.4 Conclusion

This section has illustrated how some of the tools of dynamical systems theory can be applied to the analysis of an agent interacting with its environment. For example, we have been able to explain why some locomotion controllers are robust to loss of sensory feedback and others are not in terms of the appropriateness or inappropriateness of their autonomous dynamics to the walking task. Furthermore, we have been able to gain significant insight into the specific nature of the interaction between the network dynamics and the body that gave rise to a walking pattern in each of the three controllers analyzed. For example, while the reflexive controllers make use of the body dynamics in a fundamental way in the generation of the limit cycle necessary for walking, the CPGs are capable of generating appropriate limit cycles completely autonomously and the mixed controllers use rhythmic sensory feedback to fine-tune autonomous limit cycles. Along the way, we discovered that, because it is entrained by sensory feedback, the mixed controller can adapt its motor output to a changing periphery.

What general conclusions can we draw from this analysis? One is struck by the variety of agent dynamics which evolved. Not only are the actual network parameters of each controller different, but the underlying dynamics vary widely. Yet they all lead to virtually indistinguishable walking behavior when coupled to the body under normal conditions. Furthermore, lesion studies of these controllers (not described here) have demonstrated that their operation is dynamically distributed, usually making it impossible to assign specific functional roles to individual interneurons. About the only thing that can be said about all of these controllers is that the coupled agent-environment systems in which they are embedded do what we asked them to do under the conditions in which they evolved. Indeed, as in natural evolution, this is all that they were selected for in the first place. We are thus led to conclude that it is simply inappropriate in general to attempt to impose our functional preconceptions on the organization of evolved systems.

5 Discussion

In this paper, I have attempted to use the language of dynamical systems theory to sketch a general theoretical framework for the design and analysis of autonomous agents. The framework focuses on the problem of generating the appropriate behavior at the appropriate time as both an agent's internal state and its external environment continuously change. The two key ideas of this framework are (1) that an agent and its environment must be understood as two coupled dynamical systems whose mutual interaction is jointly responsible for the agent's behavior and (2) that the adaptive fit between an agent and its environment can be characterized in terms of the satisfaction of a given constraint on the trajectories of the coupled agent-environment system. I have particularly emphasized that an agent's behavior is, strictly speaking, a property of the coupled agent-environment system only and cannot in general be attributed to either the agent or environment individually.

A concrete application of these ideas to the synthesis and analysis of a walking behavior for a six-legged agent was used to illustrate the framework. While I feel no particular commitment to either continuous-time recurrent neural networks or genetic algorithms, they represent at least one way in which agent dynamics satisfying a given constraint on the coupled agent-environment system can be designed. Such an "evolutionary" approach to agent design allows the agent's organization to be tailored to the particular dynamical and statistical structure of its environment and leads to remarkably adaptive, robust and compact controllers. I have also demonstrated that, despite the fact that they often exhibit no clean functional organization, the operation of these evolved systems can be understood from the perspective of interacting dynamical systems. Furthermore, this perspective can provide significant insight into the specific nature of the interaction between the agent and its environment that gives rise to the observed walking behavior in the various controllers.

5.1 Related work

There is currently a growing interest in dynamical explanations in the behavioral and brain sciences. The central idea dates back at least to cybernetics [6,63]. More recently, concepts from dynamical systems theory have been making a substantial impact in such fields as neuroscience, cognitive science and mobile robotics. Within neuroscience, dynamical analyses have been applied to single neurons (e.g., [55]), small circuits (e.g., [62]) and complete brain systems (e.g., the model of olfactory cortex formulated by Skarda and Freeman [58], in which a chaotic attractor plays a central role). The concepts of dynamical systems are also beginning to play a major role in understanding the biological control of movement (e.g., [57]). Connectionism has made dynamics one of its founding principles [60] (though it is not clear that the full implications of this principle have yet been appreciated in connectionist research [36]) and has, for example, begun to propose theories of language in its terms [27, 53]. Both van Gelder [61] and Giunti [30] have begun to formulate a dynamical conception of cognition in cognitive science more generally. Finally, Smithers [59] has recently argued for a role for dynamical ideas in mobile robot research.

Within the autonomous agents literature, the theoretical framework that I have proposed is perhaps most closely related to Rosenschein's work on situated automata [56]. He models an agent and its environment as two interacting automata and he has emphasized that knowledge need not be explicitly encoded within an agent in order for it to engage in sophisticated interactions with its environment. He has used concepts from automata and formal language theory to characterize the behavior of such systems. In a sense, I have generalized this perspective to arbitrary dynamical systems and demonstrated how concepts from dynamical systems theory can be used to characterize the behavior of such systems, especially emphasizing continuous systems. On the other hand, while Rosenschein's major concern has been how propositional content can be assigned to correlations between an agent's internal states and the states of its environment, my interest is in how an agent can generate the appropriate behavior at the appropriate time.

5.2 Assumptions and extensions

This paper has focused on continuous, deterministic, convergent and low-dimensional dynamical systems as models for agents and their environments. In this section, I briefly consider the motivation behind these assumptions, their impact on the framework, and a number of ways in which they might be relaxed.

5.2.1 Continuity

The emphasis on continuous dynamics (i.e., continuous state spaces and continuous time) in this paper is motivated by the fact that the dynamics of both nervous systems and the macroscopic physical world are continuous in nature. For example, though many nerve cells fire action potentials (a seemingly discrete event), the current flows that underlie action potentials are continuous quantities. Furthermore, it has long been known that many nerve cells do not produce action potentials but instead communicate using graded potentials [52]. Likewise, the more discrete behavioral phenomena that we observe (e.g., decision making) must eventually be explained in continuous terms. In addition, it is my belief that the versatility and robustness of animal behavior resides in the rich dynamical possibilities of continuous state spaces.

However, it should be noted that any system with finite state which evolves deterministically can be described using the concepts of dynamical systems. Most of the concepts we have used hold in discrete-time systems as well, and many also hold in systems defined on discrete state spaces. For example, the transition table of a finite state machine defines a flow on a discrete state space. The lack of a metric on this state space limits the dynamical behavior that a finite state machine can exhibit, but such concepts as initial state, trajectory, flow, attractor, equilibrium point, limit cycle, basin of attraction, autonomous and nonautonomous still apply. Thus the present framework may still be useful even if the continuity assumption should turn out to be inappropriate.

5.2.2 Determinism

The theoretical framework sketched in this paper is purely deterministic in nature. This determinism derives from the common assumption in science that the macroscopic physical world is in principle completely determined by a knowledge of its state and the dynamical laws that govern its evolution. However, we often say that real environments, real sensors, etc. are some-what unpredictable. What this usually means is that, because we have only incomplete knowledge of a system's state and laws, we are forced to use stochastic models to describe its behavior. In other words, regardless of whether or not the macroscopic physical world is deterministic in principle, we must sometimes treat it as stochastic in practice.

It should be noted that continuous-time recurrent neural networks show every sign of being robust in the face of unpredictable environmental contingencies. The locomotion controllers can often tolerate the loss of an interneuron or the loss of sensory feedback, and preliminary studies indicate that they are extremely robust to noise on the sensory feedback signal as well. However, regardless of the robustness of these controllers, the question naturally arises as to how the theoretical framework itself might be applied to unpredictable systems.

As I see it, there are two possibilities, depending upon whether a deterministic or stochastic model of unpredictability is adopted. Recall that nonlinear dynamical systems can exhibit dynamics that is completely deterministic in principle but unpredictable in practice (so-called chaotic dynamics). Significant progress has been made on extending the qualitative theory of dynamical systems to the analysis of chaotic dynamics [66]. If the unpredictability of a given system can be modeled with chaotic dynamics, then such techniques can be applied.

Otherwise, we must deal with a fundamentally stochastic model of unpredictability. In this case, we must consider stochastic dynamical systems (see, for example, [7]). Typical concerns in stochastic dynamical systems are understanding how some probability density function over the states of the system evolves with time and determining the asymptotic form of this distribution. The application of such techniques to autonomous agent problems is clearly an important research direction for the future development of the framework.

245

5.2.3 Convergence

In this paper, I have assumed that both the agent and environment dynamics are convergent, that is, the values of their state variables eventually converge to limit sets rather than diverging to infinity. In fact, even a flow that contains divergent regions is acceptable as long as the dynamics of interaction between the agent and environment never enters such a region. Divergent dynamical systems are a mathematical abstraction anyway. Due to resource limitations and saturation effects, no real physical system is truly divergent. Thus, the assumption of convergent dynamics is, I think, a fairly reasonable one.

However, it is important not to confuse this convergence assumption with the claim that the dynamics of agents and environments must settle onto limit sets before the framework applies. Indeed, the dynamics of the reflexive and mixed pattern generators never settle on an autonomous attractor, but instead are always in a transient because their flow is constantly perturbed by the sensory feedback that they receive. Of course, the dynamics of the coupled agent-environment system in these examples does eventually settle into a limit cycle, but even this need not be the case in general. If either the environment or the agent contains dynamics on time scales that are long relative to the lifetime of the agent, then the entire trajectory of interaction between them will take place on an extended transient.

Even in the case of an extended transient, however, the framework described in this paper still applies. The dynamics of interaction between the agent and its environment is still determined by the global structure of the flow of the coupled system and this structure is itself largely determined by the types and locations of its limit sets. Furthermore, in a system with multiple time scales, there may be a great deal of recurrence to the system's behavior over sufficiently short time scales. Under such conditions, it is often possible to treat the slower state variables as being approximately constant parameters of the faster dynamics and to study the dynamics of this reduced system. Though the attractors of this reduced system are not true attractors of the full system (because the slower state variables are in fact changing), they represent patterns of interaction that may show up repeatedly over sufficiently short time scales (cf. Agre and Chapman's notion of *routines* [3]).

5.2.4 Low dimensionality

Our ability to visualize the dynamics of the leg controllers described in Section 4 depended strongly on their relatively low dimensionality. Clearly, we will often need to analyze systems whose dimensionality makes direct visualization of the complete flow impossible. In this case, we must find ways to simplify the dynamics or rely upon nonvisual techniques. One obvious approach (utilized in Section 4) is to visualize higher dimensional dynamics with a set of carefully selected lower dimensional projections. More generally, one can sometimes find a series of coordinate transformations that map the dynamics of a higher dimensional system to a lower dimensional system while preserving most of its global structure. For example, such a technique has been used to reduce the four-dimensional Hodgkin-Huxley model of action potential generation to a two-dimensional system that preserves not only the qualitative behavior of the original system, but most of its quantitative behavior as well [43].

A number of other techniques are available for simplifying dynamical systems by reducing either their dimensionality or complexity in some spatial or temporal region of interest (e.g., Poincaré maps, center manifolds, normal forms, symbolic dynamics and the use of symmetries [66]). In addition, many of the analytical techniques of dynamical systems theory (e.g., computing limit sets, stability analysis, computation of Lyapunov exponents, etc.) do not require a global visualization of the flow. Finally, it should be pointed out that some progress has even been made on extending the qualitative theory of dynamical systems to infinite-dimensional systems (e.g., those arising from sets of partial differential, delay-differential and integro-differential equations; [34]). These and other techniques will undoubtedly need to be explored as larger systems are studied.

5.3 Modularity and design

Because the only requirement on an agent's dynamics is that the coupled agent-environment system satisfy a given constraint, there is a great deal of freedom both in how a desired dynamics of interaction is divided between the agent and its environment and in the internal organization of the agent's dynamics. We saw examples of this freedom in our analysis of the evolved leg controllers where, despite the fact that both their individual dynamics and the nature of their interaction with the body vary widely, all of these leg controllers produce virtually indistinguishable walking behavior when coupled to the body under normal conditions. Likewise, there is a growing realization within neuroscience that the neural circuits mediating nontrivial behaviors in even simpler animals are highly distributed and nonhierarchical and that traditional engineering principles may not apply to their design [4].

Because evolution only directly selects *against* agent dynamics that do not satisfy their constraint (rather than selecting *for* some optimal design), evolution tends to produce designs that take full advantage of the available freedom. This can lead to designs whose organization is very different from engineered systems. When an engineer designs a complex system, he or she typically performs a hierarchical decomposition of the problem to be solved, resulting in simpler subsystems with clean, well-defined functions and interfaces. Such a modular decomposition is necessary to ensure a correct, reliable and maintainable implementation, and it also appeals to a certain aesthetic sense of parsimony on the part of the designer. Evolution, however, operates under no such constraints. Natural selection preserves those animals that, as a package, work and discards those that do not. Of course, this is not to say that evolved systems are completely unstructured. Certainly, evolved systems exhibit modularity and it is likely that evolution would be unable to produce systems with the complexity of animals without it. However, because the internal organization of an evolved system does not reflect the conceptualization of any designer, whatever modules do exist are under no requirement to exhibit the sort of clean functional organization that we expect from an engineered system.

One might argue that this "messiness" is really just an implementation detail reflecting the blindness of evolution and not a fundamental part of the design. For example, we might be tempted to describe the leg controller dynamics as "really" just implementing a simple finite state machine that switches between two states labeled "swing phase" and "stance phase". However, it is important to realize that this is not a predictive explanation of these networks, but merely a descriptive summary of their normal operation. The predictive (and therefore explanatory) power of this summary is severely limited by the fact that it fails to capture the underlying dynamical laws that actually govern the system's operation. For example, the temporal patterns of motor neuron activations required to actually make the leg walk are not deducible from such a description. It also fails to capture how sensory feedback is capable of fine-tuning a walking pattern, or why some networks are robust to sensor loss while others are not. Yet these and other features are completely and succinctly explained by the qualitative dynamical analysis summarized in Figs. 8, 9, 10 and 11.

The fact that evolution can produce such messy designs is typically viewed as a shortcoming. However, it is also a source of freedom to cobble together counterintuitive but highly effective, versatile, robust and compact designs. Furthermore, this negative assessment overlooks a crucial difference between the task of an engineer and that of evolution. Engineers solve well-defined problems, and it is the detailed *a priori* specifications of those problems that allow modular solutions to be designed and their parsimony or optimality to be evaluated. In contrast, evolution has no clear specification of the "problem" that any given animal should solve. Even if such a specification existed, it would do little good since the "problem" itself is constantly evolving as the physical environment changes and the coevolution of conspecifics and other species modifies the relationship between behavior and reproductive success. Designing an artificial agent capable of autonomously accomplishing open-ended tasks in an unconstrained real-world environment is much closer to the sort of "problem" solved by evolution than it is to the problems for which traditional engineering methods have been successful.

While evolutionary design shows great promise as a practical method for designing autonomous agents, it is well known that the performance of the standard genetic algorithm does not scale well with the size of the parameter space using the direct encoding of neural network parameters employed here. These scaling problems will need to be addressed before such techniques can be applied to the design of more complicated agents. Toward that end, many different parameter encodings and many different variations of the basic genetic algorithm have been proposed (e.g., [16]) and their application to autonomous agent design needs to be explored. Where appropriate, other search techniques, such as simulated annealing and gradient techniques, should also be explored. When possible, biological data and symmetry considerations can be used to reduce the number of parameters to be searched, as in the adjacent coupling of the leg controllers in the full locomotion controller described in Section 4.1. Another strategy is to search not the parameter space of the agent's dynamics directly, but rather the parameter space of a developmental process that constructs the agent's dynamics (e.g., [35, 50]).

Yet another approach to the scaling problem is to evolve a complex agent dynamics incrementally. One possibility is to decompose a complex task into a set of simpler subtasks and to independently evolve solutions to these. A complete solution can then be obtained by evolving the coupling between these subnetworks on the original task. Another possibility is to evolve solutions to a simpler version of a difficult problem, successively increase the problem complexity, and then re-evolve the controllers to solve the harder versions of the problem. Finally, attempts to evolve controllers for physical robots instead of simulated agents introduce additional problems, since evolutionary search can only be carried out in simulation at present and there are nontrivial issues involved in transferring controllers from simulated to physical environments [21,40].

5.4 Internal state and representation

Due to its emphasis on the unpredictable nature and real-time requirements of the real world, a great deal of recent work on autonomous agents has focused on the development of reactive agents whose actions are completely determined by their immediate situation. A purely reactive agent is a degenerate case of the present framework because it maintains no internal state. Rather, it is simply a function from sensory inputs to motor outputs. A reactive agent has no true autonomy because it is constantly pushed around by its environment.

In contrast, a dynamical systems perspective on autonomous agents emphasizes the importance of internal state to an agent's operation. Unlike a reactive agent, an agent with internal state can initiate behavior independently from its immediate circumstances and organize its behavior in anticipation of future configurations of its environment. This ability relies upon the fact that, while it is true that the real world is complicated and somewhat unpredictable, natural environments also exhibit a great deal of structure that a properly designed agent can depend upon and even actively exploit [39]. As a simple example, consider the way in which the reflexive controllers exploit the structure of the body dynamics to achieve walking.

The importance of internal state in the present framework raises an interesting question: Does the framework imply a commitment to internal representation? Much of the debate between proponents and critics of situated agent research has tacitly assumed the equation of internal state with representation, with proponents using criticisms of representation to argue the need for reactivity and critics using the limitations of state-free systems to argue the need for representation (e.g., [20,44]). But are internal state and representation the same thing? Though this question clearly deserves a more detailed treatment than I can give it here, let me briefly explain why I believe that the answer must be no.

The problem with equating internal state and representation is that computationalism, the theoretical claim that a system's behavior derives from its instantiation of appropriate representations and computational processes [28,51,54], then becomes a tautological theoretical position. A scientific hypothesis must be falsifiable, that is, it must be formulated sufficiently clearly to be empirically tested and it must be possible that the test will come out negative. But all physical systems possess internal state on a variety of timescales. We would presumably hesitate in accepting, say, the temperature of the fuel-air mixture in a cylinder of an automobile engine as a representation of anything, or a thunderstorm as performing any computation. If, on the other hand, we did admit such a broad definition of representation and computation, then computationalism would become true by definition rather than by demonstration and would therefore be making no interesting theoretical claim about the nature of the processes underlying behavior. Similar problems exist with other commonsense notions of representation (e.g., correlation) and computation (e.g., systematicity of the relationship between input and output). For a more detailed discussion of these issues, see [12].

For this reason, representation must require additional conditions above and beyond the mere possession of internal state (or correlation, etc.) and computational systems must therefore be special cases of dynamical systems more generally [30,61]. There is a great deal of controversy about the particular form of these extra conditions, but the details fortunately need not concern us here. What matters is that the framework's emphasis on internal state, while allowing it to transcend the limitations of purely reactive systems, does not necessarily imply a commitment to internal representation. Rather, the question of whether or not the notion of representation is appropriate for understanding the operation of any particular agent must be settled by an empirical investigation of the internal organization of that particular agent's dynamics. The framework is thus, strictly speaking, agnostic about the theoretical roles of representation and computation in the design and analysis of autonomous agents.

5.5 *Conclusion*

This paper has largely been presenting an argument about language, namely the language that we use to talk about autonomous agents and their environments. In particular, my primary goal has been to demonstrate that many of the ideas emerging from recent work on autonomous agents (as well as work on the neural basis of animal behavior, though I have not emphasized this aspect here) can be naturally cast into the language of dynamical systems theory.

One must never underestimate the power of language in shaping the way we think about the world. Our theoretical languages provide the metaphors we use to conceptualize the very phenomena we seek to understand. A computational language invites us to think about representations and their manipulations. Using this language, we become concerned with the structure of representations, where they are stored, how they are retrieved, what they mean, etc. From a computational perspective, observed regularities in an agent's behavior become windows into its program. If, for example, an agent persistently acts toward some end, then, computationalism tells us, it must be by virtue of possessing an internal representation of that goal. From a computational perspective, perception becomes a problem of reconstructing an accurate internal representation of the external environment. Taking action becomes a problem of constructing and executing representations of the actions to be performed. Learning becomes a problem of modifying existing representations and accumulating new ones. And so on.

This paper has only just begun the difficult task of developing a dynamical language for these and other phenomena exhibited by autonomous agents. A great deal of work remains to be done in developing this framework into a full-fledged theory. If this framework is to succeed in providing a foundation for our understanding of autonomous agents, then specific dynamical accounts of perception, action, goal-oriented behavior, decision-making, sequential behavior, learning, etc. will need to be developed and these accounts will need to be applied to specific agents, both natural and artificial. I strongly suspect that a dynamical perspective on these phenomena will significantly change the way we think about them.

Ultimately, like all work on embodied agents, the framework must face the fact that people can deliberately form and reason with conceptual representations. While I have taken the position that such intellectual capabilities are relatively recent elaborations of a far more fundamental capacity for situated action (and are therefore not nearly so crucial as is usually assumed for even highly complex but nondeliberative behavior), they must nevertheless eventually be explained. Will attempts to extend a dynamical perspective to such cognitive behavior as language and abstract reasoning turn out to require the implementation of computational processes on top of the dynamical substrate responsible for situated action? Or will the very way we think about such cognitive behavior, and the notions of representation and computation that currently seek to underwrite it, also have to change in the process?

Acknowledgments

I would like to thank Phil Agre, Hillel Chiel, John Gallagher, Ken Loparo, Leslie Picardo, and Beth Preston for many useful discussions and for their comments on earlier drafts of this paper. I would also like to thank the reviewers, as well as the attendees of the Workshop on Computational Theories of Interaction and Agency, for their many helpful suggestions. The simulation experiments reviewed in Section 4 were carried out in collaboration with John Gallagher. This work was supported by grant N00014-90-J-1545 from the Office of Naval Research. Additional support was provided by the Howard Hughes Medical Institute and the Cleveland Advanced Manufacturing Program through the Center for Automation and Intelligent Systems Research.

Notes

1 This is a technical term in dynamical systems theory whose meaning is unrelated to its use in the term "autonomous agents".
2 An autopoietic (lit. self-producing) system is a network of component-producing processes with the property that the interactions between the components produced generate the very same network of interactions that produced them.
3 We employed a public GA simulator known as GAucsd (version 1.1). At the time of this writing, the latest version of GAucsd is available by anonymous ftp from cs.ucsd.edu in the pub/GAucsd directory. All network parameters were encoded in four bits, with time constants in the range [0.5, 10] and both thresholds and connection weights in the range [− 16,16]. The crossover rate was set to 0.6 and the mutation rate was set to 0.0001. Population sizes of 500 were used and good locomotion controllers typically took on the order of 100 generations to evolve. Full details of these experiments can be found in [13].
4 Because GAucsd is formulated to minimize an error measure rather than maximize a fitness measure, the actual measure used was the square of the difference between the maximum attainable distance and the actual distance covered in a given length of time.

References

[1] R.H. Abraham and C.D. Shaw, *Dynamics—The Geometry of Behavior* (Addison-Wesley, Redwood City, CA, 2nd ed., 1992).
[2] P. Agre, The dynamic structure of everyday life, Technical Report 1085, MIT AI Lab., Cambridge, MA (1988).

[3] P.E. Agre and D. Chapman, Pengi: an implementation of a theory of activity, in: *Proceedings AAAI-87*, Seattle, WA (1987) 268–272.

[4] J.S. Altman and J. Kien, Highlighting *Aplysia's* networks, *Trends Neurosci*, **13** (3) (1990) 81–82.

[5] M.A. Arbib and J.-S. Liaw, Sensorimotor transformations in the worlds of frogs and robots, *Artif. Intell.* **72** (1995) 53–79.

[6] W.R. Ashby, *Design for a Brain* (Wiley, New York, 2nd ed., 1960).

[7] K.J. Åström, *Introduction to Stochastic Control Theory* (Academic Press, New York, 1970).

[8] D.H. Ballard, Animate vision, *Artif. Intell.* **48** (1991) 57–86.

[9] A.G. Barto, S.J. Bradtke and S.P. Singh, Learning to act using real-time dynamic programming, *Artif. Intell.* **72** (1995) 81–138.

[10] K. Basye, T. Dean and L.P. Kaelbling, Learning dynamics: system identification for perceptually challenged agents, *Artif. Intell.* **72** (1995) 139–171.

[11] R.D. Beer, *Intelligence as Adaptive Behavior: An Experiment in Computational Neuroethology* (Academic Press, San Diego, CA, 1990).

[12] R.D. Beer, Computational and dynamical languages for autonomous agents, in: T. van Gelder and R. Port, eds., *Mind as Motion* (MIT Press, Cambridge, MA, to appear).

[13] R.D. Beer and J.C. Gallagher, Evolving dynamical neural networks for Adaptive behavior, *Adaptive Behav.* **1** (1992) 91–122.

[14] R.D. Beer, R.E. Ritzmann and T. McKenna, eds., *Biological Neural Networks in Invertebrate Neuroethology and Robotics* (Academic Press, San Diego, CA, 1993).

[15] R.D. Beer, H.J. Chiel, R.D. Quinn, K.S. Espenschied and P. Larsson, A distributed neural network architecture for hexapod robot locomotion, *Neural Comput.* **4** (3) (1992) 356–365.

[16] R.K. Belew and L.B. Booker, eds., *Proceedings of the Fourth International Conference on Genetic Algorithms* (Morgan Kaufmann, San Mateo, CA, 1991).

[17] L.B. Booker, Classifier systems that learn internal world models, *Mach. Learn.* **3** (1988) 161–192.

[18] R.A. Brooks, A robust layered control system for a mobile robot, *IEEE Trans. Rob. Autom.* **2** (1986) 14–23.

[19] R.A. Brooks, A robot that walks: emergent behaviors from a carefully evolved network, *Neural Comput.* **1** (2) (1989) 253–262.

[20] R.A. Brooks, Intelligence without representation, *Artif. Intell.* **47** (1991) 139–159.

[21] R.A. Brooks, Artificial life and real robots, in: *Toward a Practice of Autonomous Agents: Proceedings of the First European Conference of Artificial Life*, Paris, France (1992) 3–10.

[22] D. Chapman, *Vision, Instruction and Action* (MIT Press, Cambridge, MA, 1991).

[23] D. Chapman and L.P. Kaelbling, Input generalization in delayed reinforcement learning: an algorithm and performance comparisons, in: *Proceedings IJCAI-91*, Sydney, Australia (1991) 726–731.

[24] D. Cliff, Computational neuroethology: a provisional manifesto, in: *From Animals to Animals: Proceedings of the First International Conference on Simulation of Adaptive Behavior*, Paris, France (1991) 29–39.

[25] F. Delcomyn, Neural basis of rhythmic behavior in animals, *Science* 210 (1980) 492–498.

[26] M. Donner, *Real-Time Control of Walking* (Birkhauser, Boston, MA, 1987).

[27] J.L. Elman, Distributed representations, simple recurrent networks and grammatical structure, *Mach. Learn.* 7 (1991) 195–225.

[28] J.A. Fodor, *The Language of Thought* (Harvard University Press, Cambridge, MA, 1975).

[29] J.C. Gallagher and R.D. Beer, A qualitative dynamical analysis of evolved locomotion controllers, in: J.-A. Meyer, H. Roitblat and S. Wilson, eds., *From Animals to Animals 2: Proceedings of the Second International Conference on the Simulation of Adaptive Behavior* (MIT Press, Cambridge, MA, 1993) 71–80.

[30] M. Giunti, Computers, dynamical systems, phenomena and the mind, Ph.D. Thesis, Indiana University, Bloomington, IN (1992).

[31] D.E. Goldberg, *Genetic Algorithms in Search, Optimization and Machine Learning* (Addison-Wesley, Reading, MA, 1989).

[32] D. Graham, Pattern and control of walking in insects, *Adv. Insect Physiol.* 18 (1985) 31–40.

[33] J.K. Hale and H. Koçak, *Dynamics and Bifurcations* (Springer-Verlag, New York, 1991).

[34] J.K. Hale, L.T. Magalhaes and W.M. Oliva, *An Introduction to Infinite Dimensional Dynamical Systems—Geometric Theory* (Springer-Verlag, New York, 1984).

[35] S.A. Harp, T. Samad and A. Guha, Towards the genetic synthesis of neural networks, in: *Proceedings Third International Conference on Genetic Algorithms*, Fairfax, VA (1989) 360–369.

[36] I. Harvey, Untimed and misrepresented: connectionism and the computer metaphor, Technical Report CSRP 245, School of Cognitive and Computing Sciences, University of Sussex (1992).

[37] J.H. Holland, *Adaptation in Natural and Artificial Systems* (University of Michigan Press, Ann Arbor, MI, 1975).

[38] J.J. Hopfield, Neurons with graded response properties have collective computational properties like those of two-state neurons. *Proc. Nat. Acad. Sci.* 81 (1984) 3088–3092.

[39] I. Horswill, analysis of adaptation and environment, *Artif. Intell.* 73 (1995), to appear.

[40] P. Husbands and I. Harvey, Evolution vs. design: controlling autonomous robots, in: *Proceedings Third Annual Conference on AI, Simulation and Planning*, Perth, Australia (1992) 139–146.

[41] L.P. Kaelbling, *Learning in Embedded Systems* (MIT Press, Cambridge, MA, 1993).

[42] L.P. Kaelbling and S.J. Rosenschein, Action and planning in embedded agents, *Robotics and Autonomous Systems* 6 (1–2) (1990) 35–48.

[43] T.B. Kepler, L.F. Abbott and E. Marder, Reduction of conductance-based neuron models, *Biol. Cybern.* 66 (1992) 381–387.

[44] D. Kirsch, Today the earwig, tomorrow man?, *Artif. Intell.* 47 (1991) 161–184.

[45] P. Maes, ed., *Designing Autonomous Agents* (MIT Press, Cambridge, MA, 1990).

[46] S. Mahadevan and J. Connell, Automatic programming of behavior-based robots using reinforcement learning, in: *Proceedings AAAI-91*, Anaheim, CA (1991) 768–773.

[47] H.R. Maturana and F.J. Varela, *Autopoiesis and Cognition* (Reidel, Boston, MA, 1980).

[48] H.R. Maturana and F.J. Varela, *The Tree of Knowledge* (Shambhala, Boston, MA, 1987).

[49] J.-A. Meyer and S.W. Wilson, eds., *From Animals to Animats: Proceedings of the First International Conference on Simulation of Adaptive Behavior* (MIT Press, Cambridge, MA, 1991).

[50] G.F. Miller, P.M. Todd and S.U. Hegde, Designing neural networks using genetic algorithms, in: *Proceedings Third International Conference on Genetic Algorithms*, Fairfax, VA (1989) 379–384.

[51] A. Newell and H.A. Simon, Computer science as empirical inquiry: symbols and search, *Commun. ACM* **19** (1976) 113–126.

[52] K.G. Pearson, Nerve cells without action potentials, in: J.C. Fentress, ed., *Simpler Networks and Behavior* (Sinauer, Sunderland, MA, 1976).

[53] J.B. Pollack, The induction of dynamical recognizers, *Mach. Learn.* **7** (1991) 227–252.

[54] Z.W. Pylyshyn, *Computation and Cognition* (MIT Press, Cambridge, MA, 1984).

[55] J. Rinzel and G.B. Ermentrout, Analysis of neural excitability and oscillations, in: C. Koch and I. Segev, eds., *Methods in Neuronal Modeling* (MIT Press, Cambridge, MA, 1989).

[56] S.J. Rosenschein, Formal theories of knowledge in AI and robotics, *New Gen. Comput.* **3** (4) (1985) 345–357.

[57] G. Schöner and J.A.S. Kelso, Dynamic pattern generation in behavioral and neural systems, *Science* **239** (1988) 1513–1520.

[58] C.A. Skarda and W.J. Freeman, How brains make chaos in order to make sense of the world, *Behav. Brain Sci.* **10** (1987) 161–195.

[59] T. Smithers, Taking eliminative materialism seriously: a methodology for autonomous systems research, in: *Toward a Practice of Autonomous Systems: Proceedings of the First European Conference on Artificial Life*, Paris, France (1992) 31–40.

[60] P. Smolensky, On the proper treatment of connectionism, *Behav. Brain Sci.* **11** (1988) 1–74.

[61] T. van Gelder, What might cognition be if not computation?, Technical Report 75, Indiana University Cognitive Science, Bloomington, IN (1992).

[62] X.-J. Wang and J. Rinzel, Alternating and synchronous rhythms in reciprocally inhibitory model neurons, *Neural Comput.* **4** (1992) 84–97.

[63] N. Wiener, *Cybernetics* (MIT Press, Cambridge, MA, 2nd ed., 1961).

[64] G. Wendler, The influence of proprioceptive feedback on locust flight coordination, *J. Comput. Physiol.* **88** (1974) 173–200.

[65] G.M. Werner and M.G. Dyer, Evolution of communication in artificial organisms, in: C.G. Langton, C. Taylor, J.D. Farmer and S. Rasmussen, eds., *Artificial Life II* (Addison-Wesley, Reading, MA, 1991).

[66] S. Wiggins, *Introduction to Applied Nonlinear Dynamical Systems and Chaos* (Springer-Verlag, New York, 1990).

[67] S.W. Wilson, Knowledge growth in an artificial animal, in: K.S. Narendra, ed., *Adaptive and Learning Systems* (Plenum Press, New York, 1986).

Section 1.3: Evolutionary Artificial Intelligence

54

INTRODUCTION TO *ARTIFICIAL INTELLIGENCE THROUGH SIMULATED EVOLUTION*

L. J. Fogel, A. J. Owens and M. J. Walsh

Source: L. J. Fogel, A. J. Owens and M. J. Walsh, *Artificial Intelligence through Simulated Evolution*, John Wiley & Sons, 1966, pp. 1–10.

Definition of intelligence

Interest in intelligent decision-making has existed for a very long time. During this time, effort was first devoted to aiding the decision-maker, furnishing him with sound advice, and providing him with relevant information. Decision-making was treated as an art. Not until the latter part of the last century was any serious inquiry made into the behavioral aspects of intelligent decision-making. In the words of W. S. Jevons (1873), "Economy of mental power may be considered one of the main conditions on which our elevated intellectual position depends."[1] The attribute called "intelligence" was of concern, but it remained without precise definition.

At about this time, a new emphasis was placed upon the value of quantitative description in science. As Lord Kelvin (W. Thomson) remarked,

> "I often say that when you can measure what you are speaking about, and express it in numbers, you know something about it; but when you cannot measure it, when you cannot express it in numbers, your knowledge is of a meagre and unsatisfactory kind; it may be the beginning of knowledge, but you have scarcely, in your thoughts, advanced to the stage of science, whatever the matter may be."

The distinction between knowledge and intelligence became clear; knowledge being the useful information stored within the individual, and intelligence being the ability of the individual to utilize this stored information in some worthwhile (goal-directed) manner.

Early attempts to measure intelligence grew out of a practical need to recognize those who deserved special education. Various intelligence tests were developed, and although the testing technique was successively improved and refined in the decades that followed, the interpretation of the resulting score as a measure of intelligence still remains open to serious question. For example, it is generally recognized that the widely accepted I. Q. tests currently in use favor those individuals who come from an urban culture and those who are more prone to verbal expression. Such relative measures of intelligence do not pretend to offer insight into the fundamental nature of intellect.

In recent years, there have been a number of attempts to gain a deeper understanding into the nature of intellect. Biophysical studies have provided gross identification of the function of sections of the cortex, yet little is known concerning the nonspecific brain mechanisms.[2,3] There remains a wide gap between the current state of the art and a detailed understanding of how the physical embodiment provides intellect.

On the psychological side, efforts have been made to factor intelligent behavior into specific "components" that facilitate identification and individual measurement. Although such factors as *verbal comprehension, fluency, perception, psychomotor coordination, number, memory,* and *reasoning*[4] have been described in some detail, they are certainly not independent aspects of intelligent behavior. Intelligent behavior is also exhibited by creatures at much lower levels in the phylogenetic series. Are the foregoing factors also components of the behavior of these creatures? Such an approach to the definition of intelligence appears fraught with danger.

Such descriptions of intelligence are overly restrictive. Might it not be more meaningful to define intelligence in terms of the behavior of any goal-seeking entity, to measure the degree of intelligence in terms of the adequacy of its decision-making? Certainly, without the existence of a goal, decision-making is pointless, and the term "intelligence" has no meaning. More carefully stated, intelligence can be viewed as *the ability of any decision-making entity to achieve a degree of success in seeking a wide variety of goals under a wide range of environments.* The difficulty in carrying this definition into quantitative terms rests with the problem of defining what is meant by "degree of success," "variety of goals," and "range of environments." The decision-maker who can achieve a particular goal only in a certain environment and not in another displays little intelligence. *Versatility* is the essential ingredient of intelligent behavior. Under this definition, only a comparative evaluation of intelligence can be meaningful.

Avenues toward artificial intelligence

Interest in decision-making has steadily widened. As effort to measure the intelligence of the decision-maker has progressed, there has been a concurrent inquiry into the logical structure of intellect. This inquiry has grown out of purely philosophical speculation into the mechanization of various hypotheses with a view to demonstrating their validity. It is now generally agreed that a deeper understanding of the organization of intellect can be demonstrated by constructing a device that exhibits what is recognized to be "intelligent behavior." The last decade has seen a significant surge of interest in such mechanizations.

These efforts may be loosely classified into two groups. The first group represents investigators who recognize the human animal to be the most intelligent creature in nature. It would appear worthwhile, therefore, to replicate human intellect in some specific manner. From a biological point of view, an attempt is made to synthesize a "neural network" that exhibits properties of the nervous system. The term "bionics" is generally applied to this work.

Much of the work in bionics is based on the fundamental insight, contributed by McCulloch and Pitts in 1943,[5] that any "functioning" which can be defined logically, strictly, and unambiguously in a finite number of words can also be realized by a network of "formal neurons." Another classic paper[6] (1959) provided a demonstration of the selective properties of the retina of the frog. Extending this work, von Foerster was responsible for a clear explication of the possible property filters comprised of linearly interconnected formal neurons.[7] Such research is being carried on to gain greater understanding of data reduction and encoding at higher and higher levels in the phylogenetic series. The problem becomes significantly more difficult as the research concerns man.

Quite independently, Hebb suggested a brain model in which association cells were connected together in a complex, randomly organized network.[8] These connections existing prior to each successful decision were presumed to be made more permanent, thereby providing "memory traces." Farley and Clark simulated such a system[9] using

". . . a randomly interconnected network of nonlinear elements, each element having a threshold for incoming excitation, below which no action occurs, and above which the element 'fires.' When an element fires, its threshold immediately rises to infinity, and then, after a short refractory period, falls exponentially back toward its quiescent value. Furthermore, a short time after firing, an element transmits excitation to all other elements to which it is connected. The effectiveness of the excitation thus transmitted to a succeeding element is determined by a property of the particular connection known as its 'weight.' In general, there will be several incoming connections at any element, each having its individual weight . . . At the instant of transmission the appropriate weight is added to any excitation already present at the succeeding cell. Thereafter the excitation decays exponentially to zero. Thus the model contained both 'spatial' and 'temporal' summation. If at any time this excitation exceeds the threshold of the succeeding element, that element performs its own firing cycle and transmits its own excitations. . . . Thus the system organized itself to distinguish between two distinct input patterns."[10]

Rochester used even simpler "neurons" to obtain similar results, while attempting to realize Hebb's model more closely.[11]

In still later work, Rosenblatt considered a random network organized in a somewhat different manner.[12] His Perceptron consisted of a set of sensory elements (S-units), which are normally connected to a set of multilevel memory elements called association elements (A-units). The outputs of the A-unit are in turn randomly connected to a group of response elements (R-units), which read out the results of the pattern-recognizing operation. These R-units are connected via inhibiting lines to other R-units, and, by feedback paths, to the A-units. The experiments consist of two phases: a learning period and a test period. During the learning period, a number of stimuli are offered to the sensor, and each in turn is associated with one of the responses by forcing the appropriate subset to become dominant; that is, by artificially activating the appropriate response signal. Upon completion of the learning period, the Perceptron is shown a test stimulus and allowed to react without any control over the response. If the connectivity within the network has been sufficiently modified, the response will have a greater probability of being correct. In essence, a set of multilevel association elements is connected to the sensor and response cells. The excitation of the sensory elements by new stimulus patterns causes a particular distribution of activity in the association elements, which modifies their transfer property in some way. If, following this modification, a response element operates either spontaneously or by being forced, then a new distributed connectivity is created; so that, whenever the original stimulus pattern is again presented, it will correlate with this distribution in such a way as to favor the operation of the previous associated response.

To introduce learning into the model, it is necessary to go further and postulate that the distribution of ambient connectivity values over the network at any time represents the total experience of the system up to that time. If a system is to create a particular internal distribution in response to a combination of external stimuli and its own responses to these stimuli, it is necessary to postulate a process whereby information regarding the system's responses can be fed back to the system, this being a positive or negative reinforcement.

A fundamental limitation exists with any such device. A learned configuration of the logical network can be used to translate any symbol of the input alphabet into any symbol of the output alphabet; but as long as the learned configuration is maintained, this translation is invariant. In other words, conditional dependencies which lie beyond the alphabet of the input symbols cannot be recognized.

Of course, it is possible to construct multilayer systems that promise greater learning capability.[13] All of these, however, require instruction as to the desired stimulus-response pairs to be learned by the machine. Other techniques have been developed in which the outputs of threshold devices are combined to provide a weighted judgment of the classification of the stimulus pattern; however, in the interest of brevity we will not attempt a detailed description of them.[14,15]

Such biological modeling can indeed serve a useful purpose. It can provide greater insight into the functioning of the biological mechanisms by directing attention to new aspects that deserve observation and study. Although a distinct measure of success has already been attained in this regard, it is difficult to find biological mechanisms that serve as "natural prototypes" for the design of new engineering products, least of all machines that exhibit artificial intelligence.

This is not surprising. The hope of realizing artificially intelligent automata through direct biological modeling would appear to be particularly unpromising because of the sheer complexity of biological information-processing systems. The central nervous system of man is an immensely complex structure, containing some 15 billion neurons. Of these, about 10 billion are included in the brain proper. Each neuron has a great number of dendrites able to furnish it with information. Even gross patterns of connection in the central nervous system are difficult to trace. The detailed organization of the nervous system is far from what might be called "readily available knowledge." Until recently, the neuron was viewed as a two-state device; however, it is now widely recognized that there are graded responses at each synapse. A great deal remains unknown.

In addition to a lack of information regarding the structure of the nervous system, there are significant difficulties associated with describing its functioning. For example, neural encoding remains far from decipherable in terms of specific representations. The information storage mechanism is of great interest, yet there remains a considerable difference of opinion as to its biological embodiment. Here, for example, it might well be that an understanding of the mechanism of memory requires not only specific information regarding neuronal activity, but also the actions of the proximal glial cells, the modifications imposed upon the affected molecular structure of protein molecules, and, possibly, other aspects.

Biologists are the first to admit a serious lack of knowledge in these areas. Attempts to model specific aspects of biological information processing are certainly worthwhile as a step toward gaining additional knowledge of the mechanism. But at the same time, such models appear to be particularly unlikely to produce any artificially intelligent automata, at least within the foreseeable future.

The second group of investigators agree that man, because of his intelligence, is most worthy of modeling; however, this group prefers to view man as a psychological entity.[16] Such modeling may be accomplished in the following manner: A game situation is presented to the subject who is required to respond with a "move." His decision as to which move to make is then analyzed in order to reveal some consistent set of subquestions which facilitate his decision-making. Consistent aspects of his rationale are thus identified and these become the basis for a computer program that results in a machine capable of playing the game in a similar manner. This approach to artificial intelligence, generally called "heuristic programming," attempts to find a set of information reduction rules which, when applied to the observed data, will, in a relatively efficient manner, successfully transform these data into a desirable response. Through such analyses, the investigator hopes to find not only means for efficient data reduction through replication of the human decision-making process, but also certain features common to all these programs which might enable the design of a decision-maker which would prove to be "intelligent" even in the face of new problems and unexpected situations.

From a less specific approach, the flexible behavior of an intelligent decision-maker may be modeled in terms of adaptive servo systems[17] and sequential statistical decision procedures.[18,19]

In the case of the adaptive servo systems, the intent is to provide a hierarchy of feedback systems so that the parameters of lower-ordered systems will be suitably modified as a result of the response behavior of the higher-ordered systems. The domain of "adaptability" is constrained by the configuration of the multiloop servo system and the allowable range of each variable.[20] With regard to the statistical decision procedures, optimal rules for decision are derived for certain classes of environments and for specific criteria. The problem is "solved" only if the experienced environment falls into a suitable class and the goal can be expressed by one of the available criteria.[21,22] Considerable interest has been shown in nonparametric statistical inference; however, here again stationarity of environment is assumed.[23] A wide literature exists concerning optimization techniques. Some of these techniques may be viewed as being largely heuristic in that the solution is constructed on the basis of the demonstrated worth of methods in solving simpler problems.[24,25]

Although heuristic modeling has been applied to a relatively wide range of human decision-making activities, it would appear constrained to remain within the capability of the human operator. Thus far, it has been difficult to realize, through this procedure, any new insight into the fundamental nature of intellect. The performance of each specific program is limited in "skill" to that of the programmer and the subject being modeled (even though a program's performance may demonstrate far greater speed and accuracy). In situations where the machine is allowed to play against other similarly programmed machines (or against itself), its ability may be further improved; however, this results only from the increase of experience, and *not* from a gain of new insight into the essential organization of intellect. *Artificial intelligence is realized only if an inanimate machine can solve problems that have, thus far, resisted solution by man; not because of the machine's sheer speed and accuracy, but because it can discover for itself new techniques for solving the problem at hand.*

A third approach toward artificial intelligence is possible. From a less egocentric standpoint, the human animal may be viewed as but a single artifact of the natural experiment called evolution. Though, certainly, man is an intelligent creature, there is no reason to believe that he is the most intelligent creature that could possibly exist. Nature's experiment is continuing, and, in view of its past success in generating creatures of successively greater intellect, it would appear quite reasonable to anticipate that some future creatures will possess far greater intelligence than contemporary man. In this light, it would appear worthwhile to replace the process of modeling man as he now exists with the process of modeling evolution. This process would be carried out in the hope of reaching a greater understanding of the essential properties of intellect and, through this insight, gaining means for the synthesis of machines that display greater intelligence than has thus far been found in nature.[26]

In a sense, the evolutionary approach asks, "What might intellect be like some time in the distant future?" Although this question implies an outgrowth from man, the inquiry is intended to be far more general. For instance, there is no reason to believe that logical programs which result from modeling the process of evolution will bear any resemblance to the intellect of the actual progeny of contemporary man. (And yet, if the modeling of evolution can open the door to the design of greater intellect, it might also offer a significant step toward the solution of some of the important problems which face mankind today and, thereby, provide an indirect influence on the outcome of the continuing process of natural evolution.)

Modeling the natural process of evolution must be done with caution. As far as is known, this "experiment" of nature has occurred only once. The observed variability makes it difficult to believe that if the experiment were rerun, the outcome would be the same. The domain of possibilities is so great that it is highly unlikely that the human animal would be recreated even in a large number of similar evolutionary experiments. Thus, there appears to be an essential difficulty in replicating the evolutionary process. The investigator must identify those aspects of nature he considers to be fundamentally invariant properties of the environment; that is, properties that remain unaffected by the evolving creatures. In making this distinction, the investigator exercises his "freedom of design" through the selection of a set of underlying assumptions. On this basis, he may proceed to inquire into what evolution could be like: What kind of process will maximize the probability of success of those creatures that remain with respect to the challenge of their environment?

Both the bionic and heuristic programming approaches to artificial intelligence are primarily descriptive; that is, there is an attempt to model nature as it is observed to exist. In contradistinction, the evolutionary approach is primarily normative, in that it is an attempt to model evolutionary processes as they *might* occur in nature; to describe what *ought to be* rather than what *is*. The scientist does to know, while the engineer knows to do. In the evolutionary approach, the investigator takes an engineering attitude in his conceptual synthesis of the model.

It is recognized that there is no sharp distinction between descriptive and normative science. Descriptive science always includes an effect resulting from the orientation of the investigator in his search for what appears worthwhile to him. This is an ever-present normative influence. In a similar manner, normative science is carried out by an investigator who can understand nature only in terms that relate to his previous knowledge. Thus, his attempts to understand the limitations of what might exist in nature are always flavored by his descriptive outlook.

Various "organisms" might be used in the modeling of evolutionary processes; an increase in their intrinsic complexity offers, in turn, the benefit of an increase in the probability of the modeling being a success. (See Chapters 2 and 6.) But even after considering various combinations of mutation, selection, and recombination of these organisms, additional advantage may still be gained by injecting logical concepts derived from higher levels of abstraction. By analogy, model organisms may "move" on wheels, even though nature has not yet "invented" the wheel as a means for transport of living species.

Normative science specifically encourages the introduction of, and benefit from, optimal procedures whenever these are available and prove worthy of incorporation into the model. Similarly, models of decision-making processes may include optimal automated subroutines so as to benefit from the joint efforts of man and machine. Hopefully, the required decisions may be structured in terms of a hierarchy of subdecisions so that the mechanization of lower-level subdecisions allows the human operator to devote his full attention to higher-level tasks. It is expected that, as such man-machine-systems evolve, automatic subroutines will take their place at increasing levels within the hierarchy. Inquiry into methods for the worthwhile organization of decision-making automata will gain in recognition as fruits of the search for artificial intelligence materialize.

266

Notes

1 From *The Principles of Science; A Treatise on Logic and Scientific Method* (originally published 1874). Reprint, Dover Publications, New York, 1958.

2 *Biological and Biochemical Bases of Behavior*, edited by H. F. Harlow and C. N. Woolsey, The University of Wisconsin Press, Madison, 1958.

3 D. E. Wooldridge, *The Machinery of the Brain*, McGraw-Hill, New York, 1963.

4 B. F. Green, Jr., "Intelligence in Computer Simulation," *Transactions of the New York Academy of Sciences*, Serial II, Vol. 27, November, 1964, pp. 55–63.

5 W. S. McCulloch and W. H. Pitts, "A Logical Calculus of the Ideas Immanent in Nervous Activity," *Bulletin of Mathematics and Biophysics*, Vol. 5, 1943, p. 115.

6 J. Y. Lettvin, H. R. Maturana, W. S. McCulloch, and W. H. Pitts, "What the Frog's Eye Tells the Frog's Brain," *Proceedings of the IRE*, Vol. 47, November, 1959, pp. 1940–1951.

7 H. von Foerster, "Bio-Logic," in *Biological Prototypes and Synthetic Systems*, Vol. 1, edited by E. E. Bernard and M. R. Kare, Plenum Press, New York, 1962, pp. 1–13.

8 D. O. Hebb, *The Organization of Behavior*, John Wiley and Sons, New York, 1949.

9 B. G. Farley and W. A. Clark, "Simulation of Self-Organizing Systems by Digital Computer," *Transactions of the IRE*, Vol. PGIT-4, 1954, pp. 76–84.

10 G. G. Farley, "Self-Organizing Models for Learned Perception," in *Self-Organizing Systems*, edited by M. C. Yovits and S. Cameron, Pergamon Press, New York, 1960, pp. 7–31.

11 N. Rochester, J. H. Holland, L. H. Harbt, and W. L. Duda, "Tests on a Cell Assembly Theory of the Action of the Brain, Using a Large Digital Computer," *Transcription of the IRE*, Vol. PGIT-2, 1956, p. 80.

12 F. Rosenblatt, "The Perceptron: A Probabalistic Model for Information Storage and Organization in the Brain," *Psychological Review*, Vol. 65, 1958, p. 386.

13 F. Rosenblatt, *Principles of Neurodynamics*, Spartan Books, Washington, D. C., 1962.

14 G. S. Sebestyen, *Decision-Making Processes in Pattern Recognition*, The Macmillan Co., New York, 1962.

15 B. Widrow, "Generalization and Information Storage in Networks of Adeline 'Neurons'" in *Self-Organizing Systems – 1962*, edited by M. C. Yovtiz, G. T. Jacobi, and G. D. Goldstein, Spartan Books, Washington, D. C., 1962, pp. 435–462.

16 In many situations, replication of specific details may prove to be less effective than the modeling of overall logical properties; note the fact that although modern aircraft obey the same aerodynamic laws as do birds, they are not ornithopters and do not use feathers.

17 W. R. Ashby, *Design for a Brain*, John Wiley and Sons, New York, 1952 (rev. ed. 1960).

18 K. S. Fu, "A Sequential Decision Model for Optimum Recognition," in *Biological Prototypes and Synthetic Systems*, Vol. I, edited by E. E. Bernard and M. R. Kare, Plenum Press, New York, 1962, pp. 270–277.

19 R. A. Wiesen and E. H. Shuford, "Bayes Strategies as Adaptive Behavior," in *Biological Prototypes and Synthetic Systems*, Vol. I, edited by E. E. Bernard and M. R. Kare, Plenum Press, New York, 1962, pp. 303–310.

20 S. S. L. Chang, *Syntheses of Optimal Control Systems*, McGraw-Hill, New York, 1961.

21 A. Wald, *Statistical Decision Functions*, John Wiley and Sons, New York, 1950.

22 H. Raiffa and R. Schlaifer, "Applied Statistical Decision Theory," Division of

Research, Graduate School of Business Administration, Harvard University, Boston, 1961.

23 S. Siegel, *Nonparametric Statistics for the Behavioral Sciences*, McGraw-Hill, New York, 1956.

24 R. Bellman, *Dynamic Programming*, Princeton University Press, Princeton, New Jersey, 1957.

25 G. Leitmann, *Optimization Techniques with Application to Aerospace Systems*, Academic Press, New York, 1962.

26 L. J. Fogel, A. J. Owens, and M. J. Walsh, "Artificial Intelligence Through a Simulation of Evolution," in *Biophysics and Cybernetic Systems*, edited by M. Maxfield, A. Callahan, and L. J. Fogel, Spartan Books, Washington, D. C., 1965.

55

ARTIFICIAL EVOLUTION

A new path for artificial intelligence?

P. Husbands, I. Harvey, D. Cliff and G. Miller

Source: *Brain and Cognition* 34, 1997: 130–59.

Recently there have been a number of proposals for the use of artificial evolution as a radically new approach to the development of control systems for autonomous robots. This paper explains the artificial evolution approach, using work at Sussex to illustrate it. The paper revolves around a case study on the concurrent evolution of control networks and visual sensor morphologies for a mobile robot. Wider intellectual issues surrounding the work are discussed, as is the use of more abstract evolutionary simulations as a new potentially useful tool in theoretical biology.

© 1997 Academic Press

1. Introduction

This paper discusses and attempts to justify a particular approach to the development of autonomous agents with sensorimotor capabilities. The topic is treated from the standpoint of practical Artificial Intelligence, although potential wider implications are indicated. The method advocated is artificial evolution. Populations of agents are interbred under the influence of a task-based selection pressure. Starting from a population of random individuals, agents capable of performing the task well emerge.

The aim of this paper is to introduce some of the motivations underlying the use of artificial evolution and some of the key technical issues involved in implementing it. Little or no familiarity with the approach is assumed. In order to make much of the discussion more concrete, the central section of the paper (Section 5) is concerned with one particular experiment in evolutionary robotics.

Before discussing artificial evolution in some detail, the orientation of the work in relation to other areas of artificial intelligence will be dealt with. First, what do we mean by an autonomous agent? Simply this: a self-governing system that makes its own way in the world; there are no hidden leads or radio links connecting it to an operator. This is a rather large class, but, for reasons that will become clear shortly, we will restrict ourselves to those autonomous systems with sensorimotor capabilities.

The perspective taken on Artificial Intelligence (AI) is as follows. AI is regarded as the study of intelligence in natural and artificial systems through the construction of intelligence generating mechanisms. Along with Brooks and others (Brooks, 1991; Varela, Thompson, & Rosch, 1991) we regard the proper study of intelligence as an investigation into the interactions between autonomous agents and their environments. This involves the study of entire nervous systems; perception cannot be separated from action. Indeed, from our perspective nervous systems, natural and artificial, should be regarded as rather complex control systems. We agree with Brooks that the most sensible way to pursue such a study is through the construction of autonomous robots to act in complex, uncertain, dynamic environments. This follows from the belief that the greater part of intelligent behavior in animals (including humans) is bound up with sensorimotor coordination and "every day" survival skills. It is very hard to simulate in any detail an agent's sensory and motor couplings with its environment. Although more abstract computer models have their uses, as discussed later, they cannot reflect many of the messy real-time constraints imposed on embodied agents. To take these into account, it is frankly easier to use robots situated in the real world than it is to try and build some all encompassing super-simulation. Intelligence is a vague relative term used to label many adaptive behaviors (behaviors that tend to improve an organism's chance of survival—see (Ashby, 1952) for a good more precise definition). The old-fashioned human-centered notions of intelligence commonly used in the AI community until recently (Boden, 1977), with their stifling focus on abstract problem solving and deliberative thought, are here regarded as far too restrictive. Insects are intelligent. Humans are intelligent. The interesting questions are what mechanisms underly this intelligence and how can we build a robot that exhibits intelligence in this sense?

The kind of research described later is often placed under the ever wider umbrella of Artificial Life. However, most of this work fits neatly into the more specific field of Animat (artificial animals) research. However, since it is mainly concerned with developing mechanisms to generate intelligent behaviors, it can quite validly be regarded as a new approach to AI (Wilson, 1991).

Having provided some context, this paper continues with an argument for the use of artificial evolution in autonomous agent research, this is followed by a more detailed exposition of genetic algorithms, artificial evolution, and evolutionary robotics. The central section of the paper is concerned with a case study on the evolution of visually guided behaviors on a specialized mobile robot. The paper continues with a discussion of some of the more advanced aspects of evolutionary robotics. We advocate the use of artificial neural network based robot controllers, which in turn means that issues to do with the genetic encoding of the networks become central to the endeavor. We outline a set of desirable properties for such encodings. A number of encoding schemes developed by other researchers are reviewed, and we present new methods of our own. Next a number of the most pertinent issues in evolutionary robotics are outlined. There follows a discussion of the possibility of using artificial evolutionary techniques to help tackle more specifically scientific questions about natural sensorimotor systems.

2. Why evolve?

Animals that we often think of as rather simple (e.g., arthropods—that class of invertebrates including insects) in fact display a range of sophisticated adaptive behaviors, involving complex sensorimotor coordination (Young, 1989). These behaviors are generated by remarkably few nerve cells, which might suggest that they are based on simple mechanisms. However, in general this does not appear to be the case (Ewert, 1980). Despite their size, the dynamics of arthropod nervous systems are intricate.

Under present technological constraints, control systems for autonomous robots will necessarily involve relatively small numbers of "components," be they implemented in hardware or software. This suggests an analogy with arthropods: it is very likely that it will be necessary to develop complicated dynamical systems to control autonomous robots acting in uncertain complex environments.

Forty years of autonomous robotics research has taught us that generating the degree of sensorimotor coordination needed to sustain adaptive behavior in the real world is no easy matter (Moravec, 1983). We believe this is because the control systems needed will be of the complex dynamical systems variety, and these are inherently extremely difficult to design by traditional means. Indeed, the situation is even worse than is often expected; suitable sensor and actuator properties (including morphologies) are inextricably bound to the most appropriate "internal" dynamics of the control system and vice versa. Imposing the simplifying constraint of cleanly dividing the system's operation into a pipeline of sensing, internal processing, and acting now appears to be far too restrictive (Brooks, 1991; Beer, 1990).

To put it in slightly more abstract terms, we strongly suspect (along with Brooks, many biologists, and increasing numbers of cognitive scientists (Sloman, 1993)) that useful control systems to generate interesting behavior in autonomous robots will necessarily involve many emergent interactions between the constituent parts (even though there may be hierarchical functional decomposition within some of these parts). However, we go further

271

by claiming that there is no evidence that humans are capable of designing systems with these characteristics using traditional analytical approaches. We are very good at designing highly complex systems if we can divide them up into almost insulated subsystems with well defined interactions. However, when the number of interactions between modules increases exponentially with the addition of new modules, the design problem becomes intractable.

We, and a number of other authors, have suggested that the use of artificial evolution to fully, or partially, automate the design process may be a way forward (Cliff, Harvey, & Husbands, 1993; Beer & Gallagher, 1992). A number of research projects are now actively exploring this possibility. This new area is often referred to as evolutionary robotics.

The artificial evolution approach maintains a population of viable genotypes (chromosomes), coding for control architectures. The genotypes are interbred according to a selection pressure, much as in standard genetic algorithm work. This is controlled by a task-oriented evaluation function: the better the robot performs its task the more evolutionarily favored is its control architecture. Rather than attempting to hand design a system to perform a particular task or range of tasks well, the evolutionary approach allows their gradual emergence. There is no need for any assumptions about means to achieve a particular kind of behavior, as long as this behavior is directly or implicitly included in the evaluation function.

3. Genetic algorithms and artificial evolution

Genetic algorithms (GAs) are adaptive search strategies based on a highly abstract model of biological evolution (Holland, 1975). They can be used as an optimization tool or as the basis of more general adaptive systems. The fundamental idea is as follows. A population of structures, representing candidate solutions to the problem at hand, is produced. Each member of the population is evaluated according to some fitness function. Fitness is equated with goodness of solution. Members of the population are selectively interbred in pairs to produce new candidate solutions. The fitter a member of the population the more likely it is to produce offspring. Genetic operators are used to facilitate the breeding; that is, operators which result in offspring inheriting properties from both parents (sexual reproduction). The offspring are evaluated and placed in the population, quite possibly replacing weaker members of the last generation. The process repeats to form the next generation. This form of selective breeding quickly results in those properties which promote greater fitness being transmitted throughout the population: better and better solutions appear. Normally some form of random mutation is also used to allow further variation. A simple form of this algorithm is as follows.

1. Create initial population of strings (genotypes). Each string of symbols (genes) is a candidate solution to the problem.

2. Assign a fitness value to each string in the population.

3. Pick a pair of (parent) strings for breeding. The fitter the string the more likely it is to be picked.

4. Put offspring produced in a temporary population.

5. Is the temporary population full? If yes, go to 3, else go to 6.

6. Replace the current population with the temporary population.

7. Has some stopping criteria been fulfilled? If yes, exit, if no, go to 2.

This population-based survival of the fittest scheme has been shown to act as a powerful problem solving method over a wide range of complex domains (Grefenstette, 1985, 1987; Schaffer, 1989; Belew & Booker, 1991; Davis, 1990).

The loose analogies between GAs and natural evolution should be clear. The structures encoding a solution to the problem (often strings of characters) can be thought of as the genotypes or artificial DNA. There will be some process for interpreting the structure as a solution: the phenotype. The interpretation is often implicitly embedded in the evaluation function and can be complex. When the encoding and the evaluation function are static (search space of fixed dimensions, a single well-defined evaluation function), we are in the realms of optimization. When they are not, the GA can be used to build adaptive systems; systems that are able to cope with a changing environment. The latter scenario is closer to the situation existing in natural evolution and is exploited in evolutionary robotics, as will be made clear in the next section.

There are many different implementations of this idea, varying markedly in their specifics, for further details see Holland (1975), Goldberg (1989) and Mitchell (1996). The breeding phase, where offspring are produced from parents, can make use of a number of different "genetic" operators. Crossover is most often used. With this operator, sections of the parental genotype strings are exchanged to form new genotypes. Mutation is very common and involves randomly changing single genes (characters on the genotype string) to new legal values.

3.1. Evolutionary Robotics

The basic notion of Evolutionary Robotics is captured in Fig. 1. The evolutionary process, based on a genetic algorithm, involves evaluating, over many generations, whole populations of control systems specified by artificial genotypes. These are interbred using a Darwinian scheme in which the fittest individuals are most likely to produce offspring. Fitness is measured in terms of how good a robot's behavior is according to some evaluation criterion.

Just as natural evolution involves adaptations to existing species, we believe GAs should be used as a method for searching the space of possible adaptations of an existing robot, not as a search through the complete space of robots: successive adaptations over a long timescale can lead to long-term

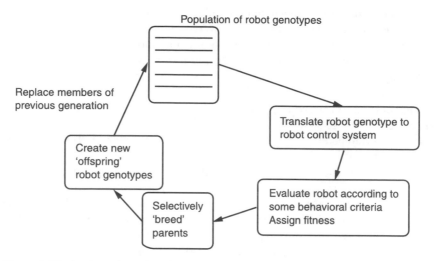

Figure 1 The basic notion of evolutionary robotics.

increases in complexity. For this reason, whereas most GAs operate on fixed-length genotypes, we believe it is necessary to work instead with variable-length genotypes. This leads to an incremental approach. A series of gradually more demanding task-based evaluation schemes are used. In this way new capabilities are built on existing ones and the search space is always constrained enough to be manageable.

The basis for extending standard GAs to cope with this has been worked out by Harvey (1992b, 1994, 1992a), who describe the *Species Adaptation Genetic Algorithm* (SAGA). In SAGA, the population being evolved is always a fairly genetically converged species; and increases in genotype length (or other metric of expressive power), associated with increases in complexity, can happen only very gradually.

4. Evolve networks

Much of the work described in this paper uses artificial neural networks of some variety as the basic building blocks of the control systems being developed. We believe this is the most appropriate choice. For reasons given in Cliff et al. (1993), network search spaces are generally smoother than spaces of explicit control programs. Networks are naturally amenable to open-ended approaches and allow the researcher to work with very low-level primitives, thereby avoiding incorporating too many preconceptions about suitable control system properties. We advocate unrestricted recurrent real-time dynamical networks as one of the most general class of behavior generating systems. However, such systems are far too unconstrained, with a great many potential free parameters (such as neuron time constants and thresholds and connection delays and weights) to admit hand design. Therefore, this class of intrinsically very powerful systems can only really be explored with the help of automated techniques, of which artificial evolution is a front runner.

5. An example experiment

This section makes much of the surrounding discussion more concrete by focusing on a particular experiment to evolve a network-based control system for a mobile robot engaged in visually guided tasks of increasing complexity.

There are many different ways of realizing each stage of the cycle shown in Fig. 1. A crucial decision is whether or not to use simulation at the evaluation stage, transferring the end results to the real world. Since an evolutionary approach potentially requires the evaluation of populations of robots over many generations, a natural first thought is that simulations will speed up the process, making it more feasible. Despite initial scepticism (Brooks, 1992), it has recently been shown that control systems evolved in carefully constructed simulations, with an appropriate treatment of noise, transfer extremely well to reality, generating almost identical behaviors in the real robot (Jakobi, Husbands, & Harvey, 1995; Thompson, 1995). However, both of these examples involved relatively simple robot-environment interaction dynamics. Once even low-bandwidth vision is used, simulations become altogether more problematic. They become difficult and time consuming to construct and computationally very intensive to run. Hence evolving visually guided robots in the real world becomes a more attractive option. The case study described in this section revolves around a piece of robotic equipment specially designed to allow the real-world evolution of visually guided behaviors—the Sussex gantry robot.

5.0.1. Concurrent evolution of visual morphologies and control networks

Rather than imposing a fixed visual sampling morphology, we believe a more powerful approach is to allow the visual morphology to evolve along with the rest of the control system. Hence we genetically specify regions of the robot's visual field to be subsampled, these provide the only visual inputs to the control network. It would be desirable to have many aspects of the robot's morphology under genetic control, although this is not yet technically feasible.

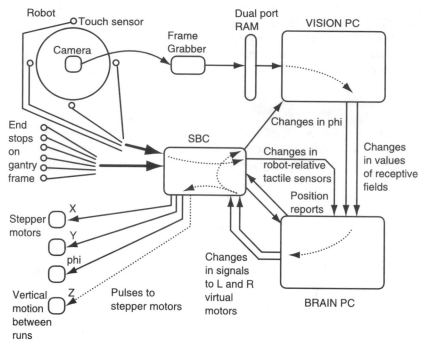

Figure 2 The different roles of the Vision computer, the Brain computer and the SBC.

5.0.2. The gantry robot

The gantry robot is shown in Fig. 3. The robot is cylindrical, some 150 mm in diameter. It is suspended from the gantry frame with stepper motors that allow translational movement in the X and Y directions, relative to a coordinate frame fixed to the gantry. The maximum X (and Y) speed is about 200 mm/sec. Such movements, together with appropriate rotation of the sensory apparatus, correspond to those which would be produced by left and right wheels. The visual sensory apparatus consists of a CCD camera pointing down at a mirror inclined at 45° to the vertical (see Fig. 4). The mirror can be rotated about a vertical axis so that its orientation always corresponds to the direction the "robot" is facing. The visual inputs undergo some transformations en route to the control system, described later. The hardware is designed so that these transformations are done completely externally to the processing of the control system.

The control system for the robot is run off-board on a fast personal computer, the "Brain PC." This computer receives any changes in visual input by interrupts from a second dedicated "Vision PC." A third (single-board)

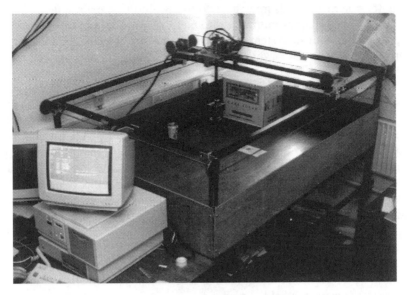

Figure 3 The Gantry viewed from above. The horizontal girder moves along the side rails, and the robot is suspended from a platform which moves along this girder.

Figure 4 The gantry robot. The camera inside the top box points down at the inclined mirror, which can be turned by the stepper motor beneath. The lower plastic disk is suspended from a joystick, to detect collisions with obstacles.

computer, the SBC, sends interrupts to the Brain PC signaling tactile inputs resulting from the robot bumping into walls or physical obstacles. The only outputs of the control system are motor signals. These values are sent, via interrupts, to the SBC, which generates the appropriate stepper motor movements on the gantry.

The roles of the three computers are illustrated in Fig. 2. Continuous visual data is derived from the output of the small monochrome CCD camera. A purpose-built Frame Grabber transfers a 64 × 64 image at 50 Hz into a highspeed 2 K CMOS dual-port RAM, completely independently and asynchronously relative to any processing of the image by the Vision PC. The Brain PC runs the top-level genetic algorithm and during an individual evaluation, it is dedicated to running a genetically specified control system for a fixed period. At intervals during an evaluation, a signal is sent from the Brain PC to the SBC requesting the current position and orientation of the robot. These are used in keeping score according to the current fitness function. The Brain PC receives signals, to be fed into the control system, representing sensory inputs from the Vision PC and the SBC. The visual signals are derived from averaging over genetically specified circular receptive patches in the camera's field of view.

This setup, with off-board computing and avoidance of tangled umbilicals, means that the apparatus can be run continuously for long periods of time—making artificial evolution feasible.

A top-level program automatically evaluates, in turn, each member of a population of control systems. A new population is produced by selective interbreeding and the cycle repeats. For full technical details of the system see Harvey et al. (1994).

5.0.3. The artificial neural networks

The artificial neurons used have separate channels for excitation and inhibition. Real values in the range [0,1] propagate along excitatory links subject to delays associated with the links. The inhibitory (or veto) channel mechanism works as follows. If the sum of excitatory inputs exceeds a threshold, T_v, the value 1.0 is propagated along any inhibitory output links the unit may have, otherwise a value of 0.0 is propagated. Veto links also have associated delays. Any unit that receives a non zero inhibitory input has its excitatory output reduced to zero (i.e., is vetoed). In the absence of inhibitory input, excitatory outputs are produced by summing all excitatory inputs, adding a quantity of noise, and passing the resulting sum through a simple linear threshold function, $F(x)$, given below. Noise was added to provide further potentially interesting and useful dynamics. The noise was uniformly distributed in the real range $[-N, +N]$.

$$F(x) = \begin{cases} 0, & \text{if } x \leq T_1 \\ \dfrac{x - T_1}{T_2 - T_1}, & \text{if } T_1 < x < T_2. \\ 1, & \text{if } x \geq T_2 \end{cases} \tag{1}$$

The networks' continuous nature was modeled by using very fine time slice techniques. In the experiments described in this paper the following neuron parameter settings were used: $N = 0.1$, $T_v = 0.75$, $T_1 = 0.0$, and $T_2 = 2.0$. The networks are hardwired in the sense that they do not undergo any architectural changes during their lifetime, they all had unit weights and time delays on their connections. These networks are just one of the class we are interested in investigating.

5.0.4. The genetic encoding

Two "chromosomes" per robot are used. One of these is a fixed length bit string encoding the position and size of three visual receptive patches as described above. Three eight-bit fields per patch are used to encode their radii and polar coordinates in the camera's circular field of view. The other chromosome is a variable-length character string encoding the network topology. The genetic encoding used for the control network is illustrated in Fig. 5.

The network chromosome is interpreted sequentially. First the input units are coded for, each preceded by a marker. For each node, the first part of its gene can encode node properties such as threshold values; there then follows a variable number of character groups, each representing a connection from that node. Each group specifies whether it is an excitatory or veto connection, and then the target node is indicated by jump type and jump size. In a manner similar to that used in Harp and Samad (1992), the jump type allows for both relative and absolute addressing. Relative addressing is provided by jumps forward or backward along the genotype order; absolute addressing is relative to the start or end of the genotype. These modes of addressing mean that offspring produced by crossover will always be legal. There is one input node for each sensor (three visual, four tactile).

The internal nodes and output nodes are handled similarly with their own identifying genetic markers. Clearly this scheme allows for any number of internal nodes. The variable length of the resulting genotypes necessitates a careful crossover operator which exchanges homologous segments. In keeping with SAGA principles, when a crossover between two parents can result in an offspring of different length, such changes in length (although allowed) are restricted to a minimum (Harvey, 1992a). There are four output neurons, two per motor. The outputs of each pair are differenced to give a signal in the range [− 1,1].

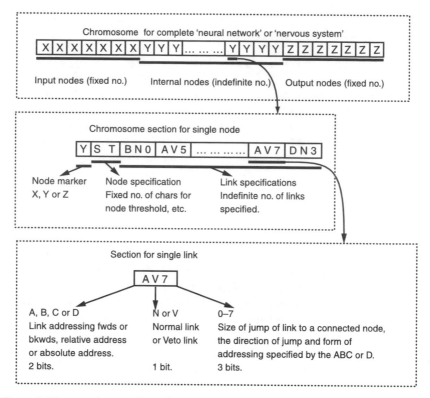

Figure 5 The genetic encoding scheme.

5.0.5. Experimental setup

In each of the experiments a population size of 30 was used with a genetic algorithm employing a linear rank-based selection method, ensuring the best individual in a population was twice as likely to breed as the median individual. Each generation took about 1.5 hr to evaluate. The most fit individual was always carried over to the next generation unchanged. A specialized crossover allowing small changes in length between offspring and parents was used (Cliff et al., 1993). Mutation rates were set at 1.0 bit per vision chromosome and 1.8 bits per network chromosome.

With the walls and floor of the gantry environment predominantly dark, initial tasks were navigating toward white paper targets. In keeping with the incremental evolutionary methodology, deliberately simple visual environments are used initially, as a basis to moving on to more complex ones. Illumination was provided by fluorescent lights in the ceiling above, with the gantry screened from significant daylight variations. However, the dark surfaces did not in practice provide uniform light intensities, neither over space nor over time. Even when the robot was stationary, individual pixel values would fluctuate by up to 13%.

5.1. Results

5.1.1. Big target

In the first experiment, one long gantry wall was covered with white paper. The evaluation function ϵ_1, to be maximized, implicitly defines a target locating task, which we hoped would be achieved by visuo-motor coordination

$$\epsilon_1 = \sum_{i=1}^{i=20} Y_i, \tag{2}$$

where Y_i are the perpendicular distances of the robot from the wall opposite that to which the target is attached, sampled at 20 fixed-time intervals throughout a robot trial which lasted a total of about 25 sec. The closer to the target the higher the score. For each robot architecture four trials were run, each starting in the same distant corner, but facing in four different partially random directions, to give a range of starts facing into obstacle walls as well as toward the target. As the final fitness of a robot control architecture was based on the *worst* of the four trials (to encourage robustness), and since in this case scores accumulated monotonically through a trial, this allowed later trials among the four to be prematurely terminated when they bettered previous trials. In addition, any control systems that had not produced any movement by 1/3 of the way into a trial was aborted and given zero score.

The run was started from a converged population made entirely of clones of a single randomly generated individual picked out by us as displaying vaguely interesting behavior (but by no means able to do anything remotely like locate and approach the target). In two runs using this method very fit individuals appeared in less than 10 generations. From a start close to a corner, they would turn, avoiding contact with the walls by vision alone, then move straight toward the target, stopping when they reached it.

5.1.2. Small target

The experiment continued from the stage already reached, but now using a much narrower target placed about 2/3 of the way along the same wall the large target had been on, and away from the robot's starting corner (see Fig. 6), with evaluation ϵ_2

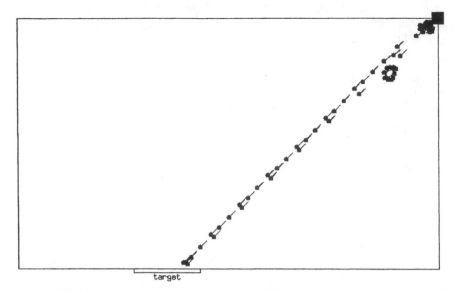

target

Figure 6 Behavior of the best of a later generation evolved under second evaluation function. The dots and trailing lines show the front of the robot and its orientation. Coarsely sampled positions from each of four runs are shown, starting in different orientations from the top right corner.

$$\epsilon_2 = \sum_{i=1}^{i=20} (-d_i), \tag{3}$$

where d_i is the distance of the robot from the center of the target at one of the sampled instances during an evaluation run. Again, the fitness of an individual was set to the worst evaluation score from four runs with starting conditions as in the first experiment. The initial population used was the 12th generation from a run of the first experiment (i.e., we incrementally evolved on top of the existing behaviors).

Within six generations a network architecture and visual morphology had evolved displaying the behavior shown in Fig. 6. This control system was tested from widely varying random starting positions and orientations, with the target in different places, and with smaller and different-shaped targets. Its behavior was general enough to cope with all these conditions for which it had not explicitly been evolved. It was also able to cope well with moving targets as shown in Figs. 7 and 8.

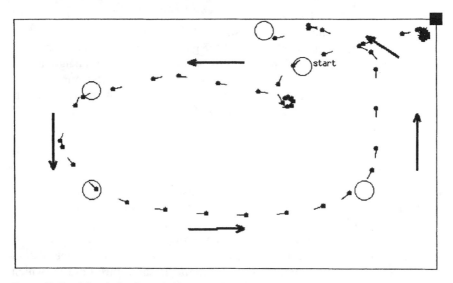

Figure 7 Tracking behavior of the control system that generated the behavior shown in Fig. 6. The unfilled circles show the position of the target at a number of points on its path (starting position indicated). The arrows roughly indicate the path of the target.

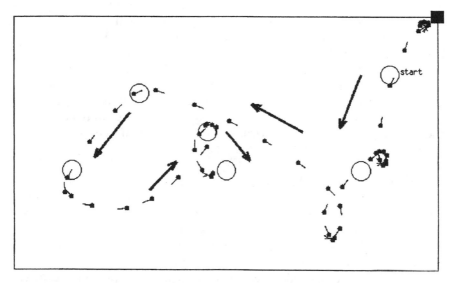

Figure 8 Further tracking behavior of the control system that generated the behavior shown in Fig. 7.

5.1.3. Rectangles and triangles

The experiment continued with a distinguish-between-two-targets task. Two white paper targets were fixed to one of the gantry walls: one was a rectangle, the other was an isosceles triangle with the same base width and height as the rectangle. The robot was started at four positions and orientations near the opposite wall such that it was not biased toward either of the two targets. The evaluation function ϵ_3, to be maximized, was

$$\epsilon_3 = \sum_{i=1}^{i=20} [\beta(D_{1_i} - d_{1_i}) - \sigma\,(D_{2_i}, d_{2_i}], \tag{4}$$

where D_1 is the distance of target 1 (in this case the triangle) from the gantry origin; d_1 is the distance of the robot from target 1; and D_2 and d_2 are the corresponding distances for target 2 (in this case the rectangle). These are sampled at regular intervals, as before. The value of β is $(D_1 - d_1)$ unless d_1 is less than some threshold, in which case it is $3 \times (D_1 - d_1)$. The value of σ (a penalty function) is zero unless d_2 is less than the same threshold, in which case it is $I - (D_2 - d_2)$, where I is the distance between the targets; I is more than double the threshold distance. High fitnesses are achieved for approaching the triangle but ignoring the rectangle. It was hoped that this experiment might demonstrate the efficacy of concurrently evolving the visual sampling morphology along with the control networks.

After about 15 generations of a run using as an initial population the last generation of the incremental small target experiment, fit individuals emerged capable of approaching the triangle, but not the rectangle, from each of the four widely spaced starting positions and orientations. The behavior generated by the fittest of these control systems is shown in Fig. 9. When started from many different positions and orientations near the far wall, and with the targets in different positions relative to each other, this controller repeatedly exhibited very similar behaviors to those shown.

The active part of the evolved network that generated this behavior is shown in Fig. 10. The evolved visual morphology for this control system is shown in the inset. Only receptive fields 1 and 2 were used by the controller.

Detailed analyses of this evolved system can be found in Harvey, Husbands, & Cliff (1994) and Husbands (1996). To crudely summarize, unless there is a difference in the visual inputs for receptive fields 1 and 2, the robot makes rotational movements. When there is a difference it moves in a straight line. The visual sensor layout and network dynamics have evolved such that it fixates on the sloping edge of the triangle and moves toward it.

The case study described above has been included to provide a concrete focus to the issues discussed in this paper. However, this is only one experiment of many, making use of one particular type of network, genetic encod-

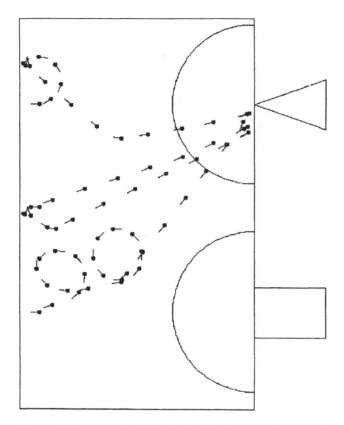

Figure 9 Behavior of a fit individual in the two target environment. The rectangle and triangle indicate the positions of the targets. The semicircles mark the "penalty" (near rectangle) and "bonus score" (near triangle) zones associated with the fitness function. In these four runs the robot was started directly facing each of the two targets, and twice from a position midway between the two targets: once facing into the wall and once facing out.

ing, and experimental setup. The rest of this paper introduces other aspects of such research.

6. Genetic encodings and developmental schemes

Once the decision to evolve network-based systems has been taken, the question of how to encode the networks on an artificial genotype becomes crucially important. Without a suitable encoding scheme little progress can be made. In the simplest schemes the genotype is a direct description of the network wiring. An example of that kind of scheme is the genetic encoding

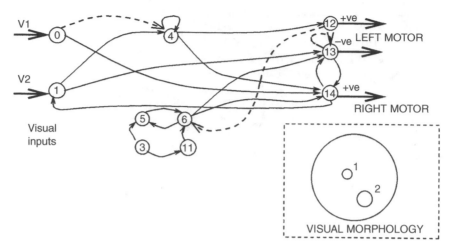

Figure 10 Active part of the control system that generated fit behavior for the rectangle and triangle experiment. Visual morphology shown in the inset.

used with the gantry robot and described in the previous section. Such encodings will necessarily be restrictive. Much more powerful approaches, allowing complete open-endedness and modularity through the repeated use of genotype sections, must involve a more complex interpretive process.[1] This can be thought of as being loosely analogous to the developmental processes that occur in nature to produce a phenotype from a genotype. Since we regard encoding issues as being central to evolutionary development of control systems, this and the following section concentrate on this area.

Gruau (1992) defines seven properties of genetic encoding of neural networks that should be considered. These include: *completeness*, any NN architecture should be capable of being encoded; *compactness*, one encoding scheme is more compact than the second if for any NN architecture the first genetic encoding is shorter than that given by the second; *closure*, implies that any genotype encodes some architecture; *modularity*, a genetic encoding would be modular if parts of the genotype specify subnetworks of the complete network, and other parts specify the connections between such subnetworks, this decomposition could be recursive. We endorse all these considerations, especially modularity which would seem necessary for sensorimotor systems employing vision. Additional points are: *smooth interaction with genetic operators*, the encoding should allow relatively smooth movements around the search space; the encoding should *not presuppose the dimensionality of the search space*, incremental evolution requires an openended approach in which the dimensionality of the search space cannot be specified in advance, the encoding should allow variable numbers of neurons and connections; the encoding must allow *specification of sensory and motor properties* as well as that of a control network.

Kitano (1990) developed an early method for encoding networks which took into account some of the issues raised above. Although his technique was not specifically developed for sensorimotor systems, it can be applied to them. The genotype was used to encode a graph generation grammar. Kitano's system allows a linear genotype to operate on a square matrix of characters, initially 1×1. Each act of rewriting expands the matrix into four quadrants each the same size as the previous matrix, with the contents of each quadrant specified by the genotype. At the end of a succession of n such rewriting steps, a network connection matrix of size $2^n \times 2^n$ is produced. In this way scalability and modularity start to be implemented in a compact genetic encoding of large regular networks.

Gruau (1992) discusses Kitano's work and also acknowledges earlier work by Wilson (1987). Gruau's cellular encoding is a form of "neural network machine language," which he claims has all the above desirable properties. This is a form of rewriting grammar, where the rewriting is considered as a form of developmental process involving "rewriting neurons" or "cells." Rewriting operators include PAR which divides a cell into two cells that inherit the same input and output links as their parent, CLIP which can cut links, WAIT which delays rewriting operations so as to change the order in which later operations are carried out. Further operators SPLIT and CLONE allow for the desirable property of modularity to be achieved. In total 13 operators are used. Although it has not yet been done, he proposes using his method for the development of sensorimotor control systems.

7. Developmental schemes for sensorimotor systems

This section outlines three schemes recently developed at Sussex for encoding network-based sensorimotor control systems. They take into account the issues listed earlier and are specifically aimed at encoding whole control systems: that is, control networks along with sensor and motor morphologies.

7.1. A language and compiler scheme

Experience with the primitive encoding we used in our early evolutionary robotics simulation studies (Cliff et al., 1993) led us to develop a language- and compiler-type genetic encoding scheme which is tailored to the demands of evolving sensory–motor coordination morphologies and in particular to encoding repeated structures as are commonly found necessary in dealing with visual sensory processing. As with genetic programming, the genome is a program, which is expressed as a 1D string—although at the conceptual level a higher-dimensional space offers a more appropriate descriptive framework. The encoding scheme is essentially a new programming language, called "NCAGE" (from "Network Control Architecture Genetic Encoding"); NCAGE allows for specifying sensory–motor controller morphologies based on "neural network" parallel-distributed processing architectures. The artificial genomes are interpreted as NCAGE programs which are "compiled" in a "morphogenesis" process to create controller structures. It is important to note that we do not consider the DNA-encoded genomes of biological systems as programs and neither do we consider biological morphogenesis as comparable to compiling or executing a computer program. The notions of "genome-as-program" and "morphogenesis-as-compilation" used here are nothing more than metaphors invoked in the exposition of what is at present essentially an engineering endeavor.

It is beyond the scope of this paper to fully describe this new encoding scheme: a brief description of its key features is given below.

> The NCAGE language draws on elementary vector-graphics programming facilities found in many graphics languages (and in platform-specific vector graphic extensions to general programming languages). It thus bears superficial similarities to turtle-graphics languages such as LOGO. Essentially, the genome is interpreted as a sequence of subroutine specifications and subroutine calls. Subroutines may call other subroutines including themselves. Subroutine calls are made from "positions" in a high-dimensional space (typically conceptualized as one of a number of distinct but super-positioned Euclidian 2 spaces or 3 spaces). Calls may reposition a "cursor" (cf. turtle) or may place one or more "neurons" of differing types at a position specified relative to the current cursor position.

The encoding scheme is modular, has varying resolution of numeric values, is robust with respect to crossover and mutation, allows for recursively repeatable structures (with systematic variations where necessary), and has inbuilt symmetry and symmetry-breaking facilities. Structure specifications are largely independent of their position on the genome, and so a transposition operator can be used to good effect. An inversion operator is also used, but because the genome is read left-to-right, inversion does not preserve structure specifications and is used primarily as an operator for achieving extremely high mutation rates within a localized sequence on the genome, while preserving the statistical distribution of characters on the inverted portion of the genome.

Because the encoding has to satisfy requirements imposed by the genetic operators, NCAGE differs significantly from traditional computer programming languages. The most marked difference is that portions of the genome may be interpreted "junk" or "silent" code: while many programming languages allow for the specification of subroutines which are never called, most will generate terminal error conditions when the subroutines are partially complete or nonexistent. The NCAGE interpreter does not generate an error when it encounters calls to unspecified subroutines (such calls are simply ignored), and sequences of instructions which cannot be parsed as generating useful structures are likewise ignored.

The genomes are expressed in a three-character alphabet, although in principle a binary alphabet could be employed at the cost of proportionately longer strings. Under the three-character scheme, two characters are used as bits for data, and the third is a "stop" control character used for terminating specifications at varying levels in the genome interpretation process. Theoretically, any sufficiently long random string over the chosen alphabet will be interpretable as a specification of a controller architecture. However, practical considerations entail that some structure (i.e., high-order correlations) are introduced in the generation of initial random genomes, to reduce their length. Experience with the encoding indicates that the inclusion of junk code on the genome increases the robustness of the encodings with respect to the genetic operators employed.

7.2. A force field development scheme

A second, contrasting, scheme makes use of a highly implicit dynamical process governed by a system of ordinary differential equations, the parameters of which are encoded on the genotype. This process describes the growth of a network-based sensorimotor control system. Again, in no way is this scheme intended to be a model of any biological process. It was developed simply as a method having the properties we believe are desirable for artificial evolution.

In this force field scheme, "neurons" are positioned across a two-dimensional plane where they exert attractive forces on the free ends of "dendrites" growing out from themselves and other neurons. The ends of the dendrites move under the influence of the force field created by the distribution of neurons. If a dendrite end moves to be within a small distance, ϵ, from a neuron it stops growing and connects to that neuron (which may be its parent). Dendrites do not affect each other and may cross in arbitrary ways. The equations of motion of the dendrite ends are given by ordinary differential equations of the form shown in Eq. (5).

$$\frac{d^2\vec{R}_{ij}}{dt^2} = \sum_{k=0}^{N} \vec{F}_{ijk} - K\frac{d\vec{R}_{ij}}{dt} + \frac{G_{ij}}{l_{ij}^3 \left|\frac{d\vec{R}_{ij}}{dt}\right|}\frac{d\vec{R}_{ij}}{dt}, \tag{5}$$

where $\vec{R}_{ij}$ is the position vector of the end of the jth dendrite of the ith neuron (henceforth referred to as end_{ij}). The first term on the RHS of Eq. (5) represents the vector sum of the attractive forces exerted on end_{ij} by all neurons. These forces are of the form given in Eq. (6).

$$\vec{F}_{ijk} = \frac{GS_i AS_k \vec{r}_{ijk}}{|\vec{r}_{ijk}|^3},$$ (6)

where $\vec{r}_{ijk}$ is the vector from end_{ij} to the center of neuron k. GS_i and AS_k are genetically determined constants. The second term in Eq. (5) is a "viscous" resistive force to prevent dendrites sailing off into outerspace. The third term provides a force in the direction of motion of the dendrite end and is inversely proportional to the cube of l_{ij}, the current length of the dendrite. This force drops off very rapidly but encourages dendrites to, at least initially, escape from the influence of their parent neuron. G_{ij} is a genetically encoded constant. In the computational implementation of the scheme, the differential equations were approximately integrated using the Euler method with an adaptive time step. One feature of this method is that the lengths of the resulting dendrite paths can be translated into time delays or weights for use in the operation of the network.

A genotype to be used with this scheme must encode the parameters of the equations, along with the positions of the neurons and the initial directions of growth of the dendrites. In principle, a large number of different encodings would suffice. However, as already discussed, it is preferable to use an encoding exhibiting the desirable properties outlined in Section 7. A particular encoding meeting these requirements, and specially developed for the force field method, is briefly outlined below.

In this method a bit string is used as a neutral encoding medium. That is, any bit string can be interpreted as a control system (although it may be an empty one). The core of the interpreting algorithm is as follows. The string is scanned from left to right until a particular type of marker (short bit pattern) is found. If the marker bounds the start of a valid string section, sequences of bits are read and turned into "neuron" parameter values for use with the force field development scheme. As with the previously described language and compiler model, each of these read operations counts the number of 1s in a sequence and uses that number to map to the parameter value. The algorithm rewinds back to the start-section marker and then searches forward to the next occurrence of a second type of marker. This signals a new "mode" of interpretation in which dendrite properties are determined. This is repeated until yet another form of marker is encountered. The algorithm then moves back to the first marker and searches forward to the next occurrence of a start-section marker. The whole process then repeats. This "looping back" behavior means the algorithm can potentially reuse parts of the string many times. This results in the encoding of relatively large parts of the networks being localized on the string. This produces a form of modularity, where repeated patterns are formed by the reexpression of parts of the genotype.

The position of a neuron is described by genetically determined distance and direction from the last neuron to be laid down. The existence or otherwise of a particular marker determines whether or not a neuron acts as a visual receptor. If it is a visual receptor, its position on the plane is mapped onto a position within the robot's receptive field. In the scheme currently being used, two special motor neurons are placed near the center of the plane. The network then develops around them. This is convenient for a two motor system, but many other ways of handling motor neurons can be incorporated into the method.

7.3. A cell division method

In this proposal, a naive model is used of the development of a multicellular organism by cell division from a single initial cell. Every cell contains the same DNA, the genotype, which acts as a constraint on an intracellular dynamics of transcription and translation of "enzymes" which themselves initiate or repress the production of further enzymes. The genotype and also the enzymes are bit strings.

Within one cell, any initial enzymes are template-matched against the genotype; wherever matches occur, transcription from the genotype starts and produces further enzymes. The ensuing intracellular dynamics can be influenced by intercellular "signals" received from neighboring cells. The production of particular enzymes initiates cell-splitting; other particular enzymes, when they are first produced, signal the completion of the developmental process.

In this way, from an initial single cell with a genotype, development produces a number of cells that can be considered as positioned in some space with neighborhood relations. Although all containing the same DNA, the cells can be differentiated into different classes by the particular distinctive internal dynamics of their enzyme production process. Thus at this stage the whole group of cells can be interpreted as a structure with organization; for instance, as a neural network with different cells being "neurons" with specific characteristics, and with connections specified between them.

8. Some related work on evolutionary development of sensorimotor control systems

This section provides a brief high-level review of research into the use of genetic algorithm based techniques for the development of sensorimotor control systems for autonomous agents.

In a traditional autonomous robotics context, mention is made of a

291

proposed evolutionary approach in Barhen, Dress, & Jorgensen (1987). A student of Brooks discussed some of the issues involved, with reference to subsumption architectures, in Viola (1988). De Garis (1992) proposed using GAs for building behavioral modules for artificial nervous systems, or "artificial embryology." However, it is only recently that more complete proposals have been made to use evolutionary approaches in robotics (Brooks, 1992; Husbands & Harvey, 1992).

Brooks (1992) outlines an approach based on Koza's genetic programming techniques (Koza, 1992). He acknowledged that time constraints would probably necessitate the use of simulations. However, he stressed the dangers of using simulated worlds rather than real worlds. He proposed that by evolving the control program incrementally the search space can be kept small at any time. He noted that symmetries or repeated structures should be exploited so that only a single module needs to be evolved, which is then repeatedly used. Brooks proposed a high-level language, GEN, which could be evolved, and then compiled down into BL (Behavior Language) and further on down onto the actual robot hardware.

Important work on an evolutionary approach to agent control using neural networks has been done by Beer and Gallagher (1992). They explore the evolution of continuous-time recurrent neural networks as a mechanism for adaptive agent control, using as example tasks chemotaxis, and locomotion-control for a six-legged insect-like agent. The networks are based on the continuous Hopfield model (Hopfield, 1982), but allow arbitrary recurrent connections. They used a standard genetic algorithm to determine neuron time constants and thresholds and connection weights. A fixed number of network parameters are encoded in a straightforward way on bitstring "genotypes." They report success in their objectives; in the case of locomotion control, controllers were evolved that in practice generated a tripod gait (front and back legs on one side in phase with the middle leg on the opposite side). This was achieved both with and without the use of sensors which measured the angular position of each leg.

Beer and Gallagher (1992) develop a dynamical systems perspective on control systems for autonomous agents, influenced by early work in Cybernetics (Ashby, 1952). In further developments of their evolutionary approach, Yamauchi and Beer (1994) evolve networks which can control autonomous agents in tasks requiring sequential and learning behavior.

Colombetti and Dorigo (1992) use Classifier Systems (CSs) for robot control. In this work the ALECSYS implementation is used to build a hierarchical architecture of CSs—one for each desired behavior, plus a coordinating CS. Results are reported which have been generated in simulations and then transferred to a real robot.

Parisi, Nolfi, and Cecconi (1992) investigated the relationship between learning and evolution in populations of back-propagation networks; these networks were the "brains" of animals that received sensory input from a simple cellular world in which the task was to collect "food." This work made use of abstract computer models rather than real robots.

Koza successfully used the technique of genetic programming to develop subsumption architectures (Brooks, 1986) for simulated robots engaged in wall-following and box-moving tasks (Koza, 1992).

Craig Reynolds (1993) uses genetic programming to create control programs which enable a simple simulated moving vehicle to avoid collisions. He comments that these solutions are brittle, vulnerable to any slight changes or to noise. In further work where the fitness-testing includes noise, he reports that the brittleness problem is overcome, and only compact robust solutions survive (Reynolds, 1994).

Floreano and Mondada (1994) were able to run a GA on a real robot in real time, rather than a simulation. The GA set the weights and thresholds in a simple recurrent network where every sensory input was connected to both motor outputs. The task was to traverse a circular corridor while avoiding obstacles, and this work demonstrates that with well-designed equipment it is possible to avoid the problems associated with simulations.

9. Some common objections

One common objection to the use of artificial evolution is the amount of time it is likely to take to evolve anything useful. This is difficult to answer. However, work done so far has shown that it is possible to evolve simple control systems in simulation in a matter of 2 or 3 hr (Jakobi et al., 1995) and in the real world in about 1 day (Harvey et al., 1994). It is too early to say how things will scale up as more complex tasks are used.

Another complaint is that the entire morphology of the robot, as well as its control system, should be evolved. This is a valid criticism. Successful adaptive behavior depends on harmonious relationships between body morphology and nervous system dynamics. However, some progress is being made in this direction in the work of Harvey, Husbands, and others where the visual morphology of a real robot is concurrently evolved along with a control network (Harvey et al., 1994). As described earlier, this is done by allowing the subsampling pattern (position and size of receptive fields) of a video camera image to be under evolutionary control (see Section 5).

Sometimes it is stated that as more complex tasks are investigated, it will become extremely difficult to design evaluation functions. Opinion is divided over this issue. One of the implicit assumptions of the field is that it is generally much easier to produce a criteria for deciding how well a robot achieved a task than it is to specify how the task should be achieved. Evaluation functions can be very implicit. For instance, tasks such as exploration and foraging can be set up as straight survival tests. Only those robots that maintain viability for sufficiently long get a chance to breed. Maintaining viability will involve finding and exploiting energy sources. However, issues relating to evaluation, both explicit and implicit, are likely to become increasingly important as attempts are made to evolve more complex behaviors.

Finally, a common assumption is that the evolved systems will be impossible to understand. There are two answers to this. The first is that there is no evidence to suggest that the systems will be impenetrable. The second is that even if they are, so what. One of the aims of this kind of work is to develop mechanisms to generate certain sorts of behaviors and then to gain insight by analyzing these mechanisms. Both Beer and Gallagher (1992) and Husbands et al. (1995) have used dynamical systems approaches to analyzing evolved controllers. They have both demonstrated ways to choose a state space at the appropriate level to allow a clear picture of the internal mechanisms. Husbands et al. also show how to incorporate an understanding of agent–environment coupling into the analysis. So far these kinds of analysis have been for relatively simple systems. It is possible that as things become more complex, state spaces at a tractable level of abstraction will not be found. However, if the robot works, and is robust and reliable, an important aspect of the research would still be successful.

10. Evolutionary simulations as science: tracing the origins and effects of sensorimotor systems in nature

While much of the work mentioned so far is biologically informed and inspired, most of it has a strong engineering characteristic. In other words, the primary goal is to develop working control systems for autonomous mobile robots and then to understand their underlying mechanisms. However, this field can potentially offer new tools and methods for investigating more specifically scientific topics. That is the focus of this section, where the use of artificial evolution in the context of more abstract computer studies will be discussed.

Very little is known about the evolutionary origins and effects of basic sensorimotor systems in nature. Brains and behaviors do not fossilize well, so normal paleontological methods cannot generally be used to trace the evolution of sensorimotor systems. Behavioral ecologists can construct optimality or game theoretic models of how behavioral strategies evolve, but these models are usually too abstract to explain the evolution of specific sensorimotor systems in specific species. Even experimental studies in fast-breeding species cannot study sensorimotor evolution for more than a few dozen generations. Neuroethologists can derive phylogenies and probable selective pressures by comparing sensorimotor adaptations across species, but cannot test evolutionary hypotheses very directly. Because of these methodological problems, evolutionary computer simulations are our only real hope for understanding the long-term adaptation of sensorimotor systems to habitats and econiches and the long-term coevolution of sensorimotor systems interacting within and between species.

This gap in our scientific understanding of sensorimotor evolution is important because (1) sensorimotor control is the essence of "adaptive agency," and the evolution of sensorimotor control is fundamental to the success of all animal species, and (2) sensorimotor systems, once evolved, can in turn exert strong selection pressures on other organisms, resulting in the evolution of camouflage, warning coloration, mimicry, lures, protean behavior, sexual displays, communication, and many other forms of adaptive display. This second phenomenon has received increasing attention in the last few years and has been termed "psychological selection" (Miller, 1993; Miller & Freyd, 1993), "sensory drive" (Endler, 1992), "sensory exploitation" (Ryan, 1990), "signal selection" (Zahavi, 1991), and "the influence of receiver psychology on the evolution of animal signals" (Guilford & Dawkins, 1991). In such cases of "sensory exploitation," where behavioral adaptations in one animal evolve to exploit particular sensory biases in other animals, we clearly cannot understand the co-evolution without simulating the relevant sensorimotor systems in some detail.

Genetic algorithms offer a general, openended method for simulating the evolutionary origins and effects of sensorimotor systems, because such systems can be modeled at almost any size and any level of description, from detailed neural network designs (as we have used in our evolutionary robotics work), up to abstract parameters of behavioral strategies, and because such systems can be left to evolve in any simulatable habitat or ecosystem. Since different scientific problems require simulations at quite different scales and levels of description, we must be explicit about our research goals and careful about finding the right simulation methods for those goals. For example, studying the phylogeny of visual circuits in a particular genus of beetle might require evolving quite detailed neural networks under particular ecological conditions, but studying the general influence of visual associative learning on the evolution of warning coloration might require much more general models of vision in predators and coloration in prey. In general, engineering research needs more detailed, lower-level simulations of sensorimotor systems than almost any scientific research would require, because sensorimotor systems for autonomous robots must actually work, whereas sensorimotor models of animals need only fit the neuroethological data.

Even if one's scientific goal is to understand neural development, learning, perception, or the mechanisms of dynamic behavior, rather than evolution itself, there is still considerable benefit to parameterizing one's model of the phenomenon in a way that allows alternative models to evolve through GA methods. Simulated evolution can be used to test the plausibility, robustness, and evolutionary stability of models of development and behavior just as real evolution tested the actual mechanisms of development and behavior that are being modeled. Human imagination is poor at envisioning alternatives to one's cherished model of some behavioral phenomenon; simulated evolution can act as a constructive critic that generates alternative hypotheses which can then be tested by observation and experimentation.

In the future, we envision a more integrated science of sensorimotor evolution that combines data and methods from cladistics, experimental psychology, neuroethology, behavioral ecology, population genetics, and computer simulation. Evolutionary simulation is unusually exciting, colorful, and fast as an empirical research method, but ideally, it will be absorbed into the scientific mainstream as just one means among many for studying natural evolutionary processes.

11. Conclusions

Using artificial evolution as a new approach to AI has been discussed. More specifically it has been advocated for the development of network-based controllers for autonomous robots, autonomous robotics being seen as the most appropriate vehicle for AI research. It has been argued that it has at least the following advantages.

- It allows the exploration of areas of design space that are not amenable to traditional rational analytic hand-design methods.
- It allows the concurrent exploration of control architectures and sensor morphologies in a principled way.
- It enables us to work with very low-level primitives and helps to throw away as many preconceptions as possible about how behaviors should be generated.

Some discussion of the role of artificial evolution in more abstract studies of potential benefit to theoretical biology has also been given.

Address reprint requests to P. Husbands, School of Cognitive & Computing Sciences, University of Sussex, Brighton, BN1 9QH, United Kingdom. E-mail: philh or inmanh or davec or geoffm@cogs.susx.ac.uk.

Note

1 In this context modularity refers to a developmental process analogous to the use of subroutines in programs. For instance, the left limbs and right limbs of animals will not be independently "coded for" in DNA, but rather generated by the same genetic information expressed more than once.

References

Ashby, W. R. 1952. *Design for a brain*. London: Chapman & Hall.
Barhen, J., Dress, W. B., & Jorgensen, C. C. 1987. Applications of concurrent neuromorphic algorithms for autonomous robots. In R. Eckmiller and C.v.d. Malsburg (Eds.), *Neural computers*. New York/Berlin: Springer–Verlag. Pp. 321–333.

Beer, R. 1990. *Intelligence as adaptive behaviour: An experiment in computational neuroethology*. New York: Academic Press.

Beer, R., & Gallagher, J. C. 1992. Evolving dynamic neural networks for adaptive behavior. *Adaptive Behavior*, **1**(1), 91–122.

Belew, R., & Booker, L. 1991. *Proceedings of the 4th International Conference on Genetic Algorithms*. Morgan Kaufmann.

Boden, M. 1977. *AI and natural man*. Brighton: Harvester Press.

Brooks, R. A. 1986. A robust layered control system for a mobile robot. *IEEE J. Rob. Autom.*, **2**, 14–23.

Brooks, R. A. 1991. Intelligence without representation. *Artificial Intelligence*, **47**, 139–159.

Brooks, R. A. 1992. Artificial life and real robots. In F. J. Varela & P. Bourgine (Eds.), *Proceedings of the First European Conference on Artificial Life*. Cambridge, MA: MIT Press/Bradford Books. Pp. 3–10.

Cliff, D., Harvey, I., & Husbands, P. 1993. Explorations in evolutionary robotics. *Adaptive Behavior*, **2**(1), 73–110.

Colombetti, M., & Dorigo, M. 1992. Learning to control an autonomous robot by distributed genetic algorithms. In J.-A. Meyer, H. Roitblat, S. Wilson (Eds.), *from animals to animats 2, Proc. of 2nd Intl. Conf. on Simulation of Adaptive Behavior, SAB'92*. Cambridge, MA: MIT Press/Bradford Books. Pp. 305–312.

Davis, L. 1990. *The handbook of genetic algorithms*. Princeton, NJ: Van Nostrand-Reinhold.

de Garis, H. 1992. The genetic programming of steerable behaviors in genNets. Toward a practice of autonomous systems. In F. J. Varela & P. Bourgine (Eds.), *Proceedings of the First European Conference on Artificial Life*. Cambridge, MA: MIT Press/Bradford Books, Pp. 272–281.

Endler, J. A. 1992. Signals, signal conditions, and the direction of evolution. *American Naturalist*, **139**, 125–153.

Ewert, J.-P. 1980. *Neuroethology*. New York/Berlin: Springer-Verlag.

Floreano, D., & F. Mondada. 1994. Automatic creation of an autonomous agent: Genetic evolution of a neural-network driven robot. In D. Cliff, P. Husbands, J.-A. Meyer, & S. Wilson (Eds.), *From animals to animats 3, Proc. of 3rd Intl. Conf. on Simulation of Adaptive Behavior, SAB'94*. Cambridge, MA: MIT Press/Bradford Books.

Goldberg, D. E. 1989. *Genetic Algorithms in search, optimization and machine learning*, Reading, MA: Addison–Wesley.

Gruau, F. 1992. *Cellular encoding of genetic neural networks*. TR.92–21, Laboratoire de l'Informatique du Parallelisme, Ecole Normale Superieure de Lyon.

Grefenstette, J. 1985. *Proceedings of an International Conference on GAs*. Hillsdale, NJ: Erlbaum.

Grefenstette, J. 1987. *Proceedings of the 2nd International Conference on GAs*. Hillsdale, NJ: Erlbaum.

Guilford, T., & Dawkins, M. S. 1991. Receiver psychology and the evolution of animal signals. *Animal Behavior*, **42**, 1–14.

Harp, S. A., & Samad, T. 1992. Genetic synthesis of neural network architecture. In L. Davis (Ed.), *Handbook of genetic algorithms*. Princeton, NJ: Van Nostrand–Reinhold. Pp. 202–221.

Harvey, I. 1992a. The SAGA cross: The mechanics of crossover for variable-length genetic algorithms. In R. Manner & B. Manderick (Eds.), *Proc. PPSN 2*. Amsterdam: North Holland. Pp. 269–278.

Harvey, I. 1992b. Species adaptation genetic algorithms: The basis for a continuing SAGA. In F.J. Varela & P. Bourgine (Eds.), *Proceedings of the First European Conference on Artificial Life*. Cambridge, MA: MIT Press/Bradford Books. Pp. 346–354.

Harvey, I. 1994. Evolutionary robotics and SAGA: The case for hill crawling and tournament selection. In C. Langton (Ed.), *Artificial life III*. Redwood City, CA: Addison–Wesley. Pp. 299–326. Santa Fe Institute Studies in the Sciences of Complexity. Proceedings Vol. XVI.

Harvey, I., Husbands, P., & Cliff, D. 1994. Seeing the light: Artificial evolution, real vision. In D. Cliff, P. Husbands, J.-A. Meyer & S. Wilson (Eds.), *From animals to animats 3, Proc. of 3rd Intl. Conf. on Simulation of Adaptive Behavior, SAB'94*. Cambridge; MA: MIT Press/Bradford Books. Pp. 392–401.

Holland, J. 1975. *Adaptation in natural and artificial systems*. Ann Arbor, MI: University of Michigan Press.

Hopfield, J. 1982. Neural networks and physical systems with emergent collective computational abilities. *Proceedings of the National Academy of Sciences*, **79**, 2554–2558.

Husbands, P. 1996. Rectangles, robots, triangles and transients. In M. Sugisaka (Ed.). *Proceedings of International Symposium on Artificial Life and Robotics, Oita, Japan*. Pp. 252–255.

Husbands, P., & Harvey, I. 1992. Evolution versus design: Controlling autonomous robots, integrating perception, planning and action. *Proceedings of 3rd Annual Conference on Artificial Intelligence, Simulation and Planning*. New York: IEEE Press. Pp. 139–146.

Husbands, P., Harvey, I., Cliff, D., & Miller, G. 1994. The use of genetic algorithms for the development of sensorimotor control systems. In P. Gaussier, & J.-D. Nicoud (Eds.), *Proceedings of from Perception to Action Conference*. Washington, DC: IEEE Comput. Soc. Pp. 110–121.

Husbands, P., Harvey, I., & Cliff, D. 1995. Circle in the round: State space attractors for evolved sighted robots. *Robotics and Autonomous Systems*, **15**, 83–106.

Jakobi, N., Husbands, P., & Harvey, I. 1995. Noise and the reality gap: The use of simulation in evolutionary robotics. In F. Moran, A. Moreno, J. J. Merelo, & P. Chacon (Eds.). *Advances in Artificial Life: Proc. 3rd European Conference on Artificial Life*. Berlin: Springer–Verlag. Lecture Notes in Artificial Intelligence. Vol. 929. Pp. 704–720.

Kitano, H. 1990. Designing neural networks using genetic algorithms with graph generation system. *Complex Systems*, **4**, 461–476.

Koza, J. 1992. *Genetic programming: On the programming of computers by means of natural selection*. Cambridge, MA: MIT Press.

Miller, G. F. 1993. *Evolution of the human brain through runaway sexual selection: The mind as a protean courtship device*. Ph.D. thesis, Stanford University Psychology Department.

Miller, G. F., & Cliff, D. 1994. Protean behavior in dynamic games: Arguments for the co-evolution of pursuit-evasion tactics in simulated robots. *From animals to animats 3, Proceedings of the Third International Conference on Simulation of Adaptive Behavior*. Cambridge, MA: MIT Press.

Miller, G. F., & Freyd, J. J. 1993. *Dynamic mental representations of animate motion: The interplay among evolutionary, cognitive, and behavioral dynamics.* Cognitive Science Research Paper CSRP-290; University of Sussex.

Mitchell, M. 1996. *An introduction to genetic algorithms.* Cambridge, MA: MIT Press/ Bradford Books.

Moravec, H. 1983. The stanford cart and the CMU rover. *Proceedings of the IEEE*, **71**, 872–884.

Parisi, D., Nolfi, S., & Cecconi, F. 1992. Learning, behavior, and evolution. Toward a practice of autonomous systems. In F. J. Varela & P. Bourgine (Eds.), *Proceedings of the First European Conference on Artificial Life.* Cambridge, MA: MIT Press/ Bradford Books. Pp. 207–216.

Reynolds, C. 1993. *An evolved, vision-based model of obstacle avoidance behavior. Artificial life III.* C. Langton (Ed.), Santa Fe Institute Studies in the Sciences of Complexity, Proceedings Vol. XVI. Reading, MA: Addison-Wesley.

Reynolds, C. 1994. Evolution of corridor following behavior in a noisy world. In D. Cliff, P. Husbands, J.-A. Meyer, & S. Wilson (Eds.), *From animals to animats 3, Proc. of 3rd Intl. Conf. on Simulation of Adaptive Behavior, SAB'94.* Cambridge, MA: MIT Press/Bradford Books.

Ryan, M. J. 1990. Sexual selection, sensory systems, and sensory exploitation. *Oxford Surveys of Evol. Biology*, **7**, 156–195.

Schaffer, J. 1989. *Proceedings of the 3rd International Conference on GAs.* Los Altos, CA: Kaufmann.

Sloman, A. 1993. The mind as a control system. Inc. Cambridge: Hookway & D. Peterson (Eds.), *Philosophy and the cognitive sciences.* CUP.

Smithers, T. 1994. On why better robots make it harder. In D. Cliff, P. Husbands, J.-A. Meyer, & S. Wilson (Eds.), *From animals to animats 3, Proc. of 3rd Intl. Conf. on Simulation of Adaptive Behavior, SAB'94.* Cambridge, MA: MIT Press/Bradford Books. Pp. 54–72.

Thompson, A. 1995. Evolving electronic robot controllers that exploit hardware resources. In F. Moran, A. Moreno, J. J. Merelo, & P. Chacon (Eds.), *Advances in Artificial Life: Proc. 3rd European Conference on Artificial Life.* Berlin: Springer-Verlag. Lecture Notes in Artificial Intelligence. Vol. 929. Pp. 640–656.

Varela, F., Thompson, E., & Rosch, E. 1991. *The embodied mind.* Cambridge, MA: MIT Press.

Viola, P. 1988. *Mobile robot evolution.* Bachelors Thesis, MIT.

Wilson, S. 1987. The genetic algorithm and biological development. In J. J. Grefenstette (Ed.), *Genetic algorithms and their applications: Proceedings of the Second Intl. Conf. on Genetic Algorithms.* Hillsdale, NJ: Erlbaum. Pp. 247–251.

Wilson, S. 1991. The animat path to AI. In J.-A. Meyer & S. Wilson (Eds.), *From Animals to Animats.* Cambridge, MA: MIT Press.

Yamauchi, B., & Beer, R. 1994. Integrating reactive, sequential, and learning behavior using dynamical neural networks. In D. Cliff, P. Husbands, J.-A. Meyer & S. Wilson (Eds.), *From animals to animats 3, Proc. of 3rd Intl. Conf. on Simulation of Adaptive Behavior, SAB'94.* Cambridge, MA: MIT Press/Bradford Books. Pp. 382–391.

Young, D. 1989. *Nerve cells and animal behaviour.* Cambridge: CUP.

Zahavi, A. 1991. On the definition of sexual selection, Fisher's model, and the evolution of waste and of signals in general. *Animal Behaviour*, **42**(3), 501–503.

Part II

CRITIQUES AND
STUMBLING BLOCKS

Section 2.1: Diagonalisation
Section 2.2 : Phenomenology
Section 2.3 : The Lighthill Report
Section 2.4 : The Frame Problem

INTRODUCTION

Critiques of Artificial Reason

Ronald Chrisley

Much of the development of the concept of artificial intelligence has been the result of a dialectical interplay between protagonists of the idea and its opponents. Although in the proceeding sections we have already seen criticisms of one approach in the service of another, what is contained here are criticisms that are, or were intended to be, criticisms of the entire enterprise of constructing an intelligent artefact. These are, then, criticisms "from the outside", even though some of the critics were themselves once researchers in artificial intelligence.

For example, Weizenbaum is the creator of the infamous program Eliza, which, although very simple in structure, convinced many people who interacted with it that they were having a discussion with a psychoanalyst – which in turn prompted many at the time to wonder if this counted as a machine passing the Turing Test. In his included paper, however, Weizenbaum questions the claim that machines can be intelligent. He blames belief in this possibility on the Western view of intelligence as a uni-dimensional, context- and culture-independent commodity. Against the possibility he argues that intelligence cannot be reduced to knowing a set of communicable facts, which the methodology of symbolic artificial intelligence requires. This is supported by a discussion of left vs. right hemisphere specialisation; Weizenbaum's contention is that symbolic artificial intelligence models only the capacities of the left hemisphere, and yet the functions of the right are also crucial. Likewise for the unconscious. He further argues that since machines do not face the same problems that humans do, they could never be intelligent in the same way that we are. Thus, he allows that some kind of "machine intelligence" might be possible, but it would be of an "alien" sort (thus recalling Wittgenstein's "if a lion could speak, we would not understand it"). He also implicitly concedes that one might make a machine humanly intelligent by simulating the human brain, but such approaches are not his target, and are anyway impractical, given their intractability and our ignorance of neurophysiology.

Although the title of the included panel discussion is "Has Artificial Intelligence Research Illuminated Human Thinking?", what ensues is primarily a discussion of Searle's, and to a lesser extent, Dreyfus', critique of whether artificial intelligence is possible. While Dreyfus' critique is covered thoroughly in section 2, Part II this Volume, Searle's critique is only given substantial airing here. This is partly because the wide availability of papers on his Chinese Room argument would make their presence here redundant. But more importantly, the Chinese Room argument is less relevant than might be supposed to the concerns of this work since Searle concedes much of what is at issue here: he concedes that machines can be intelligent (a point of dissimilarity between his argument and the otherwise similar analogy of the mill in Leibniz; cf. the Introduction to Volume I, Part II), that digital computers can be intelligent, even that a digital computer could behave indistinguishably from a human. What he denies is that a digital computer could *understand* anything *solely by virtue of* running the right *program*. Since the predominant concern of the thinkers presented in this set is with the idea of getting a machine to behave intelligently, which Searle concedes is possible, his critique is only of relevance when discussing the broader aspects of artificial intelligence in Volume IV, Part II, and especially in section 1 (there is a discussion of Searle's position in the Bechtel paper in that section).

Of considerable interest, however, is Searle's interpretation of artificial intelligence as heir to the dualism of Descartes. Rather than seeing artificial intelligence as an extension of the Hobbesian materialist view of mind, Searle contends that its analysis of mentality in terms of functional states which are multiply-realisable and biology-independent renders it the "last gasp of Cartesian metaphysics". The interesting twist here is that whereas the conventional story says that artificial intelligence relies on a world view that renders the mind to be just another physically realisable phenomenon, Searle's interpretation is that artificial intelligence relies on mind being very different from physical processes in believing that mentality, unlike a rainstorm, can be realised in any medium whatsoever, solely by reproducing its formal aspects.

1 Diagonalisation

One of the major intellectual achievements of the twentieth century was Gödel's incompleteness proof, which showed that any finitely axiomatisable formal system at least as powerful as arithmetic is either incomplete or inconsistent (Gödel 1931). There will always be a sentence (specifically, one which in effect says "This sentence cannot be proved in arithmetic") which, under the standard interpretation of arithmetic, is true, but by that very token (given what it says) must not be provable on pain of inconsistency. The paradox of the liar was also used, by Turing, to establish a similar limitation of formal automata, the uncomputability of the halting problem. (It will be useful to depart from the original formulation of the halting problem and the proof of its uncomputability, both for reasons of clarity, and to better reflect the formulation that critics of artificial intelligence have used.) The question in the halting problem is: given an enumeration of Turing machines, and given arbitrary m and n, will Turing machine number m not halt when given n as input? No Turing machine can answer this correctly for all m and n, because in particular no machine can answer correctly when m = n = its own number in the enumeration. The convention is that a Turing machine can only count as giving an affirmative answer to a question it is computing if it halts. So a Turing machine k, given k as input, can only answer "yes" to the halting problem question by halting, but that "yes" is meant to indicate that machine k, itself, does not halt – a contradiction. So if the machine is to be sound (never give a false answer), it must not halt when given k as input. But then there exists a number – k – for which Turing machine k cannot give the correct answer to the halting problem. And so it goes for every Turing machine which attempts to answer this halting question.

Since, from the start, formality has played a central role in theories of computation, it is unsurprising that some (e.g. Lucas, and some thirty years later, Penrose 1990, 1994) have taken any limitation of formal systems *ipso facto* to be a limitation of computers. Further, it is argued that from the very fact that humans can recognise these limitations in formal systems, it follows that we are not so limited. Thus, human intelligence cannot even be simulated by a computer, since there are things which we can do which a computer cannot. Lucas' paper responds to five kinds of objections to this argument, dealing with the issues of idealisation, modality and finitude, transfinite arithmetic, the formalisability of the rational, and consistency. But there seem to be some telling objections that do not fall into any of these categories. One is to note that even if Lucas' conclusion is correct, it only defeats a certain kind of artificial intelligence – that which aspires to make computers do everything and perhaps more than a human can do. Thus, it says nothing against non-formalisable machines (indeed, it may be that computers, by virtue of being physical and embodied, are not truly formalisable, not completely captured by the abstractions of automata theory, etc.). It also says nothing against machine intelligence: many readers will be pleased to hear that a human that cannot follow Gödel's proof is not thereby deemed unintelligent. So why should the lack of that ability render a machine unintelligent? In fact, Lucas' argument leaves open the possibility that computers could surpass us in intelligence in all other respects, save tricky self-referential proofs.

But at this point one smells a rat. Why should a computer be our equal or better in every aspect except this recherché case? The fact is, diagonalisation is something *no* entity can escape. In particular, we fall afoul of the same paradox. Consider what might be called the "person halting problem".

Suppose we enumerate all persons, and all "yes or no" questions of English. Then, is there any person who can answer the following question correctly for all values of m and n?

Is the mth person's answer to the nth question "no"?

No, there is no such person, and for the same diagonalising reasons as for the traditional halting problem. But notice that there is no non-question-begging argument against the possibility of a single Turing machine being able to answer all those questions. Since Turing machines are not mentioned in those questions, there is no way of tripping a Turing machine up on a case of contradictory self-reference. So in some sense, we can do things Turing machines cannot (answer all halting problem questions), and Turing machines can do things we cannot (answer all person halting problem questions). But actually, this seems to be exactly the same limitation, just indexicalised to the case of Turing machines, and people, respectively. No one will be impressed by your claim to be able to do things I cannot when you explain it by pointing out that you, but not I, can touch the middle of my back with a (or even worse: your!) finger, or that you, but not I, can look at my eyes directly, unaided by a reflective surface. But if what has been just said about the person halting problem is correct, this is precisely the situation with Lucas' argument against artificial intelligence.

2 Phenomenology

Dreyfus' 1965 critique begins with a description of the initial promise in, but subsequent stagnation of, four areas of symbolic artificial intelligence research at the time: game playing, problem solving, translation, and pattern recognition. The relevant researchers were, with hindsight, extremely overconfident and optimistic, making them easy targets for Dreyfus' attack. However, Dreyfus' own remarks about the impossibility of getting a computer to play chess well, go, with hindsight, to the other, pessimist extreme. But despite the recent success of Deep Blue and other programs, Dreyfus' points concerning computer chess still have some validity. Even today's winning programs succeed, when they do, through a brute-force consideration of millions of possibilities; yet, as Newell, Shaw and Simon admit, human players consider only one hundred or so positions in the analysis of a move. This ability to determine a good move without explicitly considering millions of positions is what marks out the human player as intelligent. The idea is that in domains unlike chess, where the possibilities may be just as numerous but difficult to formalise and evaluate, human intelligence will succeed where the brute force approach will not. This raises the question of whether intelligence should be defined in terms of the kind of open-ended environments which we have evolved to cope with, or whether there can be alternate forms of intelligence which deal with formal environments which are suitable to pure symbolic reason. The fact that such environments would no doubt be human-made is beside the point; the fact that they are becoming more numerous, pervasive and significant is not.

Dreyfus credits our superior heuristic performance to what William James called "the fringes of consciousness", and believes the lack of this feature in artificial intelligence systems is partly to blame for their brute-force stupidity. He concludes that the slowdowns and setbacks that artificial intelligence was encountering at the time of writing were indicative of a completely wrong-headed approach. An enduring image summarising his view of the situation is provided when he asks: "Are we pushing out on a continuum like that of velocity, such that progress becomes more and more difficult as we approach the speed of light, or are we instead facing a discontinuity, like the tree climbing man who reaches for the moon?" A standard defence against phenomenological arguments of this sort is to say that many or most of the operations in an artificial intelligence system do not match our own experience of, e.g. playing chess, because they are unconscious. Dreyfus' attempts to counter this reply are not persuasive.

Dreyfus claims that there are two other aspects to human intelligence that symbolic approaches cannot replicate or explain: the ability to distinguish the essential from the accidental, and the capacity to tolerate ambiguity in a context-dependent way. In arguing for this claim, Dreyfus employs Wittgenstein's point that a shared form of life is necessary for learning (especially language acquisition) – an idea that the situated approach would take to heart, as we have seen (Part I, section 1 of this Volume). A footnote midway through the paper reveals that Dreyfus limits his attack to completely digital machines, conceding that a digital machine which incorporates analogue transducers/pre-processing is not subject to his criticism regarding machine perception.

Dreyfus could have stopped at this point, but instead he continues with an analysis of what led researchers to greatly overestimate the prognosis of the symbolic/digital approach. In particular, he blames it on a background of Associationism, that dates back at least as far as Hume. This label may be puzzling, since his symbolist tablets tarred their connectionist opponents with the same brush. The explanation lies in the fact that all that Dreyfus means by Associationism is the belief that "*thinking must be analyzable into simple determinate operations*". He rejects arguments for the Associationist assumption as (1) based on an unscientific use of protocol statements; (2) assuming without argument that every process can be analysed into discrete computational steps; and (3) as assuming that if a behaviour *can* be analysed into discrete steps, then that is how it is generated.

Like Searle after him, Dreyfus turns the historical tables by deeming artificial intelligence research to be following in the steps of Descartes – only it is the emphasis on clear and distinct ideas, and not dualism, that makes the link (although Dreyfus confusingly cites the passage in Descartes (cf.

Volume I, Part II) that claims that machines could never behave like people).
He concludes by identifying four areas of human intelligence, only two of
which can be "programmed". In a statement that foreshadows the expert system work that would follow, he suggests that artificial intelligence might best
be conceived as a symbiosis between human and machine. Finally, the use of
the alchemical metaphor as a way to express the inchoate status of current
artificial intelligence research is echoed later in Smith's (Part I, article 49 in
this Volume) comparison of the field to pre-Newtonian physics/astrology.

Following Dreyfus and others, Winograd makes the link between modern
artificial intelligence research and the intellectual tradition of Descartes,
Leibniz and Hobbes. But making clear where this connection succeeds and
fails requires making a distinction between the object and meta levels of
artificial intelligence research, which may come apart. Thus, whereas Dreyfus
claims that the field of artificial intelligence and Descartes shared an interest
in the study of "clear and distinct ideas", this is understood as a claim about
the object level: what intelligence is. Winograd claims that the same issue
(also?) creates a discrepancy on the meta level: artificial intelligence does not
go about its business in a rationalist manner. But he also claims that there is
a similar departure from the empiricist tradition – not only on the meta level,
since the field does not employ strict empiricist criteria in going about its
work, but also on the object level: to its credit, it does not view human
cognition as logically rigid and formal (it would appear that Winograd does
not mean for his discussion to cover the logicist approach of McCarthy and
others).

Winograd's analysis of the symbolic approach as relying on emergence of
appropriate behaviour from the interaction of rules (unintentionally) casts
doubt on a standard way of distinguishing the symbolic and subsymbolic
approaches on the basis that the latter, and not the former, gives emergence a
prominent role. In particular, Minsky's Society of Mind programme (see
articles 33, and 45 in Volume II) is criticised for thinking that "conflict,
consciousness, genius and freedom of the will" will emerge from the simple
mechanisms that work for toy domains.

Winograd questions the idea of viewing knowledge as a commodity, and,
following phenomenologists such as Heidegger, denies that all knowledge,
especially tacit knowledge and skills, can be explicitly articulated in symbols.
He blames the brittleness of expert systems on the inability of the designers
to anticipate all situations, the blindness of the representations used, and the
restriction of the domains in which they operate. The inflexibility and
irresponsibility that results could be better termed a "bureaucracy of mind".

Like those he criticises, Winograd does not distinguish between communicative and cognitive representations. Thus, he sees computers as "language
machines" rather than thinking machines. But once this is recognised, their
performance can be enhanced through a proper understanding of language,
which Winograd takes to be given by hermeneutics and phenomenology

(Heidegger and Gadamer), the work of Wittgenstein, and the speech act theories of Austin, Searle and Habermas. The result is a view similar to that expressed at the end of Dreyfus' 1965 critique: computers will augment our intelligence by being sophisticated resources with which we can interact, not because they themselves think or understand.

Winograd's rejection of artificial intelligence was greatly influenced by Dreyfus' phenomenological critique. Developing the ideas in his 1965 paper *What Computers Can't Do*, Dreyfus contends that symbolic artificial intelligence is what Lakatos has termed a "degenerating research programme": a field that displays initial success in limited areas, but fails to extend this promise in a substantial and systematic way. A key argument appeals to the phenomenology of master chess playing, or of any other expert activity. Although the initial stages of competence may involve the explicit application of rules and search through symbolic spaces, by the time of attaining expert mastery there is little or nothing left of this. The phenomenology of expert performance is simply a matter of perceiving what is relevant, and acting accordingly. Thus, Dreyfus takes the view (to borrow an image from Wittgenstein's *Tractatus*) that after achieving a skill the ladder can be kicked away – a view usually used to justify symbolic approaches over more developmental or biological work.

In the introduction to the MIT press edition of the book (entitled *What Computers Still Can't Do*), Dreyfus assesses its relevance in the context of the recent developments in artificial intelligence, singling out CYC (see article 36 in Volume II and article 49 in this Volume) as the state-of-the-art in the symbolic approach. Bolstering his position with appeals to Merleau-Ponty and Bourdieu, he finds the CYC enterprise untenable for pretty much the same reasons as its predecessors. He admits that connectionism does address some of his criticisms, in that it acquires its own world view, rather than being given one by a programer. However, even the subsymbolic approach attracts his doubts. For one thing, there is the human intervention required by supervised learning, although he admits this difficulty might be avoided by using the reward-and-punishment techniques of reinforcement learning. More seriously are the problems having to do with generalisation and relevance: he speculates that a machine might have to be prohibitively similar to us before it could attend to the features of the world that would allow it to learn in a way that we could recognise as intelligent.

3 The Lighthill report

The Lighthill report had a devastating effect on the funding of artificial intelligence research in the United Kingdom and, to a lesser extent, elsewhere. Lighthill breaks the field down into its ABCs: Advanced Automation, and Computer modelling of the Central nervous system sandwiching the Bridging research of Building robots. It is this middle realm of building robots, which of the three best represents the enterprise of artificial intelligence as envisioned by this set, which Lighthill finds to be most disappointing, Winograd's groundbreaking PhD thesis not withstanding. Although he correctly identifies the well-known problem of combinatorial explosion, Lighthill's idiosyncratic characterisation of the field he is attacking weakens and misdirects his analysis; thus, the report is included here primarily for historical reference. However, Lighthill's speculation as to the motives of researchers in artificial intelligence is worth noting. The suggestion that they were motivated by a form of womb-envy may have infuriated said researchers at the time, but the comparison and contrast between artificial intelligence and childbearing is intellectually valuable, as discussed in the general introduction, regardless of whether it played or plays a conscious or subconscious role in the psychology of artificial intelligence practitioners.

Perhaps of more value is McCarthy's response to the report, in which we get an insider's view of the limitations of the field (as opposed to the concept) of artificial intelligence at the time: lack of scientific structure to research, the overemphasis on that which is currently mathematically characterisable (no longer a problem, it would seem!), unrealistic claims about the universality of new formalisms, and a lack of a comprehensive review of the field.

4 The frame problem

Workers in artificial intelligence soon stumbled across a problem of surprising generality and intractability: when acting in the world, how does an agent come to have the correct expectations that *this* will change but *that* will not? Called the "frame" problem (because the challenge is to be able to put a metaphorical frame around that which stays constant when a particular action is taken), the problem appears to be pernicious enough to threaten the very possibility of artificial intelligence. But its generality makes it less formidable in a way: since it applies not only to robots but also to humans, yet we obviously manage to overcome it, presumably an artefact could overcome it as well. But the problem seems to be a particular bugbear for the symbolic, sentential approach: the more one knows, the more sentences will be in one's knowledge base, and thus more time will have to be spent checking to see if one's knowledge is affected by a particular action or event. Yet phenomenologically, it seems that our thinking does not slow down with more knowledge – if anything, we find it easier to respond to familiar domains, taking less time to respond to changes. In his philosophical introduction to the problem, Dennett does not advance his own solution to it (he doesn't have one), but instead briefly covers the proposals of others, including the STRIPS formalism, non-monotonic logics (see the later McCarthy paper in Volume II, article 34), and, fittingly, frames. One might think that non-sentential approaches can avoid the problem, but Dreyfus' 1992 comments (article 61 in this Volume) are germane: if we are to avoid the problems of symbolism through the generalisation capacities of connectionism, how do we ensure that our networks will generalise in the right way? Whatever the solution is, it is not simply a solution to Hume's riddle of induction, as some have believed. Dennett's commentary becomes less relevant near the end, as it is revealed that the phrase "cognitive wheels" is meant to be a criticism of artificial intelligence as psychology, not as an engineering enterprise: the phrase is meant to poke fun at solutions which have no counterpart in nature. Finally, Dennett explicitly compares the task of artificial intelligence with that of the Creation (while also kicking away Wittgenstein's ladder): "After all, if God made Adam as an adult who could presumably solve the midnight snack problem *ab initio*, AI agent-creators can in principle make an 'adult' agent who is equipped with worldly knowledge *as if* it had laboriously learned all the things it needs to know."

Fodor agrees with Dennett that the frame problem is important and as yet unsolved (in artefacts, that is). It is important because it is an unavoidable side-effect of being truly intelligent in a robust way, as opposed to being able to perform fast calculations in a modularised domain. However, Fodor disagrees with Dennett concerning the relationship of the frame problem to induction: "The frame problem and the problem of formalizing our intuitions about inductive relevance are, in every important respect, THE SAME THING" (original emphasis). The upshot is that a solution to the frame problem will require philosophical work, not just code writing. But this seems to overstate the case. Even if one assumes a formalist, symbolic approach to artificial intelligence, it seems that one might be able to get a robot to solve the frame problem without formalising our intuitions about inductive relevance. That is, Fodor concedes that we reliably ignore what is irrelevant, and that this could be due to the fact that we employ concepts that, unlike his "kooky" notion of a "fridgeon" (see the text), allow one to "assume that nothing changes unless you have a special reason for changing it". The problem, Fodor claims, is that to give these concepts to a robot requires one to formalise the distinction between "kooky" facts and tractable ones "IN VIRTUE OF THE FORM OF THEIR CANONICAL REPRESENTATIONS" (original emphasis), and no one knows how to do that. But this confuses the knowledge of which concepts are good ones to use (which we do have) with the meta knowledge of what it is about those concepts that makes them so handy/allows them to support inference. Since we know that the concept "chair" works better than "fridgeon" with respect to reasoning about the world, we can give the former to a robot and not the latter, even though we do not know why "chair" is better, and more importantly even though we do not have a way of distinguishing the kosher concepts from the non-kosher ones on the basis of their canonical form alone. The canonical form must be such that it allows the robot to *act appropriately*, yes; the form need not, in addition, permit the robot to frame (sorry) the "solves the frame problem"/"does not solve the frame problem" distinction.

References

Gödel, K. (1931) "Über Formal Unentscheidbare Sätze der Principia Mathematica und Verwandter Systeme", *Monatshefte für Mathematik und Physik* 38: 173–98.

Penrose, R. (1990) *The Emperor's New Mind: Concerning Computers, Minds, and the Laws of Physics*, Oxford: Oxford University Press.

Penrose, R. (1994) *Shadows of the Mind. A Search for the Missing Science of Consciousness*, Oxford: Oxford University Press.

Turing, A.M. (1936) "On Computable Numbers, with an Application to the Entscheidungsproblem", *Proceedings of the London Mathematical Society, Series 2* 42: 230–65.

56

ARTIFICIAL INTELLIGENCE

Joseph Weizenbaum

Source: J. Weizenbaum, *Computer Power and Human Reasoning: From Judgment to Calculation*, W. H. Freeman, 1976, pp. 202–28.

When Roger Schank expressed the hope that we will be able to build a program that can learn as a child does, he was echoing words spoken by H.A. Simon over ten years earlier:

> "If GPS is a theory of how a machine can bootstrap itself into higher intelligence or how people learn language, then let it bootstrap itself, and let it learn language. This is an entirely appropriate obligation to impose . . . Not just on behalf of myself, but on behalf of the entire group of people working in the field, I accept the obligation and hope that one of us will produce the requisite programs before too long."[1]

Both Simon and Schank have thus given expression to the deepest and most grandiose fantasy that motivates work on artificial intelligence, which is nothing less than to build a machine on the model of man, a robot that is to have its childhood, to learn language as a child does, to gain its knowledge of the world by sensing the world through its own organs, and ultimately to contemplate the whole domain of human thought. (It is worth noting, though only by the way for now, that should this dream be realized, we will have a language-understanding machine but still no theory of language understanding as such, for observing a machine "learning as a child does" does not in itself constitute an understanding of the language-acquisition process).

Whether or not this program can be realized depends on whether man really is merely a species of the genus "information-processing system" or whether he is more than that. I shall argue that an entirely too simplistic notion of intelligence has dominated both popular and scientific thought, and that this notion is, in part, responsible for permitting artificial intelligence's perverse grand fantasy to grow. I shall argue that an organism is defined, in large part, by the problems it faces. Man faces problems no machine could possibly be made to face. Man is not a machine. I shall argue that, although man most certainly processes information, he does not necessarily process it in the way computers do. Computers and men are not species of the same genus.

Few "scientific" concepts have so thoroughly muddled the thinking of both scientists and the general public as that of the "intelligence quotient" or "I.Q." The idea that intelligence can be quantitatively measured along a simple linear scale has caused untold harm to our society in general, and to education in particular. It has spawned, for example, the huge educational-testing movement in the United States, which strongly influences the courses of the academic careers of millions of students and thus the degrees of certification they may attain. It virtually determines what "success" people may achieve in later life because, in the United States at least, opportunities to "succeed" are, by and large, open only to those who have the proper credentials, that is, university degrees, professional diplomas, and so on.

When modern educators argue that intelligence tests measure a subject's ability to do well in school, they mean little more than that these tests "predict" a subject's ability to pass academic-type tests. This latter ability leads, of course, to certification and then to "success." Consequently, any correlation between the results of such tests and people's "success", as that term is understood in the society at large, must necessarily be an artifact of the testing procedure. The test itself has become a criterion for that with which it is to be correlated! "Psychologists should be ashamed of themselves for promoting a view of general intelligence that has engendered such a testing program."[2]

My concern here is that the mythology that surrounds I.Q. testing has led to the widely accepted and profoundly misleading conviction that intelligence is somehow a permanent, unalterable, and culturally independent attribute of individuals (somewhat like, say, the color of their eyes), and moreover that it may even be genetically transmittable from generation to generation.

The trouble with I.Q. testing is not that it is entirely spurious, but that it is incomplete. It measures certain intellectual abilities that large, politically dominant segments of western European societies have elevated to the very stuff of human worth and hence to the *sine qua non* of success. It is incomplete in two ways: first, in that it fails to take into account that human creativity depends not only on intellect but also crucially on an interplay between intellect and other modalities of thought, such as intuition and wisdom; second, in that it characterizes intelligence as a linearly measurable phenomenon that exists independent of any frame of reference.

Einstein taught us that the idea of motion is meaningless in and of itself, that we can sensibly speak only of an object's motion relative to some frame of reference, not of any *absolute* motion of an object. When, in speaking informally, we say that a train moved, we mean that it moved relative to some fixed point on the earth. We need not emphasize this in ordinary conversation, because the earth (or our body) is to us a kind of "default" frame of reference that is implicitly assumed and understood in most informal conversation. But a physicist speaking as a physicist cannot be so sloppy. His equations of motion must contain terms specifying the coordinate system with respect to which the motion they describe takes place.

So it is with intelligence too. Intelligence is a meaningless concept in and of itself. It requires a frame of reference, a specification of a domain of thought and action, in order to make it meaningful. The reason this necessity does not strike us when we speak of intelligence in ordinary conversation is that the required frame of reference—that is, our own cultural and social setting with its characteristic domains of thought and action—is so much with us that we implicitly assume it to be understood. But our culture and our social milieu are in fact neither universal nor absolute. It therefore behooves, us, whenever we use the term "intelligence" as scientists or educators, to make explicit the domain of thought and action which renders the term intelligible.

Our own daily lives abundantly demonstrate that intelligence manifests itself only relative to specific social and cultural contexts. The most unschooled mother who cannot compose a single grammatically correct paragraph in her native language—as, indeed, many academics cannot do in theirs—constantly makes highly refined and intelligent judgments about her family. Eminent scholars confess that they don't have the kind of intelligence required to do high-school algebra. The acknowledged genius is sometimes stupid in managing his private life. Computers perform prodigious "intellectual feats," such as beating champion checker players at their own game and solving huge systems of equations, but cannot change a baby's diaper. How are these intelligences to be compared to one another? They cannot be compared.

Yet forms of the idea that intelligence is measurable along an absolute scale, hence that intelligences are comparable, have deeply penetrated current thought. This idea is responsible, at least in part, for many sterile debates about whether it is possible "in principle" to build computers more intelligent than man. Even as moderate and reasonable a psychologist as George A. Miller occasionally slips up, as when he says, "I am very optimistic about the eventual outcome of the work on machine solution of intellectual problems. Within our lifetime machines may surpass us in general intelligence."[3]

The identification of intelligence with I.Q. has severely distorted the primarily mathematical question of what computers can and cannot do into the nonsensical question of "how much" intelligence one can, again "in principle," give to a computer. And, of course, the reckless anthropomorphization of the computer now so common, especially among the artificial intelligentsia, couples easily to such simpleminded views of intelligence. This joining of an illicit metaphor to an ill-thought-out idea then breeds, and is perceived to legitimate, such perverse propositions as that, for example, a computer can be programmed to become an effective psychotherapist.

I had once hoped that it would be possible to prove that there is a limit, an upper bound, on the intelligence machines could achieve, just as Claude Shannon, the founder of modern information theory, proved that there is an upper bound on the amount of information a given information channel can transmit. Shannon proved that, for example, a specific telephone cable can carry at most a certain number of telephone conversations at any one time. However, before he could even sensibly formulate his now justly famous result, he had to have some way to quantify information. Else how could he speak of a channel's capacity to handle this "much" information but no "more"? Indeed, his design of an information measure itself constitutes an important contribution to modern science. (Given, of course, that he also founded a cogent theory within which his measure plays a decisive role.) It is now clear to me that, since we can speak of intelligence only in specific domains of thought and action, and since these domains are themselves not measurable, we can have no Shannon-like measure of intelligence and therefore no theorem of the kind I had hoped for. In plain words: we may express the wish, even the opinion, that there is a limit to the intelligence machines can attain, but we have no way of giving it precise meaning and certainly no way of proving it.

Does our inability to compute an upper bound on machine intelligence provide grounds either for the "optimistic" conclusion that "machines may surpass us in general intelligence" or for the very same "pessimistic" conclusion?* Neither. We learn instead that any argument that calls for such a conclusion, or for its denial, is itself ill-framed and therefore sterile.

These considerations shed additional light on a question alluded to in Chapter VII (p. 193), where I spoke of "objectives that are inappropriate for machines." Many people would argue that it is not reasonable to speak of machines as having objectives in the first place. But such a rhetorical quibble, if taken seriously, only begs the question, for it ignores the fact that people do in fact delegate responsibility to computers and give them objectives and purposes.

The question I am trying to pursue here is, "What human objectives and purposes may not be appropriately delegated to computers?" We can design an automatic pilot, and delegate to it the task of keeping an airplane flying on a predetermined course. That seems an appropriate thing for machines to do. It is also technically feasible to build a computer system that will interview patients applying for help at a psychiatric out-patient clinic and produce their psychiatric profiles complete with charts, graphs, and natural-language commentary. The question is not whether such a thing *can* be done, but whether it is appropriate to delegate this hitherto human function to a machine.

The artificial intelligentsia argue, as we have seen, that there is no domain of human thought over which machines cannot range. They take for granted that machines can think the sorts of thoughts a psychiatrist thinks when engaged with his patient. They argue that efficiency and cost considerations dictate that machines ought to be delegated such responsibilities. As Professor John McCarthy once put it to me during a debate, "What do judges know that we cannot tell a computer?" His answer to the question—which is really just our question again, only in different form—is, of course, "Nothing." And it is, as he then argued, perfectly appropriate for artificial intelligence to strive to build machines for making judicial decisions.

The proposition that judges and psychiatrists know nothing that we cannot tell computers follows from the much more general proposition subscribed to by the artificial intelligentsia, namely, that there is nothing at all which humans know that cannot, at least in principle, be somehow made accessible to computers.

Not all computer scientists are still so naive as to believe, as they were once charged with believing, that knowledge consists of merely some organization of "facts." The various language-understanding and vision programs, for example, store some of their knowledge in the form of assertions, i.e., axioms and theorems, and other of it in the form of processes. Indeed, in the course of planning and executing some of their complex procedures, these programs compose subprograms, that is, generate new processes, that were not explicitly supplied by human programmers. Some existing computer systems, particularly the so-called hand-eye machines, gain knowledge by directly sensing their environments. Such machines thus come to know things not only by being told them explicitly, but also by discovering them while interacting with the world. Finally, it is possible to instruct computers in certain skills, for example, how to balance a broomstick on one of its ends, by showing them how to do these things even when the instructor is himself quite incapable of verbalizing how he does the trick. The fact, then, and it *is* a fact, that humans know things which they cannot communicate in the form of spoken or written language is not by itself sufficient to establish that there is some knowledge computers cannot acquire at all.

But lest my "admission" that computers have the power to acquire knowledge in many diverse ways be taken to mean more than I intend it to mean, let me make my position very clear:

First (and least important), the ability of even the most advanced of currently existing computer systems to acquire information by means other than what Schank called "being spoon-fed" is still extremely limited. The power of existing heuristic methods for extracting knowledge even from natural-language texts directly "spoonfed" to computers rests precariously on, in Winograd's words, "the tiniest bit of relevant knowledge." It is simply absurd to believe that any currently existing computer system can come to know in any way whatever what, say, a two-year-old child knows about children's blocks.

Second, it is not obvious that all human knowledge is encodable in "information structures," however complex. A human may know, for example, just what kind of emotional impact touching another person's hand will have both on the other person and on himself. The acquisition of that knowledge is certainly not a function of the brain alone; it cannot be simply a process in which an information structure from some source in the world is transmitted to some destination in the brain. The knowledge involved is in part kinesthetic; its acquisition involves having a hand, to say the very least. There are, in other words, some things humans know by virtue of having a human body. No organism that does not have a human body can know these things in the same way humans know them. Every symbolic representation of them must lose some information that is essential for some human purposes.

Third, and the hand-touching example will do here too, there are some things people come to know only as a consequence of having been treated as human beings by other human beings. I shall say more about this in a moment.

Fourth, and finally, even the kinds of knowledge that appear superficially to be communicable from one human being to another in language alone are in fact not altogether so communicable. Claude Shannon showed that, even in abstract information theory, the "information content" of a message is not a function of the message alone but depends crucially on the state of knowledge, on the expectations, of the receiver. The message "Am arriving on 7 o'clock plane, love, Bill" has a different information content for Bill's wife, who knew he was coming home, but not on precisely what airplane, than for a girl who wasn't expecting Bill at all and who is surprised by his declaration of love.

Human language in actual use is infinitely more problematical than those aspects of it that are amenable to treatment by information theory, of course. But even the example I have cited illustrates that language involves the histories of those using it, hence the history of society, indeed, of all humanity generally. And language in human use is not merely functional in the way that computer languages are functional. It does not identify things and words only with immediate goals to be achieved or with objects to be transformed. The human use of language manifests human memory. And that is a quite different thing than the store of the computer, which has been anthropomorphized into "memory." The former gives rise to hopes and fears, for example. It is hard to see what it could mean to say that a computer hopes.

These considerations touch not only on certain technical limitations of computers, but also on the central question of what it means to be a human being and what it means to be a computer.

I accept the idea that a modern computer system is sufficiently complex and autonomous to warrant our talking about it as an organism. Given that it can both sense and affect its environment, I even grant that it can, in an extremely limited sense, be "socialized," that is, modified by its experiences with its world. I grant also that a suitably constructed robot can be made to develop a sense of itself, that it can, for example, learn to distinguish between parts of itself and objects outside of itself, that it can be made to assign a higher priority to guarding its own parts against physical damage than to similarly guarding objects external to itself, and that it can form a model of itself which could, in some sense, be considered a kind of self-consciousness. When I say therefore that I am willing to regard such a robot as an "organism," I declare my willingness to consider it a kind of animal. And I have already agreed that I see no way to put a bound on the degree of intelligence such an organism could, at least in principle, attain.

I make these stipulations, as the lawyers would call them, not because I believe that what any reasonable observer would call a socialized robot is going to be developed in the "visible future"—I do not believe that—but to avoid the unnecessary, interminable, and ultimately sterile exercise of making a catalogue of what computers will and will not be able to do, either here and now or ever. That exercise would deflect us from the primary question, namely, whether there are objectives that are not appropriately assignable to machines.

If both machines and humans are socializable, then we must ask in what way the socialization of the human must necessarily be different from that of the machine. The answer is, of course, so obvious that it makes the very asking of the question appear ludicrous, if indeed not obscene. It is a sign of the madness of our time that this issue has to be addressed at all.

Every organism is socialized by the process of dealing with problems that confront it. The very biological properties that differentiate one species from another also determine that each species will confront problems different from those faced by any other. Every species will, if only for that reason, be socialized differently. The human infant, as many observers have remarked, is born prematurely, that is, in a state of utter helplessness. Yet the infant has biological needs which, if he is to survive at all, must be satisfied by others. Indeed, many studies of orphanages have shown that more than his merely elementary physical needs must be satisfied; an infant will die if he is fed and cleaned but not, from the very beginning of his life, fondled and caressed—if, in other words, he is not treated as a human being by other human beings.[4]

A catastrophe, to use Erik Erikson's expression for it, that every human being must experience is his personal recapitulation of the biblical story of paradise. For a time the infant demands and is granted gratification of his every need, but is asked for nothing in return. Then, often after the infant has developed teeth and has bitten the breast that has fed him, the unity between him and his mother is broken. Erikson believes this universal human drama to be the ontogenetic contribution to the biblical saga of the Garden of Eden. So important is this period in the child's life that

"a drastic loss of accustomed mother love without proper substitution at this time can lead [under otherwise aggravating conditions] to acute infantile depression or to a mild but chronic state of mourning which may give a depressive undertone to the whole remainder of life. But even under the most favorable circumstances, this stage leaves a residue of a primary sense of evil and doom and of a universal nostalgia for a lost paradise."

[These early stages] "then, form in the infant the springs of the basic sense of trust and the basic sense of mistrust which remain the autogenic source of both primal hope and of doom throughout life."[5]

Thus begins the individual human's imaginative reconstruction of the world. And this world, as I said earlier, is the repository of his subjectivity, the stimulator of his consciousness, and ultimately the constructor of the apparently external forces he is to confront all his life.

"As the child's radius of awareness, co-ordination, and responsiveness expands, he meets the educative patterns of his culture, and thus learns the basic modalities of human existence, each in personally and culturally significant ways . . . *To get* . . . means to receive and to accept what is given. This is the first social modality learned in life; and it sounds simpler than it is. For the groping and unstable newborn organism learns this modality only as it learns to regulate its organ systems in accordance with the way in which the maternal environment integrates its methods of child care . . .

"The optimum total situation implied in the baby's readiness to get what is given is his mutual regulation with a mother who will permit him to develop and coordinate his means of getting as she develops and co-ordinates her means of giving . . . The mouth and the nipple seem to be the mere centers of a general aura of warmth and mutuality which are enjoyed and responded to with relaxation not only by these focal organs, but by both total organisms. The mutuality of relaxation thus developed is of prime importance for the first experience of friendly otherness. One may say . . . that in thus *getting what is given*, and in learning to *get somebody to do* for him what he wishes to have done, the baby also develops the necessary ego groundwork *to get to be* a giver."[6]

What these words of Erikson's make clear is that the initial and crucial stages of human socialization implicate and enmesh the totality of two organisms, the child and its mother, in an inseparable mutuality of service to their deepest biological and emotional needs. And out of this problematic reunification of mother and child—problematic because it involves inevitably the trauma of separation—emerge the foundations of the human's knowledge of what it means to give and to receive, to trust and to mistrust, to be a friend and to have a friend, and to have a sense of hope and a sense of doom.

Earlier, when speaking of theories (p. 140), I said that no term of a theory can ever be fully and finally understood. We may say the same thing about words generally, especially about such words as trust and friendship and hope and their derivatives. Erikson teaches us that such words derive their meanings from universal, primal human experiences, and that any understanding of them must always be fundamentally metaphoric. This profound truth also informs us that man's entire understanding of his world, since it is mediated by his language, must always and necessarily be bounded by metaphoric descriptions. And since the child "meets the educative patterns of his culture," as Erikson says, "and thus learns the basic modalities of human existence, each in personally and culturally-significant ways," each culture, indeed, each individual in a culture, understands such words and language, hence the world, in a culturally and personally idiosyncratic way.

I could go on to describe the later stages of the socialization of the individual human, the effects of schooling, marriage, imprisonment, warfare, hates and loves, the experiences of shame and guilt that vary so radically among the cultures of man, and so on. But that could be of no help to anyone who is not already convinced that any "understanding" a computer may be said to possess, hence any "intelligence" that may be attributed to it, can have only the faintest relation to human understanding and human intelligence. We, however, conclude that however much intelligence computers may attain, now or in the future, theirs must always be an intelligence *alien* to genuine human problems and concerns.

Still, the extreme or hardcore wing of the artificial intelligentsia will insist that the whole man, to again use Simon's expression, is after all an information processor, and that an information-processing theory of man must therefore be adequate to account for his behavior in its entirety. We may agree with the major premise without necessarily drawing the indicated conclusion. We have already observed that a portion of the information the human "processes" is kinesthetic, that it is "stored" in his muscles and joints. It is simply not clear that such information, and the processing associated with it, can be represented in the form of computer programs and data structures at all.

It may, of course, be argued that it is in principle possible for a computer to simulate the entire network of cells that constitutes the human body. But that would introduce a theory of information processing entirely different from any which has so far been advanced. Besides, such a simulation would result in "behavior" on such an incredibly long-time scale that no robot built on such principles could possibly interact with human beings. Finally, there appears to be no prospect whatever that mankind will know enough neuro-physiology within the next several hundred years to have the intellectual basis for designing such a machine. We may therefore dismiss such arguments.

There is, however, still another assumption that information-processing modelers of man make that may be false, and whose denial severely under-mines their program: that there exists one and only one class of information processes, and that every member of that class is reducible to the kind of information processes exemplified by such systems as GPS and Schank-like language-understanding formalisms. Yet every human being has the impres-sion that he thinks at least as much by intuition, hunch, and other such informal means as he does "systematically," that is by means such as logic. Questions like "Can a computer have original ideas? Can it compose a meta-phor or a symphony or a poem?" keep cropping up. It is as if the folk wis-dom knows the distinction between computer thought and the kind of thought people ordinarily engage in. The artificial intelligentsia, of course, do not believe there need be any distinction. They smile and answer "unproven."

Within the last decade or so, however, neurological evidence has begun to accumulate that suggests there may be a scientific basis to the folk wisdom.[7] It has long been known that the human brain consists of two so-called hemi-spheres that appear, superficially at least, to be identical. These two halves, which we will call LH (Left Hemisphere) and RH (Right Hemisphere), have, however, quite distinct functions. In righthanded people—and for simplicity, we can restrict our discussion to them—the LH may be said, at least roughly, to control the right half of the body, and the RH the left half. (Actually, the connectivities are somewhat more complex, particularly between the two brain halves and the eyes, but I will not go into such details here.) Most importantly, the two halves of the brain appear to have two quite distinct modalities of thought. The LH thinks, so to speak, in an orderly, sequential, and, we might call it, logical fashion. The RH, on the other hand, appears to think in terms of holistic images. Language processing appears to be almost exclusively centered in the LH, for example, whereas the RH is deeply involved in such tasks as spatial orientation, and the production and appreciation of music.

The distinct functions of the hemispheres of the brain began to be dramat-ically illustrated by patients who, after suffering from extremely severe forms of epilepsy, had their two brain halves surgically separated. In normal people, the two hemispheres are connected by a part of the brain called the corpus callosum. When this is cut, no direct communication between the two halves remains possible. It was found that when a so-called split-brain patient's hands were visually hidden from him and he was given, say, a pencil in his left hand, he could not say what had been given to him, but he could *show* that it was a pencil by drawing a picture of it or by selecting a picture of a pencil from among pictures of many different objects. However, when the experiment was repeated, only with the right hand receiving the pencil, then he could say it was a pencil but could not produce or recognize its pictorial representation. In the first situation, the RH received the "image" of the pencil and was able to encode it into pictorial representations, but not into linguistic structures. In the second, the LH received the "image" of the pencil and was able to encode it linguistically, but not pictorially.

There is also considerable evidence, which I will not detail here, that the RH is essentially the seat of intuition, and that it thinks quite independently of the LH. One way of characterizing intuitive thought is to say that, although it is logical, the standards of evidence it uses to make judgments are very different from the standards we normally associate with logical thought. In ordinary discourse, for example, when we say that two things are the same, we mean that they are identical in almost every respect; the standard of evidence we demand to justify such a judgment is extremely demanding. But when we construct a metaphor, e.g., the overseas Chinese are the Jews of the Orient, we pronounce two things to be the same in a very different sense. Metaphors are simply not logical; when taken literally, they are patently absurd. The RH, in other words, has criteria of absurdity that are far different from those of the logical LH.

The history of man's creativity is filled with stories of artists and scientists who, after working hard and long on some difficult problem, consciously decide to "forget" it, in effect, to turn it over to their RH. After some time, often with great suddenness and totally unexpectedly, the solution to their problem announces itself to them in almost complete form. The RH appears to have been able to overcome the most difficult logical and systematic problems by, I would conjecture, relaxing the rigid standards of thought of the LH. Given the looser standards the RH employs, it was perhaps able to design thought experiments which the LH simply could not, because of its rigidity, conceive. The RH is thus able to hit upon solutions which could then, of course, be recast into strictly logical terms by the LH. We may conjecture that in children the communication channel between the two brain halves is wide open; that is, that messages pass between the two halves quite freely. That may be why children are so incredibly imaginative; e.g., for them a cigar box is an automobile one moment and a house the next. In adults, the channel has been severely narrowed—whether by education or by physiological maturational processes or by both, I cannot guess. But it is clearly more open during the dream state. I may also conjecture that psychoanalysis, quite apart from its function as psychotherapy, trains people in the use of the channel. In *psychoanalysis* one learns, in Theodore Reik's happy phrase, to listen with the third ear, to attend, that is, to what the unconscious is "saying." Perhaps the various meditative disciplines serve the same purpose.

These are clearly conjectures, from which we are not entitled to draw any conclusions about how either humans or computers process information. Even as a mere possibility, however, they do raise a serious question about the universality of the mode of information processing we normally associate with logical thought and with computer programs.

That the right hemisphere of the brain is, loosely speaking, the "seat of intuition" is a hypothesis in favor of which evidence appears to be accumulating. Neither philosophers nor psychologists have yet been sufficiently persuaded by the existing evidence to confidently incorporate this hypothesis into their theories of mind. But this much is firmly established: the two hemispheres of the human brain think independently of one another; they think simultaneously; and they think in modes different from one another. Furthermore, we can say something about these two distinct modes.

The great mathematician Henri Poincaré, in his celebrated essay *Mathematical Creation*,[8] wrote

> "The conscious self is narrowly limited, and as for the subliminal self we know not its limitations . . . calculations . . . must be made in the . . . period of conscious work, that which follows the inspiration, that in which one verifies the results of this inspiration and deduces their consequences. The rules of these calculations are strict and complicated. They require discipline, attention, will, and therefore consciousness. In the subliminal self, on the contrary, reigns what I should call liberty, if we might give this name to the simple absence of discipline . . . the privileged unconscious phenomena, those susceptible of becoming conscious, are those which, directly or indirectly, affect most profoundly our emotional sensibility. . . . The role of this unconscious work in mathematical invention appears to me incontestable, and traces of it would be found in other cases where it is less evident."

Of course, Poincaré, writing at the beginning of the twentieth century, knew nothing of the findings of the now-active brain researchers. And we are jumping to a conclusion when we identify what he calls the conscious and the subliminal selves with the left and right hemispheres of the brain, respectively. But our assertion here is that there are two distinct modes of human thought that operate independently and simultaneously. And that assertion Poincaré supports.

A most highly respected scientist who is now working, the psychologist Jerome Bruner, writes on this same topic from a slightly different perspective (recall that the right hand corresponds to the left hemisphere and the left hand to the right, or "intuitive," hemisphere):

> "As a right-handed psychologist, I have been diligent for fifteen

years in the study of the cognitive processes: how we acquire, retain, and transform knowledge of the world in which each of us lives—a world in part 'outside' us, in part 'inside.' The tools I have used have been those of the scientific psychologist studying perception, memory, learning, thinking, and (like a child of my times) I have addressed my inquiries to the laboratory rat as well as to human beings. At times, indeed, I have adopted the role of the clinician and carried out therapy with children. . . . There have been times when, somewhat discouraged by the complexities of the psychology of knowing, I have sought to escape through neurophysiology, to discover that the neurophysiologist can help only in the degree to which we can ask intelligent psychological questions of him.

"One thing has become increasingly clear in pursuing the nature of knowing. It is that the conventional apparatus of the psychologist—both his instruments of investigation and the conceptual tools he uses in the interpretation of his data—leaves one approach unexplored. It is an approach whose medium of exchange seems to be the metaphor paid out by the left hand. It is a way that grows happy hunches and 'lucky' guesses, that is stirred into connective activity by the poet and the necromancer looking sidewise rather than directly. Their hunches and intuitions generate a grammar of their own—searching out connections, suggesting similarities, weaving ideas loosely in a trial web . . .

"[The psychologist] too searches widely and metaphorically for his hunches. He reads novels, looks at and even paints pictures, is struck by the power of myth, observes his fellow men intuitively and with wonder. In doing so, he acts only part-time like a proper psychologist, racking up cases against the criteria derived from hypothesis. Like his fellows, he observes the human scene with such sensibility as he can muster in the hope that his insight will be deepened. If he is lucky or if he has subtle psychological intuition, he will from time to time come up with hunches, combinatorial products of his metaphoric activity. If he is not fearful of these products of his own subjectivity, he will go so far as to tame the metaphors that have produced the hunches, tame them in the sense of shifting them from the left hand to the right hand by rendering them into notions that can be tested. It is my impression from observing myself and my colleagues that the forging of metaphoric hunch into testable hypothesis goes on all the time."[9]

That, of course, is my impression as well. Here Bruner speaks explicitly of the left hand, that is, the right hemisphere of the brain, as the artistic, the intuitive, and so on, and of the right hand, the left brain hemisphere, as the "conventional apparatus of the psychologist," and he speaks of the inadequacy of his "conceptual tools."

We learn from the testimony of hundreds of creative people, as well as from our own introspection, that the human creative act always involves the conscious interpretation of messages coming from the unconscious, the shifting of ideas from the left hand to the right, in Bruner's phrase.

The unconscious is, of course, unconscious. It is like a seething, stormy sea within us. Its waves lap on the borders of our consciousness. And what we learn from it or about it, we construct from inferences we make about the meanings of the swells and surges, the breakers and ripples that wash the fringes of our consciousness. Occasionally we wander more deeply into the surf, as when we are in that semi-hypnagogic trance that divides sleep from wakefulness. But then we experience only chaos. Our thought modalities are maximally confused. And if we rip ourselves into waking, we cannot tell, we cannot translate or transform into linguistic modalities, what we had thought.

Does not the undoubted reality of this confusion, when placed alongside all the other available evidence to which I have alluded, lend weight to the altogether plausible conjecture that the forms of information manipulated in the right hemisphere of the brain, as well as the corresponding information processes, are simply different from those of the left hemisphere? And may it not be that we can in principle come to know those strange information forms and processes only in terms that are fundamentally irrelevant to the kind of understanding we seek? When, in the distant future, we come to know in detail how the brain functions on the neurophysiological level, we will, of course, be able to give an ultimately reductionist account of the functioning of the right hemisphere. But that would not be understanding in the sense we mean here, anymore than detailed knowledge of the electrical behavior of a running computer is, or even leads to, an understanding of the program the computer is running. On the other hand, a higher-level account of the functioning of the right hemisphere may always miss its most essential features, namely, those that differentiate it from the functioning of the left hemisphere. For we are constrained by our left-hemisphere thought modalities to always interpret messages coming from the right in left-hemisphere terms.

Perhaps the LH modality of thought is GPS-like, which is to say only that perhaps it can in principle be somehow formulated (not that GPS is even a candidate for a possible formulation). Perhaps it converts a problem like

Tom has twice as many fish as Mary has guppies. If Mary has three guppies, how many fish does Tom have?

into its own terms, for example into

$$x = 2y; y = 3,$$

and solves it using information processing and symbol-manipulation techniques characteristic of GPS-like "thought." But it is then not possible for such a mechanism to have any idea of what fishes and guppies are, or of what it can mean to be a boy named Tom, and so on. Nor can the symbolic representation of the given problem be reconverted into the original problem statement. But human problem solving, perhaps even of the apparently most routine and mechanical variety, involves both left and right modes of thought. And certainly, direct human communication crucially involves the two hemispheres.

It is much too easy, especially for computer scientists, to be hypnotized by the "fact" that linguistic utterances are representable as linear strings of symbols. From this "fact" it is easy to deduce that linguistic communication is entirely a left-hemisphere affair. But human speech also has melody, and its song communicates as well as its libretto. Music is the province of the right hemisphere, as is the appreciation of gestures. As for written communication, its function is surely, at least in large part, to stimulate and excite especially the auditory imaginations of both the writer and the reader.

We may never know whether the conjecture that a part of us thinks in terms of symbolic structures that can be only sensed but not usefully explicated is true or false. Scientists, of course, abhor hypotheses that appear not to be falsifiable. Yet it may be that, under some profound conception of truth, the hypothesis is true. Perhaps it helps to explain why we remain lifelong strangers to ourselves and to each other, why every word in our lexicon is enveloped in at least some residual mystery, and why every attempt to solve life's problems by entirely rational means always fails.

But the inference that I here wish to draw from my conjecture is that, since we cannot know that it is false any more than that it is true, we are not entitled to the hubris so bombastically exhibited by the artificial intelligentsia. Even calculating reason compels the belief that we must stand in awe of the mysterious spectacle that is the whole man—I would even add, that is the whole ant.

There was a time when physics dreamed of explaining the whole of physical reality in terms of one comprehensive formalism. Leibnitz taught that if we knew the position and velocity of every elementary particle in the universe, we could predict the universe's whole future course. But then Werner Heisenberg proved that the very instruments man must use in order to measure physical phenomena disturb those phenomena, and that it is therefore impossible in principle to know both the exact position and the velocity of even a single elementary particle. He did not thereby falsify Leibnitz's conjecture. But he did show that its major premise was unattainable. That, of course, was sufficient to shatter the Leibnitzian dream. Only a little later, Kurt Gödel exposed the shakiness of the foundations of mathematics and logic itself by proving that every interesting formal system has some statements whose truth or falsity cannot be decided by the formal means of the system itself, in other words, that mathematics must necessarily be forever incomplete. It follows from this and others of Gödel's results that "The human mind is incapable of formulating (or mechanizing) all its mathematical intuitions. I.e.: If it has succeeded in formulating some of them, this very fact yields new intuitive knowledge."[10]

Both Heisenberg's so-called uncertainty principle and Gödel's incompleteness theorem sent terrible shock-waves through the worlds of physics, mathematics, and philosophy of science. But no one stopped working. Physicists, mathematicians, and philosophers more or less gracefully accepted the undeniable truth that there are limits to how far the world can be comprehended in Leibnitzian terms alone.

Much too much has already been made of the presumed implications of Heisenberg's and Gödel's results for artificial intelligence. I do not wish to contribute to that discussion here. But there is a sense in which psychology and artificial intelligence may usefully follow the example of the new-found humility of modern mathematics and physics: they should recognize that "while the constraints and limitations of logic do not exert their force on the things of the world, they do constrain and limit what are to count as defensible descriptions and interpretations of things."[11] Were they to recognize that, they could then take the next liberating step of also recognizing that truth is not equivalent to formal provability.

The lesson I have tried to teach here is not that the human mind is subject to Heisenberg uncertainties—though it may be—and that we can therefore never wholly comprehend it in terms of the kinds of reduction to discrete phenomena Leibnitz had in mind. The lesson here is rather that the part of the human mind which communicates to us in rational and scientific terms is itself an instrument that disturbs what it observes, particularly its voiceless partner, the unconscious, between which and our conscious selves it mediates. Its constraints and limitations circumscribe what are to constitute rational—again, if you will, scientific—descriptions and interpretations of the things of the world. These descriptions can therefore never be whole, anymore than a musical score can be a whole description or interpretation of even the simplest song.

But, and this is the saving grace of which an insolent and arrogant scientism attempts to rob us, we come to know and understand not only by way of the mechanisms of the conscious. We are capable of listening with the third ear, of sensing living truth that is truth beyond any standards of provability. It is *that* kind of understanding, and the kind of intelligence that is derived from it, which I claim is beyond the abilities of computers to simulate.

We have the habit, and it is sometimes useful to us, of speaking of man, mind, intelligence, and other such universal concepts. But gradually, even slyly, our own minds become infected with what A. N. Whitehead called the fallacy of misplaced concreteness. We come to believe that these theoretical terms are ultimately interpretable as observations, that in the "visible future" we will have ingenious instruments capable of measuring the "objects" to which these terms refer. There is, however, no such thing as mind; there are only individual minds, each belonging, not to "man," but to individual human beings. I have argued that intelligence cannot be measured by ingeniously constructed meter sticks placed along a one-dimensional continuum. Intelligence can be usefully discussed only in terms of domains of thought and action. From this I derive the conclusion that it cannot be useful, to say the least, to base serious work on notions of "how much" intelligence may be given to a computer. Debates based on such ideas—e.g., "Will computers ever exceed man in intelligence?"—are doomed to sterility.

I have argued that the individual human being, like any other organism, is defined by the problems he confronts. The human is unique by virtue of the fact that he must necessarily confront problems that arise from his unique biological and emotional needs. The human individual is in a constant state of becoming. The maintenance of that state, of his humanity, indeed, of his survival, depends crucially on his seeing himself, and on his being seen by other human beings, as a human being. No other organism, and certainly no computer, can be made to confront genuine human problems in human terms. And, since the domain of human intelligence is, except for a small set of formal problems, determined by man's humanity, every other intelligence, however great, must necessarily be alien to the human domain.

I have argued that there is an aspect to the human mind, the unconscious, that cannot be explained by the information-processing primitives, the elementary information processes, which we associate with formal thinking, calculation, and systematic rationality. Yet we are constrained to use them for scientific explanation, description, and interpretation. It behooves us, therefore, to remain aware of the poverty of our explanations and of their strictly limited scope. It is wrong to assert that any scientific account of the "whole man" is possible. There are some things beyond the power of science to fully comprehend.

The concept of an intelligence alien to certain domains of thought and action is crucial for understanding what are perhaps the most important limits on artificial intelligence. But that concept applies to the way humans relate to one another as well as to machines and their relation to man. For human socialization, though it is grounded in the biological constitution common to all humans, is strongly determined by culture. And human cultures differ radically among themselves. Countless studies confirm what must be obvious to all but the most parochial observers of the human scene: "The influence of culture is universal in that in some respects a man learns to

329

become like all men; and it is particular in that a man who is reared in one society learns to become in some respects like all men of his society and not like those of others."[12] The authors of this quotation, students of Japanese society who lived among the Japanese for many years, go on to make the following observations:

"In normal family life in Japan there is an emphasis on interdependence and reliance on others, while in America the emphasis is on independence and self-assertion. . . . In Japan the infant is seen more as a separate biological organism who from the beginning, in order to develop, needs to be drawn into increasingly interdependent relations with others. In America, the infant is seen more as a dependent biological organism who, in order to develop, needs to be made increasingly independent of others.

"The Japanese baby seems passive, and he lies quietly with occasional unhappy vocalizations, while his mother, in her care, does more lulling, carrying, and rocking of her baby. She seems to try to soothe and quiet the child, and to communicate with him physically rather than verbally. On the other hand, the American infant is more active, happily vocal, and exploring of his environment, and his mother, in her care, does more looking at and chatting to her baby. She seems to stimulate the baby to activity and to vocal response. It is as if the American mother wanted to have a vocal, active baby, and the Japanese mother wanted to have a quiet, contented baby. In terms of styles of caretaking of the mothers in the two cultures, they get what they apparently want . . . a great deal of cultural learning has taken place by three-to-four months of age . . . babies have learned by this time to be Japanese and American babies in relation to the expectations of their mothers concerning their behavior.

"[Adult] Japanese are more 'group' oriented and interdependent in their relations with others, while Americans are more 'individual' oriented and independent . . . Japanese are more self-effacing and passive in contrast to Americans, who appear more self-assertive and aggressive. . . . Japanese are more sensitive to, and make conscious use of, many forms of nonverbal communication in human relations through the medium of gestures and physical proximity in comparison with Americans, who predominantly use verbal communication within a context of physical separateness.

"If these distinct patterns of behavior are well on the way to being learned by three-to-four months of age, and if they continue over the life span of the person, then there are very likely to be important areas of difference in emotional response in people of one culture when compared with those in another. Such differences are not easily

330

subject to conscious control and, largely out of awareness, they accent and color human behavior. These differences . . . can also add to bewilderment and antagonism when people try to communicate across the emotional barriers of culture."[13]

Such profound differences in early training crucially affect the entire societies involved. And they are, of course, transmitted from one generation to the next and thus perpetuated. They must necessarily also help determine what members of the two societies know about their worlds, what are to be taken as "universal" cultural norms and values, hence what in each culture is and is not to be counted as fact. They determine, for example (and this is particularly relevant to the contrast between Japanese and American social norms), what are private as opposed to public conflicts, and hence what modes of adjudication are appropriate to the defense of what human interests. The Japanese traditionally prefer to settle disputes, even those for which relief at law is statutorily available, by what Westerners would see as informal means. Actually, these means are most often themselves circumscribed by stringent ritualistic requirements that are nowhere explicitly codified but are known to every Japanese of the appropriate social class. This sort of knowledge is acquired with the mother's milk and through the whole process of socialization that is itself so intimately tied to the individual's acquisition of his mother tongue. It cannot be learned from books; it cannot be explicated in any form but life itself.

An American judge, therefore, no matter what his intelligence and fair-mindedness, could not sit in a Japanese family court. His intelligence is simply alien to the problems that arise in Japanese culture. The United States Supreme Court actively recognized this while it still had jurisdiction over distant territories. For example, in the case of Diaz v. Gonzales, which was originally tried in Puerto Rico, the court refused to set aside the judgment of the court of original jurisdiction, that is, of the native court. Justice Oliver W. Holmes, writing the opinion of the Court, stated,

> "This Court has stated many times the deference due to understanding of the local courts upon matters of purely local concern. This is especially true when dealing with the decisions of a Court inheriting and brought up in a different system from that which prevails here. When we contemplate such a system from the outside it seems like a wall of stone, every part even with all the others, except so far as our own local education may lead us to see subordinations to which we are accustomed. But to one brought up within it, varying emphasis, tacit assumptions, unwritten practices, a thousand influences gained only from life, may give to the different parts wholly new values that logic and grammar never could have got from the books."[14]

Every human intelligence is thus alien to a great many domains of thought and action. There are vast areas of authentically human concern in every culture in which no member of another culture can possibly make responsible decisions. It is not that the outsider is unable to decide at all—he can always flip coins, for example—it is rather that the *basis* on which he would have to decide must be inappropriate to the context in which the decision is to be made.

What could be more obvious than the fact that, whatever intelligence a computer can muster, however it may be acquired, it must always and necessarily be absolutely alien to any and all authentic human concerns? The very asking of the question, "What does a judge (or a psychiatrist) know that we cannot tell a computer?" is a monstrous obscenity. That it has to be put into print at all, even for the purpose of exposing its morbidity, is a sign of the madness of our times.

Computers can make judicial decisions, computers can make psychiatric judgments. They can flip coins in much more sophisticated ways than can the most patient human being. The point is that they *ought* not be given such tasks. They may even be able to arrive at "correct" decisions in some cases—but always and necessarily on bases no human being should be willing to accept.

There have been many debates on "Computers and Mind." What I conclude here is that the relevant issues are neither technological nor even mathematical; they are ethical. They cannot be settled by asking questions beginning with "can." The limits of the applicability of computers are ultimately statable only in terms of oughts. What emerges as the most elementary insight is that, since we do not now have any ways of making computers wise, we ought not now to give computers tasks that demand wisdom.

Notes

* The optimist says, "This is the best of all possible worlds!" The pessimist answers, "That's right."

1 In M. Greenberger, ed., *Management and the Computer of the Future* (Cambridge, Mass.: The M.I.T. Press, 1962), p. 123.

2 David C. McClelland, "Testing for Competence Rather Than for 'Intelligence,'" *American Psychologist*, vol. 28, no. 1 (January 1973), pp. 1–14.

3 From Greenberger, *op. cit.*, p. 118.

4 See especially the work of R. A. Spitz, "Hospitalism," in *Psychoanalytic Study of the Child*, vol. 1, 1945.

5 E. Erikson, *Childhood and Society* (New York: W. W. Norton, 2d ed., 1963), pp. 79, 80.

6 *Ibid.*, pp. 75–76.

7 For an account of the findings in this area, see Robert E. Ornstein, *The Psychology of Consciousness* (San Francisco, Calif.: W. H. Freeman and Co., 1972). Chapter III is particularly relevant to the present discussion. It is written in plain English. The references it cites open the door to the entire area of research.

8 Reprinted in *The World of Mathematics* (New York: Simon and Schuster, 1956), vol. IV, pp. 2041–2050. This important essay is very much worth a trip to the library, as is the set of volumes in which it appears.

9 J. Bruner, *On Knowing* (New York: Atheneum, 1973), pp. 3–5.

10 H. Wang, *From Mathematics to Philosophy* (New York: Humanities Press, 1974), p. 324. Kurt Gödel himself referred to this in December 1951 as one of "the two most interesting rigorously proved results about minds and machines." The other is that either there exist certain formal questions which neither humans nor machines can answer, or the human mind can answer some formal questions that machines cannot.

11 D. C. Denett, "The Abilities of Men and Machines." Paper delivered to the American Philosophical Association, December 29, 1970.

12 W. Caudill and H. Weinstein, "Maternal Care and Infant Behavior in Japan and in America," reprinted in C. S. Lavatelli and F. Stendler, eds., *Readings in Child Behavior and Development* (New York: Harcourt Brace Jovanovich, 3d ed., 1972), p. 78.

13 *Ibid.*, pp. 80 *et seq.*

14 Diaz v. Gonzales, 261 U.S. 102 (1923), Per Holmes, O. W. I owe this reference to Professor Paul Freund of the Law School of Harvard University.

57

PANEL DISCUSSION

Has artificial intelligence research illuminated human thinking?

Heinz R. Pagels

Panel Members: H. L. Dreyfus, J. McCarthy, M. L. Minsky, S. Papert and J. Searle

Source: H. Pagels, *Computer Culture: The Scientific, Intellectual and Social Impact of the Computer*, Annals of the New York Academy of Sciences, 1984, pp. 138–60.

H. R. PAGELS [*The New York Academy of Sciences*, New York, N.Y.]: A few years ago, I asked a colleague of mine at Harvard what was the future of artificial intelligence. He simply said: "Heinz, if you took the smartest two dozen people of the eleventh century and put them in a room together and instructed them to put together a model of the physical universe, there's no question that they would come out with something that would be absolutely brilliant. But it would be all wrong, because the concepts were not to be invented until several centuries in the future. That's similar to the case for the AI proponents—they are very smart people, but the right concepts are not yet available."

People who work in artificial intelligence research have to contend with critics of that kind, and I'm sure we'll hear a good deal about that. I once asked Marvin Minsky why this field of study was ever called artificial intelligence. I said, "Why didn't you call it something more general, like cognitive science?" And Marvin responded: "If we ever called it anything other than artificial intelligence, we wouldn't have gotten into the universities. Now that we're in, and the philosophers and the psychologists know that we're the enemy, it's too late."

Some of the topics we're going to discuss here revolve around the issue of consciousness. There is a problem with regard to consciousness which can be stated very simply. I know that I'm conscious. I'm a thinking, experiencing being. I can close my eyes and think; I can dream; I know that I'm conscious. But as philosophers have shown in debate over the centuries, there's absolutely no way that I can prove to you that I am a conscious being. You wouldn't know, for example, that I wasn't a mindless machine put together molecule by molecule by an extraterrestrial civilization and sent here to confound you. Even if you knew what was going on in every single neuron in my brain, you could not prove that I was a conscious being.

Some people on this panel may contest that, but the real question is, Can we determine whether or not machines are conscious? Many decades ago Alan Turing addressed that question and came up with the famous Turing test, a purely behavioral model, and I'm sure some of the panelists here will allude to that test.

I want to emphasize that artificial intelligence does not have to do with the technology—with the microchips and the miracles being performed by electronics engineers. Artificial intelligence as viewed by its proponents is really a philosophy, almost "the world view." And in many ways, it's competing with other, older world views and confronting philosophical problems that have been with us for a long time.

I want to point out that the speakers are not divided into two classes—those in favor of AI and those in opposition. The individuals who are here all differ among themselves. At this point each of our panelists will very briefly describe his position and outlook on artificial intelligence and the question before us: "Has AI research illuminated human thinking?" And then we will engage in an open discussion. Professor Minsky will begin.

M. MINSKY [*Artificial Intelligence Laboratory, Massachusetts Institute of Technology, Cambridge, Mass.*]: I believe the question that we're trying to discuss is, If you made a machine that looks as if it thinks, would it really think? And there are two parts to that. There's the "if"—Can you make a machine that appears to be intelligent? We don't know the answer to that of course, but I think it will be yes, and that after a long time, when we solve such problems as commonsense reasoning and representation of knowledge, the computer programs and machines that are built according to those principles will get smarter and smarter and more lifelike in some ways.

Then there are other issues about how similar the machines will be to humans and how much they'll resemble us. There's another question yet, which is, What does it feel like inside them? These issues are complicated. For example, one of the things that I've worked on recently is the theory of jokes and humor. Many people will say they can see how you could make a machine intelligent, but not how you could make it understand humor or fear. Well, those people are wrong. They can't see how to make a machine intelligent, yet they think somehow that it's easy and that it's the emotional aspects that are difficult. This just isn't true; it's a major superstition of our culture that feeling an emotion is very deep and hard and difficult to understand, whereas intellect—how we get ideas, how we think—is easy to understand. In that perspective, many of the issues that we're about to discuss here will seem silly to me because they're missing the point of what's hard.

Say, somebody tells you he just got an idea. He could build a car with eight wheels and it would go over bumps easier. Instead of criticizing the idea, suppose you ask him how he got that idea. What will he say? He might say it just popped into his head or he just thought of it, or it came to him. Isn't that shocking? Yet if he says he feels bad and you ask him why, then he'll tell you something pretty interesting and simple—"Well this room I went into reminded me of the one that my sick friend was in." He'll tell you why he felt. I believe that's why Freud worked on emotions, not because he thought they were deeper, but because he thought they were shallower.

So everybody's got it wrong. It seems to me that we understand emotions rather well. But when it comes to ideas, my image is that people see themselves living in a world of thoughts with a brain that has an almost impermeable shield around it, but that every now and then some idea leaks through and gets in—and that's about it. The problem with these people who say that you could make a machine think but it wouldn't really feel like us is that they don't seem to have thought about the real problem. I'll end with that.

S. PAPERT (*Artificial Intelligence Laboratory, Massachusetts Institute of Technology, Cambridge, Mass.*): The question that I would like to talk about is, Has what's been done in artificial intelligence led to deeper understanding of better ways to think about human intelligence? And by human intelligence I mean everything that happens in the human mind, in the broad sense to include jokes and feelings as much as reasoning.

First, I want to make the distinction that the question of whether artificial intelligence has illuminated human intelligence is very different from the question of how intelligent machines really are or ever will be, or whether they work the same as people do, and so on. It's quite clear, for example, that one way to illuminate human intelligence is by contrast. In a sense it could well be that the more machines think in different ways from people, the more valuable they will be as means of illuminating our understanding of ourselves. To understand something, you want to know what else it's like, but you also want to know what else it's different from.

Clearly, until very recently, attempts to understand the human mind in terms of what it's different from have been of two types: one is by comparison with animals, and the other by comparison with various mythical, invented beings such as gods and other mythical creatures.

We now have a third point of comparison, namely, computers. And I do think that, at the very least, we have been led to be much more precise in a lot of the thinking about our own minds by having this new point of comparison, by being able to discuss whether we are like or unlike these machines, irrespective of whether the answer is yes or no.

I would push that a little further and say that one of the effects of artificial intelligence has been to introduce more structure into our thinking about human thinking. Because if you think of thinking only as one kind of thing, you can't get your teeth into very much. To be specific, what I think is probably the best-developed, detailed attempt to make a theory of human thinking that actually matches the way people think is Newell and Simon's attempts to simulate the solving of certain puzzles and the playing of chess. Well is this a good model of how people think?

There's a terrible pun in that. I believe it's pretty obvious what the answer is, that sometimes people think like Newell and Simon describe and sometimes, most often, not. I don't believe I'm thinking like that now, for example. But the fact that they have described this particular model of one particular way of thinking in a lot of detail means I can talk in a much more dense and technical way about other ways of thinking and so put more structure into comparative ways of thinking. This is the most fruitful way in which AI has illuminated human intelligence, by enabling us to be more specific about different ways in which the mind might work. Before AI, there was very little structured classification of ways of thinking.

I would like to push that in another direction. I take it that the question Has artificial intelligence illuminated the human intelligence? means Has AI acted as a searchlight for psychologists or other people to understand better how human intelligence works? But you could twist those same words around and ask whether it has made human intelligence work any better than it did before. I believe that this might be as much of a contribution of artificial intelligence to the world as the making of robots. I've seen some examples of this working with children. Giving children very simple AI models—extremely simple models of how the thought process works in certain situations—enables them to think more clearly about their own thinking and so be more critical about themselves and so be more constructive in taking the next step further. I choose and emphasize this example of children because I think it pushes to an extreme a remark I made at the beginning. These models of thinking that we give to these children have no pretention to be universal and complete models of how the mind works. They are only a little theoretical model that captures enough of what's happening there for you to think about it.

Now ultimately all theoretical models are of that sort. By simplifying reality and pulling out some aspect of it that you really want to think about now, they enable you to think better about reality. And I do think that artificial intelligence has done this quite irrespective of whether we think that present machines are suitable models for the whole human intelligence (which they certainly aren't), or even of whether we think they ever will be. That's the main point I wanted to make to take some sort of position for discussion.

I would now like to make a brief comment on a point raised by Marvin Minsky about whether feelings are harder to understand than thinking. I'd like to make two remarks about that. The first is that, when he expressed such an unpopular position, it reminded me that we are all very inhibited and often embarrassed about expressing what we really think about our own minds and what goes on in them. I believe this very much colors discussion on these issues and that, very likely, the attempt to make explicit models breaks down these inhibitions. This is another way in which AI is helping, by provoking us to let people see more into how we think and lay it out more than we used to.

The second is that I don't think emotions are harder to understand than ideas are, but consider the following. If you made a machine that simulated intelligence, I think it's obvious that we could argue about whether it is intelligent. And I think that most people would go along with the assumption that simulated intelligence is at least some kind of intelligence. I'm going to contrast this with the question that simulated feelings are in a very different state, that is, whereas most people would go along with the statement that simulated thinking is thinking, simulated reason is reason, most people would have serious doubts about whether to go along with the statement that simulated feelings are feelings. And yet I think this difference, which is a matter of house psychology, has very little to do with the substance of what machines can do and what they can't do.

J. McCarthy (*Department of Computer Science, Stanford University, Stanford Calif.*): The question is whether AI has illuminated human intelligence, and I think the answer is obviously yes. AI and psychology influenced by AI are responsible for destroying behaviorism as a serious approach to psychology and turning psychologists toward information processing models. Presumably a psychologist would be more competent than an AI person to speak about that influence.

Now I want to deal with the issue about whether a machine really thinks or believes. This is an elaboration of a point I made in my paper. Namely, we will find it necessary to use mentalistic terminology in describing what we know about machines. Of course, if we understand how a thermostat works, we don't have to adopt the mentalistic stance of saying that the thermostat thinks the room is too warm.

Indeed I picked the thermostat example precisely because we can understand it both ways—mechanistically and mentalistically. Just because we can understand its mechanism is not a reason to bar the use of mentalistic terms. There's an illuminating analogy with the number system and its historical development. Suppose someone said that he didn't think that one is a number, arguing that if you have only one thing you don't have to count. Indeed most languages treat one differently from the other numbers. Some treat two differently also, and in Russian numbers up to four take the genitive case. The introduction of zero to the number system is even more recent, and I believe it was controversial. The justification is that the number system as a system makes more sense if both zero and one are included. Likewise, a systematic treatment of belief by machines will have to start with the easy cases.

A more complex case arises when we say that a dog wants to go out. We cannot practically reduce this to a propensity to behave in a certain way, because we may not know what the dog will do to further this desire. It may scratch the door or yelp or whatever. Secondly, we may not know the evidence that the dog wants to go out. Therefore, the fact that the dog wants to go out is best treated as primary.

Another useful idea comes from Dan Dennett—the notion of the "design stance." Suppose we are designing a dog as an artificial intelligence. It will be convenient to design in the desire to go out as a possible state. We have a variety of choices as to what will cause this state and what our dog will do to realize the desire. In designing computer systems, we will also find this notion of *wanting* a useful intermediate point.

As far as I can see, the purely intellectual terms are easier to handle for machines than are some of the emotional terms. "It believes" is easier than "it hopes," which is easier than "it likes me" or "it doesn't like me." And as to whether the machine is suffering, all I can say is that it complains a lot.

When we ask whether it is conscious, there are a lot of criteria for saying no. No, because it doesn't know about its physical body. No, it doesn't even refer to itself. On the other hand it might claim to be alienated, but it has just read Marcuse. Well that's how most people who claim to be alienated come to claim it. It's something they read about.

H. L. DREYFUS (*Department of Philosophy, University of California, Berkeley, Calif.*): I want to respond to both these questions: Where are we in artificial intelligence? and What has the work in artificial intelligence taught us about thinking? I agree with Seymour Papert that it has taught us a lot, if in no other way than by contrast.

But first, I want to catch up on what was happening this morning, because I want to take off from what we heard about expert systems. As Marvin Minsky said, expert systems only work in microworlds. Microworlds have bracketed off all of commonsense knowledge. I think that's a very important remark to enable us to see where the interesting and essential problems arise for an attempt to understand the mind on an information processing or computer model.

Now the successful expert systems are in a way like games. They operate in a circumscribed domain where what's relevant or not relevant has been settled before the game starts. The easiest way to see that is to think about a game like chess, which is a microworld. It's always relevant where each piece is placed, what kind of piece it is (whether it's a rook or a bishop), and whether it's white or black. It's never relevant how heavy the piece is, what temperature it is, whether it's fancy, carved, or plain, whether it's in the middle of the square or on the side, whether it's clean or dirty, etc. In the same way, DENDRAL, the program that is an expert in spectrograph analysis, deals only with spectral lines—a problem that relates to human beings can never arise. That is a completely circumscribed microworld or domain. Even a program like MYCIN, which looks like it deals with human beings, deals specifically only with objective scores on blood tests. It doesn't connect up with everyday human activity.

When you do connect up with everyday human activity, when you try to make an expert system that captures the expertise of ordinary people, then you get out of microworlds and into the problem of what's called commonsense knowledge. Commonsense knowledge deals not only with facts about the everyday world such as the physics of the everyday world, but also with exceptions—the *ceteris paribus* rules of the everyday world. That's a fancy way of saying rules that say, "everything else being equal, then such and such." Marvin Minsky gave a good example of that—as a rule, birds are animals that can fly; and when people talk about birds, you can assume that they're talking about birds that fly. But if their wings are broken, as Minsky said, or if they are toys, or even if they're penguins, then birds can't fly.

A way to connect this with the talk this morning about expert systems is to use as an example the problems that arise when you try to automate a travel agent. The travel agent is an interesting area in which the microworld, or isolated domain, where expert systems have worked and will do important things shades over into the everyday world. You can give your automated travel agent lots of facts. You can tell it about airports, rates, and distances. You can also give it the kind of facts that expert travel agents know. Facts like, Don't try to go to another airline terminal when changing planes at an airport if you only have half an hour, etc.

But there's something else which is harder and so will give you an idea of what I mean by commonsense knowledge. If for instance you say to this automated travel agent, "I'd like a flight to San Francisco leaving at around 6:00." And it tells you that there's a flight leaving Kennedy at 6:30. Then you say, "No, I'd like something a little bit earlier." And it looks up its schedules and says, "There is a flight leaving at 6:29." Something has gone wrong: 6:29 is a little bit earlier than 6:30 alright, but it's not something any human being would want to know. The automated travel agent doesn't contain any knowledge of human temporality—what spans of time are important to human beings.

Now you might think that you could just fix that. But it's not so easy. You can't just give it a rule like "a little bit earlier means at least 15 minutes earlier," because that is a *ceteris paribus* rule, the kind of rule human beings could use if they were travel agents. But everything else often isn't equal. Sometimes you really do need a flight ten minutes earlier if it's a tight connection. And sometimes even an hour earlier might be okay, if you're flying to Australia for example. So what you need is some sense of the background of everyday needs and experience that human beings bring to the question, Do you have something a little bit earlier? And that means you not only have to put into your expert system all the facts about airports and airplanes, but something like the facts about what it is to be a human being. Because a computer hasn't the slightest idea of what it is to be a human being. You have to tell it everything that there is to know about human beings if it's going to have the kind of commonsense background knowledge that human beings have.

Now of course, it won't need to know *everything* before it gets pretty good. Indeed, if you really tried to tell it everything, it would be an infinite task. There's a general agreement between John McCarthy and Marvin Minsky that it might take, say, 300 years before you get commonsense knowledge into a machine. What they mean is that in 300 years we might get enough of the facts about human beings into the machine so it will begin to be able to behave intelligently, and we could then get expert systems out of microworlds into the real world and start capturing the kind of expertise that travel agents and bankers and literary agents have, which is always an expertise that opens out into the rest of human common sense.

That's the first half of what I have to say. Now I want to talk about how human thinking differs from computer thinking, because the question before this panel comes down to, How do humans deal with common sense and is their way different from the way computers would deal with common sense?

My view is that if commonsense understanding were just knowledge, then programming it would only be an infinite task and we could get on with it and maybe we'd be somewhere with it in 300 years. But I think commonsense understanding isn't a kind of knowledge at all. And that's where I want to agree with Seymour Papert that we can learn a lot by contrasting computer "thinking" and human thinking. What we will learn by contrast is that people don't have a lot of facts and rules in their minds for understanding the everyday world. They've got a kind of skill for coping with things. Therefore, as Minsky says, the right action usually just pops into their head. They're able to see what the issues are and to see what's relevant in a situation.

This ability that people have, to see what's relevant and to have the right thing pop into their head, presupposes something like knowing what matters. But I don't think computers as we now understand them have anything like mattering or concern. It also requires having images and having memories since it involves seeing the current situation as resembling earlier situations, where resembling is a tricky notion because resembling doesn't mean identical with respect to any particular features, which is the way machines always have to analyze resemblance, but simply overall similarity.

Since human intelligence is not a matter of knowledge but a matter of understanding. AI is not even moving in the right dimension. To work at the commonsense knowledge problem is like trying to get to the moon by climbing higher and higher in a tree. You're just not going to get there that way although you are getting a little bit closer.

Now we don't need commonsense *knowledge* to be intelligent and know what matters to our kind of being because we *are* it. We don't need to *know* about bodies because we are bodies, and the same for emotions and situations. That is, we are our bodies, we have emotions, and we're in situations whereas computers are outside and have to be given knowledge of all that. That, I think, poses an insurmountable problem for AI as it's now practiced and lets us see how our kind of thinking is totally different from the computer's kind of thinking.

J. SEARLE (*Department of Philosophy, University of California, Berkeley, Calif.*): Well I'm distressed to find that I agree with a lot that everybody said. However, I'm going to try to state some positions where I disagree with what I take to be certain common tendencies in artificial intelligence.

I want to remark that the question we're supposed to be talking about got subtly rewritten. It says, Does AI illuminate human thinking? At some level, that means the kind of stuff that's going on in us now. Not all of our thinking is conscious, of course, but some is and some of it's unconscious. I want to focus a little bit on the question of what sorts of significance we should attach to artificial intelligence research into thought processes, conscious and unconscious.

In doing that, it seems to me we ought to make some distinctions. The computer is a terrific tool and there's no question but that it's going to be a useful tool in studying human beings and human thought processes just as it's a terrific tool in studying fires or patterns of crime or the marginal propensity to consume or all sorts of other things. But when you read the AI literature, you discover something amazing. There are a lot of people who don't think we can just use the computer to study understanding the way we can use the computer to study five-alarm fires and big rain storms in California. Rather, it turns out that they think the appropriately programmed computer literally does think in exactly the same sense that you and I think—that it literally has the kind of mental processes that you and I are having. So I want to distinguish what I call "weak AI," which is the view that says, "Sure, use the computer; it's a terrific tool," from a much stronger view that says: "It isn't just that we're simulating thinking or studying thinking. Our appropriately programmed computers with the right inputs and outputs will literally have thought processes, conscious and otherwise, in the same sense that you and I do." I call this view "strong AI."

Now I like that thesis because it's clear that we know exactly what somebody's saying when he says, "Look, my machine or the machine we're going to eventually build has thought processes in exactly the same sense that you and I have thought processes." It's clear, and it is false, and it is demonstrably false. I'm going to take a couple of minutes to demonstrate its falsity, so there won't be any illusion that we're all one big community of agreement.

The way I like to demonstrate the falsity of strong AI is to get you to imagine yourself instantiating a computer program for a certain kind of thought process. It's very important in these discussions to take the first-person point of view, to ask, What would it be like for me? Because that's what we know of being conscious and having thought processes. So imagine that there's a computer program for understanding Chinese, so that if you punch a question in Chinese into the computer, the computer can give out the right sort of answer. It has the right sort of data base and the right kind of program so that it can process questions in Chinese and give the right answers.

Now imagine that you *are* the computer. You're locked in a room and a lot of Chinese symbols are in the room together with a whole lot of rule books for shuffling these Chinese symbols around. This will only work if you don't know Chinese. Like me; I don't know a word of Chinese. I don't know what any of these symbols mean. So there I am in the room shuffling these symbols around. The questions come in. I look up what I'm supposed to do when I get a squiggle squiggle sign and I go and match it with a squaggle squaggle sign. That is called a computational process over a purely formally specified element. These are what Simon and Newell called physical symbols; and I am now acting as a physical symbol system.

Let's suppose these guys get good at writing the programs. I get good at shuffling the symbols. The questions come in, and I give out the right answers. One guy in responding to me said, "Suppose one of the questions is 'Do you understand Chinese?'" And I shuffle around—now I don't know what any of these symbols mean—and put out the symbol that says: "You bet I understand Chinese. And how! What could be more obvious? Why do you keep asking me these dumb questions?" What I want to say is that it's quite obvious, once you look at it from the first-person point of view, that I don't understand a word of Chinese and I wouldn't learn Chinese from instantiating the Chinese understanding program.

Why not? What is it that I have in English that the computer doesn't have in Chinese? Notice that if I don't understand Chinese in that story, then neither does any other computer program understand Chinese, because the program hasn't got anything that I haven't got in the story. What is it that I've got for English that the computer program doesn't have? Well I like commonsense answers. The difference is that in English, I know the meanings of the words, and in Chinese, I don't know the meanings of the words— all I've got is a set of formal symbols with a set of computational rules for manipulating the formal symbols.

The point of the parable about the Chinese room is to reveal a deep point about the character of artificial intelligence research and human thinking. This is the point I want to leave you with, that is, from syntax alone you can't get semantics. From purely formal, symbolic operations, you can't get the mental content. So what I'm trying to remind you of with this story about the Chinese room is something we know independently anyway, namely, what the computer has as a computer is a purely formal level of operation. That's its great appeal. The same program can be put in a complete variety of different kinds of substances, in different kinds of hardware. But as far as we know anything about how the real world works, the world in which we live, our mental states have to be something much more than just a set of syntactical processes because we actually do have thoughts and feelings. We actually have mental contents.

Why is it that the computer doesn't have those in the sense that we do? Let's take the case of thirst, because I'm now thirsty. As far as we know anything about it, thirst is produced in the hypothalamus by the action of angiotensin, which is synthesized by the secretions of renin from the kidneys. The point is that there's a quite specific story about how it works, and the result is that I now feel thirsty. Now think about what an AI program would do. An AI program would say, "Well look, there's just a set of formal syntactical processes; that's all there is to feeling thirsty." The way to see that this can't be right from what we know about how the world works is to imagine that we put the thirst feeling program in some completely different sort of system. Make your computer out of old beer cans, take millions of old cans and let them bang together to simulate the neuron firings of the synapses. Now notice what strong AI has to claim. It can't be just claiming: "Well who knows, maybe the system of beer cans is thirsty. I mean do we know so much about what it's like to be a beer can that we're sure that the beer can isn't thirsty?" That's not the claim. The claim has to be that the system must be thirsty because all there is to being thirsty is instantiating the formal computer program for being thirsty. I want to say that if we know anything to be false, we know that to be false. We know it quite independently of these discussions because we know that from a formal level of symbol manipulation by itself, you don't get semantic content.

Well why do people get in this bind? I mean why would anybody want to maintain these views? There are a couple of reasons. One is the constant adoption of a third-person point of view. We're always asked how would we know that some other system was thirsty or understood Chinese. That's the whole point of the Turing test—take the third-person point of view. But I want to tell you something about the mind. At some point, you'll only understand what a mind is and what it's like to have a mind by having one, by being one, by adopting the first-person point of view.

So there is this objectivizing tendency. It's part of modern life that we think all of knowledge must be described from a third-person point of view. But it's obviously false, if you think about the character of our mental states.

The second feature—and this is a kind of linguistic problem that gets into these discussions—is that we find it completely natural to use mental terms in a metaphorical extended sense. It seems to me we do that all the time. I mean I apply all kinds of mental vocabulary to my car, and sometimes not very sympathetic when the thing won't start. But we don't take it seriously in supposing that the car has mental states in the same way that we do. I want to say the same thing about my computer. I ascribe all kinds of mental properties to it. It's completely natural. The mistake is if we suppose that those are to be taken at face value.

But a third and really important reason, and I think the deepest reason, that leads to this mistake is oddly enough that in all of these discussions with all of their technical vocabulary, there is an old-style philosophical mistake that goes back to the seventeenth century—it goes back to Descartes, and frankly it goes back to Plato. This is the mistake—it is the refusal to think that the mind is just a biological phenomenon like any other. That is, in all of these discussions you get the idea that intelligence is something very abstract, that it can't be just a fact of biology like digestion, or the secretion of bile, or mitosis or meiosis.

I want to say that it is a kind of contempt for biology or a willingness to ignore the obvious facts of biology that leads to what is essentially the dualist view that mental states and minds are just programs.

M. L. MINSKY: I'd like to say a couple of words about the things Dr. Searle said. This consciousness thing is a very complicated business. And Searle is imagining a machine that looks up rules and executes them, and he's saying, "Well how would it feel?" But I think he's confusing what's going on in the process with what somebody else might feel when he's looking at it. Of course, if you look at somebody's brain cells with the right instrument, you'll see the nervous impulses going around, and you can say it's just adding and subtracting or whatever it's doing with those electric currents. To think that you know what it feels like to be a typewriter and that if you were a typewriter, you wouldn't feel anything, and to assume from that that if you were a machine a billion times as complex as a typewriter, you wouldn't feel anything is an extraordinary extrapolation. It seems to me this is very similar to his remarks at the end about consciousness and digestion being biological. Everybody knows that there's no vital mystery to digestion if you just know how the enzymes work. There isn't, in a certain reductionist sense, any such thing as digestion.

Now you might say that I'm missing the point because that would mean there isn't any such thing as consciousness. But my complaint is that the people who think there is such a thing as consciousness are trying to simplify it so much. Suppose I ask myself if I was aware four seconds ago of saying the word consciousness. What is consciousness to me? What does it mean to be self-aware? Now think of that Chinese machine that interpreted and answered questions in Chinese without knowing it. Suppose I asked it the question in Chinese, "Were you aware that four seconds ago you translated the word kumquat into mandarin orange or some erroneous such thing?" The machine, if it said yes—and Searle has to grant it says yes because he's assuming that it did all of the things it needed to do to translate correctly—it certainly would have said, "Yes, I was conscious." What does it mean to say that? If I say that I was conscious of doing something a few minutes ago, that means that somewhere in my data processing, I must have made a pale copy of the state of the machine. So you see it's true that if the machine had no trace of its past state, like the old typewriters, then it can't answer questions about how it felt and it wouldn't mean anything to ask it such a question because you know that it's amnesic—every second is disconnected from the next, there's no trace. But if I translate a word and if I can say later. "Yes, I knew I did that," I could only answer that if I made little fuzzy copies. What I'm saying is that the mind is very complicated. When I say I and when Searle says first person, there's no such thing as first person. There are a lot of processes going on. If I ask how did I feel when I met so and so and an hour ago, I go back and I run these processes, but it's not that there was a way I felt. If you've read anything about the mind, you know that there are many parts of my mind, some of which I don't know about for years, some of which I know right away. And what do I mean by I? You see, I'm falling into the trap. There are five parts of the mind. This one has some copy of the state of that one a while ago, this of that, this of that. When you say first person, when you say I felt, a little piece of machinery inside of all this that's connected to the mouth and won't stop, is pretending that it knows what happened there. That it was conscious. That it could be responsible for the things that went on in all the other parts. Well this is all so absurd. A thing like saying a machine can't feel pain really gets you into very complicated issues. It's no use to say a syntactic process can't feel because syntax is in fact the technical word for describing what doesn't happen in a process.

S. PAPERT: One might have said that watches are definitionally made up of wheels turning, and something that doesn't have wheels turning isn't a watch. If one had a commitment to this point of view, obviously these digital things that many people are wearing would not be watches. They'd be simulations of watches. And they wouldn't keep time. They'd do something like seeming to keep time.

Obviously, machines think not in the same way exactly as people think. And obviously people are biological. And when we say Is it true that machines think? we're asking whether we would like to extend the notion of thinking to include what machines might do. That's the only meaningful sense of the question, Do machines think? Newton said the sun exerts a force on the earth. And one might have said, "No, forces are what you do with your muscles, it's biological," but we'd be missing the point. Newton was introducing a new technical concept of force. And AI, if it's going to be taken seriously, is introducing a new technical concept of thinking, one that is not the same as the concept of thinking that's existed since Aristotle and before.

So I've got to agree, of course, that surely machines don't think in exactly the same way as I do. I'm not sure Searle thinks in exactly the same way I do either, or whether any two people think in exactly the same way. But what is obvious to me is that machines don't think in exactly the same way as me or in exactly the same way as one another. And one would deliberately—in working with artificial intelligence—try to make machines think in very different ways so as to have a comparative study of the different ways that this sort of function that we're all interested in can operate.

So I think that Searle's conclusion is true, but I don't know what it's relevant to. Of course it might be that if you poke around in the artificial intelligence literature as he says, there really are some people who have said machines think in exactly the same way as people do. Maybe they meant it, maybe they didn't mean it. Maybe this was a slip of the tongue. Maybe they were philosophically naive. All this is rather irrelevant I think to any fundamental considerations about the nature of thinking and whether something that is shared by us and potential machines is a more coherent, more useful, more powerful notion than this pretechnical sense of thinking that's rooted in the biological.

H. R. PAGELS: Dr. Papert, I'm a little confused. Your remarks make a strong distinction between the kind of "thinking" that a computer might do and the kind of thinking that a human being does. You seem to suggest that these two kinds of thinking have nothing to do with one another. In other words, AI-type thinking has nothing to do with human thinking. But that was not the impression that I got from your earlier remarks.

S. PAPERT: Well let's take the example of Newton expanding the concept of force from someone pushing to something that the sun might do to the earth. He has extended the notion of force, he has changed it. To go from that to saying that his notion of force has nothing to do with what might happen when I push the table is absurd. I think that this is what the theory of intelligence is about, that we are constantly extending the theory or thinking, whether it's in the psychology lab or in the philosophy seminar or in making machines. We are constantly extending and defining our notion of thinking and making new notions of thinking—technical ones. It's not true to say they have nothing to do with the previous ones. So I don't think that there's anything in Searle's argument that could be construed as trying to prove that what happens in the machine has nothing to do with what happens in the person. What he has argued for—and I'm accepting this for the sake of argument—is that it's not exactly the same thing. And I think his argument depends essentially on the attempt to want it to be exactly the same thing.

H. R. PAGELS: So if I understand you, there is a more general idea of thinking which includes both machine thinking and human thinking.

S. PAPERT: And the theoretical enterprise is trying constantly to extend.

J. MCCARTHY: I'd like to go back to the Chinese room. There is a confusion between the system consisting of the person and the person himself. I agree with Robert Wilensky who made the same point earlier. The system knows Chinese, but the person who is executing the system may not. This is analogous to an interpreter running in a computer, the interpreted program often has capabilities the interpreter does not. It's just that we don't have experience with systems in which a person carries out a mental process that has properties different from those of the person himself. We get the same

347

confusion with computers. Someone asks me whether LISP can do calculus problems. No, LISP cannot do calculus, but some LISP programs can.

The example of thirst is different. A program that simulates thirst is not going to be thirsty. For example, there is no way to relieve it with real water.

Searle has said that the people in AI take the third-person view of mental qualities. That's correct. We do, and we'll claim that it's a virtue. He says we consider the problem of intelligence as distinct from biology. Yes, we hold that intelligence is something that can be dealt with abstractly just as computation can be discussed and dealt with abstractly. One can ask whether a computer calculates the sum of 3 and 5 to be 8 in the same sense as a human does. I suppose Searle would agree that "calculate" is being used in the same sense for both human and machine in this case.

Now there's the point Dreyfus made about it taking 300 years. I have been saying that human-level AI will take between 5 and 500 years. The problem isn't that it will take a long time to enter data into a computer. It is rather that conceptual advances are required before we can implement human-level artificial intelligence—just as conceptual advances were required beyond the situation in 1900 before we could have nuclear energy.

Pursuing the nuclear energy analogy, the question is whether the present AI situation corresponds to 1900 or to 1938 when Rutherford, the leading nuclear physicist, declared nuclear energy impossible. The situation of 1938 is interesting in that experiments exhibiting nuclear fission had already been done but had been misinterpreted. Perhaps someone has already done experimental research that, when properly interpreted, will make possible human-level AI. I would be very surprised. When we talk about future conceptual advances, we don't know where we stand at present.

Dreyfus made a point about a reservation machine not knowing whether 6:25 will do as a little earlier than 6:30. The program would have the same problem if it were making a reservation for a robot. Whether even a 6:29 reservation will do depends on circumstances. So the fact that the reservation is for humans isn't the problem.

Finally, let me defend Searle on one point. He was discussing whether a computer can think in the same sense as a human—not does it think in the same way. In my opinion the thermostat thinks the room is too warm in the same sense as a human might, and he would disagree. Likewise about whether the dog simulation wants to go out.

H. L. DREYFUS: I want to be very brief because I think there are two separate issues and the bulk of the questions have been directed at John Searle's issue. Let's distinguish the issues. That will help people be clear what's going on. There's the question of whether programmed computers of the sort that we now have with the sorts of programs that we now have could ever behave like human beings. And I want to say they can't. And then there's the question, Even if computers behaved exactly like human beings, would they be thinking? Would they be intelligent? Would they have meaningful mental states? Searle wants to grant the first point hypothetically, i.e., that programmed as at present, computers could be intelligent, and then to say even if they behave exactly like human beings, that still wouldn't tell us anything about thinking because such machines wouldn't be thinking.

To return to issue one, McCarthy brought up the conceptual advances required before we reach the level of commonsense artificial intelligence. I agree we need some breakthroughs, but it all hinges on what you mean by conceptual advances. I think we're not in the same position as we were with respect to atomic energy in 1900 or in 1938, but more like the alchemists were with respect to atomic energy. That is, it's not just a question of the right conceptual advances. We're not even in the right dimension. We're trying to use computers that have programs. And the programs operate using facts and rules stored in complicated data structures. I just think that that's not going to get us common sense because that's not the kind of knowledge that gives us common sense. It seems to me highly unlikely that we could ever cash what gives us common sense into enough knowledge to make a computer seem to have common sense.

The travel agent might have the same sort of problem I mentioned with Martians as with robots. Of course, if Martians were enough like us, the travel agent would not have the same problem, but if they lived 100 times faster, or died in a day like may flies, then their concerns about a little earlier and a little later would be very different from ours. And so you have to understand how human beings live in time or how any other kind of creature lives in time to see what kind of problems it has and the best way to know how it experiences time is to be of the same species.

J. SEARLE: Can a machine think? Well I want to tell you that's a fairly tricky question. So let's slow down and go through it. There is a sense in which each of us is a machine. We're each a material system. We just have an awful lot of neurons up there. And in that sense, it seems to me the answer to the question is obvious—of course machines can think; we are thinking machines.

So maybe we're trying to ask another question. We're trying to ask the question, Could an artifact think? Could you make a thinking machine? But there again, I don't see any difficulty in principle. Suppose we got the billions of neurons with their axons and their dendrites and synaptic clefts, and neurotransmitters and all the rest of it. If you can duplicate the causes, then you can duplicate the effects. So that wasn't the question we're trying to ask.

Here's another version of the question—Could a digital computer think? We're getting closer now. Even that's a little bit tricky because we want to say just about any system has a level of description where you can describe it as a digital computer. You can describe it as instantiating a formal program. So in that sense, I suppose, all of our brains are digital computers, and in that sense a digital computer can think.

The question we're driving at is this—and that is really the heart of the matter—Could a system think solely by virtue of being a digital computer? That is to say, solely by virtue of instantiating the right program with the right inputs and the right outputs? And there the answer is no. And it has to be no for the reasons that I said earlier. Namely, the purely formal processes can't by themselves give you the content. The same formal processes can be instantiated in any number of different kinds of substances which have quite different biochemical features, most of which will simply be incapable of duplicating the powers of the brain.

There are two very simple axioms on which my whole argument rests. One, the brain causes mental states. And just as a slogan, "brains cause minds." If we know anything about the world, we know that much about how it works.

Two, formal processes by themselves are not sufficient for semantic or mental content. I put that in the slogan by saying "From syntax, you can't get semantics." I don't mean to confine it to linguistics. That's just a mnemonic for reminding us of the difference between the formal, the purely formal, and the content.

So the question we were trying to ask was, Could a system think solely by virtue of being a digital computer? And the answer to that question has to be no. But now we can make a derivation from these two axioms—number one, brains cause minds, and number two, from syntax alone, you don't get semantics. What follows is that the way the brain does it can't be by instantiating a computational program alone. It can't. When we explain how the brain produces mental states, we will not be able to do it entirely by the fact that the brain instantiates formal programs. And indeed, where we actually know something about the operations of the brain, we don't have to appeal to a formal or abstract level. What we do appeal to is quite specific biochemical facts about the operation of the brain as we appeal to quite specific biochemical facts about the operation of the digestion or the operation of the liver or the pancreas or anything else.

Now there are two other little points I want to take up. Throughout these discussions, we tend to think there must be some technical solution to this problem. If you watch the discussion, people will often say that we get so far with computers, but there's always that extra little bit we can't go. So they will say, "Can you program a computer that will fall in love, have a sense of humor, or whatever?" But I want to say that that really misses the point. The point is not that the digital computer doesn't get quite all the way to having a mind, it doesn't get started. It's not in that line of business.

You can always say, of course, "Well it's just an extended notion of thinking. Why not have a larger notion of thinking?" I have no objection to using words in an extended sense provided you make clear the extension. Now I want to say computers think and have thoughts and feelings and consciousness in the same extended sense of feelings, consciousness, and thought that computer simulations of rainstorms leave us all drenched, or computer simulations of five-alarm fires burn all the buildings down. It's only an extended sense of leaving us all wet or burning the building down. I have no objections to that kind of talk, provided you realize that there is a sense in which it just abandons the claim of strong AI.

Indeed, I want to conclude by saying, why does anybody feel tempted to adopt strong AI? That is, McCarthy has written, and I quote this verbatim because it made a big impression on me, "Even a machine as simple as a thermostat can be said to have beliefs." And he means that quite literally— beliefs in the same sense that you and I have. I've discussed this with McCarthy enough to know that he thinks the thermostat literally has beliefs. I once asked him what beliefs. It believes it's too cold in here, it's too hot in here, and it's just right in here.

What I want to conclude with is this—it seems to me unnecessary, in order to pursue what I think is the really fruitful part of artificial intelligence, for people to adopt strong AI. I mean the computer is a wonderfully exciting tool. And computer science is a very exciting field of human investigation. It isn't necessary either for the success of artificial intelligence or even for the getting of substantial research grants that we should make exaggerated claims.

H. R. PAGELS: I want to move the discussion in a different direction. I'd like to know the panelists' viewpoints on where this discussion might be in 5 or 10 years. Is it possible that an advance in neurobiology, computer design, or the conceptual foundations of artificial intelligence research might resolve this issue one way or the other?

Another area we might discuss is potential collaboration between philosophers and people working in artificial intelligence research.

M. L. MINSKY: I don't have much to say about that. I think as things are discovered and demonstrated, then—barring paradigm shifts of very large magnitude—attitudes will drift a little bit when machines seem more intelligent, people will tend to think that they're more intelligent or that they'll think.

But there are things that never change until there's a paradigm change. For example, very often someone will ask me, "What is intelligence?" And I'll say, "Well I don't know—I'm trying to find out." And they'll say: "Well I didn't mean that. I mean how do you define it? How do you define intelligence?" And I go back and say, "Well how do you define life?" The word "life" doesn't have much place anymore in science, as many of you know. There's a sort of continuum. We know that crystals can copy certain patterns and that a million billion years ago, events started to happen where these very complicated systems started appearing. And if you ask a biologist what he's studying, he'll say he's trying to study some facet of the digestion microworld. To develop a theory to understand a complicated system, we have to cover very small areas until it's all covered up and then sew it all together with exceptions or other theories. I think what will happen in artificial intelligence is that to a large extent, these side issues will decay.

Obviously the machines that we have now, whether they think or not in the weakest sense that John McCarthy suggested, are nothing at all like us. They can't remember why they did things. People put in programs to help them. And so it makes very little sense to talk about them having much in the way of consciousness or sensitivity or whatever.

As for 10 years or 200 from now, we don't know. I want to point out that we don't have to spend all the time of the future figuring out what common sense is. We may be able to make learning machines that will cleverly watch their own behavior and decide that certain principles they're using don't work and edit them.

Gradually, the attitude and the respect for intelligent machines will change as they become more intelligent. But in our culture, until there's a revolution, the idea will persist that they're just simulations. People will say, "It's crying terribly out there, that robot. Don't you think you should let it in?" And other people will say, "No it's just simulating. It doesn't really feel bad." I wonder if Searle thinks that the brain gets wet when it thinks about rain. Whatever the process is, why should it matter what the substance is as long as the impulses are there. When we look at a picture of a pretty girl, let's face the fact that we're not seeing a pretty girl, we're only seeing a lot of little colored dots on the retina. And then let's face the next fact, when we see a real pretty girl, we're still just seeing little dots on the retina, if you confine the system to that. I think that's what one means by you can't just look at the interpretation process, you have to look at the system of the person carrying out the rules. We never see anything. Does that mean that we do never see anything? It just depends on the size of the system to which you make this attribution.

So unless there's a revolution that says words like "life" should be removed, everybody will still feel there's a difference. That these robots are maybe intelligent but not alive, or that they have pseudointelligence but not real. And the attributions that you use there will depend on your purposes. Are you worrying about them getting legal rights and inheriting your property? Are you worried about having to share? Are you worried about feeling guilty that they might have the same feelings as you although maybe John Searle is right and one could never prove such a thing? Because it's just a style of thought itself. These questions will depend on too much to answer.

S. PAPERT: I'd like to say something about the question of where we are going, and maybe this is relevant to what kind of cooperation there might be between AI and the different kind of philosopher—a philosopher concerned with reality, with social reality and with people's concerns.

I'd like to put this into a different context. Can machines be intelligent? Can they think? There's a certain form of this question that is of very vital concern to all of us, because there will be machines that will be better than people at doing whatever their jobs are. If your job is being a doctor, there will be a machine that can make a better diagnosis and decide on a better treatment of your patient than you can. Or if you want to invest in the stock exchange, rather than go and ask a human advisor, you should get a machine. The machine will know much better than you—probably will have made millions of dollars already. I think that most people are more concerned about this than they are willing to admit. Because it really is frightening.

Now given that people think this is even slightly likely, they might want to be reassured. And I believe that a lot of people have found reassurance in the writings of Dreyfus and Searle. They read what these philosophers say as somehow reassuring that this isn't going to happen, that people are always going to keep their unique special position in the universe, that maybe the diggers of ditches and the drivers of horses have had their jobs taken away from them, but we intellectuals will always have our jobs and prestige and all the things that come with our particular kind of work.

Can machines ever make us intellectuals obsolete? Dreyfus has said no, they can't because there are certain things that machines will never be. And Searle takes a slightly different position, saying that whatever machines do, we won't call it thinking but we can't define what they'll do or won't do from the outside.

I think it's a little bit chancy to make predictions about what machines can't do, because some clever engineer will come along and make the machine do that thing. So I think a lot of people would rather have something like the Chinese room argument which doesn't depend on competing with the technicians about what is technically possible. Undoubtedly this kind of argument has acquired a certain social popularity for that reason.

But I would like to say, concerning the consequences, that I feel that this is a very dangerous situation. I think it's socially dangerous for people to be lulled into a sense of security that there won't be machines to threaten their positions. I think that these are important issues of what it really means to our sense of ourselves to allow ourselves to face the social issue of what machines will be doing out there—what life will be like—after 300 years or 3 years or whatever.

To go back to a point I made at the beginning—that machines are changing the way people think because machine thinking is often useful as a model for human thinking. It's also sometimes dangerous as a model. For example if you think that Newell and Simon machine that solves puzzles in a certain way is a good model for us to follow, you might be concerned about whether this is a good model for our children to follow. Finding the appropriate context for discussing that is a matter of vital social concern, and it's not dealt with—it's only covered over—by saying, "Well that machine is not thinking because it's not biological, or because it's just following rules, or because it's not semantic." The point is, you give it a problem, it gives you an answer. You ask it why it did this and it gives you reasons. And then you're going to tend to follow that kind of reason or not follow that kind of reason. Or pass them on to your children or not pass them on to your children. I'm just suggesting this as somewhere that AI is going. And the kinds of consideration that have come up here can be dangerously misleading if we don't keep them rigorously separated from all issues of this kind.

J. McCarthy: The question is, What will be the situation 5 to 10 years from now? Let me make it 10 or 15. I think there'll be a paradigm shift among the public that will give John Searle the following problem. He will want to come to the symposium to correct our use of mental terms, but he won't even get here, because he'll have to correct his secretary who will tell him, "It promised to process your travel advance, but I don't think it will, because it's puzzled about whether the expenditure for flowers was intended and necessary for the business's goals."

Thus in 10 or 15 years, quite mundane systems used for business and personal purposes will require the use of a certain amount of mental terminology in order to be used effectively.

Also let me repeat my warning to philosophers that if they insist on discussing commonsense reasoning only at the general level of today's discussion, they will lose the jurisdiction. We need to consider the conditions for the ascription of particular mental qualities, and this may require collaboration among philosophers and artificial intelligence researchers.

We attempted such a collaboration several years ago, but I think the particular attempt was unsuccessful largely because it considered overly general questions. This was partly because the AI people succumbed to the temptation to become amateur philosophers rather than raising the AI issues to which philosophy is relevant.

H. L. Dreyfus: I think that I'm the one, not John Searle, who's lulling people into a sense of security. I just think it's not a *false* sense of security. I think that you should be confident and trust your natural intuitions and your grandmother's natural intuitions that you are not a machine. Not that you are not a material thing, you certainly are. But you are not the sort of machine that, by using a program manipulating facts by way of rules, produces the kind of behavior we call intelligent.

Now I want to make clear that that's not to say—as people have rightly said—that computers won't fall in love, etc. A recent *Time Magazine* essay, claiming to be giving my views, said that I think that computers won't be able to pray, won't be able to look you in the eye while shaking hands, and so forth. Of course I think that. But that's not important. What I want to say is that even though computers can do really complicated things like analyze spectrograms and play chess, computers as we now understand them and program them can't even understand the sort of stories that four-year-old children understand. Moreover, I think they will never be able to understand the sort of stories that four-year-old children understand because such stories involve emotions like jealousy, everyday practices, seeing one situation as similar to another situation, and the sort of rules that include a clause saying "everything else being equal," without spelling out what everything else is, or what counts as being equal. It's that sort of thing, it seems to me, that the current way of trying to produce artificial intelligence will never achieve. And so I don't think computers will ever behave like human beings if the current direction of research continues. And you can be secure that there won't be the sort of robots around doing the sort of things we do and thinking like we do in your lifetime or even in the foreseeable future.

Let me take the rest of my time to try to answer Dr. Pagel's question, Where will we be in 10 years? When I wrote *What Computers Can't Do* 10 years ago, nobody seemed to think that the problem of making computers intelligent required programming commonsense knowledge. People were trying to use shortcuts to get computers that seemed to be intelligent. Now, 10 years later, everyone thinks there is a big problem concerning commonsense knowledge. Where will we be 10 years from now? I think 10 years from now people might realize that it's not a question of commonsense knowledge at all. That common sense includes feelings, having a body, having images, responding to similarities, etc. Then maybe the field will switch to something that I feel would be more promising, simulating the brain by neural nets with changing thresholds rather than storing facts and rules. And in that new dimension, in x number of years, maybe we'd get somewhere. But I don't think we'll get somewhere by trying to treat our commonsense understanding as if it were knowledge.

J. SEARLE: I always have the disconcerting sense in these discussions that I'm busy saying over and over, "Look, 2 plus 2 is really just 4," while other people are saying, "Yes, but if 2 plus 2 were 5 or 7, think of the terrific derivations that we could make."

Now what will this discussion look like in 10 or in x number of years? I have very great confidence in human rationality. People are going to say, "Yes, 2 plus 2 is just plain 4." And the specific form I think that's going to take is this. Mentality is a biological phenomenon. We don't know an awful lot about how it works in the brain, but suppose we really did know how it worked. Suppose we had a perfect science of the brain or even a pretty good science of the brain. Suppose we were able to explain how the behavior at the neuronal level caused consciousness and thought processes at the same degree that we can now explain how the behavior of H_2O molecules causes the liquidity of the water in this glass.

Once we get to that point, then nobody will make these confusions. Ignorance is one of the reasons that lead to strong AI. Notice what the strong AI partisans are saying. They're saying the brain doesn't matter. And that is literally incredible. It is incredible to suppose that the brain doesn't matter to the mind, that any system whatever, whether it's beer cans or, as Weizenbaum said, rolls of toilet paper with stones laid on the squares, any system at all will have to have mental states in exactly the same sense that you and I do because all there is to having mental states is instantiating the right program.

I believe this discussion will peter out when people realize that that's a preposterous view.

Another reason that it's still possible to propound strong AI is that there's still a certain mystique surrounding the computer. We're not as at home with the computer as we are with cars and telephones and so on. It still seems for most of us a kind of mysterious object, and that leads to a kind of mystification. And that will peter out as the computer becomes more common.

So my answer to the question of what is likely to happen over the years is that people will see that strong AI, the idea that the computer program is sufficient for having mental states, is in a way a last gasp of a Cartesian metaphysics. The last gasp for the idea that the mind is something special. That it isn't part of the biological universe like the rest of the biological facts about our life.

I'd like to end on a more constructive note. I do see enormous possibilities for collaboration between AI and the sort of philosopher that I am. In fact, I've engaged in some of this. And this seems to me the real world of AI. Suppose you have a language and certain rules for speech acts and you also have rules for understanding indirect speech acts, that is, rules for understanding how it is that when a guy says "You're standing on my toe," you know perfectly well that's not just a remark about your geographical location. He's actually trying to get you to do something about it. I think those are rational processes. Now the beauty of AI, and this I really do admire, is that it forces you to pose those questions precisely and forces you to state your theory precisely. In fact the things I've written about—metaphors and indirect speech acts and so on—a great deal of it has been programmed by people working in various AI labs. So I think, in fact, that AI is an immensely useful tool in the study of language and the study of the mind, just as it's a useful tool in the study of rainstorms or the economy or anything else. I feel fairly confident that in the end, the exaggerated and I think implausible and preposterous kinds of strong AI will be abandoned.

What McCarthy says is surely right, we will come to make all these attributions of intentional states to computers as we now make attributions of mental states to cars and adding machines and photoelectric cells and so on. It's quite harmless. Nobody supposes that his car literally has thoughts and feelings. And in the same way, we will come to the point where we realize that our PDP-10 or even our beloved Apple II doesn't actually have thoughts and feelings. And when that happens, then we'll be able to see what is really useful in AI, namely, it is itself a tremendous intellectual advance in the development of computer science and, even more important, it enables us to make further intellectual advances in other fields.

Section 2.1: Diagonalisation

58

MINDS, MACHINES AND GÖDEL

A retrospect

J. R. Lucas

Source: P. J. R. Millican and A. Clark, *Machines and Thought: The Legacy of Alan Turing*, Princeton University Press, 1996, pp. 103–24.

I must start with an *apologia*. My original paper, "Minds, Machines and Gödel", was written in the wake of Turing's 1950 paper in *Mind*, and was intended to show that minds were not Turing machines. Why, then, didn't I couch the argument in terms of Turing's theorem, which is easyish to prove and applies directly to Turing machines, instead of Gödel's theorem, which is horrendously difficult to prove, and doesn't so naturally or obviously apply to machines? The reason was that Gödel's theorem gave me something more: it raises questions of truth which evidently bear on the nature of mind, whereas Turing's theorem does not; it shows not only that the Gödelian well-formed formula is unprovable-in-the-system, but that it is true. It shows something about reasoning, that it is not completely rule-bound, so that we, who are rational, can transcend the rules of any particular logistic system, and construe the Gödelian well-formed formula not just as a string of symbols but as a proposition which is true. Turing's theorem might well be applied to a computer which someone claimed to represent a human mind, but it is not so obvious that what the computer could not do, the mind could. But it is very obvious that we have a concept of truth. Even if it is not the *summum bonum*, it is a *bonum*, and one it is characteristic of minds to value. A representation of the human mind which could take no account of truth would be inherently implausible. Turing's theorem, though making the same negative point as Gödel's theorem, that some things cannot be done by even idealized computers, does not make the further positive point that we, inasmuch as we are rational agents, can do that very thing that the computer cannot. I have, however, sometimes wondered whether I could not construct a parallel argument based on Turing's theorem, and have toyed with the idea of a von Neumann machine. A von Neumann machine was a black box, inside which was housed John von Neumann. But although it was reasonable, on inductive grounds, to credit a von Neumann machine with the power of solving any problem in finite time—about the time taken to get from New York to Chicago by train—it did not have the same edge as Gödel's proof of his own first incompleteness theorem. I leave it therefore to the reader to consider further how Turing's theorem bears on mechanism, and whether a Turing machine could plausibly represent a mind, and myself return to the argument I actually put forward.

I argued that Gödel's theorem enabled us to devise a schema for refuting the various different mechanist theories of the mind that might be put forward. Gödel's theorem is a sophisticated form of the Cretan paradox posed by Epimenides. Gödel showed how we could represent any reasonable mathematical theory within itself. Whereas the original Cretan paradox, "This statement is untrue" can be brushed off on the grounds that it is viciously self-referential, and we do not know what the statement is, which is alleged to be untrue, until it has been made, and we cannot make it until we know what it is that is being alleged to be false, Gödel blocks that objection. But in order to do so, he needs not only to represent within his mathematical theory some means of *referring* to the statement, but also some means of expressing mathematically what we are saying about it. We cannot in fact do this with "true" or "untrue": could we do that, a direct inconsistency would ensue. What Gödel was able to do, however, was to express within his mathematical system the concept of being *provable-*, and hence also *unprovable-*, in-that-system. He produced a copper-bottomed well-formed formula which could be interpreted as saying "This well-formed formula is unprovable-in-this-system." It follows that it must be both unprovable-in-the-system and none the less true. For if it were provable, and provided the system is a sound one in which only well-formed formulae expressing true propositions could be proved, then it would be true, and so what it says, namely that it is unprovable-in-the-system, would hold; so that it would be *un*provable-in-the-system. So it cannot be provable-in-the-system. But if it is unprovable-in-the-system, then what it claims to be the case is the case, and so it is true. So it is true but unprovable-in-the-system. Gödel's theorem seemed to me to be not only a surprising result in mathematics, but to have a bearing on theories of the mind, and in particular on mechanism, which is as much a background assumption of our age as classical materialism was towards the end of the last century in the form expressed by Tyndale. Mechanism claims that the workings of the mind can be entirely understood in terms of the working of a definite finite system operating according to definite deterministic laws. Enthusiasts for artificial intelligence are often mechanists, and are inclined to claim that in due course they will be able to simulate all forms of intelligent behaviour by means of a sufficiently complex computer garbed in sufficiently sophisticated software. But the operations of any such computer could be represented in terms of a formal logistic calculus with a definite

finite number (though enormously large) of possible well-formed formulae and a definite finite number (though presumably smaller) of axioms and rules of inference. The Gödelian formula of such a system would be one that the computer, together with its software, would be unable to prove. We, however, could. So the claim that a computer could in principle simulate all our behaviour breaks down at this one, vital point.

The argument I put forward is a two-level one. I do not offer a simple knock-down proof that minds are inherently better than machines, but a schema for constructing a *dis*proof of any plausible mechanist thesis that might be proposed. The disproof depends on the particular mechanist thesis being maintained, and does not claim to show that the mind is uniformly better than the purported mechanist representation of it, but only that it is one respect better and therefore different. That is enough to refute that particular mechanist thesis. By itself, of course, it leaves all others unrefuted, and the mechanist free to put forward some variant thesis which the counter-argument I constructed does not immediately apply to. But I claim that it can be adjusted to meet the new variant. Having once got the hang of the Gödelian argument, the mind can adapt it appropriately to meet each and every variant claim that the mind is essentially some form of Turing machine. Essentially, therefore, the two parts of my argument are first a hard negative argument, addressed to a mechanist putting forward a particular claim, and proving to him, by means he must acknowledge to be valid, that his claim is untenable; and secondly a hand-waving positive argument, addressed to intelligent men, bystanders as well as mechanists espousing particular versions of mechanism, to the effect that some sort of argument on these lines can always be found to deal with any further version of mechanism that may be thought up.

I read the paper to the Oxford Philosophical Society in October 1959 and subsequently published it in *Philosophy*,[1] and later set out the argument in more detail in *The Freedom of the Will*.[2] I have been much attacked. Although I argued with what I hope was becoming modesty and a certain degree of tentativeness, many of the replies have been lacking in either courtesy or caution. I must have touched a raw nerve. That, of course, does not prove that I was right. Indeed, I should at once concede that I am very likely not to be entirely right, and that others will be able to articulate the arguments more clearly, and thus more cogently, than I did. But I am increasingly persuaded that I was not entirely wrong, by reason of the very wide disagreement among my critics about where exactly my arguments fail. Each picks on a different point, allowing that the points objected to by other critics, are in fact all right, but hoping that his one point will prove fatal. None has, so far as I can see. I used to try and answer each point fairly and fully, but the flesh has grown weak. Often I was simply pointing out that the critic was not criticizing any argument I had put forward but one which he would have liked me to put forward even though I had been at pains to discount it. In recent years I have been less zealous to defend myself, and often miss articles altogether.[3] There may be some new decisive objection I have altogether overlooked. But the objections I have come across so far seem far from decisive.

To consider each objection individually would be too lengthy a task to attempt here. I shall pick on five recurrent themes. Some of the objections question the idealization implicit in the way I set up the contest between the mind and the machine; some raise questions of modality and finitude; some turn on issues of transfinite arithmetic; some are concerned with the extent to which rational inferences should be formalizable; and some are about consistency.

Many philosophers question the idealization implicit in the Gödelian argument. A context is envisaged between "the mind" and "the machine", but it is an idealized mind and an idealized machine. Actual minds are embodied in mortal clay, actual machines often malfunction or wear out. Since actual machines are not Turing machines, not having an infinite tape, that is to say an infinite memory, it may be held that they cannot be automatically subject to Gödelian limitations. But Gödel's theorem applies not only to Peano Arithmetic, with its infinitistic postulate of recursive reasoning, but to the weaker Robinson Arithmetic Q, which is only potentially, not actually infinite, and hardly extends beyond the range of plausible computer progress. In any case, limitations of finitude reduce, rather than enhance, the plausibility of some computer's being an adequate representation of a mind. Actual minds are embodied in mortal clay. In the short span of our actual lives we cannot achieve all that much, and might well have neither the time nor the cleverness to work out Gödelian formulae. Hanson points out that there could be a theorem of Elementary Number Theory that I cannot prove because a proof of it would be too long or complex for me to produce.[4] Any machine that represented a mind would be enormously complicated, and the calculation of its Gödel sentence might well be beyond the power of any human mathematician.[5] But he could be helped. Other mathematicians might come to his aid, reckoning that they also had an interest in the discomfiture of the mechanical Goliath.[6] The truth of the Gödelian sentence under its intended interpretation in ordinary informal arithmetic is a mathematical truth, which even if pointed out by other mathematicians would not depend on their testimony in the way contingent statements do. So even if aided by the hints of other mathematicians, the mind's asserting the truth of the Gödelian sentence would be a genuine ground for differentiating it from the machine.

Some critics of the Gödelian argument—Dennett, Hofstadter, and Kirk—complain that I am insufficiently sensitive to the sophistication of modern computer technology, and that there is a fatal ambiguity between the fundamental level of the machine's operations and the level of input and output that is supposed to represent the mind: in modern parlance, between the

362

machine code and the programming language, such as Prolog. But although there is a difference of levels, it does not invalidate the argument. A compiler is entirely deterministic. Any sequence of operations specified in machine code can be uniquely specified in the programming language, and vice versa, hence it is quite fair to characterize the capacity of the mechanist's machine in terms of a higher-level language. In order to begin to be a representation of a mind it must be able to do simple arithmetic. And then, at this level, Gödel's theorem applies. The same counter applies to Dennett's complaint that the comparison between men and Turing machines is highly counter-intuitive because we are not much given to wandering round uttering obscure truths of ordinary informal arithmetic. Few of us are capable of asserting a Gödelian sentence, fewer still of wanting to do so. "Men do not sit around uttering theorems in a uniform vocabulary. They say things in earnest and in jest, make slips of the tongue, speak several languages, signal agreement by nodding or otherwise acting nonverbally, and—most troublesome for this account—utter all kinds of nonsense and contradictions, both deliberately and inadvertently."[7] Of course, men are unmachine-like in these ways, and many philosophers have rejected the claims of mechanism on these grounds alone. But mechanists claim that this is too quick. Man, they say, is a very complicated machine, so complicated as to produce all this unmachinelike output. We may regard their contention as highly counter-intuitive, but should not reject it out of hand. I therefore take seriously, though only in order to refute it, the claim that a machine could be constructed to represent the behaviour of a man. If so, it must, among other things, represent a man's mental behaviour. Some men, many men, are capable of recognizing a number of basic arithmetical truths, and, particularly when asked to (which can be viewed as a particular input) can assert them as truths. Although "a characterization of a man as a certain sort of theorem-proving machine"[8] would be a less than complete characterization, it would be an essential part of a characterization of a machine if it was really to represent a man. It would have to be able to include in its output of what could be taken as assertions the basic truths of arithmetic, and to accept as valid inferences those that are validated by first-order logic. This is a minimum. Of course it may be able to do much more—it may have in its memory a store of jokes for use in after-dinner speeches, or personal reminiscences for use on subordinates—but unless its output, for suitable questions or other input, includes a set of assertions itself including Elementary Number Theory, it is a poor representation of some human minds. If it cannot pass O-level maths, are we really going to believe a mechanist when he claims that it represents a graduate?

Actual minds are finite in what they actually achieve. Wang and Boyer see difficulties in the infinite capabilities claimed for the mind as contrasted with the actual finitude of human life. Boyer takes a post-mortem view, and points out that all of the actual output of Lucas, Astaire, or anyone else can be represented *ex post facto* by a machine.[9] Actual achievements of mortal men are finite, and so simulable. When I am dead it would be possible to program a computer with sufficient graphic capacity to show on a video screen a complete biographical film of my life. But when I am dead it will be easy to outwit me. What is in issue is whether a computer can copy a living me, when I have not as yet done all that I shall do, and can do many different things. It is a question of potentiality rather than actuality. Wang concedes this, and allows that we are inclined to say that it is logically possible to have a mind capable of recognizing any true proposition of number theory or solving a set of Turing-unsolvable problems, but life is short.[10] In a finite lifespan only a finite number of the propositions can be recognized, only a finite set of problems can be solved. And a machine can be programmed to do that. Of course, we reckon that a man *can* go on to do more, but it is difficult to capture that sense of infinite potentiality. This is true. It *is* difficult to capture the sense of infinite potentiality. But infinite potentiality is an essential part of the concept of mind, and a modally "flat" account of a mind in terms only of what it has done is as unconvincing as an account of a cause which considers only constant conjunction, and not what would have been the case had circumstances been different. In order to capture this sense of potentiality, I set out my argument in terms of a challenge which leaves it open to the challenger to meet it in any way he likes. Two-sided, or "dialectical", arguments often succeed in encapsulating concepts that elude explication in purely monologous terms: the epsilon-delta exegesis of infinitesimals is best conveyed thus, and more generally any alternation of quantifiers, as in the EA principles suggested by Clark Glymour for the ultimate convergence of theories on truth (in his contribution to this volume, pp. 265–91).

Although some degree of idealization seems allowable in considering a mind untrammelled by mortality and a Turing machine with infinite tape, doubts remain as to how far into the infinite it is permissible to stray. Transfinite arithmetic underlies the objections of Good and Hofstadter. The problem arises from the way the contest between the mind and the machine is set up. The object of the contest is not to prove the mind better than the machine, but only different from it, and this is done by the mind's Gödelizing the machine. It is very natural for the mechanist to respond by including the Gödelian sentence in the machine, but of course that makes the machine a different machine with a different Gödelian sentence all of its own, which it cannot produce as true but the mind can. So then the mechanist tries adding a Gödelizing operator, which gives in effect a whole denumerable infinity of Gödelian sentences. But this, too, can be trumped by the mind, who produces the Gödelian sentence of the new machine incorporating the Gödelizing operator, and out-Gödelizes the lot. Essentially this is the move from ω, the infinite sequence of Gödelian sentences produced by the Gödelizing operator, to $\omega + 1$, the next transfinite ordinal. And so it goes on. Every now and again the mechanist loses patience, and incorporates in his machine a further operator designed to produce in one fell swoop all the Gödelian sentences the mentalist is trumping him with: this is in effect to produce a new limit ordinal. But such ordinals, although they have no predecessors, have successors just like any other ordinal, and the mind can out-Gödel them by producing the Gödelian sentence of the new version of the machine, and seeing it to be true, which the machine cannot. Hofstadter thinks there is a problem for the mentalist in view of a theorem of Church and Kleene on Formal Definitions of Transfinite Ordinals.[11] They showed that we cannot program a machine to produce names for all the ordinal numbers. Every now and again some new, creative step is called for, when we consider all the ordinal numbers hitherto named, and we need to encompass them all in a single set, which we can use to define a new sort of ordinal, transcending all previous ones. Hofstadter thinks that, in view of the Church-Kleene theorem, the mind might run out of steam, and fail to think up new ordinals as required, and so fail in the last resort to establish the mind's difference from some machine. But this is wrong on two counts. In the first place it begs the question, and in the second it misconstrues the nature of the contest.

Hofstadter assumes that the mind is subject to the same limitations as the machine is, and that since there is no mechanical way of naming all the ordinals, the mind cannot do it either. But this is precisely the point in issue. Gödel himself rejected mechanism on account of our ability to think up fresh definitions for transfinite ordinals (and ever stronger axioms for set theory) and Wang is inclined to do so too.[12] Here, it is pertinent to note that Turing himself was, on this question, of the same mind as Gödel. He was led "to ordinal logics as a way to 'escape' Gödel's incompleteness theorems",[13] but recognized that although "in pre-Gödel times it was thought by some that it would probably be possible to carry this programme to such a point that . . . the necessity for intuition would then be entirely eliminated", as a result of Gödel's incompleteness theorems one must instead "turn to 'non-constructive' systems of logic with which not all the steps in a proof are mechanical, some being intuitive."[14] Turing concedes that the steps whereby we recognize formulae as ordinal formulae are intuitive, and goes on to say that we should show quite clearly when a step makes use of intuition, and when it is purely formal, and that the strain put on intuition should be a minimum. He clearly, like Gödel, allows that the mind's ability to recognize new ordinals outruns the ability of any formal algorithm to do so, though he does not draw Gödel's conclusion. It may be, indeed, that the mind's ability to recognize new ordinals is the issue on which battle should be joined; Good claimed as much[15]—though disputes about the notation for ordinals lack the sharp edge of the Gödelian argument. But whatever the merits of different battlefields, it is clear that they are contested areas in the same conflict, and undisputed possession of the one cannot be claimed in order to assert possession of the other.

In any case Hofstadter misconstrues the nature of the contest. All the difficulties are on the side of the mechanist trying to devise a machine that cannot be out-Gödelized. It is the mechanist who resorts to limit ordinals, and who may have problems in devising new notations for them. The mind needs only to go on to the next one, which is always an easy, unproblematic step, and out-Gödelize whatever is the mechanist's latest offering. Hofstadter's argument, as often, tells against the position he is arguing for, and shows up a weakness of machines: there is no reason to suppose that it is shared by minds, and in the nature of the case it is a difficulty for those who are seeking to evade the Gödelian argument, not those who are deploying it.

Underlying Hofstadter's argument is a rhetorical question that many mechanists have raised. "How does Lucas know that the mind can do this, that, or the other?" It is no good, they hold, that I should opine it or simply assert it; I must prove it. And if I prove it, then since the steps of my proof can be programmed into a machine, the machine can do it too. Good puts the argument explicitly:

> What he must prove is that he personally can always make the improvement: it is not sufficient to *believe* it since belief is a matter of probability and Turing machines are not supposed to be capable of probability judgements. But no such proof is possible since, if it were given, it could be used for the design of a machine that could always do the improving. (Good, "Gödel's Theorem is a Red Herring", *BJPS* 19(1969): 357)

The same point is made by Webb in his sustained and searching critique of the Gödelian argument:

> [It is only because Gödel has given an effective method of constructing the Gödelian sentence that Lucas feels confident that] he can find the Achilles' heel of any machine . . . But . . . then . . . if Lucas can effectively stump any machine, . . . there must be a machine which does this too! . . . [This] is the basic dilemma confronting antimechanism: just when the constructions used in its arguments become effective enough to be sure of, [the result that every humanly effective computation procedure can be simulated by a Turing machine] then implies that a machine can simulate them. In particular, it implies that our very behavior of applying Gödel's argument to arbitrary machines—in order to conclude that we cannot be modelled by a machine—can indeed be modelled by a machine. Hence any such conclusion must fail, or else we will have to conclude that certain machines cannot be modelled by any machine! In short, antimechanist arguments must either be ineffective, or else unable to show that their executor is not a machine.[16]

The core of this argument is an assumption that every informal argument

366

must either be formalisable or else invalid. Such an assumption undercuts the distinction I have drawn between two senses of Gödelian argument: between a negative argument according to an exact specification, which a machine could be programmed to carry out, and on the other hand a certain style of arguing, similar to Gödel's original argument in inspiration, but not completely or precisely specified, and therefore not capable of being programmed into a machine, though capable of being understood and applied by an intelligent mind. Admittedly, we cannot *prove* to a hide-bound mechanist that we can go on. But we may come to a well-grounded confidence that we can, which will give us, and the erstwhile mechanist if he is reasonable and not hide-bound, good reason for rejecting mechanism.

Against this claim of the mentalist that he has got the hang of doing something which cannot be described in terms of a mechanical program, the mechanist says "Sez you" and will not believe him unless he produces a program showing how he would do it. It is like the argument between the realist and the phenomenalist. The realist claims that there exist entities not observed by anyone: the phenomenalist demands empirical evidence; if it is not forthcoming, he remains sceptical of the realist's claim; if it is, then the entity is not unobserved. In like manner the mechanist is sceptical of the mentalist's claim, unless he produces a specification of how he would do what a machine cannot: if such a specification is not forthcoming, he remains sceptical; if it is, it serves as a basis for programming a machine to do it after all. The mechanist position, like the phenomenalist, is invulnerable but unconvincing. I cannot prove to the mechanist that anything can be done other than what a machine can do, because he has restricted what he will accept as a proof to such an extent that only "machine-doable" deeds will be accounted doable at all. But not all mechanists are so limited. Many mechanists and many mentalists are rational agents wondering whether, in the light of modern science and cybernetics, mechanism is, or is not, true. They have not closed their minds by so redefining proof that none but mechanist conclusions can be established. They can recognize in themselves their having "got the hang" of something, even though no program can be written for giving a machine the hang of it. The parallel with the *sorites* argument is helpful. Arguing against a finitist, who does not accept the principle of mathematical induction, I may see at the metalevel that if he has conceded $F(0)$ and $(\forall x)(F(x) \rightarrow F(x + 1))$ then I can claim without fear of contradiction $(\forall x)F(x)$. I can be quite confident of this, although I have no finitist proof of it. All I can do, *vis-à-vis* the finitist, is to point out that *if* he were to deny my claim in any specific instance, I could refute him. True, a finitist could refute him too. But I have generalized in a way a finitist could not, so that although each particular refuting argument is finite, the claim is infinite. In a similar fashion each Gödelian argument is effective, and will convince even the mechanist that he is wrong; but the generalization from individual tactical refutations to a strategic claim does not have to be effective in the same sense, although it may be entirely rational for the mind to make the claim.

Nevertheless an air of paradox remains. The idea of a totally intuitive, unformalizable argument arouses suspicion: if it can convince, it can be conveyed, and if it can be conveyed, it can be formulated and expressed in formal terms. Let me therefore stress that I am not claiming that my, or any, argument is absolutely unformalizable. Any argument can be formalized, but, as the Tortoise proved to Achilles, the formal axiom or rule of inference invoked will be no more convincing than the original unformalized argument. I am not claiming that the Gödelian argument cannot be formalized, but that, whatever formalization we adopt, there are further arguments which are clearly valid though not captured by that formalization. Not only, again as the Tortoise proved to Achilles, must we always be ready to recognize some rules of inference as applying and some inferences as valid without more ado, but we shall be led, if we are rational, to extend our range of acknowledged valid inferences beyond any antecedently laid-down bounds. This does not preclude our subsequently formalizing them, but only our supposing that any formalization is inferentially complete.

But we always can formalize; in particular, we can formalize the argument that Gödel uses to prove that the Gödelian formula is unprovable-in-the-system but none the less true. At first sight there seems to be a paradox. Gödel's argument purports to show that the Gödelian sentence is unprovable but true. But if it shows that the Gödelian sentence is true, surely it has proved it, so that it is provable after all. The paradox in this case is resolved by distinguishing provability-in-the-formal-system from the informal provability given by Gödel's reasoning. But this reasoning can be formalized. We can go over Gödel's argument step by step, and formalize it. If we do so we find that an essential assumption for his argument that the Gödelian sentence is unprovable is that the formal system should be consistent. Else every sentence would be provable, and the Gödelian sentence, instead of being unprovable and therefore true, could be provable and false. So what we obtain, if we formalize Gödel's informal argumentation, is not a formal proof within Elementary Number Theory (ENT for short) that the Gödelian sentence, G is true, but a formal proof within Elementary Number Theory

$$\vdash Cons(ENT) \rightarrow G,$$

where Cons(ENT) is a sentence expressing the consistency of Elementary Number Theory. Only if we also had a proof in Elementary Number Theory yielding

$$\vdash Cons(ENT)$$

would we be able to infer by *modus ponens*

⊢ G.

Since we know that

⊬ G,

we infer also that

⊬ Cons(ENT).

This is Gödel's second theorem. Many critics have appealed to it in order to fault the Gödelian argument. Only if the machine's formal system is consistent and we are in a position to assert its consistency, are we really able to maintain that the Gödelian sentence is true. But we have no warrant for this. For all we know, the machine we are dealing with may be inconsistent, and even if it is consistent we are not entitled to claim that it is. And in default of such entitlement, all we have succeeded in proving is

⊢ Cons(ENT) → G,

and the machine can do that too.

These criticisms rest upon two substantial points: the consistency of the machine's system *is* assumed by the Gödelian argument and *cannot* be always established by a standard decision-procedure. The question "By what right does the mind assume that the machine is consistent?" is therefore pertinent. But the moves made by mechanists to deny the mind that knowledge are unconvincing. Paul Benacerraf suggests that the mechanist can escape the Gödelian argument by not staking out his claim in detail.[17] The mechanist offers a "black box" without specifying its program, and refuses to give away further details beyond the claim that the black box represents a mind. But such a position is both vacuous and untenable: vacuous because there is no content to mechanism unless some specification is given—if I am presented with a black box but "told not to peek inside" then why should I think it contains a machine and not, say, a little black man? The mechanist's position is also untenable: for although the mechanist has refused to specify what machine it is that he claims to represent the mind, it is evident that the Gödelian argument would work for any consistent machine and that an inconsistent machine would be an implausible representation. The stratagem of playing with his cards very close to his chest in order to deny the mind the premisses it needs is a confession of defeat.

Putnam contends that there is an illegitimate inference from the true premiss

I can see that (Cons(ENT) → G)

to the false conclusion

$$\text{Cons(ENT)} \rightarrow \text{I can see that (G).}^{18}$$

It is the latter that is needed to differentiate the mind from the machine, for what Gödel's theorem shows is

$$\text{Cons(ENT)} \rightarrow \text{ENT machine cannot see that (G),}$$

but it is only the former, according to Putnam, that I am entitled to assert. Putnam's objection fails on account of the dialectical nature of the Gödelian argument. The mind does not go round uttering theorems in the hope of tripping up any machines that may be around. Rather, there is a claim being seriously maintained by the mechanist that the mind can be represented by some machine. Before wasting time on the mechanist's claim, it is reasonable to ask him some questions about his machine to see whether his seriously maintained claim has serious backing. It is reasonable to ask him not only what the specification of the machine is, but whether it is consistent. Unless it is consistent, the claim will not get off the ground. If it is warranted to be consistent, then that gives the mind the premiss it needs. The consistency of the machine is established not by the mathematical ability of the mind but on the word of the mechanist. The mechanist has claimed that his machine is consistent. If so, it cannot prove its Gödelian sentence, which the mind can none the less see to be true: if not, it is out of court anyhow.

Wang concedes that it is reasonable to contend that only consistent machines are serious candidates for representing the mind, but then objects it is too stringent a requirement for the mechanist to meet because there is no decision-procedure that will always tell us whether a formal system strong enough to include Elementary Number Theory is consistent or not.[19] But the fact that there is no decision-*procedure* means only that we cannot always tell, not that we can never tell. Often we can tell that a formal system is not consistent, e.g. it proves as a theorem:

$$\vdash p \,\&\, \neg p$$

or,

$$\vdash 0 = 1.$$

Also, *we* may be able to tell that a system *is* consistent. We have finitary consistency proofs for propositional calculus and first-order predicate calculus, and Gentzen's proof, involving transfinite induction, for Elementary Number Theory. We are therefore not asking the impossible of the mechanist in requiring him to do some preliminary sorting out before presenting

370

candidates for being plausible representations of the mind. Unless they satisfy the examiner—the mechanist—in prelims on the score of consistency, they are not eligible to enter for finals, and all those that are thus qualified can be sure of failing for not being able to assert their Gödelian sentence.

The two-stage examination is thus able to sort out the inconsistent sheep who fail the qualifying examination from the consistent goats who fail their finals, and hence enables us to take on all challenges even from inconsistent machines without pretending to possess superhuman powers. Although all machines are entitled to enter for the mind-representation examination, only relatively few machines are plausible candidates for representing the mind, and there is no need to take a candidate seriously just because it is a machine. If the mechanist's claim is to be taken seriously, some recommendation will be required, and at the very least a warranty of consistency would be essential. Wang protests that this is to expect superhuman powers of him, and in a response to Benacerraf's "God, The Devil and Gödel", I picked up his suggestion that the mechanist might be no mere man but the Prince of Darkness himself to whom the question of whether the machine was consistent or not could be addressed in expectation of an answer.[20] Rather than ask high-flown questions about the mind we can ask the mechanist the single question whether or not the machine that is proposed as a representation of the mind would affirm the Gödelian sentence of its system. If the mechanist says that his machine will affirm the Gödelian sentence, the mind then will know that it is inconsistent and will affirm anything, quite unlike the mind which is characteristically selective in its intellectual output. If the mechanist says that his machine will not affirm the Gödelian sentence, the mind then will know since there was at least one sentence it could not prove in its system it must be consistent; and knowing that, the mind will know that the machine's Gödelian sentence is true, and thus will differ from the machine in its intellectual output. And if the mechanist is merely human, and moreover does not know what answer the machine would give to the Gödelian question, he has not done his homework properly, and should go away and try to find out before expecting us to take him seriously.

In asking the mechanist rather than the machine, we are making use of the fact that the issue is one of principle, not of practice. The mechanist is not putting forward actual machines which actually represent some human being's intellectual output, but is claiming instead that there could in principle be such a machine. He is inviting us to make an intellectual leap, extrapolating from various scientific theories and skating over many difficulties. He is quite entitled to do this. But having done this he is not entitled to be coy about his in-principle machine's intellectual capabilities or to refuse to answer embarrassing questions. The thought-experiment, once undertaken, must be thought through. And when it is thought through, it is impaled on the horns of a dilemma. Either the machine can prove in its system the Gödelian sentence or it cannot: if it can, it is inconsistent, and not equivalent to a mind; if it cannot, it is consistent, and the mind can therefore assert the Gödelian sentence to be true. Either way the machine is not equivalent to the mind, and the mechanist thesis fails.

A number of thinkers have chosen to impale themselves on the inconsistency horn of the dilemma. We are machines, they say, but very limited, fallible and inconsistent ones. In view of our many contradictions, changes of mind and failures of logic, we have no warrant for supposing the mind to be consistent, and therefore no ground for disqualifying a machine for inconsistency as a candidate for being a representation of the mind. Hofstadter thinks it would be perfectly possible to have an artificial intelligence in which propositional reasoning emerged as consequences rather than as being pre-programmed. "And there is no particular reason to assume that the strict propositional calculus, with its rigid rules and the rather silly definition of consistency that they entail, would emerge from such a program."[21]

None of these arguments goes any way to making an inconsistent machine a plausible representation of a mind. Admittedly the word "consistent" is used in different senses, and the claim that a mind is consistent is likely to involve a different sense of consistency and to be established by different sorts of arguments from those in issue when a machine is said to be consistent. If this is enough to establish the difference between minds and machines, well and good. But many mechanists will not be so quickly persuaded and will maintain that a machine can be programmed, in some such way as Hofstadter supposes, to emit mind-like behaviour. In that case it is machine-like consistency rather than mind-like consistency that is in issue. Any machine, if it is to begin to represent the output of a mind must be able to operate with symbols that can be plausibly interpreted as negation, conjunction, implication, etc., and so must be subject to the rules of some variant of the propositional calculus. Unless something rather like the propositional calculus with some comparable requirement of consistency emerges from the program of a machine, it will not be a plausible representation of a mind, no matter how good it is as a specimen of artificial intelligence. Of course, any plausible representation of a mind would have to manifest the behaviour instanced by Wang, constantly checking whether a contradiction had been reached and attempting to revise its basic axioms when that happened. But this would have to be in accordance with certain rules. There would have to be a program giving precise instructions how the checking was to be undertaken, and in what order axioms were to be revised. Some axioms would need to be fairly immune to revision. Although some thinkers are prepared to envisage a logistic calculus in which the basic inferences of propositional calculus do not hold (e.g. from p & q to p), or the axioms of Elementary Number Theory have been rejected, any machine which resorted to such a stratagem to avoid contradiction would also lose all credence as a representation of a mind. Although we sometimes contradict ourselves and change our minds, some parts of our conceptual structure are very stable, and immune to revision. Of course it is not an absolute immunity. One can allow the Cartesian possibility of conceptual revision without being guilty, as Hutton supposes,[22] of inconsistency in claiming knowledge of his own consistency. To claim to know something is not to claim infallibility, but only to have adequate backing for what is asserted. Else all knowledge of contingent truths would be impossible. Although one cannot say "I know it, although I *may* be wrong", it is perfectly permissible to say "I know it, although I *might conceivably* be wrong." So long as a man has good reasons, he can responsibly issue a warranty in the form of a statement that he knows, even though we can conceive of circumstances in which his claim would prove false and would have to be withdrawn. So it is with our claim to know the basic parts of our conceptual structure, such as the principles of reasoning embodied in the propositional calculus or the truths of ordinary informal arithmetic. We have adequate, more than adequate, reason for affirming our own consistency and the truth, and hence also the consistency, of informal arithmetic, and so can properly say that we know, and that any machine representation of the mind must manifest an output expressed by a formal (since it is a machine) system which is consistent and includes Elementary Number Theory (since it is supposed to represent the mind). But there remains the Cartesian possibility of our being wrong; and that we need now to discuss. Some mechanists have conceded that a consistent machine could be out-Gödeled by a mind, but have maintained that the machine representation of the mind is an inconsistent machine, but one whose inconsistency is so deep that it would take a long time ever to come to light. It therefore would avoid the quick death of non-selectivity. Although in principle it could be brought to affirm anything, in practice it will be selective, affirming some things and denying others. Only in the long run will it age—or mellow, as we kindly term it—and then "crash" and cease to deny anything; and in the long run we die—usually before suffering senile dementia. Such a suggestion chimes in with a line of reasoning which has been noticeable in Western thought since the eighteenth century. Reason, it is held, suffers from certain antinomies, and by its own dialectic gives rise to internal contradictions which it is quite powerless to reconcile, and which must in the end bring the whole edifice crashing down in ruins. If the mind is really an inconsistent machine then the philosophers in the Hegelian tradition who have spoken of the self-destructiveness of reason are simply those in whom the inconsistency has surfaced relatively rapidly. They are the ones who have understood the inherent inconsistency of reason, and who, negating negation, have abandoned hope of rational discourse, and having brought mind to the end of its tether, have had on offer only counsels of despair.

Against this position the Gödelian argument can avail us nothing. Quite other arguments and other attitudes are required as antidotes to nihilism. It has long been sensed that materialism leads to nihilism, and the Gödelian argument can be seen as making this *reductio* explicit. And it is a *reductio*.

For mechanism claims to be a rational position. It rests its case on the advances of science, the underlying assumptions of scientific thinking, and the actual achievements of scientific research. Although other people may be led to nihilism by feelings of *angst* or other intimations of nothingness, the mechanist must advance arguments or abandon his advocacy altogether. On the face of it we are not machines. Arguments may be adduced to show that appearances are deceptive, and that really we are machines, but arguments presuppose rationality, and if, thanks to the Gödelian argument, the only tenable form of mechanism is that we are inconsistent machines, with all minds being ultimately inconsistent, then mechanism itself is committed to the irrationality of argument, and no rational case for it can be sustained.

Notes

1 J. R. Lucas (1961), "Minds, Machines and Gödel", *Philosophy 36*: 112–27; repr. in Kenneth M. Sayre and Frederick J. Crosson (eds.), *The Modeling of Mind*, Notre Dame: University of Notre Dame Press (1963), 255–71; and in A. R. Anderson, *Minds and Machines*, Englewood Cliffs: Prentice-Hall (1964), 43–59.
2 Lucas (1970), *The Freedom of the Will*, Oxford: Oxford University Press.
3 I give at the end a list of some of the major criticisms I have come across, and most of the references in the following notes are to the items on that list.
4 W. H. Hanson (1971), 12; cf. D. R. Hofstadter (1979), 475.
5 R. Rucker (1985), 168.
6 I owe this suggestion to M. A. E. Dummett, at the original meeting of the Oxford Philosophical Society on 30 Oct., 1959. A similar suggestion is implicit in H. Wang (1974), 316.
7 D. C. Dennett (1972), 530.
8 Ibid., 527.
9 D. L. Boyer (1983).
10 Wang (1974), 315.
11 Hofstadter (1979), 475.
12 Wang (1974), 324–6.
13 Solomon Feferman (1988), "Turing in the Land of O(z)", in Rolf Herken (ed.), *The Universal Turing Machine*, Oxford: Oxford University Press, 113–47.
14 A. M. Turing (1939), "Systems of Logic Based on Ordinals", *Proceedings of the London Mathematical Society* 2/45: 161–228; repr. in M. Davis (ed.), *The Undecidable*, New York: Raven Press (1965), 155–222; quotations from pp. 209 and 210 (of Davis), also quoted by Feferman (1988) "Turing in the Land of O(z)", 129.
15 I. J. Good (1969), 357–8.
16 J. C. Webb (1980), 230–2.
17 P. Benacerraf (1967).
18 H. Putnam (1960).
19 Wang (1974), 317.
20 Benacerraf (1967), 22–3; Lucas (1968), "Satan Stultified", *The Monist* 52: 145–58.
21 Hofstadter (1979), 578; cf. C. S. Chihara (1972), 526.
22 A Hutton (1976).

References

Benacerraf, Paul (1967), "God, the Devil and Gödel", *The Monist* 51: 9–32.

Bostock, David (1984), "Gödel and Determinism", private communication, Nov. 1984.

Bowie, G. Lee (1982), "Lucas' Number is Finally Up", *Journal of Philosophical Logic* 11: 279–85.

Boyer, David L. (1983), "J.R. Lucas, Kurt Gödel, and Fred Astaire", *Philosophical Quarterly* 33: 147–59.

Chihara, Charles S. (1972), "On Alleged Refutations of Mechanism using Gödel's Incompleteness Results", *Journal of Philosophy* 69/17: 507–26.

Coder, David (1969), "Goedel's Theorem and Mechanism", *Philosophy* 64: 234–7, esp. 236.

Dennett, D. C. (1972), review of *The Freedom of the Will* (Lucas 1970), *Journal of Philosophy* 59: 527–31.

Fernando, Emmanuel Q. (1980), "Mathematical and Philosophical Implications of the Gödel Incompleteness Theorems", MA thesis, College of Arts and Sciences, University of the Philippines, Quezu City, Sept. 1980.

Glover, Jonathan (1970), *Responsibility*, London: Routledge & Kegan Paul, 31.

Good, I.J. (1967), "Human and Machine Logic", *British Journal for the Philosophy of Science* 18: 144–7.

—— (1969), "Gödel's Theorem is a Red Herring", *British Journal for the Philosophy of Science* 19: 357–8.

Hanson, William H. (1971), "Mechanism and Gödel's Theorems", *British Journal for the Philosophy of Science* 22: 9–16.

Hofstadter, Douglas R. (1979), *Gödel, Escher, Bach*, New York: Basic Books, 475.

Hutton, Anthony (1976), "This Gödel is Killing Me", *Philosophia* 6/1: 135–44.

Kenny, A. J. P. (1972), in A. J. P. Kenny, H. C. Longuet-Higgins, J. R. Lucas, and C. H. Waddington, *The Nature of Mind*, Edinburgh: Edinburgh University Press, 75–87.

Kirk, Robert (1986), "Mental Machinery and Gödel", *Synthese* 66: 437–52.

Lewis, David (1969), "Lucas against Mechanism", *Philosophy* 64: 231–3.

—— (1979), "Lucas against Mechanism II", *Canadian Journal of Philosophy* 9: 373–6.

Mackie, J. L. (1977), *Ethics: Inventing Right and Wrong*, Harmondsworth: Penguin, 219.

Putnam, Hilary (1960), "Minds and Machines", in Sidney Hook (ed.), *Dimensions of Mind: A Symposium*, New York: New York University Press, 138–64; repr. in A. R. Anderson (ed.), *Minds and Machines*, Englewood Cliffs: Prentice-Hall (1964), 72–97.

Rucker, Rudy (1985), "Gödel's Theorem: The Paradox at the Heart of Modern Man', *Popular Computing*, Feb. 1985, 168.

Sleazak, P. (1982), "Gödel's Theorem and the Mind", *British Journal for the Philosophy of Science* 33: 41–52.

Smart, J. J. C. (1961), "Gödel's Theorem, Church's Theorem, and Mechanism", *Synthese* 13: 105–110.

—— (1963), "Man as a Physical Mechanism", ch. 6 in his *Philosophy and Scientific Realism*, London: Routledge & Kegan Paul.

Thorp, J. W. (1976), "Free Will and Neurophysiological Determinism", Oxford D.Phil. thesis, 79.

Wang, Hao (1974), *From Mathematics to Philosophy*, London: Routledge & Kegan Paul, 319–26.

Webb, Judson C. (1980), *Mechanism, Mentalism and Meta-mathematics: An Essay on Finitism*, Dordrecht: D. Reidel, 230.

Whiteley, C. H. (1962), "Minds, Machines and Gödel: A Reply to Mr Lucas", *Philosophy* 37: 61–2.

Other works are cited in J. R. Lucas (1970), *The Freedom of the Will*, Oxford: Oxford University Press, 174–6.

Section 2.2: Phenomenology

59

ALCHEMY AND ARTIFICIAL INTELLIGENCE[1]

Hubert L. Dreyfus

Source: *Rand Organization*, 1965, 1–90.

Summary Early successes in programming digital computers to exhibit simple forms of intelligent behavior, coupled with the belief that intelligent activities differ only in their degree of complexity, have led to the conviction that the information processing underlying any cognitive performance can be formulated in a program and thus simulated on a digital computer. Attempts to simulate cognitive processes on computers have, however, run into greater difficulties than anticipated.

An examination of these difficulties reveals that the attempt to analyze intelligent behavior in digital computer language systematically excludes three fundamental human forms of information processing (fringe consciousness, essence/accident discrimination, and ambiguity tolerance). Moreover, there are four distinct types of intelligent activity, only two of which do not presuppose these human forms of information processing and can therefore be programmed. Significant developments in artificial intelligence in the remaining two areas must await computers of an entirely different sort, of which the only existing prototype is the little-understood human brain.

The difference between the mathematical mind (*esprit de géométrie*) and the perceptive mind (*esprit de finesse*): the reason that mathematicians are not perceptive is that they do not see what is before them, and that, accustomed to the exact and plain principles of mathematics, and not reasoning till they have well inspected and arranged their principles, they are lost in matters of perception where the principles do not allow for such arrangement . . . These principles are so fine and so numerous that a very delicate and very clear sense is needed to perceive them, and to judge rightly and justly when they are perceived, without for the most part being able to demonstrate them in order as in mathematics; because the principles are not known to us in the same way, and because it would be an endless matter to undertake it. We must see the matter at once, at one glance, and not by a process of reasoning, at least to a certain degree . . . Mathematicians wish to treat matters of perception mathematically, and make themselves ridiculous . . . the mind . . . does it tacitly, naturally, and without technical rules.

(Pascal, Pensées)

Introduction

Research dedicated to the construction of intelligent artifacts has, from its inception, intrigued philosophers, but thus far their discussions have been remarkably out of touch with the work actually being done. Analytic philosophers, such as Putnam, Scriven, and Ziff, use the present interest in "mechanical brains" to recast the conceptual issues dividing behaviorists from Cartesians. They assume that robots will eventually be built whose behavior will be indistinguishable from that of humans, and ask under what conditions we would be justified in saying that such an artifact was thinking. On the other hand, moralists and theologians evoke certain highly sophisticated forms of behavior – moral choice, love, creative abstraction, etc. – which they claim are beyond the powers of any machine. Neither side defines what sort of machine it has in mind nor tries to show that a machine can or cannot exhibit the behavior in question. Both parties credulously assume that highly intelligent artifacts have already been developed.

If such artifacts have been or are about to be produced, their operation will depend on the only high-speed, all-purpose information processing device which now exists – the digital computer. Thus, the only question which can reasonably be discussed at present is not whether robots can fall in love, or whether if they did we would say they were conscious, but rather to what extent a digital computer can be programmed to exhibit the sort of simple intelligent behavior characteristic of children and sometimes animals, such as playing games, solving simple problems, reading sentences, and recognizing patterns. Philosophers have failed to raise this modest question. Instead, they approach the subject in terms of man's highest capacities, presumably because they are under the impression, fostered by the press and some artificial intelligence researchers, that these simple feats have been or are about to be performed. To begin with, then, these claims must be examined.

It is fitting to begin with a statement made in 1957 by H. A. Simon, one of the originators of the field of artificial intelligence:

> It is not my aim to surprise or shock you – if indeed that were possible in an age of nuclear fission and prospective interplanetary

travel. But the simplest way I can summarize is to say that there are now in the world machines that think, that learn and that create. Moreover, their ability to do these things is going to increase rapidly until – in a visible future – the range of problems they can handle will be co-extensive with the range to which the human mind has been applied.

The speaker makes the following predictions:

1) That within ten years a digital computer will be the world's chess champion, unless the rules bar it from competition.
2) That within ten years a digital computer will discover and prove an important new mathematical theorem.
3) That within ten years a digital computer will write music that will be accepted by critics as possessing considerable aesthetic value.
4) That within ten years most theories in psychology will take the form of computer programs, or of qualitative statements about the character- istics of computer programs [34:7, 8].[2]

Let us hope that in November 1967, the tenth anniversary of this historic talk, workers in the field of artificial intelligence will meet to measure their vision against reality. Meanwhile, though it is too early to definitively test these claims, enough time has elapsed to allow a significant confrontation of these predictions with actual progress in the field.

Recent publications suggest that the first of Simon's forecasts has already been half-realized and that considerable progress has been made in fulfilling his second prediction. In a review of Feigenbaum and Feldman's anthology, *Computers and Thought*, W. R. Ashby (one of the leading authorities in the field) hailed the mathematical power of the properly programmed com- puter: "Gelernter's theorem-proving program has discovered a new proof of the *pons asinorum* that demands no construction." This proof, Professor Ashby goes on to say, is one which "the greatest mathematicians of 2000 years have failed to notice . . . which would have evoked the highest praise had it occurred" [2:2].

The theorem sounds important and the naive reader cannot help sharing Ashby's enthusiasm. A little research, however, reveals that the *pons asino- rum*, or ass's bridge, is the first theorem to be proved in Euclidian geometry, *viz.*, that the opposite angles of an isosceles triangle are equal. Moreover, the proof requiring the construction of a perpendicular to the base of the tri- angle (still taught in high schools) was introduced as late as the 19th century, presumably as a pedagogical device. The first announcement of the "new" proof "discovered" by the machine is attributed to Pappus (300 A.D.) [37:284]. There is a striking disparity between Ashby's excitement and the antiquity and triviality of this proof. We are still a long way from "the important mathematical theorem" to be found by 1967.

The chess-playing story is more involved and might serve as a model for a study of the production of intellectual smog in this area. The story began in 1955 with Allen Newell's sober survey of the problems posed by the game of chess and suggestions as to how they might be met. He found that "these [suggested] mechanisms are so complicated that it is impossible to predict whether they will work" [18:89].

The next year (a year before Simon makes his predictions) brought startling success. A group at Los Alamos produced a program which played poor but legal chess on a reduced board. In a review of this work, Newell, J. C. Shaw, and H. A. Simon concluded: "With very little in the way of complexity, we have at least entered the arena of human play – we can beat a beginner" [22:48]. In 1957, the year of the great prediction, the Bernstein program for the IBM 704 entered the arena, and played two "passable amateur games" [22:45].

The following year, Newell, Shaw, and Simon (NSS) presented an elaborate chess-playing program. As described in their classic paper, "Chess Playing and the Problem of Complexity," their program was "not yet fully debugged," so that one "cannot say very much about the behavior of the program" [22:60]. Still, it is clearly "good in the opening." This is the last detailed published report on the program. In the same year, however, NSS announced: "We have written a program that plays chess" [21:6] and Simon, on the basis of this success, revised his earlier prediction.

> In another place, we have predicted that within ten years a computer will discover and prove an important mathematical theorem, and compose music that is regarded as aesthetically significant. On the basis of our experience with the heuristics of logic and chess, we are willing to add the further prediction that only moderate extrapolation is required from the capacities of programs already in existence to achieve the additional problem-solving power needed for such simulation [21:78].

In fact, in its few recorded games, the NSS program played poor but legal chess, and in its last official bout (October 1960) was beaten in 35 moves by a ten-year old novice. Fact, however, had ceased to be relevant. Newell, Shaw, and Simon's claims concerning their still bugged program had launched the chess machine into the realm of scientific mythology. In 1959, Norbert Wiener, whose optimism was strengthened by the claim that the program was "good in the opening," informed the N.Y.U. Institute of Philosophy that "chess-playing machines as of now will counter the moves of a master game with the moves recognized as right in the text books, up to some point in the middle game" [41:110]. In the same symposium, Michael Scriven moved from the ambiguous claim that "machines now play chess" to the positive assertion that "machines are already capable of a good game" [32:128].

While their program was losing its five or six poor games – and the myth they had engendered was holding its own against masters in the middle game – Newell, Shaw, and Simon kept silent. When they speak again, three years later, they do not report their difficulties and disappointment. Rather, as if to take up where the myth had left off, Simon published an article in *Behavioral Science* announcing a program which will play "highly creative" chess end games involving "combinations as difficult as any that have been recorded in chess history" [36:429]. That the program restricts these end games to dependence on continuing checks, so that the number of relevant moves is greatly reduced, is mentioned but not emphasized. On the contrary, it is misleadingly implied that similar simple heuristics would account for master play even in the middle game. Thus, the article gives the impression that the chess prediction is almost realized. With such progress, the chess championship may be *claimed* at any moment. Indeed, a Russian cyberneticist, upon hearing of Simon's ten-year estimate, called it "conservative" [1:405]. And Fred Gruenberger at RAND has suggested that a world champion is not enough – that we should aim for "a program which plays better than any man could" [11:6]. This output of confusion makes one think of the French mythical beast which is supposed to secrete the fog necessary for its own respiration.

I propose first to clear the air by reviewing the present state of artificial intelligence. The field has many divisions and subdivisions, but the most important work can be classified into four areas: a) game playing, b) problem solving, c) language translation and learning, and d) pattern recognition.

Part I will simply report the progress and difficulties in each area. Part II will show the common source of these seemingly unconnected difficulties and clarify certain conceptual confusions which hide the gravity of the situation these difficulties reveal. Part III will consider certain essential limitations on the information which can be processed by digital computers. Then, by classifying intelligent behavior in the light of these limitations, Part III will indicate which areas of behavior are susceptible to simulation and which areas lie beyond the capacities of digital computer programs.

Part I

The current state of the field of artificial intelligence

The field of artificial intelligence exhibits a recurrent pattern: early, dramatic success followed by sudden unexpected difficulties. Let us explore this pattern in detail.

Signs of stagnation

Game playing

The first years produced very impressive work – perhaps the most impressive work in the whole field of artificial intelligence. By 1955 Samuel had a checker program which could play "a fairly interesting game" [29:73]. After several improvements, including a learning program, Samuel's program was able to beat a former Connecticut checkers champion. Samuel's program does not attempt to simulate human information processing nor use heuristic search techniques. A tree of moves is searched to a depth which depends on the final position, and then, on the basis of an evaluation of certain parameters, a move is chosen.

This method is less successful in chess where the number of possible moves and responses is so great, the problem of exponential growth so acute, that the search tree must be pruned at each stage. Still, chess programs attained early success with simple limited search. The Los Alamos program, using no heuristics, could play a legal game on a reduced board. A year later, the Bernstein program using search pruning heuristics did as well on a full eight-by-eight board. Then came the program developed by Newell, Shaw, and Simon, followed by the optimistic claims and predictions.

No one noted the unexpected difficulties. The initial NSS chess program was poor and, in the last five years, remains unimproved. Burton Bloom at M.I.T. has made the latest attempt to write a chess program; like all the others, it plays a stupid game. In fact, in the nine years since the Los Alamos program beat a weak player, in spite of a great investment of time, energy, and ink, the only improvement seems to be that a machine now plays poorly on an eight-by-eight rather than a six-by-six board. According to Newell, Shaw, and Simon themselves, evaluating the Los Alamos, the IBM, and the NSS program: "All three programs play roughly the same quality of chess (mediocre) with roughly the same amount of computing time" [20:14]. Still no chess program can play even amateur chess, and the world championship tournament is only two years away.

Problem solving

Again an early success: In 1957 Newell, Shaw, and Simon's Logic Theorist, using heuristically guided trial-and-error, proved 38 out of 52 theorems from *Principia Mathematica*. (Significantly, the greatest achievement in the field of mechanical theorem-proving, Wang's theorem-proving program, which proved in less than five minutes all 52 theorems chosen by Newell, Shaw, and Simon, does not use heuristics.) Two years later, the General Problem Solver (GPS), using more sophisticated means-ends analysis, solved the "cannibal and missionary" problem and other problems of similar complexity [22:15].

In 1961, after comparing a machine trace with a protocol which matched the machine output to some extent, Newell and Simon concluded rather cautiously:

> The fragmentary evidence we have obtained to date encourages us to think that the General Problem Solver provides a rather good *first approximation* to an information processing theory of *certain kinds* of thinking and problem solving behavior. The processes of "thinking" can no longer be regarded as completely mysterious (my italics) [24:19].

Soon, however, Simon gave way to more enthusiastic claims:

> Subsequent work has tended to confirm [our] initial hunch, and to demonstrate that heuristics, or rules of thumb, form the integral core of human problem-solving processes. As we begin to understand the nature of the heuristics that people use in thinking, the mystery begins to dissolve from such (heretofore) vaguely understood processes as "intuition" and "judgment" [33:12].

But, as we have seen in the case of chess, difficulties have an annoying way of reasserting themselves. This time, the "mystery" of judgment reappears in terms of the organizational aspects of the problem-solving programs. In "Some Problems of Basic Organization in Problem-Solving Programs" (December 1962), Newell discusses some of the problems which arise in organizing the Chess Program, the Logic Theorist, and especially the GPS, with a candor rare in the field, and admits that "most of them are unsolved to some extent, either completely, or because the solutions that have been adopted are still unsatisfactory in one way or another" [19:4]. No further progress has been reported toward the resolution of these problems.

This curve from success to optimism to disappointment can be followed in miniature in the case of Gelernter's Geometry Theorem Machine (1959). Its early success with theorems like the *pons asinorum* gave rise to the first prediction sufficiently short-range to have already been totally discredited. In an article published in 1960, Gelernter explains the heuristics of his program and then concludes: "Three years ago, the dominant opinion was that the geometry machine would not exist today. And today, hardly an expert will contest the assertion that machines will be proving interesting theorems in number theory three years hence," i.e., in 1963 [9:160]. No more striking example exists of an "astonishing" early success and the equally astonishing failure to follow it up.

Language translation

This area had the earliest success, the most extensive and expensive research, and the most unequivocal failure. It was clear from the start that a mechanical dictionary could easily be constructed in which linguistic items, whether they were parts of words, whole words, or groups of words, could be processed independently and converted one after another into corresponding items in another language. As Richard See notes in his article in *Science*, May 1964: "Successful processing at this most primitive level was achieved at an early date" [30:622], and Oettinger, the first to produce a mechanical dictionary (1954), recalls this early enthusiasm: "The notion of ... fully automatic high quality mechanical translation, planted by over-zealous propagandists for automatic translation on both sides of the Iron Curtain and nurtured by the wishful thinking of potential users, blossomed like a vigorous weed" [27:18]. This initial success and the subsequent disillusionment provides a sort of paradigm for the field. It is aptly described by Bar-Hillel in his report on "The Present Status of Automatic Translation of Languages."

> During the first year of the research in machine translation, a considerable amount of progress was made ... It created among many of the workers actively engaged in this field the strong feeling that a working system was just around the corner. Though it is understandable that such an illusion should have been formed at the time, it was an illusion. It was created ... by the fact that a large number of problems were rather readily solved ... It was not sufficiently realized that the gap between such output ... and high quality translation proper was still enormous, and that the problems solved until then were indeed many but just the simplest ones whereas the "few" remaining problems were the harder ones – very hard indeed [3:94].

During the ten years since the development of a mechanical dictionary, five government agencies have spent about 16 million dollars on mechanical translation research [30:625]. In spite of journalistic claims at various moments that machine translation was at last operational, this research produced primarily a much deeper knowledge of the unsuspected complexity of syntax and semantics. As Oettinger remarks, "The major problem of selecting an appropriate target correspondent for a source word on the basis of context remains unsolved, as does the related one of establishing a unique syntactic structure for a sentence that human readers find unambiguous" [27:21]. Oettinger concludes: "The outlook is grim for those who still cherish hopes for fully automatic high-quality mechanical translation" [27:27]. Acting on Oettinger's realization, the Harvard Computation Laboratory decided to concentrate its work on English syntax and dropped all work on Russian.

Pattern recognition

This field is discussed last because the resolution of the difficulties which have arrested development in game playing, problem solving, and language translation all presuppose success in the field of pattern recognition (which in turn suffers from each of the difficulties encountered in the other fields). As Selfridge and Neisser point out in their classic article, "Pattern Recognition by Machine,"

> . . . a man is continually exposed to a welter of data from his senses, and abstracts from it the patterns relevant to his activity at the moment. His ability to solve problems, prove theorems and generally run his life depends on this type of perception. We suspect that until programs to perceive patterns can be developed, achievements in mechanical problem-solving will remain isolated technical triumphs [31:238].

As one might expect, this field experienced no simple early successes. Selfridge and Neisser allow that "developing pattern recognition programs has proved rather difficult" [31:238]. There has indeed been some excellent work. The Lincoln Laboratory group under Bernard Gold produced a program for transliterating hand-sent Morse code. And there are several operational programs that can learn to recognize hand-printed alphabetic characters of variable sizes and rotations. Still, as Selfridge and Neisser remark, "At present the only way the machine can get an adequate set of features is from a human programmer" [31:244]. And they conclude their survey of the field with a challenge rather than a prediction:

> The most important learning process of all is still untouched: No current program can generate test features of its own. The effectiveness of all of them is forever restricted by the ingenuity or arbitrariness of their programmers. We can barely guess how this restriction might be overcome. Until it is, "artificial intelligence" will remain tainted with artifice [31:250].

Even these remarks may be too optimistic, however, in their supposition that the present problem is feature-generation. The relative success of the Uhr-Vossler program, which generates and evaluates its own operators, shows that this problem is partially soluble. However, as Part II demonstrates, mechanical recognition still remains a rigid process of brute-force enumeration. No pattern recognition program, even Uhr-Vossler's, incorporates the flexibility of the human tacit pattern-recognition processes.

Thus the disparity between prediction and performance which is characteristic of artificial intelligence reappears, for example, in the case of the print reader. Bar-Hillel, who also likes to collect unfulfilled prophesies, quoted in 1959 a claim by Edwin Reifler that "in about two years [from August 1957] we shall have a device which will at one glance read a whole page." Bar-Hillel, who presumably has been cured of over-optimism, then went on to make a more modest claim. "The best estimates I am aware of at present mention five years as the time after which we are likely to have a reliable and versatile print reader . . . " [3:104].

Over five years have elapsed since Bar-Hillel made this conservative estimate. At that time, flight to the moon was still science fiction and the print reader was just around the corner. Now the moon project is well underway while, according to Oettinger in 1963, no versatile print reader is in sight: "In the foreseeable future, automatic print reading devices will handle only materials with great uniformity of layout and type design, such as, for example, ordinary typewritten material" [27:20]. Books and journals with registered margins seem to be over the horizon, and the horizon seems to be receding at an accelerating rate.

Comments and conclusions

An overall pattern is taking shape: an early, dramatic success based on the easy performance of simple tasks, or low-quality work on complex tasks, and then diminishing returns, disenchantment, and, in some cases, pessimism. The pattern is not caused by too much being demanded too soon by eager or skeptical outsiders. The failure to produce is measured solely against the expectations of those working in the field.

When the situation is grim, however, enthusiasts can always fall back on their own optimism. This tendency to substitute long-range for operational programs slips out in Feigenbaum and Feldman's claim that "the forecast for progress in research in human cognitive processes is most encouraging" [8:276]. The forecast always has been, but one wonders: how encouraging are the prospects?

Feigenbaum and Feldman claim that tangible progress is indeed being made and they define progress very carefully as "displacement toward the ultimate goal" [8:vi]. According to this definition, the first man to climb a tree could claim tangible progress toward flight to the moon.[3]

Part II

The underlying significance of current difficulties

Negative results can be interesting, provided one recognizes them as such. The diminishing achievement, instead of the predicted accelerating success, perhaps indicates some unexpected phenomenon. Are we pushing out on a continuum like that of velocity, such that progress becomes more and more difficult as we approach the speed of light, or are we instead facing a discontinuity, like the tree-climbing man who reaches for the moon?

It seems natural to take stock of the field at this point, yet surprisingly no one has done so. If someone had, he would have found that each of the four areas considered has a corresponding specific form of human information processing which enables human subjects in that area to avoid the difficulties which an artificial subject must confront. The section below will isolate these four human forms of information processing and contrast them with their machine surrogates. The following section will formulate and criticize the assumption shared by workers in artificial intelligence that human subjects face the same difficulties as artificial subjects and that therefore these difficulties obviously can be overcome.

Human vs. machine information processing

Fringe consciousness vs. heuristically guided search

It is common knowledge that a certain class of games are decidable on present-day computers with present-day techniques – games like nim and tic-tac-toe can be programmed so that the machine will win or draw every time. Other games, however, cannot be decided in this way on present-day computers, and yet have been successfully programmed. In checkers, for example, because only two kinds of moves are possible, the captures are forced, and pieces block each other, one can explore all possibilities to a depth of as many as twenty moves, which proves sufficient for playing a good game.

Chess, however, presents the problem inevitably connected with choice mazes: exponential growth. We cannot run through all the branching possibilities even far enough to form a reliable judgment as to whether a given branch is sufficiently promising to merit further exploration. Newell notes that it would take much too long to find an interesting move if the machine had to examine the pieces on the board one after another. He is also aware that, if this is not done, the machine may sometimes miss an important and original combination. "We do not want the machine to spend all its time examining the future actions of committed men; yet if it were never to do this, it could overlook real opportunities . . . " [18:80].

His first solution was "the random element . . . The machine should rarely [i.e., occasionally] search for combinations which sacrifice a Queen ... " [18:80]. But this solution is unsatisfactory, as Newell himself presumably now realizes. The machine should not look just every once in a while for a Queen sacrifice but, rather, look in those situations in which such a sacrifice would be relevant. This is what the right heuristics are supposed to assure, by limiting the number of branches explored while retaining the more promising alternatives.

No such heuristics have as yet been found. All current heuristics either exclude some possibly good moves or leave open the risk of exponential growth. Simon is nonetheless convinced, for reasons discussed below, that chess masters use such heuristics, and so he is confident that if we listen to their protocols, follow their eye movements, perhaps question them under bright lights, we can eventually discover these heuristics and build them into our program – thereby pruning the exponential tree. But let us examine more closely the evidence that chess playing is governed by the use of heuristics.

Consider the following protocol quoted by Simon, noting especially how it begins rather than how it ends. The player says,

> Again I notice that one of his pieces is not defended, the Rook, and there must be ways of taking advantage of this. Suppose now, if I push the pawn up at Bishop four, if the Bishop retreats I have a Queen check and I can pick up the Rook. If, etc., etc. [24:15].

At the end we have an example of what I shall call "counting out" – thinking through the various possibilities by brute-force enumeration. We have all engaged in this process, which, guided by suitable heuristics, is supposed to account for the performance of chess masters. But how did our subject notice that the opponent's Rook was undefended? Did he examine each of his opponent's pieces and their possible defenders sequentially (or simultaneously) until he stumbled on the vulnerable Rook? Impossible! As Newell, Shaw, and Simon remark, "The best evidence suggests that a human player considers considerably less than 100 positions in the analysis of a move" [22:47], and our player must still consider many positions in evaluating the situation once the undefended Rook has been discovered.

We need not appeal to introspection to discover what a player in fact does before he begins to count out; the protocol itself indicates it: the subject "zeroed in" on the promising situation ("I notice that one of his pieces is not defended"). Often, of course, locating the promising or threatening area involves more than simply noticing that a Rook is undefended. It may involve noticing that "here something interesting seems to be going on"; "he looks weak over here"; "I look weak over there"; etc. Only *after* the player has zeroed in on an area does he begin to count out, to test, what he can do from there.

The player need not be aware of having explicitly considered or explicitly excluded from consideration any of the hundreds of possibilities that would have had to be enumerated in order to have arrived at this particular area by counting out. Still, the specific portion of the board which finally attracts the subject's attention depends on the overall configuration. To understand how this is possible, consider what William James has called "the fringes of consciousness": the ticking of a clock which we notice only if it stops provides a simple example of this sort of marginal awareness. Our vague awareness of the faces in a crowd when we search for a friend is another, more complex and more nearly appropriate, case.

But in neither of these cases does the subject make positive use of the information resting on the fringe. The chess case is best understood in terms of Polanyi's description of the power of the fringes of consciousness to concentrate information concerning our peripheral experience.

> This power resides in the area which tends to function as a background because it extends indeterminately around the central object of our attention. Seen thus from the corner of our eyes, or remembered at the back of our mind, this area compellingly affects the way we see the object on which we are focusing. We may indeed go so far as to say that we are aware of this subsidiarily noticed area mainly in the appearance of the object to which we are attending [28:214].

Once familiar with a house, for example, the front *looks* thicker than a facade, because one is marginally aware of the house behind. Similarly, in chess, cues from all over the board, while remaining on the fringes of consciousness, draw attention to certain sectors by making them appear promising, dangerous, or simply worth looking into.

If information, rather than being explicitly considered, can remain on the fringes of consciousness and be implicitly taken into account through its effect on the appearance of the objects on which our attention is focused, *then* there is no reason to suppose that, in order to discover an undefended Rook, our subject must have counted out rapidly and unconsciously until he arrived at the area in which he began consciously counting out. Moreover, there are good reasons to reject this assumption, since it raises more problems than it solves.

If the subject has been unconsciously counting out thousands of alternatives with brilliant heuristics to get to the point where he focuses on that Rook, why doesn't he carry on with that unconscious process all the way to the end, until the best move just pops into his consciousness? Why, if the *unconscious* counting is rapid and accurate, does he resort at the particular point where he spots the Rook to a cumbersome method of slowly, awkwardly, and consciously counting things out? Or if, on the other hand, the unconscious counting is *inadequate*, what is the advantage of switching to a conscious version of the same process?

It seems that "unconsciously" the subject is engaged in a sort of information processing which differs from counting out, and conscious counting begins when he has to refine this global process in order to deal with details. Moreover, even if he does unconsciously count out, using unconscious heuristics – which there is no reason to suppose and good reason to doubt – what kind of program could convert this unconscious counting into the kind of fringe-influenced awareness of the centers of interest, which is the way zeroing-in presents itself in our experience? Why has no one interested in cognitive simulation been interested in this conversion process?

There is thus no evidence, behavioral or introspective, that counting out is the only function of thought involved in playing chess, that "the essential nature of the task [is] search in a space of exponentially growing possibilities" [22:65]. On the contrary, all protocols testify that chess involves two kinds of behavior: *zeroing in* on an area formerly on the fringes of consciousness, which other areas still on the fringes of consciousness make interesting; and *counting out* explicit alternatives.

This distinction clarifies the early success and the later failure of work in artificial intelligence. In all game-playing programs, early success is attained by working on those games or parts of games in which counting out is feasible; failure occurs when global awareness is necessary to avoid exponential growth.

Essence / accident discrimination vs. trial and error

Work in problem solving also encounters two functions of thought – one, elementary and associationistic, accounts for the early success in the field; another, more complex and requiring insight, has proved intractable to step-wise programs such as the GPS.

If a problem is set up in a simple, completely determinate way, with an end and a beginning and rules for getting from one to the other (in other words, if we have what Simon calls a "simple formal problem"), then GPS can successfully bring the end and the beginning closer and closer together until the problem is solved. But even this presents many difficulties. Comparing the trace of a GPS solution with the protocol of a human solving the same problem reveals steps in the machine trace (explicit searching) which do not appear in the subject's protocol. And we are again asked to accept the dubious assumption that "many things concerning the task surely occurred without the subject's commenting on them (or being aware of them)" [26:288], and the even more arbitrary assumption that these further operations were of the same elementary sort as those verbalized. In fact, certain details of Newell and Simon's article, "GPS: A Program that Simulates Human Thought," suggest that these further operations are not like the programmed operations at all.

At a point in the protocol analyzed in this article, the subject applies the rule $(A \cdot B \rightarrow A, A \cdot B \rightarrow B)$, to the conjunction $(-R \; v - P) \cdot (R \; v \; Q)$. Newell and Simon note:

> The subject handled both forms of rule 8 together, at least as far as his comment is concerned. GPS, on the other hand, took a separate cycle of consideration for each form. Possibly the subject followed the program covertly and simply reported the two results together [26:289].

Probably, however, the subject grasped the conjunction as symmetric with respect to the transformation operated by the rule, and so in fact applied both forms of the rule at once. Even Newell and Simon admit that they would have preferred that GPS apply both forms of the rule in the same cycle. They wisely refrain, however, from trying to write a program which could discriminate between occasions when it was appropriate to apply both forms of the rule at once and those when it was not. Such a program, far from eliminating the above divergence, would require further processing not reported by the subject, thereby increasing the discrepancy between the program and the protocol. Unable thus to eliminate the divergence and unwilling to try to understand its significance, Newell and Simon dispose of the discrepancy as "an example of parallel processing" [26:290].

Another divergence noted by Newell and Simon, however, does not permit such an evasion. At a certain point, the protocol reads: " . . . I should have used rule 6 on the left-hand side of the equation. So use 6, but only on the left-hand side." Simon notes:

> Here we have a strong departure from the GPS trace. Both the subject and GPS found rule 6 as the appropriate one to change signs. At this point GPS simply applied the rule to the current expression; whereas the subject went back and corrected the previous application. Nothing exists in the program that corresponds to this. The most direct explanation is that the application of rule 6 in the inverse direction is perceived by the subject as undoing the previous application of rule 6 [26:291].

This is indeed the most direct explanation, but Newell and Simon do not seem to realize that this departure from the trace, which cannot be explained away by parallel processing, is as serious as the planetary discrepancies which alerted modern astronomers to the inadequacies of the Ptolemaic system. Some form of thinking other than searching is taking place.

Newell and Simon note the problem: "It clearly implies a mechanism [maybe a whole set of them] that is not in GPS" [26:292], but, like the ancient astronomers, they try to save their theory by adding a few epicycles. They continue to suppose, without any evidence, that this mechanism is just a more elaborate search technique which can be accommodated by providing GPS with "a little continuous hindsight about its past actions" [26:292]. They do not realize that their subject's decision to backtrack must be the result of a very *selective* checking procedure. Otherwise, all past steps would have to be rechecked at each stage, which would hopelessly encumber the program.

A more scientific approach would be to explore further the implications of the five discrepancies noted in the article, in order to determine whether or not a different form of information processing might be involved. For example, Wertheimer points out in his classic work, *Productive Thinking*, that the associationist account of problem solving excludes the most important aspect of problem solving behavior, *viz.*, a grasp of the essential structure of the problem, which he calls "insight" [40:202]. In this operation, one breaks away from the surface structure and sees the basic problem – what Wertheimer calls the "deeper structure" – which enables one to organize the steps necessary for a solution.

This gestaltist conception may seem antithetical to the operational concepts demanded in artificial intelligence, but in fact this restructuring is surreptitiously pre-supposed by the work of Newell, Shaw, and Simon themselves. In *The Processes of Creative Thinking*, they introduce "the heuristics of planning" to account for characteristics of the subject's protocol lacking in a simple means-end analysis.

> We have devised a program . . . to describe the way some of our subjects handle O. K. Moore's logic problems, and perhaps the easiest way to show what is involved in planning is to describe that program. On a purely pragmatic basis, the twelve operators that are admitted in this system of logic can be put in two classes, which we shall call "essential" and "inessential" operators, respectively. Essential operators are those which, when applied to an expression, make "large" changes in its appearance – change "PvP" to "P", for example. Inessential operators are those which make "small" changes – e.g., change "PvQ" to "QvP". As we have said, the distinction is purely pragmatic. Of the twelve operators in this calculus, we have classified eight as essential and four as inessential . . .
>
> Next, we can take an expression and abstract from it those features that relate only to essential changes. For example, we can abstract from "PvQ" the expression (PQ), where the order of the symbols in the latter expression is regarded as irrelevant. Clearly, if inessential operations are applied to the abstracted expressions, the expressions will remain unchanged, while essential operations can be expected to change them . . .
>
> We can now set up a correspondence between our original expressions and operators, on the one hand, and the abstracted expressions

and essential operators, on the other. Corresponding to the original problem of transforming a into b, we can construct a new problem of transforming a' into b', where a' and b' are the expressions obtained by abstracting a and b respectively. Suppose that we solve the new problem, obtaining a sequence of expressions, $a'c'd' \ldots b'$. We can now transform back to the original problem space and set up the new problems of transforming a into c, c into d, and so on. Thus, the solution of the problem in the planning space provides a plan for the solution of the original problem [21:43,44].

No comment is necessary. One merely has to note that the actual program description begins in the second paragraph. The classification of the operators into essential and inessential, the function Wertheimer calls "finding the deeper structure" or "insight," is *introduced by the programmers* before the actual programming begins.

This human ability to distinguish the accidental from the essential accounts for the divergence of the protocol of the problem-solving subjects from the machine trace. We have already suggested that the subject applies both forms of rule 8 together because he realizes that, at this initial stage, both sides of the conjunction are functionally equivalent. Likewise, because he has grasped the essential function of rule 6, the subject can see that the present application of the rule simply neutralizes the previous one. As Wertheimer notes:

> The process [of structuring a problem] does not involve merely the given parts and their transformations. It works in conjunction with material that is structurally relevant but is selected from past experience . . . [40:195].

No one has even tried to suggest how a machine could perform this structuring operation or how it could be learned, since it is one of the conditions for learning from past experience. The ability to distinguish the essential from the inessential seems to be a uniquely human form of information processing not amenable to the mechanical search techniques, which may operate once this distinction has been made. It is precisely this function of intelligence which resists further progress in the problem-solving field.

In the light of their frank recourse to the insightful predigesting of their material, there seems to be no foundation for Newell, Shaw, and Simon's claim that the behavior vaguely labeled cleverness or keen insight in human problem solving is really just the result of the judicious application of certain heuristics for narrowing and guiding the search for solutions. Their work on GPS, on the contrary, demonstrates that all searching, unless directed by a preliminary structuring of the problem, is merely a blind muddling through.

Ironically, research in cognitive simulation is the only example of so-called intelligent behavior which proceeds like the unaided GPS. Here one finds the kind of muddling through and *ad hoc* patching up characteristic of a fascination with the surface structure – a sort of tree-climbing with one's eyes on the moon. Perhaps because the field provides no example of insight, some people in cognitive simulation have mistaken the operation of GPS for intelligent behavior.

Ambiguity tolerance vs. exhaustive enumeration

Work on game playing revealed the necessity of processing information which is not explicitly considered or rejected, i.e., information on the fringes of consciousness. Problem solving research demonstrated that a distinction between the essential and the accidental is presupposed in attacking a problem. Work in language translation has been halted by the need for a third, non-programmable form of information processing.

We have seen that Bar-Hillel and Oettinger, two of the most respected and best informed workers in the field of automatic language translation, have been led to similar pessimistic conclusions concerning the possibility of further progress in the field. They have each realized that, in order to translate a natural language, more is needed than a mechanical dictionary, no matter how complete, and the laws of grammar, no matter how sophisticated. The order of the words in a sentence does not provide enough information to enable a machine to determine which of several possible parsings is the appropriate one, nor does the context of a word indicate which of several possible meanings is the one the author had in mind.

As Oettinger says in discussing systems for producing all parsings of a sentence acceptable to a given grammar:

> The operation of such analyzors to date has revealed a far higher degree of legitimate *syntactic* ambiguity in English and in Russian than has been anticipated. This, and a related fuzziness of the boundary between the grammatical and the non-grammatical, raises serious questions about the possibility of effective fully automatic manipulation of English or Russian for any purposes of translation or information retrieval [27:26].

Instead of claiming, on the basis of his early partial success with a mechanical dictionary, that, in spite of a few exceptions and difficulties, the mystery surrounding our understanding of language is beginning to dissolve, Oettinger draws attention to the "very mysterious semantic processes that enable most reasonable people to interpret most reasonable sentences unequivocally most of the time . . ." [27:26].

Here is another example of the importance of the fringe effect. Obviously, the user of a natural language is not aware of many of the cues to which he responds in determining the intended syntax and meaning. On the other hand, nothing indicates that he considers each of these cues unconsciously. In fact, two considerations suggest that these cues are not the sort that *could be* taken up and considered by a sequential or even parallel list-searching program.

First, too many possibly relevant cues exist, as Bar-Hillel concludes in an argument "which amounts to an almost full-fledged demonstration of the unattainability of fully automatic high quality translation, not only in the near future but altogether" [3:94]. The argument is sufficiently important to merit quoting at some length.

> I shall show that there exist extremely simple sentences in English – and the same holds, I am sure, for any other natural language – which, within certain linguistic contexts, would be uniquely (up to plain synonymy) and unambiguously translated into any other language by anyone with a sufficient knowledge of the two languages involved, though I know of no program that would enable a machine to come up with this unique rendering unless by a completely arbitrary and *ad hoc* procedure whose futility would show itself in the next example.

A sentence of this kind is the following:

> *The box was in the pen.*

The linguistic context from which this sentence is taken is, say, the following:

> Little John was looking for his toy box. Finally he found it.
> The box was in the pen. John was very happy.

> Assume, for simplicity's sake, that *pen* in English has only the following two meanings: (1) a certain writing utensil, (2) an enclosure where small children can play. I now claim that no existing or imaginable program will enable an electronic computer to determine that the word *pen* in the given sentence within the given context has the second of the above meanings, whereas every reader with a sufficient knowledge of English will do this "automatically" [3:158,159].

What makes an intelligent human reader grasp this meaning so unhesitatingly is, in addition to all the other features that have been discussed by MT workers . . . , his *knowledge* that the relative sizes of pens, in the sense of writing implements, toy boxes, and pens, in the sense of playpens, are such that when someone writes under ordinary circumstances and in something like the given context, "The box was in the pen," he almost certainly refers to a playpen and most certainly not to a writing pen [3:160].

And, as Bar-Hillel goes on to argue, the suggestion that a computer used in translating be supplied with a universal encyclopedia is "utterly chimerical." "The number of facts we human beings know is, in a certain very pregnant sense, infinite" [3:160]. Even if the number of facts was only very large and even if all these facts could be stored in an enormous list in our memory or in a machine, neither we nor the machine could possibly search such a list in order to resolve semantic and syntactic ambiguities.

Second, even if a manageable number of relevant cues existed, they would not help us: in order to use a computer to interpret these cues, we would have to formulate syntactic and semantic criteria in terms of strict rules; and our use of language, while precise, is not strictly rule-like. Pascal already noted that the perceptive mind functions "tacitly, naturally, and without technical rules." Wittgenstein has spelled out this insight in the case of language.

> We are unable clearly to circumscribe the concepts we use; not because we don't know their real definition, but because there is no real "definition" to them. To suppose that there *must* be would be like supposing that whenever children play with a ball they play a game according to strict rules [43:25].[4]

A natural language is used by people involved in situations in which they are pursuing certain goals. These extra-linguistic goals, which need not themselves be precisely stated or statable, provide the cues which reduce the ambiguity of expressions as much as is necessary for the task at hand. A phrase like "stand near me" can mean anything from "press up against me" to "stand one mile away," depending upon whether it is addressed to a child in a crowd or to a fellow scientist at Los Alamos. Even in context its meaning is imprecise, but it is precise enough to get the intended result.

Our ability to use a global context to *sufficiently reduce ambiguity* without having to formalize (i.e., eliminate ambiguity altogether), reveals a third fundamental form of human information processing, which presupposes the other two. Fringe consciousness makes us aware of cues in the context which are too numerous to be made explicit. A pragmatic sense of what is essential in a given context allows us to ignore as irrelevant certain possible parsings of sentences and meanings of words which would be included in the output of a machine. Ambiguity tolerance then allows us to use this information about goals and context to narrow down the remaining spectrum of possible parsings and meanings as much as the situation requires without requiring the resulting interpretation to be absolutely unambiguous.

Since understanding a sentence in a natural language requires a knowledge of extra-linguistic facts and a grasp of the sentence's context-dependent use – neither of which we learn from explicit rules – the only way to make a computer which could understand and translate a natural language is to program it to learn about the world. Bar-Hillel remarks: "I do not believe that machines whose programs do not enable them to learn, in a sophisticated sense of this word, will ever be able to consistently produce high-quality translations" [3:105,106].[5]

In the area of language-learning, the only interesting and successful program is Feigenbaum's EPAM (Elementary Perceiver and Memorizer). EPAM simulates the learning of the association of nonsense syllables, which Feigenbaum calls "a simplified case of language learning" [7:289].

The interesting thing about nonsense syllable learning, however, is that it is not a case of *language* learning at all. Learning to associate nonsense syllables is in fact acquiring a Pavlovian conditioned reflex. The machine could exhibit "DAX" then "JIR" or it could flash red and then green lights; as long as two such events were associated frequently enough, one would learn to anticipate the second member of the pair. In such an experiment, the subject is supposed to be completely passive. In a sense, he isn't really learning anything, but is having something done to him. Whether the subject is an idiot, a child, or a genius should ideally make no difference in the case of nonsense syllable learning. Ebenhouse, at the end of the 19th century, proposed this form of conditioning precisely to eliminate any use of meaningful grouping or appeal to a context of previously learned associations.

It is no surprise that subject protocol and machine trace most nearly match in this area. But it is a dubious triumph: the only successful case of cognitive simulation simulates a process which does not involve comprehension and so is not genuinely cognitive.

What is involved in learning a language is much more complicated, and more mysterious, than the sort of conditioned reflex involved in learning to associate nonsense syllables. To teach someone the meaning of a new word, we can sometimes point at the object which the word names. Since Augustine's *Confessions*, it has been assumed that this is the way we teach language to children. But Wittgenstein pointed out that if we simply point at a table, for example, and say "brown," a child may not know if brown is the color, the size or the shape of the table, the kind of object, or the proper name of the object. If the child already uses language, we can *say* that we are pointing out the color, but if he doesn't already use language, how do we ever get off the ground? Wittgenstein says that the subject must be engaged in a form of life in which he shares at least some of the goals and interests of the teacher, so that the activity at hand helps determine the meanings of the words used.

The above considerations concerning the essential role of context awareness and ambiguity tolerance in the use of a natural language should suggest why work is coming to a halt in the translating field. Furthermore, the ability to learn a language presupposes a complex combination of the uniquely human forms of information processing, so that an appeal to learning cannot be used to bypass the problems confronting this area.

Perspicuous grouping – a derivative of the above three forms

Successful recognition of even simple patterns requires each of the fundamental forms of human information processing discussed thus far; recognition of patterns as complex as artistic styles and the human face requires, in addition, a special combination of the above three. It is no wonder that work in pattern recognition has had a late start and an early stagnation.

Part I noted that a weakness of current pattern recognition programs (with the possible exception of the Uhr-Vossler program, the power of whose operators – since it only recognizes five letters – has not yet been sufficiently tested) is that they are not able to determine their own selection operators. Now, however, we shall see that this way of presenting the problem is based on assumptions which hide deeper and more difficult issues.

Insight

A first indication that human pattern recognition differs radically from mechanical recognition is seen in human (and animal) tolerance for changes in orientation and size, degrees of incompleteness and distortion, and amount of background noise.

An early artificial intelligence approach was to try to normalize the pattern and then to test it against a set of templates to see which it matched. Human recognition, on the other hand, seems to simply disregard changes in size and orientation, as well as breaks in the figure, etc. Although certain perceptual constants do achieve some normalization (apparent size and brightness do not vary as much as corresponding changes in the signal reaching the retina), clearly we do not fully normalize and smooth out the pattern, since we perceive the pattern as skewed, incomplete, large or small, etc., at the same time we recognize it.

More recent programs, rather than normalizing the pattern, seek powerful operators which pick out discriminating traits but are insensitive to distortion and noise. Human pattern recognizers do not employ these artificial expedients either. In those special cases where human pattern recognizers can articulate their cues, these turn out to be not powerful operators which include sloppy patterns and exclude noise, but rather a set of ideal traits which are only approximated in the specific instances of patterns recognized. Distorted patterns are recognized not as falling under some looser and more ingenious set of traits, but as exhibiting the same simple traits as the undistorted figures, along with certain accidental additions or omissions. Similarly, noise is not tested and excluded; it is ignored as inessential.[6] Here again we must presuppose the human ability to distinguish the essential from the inessential, which Newell, Shaw, and Simon surreptitiously introduced into their planning program.

Fringe consciousness

To determine which of a set of already-analyzed patterns a presented pattern most nearly resembles, workers have proposed analyzing the presented pattern for a set of traits by means of a decision tree; or combining the probabilities that each of a set of traits is present, as in Selfridge's Pandaemonium program. Either method uncritically assumes that a human or mechanical pattern recognizer must proceed by a classification based on the analysis of a specific list of traits. It seems self-evident to Selfridge and Neisser that: "A man who abstracts a pattern from a complex of stimuli has essentially classified the possible inputs" [31:238].

Yet, if the pattern is at all complicated and sufficiently similar to many other patterns so that many traits are needed for discrimination, the problem of exponential growth threatens. Supposing that a trait-by-trait analysis is the way any pattern recognizer, human or artificial, must proceed, leads to the assumption that there must be certain crucial traits – if one could only find them, or program the machine to find them for itself – which would make the processing manageable.

Thus one is led to look for a sort of perceptual heuristic, the "powerful operators" which no one as yet has been able to find. And just as the chess masters are not able to provide the programmer with the heuristic short cuts they are supposed to be using, Selfridge and Neisser note in the case of pattern recognition that "very often the basis of classification is unknown, even to [the analyzer]: it is too complex to be specified explicitly" [31:238]. Nevertheless, Selfridge and Neisser assume, like Newell and Simon, that unconsciously a maze is being explored – in this case, that a list of traits is being searched. But the difficulties involved in searching such a list suggest again that not all possibly relevant traits are taken up in series or in parallel and used to make some sort of decision, but that many traits crucial to discrimination are never taken up explicitly at all but remain on the fringe of consciousness.

Moreover, though in chess we are finally reduced to counting out, in perception we need never appeal to *any* explicit traits. We often recognize an object without recognizing it as one of a type or a member of a class. As Aron Gurwitsch puts it in his analysis of the difference between perceptual and conceptual consciousness:

> Perceived objects appear to us with generic determinations. . . .
> But – and this is the decisive point – *to perceive an object of a certain kind is not at all the same thing as grasping that object as representative or as a particular case of a type* [12:203].

Of course, we can sometimes make the cues explicit:

The first step in the constituting of conceptual consciousness consists in effecting a dissociation within the object perceived in its typicality. The generic traits which until then were immanent and inherent in the perceived thing are detached and disengaged from it. Rendered explicit, these traits can be seized in themselves and crystallize themselves into a new and specific object of consciousness. This object is the concept taken in comprehension. Consequent upon this dissociation, *the generic becomes the general.* From this aspect it opposes itself to the thing perceived from which it has just been disengaged, and which now is transformed into an example, a particular instance, and, in this sense, into a representative of the concept . . .

[Thus, cues] can be grasped and become themes [specific traits we are aware of] . . . , whereas previously they only contributed to the constitution of another theme [the pattern] within which they played only a mute role [12:204, 205].

This shift from perceptual to conceptual consciousness (from the perceptive to the mathematical frame of mind, to use Pascal's expression), is not necessarily an improvement. Certain victims of aphasia, studied by Gelb and Goldstein, have lost their capacity for perceptual recognition. All recognition for the patient becomes a question of classification. The patient has to resort to check lists and search procedures, like a digital computer. A typical aphasic can only recognize a figure such as a triangle by listing its traits, i.e., by counting its sides and then thinking: "A triangle has three sides. Therefore, this is a triangle." Such conceptual recognition is time-consuming and unwieldy; the victims of such brain injuries are utterly incapable of getting along in the everyday world.

Evidently, passing from implicit perceptual grouping to explicit conceptual classification – even at some final stage, as in chess – is usually disadvantageous. The fact that we need not conceptualize or thematize the traits common to several instances of the same pattern in order to recognize that pattern, distinguishes human recognition from machine recognition which only occurs on the explicit conceptual level of class membership.

Context-dependent ambiguity reduction

In the cases thus far considered, the traits defining a member of a class, while generally too numerous to be useful in practical recognition, could at least in principle always be made explicit. In some cases, however, such explicitness is not even possible. In recognizing certain complex patterns, as in narrowing down the meaning of words or sentences, the context plays a determining role. The context may simply help us notice those patterns which we can subsequently recognize in isolation. But sometimes an object or person can only be recognized in the context. The unique character of a person's eyes, for example, may depend on the whole face in such a way as to be unrecognizable if viewed through a slit. Moreover, a certain expression of the eyes may bring out a certain curve of the nose which would not be noticed if the nose were in another face; the nose in turn may give a certain twist to the smile which may affect the appearance of the eyes. In such cases, the traits necessary for recognizing these particular eyes cannot be isolated. The context not only brings out the essential features, but is reciprocally determined by them.

In some cases, however, objects recognized as belonging together need not have any traits in common at all. Wittgenstein, in his study of natural language, was led to investigate such cases.

> We see a complicated network of similarities overlapping and criss-crossing: Sometimes overall similarities, sometimes similarities of detail.
>
> I can think of no better expression to characterize these similar-ities than "family resemblances"; for the various resemblances between members of a family: build, features, color of eyes, gait, temperament, etc. etc. overlap and criss-cross in the same way. . . . We extend our concept . . . as in spinning a thread we twist fibre on fibre. And the strength of the thread does not reside in the fact that some one fibre runs through its whole length, but in the overlapping of many fibres.
>
> But if someone wishes to say: "There is something common to all these constructions – namely the disjunction of all their common properties" – I should reply: Now you are only playing with words. One might as well say: "Something runs through the whole thread – namely the continuous overlapping of these fibres" [42:32].

Those capable of recognizing a member of a "family" need not be able to list *any* exactly similar traits common to even two members, nor is there any reason to suppose such traits exist. Indeed, formalizing family resem-blance in terms of exactly similar traits would eliminate the openness to new cases which is the most striking feature of this form of recognition. No matter what disjunctive list of traits is constructed, one can always invent a new "family" member whose traits are similar to those of the given members without being *exactly* similar to any of the traits of any of them.

Here, as in narrowing down the meaning of words or sentences, the con-text plays a determining role. Recognition of a member of a "family" is made possible not by a list of traits, but by seeing the case in question in terms of its similarity to a paradigm (i.e., typical) case. For example, an unfamiliar painting is recognized as a Cézanne by thinking of a Cézanne we think to be typical. By thinking, if need be, of bridging cases, one can recognize even a deviant case.

Perspicuous grouping

The above sophisticated but nonetheless very common form of recognition employs a special combination of the three forms of information processing discussed thus far: fringe consciousness, insight, and context dependence. To begin with, the process is implicit. It uses information which remains on the fringes of consciousness.

Seeing the role of insight necessitates distinguishing the generic from the typical, although Gurwitsch uses these two terms interchangeably. Recognition of the generic depends on implicit cues which can always be made explicit. Recognition of the typical, on the other hand, as in the case of family resemblance, depends on cues which cannot be thematized. Recognition of the typical, unlike recognition of the generic, requires insight. A paradigm case serves its function insofar as it is the clearest manifestation of what (essentially) makes all members members of a given group. Finally, recognition in terms of proximity to the paradigm is a form of context dependence.

Wittgenstein remarks that "a perspicuous representation produces just that understanding which consists in seeing connections" [42:49]. Following Wittgenstein, we will call this combination of fringe consciousness, insight, and context determination "perspicuous grouping." This form of human information processing is as important as the three fundamental forms of information processing from which it is derived.

Conclusion

Human beings are able to recognize patterns under the following increasingly difficult conditions:

1) The pattern may be skewed, incomplete, deformed, and embedded in noise;
2) The traits required for recognition may be "so fine and so numerous" that, even if they could be formalized, a search through a branching list of such traits would soon become unmanageable as new patterns for discrimination were added;
3) The traits may depend upon internal and external context and are thus not isolable into lists;
4) There may be no common traits but a "complicated network of overlapping similarities," capable of assimilating ever new variations.

Any system which can equal human performance, must therefore, be able to:

1) Distinguish the essential from the inessential features of a particular instance of a pattern;
2) Use cues which remain on the fringes of consciousness;
3) Take account of the context;
4) Perceive the individual as typical, i.e., situate the individual with respect to a paradigm case.

Since the recognition of patterns of even moderate complexity may require these four forms of human information processing, work in pattern recognition has not progressed beyond the laborious recognition of a few simple patterns in situations which severely limit variation. It is not surprising, but all the more discouraging, that further progress in game playing, problem solving, and language translation awaits a breakthrough in pattern recognition research.

Misconceptions masking the seriousness of current difficulties

The problems facing workers attempting to use computers in the simulation of human intelligent behavior should now be clear. In game playing, the exponential growth of the tree of alternative paths requires a restriction on the paths which can be followed out; in complicated games such as chess, programs cannot select the most promising paths. In problem solving, the issue is not how to direct a selective search, but how to structure the problem so as to begin the search process. In language translation, even the elements to be manipulated are not clear, due to the intrinsic ambiguity of a natural language; in pattern recognition, all three difficulties are inextricably intertwined.

In spite of these grave difficulties, workers in cognitive simulation and artificial intelligence are not discouraged. In fact, they are unqualifiedly optimistic. Underlying their optimism is the conviction that human information processing must proceed by discrete steps like those of a digital computer, and, since nature has produced intelligent behavior with this form of processing, proper programming should be able to elicit such behavior from machines.

The assumption that human and mechanical information processing ultimately involve the same elementary process, is sometimes made naively explicit. Newell, Shaw, and Simon introduce one of their papers with the following remark:

> It can be seen that this approach makes no assumption that the "hardware" of computers and brains are similar, beyond the assumptions that both are general-purpose symbol-manipulating devices, and that the computer can be programmed to execute elementary

information processes functionally quite like those executed by the brain [24:9].

They do not even consider the possibility that the brain might process information in an entirely different way than a computer – that information might, for example, be processed globally the way a resistor analogue solves the problem of the minimal path through a network.

In general, workers in cognitive simulation assume that heuristically-guided search techniques reflect the way human beings resolve the difficulties inherent in discrete techniques. Workers in artificial intelligence, although uninterested in copying human information processing techniques, also assume that humans utilize discrete processes – otherwise there would be no reason to expect to find ways to mechanically achieve human results.

Yet judging from their behavior, human beings avoid rather than resolve the difficulties confronting workers in cognitive simulation and artificial intelligence by avoiding the discrete information processing techniques from which these difficulties arise. Why, in the light of this evidence, do those pursuing cognitive simulation assume that the information processes of a computer reveal the hidden information processes of a human being, and why do those working in artificial intelligence assume that there must be a digital way of performing human tasks? Strangely, no one in the field seems to have asked himself these questions.

When intelligent workers are unanimously dogmatic, there must be a reason. Some force in their assumptions must allow them to ignore the need for justification. We must now try to discover why, in the face of increasing difficulties, workers in these fields show such untroubled confidence.

The associationist assumption

The development of the high-speed digital computer has strengthened a conviction which was first expressed by Lucretius, later developed in different ways by Descartes and Hume, and finally expressed in nineteenth-century associationist or stimulus-response psychology: *thinking must be analyzable into simple determinate operations.*[7] The suitably programmed computer can be viewed as a working model of the mechanism presupposed by this theory. Artificial intelligence has in this way made associationism operational and given it a second wind.

The affinity between this venerable but somewhat outdated conception of mental processes and the presuppositions of workers in artificial intelligence is often quite explicit. As Lindsay says in his article on "Machines which Understand Natural Language,"

> A list structure is a form of associative memory, wherein each symbol is tagged by an indicator which tells the machine the location

of a related symbol. So far this corresponds to the associative bonds which are the basic concept of stimulus-response psychology [14:221].

Early success in artificial intelligence has so strengthened this associationist assumption that no one feels called upon to defend associationism in the face of mounting evidence in both experimental psychology and in the artificial intelligence field itself that, although machines do, people do not perform intelligent tasks by simple determinate steps. To determine whether the confidence exhibited by workers in cognitive simulation and artificial intelligence is justified, we must evaluate the empirical and philosophical arguments offered for associationism.

Empirical evidence for the associationist assumption: critique of the scientific methodology of cognitive simulation

The empirical justification of the associationist assumption poses a question of scientific methodology – the problem of the evaluation of evidence. Gross similarities of behavior between computers and people do not justify the associationist assumption, nor does the present inability to demonstrate these similarities alone justify its rejection. A test of the associationist assumption requires a detailed comparison of the *steps* involved in human and machine information processing. Newell, Shaw, and Simon conscientiously note the similarities and differences between human protocols and machine traces recorded during the solution of the same problem. We must now turn to their evaluation of the evidence thus obtained.

After carefully noting the exceptions to their program, Newell and Simon conclude that their work

> provide[s] a general framework for understanding problem-solving behavior . . . and finally reveals with great clarity that free behavior of a reasonably intelligent human can be understood as the product of a complex but finite and determinate set of [presumably associationist] laws [26:293].

This is a strangely unscientific conclusion to draw from a program which "provides a complete explanation of the subject's task behavior with five exceptions of varying degrees of seriousness" [26:292]. For Newell and Simon acknowledge that their specific theories – like any scientific theories – must stand or fall on the basis of their generality, that is, the range of phenomena which can be explained by the programs [24:9].

There seems to be some confusion concerning the universality of scientific laws. Scientific laws do not admit of exceptions, yet here the exceptions are honestly noted – as if the frank recognition of these exceptions mitigates their importance, as if Galileo might, for example, have presented the law of falling bodies as holding for all but five objects which were found to fall at a different rate. Not that a scientific theory must necessarily be discarded in the face of a few exceptions; there are scientifically sanctioned ways of dealing with such difficulties. One can, to begin with, hold on to the generalization as a working hypothesis and wait to announce a scientific law until the exceptions are incorporated. A working hypothesis need not explain *all* the data. When, however, one claims to present a theory, let alone a "general framework for understanding," then this theory must account for *all* the phenomena it claims to cover – either by subsuming them under the theory or by showing how, according to the theory, one would expect such exceptions.

Even without exceptions, the theory would not be general, since the available evidence has necessarily been restricted to those most favorable cases where the subject can to some extent articulate his information processing protocols (game playing and the solution of simple problems as opposed to pattern recognition and the acquisition and use of natural language). But even if we were to ignore this difficulty and require only a special theory of problem solving, ordinary scientific standards of accounting for exceptions would invalidate all cognitive simulation theories so far presented. As things stand, even after *ad hoc* adjusting of the program to bring it into line with the protocol – itself a dubious procedure – a machine trace never completely matches the protocol and the exceptions, while carefully noted, are never explained.

There is one other acceptable way of dealing with exceptions. If one knew, *on independent grounds*, that mental processes *must* be the product of discrete operations, then exceptions could be dealt with as accidental difficulties in the experimental technique, or challenging cases still to be subsumed under the law. Only then would those involved in the field have a right to call each program which simulated intelligent behavior – no matter how approximately – an achievement and to consider all set-backs nothing but challenges for sharper heuristic hunting and further programming ingenuity. The problem, then, is how to justify independently the associationist assumption that all human information processing proceeds by discrete steps. Otherwise the exceptions along with the narrow range of application of the programs and the lack of progress during the last few years, tend to deconfirm, rather than confirm, the hypothesis. The "justification" seems to have two stages.

In the early literature, instead of attempting to justify this important and questionable assumption, Newell, Shaw, and Simon present it as a postulate, a working hypothesis which directs their investigation. "We postulate that the subject's behavior is governed by a program organized from a set of elementary information processes" [24:9]. This postulate, which alone might seem rather arbitrary, is in turn sanctioned by the basic methodological principle of parsimony. This principle enjoins us to assume *tentatively* the most simple hypothesis, in this case that all information processing resembles that sort of processing which can be programmed on a digital computer. We can suppose, for example, that in chess, when our subject is zeroing in, he is unconsciously counting out. In general, whenever the machine trace shows steps which the subject did not report, the principle of parsimony allows us to suppose that the subject unconsciously performed these steps. So far this is perfectly normal. The principle of parsimony justifies picking a simple working hypothesis as a guide to experimentation. But of course the investigations must *support* the working hypothesis; otherwise it must eventually be discarded.

The divergence of the protocols from the machine trace, as well as the difficulties raised by planning, indicate that things are not so simple as our craving for parsimony leads us to hope. In the light of these difficulties, it would be natural to revise the working hypothesis, just as scientists had to give up the Bohr conception of the atom; but at this point, research in cognitive simulation deviates from acceptable scientific procedures. In a recent publication, Newell and Simon announce:

> There is a growing body of evidence that the elementary information processes used by the human brain in thinking are highly similar to a subset of the elementary information processes that are incorporated in the instruction codes of the present-day computers [35:282].

What is this growing body of evidence? Have the gaps in the protocols been filled and the exceptions explained? Not at all. The growing body of evidence seems to be the very programs whose lack of universality would cast doubt on the whole project but for the independent assumption of the associationist hypothesis. The associationist assumption must have at first been taken as independently justified, since the specific programs are presented as established theories, and yet now the assumption is recognized as an hypothesis whose sole confirmation rests on the success of the specific programs.

An hypothesis based on a methodological principle is often confirmed later by the facts. What is unusual and inadmissible is that, in this case, the hypothesis produces the evidence by which it is later confirmed. Thus, no empirical evidence exists for the associationist assumption. In fact, the supposed empirical evidence presented for the assumption tends, when considered in itself, to show that the assumption is empirically untenable.

This particular form of methodological confusion is restricted to those working in cognitive simulation, but even workers in artificial intelligence share their belief in the soundness of heuristic programs, their tendency to think of all difficulties as accidental, and their refusal to consider any setbacks as disconfirming evidence. Concluding from the small area in which search procedures are partially successful, workers in both fields find it perfectly clear that the unknown and troublesome areas are of exactly the same sort. Thus, all workers proceed as if the credit of the associationist assumption were assured, even if all do not – like those in cognitive simulation – attempt to underwrite the credit with a loan for which it served as collateral. For workers in the field, the associationist assumption is not an empirical hypothesis which can be supported or disconfirmed, but some sort of philosophical axiom whose truth is assured *a priori*.

A priori arguments for the associationist assumption: conceptual confusions underlying confidence in artificial intelligence

As stated in artificial intelligence literature, the claim that all human information processing can in principle be simulated or at least approximated on a digital computer, presupposes the validity of the associationist assumption. Feigenbaum, for example, asserts:

> . . . Human thinking is wholly information-processing activity within the human nervous system; these information processes are perfectly explicable; . . . digital computers, being general information-processing devices, can be programmed to carry out any and all of the information processes thus explicated [6:248,249].

The statement that a computer is a general information-processing device does indeed imply that a digital computer can process any information which is completely formalized, i.e., expressed in exhaustive and unambiguous form. But this is significant for work in artificial intelligence only if information processes in humans are also "perfectly explicable," i.e., reducible to discrete operations. Feigenbaum gives no argument to back up his claim.

Such an assertion, however, is by no means obvious. If it is supposed to gain plausibility from the physiological fact that the human nervous system operates with all-or-none switches like a digital computer, it is antiquated by the recent discoveries in brain physiology.

> . . . In the higher invertebrates we encounter for the first time phenomena such as the graded synaptic potential, which before any post synaptic impulse has arisen can algebraically add the several incoming presynaptic barrages in a complex way. These incoming barrages are of different value depending upon the pathway and a standing bias. Indeed, so much can be done by means of this graded and nonlinear local phenomenon prior to the initiation of any post-synaptic impulse that we can no more think of the typical synapse in integrative systems as being a digital device exclusively as was commonly assumed a few years ago, but rather as being a complex analog device . . . [4:172].

410

If this assertion (that human information processing is explicable in discrete terms) claims to be based on a description of human experience and behavior, it is even more untenable. Certain forms of human experience and behavior clearly require that some of the information being processed not be made perfectly explicit. Consider a specific example from gestalt psychology: When presented with the equal line segments in the Muller-Lyer illusion (Fig. 1), the subject cannot help but see the upper line as shorter than the lower. The lines at the end of each segment (which are not considered explicitly, but which rest on the fringes of the perceptual field) affect the appearance of the lines on which attention is centered. Now suppose a machine with some sort of electronic perceptors perceives these lines by scanning them explicitly point by point. It will simply perceive the lines as equal, with no suspicion of illusion.

Or consider the even clearer case of the Necker Cube (Fig. 2) seen as opening toward or away from the viewer. A machine could scan the figure point by point and analyze it as the projection of a cube oriented in either of two possible ways. But the machine could not interpret the figure three-dimensionally as a cube first in one, then in the other of these orientations. Such an interpretation would require the machine to focus on certain aspects of the figure while leaving others in the background, and the machine lacks precisely this figure-ground form of representation. For it, every point of the figure is equally explicit; thus the figure can only be interpreted as an ambiguous flat projection. To say that now one, now the other orientation was being presented would make no sense in such a program, although this alternation of perspectives could easily affect human behavior. Such

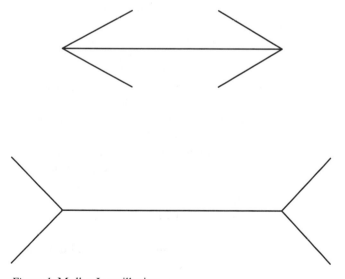

Figure 1 Muller-Lyer illusion

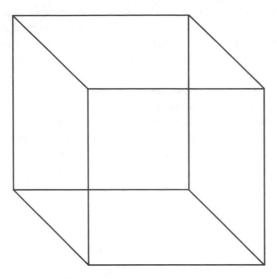

Figure 2 Necker Cube

phenomena challenge the possibility of totally formalizing human information processing. As Feigenbaum's argument stands, the case for the necessary programmability of intelligent human behavior has not been made.

Still, the associationist assumption is not so easily dismissed. After all, a device does exist which can detect the Muller-Lyer illusion and respond to the difference between the two aspects of the cube: the human brain.[8] And if this device obeys the laws of physics and chemistry, which we have every reason to suppose it does, then we ought to be able to build an analogous device which might, for example, take the form of an analogue computer using ion solutions whose electrical properties change with various local saturations.[9]

Further, knowing the solutions and how they work enables us at least in principle to write the physico-chemical equations describing such wet components and to solve these equations on a dry digital computer. Thus, given enough memory and time, any computer – even such an analogue computer – could be simulated on a digital computer. In general, by accepting the fundamental assumptions that the brain is part of the physical world and that all physical processes can be described in a mathematical formalism which can in turn be manipulated by a digital computer, one can arrive at the strong claim that all human information processing, whether formalizable or not, can be carried out on a digital machine.

This claim may well account for the simulators' smugness, but what in fact is justified by the fundamental truth that every form of information processing (even those in which *in practice* can only be carried out on an analogue

412

computer) must *in principle* be simulable on a digital computer? Does it really prove the associationist claim that, even when a human being is unaware of using discrete operations in processing information, he must nonetheless be carrying on unconscious searching, sorting, and storing?

Consider again the ion solution which might duplicate the information processing in the Muller-Lyer illusion. Does the solution, in reaching equilibrium, go through the series of discrete steps a digital computer would follow in solving the equations which describe this process? In that case, the solution is solving in moments a problem which it would take a machine centuries to solve – if the machine could solve it at all. Is the solution an ultra-rapid computer, or has it got some secret, clever heuristic like the chess master, which simplifies the problem? Obviously, neither. The fact that we can describe the process of reaching equilibrium in terms of equations and then break up these equations into discrete elements in order to solve them on a computer does not show that equilibrium is actually reached in discrete steps. Likewise, *we need not conclude from the claim that all continuous processes involved in human information processing can be formalized and calculated out discretely, that any discrete processes are actually taking place.* Once the *a priori* argument for associationism, based on the all-purpose character of the digital computer, is restated so as to be defensible, it turns out not to be an argument for associationism at all.

Conclusion

Without the associationist assumption to fall back on, what encouragement can workers in cognitive simulation and artificial intelligence draw from the argument that, even though the brain does not process information in discrete operations, we can simulate the brain on a digital computer and thus by discrete operations produce the same results the brain produces?

To begin with, what would such a computer program tell us about operations on the information-processing level? According to Newell, Shaw, and Simon, a description of operations on the information-processing level is a theory in psychology and not physiology. Psychological operations must be the sort which human beings at least sometimes consciously perform in processing information – e.g., searching, sorting, and storing – and not physicochemical processes in the organism. Thus a chess player's report as he zeroed in on his Rook, "And now my brain reaches the following chemical equilibrium, described by the following array of differential equations," would describe physiological processes no doubt correlated with information processing, but not that information processing itself.

Similarly, one must delimit what can count as information processing in a computer. A digital computer solving the equations describing an analogue information-processing device and this simulating its *function* is not thereby simulating its *information processing*. It is not processing the information

413

which is processed by the simulated analogue, but entirely different information concerning the physical or chemical properties of the analogue. Thus the strong claim that every processable form of information can be processed by a digital computer is misleading. One can only show that, for any given type of information, a digital computer can in principle be programmed to simulate a device which can process that information. This does not support Feigenbaum's assertion that human information processes are perfectly explicable, and therefore fails to show that "digital computers being general information-processing devices, they can be programmed to carry out any and all information processes."

Confidence of progress in cognitive simulation is thus as unfounded as the associationist assumption, but this realization leaves untouched the weaker claim of workers in artificial intelligence that human intelligent *behavior* – not human *information processing* – can be simulated by using digital computers. Nothing that has been said thus far suggests that digital computers could not process, in their own way, the information which human beings process. Indeed, at first sight, our results might seem encouraging for work in artificial intelligence. We have seen that, in principle, a digital computer can simulate any physical information processing system. In fact, however, no comfort can be gained from this substitute for the associationist assumption, since this "principle" cannot be realized in practice. We do not know the equations describing the physical processes in the brain, and even if we did, the solution of the equations describing the simplest reaction would take a prohibitive amount of time.

The facts that the associationist assumption cannot be defended on empirical or on *a priori* grounds, and that the simulation of the brain is in practice impossible, do not show that the task set for artificial intelligence is hopeless. However, they eliminate the only argument which suggests any particular reason for hope. The associationist assumption asserted that human and mechanical information processing proceed by discrete operations, leaving artificial intelligence the promising task of finding them. Without the defense provided by the associationist assumption, all the difficulties of artificial intelligence during the past few years take on new significance: there is no reason to deny the evidence that human and mechanical information processing proceed in entirely different ways. At best, research in artificial intelligence can write programs which allow the digital machine to *approximate*, by means of discrete operations, the results which human beings achieve by avoiding rather than resolving the difficulties inherent in discrete techniques.

Is such research realistic? Can one introduce search heuristics which enable the speed and accuracy of computers to bludgeon through in those areas where human beings use more elegant techniques? Lacking any *a priori* basis for confidence, we can only turn to the empirical results obtained thus far. That brute force can succeed to some extent is demonstrated by the early work in the field. The present difficulties in game playing, problem solving, language translation, and pattern recognition, however, indicate a limit to our ability to substitute one kind of information processing for another. Only experimentation can determine the extent to which newer and faster machines, better programming languages, and clever heuristics can continue to push back the frontier. Nonetheless, the dramatic slowdown in the fields we have considered and the general failure to fulfill earlier predictions suggest the boundary may be near.

Part III

The future of artificial intelligence

No valid empirical or *a priori* arguments have been put forward to support the associationist assumption, and therefore there is no reason to expect continuing progress in artificial intelligence. On the other hand, no arguments have been put forward to deny the possibility of such progress. Are there any reasons for denying that such continuing progress is possible? That is, are there any reasons to suppose that the unexpected difficulties which have appeared in all areas of artificial intelligence research indicate a necessary limit to what can be accomplished with digital computers in this field?

To understand these difficulties and show that they are more than temporary, we would have to show that mechanical information processing has inherent limitations from which human information processing is free. We have already considered the processing itself; here there is no way to fix a limit to the degree of approximation clever heuristics might achieve. We have not yet considered the information to be processed. I propose to show now that, near or far off, there does exist a boundary to possible progress in the field of artificial intelligence: given the nature of the information to be processed, the contribution of the uniquely human forms of information processing which we have considered are indispensable, since they alone provide access to information inaccessible to a mechanical system.

Three non-programmable forms of information

Machines are perfect Cartesians. They are able to deal only with the determinate and discrete bits of information which Descartes called "clear and distinct ideas." Newell describes GPS as "a program for accepting a task environment defined in terms of discrete objects" [20:17]; Feigenbaum and Feldman extend this basic requirement when they assert that the only constraint on the computer user "is that his statements be unambiguous and complete" [8:271]. They, like Descartes, consider this "a blessing rather than a limitation, for it forces a refreshing rigor on builders of models of human thought processes." This may well be true for cognitive simulation considered

as a branch of psychology, but it ignores the more general attempt to introduce mechanical information processing into all areas of intelligent activity
which are now the exclusive province of human beings. Simon predicts that:

> There will be more and more applications of machines to take the
> place of humans in solving ill-structured problems; just as machines
> are now being more and more used to solve well-structured problems
> [32:8].

If the machine is only able to handle unambiguous, completely structured
information, however, how can it deal with the ill-structured data of daily
life? Indeed, here the project of using digital computers to simulate or even
approximate human information processing seems to reach its absolute limit;
the computer cannot be given the information it is to process.[10]

This limit is manifest in each of the areas in which a uniquely human form
of information processing is necessary to avoid the difficulties faced by
digital computers. In these areas, if we restrict ourselves to information
which can be fed to digital computers and yet try to write a program which
rivals everyday human information processing, a contradiction develops
within the program itself.

The infinity of facts and the threat of infinite progression

In the area of game playing, as we have seen, the array of branching possibilities to be searched may become so large that heuristics are necessary to
eliminate a certain number of possible alternatives. These heuristics save the
day by pruning the search tree, but they also discard some combinations a
human player could consider, so situations will always occur in which the
machine cannot pursue the chain of moves which contains the winning combination; thus, there will always be games that people can win and machines
cannot.

Concerning formal finite games like chess, this is only a practical objection. In principle, at least, the whole maze could be calculated out; or one
could introduce a random element, as Newell once suggested which, while
complicating the program without improving the play, would answer the
objection that there were specific moves whose consideration was forbidden
to the machine.

However, in a non-formal game like playing the horses – which is still
much more systematic than the everyday ill-structured problems that Simon
predicted machines would be able to handle – an unlimited set of conditions
become relevant. In placing a bet, we can usually restrict ourselves to facts
about the horse's age, jockey, and past performance – and perhaps, restricted
to these, the machine could do fairly well, perhaps better than an average
handicapper – but there are always other factors, such as whether the horse is

allergic to goldenrod or whether the jockey has just had a fight with the owner – which *may* in some cases be decisive. These possibilities remain on the fringes of consciousness. If the machine were to examine explicitly each of these possibly relevant factors as determinate bits of information, in order to determine whether to take it into consideration or ignore it, it could never complete the calculations necessary to predict the outcome of a single race. If, on the other hand, the machine systematically excluded possibly relevant factors in order to complete its calculations, then the machine would sometimes be incapable of performing as well as an intelligent human.

Descartes, who was the first to ask whether a machine could imitate all the actions of men, comes to a similar conclusion.

> ... Although such machines could do many things as well as, or perhaps even better than, men, they would infallibly fail in certain others ... For while reason is a universal instrument which can be used in all sorts of situations, the organs [of a machine] have to be arranged in a particular way for each particular action. From this it follows that it is morally impossible that there should be enough different devices [i.e., states] in a machine to make it behave in all the occurrences of life as our reason makes us behave [5:36].

Even the appeal to a random element will not help here, since to be able to take up a sample of excluded possibilities at random so that no possibility is in principle excluded, the machine would have to be explicitly provided with a list of all such other possibly relevant facts or a specific set of routines for exploring all classes of possibly relevant facts, so that no facts were in principle inaccessible. This is just what could be done in a completely defined system such as chess, where a finite number of concepts determines totally and unequivocally the set of all possible combinations in the domain, but in the real world the list of such possibly relevant facts, or even possibly relevant classes of facts, is indefinitely large ("infinite in a pregnant sense," to use Bar-Hillel's phrase), and cannot be exhaustively listed. The ability to retain this infinity of facts on the fringes of consciousness allows human beings access to the open-ended information characteristic of everyday experience, without leading to the inconsistency of requiring an incompletable series of data-gathering operations before the data processing can begin.

The indeterminacy of needs and the threat of infinite regress

In problem solving, the contradiction takes a different form. If, using only digital programs, we try to process the ill-structured data in which real-life problems are posed, we face an infinite regress.

A problem can in principle always be solved on a digital computer, provided the data and the rules of transformation are explicit. However,

Newell, Shaw, and Simon have pointed out that – even in the case of simple logic problems – finding a path through the maze of possible combinations requires a planning program. In the case of formal problems, planning is a matter of practical necessity; in the case of ill-defined problems, it is necessary in principle. Since an indefinite amount of data may be relevant for the solution of an ill-defined problem, one cannot even in principle try all the permutations of the possibly relevant data in seeking a solution. Thus, one needs to structure the problem, to determine both which facts from the environment are relevant, and which operations bring about essential transformations.

According to Minsky, Simon's group working on GPS has set itself the goal of giving the problem-solving program the problem of improving its own operation [10:117]. This, one might hope, would enable a computer to discover the data and operations essential to the solution of a certain type of problem and write a plan for solving the problem. But a difficulty immediately arises: such a planning program itself would require a distinction between essential and inessential operators. Unless, at some stage, the programmer himself introduces this distinction, he will be forced into an infinite regress of planning programs, each one of which will require a higher-order program to structure its ill-structured data.

The nature of the essential/inessential distinction itself explains this regress. Newell, Shaw, and Simon remark that the distinction they introduce in setting up their planning program is pragmatic. Such a pragmatic distinction is made in terms of goals. These goals in turn are determined by needs, and these needs are not themselves always precise. Some needs are first experienced as an indeterminate sense that the present situation is unsatisfactory; we can determine these needs only when we discover what action reduces this uneasiness. Thus, needs and goals cannot be introduced as determinate data which can then be used in structuring the problem. Often only in structuring or solving the problem do they become precise. Only the uniquely human form of information processing which uses the indeterminate sense of dissatisfaction to pragmatically structure ill-structured problems enables us to avoid the problem-solving regress.

The reciprocity of context and the threat of circularity

The meaning of a word is determined by its context, but also contributes to the meaning of that context. As long as all the meanings in question are left somewhat ambiguous (i.e., as long as possible ambiguities are not resolved in advance, and the meanings are made only as determinate as necessary for the particular activity in question), there is no contradiction in this notion of the totality of elements determining the significance of each one. If, however (in order to describe the situation in language suited to a computer), we try to explicate the meaning of a word used in a context, then we find ourselves obliged to resolve all the ambiguities in the context. Since the meaning of each term contributes to the meaning of the context, *every* word must be made determinate before *any* word can be made determinate, and we find ourselves involved in a circle.

This situation may even arise in a completely formal system if we try to use heuristics to avoid exponential growth. In developing a heuristic program for playing chess, one must evaluate the positions arrived at. This evaluation must depend on the evaluation of parameters, which measure success in achieving certain goals. To evaluate these parameters, one must assume that any parameter can be considered independently of the others. For example, in explaining the evaluation of "Material Balance," Newell, Shaw, and Simon note that: "For each exchange square a static exchange value is computed by playing out the exchange with all the attackers and defenders *assuming no indirect consequences like pins, discovered attacks, etc.*" [22:59] (italics added).

Newell, Shaw, and Simon seem to assume that such specification, independent of the other parameters, is simply a matter of caution and ingenuity. Feigenbaum and Feldman make the same assumption when they casually remark that, "before the . . . chess model . . . could be programmed, the meaning of the words 'check' and 'danger' would have to be specified" [8:271]. What counts as "danger," however, depends not simply on whether a piece is attacked, but whether it is defended by a less valuable piece; whether, in the capturing move, a check is revealed or a forced mate is allowed. In the case of a trade, it further depends on who is ahead, the stage of the game, who is on the offensive, who has the tempo, etc. Clearly, for a more and more refined definition of danger, a larger segment of the total situation will have to be considered. Moreover, at some point the factors to be taken into account, such as tempo or possibility of a forced mate, will themselves have to be defined in terms which involve the determination of whether pieces are in danger.

It is not clear how complete such a definition would have to be for a heuristic program to be able to play good or even mediocre chess. The poor performance of chess programs may indicate that thus far evaluations have been too static and crude. Perhaps, as Newell remarks in his discussion of the difficulties in problem-solving programs, "something has been assumed fixed in order to get on with the program, and the concealed limitation finally shows itself" [19:56]. If, however, one attempts to refine the evaluation of parameters, the interdependence of such definitions will eventually be revealed by a loop, which could be eliminated only by sacrificing the flexibility of the definitions of the parameters involved. At this point, the limits of a heuristic chess program will have become a matter of principle rather than simply of practice.

The reason a human player does not go into a corresponding loop is that his definitions are neither completely flexible and sophisticated – so as to take into account all possible situations – nor are they static and crude. His definitions are adjustable. Thus he is able, for example, to define "danger" as precisely as necessary to make whatever decision the situation requires, without at the same time being obliged to try to eliminate all possible ambiguity. The human player never need make the *whole* context explicit in working out any *particular* move.

The digital computer by definition lacks this ambiguity tolerance. A program for collecting information concerning parameters must either arbitrarily isolate the area in question and restrict the definition of the parameters, or take into account all consequences, no matter how indirect. In the first case, the machine's play will be crude; in the second, the program will contain a loop and the machine will not be able to play at all.

Newell, in his thoughtful paper on the problems involved in program organization, seems on the verge of recognizing the importance of the flexibility inherent in human information processing. He remarks that "sequential processing . . . built into the basic structure of our machines . . . encourages us to envision isolated processes devoted to specific functions, each passively waiting in line to operate when its turn comes" [19:10], and he notes that "it seems a peculiar intelligence which can only reveal its intellectual powers in a fixed pattern" [19:18]. Yet Newell is still convinced that more ingenious programs or the substitution of parallel for sequential processing can remove these difficulties. He does not seem to realize that, if one attempts to use a computer which can only deal with discrete unambiguous information to process context-dependent information, the isolation of processes is necessary if one is to avoid circularity.

Only Shannon seems to be aware of the true dimensions of the problem: that by its very nature as a discrete machine, a digital computer cannot cope with intrinsic ambiguity. In a discussion of "What Computers Should Be Doing," he observes that:

> . . . Efficient machines for such problems as pattern recognition, language translation, and so on, may require a different type of computer than any we have today. It is my feeling that this computer will be so organized that single components do not carry out simple, easily described functions. . . . Can we design . . . a computer whose natural operation is in terms of patterns, concepts, and vague similarities, rather than sequential operations on ten-digit numbers? [10:309–310]

Areas of intelligent activity classified with respect to the possibility of artificial intelligence in each

This section discusses the various areas of intelligent activity which have been or might be attacked by workers in artificial intelligence, in order to determine to what extent intelligent activity in each area presupposes the three uniquely human forms of information processing. We can thus account for what success has been attained and predict what further progress can be expected. There are four distinct areas of intelligent behavior (cf. Table 1). The first and third are adaptable to digital computer simulation, while the second is totally intractable, and the fourth is amenable to only a small extent. The assumption that all intelligent behavior can be mapped on a multi-dimensional continuum has encouraged workers to generalize from success in the two promising areas to unfounded expectations of success in the other two.

Area I includes all forms of elementary associationistic behavior where meaning and context are irrelevant to the activity concerned. Learning non-sense syllables is the most perfect example of such behavior so far pro-grammed, although any form of conditioned reflex would serve as well. Also some games, such as the game sometimes called "geography" (which simply consists of finding a country whose name begins with the last letter of the previously named country), belong in this area. In language translating, this is the level of the mechanical dictionary; in problem solving, that of pure trial-and-error routines.

Area II might be called the area of non-formal behavior. This includes all our everyday activities in indeterminate situations. The most striking example of this controlled imprecision is our use of natural languages. This area also includes games in which the rules are not definite, such as guessing riddles. Pattern recognition in this domain is based on recognition of the generic or typical, and the use of the paradigm case. Problems on this level are unstructured, requiring a determination of what is relevant and insight into which operations are essential, before the problem can be attacked.[11] Techniques on this level are usually taught by example and followed intui-tively without appeal to rules. We might adopt Pascal's terminology and call Area II the home of the *esprit de finesse*.

Area III on the other hand, is the domain of the *esprit de géométrie*. It encompasses the conceptual rather than the perceptual world. Problems are completely formalized and completely calculable. For this reason, it might best be called the area of the simple-formal.

In Area III, natural language is converted into formal language, of which the best example is logic. Games have precise rules and can be calculated out completely, as in the case of nim or tic-tac-toe, or at least sufficiently to dispense with search-pruning heuristics (checkers). Pattern recognition on this level takes place according to determinate types, which are defined by a list of traits characterizing the individuals which belong to the class in ques-tion. Problem solving takes the form of reducing the distance between means and ends by recursive application of formal rules. The formal systems in this area, as we have defined it, are characteristically simple enough to be manipulated by algorithms which require no search procedure at all (for

Table 1 Classification of intelligent activities

I. Associationistic	II. Non-formal	III. Simple Formal	IV. Complex Formal
Characteristics of Activity			
Irrelevance of meaning and context.	Dependent on meaning and context, which are not explicit.	Meanings completely explicit and context-independent.	In principle, same as III; in practice, internally context-dependent, independent of external context.
Learned by repetition.	Learned by perspicuous examples.	Learned by rule (exception: checkers).	Learned by rule and practice.
Field of Activity (and Appropriate Procedure)			
Memory games, e.g., 'Geography' (association).	Ill-defined games, e.g., riddles (perceptive guess).	Computable or quasi-computable games, e.g., nim or checkers (seek algorithm or count out).	Uncomputable games, e.g., chess or go (global intuition and detailed counting out).
Maze problems (trial and error).	Structurable problems (insight).	Combinatory problems (non-heuristic means/ends analysis).	Complex combinatory problems (planning and maze calculation).
Word-by-word translation (mechanical dictionary).	Translating a natural language (understanding in context of use).	Proof of theorems in decidable math (seek algorithm).	Proof of theorems in undecidable math (intuition and calculation).
Instinctive recognition of rigid patterns (conditioned response).	Recognition of varied and distorted patterns (recognition of generic or use of paradigm case).	Recognition of simple rigid patterns, e.g., reading typed page (search for traits whose conjunction defines class membership).	Recognition of complex patterns in noise (search for regularities).
Kinds of Program			
Decision tree, list search.	None.	Algorithm or limit on growth of search tree.	Search-pruning heuristics.

example, Wang's logic program), or require search-limiting but not search-pruning procedures (Samuel's checker program). Heuristics are not only unnecessary here, they are a positive handicap, as the relative success of the NSS and the Wang logic programs have strikingly demonstrated. In this area, artificial intelligence has had its only unqualified successes.

Area IV, complex-formal systems, is the most difficult to define and has generated most of the misunderstandings and difficulties in the field. The difference between the simple-formal and the complex-formal systems need not be absolute. As used here, "complex-formal" includes systems in which exhaustive computation is impossible (undecidable domains of mathematics) as well as systems which, in practice, cannot be dealt with by exhaustive enumeration (chess, go, etc.).[12]

The literature of artificial intelligence generally fails to distinguish these four areas. For example, Newell, Shaw, and Simon announce that their logic theorist "was devised to learn how it is possible to solve difficult problems such as proving mathematical theorems [III or IV], discovering scientific laws from data [II and IV], playing chess [IV], or understanding the meaning of English prose [II]" [24:109]. This confusion has two dangerous consequences. First there is the tendency to think that heuristics discovered in one field of intelligent activity, such as theorem proving, must tell us something about the information processing in another area, such as the understanding of a natural language. Thus, certain simple forms of information processing applicable to Areas I and III are imposed on Area II, while the unique forms of information processing in this area are overlooked.

Second there is the converse danger that the informal processes used in Area II may be covertly introduced in the programs for dealing with other areas, particularly Area IV, with even more disastrous consequences. The success of artificial intelligence in Area III depends upon avoiding anything but discrete and determinate operations. The fact that, like the simple systems in Area III, the complex systems in Area IV are formalizable, leads the simulator to suppose the intelligent activities in Area IV are likewise amenable to programming on a digital computer. The difference in degree between simple and complex systems, however, turns out in practice to be a difference in kind; exponential growth becomes a serious problem. When he discovers his inability to cope with the problems of complex-formal systems, using the techniques which worked with simple-formal systems, the programmer (unaware of the differences between the four areas) may inconsistently introduce procedures borrowed from the observation of behavior in Area II – e.g., evaluation of position in chess, planning in problem solving. These procedures are useful only in conjunction with one or more of the specifically human forms of information processing – a heuristic chess program, using context-dependent evaluations, presupposes ambiguity tolerance; the introduction of planning into simple means-end analysis presupposes a distinction between essential and inessential operations, etc. The programmer, of course, does not suspect that he is treating the formal system in Area IV as if it were a non-formal system, but in fact he is introducing into the continuity between Areas III and IV a discontinuity similar to the discontinuity between Areas I and II. Thus, problems which in principle should only arise in trying to program the ill-structured and open-ended activities of daily life, arise in practice for complex-formal systems. Since Area II is just that area of intelligent behavior in which digital computers necessarily have the least success, this attempt to treat complex-formal systems as non-formal systems is doomed to failure.

Conclusion

What, then, should be the direction of work in artificial intelligence? Progress can evidently be expected in Area III. As Wang points out, we have been given a race of "persistent, plodding slaves" [39:93]; we can make good use of them in the field of simple-formal systems. This does not mean that work in Areas II and IV is wasted. The protocols collected by Newell, Shaw, and Simon suggest that human beings sometimes operate like digital computers, within the context of more global processes. This is really not surprising, since, as Shannon points out, while "most computers are either digital or analogue, the nervous system seems to have a complex mixture of both representations of data" [10:309]. Since digital machines have symbol-manipulating powers superior to those of humans, they should, so far as possible, take over the digital aspects of human information processing.

Thus, to use computers in Areas II and IV, we must couple their capacity for fast and accurate calculation with the short-cut processing made possible by the fringes of consciousness and ambiguity tolerance. A chess player who could call on a machine to count out alternatives once he had zeroed in on an interesting area or in certain parts of the endgame, would be a formidable opponent. Likewise, in problem solving, once the problem is structured and planned, a machine could take over to work out the details (as in the case of machine shop allocation or investment banking). A mechanical dictionary would be useful in translation. In pattern recognition, machines are able to recognize certain complex patterns that the natural prominences in our experience force us to exclude. Bar-Hillel, Oettinger, and Pierce have each proposed that work be done on systems which promote a symbiosis between computers and human beings. As Rosenblith put it at a recent symposium, "Man *and* computer is capable of accomplishing things that neither of them can do alone" [10:313].

Instead of trying to make use of the special capacities of computers, workers in artificial intelligence – blinded by their early success and hypnotized by the assumption that thinking is a continuum – will settle for nothing short of the moon. Feigenbaum and Feldman's anthology opens with the baldest statement of this dubious principle:

In terms of the continuum of intelligence suggested by Armer, the computer programs we have been able to construct are still at the low end. What is important is that we continue to strike out in the direction of the milestone that represents the capabilities of human intelligence. Is there any reason to suppose that we shall never get there? None whatever. Not a single piece of evidence, no logical argument, no proof or theorem has ever been advanced which demonstrates an insurmountable hurdle along the continuum [8:8].

Armer prudently suggests a boundary, but he is still optimistic:

It is irrelevant whether or not there may exist some upper bound above which machines cannot go in this continuum. Even if such a boundary exists, there is no evidence that it is located close to the position occupied by today's machines [8:392].

Current difficulties, however, suggest that the areas of intelligent activity are discontinuous and that the boundary is near. To persist in such optimism in the face of recent developments borders on self-delusion.

Alchemists were so successful in distilling quicksilver from what seemed to be dirt, that after several hundred years of fruitless effort to convert lead into gold they still refused to believe that on the chemical level one cannot transmute metals. To avoid the fate of the alchemists, it is time we asked where we stand. Now, before we invest more time and money on the information-processing level, we should ask whether the protocols of human subjects suggest that computer language is appropriate for analyzing human behavior. Is an exhaustive analysis of human intelligent behavior into discrete and determinate operations possible? Is an approximate analysis of human intelligent behavior in such digital terms probable? The answer to both these questions seems to be, "No."

Does this mean that all the work and money put into artificial intelligence has been wasted? Not at all, if, instead of trying to hide our difficulties, we try to understand what they show. The success and subsequent stagnation of cognitive simulation and of artificial intelligence in general, plus the omnipresent problem of pattern recognition and its surprising difficulty, should focus research on the three uniquely human forms of information processing. These forms are significantly irrelevant in those two areas of intelligent activity in which artificial intelligence has had its early success, but they are essential in just those areas of intelligent behavior in which artificial intelligence has experienced consistent failure. We can then view recent work in artificial intelligence as a crucial experiment disconfirming the associationist assumption that all thinking can be analyzed into discrete, determinate operations – the most important disconfirmation of this Humean hypothesis that has ever been produced. In the same way, striking evidence has been collected that not all information can be conceived of in terms of clear and distinct ideas. This technique of pushing associationism and Cartesianism until they reveal their limits suggest fascinating new areas for basic research, notably the development and programming of machines capable of global and indeterminate forms of information processing.

But if the machines for processing informal information must be, as Shannon suggests, entirely different from present digital computers, what can now be done? Nothing directly toward building machines which will be intelligent. We must think in the short run of cooperation between men and digital computers, and only in the long run of non-digital automata which would exhibit the three forms of information processing essential in dealing with our informal world. Those who feel that some concrete results are better than none, and that we should not abandon work on artificial intelligence until some more flexible device for information processing comes along, cannot be refuted. The long reign of alchemy has shown that any research which has had an early success can always be justified and continued by those who prefer adventure to patience.[13] When one insists on *a priori* proof of the impossibility of success, it is difficult to show that his research is misguided. Artificial intelligence is uniquely vulnerable along this line; still one can always retort that at least the goal can be approached. If, however, one is willing to accept empirical evidence as to whether an effort has been misdirected, he has only to look at the promises and the results.

An alchemist would surely have considered it rather pessimistic and petty to insist that, since the creation of quicksilver, he had produced many beautifully colored solutions but not a speck of gold; he would probably have considered such a critic extremely unfair. Similarly, the person who is hypnotized by the moon and is inching up those last branches toward the top of the tree would consider it reactionary of someone to shake the tree and yell, "Come down!" But if the alchemist had stopped poring over his retorts and pentagrams and had spent his time looking for the true structure of the problem, if the man had come out of the tree and started working perhaps to discover fire and the wheel, things would have been set moving in a more promising direction. After all, three hundred years later we did get gold from lead (and we have touched the moon), but only after we abandoned work on the alchemic level, and reached the chemical level or the even deeper level of the nucleus.

Notes

1 Any views expressed in this paper are those of the author. They should not be interpreted as reflecting the views of The RAND Corporation or the official opinion or policy of any of its governmental or private research sponsors. Papers are reproduced by The RAND Corporation as a courtesy to members of its staff.

This paper is based on an informal talk presented at The RAND Corporation in August 1964.

2 References are listed alphabetically in the Bibliography at the end of this Paper. They are also numbered in this alphabetical order. Citations in the text are given in a bracketed pair of numbers: the first is the number of the reference itself, the second is the page on which the citation appears.

3 An example of the absurdity to which this notion of progress leads is the suggestion that the baseball program which answers questions posed in a drastically restricted vocabulary and syntax is an "important initial step toward [the] goal . . . of discovering the information processing structure underlying the act of 'comprehending' or the process of 'understanding'" [8:205].

4 The participants in the RAND symposium on "Computers and Comprehension" suggest the psychological basis and advantage of this non-rule-like character of natural languages.

> It is crucial that language is a combinatory repertoire with unlimited possible combinations whose meanings can be inferred from a finite set of "rules" governing the components' meaning. (The so-called "rules" are learned as response sets and are only partly formalizable.) [13:12]

5 Among workers in artificial intelligence, only MacKay has made specific suggestions as to what form such "sophisticated learning" programs might take (cf., "An Internal Representation of the External World" [15]).

6 Whatever information processing the human brain employs to pick out patterns, this work is no doubt aided by the organization of human receptors. One cannot assume, however, that an organization of the input into perceptual prominences (figure and ground) can be built into the receptors of a digital machine. Such selective receptors would amount to introducing a stage of analogue processing.

7 The gestaltists claim, in opposition to this school, that thinking involves global processes which cannot be understood in terms of a sequence or even a parallel set of discrete steps. In this context, Newell, Shaw, and Simon's claims to have synthesized the contributions of associationists and gestaltists by, on the one hand, accepting behavioral measures and, on the other, recognizing that "a human being is a tremendously complex, organized system" [26:280,293] shows either a will to obscure the issues or a total misunderstanding of the contribution of each of these schools.

8 It seems self-evident that we could simulate intelligent behavior if we could build or simulate a device which functioned exactly like the human brain. But even this could be challenged if it could be shown that the body plays a crucial role in making possible intelligent behavior. This view has been developed by Maurice Merleau-Ponty in his book *Phenomenology of Perception,* and may be implicit in the work of MacKay, but will not be defended in this Paper.

9 MacKay seriously considers such a possibility: "It may well be that only a special-purpose 'analogue' mechanism could meet all detailed needs . . . We on the circuit side had better be very cautious before we insist that the kind of information processing that a brain does can be replicated in a realizable circuit. Some kind of 'wet' engineering may turn out to be inevitable" [16:16].

10 In *The Process of Creative Thinking*, Newell, Shaw, and Simon list four characteristics of creative thought, the fourth of which is: "The problem as initially posed was vague and ill defined, so that part of the task was to formulate the problem itself" [21:4]. They claim that, "a problem-solving process [presumably their own] can exhibit all of these characteristics to a greater or lesser degree . . . " [24:4]. In the light of Newell's statement that "GPS is a program for accepting a task environment defined in terms of discrete objects . . . " [20:17], one can only wonder whether, in the literature of artificial intelligence, zero counts as a lesser degree.

11 The activities found in Area II can be thought of as the sort of "milestones" asked

for by Paul Armer in his article, "Attitudes toward Intelligent Machines": "A clearly defined task is required which is, at present, in the exclusive domain of humans (and therefore incontestably 'thinking') but which may eventually yield to accomplishment by machines" [1:397]. We contend that such machines could not be digital computers; they would have to exhibit the sort of flexibility suggested by Shannon.

12 It is difficult to classify and evaluate the various one-purpose programs that have been developed for motor design, line balancing, integrating, etc. They are not clearly successful programs, until a) like the chess and checker programs they are tested against human professionals; and b) the problems attacked by these programs have, if possible, been formalized so that these heuristic programs can be compared with non-heuristic programs designed for the same purpose. (Wherever such a comparison has been made – in checkers, logic, pattern recognition, chess – the non-heuristic programs have proved either equal or superior to their heuristic counterparts.)

Programs which simulate investment banking procedures and the like have no bearing on cognitive simulation or artificial intelligence. They merely show that certain forms of human activity are sufficiently simple and sterotyped to be formalized. Intelligence was surely involved in *formulating* the rules which investors now follow in making up a portfolio of stocks, but the *formalization* of these rules only reveals them to be explicable and unambiguous, and casts no light on the intelligence involved in discovering them or in their judicious application. The challenge for artificial intelligence does not lie in such *ex post facto* formalization of a specific task, but rather in Area II in which behavior is flexible and not strictly formalizable, in Area III where the formalization is sufficiently complex to require elegant techniques in order to reach a solution, and in Area IV where the formal system is so complex that no decision procedure exists and one has to resort to heuristics.

13 Enthusiasts might find it sobering to imagine a fifteenth-century version of Feigenbaum and Feldman's exhortation: "In terms of the continuum of substances suggested by Paracelsus, the transformations we have been able to perform on baser metals are still at a low level. What is important is that we continue to strike out in the direction of the milestone, the philosopher's stone which can transform any element into any other. Is there any reason to suppose that we will never find it? None whatever. Not a single piece of evidence, no logical argument, no proof or theorem has ever been advanced which demonstrates an insurmountable hurdle along this continuum."

Bibliography

1. Armer, Paul, "Attitudes Toward Intelligent Machines," in *Computers and Thought*, Edward A. Feigenbaum and Julian Feldman (eds.), McGraw-Hill Book Company, New York, 1963, pp. 389–405.

2. Ashby, W. Ross, "Review of Feigenbaum's *Computers and Thought*," (manuscript loaned by author).

3. Bar-Hillel, Yehoshua, "The Present Status of Automatic Translation of Languages," in *Advances in Computers*, Vol. 1, F. L. Alt (ed.), Academic Press, New York, 1960, pp. 91–163.

4. Bullock, Theodore H., "Evolution of Neurophysiological Mechanisms," in *Behavior and Evolution*, Anne Roe and George Gaylord Simpson (eds.), Yale University Press, New Haven, Connecticut, 1958, pp. 165–177.

5. Descartes, René, *Discourse on Method*, L. J. Lafleur (trans.), Library of Liberal Arts, New York, 1951.

6. Feigenbaum, Edward A., "Artificial Intelligence Research," *IEEE Trans. on Information Theory*, Vol. IT-9, November 1963, pp. 248–260.

7. ———, "The Simulation of Verbal Learning Behavior," in *Computers and Thought*, Edward A. Feigenbaum and Julian Feldman (eds.), McGraw-Hill Book Company, New York, 1963, pp. 297–309.

8. Feigenbaum, Edward A., and Julian Feldman (eds.), *Computers and Thought*, McGraw-Hill Book Company, New York, 1963.

9. Gelernter, H., J. R. Hansen, and D. W. Loveland, "Empirical Explorations of the Geometry-Theorem Proving Machine," in *Computers and Thought*, Edward A. Feigenbaum and Julian Feldman (eds.), McGraw-Hill Book Company, New York, 1963, pp. 153–163.

10. Greenberger, Martin (ed.), *Computers and the World of the Future*, Massachusetts Institute of Technology Press, Cambridge, Massachusetts, 1962.

11. Gruenberger, Fred, *Benchmarks in Artificial Intelligence*, The RAND Corporation, P-2586, June 1962.

12. Gurwitsch, Aron, "On the Conceptual Consciousness," in *The Modeling of Mind*, Kenneth M. Sayre and Frederick J. Crosson (eds.), Notre Dame University Press, South Bend, Indiana, 1963, pp. 199–205.

13. Kochen, M., D. M. MacKay, M. E. Maron, M. Scriven, and L. Uhr, *Computers and Comprehension*, The RAND Corporation, RM-4065-PR, April 1964.

14. Lindsay, Robert K., "Inferential Memory as the Basis of Machines which Understand Natural Language," in *Computers and Thought*, Edward A. Feigenbaum and Julian Feldman (eds.), McGraw-Hill Book Company, New York, 1963, pp. 217–236.

15. MacKay, D. M., "Internal Representation of the External World," precirculated draft of paper for Avionics Panel, Athens, 1963.

16. ———, "A Mind's Eye View of the Brain," in *Progress in Brain Research, 17: Cybernetics of the Nervous System*, (a memorial volume honoring Norbert Wiener), Elsevier Publishing Company, Amsterdam, Holland, 1965.

17. Minsky, Marvin, "Steps toward Artificial Intelligence," *Proc. of the IRE*, Vol. 49, January 1961, pp. 8–30.

18. Newell, Allen, "The Chess Machine," in *The Modeling of Mind*, Kenneth M. Sayre and Frederick J. Crosson (eds.), Notre Dame University Press, South Bend, Indiana, 1963, pp. 73–89.

19. ———, *Some Problems of Basic Organization in Problem-Solving Programs*, The RAND Corporation, RM-3283-PR, December 1962.

20. ———, *Learning, Generality and Problem-Solving*, The RAND Corporation, RM-3285-1-PR, February 1963.

21. Newell, Allen, J. C. Shaw, and H. A. Simon, *The Processes of Creative Thinking*, The RAND Corporation, P-1320, September 16, 1958.

22. ———, "Chess-Playing Programs and the Problem of Complexity," in *Computers and Thought*, Edward A. Feigenbaum and Julian Feldman (eds.), McGraw-Hill Book Company, New York, 1963, pp. 39–70.

23. Newell, Allen, J. C. Shaw, and H. A. Simon, "Empirical Explorations with the Logic Theory Machine: A Case Study in Heuristics," in *Computers and Thought*, Edward A. Feigenbaum and Julian Feldman (eds.), McGraw-Hill Book Company, New York, 1963, pp. 109–133.

24. Newell, Allen and H. A. Simon, *Computer Simulation of Human Thinking*, The RAND Corporation, P-2276, April 20, 1961; also published in *Science*, Vol. 134, December 22, 1961, pp. 2011–2017.

25. ——, *Computer Simulation of Human Thinking and Problem Solving*, The RAND Corporation, P-2312, May 29, 1961.

26. ——, "GPS, a Program that Simulates Human Thought," in *Computers and Thought*, Edward A. Feigenbaum and Julian Feldman (eds.), McGraw-Hill Book Company, New York, 1963, pp. 279–293.

27. Oettinger, Anthony G., "The State of the Art of Automatic Language Translation: An Appraisal," in *Beitraege zur Sprachkunde und Information Verarbeitung*, Vol. 1, Heft 2, Oldenbourg Verlage, Munich, 1963, pp. 17–32.

28. Polyani, Michael, "Experience and the Perception of Pattern," *The Modeling of Mind*, Kenneth M. Sayre and Frederick J. Crosson (eds.), Notre Dame University Press, South Bend, Indiana, 1963, pp. 207–220.

29. Samuel, A. L., "Some Studies in Machine Learning Using the Game of Checkers," in *Computers and Thought*, Edward A. Feigenbaum and Julian Feldman (eds.), McGraw-Hill Book Company, New York, 1963, pp. 71–108.

30. See, Richard, "Mechanical Translation and Related Language Research," *Science*, Vol. 144, No. 3619, May 8, 1964, pp. 621–626.

31. Selfridge, Oliver G., and Ulric Neisser, "Pattern Recognition by Machine," in *Computers and Thought*, Edward A. Feigenbaum and Julian Feldman (eds.), McGraw-Hill Book Company, New York, 1963, pp. 237–250.

32. Scriven, Michael, "The Compleat Robot: A Prolegomena to Androidology," in *Dimensions of Mind*, Sidney Hook (ed.), Collier Books, New York, 1961, pp. 113–133.

33. Simon, H. A., *Modeling Human Mental Processes*, The RAND Corporation, P-2221, February 20, 1961.

34. Simon, H. A., and Allen Newell, "Heuristic Problem Solving: The Next Advance in Operations Research," *Operations Research*, Vol. 6, January–February 1958, pp. 1–10.

35. ——, "Information Processing in Computer and Man," *American Scientist*, Vol. 52, September 1964, pp. 281–300.

36. Simon, H. A., and Peter A. Simon, "Trial and Error Search in Solving Difficult Problems: Evidence from the Game of Chess," *Behavioral Science*, Vol. 7, October 1962, pp. 425–429.

37. Smith, D. E., *History of Mathematics*, Vol. II, Ginn and Company, New York, 1925.

38. Uhr, Leonard, and Charles Vossler, "A Pattern-Recognition Program that Generates, Evaluates, and Adjusts Its Own Operators," in *Computers and Thought*, Edward A. Feigenbaum and Julian Feldman (eds.), McGraw-Hill Book Company, New York, 1963, pp. 251–268.

39. Wang, Hao, "Toward Mechanical Mathematics," in *The Modeling of Mind*, Kenneth M. Sayre and Frederick J. Crosson (eds.), Notre Dame University Press, South Bend, Indiana, 1963, pp. 91–120.

40. Wertheimer, M., *Productive Thinking*, Harpers, New York, 1945.

41. Wiener, Norbert, "The Brain and the Machine (Summary), in *Dimensions of Mind*, Sidney Hook (ed.), New York University Press, New York, 1960, pp. 109–112.

42. Wittgenstein, Ludwig, *Philosophical Investigations*, Basil Blackwell, Oxford, England, 1953.
43. ——, *The Blue and Brown Books*, Basil Blackwell, Oxford, England, 1960.

60

THINKING MACHINES

Can there be? Are we?

Terry Winograd

Source: D. Partridge and Y. Wilks (eds), *The Foundations of Artificial Intelligence: A Sourcebook*, Cambridge University Press, 1990, pp. 167–89.

1 Introduction

Futurologists have proclaimed the birth of a new species, *machina sapiens*, that will share (perhaps usurp) our place as the intelligent sovereigns of our earthly domain. These "thinking machines" will take over our burdensome mental chores, just as their mechanical predecessors were intended to eliminate physical drudgery. Eventually they will apply their "ultra-intelligence" to solving all of our problems. Any thoughts of resisting this inevitable evolution is just a form of "speciesism," born from a romantic and irrational attachment to the peculiarities of the human organism.

Critics have argued with equal fervor that "thinking machine" is an oxymoron – a contradiction in terms. Computers, with their foundations of cold logic, can never be creative or insightful or possess real judgment. No matter how competent they appear, they do not have the genuine intentionality that is at the heart of human understanding. The vain pretensions of those who seek to understand mind as computation can be dismissed as yet another demonstration of the arrogance of modern science.

Although my own understanding developed through active participation in artificial intelligence research, I have now come to recognize a larger grain of truth in the criticisms than in the enthusiastic predictions. But the story is more complex. The issues need not (perhaps cannot) be debated as fundamental questions concerning the place of humanity in the universe. Indeed, artificial intelligence has not achieved creativity, insight, and judgment. But its shortcomings are far more mundane: we have not yet been able to construct a machine with even a modicum of common sense or one that can converse on everyday topics in ordinary language.

The source of the difficulties will not be found in the details of silicon micro-circuits or of Boolean logic. The basic philosophy that has guided the research is shallow and inadequate, and has not received sufficient scrutiny. It is drawn from the traditions of rationalism and logical empiricism but has taken a novel turn away from its predecessors. This new "patchwork rationalism" will be our subject of examination.

First, we will review the guiding principles of artificial intelligence and see how they are embodied in current research. Then we will look at the fruits of that research. I will argue that "artificial intelligence" as now conceived is limited to a very particular kind of intelligence: one that can usefully be likened to bureaucracy in its rigidity, obtuseness, and inability to adapt to changing circumstances. The weakness comes not from insufficient development of the technology, but from the inadequacy of the basic tenets.

But, as with bureaucracy, weaknesses go hand in hand with unique strengths. Through a re-interpretation and re-formulation of the techniques that have been developed, we can anticipate and design appropriate and valuable uses. In conclusion I will briefly introduce an orientation I call hermeneutic constructivism and illustrate how it can lead down this alternative path of design.

2 The mechanization of rationality

In their quest for mechanical explanations of (or substitutes for) human reason, researchers in artificial intelligence are heirs to a long tradition. In his "Discourse on the method of properly guiding the reason in the search of truth in the sciences" (1637), Descartes initiated the quest for a systematic method of rationality. Although Descartes himself did not believe that reason could be achieved through mechanical devices, his understanding laid the groundwork for the symbol-processing machines of the modern age.

In 1651, Hobbes described reason as symbolic calculation:

> When a man reasoneth, he does nothing else but conceive a sum total, from addition of parcels; or conceive a remainder . . . These operations are not incident to numbers only, but to all manner of things that can be added together, and taken one out of another . . . the logicians teach the same in consequences of words; adding together two names to make an affirmation, and two affirmations to make a syllogism; and many syllogisms to make a demonstration.
>
> (*Quoted in Haugeland, 1985*)

Leibniz[1] cherished through his life the hope of discovering a kind of generalized mathematics, which he called *Characteristica Universalis*, by means of which thinking could be replaced by calculation. "If we had it," he says "we should be able to reason in metaphysics and morals in much the same way as in geometry and analysis. If controversies were to arise, there would be no more need of disputation between two philosophers than between two accountants. For it would suffice to take their pencils in their hands, to sit down to their slates, and to say to each other . . . 'Let us calculate'."

Behind this program of mechanical reason was a faith in a rational and ultimately understandable universe. The model of "Let us calculate" is that of Euclidean geometry, in which a small set of clear and self-evident postulates provides a basis for generating the right answers (given sufficient diligence) to the most complex and vexing problems. Reasonable men could be relied upon to agree on the postulates and the methods, and therefore dispute could only arise from mistaken calculation.

The empiricists turned to physical experience and experiment as the true basis of knowledge. But in rejecting the a priori status of the propositions on which reasoning was based, they did not abandon the vision of rigorous (potentially mechanizable) logical procedures. For our purposes here, it will suffice to adopt a broader characterization, in which much of both rationalism and empiricism fall within a common "rationalistic tradition" (Winograd and Flores, 1986). This label subsumes the varied (and at times hotly opposed) inheritors of Descartes' legacy – those who seek to achieve rational reason through a precise method of symbolic calculation.

The electronic computer gave new embodiment to mechanical rationality, making it possible to derive the consequences of precisely specified rules, even when huge amounts of calculation are required. The first decades of computing emphasized the application of numerical techniques. Researchers in operations research and decision theory addressed policy questions by developing complex mathematical models of social and political systems and calculating the results of proposed alternatives.[2] Although these techniques work well in specialized cases (such as scheduling delivery vehicles or controlling the operations in a refinery), they proved inadequate for the broader problems to which they were applied. The "mathematization" of experience required simplifications that made the computer results – accurate as they might be with respect to the models – meaningless in the world.

Although there are still attempts to quantify matters of social import (for example in applying mathematical risk analysis to decisions about nuclear power), there is an overall disillusionment with the potential for adequately reducing human concerns to a precise set of numbers and equations (see for example, Davis and Hersh, 1986). The developers of artificial intelligence have rejected traditional mathematical modeling in favor of an emphasis on symbolic – rather than numerical – formalisms. Leibniz's "Let us calculate" is taken in Hobbes' broader sense to include not just numbers but also "affirmations" and "syllogisms."

3 The promise of artificial intelligence

Attempts to duplicate formal non-numerical reasoning on a machine date back to the earliest computers, but the endeavor began in earnest with the AI projects of the mid 1950s (see Gardner, 1985, for an overview of the historical perspective). The goals were ambitious: to fully duplicate the human capacities of thought and language on a digital computer. Early claims that a complete theory of intelligence would be achieved within a few decades have long since been abandoned, but the research has not diminished. For example, a recent book by Minsky (one of the founders of AI) offers computational models for phenomena as diverse as conflict, pain and pleasure, the self, the soul, consciousness, confusion, genius, infant emotion, foreign accents, and freedom of will (these are among the section headings in Minsky, 1986).

In building models of mind, there are two distinct but complementary goals. On the one hand is the quest to explain human mental processes as thoroughly and unambiguously as physics explain the functioning of ordinary mechanical devices. On the other hand is the drive to create intelligent tools – machines that apply intelligence to serve some purpose, regardless of how closely they mimic the details of human intelligence. At times these two enterprises have gone hand in hand, at others they have led down separate paths.

Researchers such as Newell and Simon (two other founding fathers of artificial intelligence) have sought precise and scientifically testable theories of more modest scope than Minsky suggests. In reducing the study of mind to the formulation of rule-governed operations on symbol systems, they focus on detailed aspects of cognitive functioning, using empirical measures such as memory capacity and reaction time. They hypothesize specific "mental architectures" and compare their detailed performance with human experimental results (e.g., Newell and Simon, 1972; Laird et al., 1986). It is difficult to measure the success of this enterprise. The tasks that have been examined (such as puzzle-solving and the ability to remember abbreviations for computer commands) do not even begin to approach a representative sample of human cognitive abilities, for reasons we will examine below.

On the other side lies the goal of practical system building. In the late 1970s, the field of artificial intelligence was drastically affected by the continuing precipitous drop in computing costs. Techniques that previously demanded highly specialized and costly equipment came within the reach of commercial users. A new term, "knowledge engineering," was coined to indicate a shift to the pragmatic interests of the engineer, rather than the scientists's search for theoretical knowledge.

"Expert systems," as the new programs were called, incorporate "knowledge bases" made up of simple facts and "if . . . then" rules, as illustrated in figure 1.

435

FACTS:

Tank no. 23 contains sulfuric acid.

The plaintiff was injured by a portable power saw.

RULES:

If the sulfate ion test is positive, the spill material is sulfuric acid.

If the plaintiff was negligent in the use of the product,

the theory of contributory negligence applies.

Figure 1 Rules for an expert system (from D. Waterman, 1986, p. 16)

These systems do not attempt to explain human intelligence in detail, but are justified in terms of their practical applications, for which extravagant claims have been made.

> Humans need expert systems, but the problem is they don't often believe it . . . At least one high-performance medical diagnosis program sits unused because the physicians it was designed to assist didn't perceive that they needed such assistance; they were wrong, but that doesn't matter . . . There's a manifest destiny in information processing, in knowledge systems, a continent we shall all spread out upon sooner or later.
>
> (*Feigenbaum and McCorduck, 1983*)

The high hopes and ambitious aspirations of knowledge engineering are well-documented, and the claims are often taken at face value, even in serious intellectual discussions. In fact, although a few widely-known systems illustrate specific potentials, the successes are still isolated pinnacles in a landscape of research prototypes, feasibility studies, and preliminary versions. It is difficult to get a clear picture of what has been accomplished and to make a realistic assessment of what is yet to come. We need to begin by examining the difficulties with the fundamental methods these programs employ.

4 The foundations of artificial intelligence

Artificial intelligence draws its appeal from the same ideas of mechanized reasoning that attracted Descartes, Leibniz, and Hobbes, but it differs from the more classical forms of rationalism in a critical way. Descartes wanted his method to stand on a bedrock of clear and self-evident truths. Logical empiricism sought truth through observation and the refinement of formal theories that predicted experimental results. Artificial intelligence has

436

abandoned the quest for certainty and truth. The new patchwork rational-ism is built upon mounds of "micro-truths" gleaned through common sense introspection, *ad hoc* programming and so-called "knowledge acquisi-tion" techniques for interviewing experts. The grounding on this shifting sand is pragmatic in the crude sense – "If it seems to be working, it's right."

The resulting patchwork defies logic. Minsky observes:

> For generations, scientists and philosophers have tried to explain ordinary reasoning in terms of logical principles – with virtually no success. I suspect this enterprise failed because it was looking in the wrong direction: common sense works so well not because it is an approximation of logic; logic is only a small part of our great accumulation of different, useful ways to chain things together.
>
> (*Minsky, 1986*)

In the days before computing, "ways to chain things together" would have remained a vague metaphor. But the computer can perform arbitrary symbol manipulations that we interpret as having logical import. It is easy to build a program to which we enter "Most birds can fly" and "Tweety is a bird" and which then produces "Tweety can fly" according to a regular (although logically questionable) rule. The artificial intelligence methodology does not demand a logically correct answer, but one that works sufficiently often to be "heuristically adequate."

In a way, this approach is very attractive. Everyday human thought does not follow the rigid strictures of formal deduction. Perhaps we can devise some more flexible (and even fallible) system that operates according to mechanical principles, but more accurately mirrors the mind.

But this appeal is subtly deceptive. Minsky places the blame for lack of success in explaining ordinary reasoning on the rigidity of logic, and does not raise the more fundamental questions about the nature of all symbolic representations and of formal (though possibly "non-logical") systems of rules for manipulating them. There are basic limits to what can be done with symbol manipulation, regardless of how many "different, useful ways to chain things together" one invents. The reduction of mind to the interactive sum of decontextualized fragments is ultimately impossible and misleading. But before elaborating on the problems, let us first review some assumptions on which this work proceeds:

1 Intelligence is exhibited by "physical symbol systems."
2 These systems carry out symbol manipulations that correspond to some kind of "problem solving."
3 Intelligence is embodied as a large collection of fragments of "knowledge."

4.1 The physical symbol system hypothesis

The fundamental principle is the identification of intelligence with the functioning of a rule-governed symbol-manipulating device. It has been most explicitly stated by Newell and Simon:

> A physical symbol system has the necessary and sufficient means for general intelligent action . . . By "general intelligent action" we wish to indicate the same scope of intelligence we see in human action: that in any real situation behavior appropriate to the ends of the system and adaptive to the demands of the environment can occur, within some limits of speed and complexity.
>
> (*Newell and Simon, 1976*)

This "physical symbol system hypothesis" presupposes materialism: the claim that all of the observed properties of intelligent beings can ultimately be explained in terms of lawful physical processes. It adds the claim that these processes can be described at a level of abstraction in which all relevant aspects of physical state can be understood as the encoding of symbol structures and that the activities can be adequately characterized as systematic application of symbol manipulation rules.

The essential link is *representation* – the encoding of the relevant aspects of the world. Newell lays this out explicitly:

> An intelligent agent is embedded in a *task environment*; a *task statement* enters via a *perceptual* component and is encoded in an initial *representation*. Whence starts a cycle of activity in which a *recognition* occurs . . . of a method to use to attempt the problem. The method draws upon a memory of *general world knowledge* . . . It is clear to us all what *representation* is in this picture. It is the data structures that hold the problem and will be processed into a form that makes the solution available. Additionally, it is the data structures that hold the world knowledge and will be processed to acquire parts of the solution or to obtain guidance in constructing it. [emphasis in original]
>
> (*Newell, 1982*)

Complete and systematic symbolic representation is crucial to the paradigm. The rules followed by the machine can deal only with the symbols, not their interpretation.

4.2 Problem-solving, inference, and search

Newell's and Simon's physical symbol systems aspire not to an idealized rationality, but to "behavior appropriate to the ends of the system and adaptive to the demands of the environment." This shift reflects the formulation that won Simon a Nobel prize in economics. He supplanted decision theories based on optimization with a theory of "satisficing" – effectively using finite decision-making resources to come up with adequate, but not necessarily optimal plans of action.

As artificial intelligence developed in the 1950s and 1960s, this methodology was formalized in the techniques of "heuristic search."

The task that a symbol system is faced with, then, when it is presented with a problem and a problem space, is to use its limited processing resources to generate possible solutions, one after another, until it finds one that satisfies the problem-defining test (Newell and Simon, 1976).

The "problem space" is a formal structure that can be thought of as enumerating the results of all possible sequences of actions that might be taken by the program. In a program for playing chess, for example, the problem space is generated by the possible sequences of moves. The number of possibilities grows exponentially with the number of moves, and is beyond practical reach after a small number. However, one can limit search in this space by following heuristics that operate on the basis of local cues ("If one of your pieces could be taken on the opponent's next move, try moving it . . . "). There have been a number of variations on this basic theme, all of which are based on explicit representations of the problem space and the heuristics for operating within it.

Figure 1 illustrated some rules and facts from expert systems. These are not represented in the computer as sentences in English, but as symbols intended to correspond to the natural language terms. As these examples indicate, the domains are naturally far richer and more complex than can be captured by such simple rules. A lawyer will have many questions about whether a plaintiff was "negligent," but for the program it is a simple matter of whether a certain symbolic expression of the form "Negligent(x)" appears in the store of representations, or whether there is a rule of the form "If . . . then Negligent(x)," whose conditions can be satisfied.

There has been a great deal of technical debate over the detailed form of rules, but two principles are taken for granted in essentially all of the work:

1 Each rule is true in a limited (situation-dependent), not absolute sense.
2 The overall result derives from the synergistic combination of rules, in a pattern that need not (in fact could not in general) be anticipated in writing them.

For example, there may be cases in which the "sulfate ion test is positive" even though the spill is not sulfuric acid. The overall architecture of the rule-manipulating system may lead to a conclusion being drawn that violates one of these rules (on the basis of other rules). The question is not whether each of the rules is true, but whether the output of the program as a whole is "appropriate." The knowledge engineers hope that by devising and tuning such rules they can capture more than the deductive logic of the domain.

> "While conventional programs deal with facts, expert systems handle "lore" . . . the rules of thumb, the hunches, the intuition and capacity for judgment that are seldom explicitly laid down but which form the basis of an expert's skill, acquired over a lifetime's experience."
>
> (*Michie and Johnston, 1984*)

This *ad hoc* nature of the logic applies equally to the cognitive models of Newell and Simon, in which a large collection of separate "production rules" operates on a symbolic store or "working memory." Each production rule specifies a step to be carried out on the symbols in the store, and the overall architecture determines which will be carried out in what order. The symbols don't stand for chemical spills and law, but for hypothesized psychological features, such as the symbolic contents of short-term memory. Individual rules do things like moving an element to the front of the memory or erasing it. The cognitive modeler does not build an overall model of the system's performance on a task, but designs the individual rules in hopes that appropriate behavior will emerge from their interaction.

Minsky makes explicit this assumption that intelligence will emerge from computational interactions among a plethora of small pieces.

> I'll call "Society of Mind" this scheme in which each mind is made of many smaller processes. The smaller processes we'll call agents. Each mental agent by itself can only do some simple thing that needs no mind or thought at all. Yet when we join these agents in societies – in certain very special ways – this leads to true intelligence.
>
> (*Minsky, 1986*)

Minsky's theory is quite different from Newell's cognitive architectures. In place of finely-tuned clockworks of precise production rules we find an impressionistic pastiche of metaphors. Minsky illustrates his view in a simple "micro-world" of toy blocks, populated by agents such as BUILDER (which stacks up the blocks), ADD (which adds a single block to a stack), and the like:

> for example, BUILDER's agents require no sense of meaning to do their work; ADD merely has to turn on GET and PUT. Then GET

and PUT do not need any subtle sense of what those turn-on signals "mean" – because they're wired up to do only what they're wired up to do.

(Minsky, 1986)

These agents seem like simple computer subroutines – program fragments that perform a single well-defined task. But a subsequent chapter describes an interaction between the BUILDER agent and the WRECKER agent, which are parts of a PLAY-WITH-BLOCKS agent:

> inside an actual child, the agencies responsible for BUILDING and WRECKING might indeed become versatile enough to negotiate by offering support for one another's goals. "Please, WRECKER, wait a moment more till BUILDER adds just one more block: it's worth it for louder crash!".

(Minsky, 1986)

With a simple "might indeed become versatile . . . ," we have slipped from a technically feasible but limited notion of agents as subroutines, to an impressionistic description of a society of *homunculi*, conversing with each other in ordinary language. This sleight of hand is at the center of the theory. It takes an almost childish leap of faith to assume that the modes of explanation that work for the details of block manipulation will be adequate for understanding conflict, consciousness, genius, and freedom of will.

One cannot dismiss this as an isolated fantasy. Minsky is one of the major figures in artificial intelligence and he is only stating in a simplistic form a view that permeates the field.

In looking at the development of computer technology, one cannot help but be struck by the successes at reducing complex and varied tasks to systematic combinations of elementary operations. Why not, then, make the jump to the mind. If we are no more than protoplasm-based physical symbol systems, the reduction must be possible and only our current lack of knowledge prevents us from explicating it in detail, all the way from BUILDER's clever ploy down to the logical circuitry.

4.3 Knowledge as a commodity

All of the approaches described above depend on interactions among large numbers of individual elements: rules, productions, or agents. No one of these elements can be taken as representing a substantial understandable truth, but this doesn't matter since somehow the conglomeration will come out all right. But how can we have any confidence that it will? The proposed answer is a typical one of our modern society: "More is better!" "Knowledge is power, and more knowledge is more power."

A widely-used expert systems text declares:

> It wasn't until the late 1970s that AI scientists began to realize something quite important: The problem-solving power of a program comes from the knowledge it possesses, not just from the formalisms and inference schemes it employs. The conceptual breakthrough was made and can be quite simply stated. *To make a program intelligent, provide it with lots of high-quality, specific knowledge about some problem area.* [emphasis in the original]
>
> (*Waterman, 1986*)

This statement is typical of much writing on expert systems, both in the parochial perspective that inflates homily into "conceptual breakthrough" and in its use of slogans like "high-quality knowledge." Michie (the doyen of artificial intelligence in Britain) predicts:

> [Expert systems] . . . can actually help to codify and improve expert human knowledge, taking what was fragmentary, inconsistent and error-infested and turning it into knowledge that is more precise, reliable and comprehensive. This new process, with its enormous potential for the future, we call "knowledge refining."
>
> (*Michie and Johnston, 1984*)

Feigenbaum proclaims:

> The miracle product is knowledge, and the Japanese are planning to package and sell it the way other nations package and sell energy, food, or manufactured goods . . . The essence of the computer revolution is that the burden of producing the future knowledge of the world will be transferred from human heads to machine artifacts.
>
> (*Feigenbaum and McCorduck, 1983*)

Knowledge is a kind of commodity – to be produced, refined, and packaged. The knowledge engineers are not concerned with the age-old epistemological problems of what constitutes knowledge or understanding. They are hard at work on techniques of "knowledge acquisition" and see it as just a matter of sufficient money and effort:

> We have the opportunity at this moment to do a new version of Diderot's *Encyclopedia*, a gathering up of all knowledge – not just the academic kind, but the informal, experiential, heuristic kind – to be fused, amplified, and distributed, all at orders of magnitude dif-

ference in cost, speed, volume, and *usefulness* over what we have now. [emphasis in the original]

(*Feigenbaum and McCorduck, 1983*)

Lenat has embarked on this task of "encod[ing] all the world's knowledge down to some level of detail." The plan projects an initial entry of about 400 articles from a desk encyclopedia (leading to 10,000 paragraphs worth of material), followed by hiring a large number of "knowledge enterers" to add "the last 99 percent." There is little concern that foundational problems might get in the way. Lenat *et al.* (1986) asserts that "AI has for many years understood enough about representation and inference to tackle this project, but no one has sat down and done it."

5 The fundamental problems

The optimistic claims for artificial intelligence have far outstripped the achievements, both in the theoretical enterprise of cognitive modeling and in the practical application of expert systems.

In cognitive modeling we seek to fit a model's performance with measured human behavior but the enterprise is fraught with methodological difficulty, as it straddles the wide chasm between the engineering bravado of computer science and the careful empiricism of experimental psychology. When a computer program duplicates to some degree some carefully restricted aspect of human behavior, what have we learned? It is all too easy to write a program that would produce that particular behavior, and all too hard to build one that covers a sufficiently general range to inspire confidence. As Pylyshyn (an enthusiastic participant in cognitive science) observes:

> Most current computational models of cognition are vastly underconstrained and *ad hoc*; they are contrivances assembled to mimic arbitrary pieces of behavior, with insufficient concern for explicating the principles in virtue of which such behavior is exhibited and with little regard for a precise understanding.
>
> (*Pylyshyn, 1984*)

Newell and his colleagues' painstaking attention to detailed architecture of production systems is an attempt to better constrain the computational model, in hopes that experiments can then test detailed hypotheses. As with much of experimental psychology, a highly artificial experimental situation is required to get results that can be sensibly interpreted at all. Proponents argue that the methods and theoretical foundations that are being applied to micro-behavior will eventually be extended and generalized to cover the full range of cognitive phenomena. As with Minsky, this leap from the microstructure to the whole human is one of faith.

In the case of expert systems, there is a more immediate concern. Applied AI is widely seen as a means of managing processes that have grown too complex or too rapid for unassisted humans. Major industrial and governmental organizations are mounting serious efforts to build expert systems for tasks such as air traffic control, nuclear power plant operation, and – most distressingly – the control of weapons systems. These projects are justified with claims of generality and flexibility for AI programs. They ignore or downplay the difficulties that will make the programs almost certain to fail in just those cases where their success is most critical.

It is commonplace in the field to describe expert systems as "brittle" – able to operate only within a narrow range of situations. The problem here is not just one of insufficient engineering, but is a direct consequence of the nature of rule-based systems. We will examine three manifestations of the problem: gaps of anticipation; blindness of representation; and restriction of the domain.

5.1 Gaps of anticipation

In creating a program or knowledge base, one takes into account as many factors and connections as feasible. But in any realistically complex domain, this gives at best a spotty coverage. The person designing a system for dealing with acid spills may not consider the possibility of rain leaking into the building, or of a power failure, or that a labeled bottle does not contain what it purports to. A human expert faced with a problem in such a circumstance falls back on common sense and a general background of knowledge.

The hope of patchwork rationalism is that with a sufficiently large body of rules, the thought-through spots will successfully interpolate to the wastelands in between. Having written rule A with one circumstance in mind and rule B with another, the two rules in combination will succeed in yet a third. This strategy is the justification for the claim that AI systems are more flexible than conventional programs. There is a grain of truth in the comparison, but it is deceptive. The program applies the rules blindly with erratic results. In many cases, the price of flexibility (the ability to operate in combinations of contingencies not considered by the programmer) is irreparable and inscrutable failure.

In attempting to overcome this brittleness, expert systems are built with many thousands of rules, trying to cover all of the relevant situations and to provide representations for all potentially relevant aspects of context. One system for medical diagnosis, called CADUCEUS (originally INTERNIST) has 500 disease profiles, 350 disease variations, several thousand symptoms, and 6,500 rules describing relations among symptoms. After fifteen years of development, the system is still not on the market. According to one report, it gave a correct diagnosis in only 75 per cent of its carefully selected test cases. Nevertheless, Myers, the medical expert who developed it, "believes that the addition of another 50 [diseases] will make the system workable and, more importantly, practical" (Newquist, 1987).

Human experts develop their skills through observing and acting in many thousands of cases. AI researchers argue that this results in their remembering a huge repertoire of specialized "patterns" (complex symbolic rules) that allows them to discriminate situations with expert finesse and to recognize appropriate actions. But it is far from obvious whether the result of experience can be adequately formalized as a repertoire of discrete patterns (see discussion in Dreyfus and Dreyfus, 1986). To say that "all of the world's knowledge" could be explicitly articulated in any symbolic form (computational or not) we must assume the possibility of reducing all forms of tacit knowledge (skills, intuition, and the like) to explicit facts and rules. Heidegger and other phenomenologists have challenged this, and many of the strongest criticisms of artificial intelligence are based on the phenomenological analysis of human understanding as a "readiness-at-hand" of action in the world, rather than as the manipulation of "present-at-hand" representations (see, for example Dreyfus, 1979; Winograd and Flores, 1986).

Be that as it may, it is clear that the corresponding task in building expert systems is extremely difficult, if not theoretically impossible. The knowledge engineer attempts to provide the program with rules that correspond to the expert's experience. The rules are modified through analyzing examples in which the original rules break down. But the patchwork nature of the rules makes this extremely difficult. Failure in a particular case may not be attributable to a particular rule, but rather to a chance combination of rules that are in other circumstances quite useful. The breakdown may not even provide sharp criteria for knowing what to change, as with a chess program that is just failing to come up with good moves. The problem here is not simply one of scale or computational complexity. Computers are perfectly capable of operating on millions of elements. The problem is one of human understanding – the ability of a person to understand how a new situation experienced in the world is related to an existing set of representations, and to possible modifications of those representations.

In trying to remove the potentially unreliable "human element," expert systems conceal it. The power plant will no longer fail because a reactor-operator falls asleep, but because a knowledge engineer didn't think of putting in a rule specifying how to handle a particular failure when the emergency system is undergoing its periodic test, and the backup system is out of order. No amount of refinement and articulation can guarantee the absence of such breakdowns. The hope that a system based on patchwork rationalism will respond "appropriately" in such cases is just that: a hope, and one that can engender dangerous illusions of safety and security.

5.2 *The blindness of representation*

The second problem lies in the symbol system hypothesis itself. In order to characterize a situation in symbolic form, one uses a system of basic distinctions, or terms. Rules deal with the interrelations among the terms, not with their interpretations in the world.

Consider ordinary words as an analogy. Imagine that a doctor asks a nurse "Is the patient eating?" If they are deciding whether to perform an examination, the request might be paraphrased "Is she eating at this moment?" If the patient is in the hospital for anorexia and the doctor is checking the efficacy of the treatment, it might be more like "Has the patient eaten some minimal amount in the past day?" If the patient has recently undergone surgery, it might mean "Has the patient taken any nutrition by mouth," and so on. In responding, a person interprets the sentence as having relevance in the current situation, and will typically respond appropriately without conscious choosing among meanings.

In order to build a successful symbol system, decontextualized meaning is necessary – terms must be stripped of open-ended ambiguities and shadings. A medical expert system might have a rule of the form: "IF Eating(x) THEN . . . ", which is to be applied only if the patient is eating, along with others of the form "IF . . . THEN Eating (x)" which determine when that condition holds. Unless everyone who writes or reads a rule interprets the primitive term "Eating" in the same way, the rules have no consistent interpretation and the results are unpredictable.

In response to this, one can try to refine the vocabulary. "Currently-Dining" and "Taking-Solids" could replace the more generic term, or we could add construal rules, such as "in a context of immediate action, take 'Eating' to mean 'Currently-Dining'." Such approaches work for the cases that programmers anticipate, but of course are subject to the infinite regress of trying to decontextualize context. The new terms or rules themselves depend on interpretation that is not represented in the system.

5.3 *Restriction of the domain*

A consequence of decontextualized representation is the difficulty of creating AI programs in any but the most carefully restricted domains, where almost all of the knowledge required to perform the task is special to that domain (i.e., little common-sense knowledge is required). One can find specialized tasks for which appropriate limitations can be achieved, but these do not include the majority of work in commerce, medicine, law, or the other professions demanding expertise.

Holt characterized the situation: "A brilliant chess move while the room is filling with smoke because the house is burning down does not show intelligence. If the capacity for brilliant chess moves without regard to life

446

circumstances deserves a name, I would naturally call it 'artificial intelligence.'"[3]

The brilliance of a move is with respect to a well-defined domain: the rules of chess. But acting as an expert doctor, attorney, or engineer takes the other kind of intelligence: knowing what makes sense in a situation. The most successful artificial intelligence programs have operated in the detached puzzle-like domains of board games and technical analysis, not those demanding understanding of human lives, motivations, and social inter-action. Attempts to cross into these difficult territories, such as a program said to "understand tales involving friendship and adultery" (see discussion of BORIS program in Winograd and Flores, 1986), proceed by replacing the real situation with a cartoon-like caricature, governed by simplistic rules whose inadequacy is immediately obvious (even to the creators, who argue that they simply need further elaboration).

This reformulation of a domain to a narrower, more precise one can lead to systems that give correct answers to irrelevant problems. This is of con-cern not only when actions are based directly on the output of the computer system (as in one controlling weapons systems), but also when, for example, medical expert systems are used to evaluate the work of physicians (Atha-nasiou, 1987). Since the system is based on a reduced representation of the situation, it systematically (if invisibly) values some aspects of care while remaining blind to others. Doctors whose salaries, promotions, or accredita-tions depend on the review of their actions by such a program will find their practice being subtly shaped to its mold. The attempt to encode "the world's knowledge" inevitably leads to this kind of simplification. Every explicit rep-resentation of knowledge bears within it a background of cultural orienta-tion that does not appear as explicit claims, but is manifest in the very terms in which the "facts" are expressed and in the judgment of what constitutes a fact. An encyclopedia is not a compendium of "refined knowledge," but a statement within a tradition and a culture. By calling an electronic encyclo-pedia a "knowledge base" we mystify its source and its grounding in a tradition and background.

6 The bureaucracy of mind

Many observers have noted the natural affinity between computers and bur-eaucracy. Lee argues that "bureaucracies are the most ubiquitous form of artificial intelligence . . . Just as scientific management found its idealization in automation and programmable production robots, one might consider an artificially intelligent knowledge-based system as the ideal bureaucrat" (Lee, 1985). Lee's stated goal is "improved bureaucratic software engineering," but his analogy suggests more.

Stated simply, *the techniques of artificial intelligence are to the mind what bureaucracy is to human social interaction.*

In today's popular discussion, bureaucracy is seen as an evil – a pathology of large organizations and repressive governments. But in his classic work on bureaucracy, Weber argued its great advantages over earlier, less formalized systems, calling it the "unambiguous yardstick for the modernization of the state." He notes that "bureaucracy has a 'rational' character, with rules, means-ends calculus, and matter-of-factness predominating," (Weber, 1968), and that it succeeds in "eliminating from official business love, hatred, and all purely personal, irrational, and emotional elements which escape calculation" (Weber, 1968).

> The decisive reason for the advance of bureaucratic organization has always been its purely *technical* superiority over any other form of organization. The fully developed bureaucratic apparatus compares with other organizations exactly as does the machine with the non-mechanical modes of production. Precision, speed, unambiguity, knowledge of the files, continuity, discretion, unity, strict subordination, reduction of friction and of material and personal costs – these are raised to the optimum point in the strictly bureaucratic administration. [emphasis in original]
>
> (*Weber, 1968*)

The benefits of bureaucracy follow from the reduction of judgment to the systematic application of explicitly articulated rules. Bureaucracy achieves a predictability and manageability that is missing in earlier forms of organization. There are striking similarities here with the arguments given for the benefits of expert systems, and equally striking analogies with the shortcomings as pointed out, for example, by March and Simon:

> The reduction in personalized relationships, the increased internalization of rules, and the decreased search for alternatives combine to make the behavior of members of the organization highly predictable; i.e., they result in an increase in the *rigidity of behavior* of participants [which] increases the *amount of difficulty with clients* of the organization and complicates the achievement of client satisfaction. [emphasis in original]
>
> (*March and Simon, 1958*)

Given Simon's role in artificial intelligence, it is ironic that he notes these weaknesses of human-embodied rule systems, but sees the behavior of rule-based physical symbol systems as "adaptive to the demands of the environment." Indeed, systems based on symbol manipulation exhibit the rigidities of bureaucracies, and are most problematic in dealing with "client satisfaction" – the mismatch between the decontextualized application of rules and the human interpretation of the symbols that appear in them. Bureaucracy is most successful in a world that is stable and repetitive – where the rules can be followed without interpretive judgments. Expert systems are best in just the same situations. Their successes have been in stable and precise technical areas, where exceptions are not the rule.

Michie's claim that expert systems can encode "the rules of thumb, the hunches, the intuition and capacity for judgment . . . " is wrong in the same way that it is wrong to seek a full account of an organization in its formal rules and procedures. Modern sociologists have gone beyond Weber's analysis, pointing to the informal organization and tacit knowledge that make organizations work effectively. This closely parallels the importance of tacit knowledge in individual expertise. Without it we get rigidity and occasional but irreparable failure.

The depersonalization of knowledge in expert systems also has obvious parallels with bureaucracy. When a person views his or her job as the correct application of a set of rules (whether human-invoked or computer-based), there is a loss of personal responsibility or commitment. The "I just follow the rules" of the bureaucratic clerk has its direct analog in "That's what the knowledge base says." The individual is not committed to appropriate results (as judged in some larger human context), but to faithful application of the procedures. This forgetfulness of individual commitment is perhaps the most subtle and dangerous consequence of patchwork rationality. The person who puts rules into a knowledge base cannot be committed to the consequences of applying them in a situation he or she cannot foresee. The person who applies them cannot be committed to their formulation or to the mechanics by which they produce an answer. The result belongs to no-one. When we speak here of "commitment," we mean something more general than the kind of accountability that is argued in court. There is a deep sense in which every use of language is a reflection of commitment, as we will see in the following section.

7 Alternatives

We began with the question of thinking machines – devices that mechanically reproduce human capacities of thought and language. We have seen how this question has been reformulated in the pursuit of artificial intelligence, to reflect a particular design based on patchwork rationalism. We have argued that the current direction will be inadequate to explain or construct real intelligence.

But, one might ask, does that mean that no machine could exhibit intelligence? Is artificial intelligence inherently impossible, or is it just fiendishly difficult? To answer sensibly we must first ask what we mean by "machine." There is a simple a priori proof that machines can be intelligent if we accept that our own brains are (in Minsky's provocative words) nothing but "meat machines." If we take "machine" to stand for any physically constituted device subject to the causal laws of nature, then the question reduces to one of materialism, and is not to be resolved through computer research. If, on the other hand, we take machine to mean "physical symbol system" then there is ground for a strong skepticism. This skepticism has become visible among practitioners of artificial intelligence as well as the critics.

7.1 Emergent intelligence

The innovative ideas of cybernetics a few decades ago led to two contrasting research programmes. One, which we have examined here, took the course of symbol processing. The other was based on modelling neural activity and led to the work on "perceptions," a research line that was discounted for many years as fruitless and is now being rehabilitated in "connectionist" theories, based on "massively parallel distributed processing." In this work, each computing element (analogous to a neuron) operates on simple general principles, and intelligence emerges from the evolving patterns of interaction.[4]

Connectionism is one manifestation of what Turkle calls "emergent AI" (Turkle, 1987). The fundamental intuition guiding this work is that cognitive structure in organisms emerges through learning and experience, not through explicit representation and programming. The problems of blindness and domain limitation described above need not apply to a system that has developed through situated experience.

It is not yet clear whether we will see a turn back towards the heritage of cybernetics or simply a "massively parallel" variant of current cognitive theory and symbol processing design. Although the new connectionism may breathe new life into cognitive modeling research, it suffers an uneasy balance between symbolic and physiological description. Its spirit harks back to the cybernetic concern with real biological systems, but the detailed models typically assume a simplistic representational base much closer to traditional artificial intelligence. Connectionism, like its parent cognitive theory, must be placed in the category of brash unproved hypotheses, which have not really begun to deal with the complexities of mind, and whose current explanatory power is extremely limited.

In one of the earliest critiques of artificial intelligence, Dreyfus compared it to alchemy (Dreyfus, 1965). Seekers after the glitter of intelligence are misguided in trying to cast it from the base metal of computing. There is an amusing epilogue to this analogy: in fact, the alchemists were right. Lead can be converted into gold by a particle accelerator hurling appropriate beams at lead targets. The AI visionaries may be right in the same way, and they are likely to be wrong in the same way. There is no reason but hubris to believe that we are any closer to understanding intelligence than the alchemists were to the secrets of nuclear physics. The ability to create a glistening simulacrum should not fool us either into thinking the rest is "just a matter of encoding a sufficient part of the world's knowledge" or into a quest for the philosopher's stone of "massively parallel processing."

7.2 Hermeneutic constructivism

Discussions of the problems and dangers of computers often leave the impression that on the whole we would be better-off if we could return to the pre-computer era. In a similar vein one might decry the advent of written language, which created many new problems. For example, Weber attributes the emergence of bureaucracy to the spread of writing and literacy, which made it possible to create and maintain systems of rules. Indeed, the written word made bureaucracy possible, but that is far from a full account of its relevance to human society.

The computer is a physical embodiment of the symbolic calculations envisaged by Hobbes and Leibniz. As such, it is not really a thinking machine, but a language machine. The very notion of "symbol system" is inherently linguistic and what we duplicate in our programs with their rules and propositions is really a form of verbal argument, not the workings of mind. It is tempting – but ultimately misleading – to project the image of rational discourse (and its reflection in conscious introspection) onto the design of embodied intelligence. In taking inner discourse as a model for the activity of Minsky's tiny agents, or of productions that determine what token to process next, artificial intelligence has operated with the faith that mind is linguistic down to the microscopic level.

But the utility of the technology need not depend on this faith. The computer, like writing, is fundamentally a communication medium – one that is unique in its ability to perform complex manipulations on the linguistic objects it stores and transmits. We can reinterpret the technology of artificial intelligence in a new background, with new consequences. In doing so we draw on an alternative philosophical grounding, which I will call hermeneutic constructivism.

We begin with some fundamental questions about what language is and how it works. In this we draw on work in hermeneutics (the study of interpretation) and phenomenology, as developed by Heidegger and Gadamer, along with the concepts of language action developed from the later works of Wittgenstein and through the speech act philosophy of Austin, Searle, and Habermas (see chapter 5 of Winograd and Flores, 1986).

Two guiding principles emerge:

1 People create their world through language.
2 Language is always interpreted in a tacitly understood background.

Austin pointed out that "performative" sentences do not convey information about the world, but act to change that world. "You're hired," when uttered in appropriate conditions, creates – not describes – a situation of employment. Searle applied this insight to mundane language actions such as asking questions and agreeing to do something. Habermas extended it further, showing how sentences we would naively consider statements of fact have force by virtue of an act of commitment by the speaker.

> The essential presupposition for the success of [a language] act consists in the speaker's entering into a specific engagement, so that the hearer can rely on him. An utterance can count as a promise, assertion, request, question, or avowal, if and only if the speaker makes an offer that he is ready to make good insofar as it is accepted by the hearer. The speaker must engage himself, that is, indicate that in certain situations he will draw certain consequences for action.
>
> (*Habermas, 1979*)

Descartes' descendants in the rationalistic tradition take the language of mathematics as their ideal. Terms are either primitive or can be fully defined; the grammar is unambiguous; and precise truth conditions can be established through formal techniques. But even in apparently simple and straightforward situations, human language is metaphorical, ambiguous and undefinable. What we can take as fundamental is the engagement – the commitment to make good what cannot be fully made precise.

This grounding is especially evident for statements of the kind that Roszak characterizes as "ideas rather than information" (Roszak, 1986). "All men are created equal" cannot be judged as a true or false description of the objective world. Its force resides in the commitments it carries for further characterization and further action. But it is critical to recognize that this social grounding of language applies equally to the mundane statements of everyday life. "The patient is eating" cannot be held up to any specific set of truth conditions across situations in which it may be uttered. The speaker is not reporting an objectively delineated state of affairs, but indicating the "engagement" to enter sincerely into a dialogue of articulation of the relevant background.

This unavoidable dependence of interpretation on unspoken background is the fundamental insight of the hermeneutic phenomenologists, such as Gadamer. It applies not just to ordinary language, but to every symbolic representation as well. We all recognize that in "reducing things to numbers" we lose the potential for interpretation in a background. But this is equally true of "reducing them to symbol structures."

Whenever a computer program is intended to guide or take action in a human domain, it inevitably imports basic values and assumptions. The basic nature of patchwork rationalism obscures the underlying constitutive "ideas" with a mosaic of fragmentary bits of "information." The social and political agenda concealed behind these patches of decontextualized and depersonalized belief is dangerous in its invisibility.

7.3 Language machines

Symbol structures are ultimately created by people and interpreted by people. The computer, as a language machine, manipulates symbols without respect to their interpretation. To the extent that relations among the meanings can be adequately reflected in precise rules, the computational manipulations make sense. The error is in assuming that these manipulations capture, rather than augment or reify parts of the meaning. If an expert system prints out "Give the patient penicillin" or "Fire the missiles now," room for interpretation is limited and meaning is lost. But instead we can see the computer as a way of organizing, searching, and manipulating texts that are created by people, in a context, and ultimately intended for human interpretation.

We are already beginning to see a movement away from the early vision of computers replacing human experts. For example, the medical diagnostic system described above is being converted from "Internist" (a doctor specializing in internal medicine) to an "advisory system" called "QMR" (for "Quick Medical Reference") (Newquist, 1987). The rules can be thought of as constituting an automated textbook, which can access and logically combine entries that are relevant to a particular case. The goal is to suggest and justify possibilities a doctor might not otherwise have considered. The program need not respond with an evaluation or plan for action, but is successful through providing relevant material for interpretation by an expert. Similarly, in areas of real-time control (like a nuclear power plant), an advisory system can monitor conditions and provide warnings, reports, and summaries for human review. In a similar vein, an interactive computer-based encyclopedia need not cover all of human knowledge or provide general purpose deduction in order to take advantage of the obvious computer capacities of speed, volume, and sophisticated inferential indexing.

Another opportunity for design is in the regularities of the structure of language use. As a simple example, a request is normally followed in coherent conversation by an acceptance, a rejection, or a request to modify the conditions. These in turn are followed by other language acts in a logic of "conversation for action" oriented towards completion (a state in which neither party is awaiting further action by the other). The theory of such conversations has been developed as the basis for a computer program called The Coordinator which is used for facilitating and organizing computer-message conversations in an organization (see Flores, 1982; Winograd and Flores, 1986; Winograd, 1987/88). It emphasizes the role of commitment by the speaker in each speech act and provides the basis for timely and effective action.

Howard has studied the use of computer systems by professionals evaluating loan applications for the World Bank. He argues that their use of computers while on field missions increases the "transparency" of their decision-making process, hence increasing their accountability and enhancing opportunities for meaningful negotiation. The computer serves as a medium of discourse in which different commitments and their consequences can be jointly explored.

> As a result, the dialogue between them [the bankers and their clients] suddenly becomes less about the final results – "the numbers" – and more about the assumptions behind the numbers, the criteria on which decisions are themselves based ... [quoting a bank professional] "Instead of just saying, 'I don't believe you, my opinion is X,' we explore it. We say, 'let's see what the consequences of that are.' And, sometimes, we end up changing our assumptions."
>
> (*Howard, 1986*)

Current expert systems methodologies are not well suited to this kind of dialogue. They separate the construction of the knowledge base from the use of its "expertise."

The experts (with the help of knowledge engineers) enter the knowledge in the laboratory, and the users apply it in the field to get results. But we might instead use the computer to support the discourse that creates the reality – as a tool for the cooperative articulation of the characterizations and rules that will be applied. Rather than seeing the computer as working with objectified refined knowledge, it can serve as a way of keeping track of how the representations emerge from interpretations: who created them in what context, and where to look for clarification.

8 Conclusion

The question of our title demands interpretation in a context. As developed in the paper, it might be formulated more precisely "Are we machines of the kind that researchers are building as 'thinking machines'?" In asking this kind of question we engage in a kind of projection – understanding humanity by projecting an image of ourself onto the machine and the image of the machine back onto ourselves. In the tradition of artificial intelligence, we project an image of our language activity onto the symbolic manipulations of the machine, then project that back onto the full human mind.

But these projections are like the geometric projection of a three-dimensional world onto a two-dimensional plane. We systematically eliminate dimensions, thereby both simplifying and distorting. The particular dimensions we eliminate or preserve in this exercise are not idiosyncratic accidents. They reflect a philosophy that precedes them and which they serve to amplify and extend. In projecting language as a rule-governed manipulation of symbols, we all too easily dismiss the concerns of human meaning that make up the humanities, and indeed of any socially grounded understanding of human language and action. In projecting language back as the model for thought, we lose sight of the tacit embodied understanding that undergirds our intelligence. Through a broader understanding, we can recapture our view of these lost dimensions, and in the process better understand both ourselves and our machines.

Notes

I thank Gary Chapman, Brad Hartfield and especially Carol Winograd for insightful critical readings of early drafts. I am also grateful for my continuing conversation with Fernando Flores, in which my understanding has been generated.

1   As described by Russell (1952) in *A History of Western Philosophy*.
2   One large-scale and quite controversial example was the Massachusetts Institute of Technology/Club of Rome simulation of the world social and economic future (The Limits of Growth).
3   Remarks made by Anatol Holt at the Advanced Research Project's Agency Principal Investigator's Conference, Los Angeles, February 6–8, 1974 (unpublished manuscript).
4   For a historical account and analysis of the current debates, see H. Dreyfus and S. Dreyfus, *Making a Mind vs. Modeling the Brain* (1988). For a technical view, see Rumelhart and McClelland (1986a), *Parallel Distributed Processing*. Maturana and Varela, in *The Tree of Knowledge* (1987), offer a broad philosophy of cognition on this base.

Bibliography

Athanasiou, Tom (1987). High-Tech Politics: The Case of Artificial Intelligence. *Socialist Review*, pp. 7–35.

Austin, J. L. (1962). *How to Do Things with Words*. Cambridge, MA: Harvard University Press.

Bobrow, Daniel G. (ed.) (1980). Special Issue on Nonmonotonic Logic. *Artificial Intelligence*, 13, 1.

Club of Rome (1972). *The Limits to Growth*. New York: Universe Books.

Davis, Philip J. and Hersh Reuben (1986). *Descartes' Dream: The World According to Mathematics*. San Diego: Harcourt Brace.

Dreyfus, Hubert L. (1965). Alchemy and Artificial Intelligence. *Rand Corporation Paper* (P-3244). Reference WIN

Dreyfus, Hubert L. (1972). *What Computers Can't Do: The Limits of Artificial Intelligence*. New York: Harper & Row. [Gives a sharp criticism of current AI. Judging from the harsh reaction it received from the AI community, some of the criticisms seem to be very close to the mark. The second edition, with a new preface, which appeared in 1979, is a revision of the 1972 book in which Dreyfus argues that AI has made very little progress, especially when compared to the promises made. In the revision he claims that the "results" obtained since the first edition further support his position. He feels that intelligent behavior is dependent on the total interaction between an intelligent being and its environment, therefore computers cannot have intelligence until they have the ability for this level of interaction.]

Dreyfus, Hubert L. and Stuart E. Dreyfus (1986). *Mind Over Machine: The Power of Human Intuition and Expertise in the Era of the Computer.* New York: The Free Press. [A general assault on the conventional wisdom of expert systems technology. A five-step process of acquiring expertise is presented. In particular they claim that rule following, of the type that current expert system technology (CEST) is based upon, is characteristic of the human novice rather than the expert, except in domains where there are no intuitive human experts.

Dreyfus, Hubert L. and Stuart E. Dreyfus (1987/88). *Making a Mind versus Modeling the Brain: AI Again at the Crossroads.* 117, 1, pp. 15–44. Daedalus.

Feigenbaum, Edward A. and Pamela McCorduck (1983). *The Fifth Generation: Artificial Intelligence and Japan's Computer Challenge to the World.* Reading, MA: Addison-Wesley.

Flores, C. Fernando (1982). Management and Communication in the Office of the Future. Doctoral dissertation. Berkeley, CA: University of California, Berkeley.

Gardner, Howard (1985). *The Mind's New Science: A History of the Cognitive Revolution.* New York: Basic Books. [A good history of cognitive science that concentrates on the interaction of the disciplines (such as AI) that form cognitive science.]

Habermas, Jurgen (1979). *Communication and the Evolution of Society.* (Translated by Thomas McCarthy). Boston, MA: Beacon Press.

Haugeland, John (1985). *Artificial Intelligence: The Very Idea.* Cambridge, MA: MIT Press. [A philosophically oriented discussion of the potential of AI. He characterizes formal systems and points out that much of AI focusses on such systems but that much of the subject matter of AI does not seem to be easily reducible to such formal systems. He characterizes Good Old-Fashioned AI (GOFAI) and states its two essential claims: (a) intelligence is due to our capacity to think about things reasonably; (b) thinking about things reasonably amounts to a faculty for internal "automatic" symbol manipulation.]

Haugeland, John (ed.) (1981). *Mind Design: Philosophy, Psychology, Artificial Intelligence.* Cambridge, MA: MIT Press/Bradford Books. [This book is intended to be a sequel to *Minds and Machines* (1964), edited by Alan R. Anderson (this bibliography), bringing up to date and augmenting the topics discussed in that book.]

Holt, Anatol (1974). Remarks made at US Advanced Research Projects Agency Principal Investigators' Conference. Los Angeles, February 6–8. (Unpublished manuscript).

Howard, Robert (1986). *Systems Design and Social Responsibility: The Political Implications of "Computer-Supported Cooperative Work."* Address delivered at the First Annual Conference on Computer-Supported Cooperative Work, Austin, TX, December.

Laird, John, Paul Rosenbloom, and Allen Newell (1986). *Universal Subgoaling and Chunking: The Automatic Generation and Learning of Goal Hierarchies.* Hingham, MA: Kluwer.

Lashley, K. (1985). Bureaucracy as Artificial Intelligence. In *Knowledge Representation for Decision Support Systems*, edited by L. B. Methlie and R. H. Sprague, pp. 125–132. New York: Elsevier/North-Holland.

Lenat, D. B., M. Prakash and M. Shepherd (1986). CYC: Using Common Sense

Knowledge to Overcome Brittleness and Knowledge Acquisition Bottlenecks. *The AI Magazine*, 6, 4, pp. 65–85. [The CYC project is a long-term attempt to construct a very large knowledge base in the hope that such an encyclopaedic database will be sufficient to support commonsense reasoning in AI systems.]

March, James G. and Herbert A. Simon (1958). *Organizations*. New York: Wiley.

Maturana, Humberto R. and Francisco Varela (1987). *The Tree of Knowledge*. Boston, MA: Shambhala.

Michie, Donald and Rory Johnston (1984). *The Creative Computer*. New York: Viking.

Minsky, Marvin (1986). *The Society of Mind*. New York: Simon and Schuster. [Minsky presents a theory that intelligence can be described as a "society" of unintelligent cognitive agents. The book gives a comprehensive description of the human mind in these terms.]

Newell, Allen (1982). The Knowledge Level. *Artificial Intelligence*, 18, pp. 87–127. [Argues that logic is an appropriate tool for analyzing the knowledge of an agent – under the assumption that knowledge is a "potential for action" independent of symbolic representation.]

Newell, Allen and Herbert A. Simon (1972). *Human Problem Solving*. Englewood Cliffs, NJ: Prentice-Hall.

——, (1976). Computer Science as Empirical Inquiry: Symbols and Search. *Communications of ACM*, 19, 3, pp. 113–126. Reprinted in *Mind Design*, edited by John Haugeland, pp. 35–66. Cambridge, MA: MI Press/Bradford Books, 1981. [This is the text of the tenth Turing Award Lecture. It presents Newell and Simon's view of how computer science and AI can be seen as an empirical study of symbol systems.]

Newquist, Harvey P. III (1987). The Machinery of Medical Diagnosis. *AI Expert*, 2, 5, pp. 69–71.

Pylyshyn, Zenon W. (1984). *Computation and Cognition: Toward a Foundation for Cognitive Science*. Cambridge, MA: MIT Press/Bradford Books. [Destined to be a landmark in the cognitive science literature, this book argues that cognition as computation is more than a metaphor, and that cognitive descriptions of mental states can be mechanistically framed. The point is to discover the "functional architecture" of the mind, and the sorts of representations of symbols and rules being processed.]

Roszak, Theodore (1986). *The Cult of Information: The Folklore of Computers and the True Art of Thinking*. New York: Pantheon.

Rumelhart, D. E. and J. L. McClelland (1986a). PDP Models and General Issues in Cognitive Science. In *Parallel Distributed Processing*, vol. I, edited by D. E. Rumelhart, J. L. McClelland, and the PDP Research Group, Cambridge, MA: MIT Press/Bradford Books.

Russell, Bertrand (1952). *A History of Western Philosophy*. New York: Simon and Schuster.

Simon, Herbert A. (1979). *Models of Thought*. New Haven and London: Yale University Press.

Turkle, Sherry (1987). A New Romantic Reaction: The Computer as Precipitant of Anti-mechanistic Definitions of the Human. Paper given at conference on Humans, Animals, Machines: Boundaries and Projections, Stanford University, April.

Waterman, Donald A. (1986). *A Guide to Expert Systems*. New York, Reading, MA: Addison-Wesley.

Weber, Max (1968). *Economy and Society: An Outline of Interpretive Sociology*. Berkeley, CA: University of California Press.

Winograd, Terry (1987/88). A Language/Action Perspective on the Design of Cooperative Work. *Human-Computer Interaction* 3, 1, pp. 3–30.

Winograd, Terry and C. Fernando Flores (1986). *Understanding Computers and Cognition: A New Foundation for Design*. Norwood, NJ: Ablex. Reprinted Addison-Wesley 1987.

· 61

INTRODUCTION TO THE MIT PRESS EDITION OF *WHAT COMPUTERS CAN'T DO*

Hubert L. Dreyfus

Source: H. Dreyfus, *What Computers Still Can't Do*, MIT Press, 1992, pp. ix–lii.

This edition of *What Computers Can't Do* marks not only a change of publisher and a slight change of title; it also marks a change of status. The book now offers not a controversial position in an ongoing debate but a view of a bygone period of history. For now that the twentieth century is drawing to a close, it is becoming clear that one of the great dreams of the century is ending too. Almost half a century ago computer pioneer Alan Turing suggested that a high-speed digital computer, programmed with rules and facts, might exhibit intelligent behavior. Thus was born the field later called artificial intelligence (AI). After fifty years of effort, however, it is now clear to all but a few diehards that this attempt to produce general intelligence has failed. This failure does not mean that this sort of AI is impossible; no one has been able to come up with such a negative proof. Rather, it has turned out that, for the time being at least, the research program based on the assumption that human beings produce intelligence using facts and rules has reached a dead end, and there is no reason to think it could ever succeed. Indeed, what John Haugeland has called Good Old-Fashioned AI (GOFAI) is a paradigm case of what philosophers of science call a degenerating research program.

A degenerating research program, as defined by Imre Lakatos, is a scientific enterprise that starts out with great promise, offering a new approach that leads to impressive results in a limited domain. Almost inevitably researchers will want to try to apply the approach more broadly, starting with problems that are in some way similar to the original one. As long as it succeeds, the research program expands and attracts followers. If, however, researchers start encountering unexpected but important phenomena that

459

consistently resist the new techniques, the program will stagnate, and researchers will abandon it as soon as a progressive alternative approach becomes available.

We can see this very pattern in the history of GOFAI. The program began auspiciously with Allen Newell and Herbert Simon's work at RAND. In the late 1950s Newell and Simon proved that computers could do more than calculate. They demonstrated that a computer's strings of bits could be made to stand for anything, including features of the real world, and that its programs could be used as rules for relating these features. The structure of an expression in the computer, then, could represent a state of affairs in the world whose features had the same structure, and the computer could serve as a physical symbol system storing and manipulating such representations. In this way, Newell and Simon claimed, computers could be used to simulate important aspects of intelligence. Thus the information-processing model of the mind was born.

Newell and Simon's early work was impressive, and by the late 1960s, thanks to a series of micro-world successes such as Terry Winograd's SHRDLU, a program that could respond to English-like commands by moving simulated, idealized blocks (see pp. 12–13), AI had become a flourishing research program. The field had its Ph.D. programs, professional societies, international meetings, and even its gurus. It looked like all one had to do was extend, combine, and render more realistic the micro-worlds and one would soon have genuine artificial intelligence. Marvin Minsky, head of the M.I.T. AI project, announced: "Within a generation the problem of creating 'artificial intelligence' will be substantially solved."[1]

Then, suddenly, the field ran into unexpected difficulties. The trouble started with the failure of attempts to program an understanding of children's stories (see pp. 57–62). The programs lacked the common sense of a four-year-old, and no one knew how to give them the background knowledge necessary for understanding even the simplest stories. An old rationalist dream was at the heart of the problem. GOFAI is based on the Cartesian idea that all understanding consists in forming and using appropriate symbolic representations. For Descartes, these representations were complex descriptions built up out of primitive ideas or elements. Kant added the important idea that all concepts are rules for relating such elements, and Frege showed that rules could be formalized so that they could be manipulated without intuition or interpretation. Given the nature of computers as possible formal symbol processors, AI turned this rationalist vision into a research program and took up the search for the primitives and formal rules that captured everyday knowledge. Commonsense understanding had to be represented as a huge data structure comprised of facts plus rules for relating and applying those facts. As it turned out, though, it was much harder than anyone expected to formulate, let alone formalize, the required theory of common sense. It was not, as Minsky had hoped, just a question of cataloging 10 million facts. Minsky's mood changed completely in the course of fifteen years. In 1982 he told a reporter: "The AI problem is one of the hardest science has ever undertaken."[2]

My work from 1965 on can be seen in retrospect as a repeatedly revised attempt to justify my intuition, based on my study of Martin Heidegger, Maurice Merleau-Ponty, and the later Wittgenstein, that the GOFAI research program would eventually fail. My first take on the inherent difficulties of the symbolic information-processing model of the mind was that our sense of relevance was holistic and required involvement in ongoing activity, whereas symbol representations were atomistic and totally detached from such activity. By the time of the second edition of *What Computers Can't Do* in 1979, the problem of representing what I had vaguely been referring to as the holistic context was beginning to be perceived by AI researchers as a serious obstacle. In my new introduction I therefore tried to show that what they called the commonsense-knowledge problem was not really a problem about how to represent *knowledge*; rather, the everyday commonsense background understanding that allows us to experience what is currently relevant as we deal with things and people is a kind of *know-how*. The problem precisely was that this know-how, along with all the interests, feelings, motivations, and bodily capacities that go to make a human being, would have had to be conveyed to the computer as knowledge—as a huge and complex belief system—and making our inarticulate, preconceptual background understanding of what it is like to be a human being explicit in a symbolic representation seemed to me a hopeless task.

For this reason I doubted that the commonsense-knowledge problem could be solved by GOFAI techniques, but I could not justify my suspicion that the know-how that made up the background of common sense could not itself be represented by data structures made up of facts and rules. Granted that our background knowledge consists largely of skills for dealing with things and people rather than facts about them, what I needed was an argument against those who assumed that such skills were representable in symbolic form. As it turned out, my brother Stuart provided the missing argument in his phenomenological account of skill acquisition.[3]

Skill acquisition, he pointed out, usually begins with a student learning and applying rules for manipulating context-free elements. This is the grain of truth in the information-processing model. Thus a beginner at chess learns to follow strict rules relating such features as center control and material balance. After one begins to understand a domain, however, one sees meaningful aspects, not context-free features. Thus the more experienced chess player sees context-dependent characteristics such as unbalanced pawn structure or weakness on the king side. At the next stage, a competent performer learns to set goals and then look at the current situation in terms of what is relevant to achieving those goals. A further stage of proficiency is achieved when, after a great deal of experience, a player is able to see a situation as having a certain significance tending toward a certain outcome, and certain aspects of the situation stand out as salient in relation to that end. Given an appropriate board position, for example, almost all masters would observe after a few seconds of examination that to win white must attack the king side.

Finally, after even more experience, one reaches the level where one sees immediately what must be done. A chess grandmaster, for example, not only sees the issues in a position almost immediately, but the right response just pops into his or her head. There is no reason to suppose that the beginner's features and rules, or any other features and rules, play any role in such expert performance.[4] That we once followed a rule in learning to tie our shoelaces does not show, as Edward Feigenbaum argues it does,[5] that we must still be following that same rule unconsciously whenever we tie a lace. That would be like claiming that since we needed training wheels when learning how to ride a bicycle, we must now be using invisible training wheels whenever we ride. There is no reason to think that the rules that play a role in the *acquisition* of a skill play a role in its later *application*.

When *Mind Over Machine* came out, however, Stuart and I faced the same objection that had been raised against my appeal to holism in *What Computers Can't Do*. You may have described how expertise *feels*, critics said, but our only way of *explaining* the production of intelligent behavior is by using symbolic representations, and so that must be the underlying causal mechanism. Newell and Simon resort to this type of defense of symbolic AI:

> The principal body of evidence for the symbol-system hypothesis . . .
> is negative evidence: the absence of specific competing hypotheses as
> to how intelligent activity might be accomplished whether by man or
> by machine.[6]

In order to respond to this "what else could it be" defense of the physical symbol system research program, we appealed in *Mind Over Machine* to a somewhat vague and implausible idea that the brain might store holograms of situations paired with appropriate responses, allowing it to respond to situations in ways it had successfully responded to similar situations in the past. The crucial idea was that in hologram matching one had a model of similarity recognition that did not require analysis of the similarity of two patterns in terms of a set of common features. But the model was not convincing. No one had found anything resembling holograms in the brain.

At this point, like Charlie Chaplin in *Modern Times* emerging from a manhole with a red flag just as the revolutionaries came swarming by, we happily found ourselves surrounded by the rapidly growing ranks of neural-network modelers. As the commonsense-knowledge problem continued to resist the techniques that had worked so well in problem solving, and as pattern recognition and learning turned out to be much more intractable than anticipated, this alternative way of using computers to produce intelligence reemerged as an attractive research program after a long period of dormancy. The triumphant arrival of the neural-net revolutionaries, also called connectionists, completed the degeneration of the GOFAI research program.

The proposal that we should set about creating artificial intelligence by modeling the brain's learning power rather than the mind's symbolic representation of the world drew its inspiration not from philosophy but from what was soon to be called neuroscience. It was directly inspired by the work of D. O. Hebb, who had suggested in 1949 that a mass of neurons could learn if the simultaneous excitation of neuron A and neuron B increased the strength of the connection between them.[7] This lead was followed in the late 1950s by Frank Rosenblatt, who reasoned that since it was probably going to be hard to formalize intelligent behavior, AI should instead attempt to automate the procedures by which a network of neurons learns to discriminate patterns and respond appropriately. Researchers seeking symbolic representations were looking for a formal structure that would give computers the ability to solve a certain class of problems or discriminate certain types of patterns. Rosenblatt, conversely, wanted to build a physical device, or simulate such a device on a digital computer, that could generate its own abilities.

When symbolic AI seemed to stall, Donald Norman's Parallel Distributed Processing group and others started investigating variations of Rosenblatt's project and chalked up surprising successes. Soon, frustrated AI researchers, tired of clinging to a research program that Jerry Lettvin characterized in the early 1980s as "the only straw afloat," began defecting to the revived paradigm. Rumelhart, McClelland, and the PDP Research Group's two-volume work, *Parallel Distributed Processing*, had 6000 backorders the day it went on the market in 1986, and over 45,000 sets are now in print. Like the dissolution of the Soviet Union, the speed of collapse of the GOFAI research program has taken everyone, even those of us who expected it to happen sooner or later, by surprise.[8]

Happily for Stuart and me, the neural-network modelers had a much more plausible answer to the question. If not symbols and rules, what else? Their model showed that one need not store cases at all; instead, a designer could tune a simulated multilayer perceptron (MLP) neural network[9] by training it to respond to specific situations and then having it respond to other situations in ways that are (the designer hopes) appropriate extrapolations of the responses it has learned. Indeed, the most striking difference between neural-network modeling and GOFAI is that the neural-network modeler provides not rules relating features of the domain but a history of training input-output pairs, and the network organizes itself by adjusting its many parameters so as to map inputs into outputs, that is, situations into responses. Thus computers running simulations of such nets do not count as physical symbol systems. Paul Smolensky, one of the PDP researchers, sums up the point:

Connectionist systems are large networks of extremely simple processors, massively interconnected and running in parallel. Each processor has a numerical activation value which it communicates to other processors along connections of varying strengths. The activation value for each processor constantly changes in response to the activity of the processors to which it is connected. The values of some of the processors form the input to the system, and the values of other processors form the output. The connections between the processors determine how input is transformed to output. In connectionist systems, knowledge is encoded not in symbolic structures but rather in the pattern of numerical strengths of the connections between processors.[10]

In retrospect, the stages of my critique of attempts to use computers as physical symbol systems to simulate intelligence now fell into place. My early appeal to holism, my concern with commonsense understanding as know-how, Stuart's phenomenology of everyday skills, and the capacities of simulated neural networks all added up to a coherent position—one that predicted and explained why GOFAI research should degenerate just as it had.

Here is where I would like to say "and the rest is history," but there are two issues that must be faced before we lay the whole controversy to rest. First, the GOFAI research program has refused to degenerate gracefully and is fighting on, and we have to ask why this is happening. Second, the question remains whether neural networks can be intelligent or whether network researchers, like AI researchers in the 1960s, are basing their hopes on ad hoc successes that may not be generalizable.

That GOFAI was not as dead as I believed was brought home to me by public television. Readers may have seen an impressive five-part series called "The Machine That Changed the World," one episode of which was devoted to AI. In that episode my objections to symbolic AI, and specifically my conclusion that in attempting to represent common sense GOFAI had run into a problem it could not solve, was played off against the claims of a lone AI researcher, Douglas Lenat. In 1984 Lenat had shared my sense of AI's stagnation:

> By the mid-1970s, after two decades of humblingly slow progress, workers in the new field of artificial intelligence had come to a fundamental conclusion about intelligent behavior in general: it requires a tremendous amount of knowledge, which people often take for granted but which must be spoon-fed to a computer. . . . Understanding even the easiest passages in common English, for example, requires a knowledge of the context, the speaker and the world at large that is far beyond the capabilities of present-day computer programs.[11]

And by 1991 his concern was even clearer: "Most of the current AI research we've read about is currently stalled."[12] Nevertheless, he is not discouraged. He heads a research team at the Microelectronics and Computer Technology Corporation (MCC) that is in the middle of a ten-year project aimed at formalizing consensus knowledge, that is, "the millions of abstractions, models, facts, rules of thumb, representations, etc., that we all possess and that we assume everyone else does."[13]

This is not the sort of knowledge that is in an ordinary encyclopedia. Rather, it is the taken-for-granted knowledge that is used by readers in understanding an encyclopedia article and, more generally, in understanding what goes on in the world. Consensus knowledge ranges from "George Bush is President of the United States" to "George Bush wears underwear" to "When George Bush is in Washington, his left foot is also in Washington." Lenat presents himself as the only person willing to take on the commonsense-knowledge problem as a major research program instead of trying to finesse it. And he is confident that, thanks to his research, "artificial intelligence is within our grasp."[14]

Through cross-cut interviews, the Black Knight of AI, as I have been called, met the White Knight of symbolic information processing for a final joust. Lenat claimed that his project was going well and had a 60 percent chance of success. I came across as dubious but ill-informed and made some unconvincing objections. Clearly, my claim that the GOFAI program is degenerating can be dismissed as merely reporting a transient sociological phenomenon unless I can defend my conviction that Lenat's project is doomed.

To understand my critique of the GOFAI approach to common sense, it helps to know its ancestry. Rationalists such as Descartes and Leibniz thought of the mind as defined by its capacity to form representations of all domains of activity. These representations were taken to be theories of the domains in question, the idea being that representing the fixed, context-free features of a domain and the principles governing their interaction explains the domain's intelligibility. On this view all that we know—even our general know-how for getting around in the world and coping with things and people—must be mirrored in the mind in propositional form. I shall call this view of the mind and its relation to the world "representationalism." Representationalism assumes that underlying everyday understanding is a system of implicit beliefs.

This assumption is shared by intentionalist philosophers such as Edmund Husserl and computationalists such as Jerry Fodor and GOFAI researchers. The specific AI problem of representing all this knowledge in *formal* rules and features only arises after one has already assumed that common sense derives from *a vast data base of propositional knowledge*. When, instead of developing philosophical theories of the transcendental conditions that must hold if the mind is to represent the world, or proposing psychological models of how the storage and retrieval of propositional representations works, researchers in AI actually tried to formulate and organize everyday consensus knowledge, they ran into what has come to be called the commonsense-knowledge problem. There are really at least three problems grouped under this rubric:

1. How everyday knowledge must be organized so that one can make inferences from it.
2. How skills or know-how can be represented as knowing-that.
3. How relevant knowledge can be brought to bear in particular situations.

While representationalists have written programs that attempt to deal with each of these problems, there is no generally accepted solution, nor is there a proof that these problems cannot be solved. What is clear is that all attempts to solve them have run into unexpected difficulties, and this in turn suggests that there may well be in-principle limitations on representationalism. At the very least these difficulties lead us to question why anyone would expect the representationalist project to succeed.

Lenat, however, thinks that his predecessors have simply not tried hard enough to systematize common sense. His goal is to organize commonsense knowledge using general categories that make no reference to the specific uses to which the knowledge is to be put:

> Naturally, all programs are built on some primitives (predicates, frames, slots, rules, functions, scripts).[15] But if you choose task-specific primitives, you'll win in the short run (building a program for that narrow domain) but lose in the long run (you'll find yourself painted into a corner when you try to scale the program up).[16]

Lenat relates his work to the traditional philosophical job of working out an ontology—a description of the various types of context-free entities and their relationships—and he sees that turning traditional ontology into a research program is no small task:

> A serious attempt at [capturing consensus knowledge] would entail building a vast knowledge base, one that is 10^4 to 10^5 larger than today's typical expert system, which would contain general facts and heuristics and contain a wide sample of specific facts and heuristics for analogizing as well. ... Moreover, this would include beliefs, knowledge of others' (often grouped by culture, age group, or historical era) limited awareness of what we know, various ways of representing things, knowledge of which approximations (micro-theories) are reasonable in various contexts, and so on.[17]

The data structures must represent objects and their properties, individuals, collections, space, time, causality, events and their elements, agency, institutions, and oddly, from a traditional philosophical point of view, recurrent social situations such as dinner at a restaurant or a birthday party. This data-base ontology, like any traditional rationalist ontology, must bottom out in primitive elements.

> Choosing a set of representation primitives (predicates, objects, functions) has been called *ontological engineering*—that is, defining the categories and relationships of the domain. (This is empirical, experimental engineering, as contrasted with *ontological theorizing*, which philosophers have done for millennia.)[18]

Lenat is clear that his ontology must be able to represent our commonsense background knowledge—the understanding we normally take for granted. He would hold, however, that it is premature to try to give a computer the skills and feelings required for actually coping with things and people. No one in AI believes anymore that by 2001 we will have an artificial intelligence like HAL. Lenat would be satisfied if the Cyc data base could understand books and articles, for example, if it could answer questions about their content and gain knowledge from them. In fact, it is a hard problem even to make a data base that can understand simple sentences in ordinary English, since such understanding requires vast background knowledge. Lenat collects some excellent examples of the difficulty involved. Take the following sentence:

Mary saw a dog in the window. She wanted it.[19]

Lenat asks:

> Does "it" refer to the dog or the window? What if we'd said "She *smashed* it," or "She pressed her nose up against it"?[20]

Note that the sentence seems to appeal to our ability to imagine how we would feel in the situation, rather than requiring us to consult *facts* about dogs and windows and how a typical human being would react. It also draws on know-how for getting around in the world, such as how to get closer to something on the other side of a barrier. In this way the feelings and bodily coping skills that were excluded to make Lenat's problem easier return. We need to be able to imagine feeling and doing things in order to organize the knowledge we need to understand typical sentences. There are also all the problems of "deixis," that is, the way we locate things with respect to our own locations, as "over there," "nearby," etc. All these problems point to the importance of the body. Lenat does not tell us how he proposes to capture in propositional terms our bodily sense of what is inside and outside, accessible and inaccessible, and what distance we need to be from various sorts of things to get an optimal grip on them. He just tells us dogmatically that this can be done.

> Our response—in principle and in CYC—is to describe perception, emotion, motion, etc., down to some level of detail that enables the system to understand humans doing those things, and/or to be able to reason simply about them.[21]

In our constructed television debate my claim that an intelligence needs a body was dismissed by reference to the case of Madeleine, a wheelchair-bound woman described by Oliver Sacks, who was blind from birth, could not use her hands to read braille, and yet acquired commonsense knowledge from books that were read to her. But this case does not in fact support Lenat. Madeleine is certainly not like a computer. She is an expert at speaking and interacting with people and so has commonsense social skills. Moreover, she has feelings, both physical and emotional, and a body that has an inside and outside and can be moved around in the world. Thus she can empathize with others and to some extent share the skillful way they encounter their world. Her expertise may well come from learning to discriminate many imagined cases and what typically occurs in them, not from forming a model of the world in Lenat's sense. Indeed, Sacks says that Madeleine had "an imagination filled and sustained, so to speak, by the images of others, images conveyed by language."[22] Thus the claim that Madeleine's acquisition of commonsense knowledge from books despite her inability to see and move her hands proves that a person can acquire and organize facts about the world on the model of a symbolic computer being fed rationally ordered representations ignores the possibility that a person's bodily skills and imagination are a necessary condition for acquiring common sense even from books.

Mark Johnson gives a good argument for the importance of imagination even in conscious problem solving:

> Imagination is a pervasive structuring activity by means of which we achieve coherent, patterned, unified representations. It is indispensable for our ability to make sense of our experience, to find it meaningful. The conclusion ought to be, therefore, that imagination is absolutely central to human rationality, that is, to our rational capacity to find connections, to draw inferences, and to solve problems.[23]

To assume that Madeleine's body and imagination are irrelevant to her accumulation, organization, and use of facts, and that her skills themselves are the result of just more storing and organizing of facts, begs the question.

Why should we assume that the imagination and skills Madeleine brings to the task of learning and using common sense can be finessed by giving a computer facts and rules for organizing them?

A way to see the implausibility of this claim is to ask how the computer—with its millions of facts organized for no particular purpose—might be able to retrieve just the relevant information for understanding a sentence uttered in a specific situation. This is a far harder problem than that of answering questions on the basis of stored data, which seems to be all that Lenat has considered until now. In order to retrieve relevant facts in a specific situation, a computer would have to categorize the situation, then search through all its facts following rules for finding those that could possibly be relevant in this type of situation, and finally deduce which of these facts are actually relevant in this particular situation. This sort of search would clearly become more difficult as one added more facts and more rules to guide it. Indeed, AI researchers have long recognized that the more a system knows about a particular state of affairs, the longer it takes to retrieve the relevant information, and this presents a general problem where scaling up is concerned. Conversely, the more a human being knows about a situation or individual, the easier it is to retrieve other relevant information. This suggests that human beings use forms of storage and retrieval quite different from the symbolic one representationalist philosophers and Lenat have assumed.

Lenat admits that there is a problem:

> The natural tendency of any search program is to slow down (often combinatorially explosively) as additional assertions are added and the search space therefore grows . . . [T]he key to preserving effective intelligence of a growing program lies in judicious adding of meta-knowledge.[24]

The problem is that the rules and meta-rules are just more meaningless facts and so may well make matters worse.

In the end, Lenat's faith that Cyc will succeed is based neither on arguments nor on actual successes but on the untested traditional assumption that human beings have a vast library of commonsense knowledge and somehow solve the scaling-up problem by applying further knowledge:

> We're often asked how we expect to efficiently "index"—find relevant partial matches—as the knowledge base grows larger and larger. . . . Our answer . . . often appears startling at first glance: wait until our programs *are* finding many, far-flung analogies, but inefficiently, i.e. only through large searches. Then investigate what additional knowledge *people* bring to bear, to eliminate large parts of the search space in those cases. Codify the knowledge so extracted, and add it to the system.[25]

But the conviction that people *are* storing context-free facts and using meta-rules to cut down the search space is precisely the dubious rationalist assumption in question. It must be tested by looking at the phenomenology of everyday know-how. Such an account is worked out by Heidegger and his followers such as Merleau-Ponty and the anthropologist Pierre Bourdieu. They find that what counts as the facts depends on our everyday skills. In describing a society in which gift-exchange is important, Bourdieu tells us:

> If it is not to constitute an insult, the counter-gift must be *deferred* and *different*, because the immediate return of an exactly identical object clearly amounts to a refusal. . . . It is all a question of style, which means in this case timing and choice of occasion, for the same act—giving, giving in return, offering one's services, paying a visit, etc.—can have completely different meanings at different times.[26]

Yet members of the culture have no trouble understanding what to do. Once one has acquired the necessary social skill, one does not need to *recognize* the situation objectively as having the features of one in which gift-giving is appropriate and then *decide* rationally what gift to give. Normally one simply responds in the appropriate circumstances by giving an appropriate gift. That this is the normal response is what constitutes the circumstance as a gift-giving situation. The same, of course, holds for the know-how of what gift is appropriate. One does not have to *figure out* what is appropriate, or at least not the range of what is appropriate. Everyone's skills are coordinated so that normally one is just solicited by the situation to give a certain type of gift, and the recipient, socialized into the same shared practices, finds it appropriate. Bourdieu comments:

> The active presence of past experiences . . . deposited in each organism in the form of schemes of perception, thought, and action, tend to guarantee the "correctness" of practices and their constancy over time, more reliably than all formal rules and explicit norms.[27]

This sort of experience suggests that structuring a knowledge base so as to represent all facts about gift-giving is necessary only for a stranger or spectator who does not already have the appropriate skill. Bourdieu insists that it is a mistake—one often made by anthropologists, philosophers, and, we can add, AI researchers—to read the rules we need to appeal to in breakdown cases back into the normal situation and then to appeal to such representations for a causal explanation of how a skillful response is normally produced.

The point of this example is that knowing how to give an appropriate gift at the appropriate time and in the appropriate way requires cultural *savoir faire*. So knowing what a gift is is not a bit of factual knowledge, separate from the skill or know-how for giving one. The distinction between what a gift is and what counts as a gift, which seems to distinguish facts from skills, is an illusion fostered by the philosophical belief in a nonpragmatic ontology. Since the organization and content of a gift frame presupposes gift-giving *practices*, there is no need of and no evidence for frames and slots that spell out the supposed objective features of gifts and gift-giving occasions. It is doubtful that such an exhaustive account is even possible.

There is an even deeper problem lurking in wait for Lenat. We are not only able to cope with changing events and motivations, both on the fly and in our imaginations; we are also able to project our understanding into new situations. If one is a master of a cultural practice, one can sometimes do what has not so far counted as appropriate and have it recognized in retrospect as having been just the right thing to do. Thus a master of the culture can introduce a new sort of gift or a new gift-giving occasion. This happens not only at private parties and public ceremonies but, of course, also in stories and reports about such occasions. A data base that did not share the culture's *savoir faire*, then, would not only be unable to *give* appropriate gifts—we've agreed that Lenat does not have to build a skillful robot—but would also fail as a system storing our consensus knowledge of gifts because it could not *understand* innovations in gift-giving.

Lenat sees that the ability to extend our knowledge is crucial both to exercising our knowledge and to acquiring new knowledge from experience. Indeed, the success of his program, by his own criterion, requires that it be able to extend what it knows and learn from reading books and articles rather than from "brain surgery." The question of how we project or extend what we already know therefore becomes crucial.

> Designing more proficient learning programs depends in part on finding ways to tap a source of power at the heart of human intelligence: the ability to understand and reason by analogy. . . . This source of power is only beginning to be exploited by intelligent software, but it will doubtless be the focus of future research.[28]

Granted that an intelligent person can see analogies or similarities to what he or she already knows, there are several ways to think about this basic human capacity. The classical rationalist tradition since Aristotle has tried to understand analogies as proportions. A second tradition traces analogy back to our experience of our body. A third approach has reacted to the implausibility of the classical tradition by approaching analogy in terms of extrapolating a style. Lenat, of course, belongs to the first camp; Mark Johnson and George Lakoff belong to the second; and Heidegger, Merleau-Ponty, and Bourdieu belong to the third.

Bourdieu mentions the role of style in learning and extrapolating gift exchanges. It may well be that different cultures have different styles—

aggressive, passive, controlling, etc.—and that infants pick up first on these pervasive styles, which in turn direct what the infant notices and imitates. If this is so, we would expect style to play an important role in what similarities are noticed and what metaphors are used to organize experience. Style, however, is generally neglected in GOFAI. The only AI researcher who has seen its importance is Douglas Hofstadter, but even he has not come up with any convincing proposals for dealing with it.[29]

Given that the solution of this problem is essential to the success of his system, Lenat's remarks on analogy are rather sketchy. Still, what he does say works out the rationalist approach in enough details to reveal its implausibility. Lenat's sensitivity to metaphors and analogies is arresting and persuasive.

> Almost every sentence is packed with metaphors and analogies. An unbiased example: here is the first article we saw today (April 7, 1987), the lead story in the *Wall Street Journal*: "Texaco lost a major ruling in its legal battle with Pennzoil. The Supreme Court dismantled Texaco's protection against having to post a crippling $12 billion appeals bond, pushing Texaco to the brink of a Chapter 11 filing." Lost? Major? Battle? Dismantled? Posting? Crippling? Pushing? Brink? The example drives home the point that, far from overinflating the need for real-world knowledge in language understanding, the usual arguments about disambiguation barely scratch the surface. (Drive? Home? The point? Far? Overinflating? Scratch? Surface? Oh no, I can't call a halt to this! (call? halt?))[30]

Lenat's faith that the metaphors "bottom out" in primitives, however, is not convincing, nor is it argued for. He simply asserts:

> These layers of analogy and metaphor eventually "bottom out" at physical—*somatic*—primitives: up, down, forward, back, pain, cold, inside, seeing, sleeping, tasting, growing, containing, moving, making noise, hearing, birth, death, strain, exhaustion, . . .[31]

The fact that these are *somatic* primitives does not seem to bother him at all.

Lenat, nonetheless, asks the right question: "How can a program automatically find good mappings?"[32] But he gives the simplistic rationalist answer: "If *A* and *B* appear to have some unexplained similarities, then it's worth your time to hunt for additional shared properties."[33]

This begs the question. Everything is similar to everything else in an indefinitely large number of ways. Why should we suppose that any two items should be compared? Even if two frames have many slots in common, why should we think these are the important similarities? Perhaps the important similarities cannot be symbolically represented at all. Both the defenders of the basic role of our sense of our active body with inside/outside, forward/backward, and up/down dimensions and those who hold that similarity of style is what defines what is worth comparing would hold that there is no reason to think that the constraints on similarity can be represented symbolically.

When John Searle tried to understand metaphors as proportions, he found that metaphors like "Sally is a block of ice" could not be analyzed by listing the features that Sally and a large, cold cube have in common.

> If we were to enumerate quite literally the various distinctive qualities of blocks of ice, none of them would be true of Sally. Even if we were to throw in the various beliefs that people have about blocks of ice, they still would not be literally true of Sally. . . . Being unemotional is not a feature of blocks of ice because blocks of ice are not in that line of business at all, and if one wants to insist that blocks of ice are literally unresponsive, then we need only point out that that feature is still insufficient to explain the metaphorical utterance meaning . . . because in that sense bonfires are "unresponsive" as well.[34]

Searle concludes:

> There are . . . whole classes of metaphors that function without any underlying principles of similarity. It just seems to be a fact about our mental capacities that we are able to interpret certain sorts of metaphor without the application of any underlying "rules" or "principles" other than the sheer ability to make certain associations. I don't know any better way to describe these abilities than to say that they are nonrepresentational mental capacities.[35]

So far we have only discussed the facts and metaphors that are constituted by our *social* skills. What about the facts of nature? Where a domain of facts is independent of us, as is the domain of physical objects, do we then need a theory of the domain? Not likely. The way people cope with things is sometimes called commonsense physics. This leads to the comforting illusion that just as the planets do not move around at random but obey general principles, so everyday objects do not stick, slide, fall, and bounce in an unprincipled way but obey complex and particular laws. Attempts to work out commonsense physics for the simplest everyday objects, however, lead to formal principles that are subject to many exceptions and are so complex that it is hard to believe they could be in a child's mind.[36] Lenat concludes from this that what we know concerning how everyday objects behave cannot be principles but must be a lot of facts and rules.

> [The Cyc] methodology will collect, e.g., all the facts and heuristics about "Water" that newspaper articles assume their readers already know. This is in contrast to, for instance, naive physics and other approaches that aim to somehow capture a deeper theory of "Water" in all its various forms.[37]

But granted that there is no reason to think that there can be a *theory* of commonsense physics as there is of celestial physics, that is no reason to think that our know-how for dealing with physical objects can be spelled out in some all-purpose data base concerning physical objects and their properties. Perhaps there is no set of context-free facts adequate to capture the way everyday things such as water behave. We may just have to learn from vast experience how to respond to thousands of typical cases. That would explain why children find it fascinating to play with blocks and water day after day for years. They are probably learning to discriminate the sorts of typical situations they will have to cope with in their everyday activities. For natural kinds like water, then, as well as for social kinds like gifts, common sense seems to be based on knowing-how rather than knowing-that, and this know-how may well be a way of storing our experience of the world that does not involve representing the world as symbolic AI required.

This still leaves the important question of how human beings manage to engage in purposive behavior. The traditional view, accepted by GOFAI, has been that they use their theory of the domain in question to work out a plan for accomplishing whatever they are trying to do. But rather than suggesting that people store vast numbers of facts and then plan how to use them, the phenomena, which have to be trusted until psychology or neuroscience gives us any reason to think otherwise, suggest that when one has had a great deal of experience in a domain, one simply sees what needs to be done. It seems that when a person has enough experience to make him or her an expert in any domain, the field of experience becomes structured so that one directly experiences which events and things are relevant and how they are relevant. Heidegger, Merleau-Ponty, and the gestaltists would say that objects appear to an involved participant not in isolation and with context-free properties but as things that solicit responses by their significance.

In the first edition of this book I noted that good chess players don't seem to figure out from scratch what to do each time they make a move. Instead, they zero in on a certain aspect of the current position and figure out what to do from there (pp. 102–106). In *Mind Over Machine* Stuart went further and pointed out that a mere master might need to figure out what to do, but a grandmaster just sees the board as demanding a certain move.[38]

We are all masters in our everyday world. Consider the experience of entering a familiar type of room. We know but do not appeal to the sort of facts that can be included in a room frame, such as that rooms have floors, ceilings, and walls, that walls can have windows in them, and that the floor can have furniture on it. Instead, our feeling for how rooms normally behave, a skill for dealing with them that we have developed by crawling and walking around many rooms, gives us a sense of relevance. We are skilled at not coping with the dust, unless we are janitors, and not paying attention to whether the windows are open or closed, unless it is hot, in which case we know how to do what is appropriate. Our expertise in dealing with rooms determines from moment to moment both what we cope with by using and what we cope with by ignoring (while being ready to use it should an appropriate occasion arise). This global familiarity maps our past experience of the room onto our current activity, so that what is appropriate on each occasion is experienced as perceptually salient or simply elicits what needs to be done.

In general, human beings who have had vast experience in the natural and social world have a direct sense of how things are done and what to expect. Our global familiarity thus enables us to respond to what is relevant and ignore what is irrelevant without planning based on purpose-free representations of context-free facts. Such familiarity differs entirely from our knowledge of an unfamiliar room, such as the room of a seventeenth-century nobleman. In that sort of room our knowledge resembles the sort of knowledge a data base might have. But even if a Jacobean drawing-room frame and its slots were all in place, we would still be disoriented. We would not know what to pay attention to or how to act appropriately.

Global sensibilities (or the imagination thereof) determine situational relevance because our world is organized by these preconceptual meanings. It is in terms of them that objects and events are experienced *as* something. Our everyday coping skills and the global familiarity they produce determine what counts as the facts and the relevance of all facts and so are already presupposed in the organization of the frames and slots GOFAI uses for representing these facts. That is why human beings cope more easily and expertly as they learn to discriminate more aspects of a situation, whereas, for data bases of frames and rules, retrieving what is relevant becomes more and more difficult the more they are told.

Lenat does seem to be correct in seeing the Cyc project as the last defense of the AI dream of producing broad, flexible human intelligence. Indeed, just because of its courage and ambition, the Cyc project, more than any previous one, confronts the problems raised by the idea of basing intelligence on symbolic representations. As we have just seen, the somatic and stylistic background sensitivities that determine what counts as similar to what and the background coping familiarity that determines what shows up as relevant are presupposed for the intelligent use of the facts and rules with which symbolic AI starts. The hope that these background conditions can be analyzed in terms of the features whose isolation and recognition they make possible is, on the face of it, implausible. The only arguments that are ever given in support of the physical symbol system hypothesis are the rationalist assumption that understanding equals analysis, so that all of experience must be analyzable (that is, there must be a theory of every intelligible domain), or the GOFAI response that the mind must be a symbol manipulator since no one knows what else it might be. Now that both of these arguments have lost plausibility, there remains only the pragmatic argument that GOFAI will demonstrate its possibility by producing an intelligent machine. So far that sort of claim has not been made good, and Cyc faces all the old problems in their most daunting form. The project has five more years to go, but Lenat has given us no reason to be optimistic. It seems highly likely that the rationalist dream of representationalist AI will be over by the end of the century.

For three groups of AI researchers whose work now focuses on alternative approaches, GOFAI is already over. One of these approaches, associated with the work of Philip Agre and David Chapman, attempts to produce programs that interact intelligently with a micro-world without using either context-free symbolic representations or internal model-based planning. The second, represented by the neural-network modelers, abandons representation altogether. This approach uses conventional features but produces outputs by a direct mapping from the inputs, with the mapping extrapolated from examples provided by an expert. A third new approach to AI, called reinforcement learning, aims to develop a program that dispenses with the expert and uses actual performance in the skill domain in order to find, on its own, a successful input-output rule. It is worth considering the advantages and limitations of each of these approaches.

The interactionists are sensitive to the Heideggerian critique of the use of symbolic models of the world and attempt to turn Heidegger's account of ongoing skillful coping[39] into an alternative research program. At MIT, where this approach was developed, it is sometimes called Heideggerian AI. Terry Winograd, who was the first to introduce Heidegger into his computer science courses, has described this surprising new development:

> For those who have followed the history of artificial intelligence, it is ironic that [the MIT] laboratory should become a cradle of "Heideggerian AI." It was at MIT that Dreyfus first formulated his critique, and, for twenty years, the intellectual atmosphere in the AI Lab was overtly hostile to recognizing the implications of what he said. Nevertheless, some of the work now being done at that laboratory seems to have been affected by Heidegger and Dreyfus.[40]

The AI Lab work Winograd is referring to is the influential theory of activity developed by Agre and Chapman, implemented in two programs, Pengi and Sonja, that play computer games. Agre and Chapman question the need for an internal symbolic model of the world that represents the context-free features of the skill domain. Following Heidegger, they note that in our everyday coping we experience ourselves not as subjects with mental representation over against objects with fixed properties, but rather as absorbed in our current situation, responding directly to its demands.

Interactive AI takes seriously the view I attributed to Heidegger in this book—that there is usually no need for a representation of the world in our mind since the best way to find out the current state of affairs is to look to the world as we experience it. Chapman tells us:

> If you want to find out something about the world that will affect how you should act, you can usually just look and see. Concrete activity is principally concerned with the here-and-now. You mostly don't need to worry about things that have gone before, are much in the future, or are not physically present. You don't need to maintain a world model; the world is its own best representation.[41]

Agre and Chapman also adapt another Heideggerian thesis that Stuart and I developed in *Mind Over Machine*, namely that behavior can be purposive without the agent having in mind a goal or purpose.

> In a great many situations, it's obvious what to do next given the configuration of materials at hand. And once you've done that the next thing to do is likely to be obvious too. Complex sequences of actions result, without needing a complex control structure to decide for you what to do.[42]

What is original and important in Agre and Chapman's work is that these ideas are taken out of the realm of armchair phenomenology and made specific enough to be implemented in programs. What results is a system that represents the world not as a set of objects with properties but as current functions (what Heidegger called in-order-tos). Thus, to take a Heideggerian example, I experience a hammer I am using not as an object with properties but as in-order-to-drive-in-the-nail. Only if there is some disturbance does the skilled performer notice what I have called aspects of the situation. In Heidegger's example, the carpenter notices that the hammer is too heavy. Both of the above ways of being, which Heidegger calls the available (the ready-to-hand) and the unavailable (the unready-to-hand), are to be distinguished from what he calls the occurrent (the present-at-hand) mode of being, the mode of being of stable objects. Objects can be recognized as the same even when they are used in different contexts or when some of their properties change. Such reidentifiable objects with their changing features or properties have been the only mode of being represented in GOFAI models. The interactionists seek to represent the available and the unavailable modes. Chapman speaks in this respect of "deictic representations":

The sorts of representations we are used to are *objective*: they represent the world without reference to the representing agent. *Deictic* representations represent things in terms of their relationship with the agent. The units of deictic representation are *entities*, which are things in a particular relationship to the agent, and relational *aspects* of these entities. For example, *the-cup-I-am-drinking-from* is the name of an entity, and *the-cup-I-am-drinking-from-is-almost-empty* defined in terms of an agent and the time the aspect is used. The same representation refers to different cups depending on whose representation it is and when it is used. It is defined *functionally*, in terms of the agent's purpose: drinking.[43]

The other important Heidegger-inspired innovation in interactive programming is its implementation of purposive action. A GOFAI planner searches the space of possible sequences of actions to determine how to get from a symbolic representation of the current situation to a specified goal. The interactive approach to action stipulates a mapping from situations directly to actions.

Interactive AI has implemented Heidegger's phenomenology of everyday coping but has not attempted to implement his account of the background familiarity on the basis of which certain equipment is seen as relevant and certain courses of action solicit my response. This gap shows up in Chapman's unsatisfying account of relevance. Chapman tells us that "agents represent only relevant aspects of the situation."[44] But this turns out to mean that, as in all GOFAI programs, the programmer has predigested the domain and determined for the system what are the possibly relevant features at any given moment.

So far it looks like Heideggerian AI is true to Heidegger's phenomenology in what it leaves out—long-range planning and internal representations of reidentifiable objects with context-free features—but it lacks what any intelligent system needs, namely the ability to discriminate relevant distinctions in the skill domain and to learn new distinctions from experience. To provide this crucial capability, more and more researchers are looking to simulated neural networks. We therefore turn to the question of whether such networks can exhibit what I have called familiarity or global sensitivity and, if not, whether they can cope in some other way with relevance and learning. (My use of "we" here is not royal but literal, since my brother Stuart has made indispensable contributions to the rest of this introduction.)

We have already mentioned that neural-network modeling, the fashionable answer to the what-else-could-it-be question, has swept away GOFAI and given AI researchers an optimism they have not had since the 1960s. After all, neural networks can learn to recognize patterns and pick out similar cases, and they can do this all in parallel, thus avoiding the bottleneck of serial processing. But neural networks raise deep philosophical questions. It seems that they undermine the fundamental rationalist assumption that one must have abstracted a theory of a domain in order to behave intelligently in that domain. In its simplest terms, as understood from Descartes to early Wittgenstein, finding a theory means finding the invariant features in terms of which one can map specific situations onto appropriate responses. In physical symbol systems the symbols in the representation are supposed to correspond to these features, and the program maps the features onto the response. As we saw, Lenat, the last heir to GOFAI, assumes that there must be such context-free primitives in which his ontology would bottom out. When neural networks became fashionable, traditional AI researchers assumed that the hidden nodes in a trained net would detect and learn the relevant features, relieving the programmer of the need to discover them by trial and error. But this turned out to be problematic.

The input to neural networks must, of course, be expressed in terms of stable, recognizable features of the domain. For example, a network that is to be trained to play chess would take as its inputs board positions defined in terms of types and locations of pieces. The question is whether a network that has learned to play chess has detected higher-order features, such as unbalanced pawn structure, that combine these input features in such a way that any position that shares the same higher-order features maps into the same move. If a given network architecture trained on a given set of examples could be shown to detect such higher-order features independently of its connection strengths prior to training, then it could be said to have abstracted the theory of the domain. If, for example, such features turned out to be the kinds of features chess masters actually think about, then the net would have discovered the theory of the chess domain that chess theorists and symbolic AI researchers have sought for so long. If these higher-order features were not the sort of features an expert in the domain could recognize, the belief that programmers of AI systems could invent higher-order features based on chess knowledge would of course be shaken, but the assumption that there must be a theory of any domain in which intelligent behavior is possible would not have been called into question.

The implications for rationalism, however, may be much more serious. To defend the theory theory, rationalists might well insist that, given any particular set of connection strengths as a starting point for training a network with examples, we can always identify higher-order features, even if these features cannot be used consciously by experts. Consider the simple case of layers of binary units activated by feedforward, but not lateral or feedback, connections. To construct such higher-order features from a network that has learned certain associations, we could interpret each node one level above the input nodes, on the basis of the connections to it, as detecting when any one of a certain set of identifiable input patterns is present. (Some of the patterns will be the ones used in training, and some will never have been used.) If the set of input patterns that a particular node detects is given a name (it almost certainly won't have one already), the node could be interpreted as detecting the highly abstract feature so named. Hence, every node one level above the input level could be characterized as a feature detector. Similarly, every node a level above those nodes could be interpreted as detecting a higher-order feature defined as the presence of one of a specified set of patterns among the first level of feature detectors. And so on up the hierarchy. A similar story could be constructed for neurons with graded (continuous, nonbinary) responses. One would then speak of *the extent to which* a higher-order feature is present.

The fact that intelligence, defined as the knowledge of a certain set of associations appropriate to a domain, can always be accounted for in terms of relations among a number of such highly abstract features of a skill domain does not, however, preserve the rationalist intuition that these explanatory features capture the essential structure of the domain. The critical question is whether, if several different nets with different initial connection strengths were trained to produce a given set of input/output mappings, the same higher-order features would be detectable in all of them or, at least, whether, at some level of abstraction, all of the nets could be seen as abstracting equivalent invariances.

No such invariances have been found. The most thorough search concerns a neural network called NETtalk that converts printed text into speech. NETtalk is given several pages of text plus the correct pronunciation of the middle letter of every string of seven characters in the text. The net starts with random connection strengths, and its reading of the text sounds like noise. After many hours of training using backpropagation, a technique that changes the connection strengths repeatedly, each time bringing the actual output closer to the correct output, the net learns to read the text aloud in a way that a native speaker can easily understand.[45] But careful analysis of the activity of the hidden nodes when the net was producing correct responses failed to reveal any consistent higher-order features in trials with different initial connection strengths. Thus we can say that so far neural-network research has tended to substantiate the belief that coping does not require the abstraction of a theory of the skill domain.[46] This is bad news for rationalism but gives networks a great advantage over GOFAI.

Nevertheless, the commonsense-knowledge problem resurfaces in this work and threatens its progress just as it did work in GOFAI. All multilayer perceptron neural-network modelers agree that an intelligent network must be able to generalize; for example, for a given classification task, given sufficient examples of inputs associated with one particular output, it should associate further inputs of the same type with that same output. But what counts as the same type? The network's designer usually has in mind a specific definition of "type" required for a reasonable generalization and counts it a success if the net generalizes to other instances of this type. But when the net produces an unexpected association, can one say that it has failed to generalize? One could equally well say that the net has all along been acting on a different definition of "type" and that that difference has just been revealed.

For an amusing and dramatic case of creative but unintelligent generalization, consider one of connectionism's first applications. In the early days of this work the army tried to train an artificial neural network to recognize tanks in a forest. They took a number of pictures of a forest without tanks and then, on a later day, with tanks clearly sticking out from behind trees, and they trained a net to discriminate the two classes of pictures. The results were impressive, and the army was even more impressed when it turned out that the net could generalize its knowledge to pictures that had not been part of the training set. Just to make sure that the net was indeed recognizing partially hidden tanks, however, the researchers took more pictures in the same forest and showed them to the trained net. They were depressed to find that the net failed to discriminate between the new pictures of trees with tanks behind them and the new pictures of just plain trees. After some agonizing, the mystery was finally solved when someone noticed that the original pictures of the forest without tanks were taken on a cloudy day and those with tanks were taken on a sunny day. The net had apparently learned to recognize and generalize the difference between a forest with and without shadows! This example illustrates the general point that a network must share our commonsense understanding of the world if it is to share our sense of appropriate generalization.

One might still hope that networks different from our brain will make exciting new generalizations and add to our intelligence. After all, detecting shadows is just as legitimate as detecting tanks. In general, though, a device that could not learn our generalizations and project our practices to new situations would just be labeled stupid. For example, thanks to our bodies, we normally see symmetric objects as similar. If a system consistently classified mirror images of otherwise identical objects as different but classified objects that cast the same shadows or had any red on them as similar, we would count it not as adding to our intelligence but as being unteachable or, in short, stupid as far as joining our community or giving us new insights was concerned. For an exercise in interesting but unintelligible categorization, consider Jorge Luis Borges's story of "a 'certain Chinese encyclopedia' in which it is written that 'animals are divided into: (a) belonging to the Emperor, (b) embalmed, (c) tame, (d) sucking pigs, (e) sirens, (f) fabulous, (g) stray dogs, (h) included in the present classification, (i) frenzied, (j) innumerable, (k) drawn with very fine camelhair brush, (l) et cetera, (m) having broken the water pitcher, (n) that from a long way off look like flies.'"[47]

Neural-network modelers were initially pleased that their nets were a blank slate (*tabula rasa*) until trained, so that the designer did not need to identify and provide anything resembling a pretraining intelligence. Recently, however, they have been forced by the problem of producing appropriate, human-like generalizations to the recognition that, unless the class of possible generalizations is restricted in an appropriate a priori manner, nothing resembling human generalizations can be confidently expected.[48] Consequently, after identifying in advance the class of allowable human-like generalizations appropriate to the problem (the hypothesis space), these modelers then attempt to design the architecture of their networks so that they transform inputs into outputs only in ways that are in the hypothesis space. Generalization would then be possible only on the designer's terms. While a few examples will be insufficient to identify uniquely the appropriate member of the hypothesis space, after enough examples only one hypothesis will account for all the examples. The network will then have learned the appropriate generalization principle. That is, all further input will produce what, from the designer's point of view, is the right output.

The problem here is that the designer has determined, by means of the architecture of the network, that certain possible generalizations will never be found. All this is well and good for toy problems in which there is no question of what constitutes a reasonable generalization, but in real-world situations a large part of human intelligence consists in generalizing in ways that are appropriate to a context. If the designer restricts the network to a predefined class of appropriate responses, the network will be exhibiting the intelligence built into it by the designer for that context but will not have the common sense that would enable it to adapt to other contexts as a truly human intelligence would.

Perhaps a network must share size, architecture, and initial-connection configuration with the human brain if it is to share our sense of appropriate generalization. Indeed, neural-network researchers with their occasional ad hoc success but no principled way to generalize seem to be at the stage of GOFAI researchers when I wrote about them in the 1960s. It looks likely that the neglected and then revived connectionist approach is merely getting its deserved chance to fail.

To generalize in the way that human beings do, a network's architecture would have to be designed in such a way that the net would respond to situations in terms of what are for human beings relevant features. These features would have to be based on what past experience has shown to be important and also on recent experiences that determine the perspective from which the situation is viewed. Only then could the network enter situations with perspective-based human-like expectations that would allow recognition of unexpected inputs (such as tanks in forests) as well as significant expected inputs that are not currently present in the situation. No current networks show any of these abilities, and no one at present knows or even speculates about how our brain's architecture produces them.

There is yet another fundamental problem with the route to artificial intelligence through the supervised training of neural networks. In GOFAI it has long been clear that whatever intelligence the system exhibits has been explicitly identified and programmed by the system designer. The system has no independent learning ability that allows it to recognize situations in which the rules it has been taught are inappropriate and to construct new rules. Neural networks do appear to have learning ability; but in situations of supervised learning, it is really the person who decides which cases are good examples who is furnishing the intelligence. What the network learns is merely how to capture this intelligence in terms of connection strengths. Networks, like GOFAI systems, therefore lack the ability to recognize situations in which what they have learned is inappropriate; instead, it is up to the human user to recognize failures and either modify the outputs of situations the net has already been trained on or provide new cases that will lead to appropriate modifications in behavior. The most difficult situation arises when the environment in which the network is being used undergoes a structural change. Consider, for example, the situation that occurred when OPEC instigated the energy crisis in 1973. In such a situation, it may well happen that even the human trainer does not know the responses that are now correct and that should be used in retraining the net. Viewed from this perspective, neural networks are almost as dependent upon human intelligence as are GOFAI systems, and their vaunted learning ability is almost illusory. What we really need is a system that learns on its own how to cope with the environment and modifies its own responses as the environment changes.

To satisfy this need, recent research has turned to an approach sometimes called "reinforcement learning."[49] This approach has two advantages over supervised learning. First, supervised learning requires that the device be told the correct action for each situation. Reinforcement learning assumes only that the world provides a reinforcement signal measuring the immediate cost or benefit of an action. It then seeks to minimize or maximize the total reinforcement it receives while solving any problem. In this way, it gradually learns from experience the optimal actions to take in various situations so as to achieve long-term objectives. To learn skillful coping, then, the device needs no omniscient teacher, just feedback from the world. Second, in supervised learning, any change in the skill environment requires new supervision by an expert who knows what to do in the new environment. In reinforcement learning, new conditions automatically lead to changes in reinforcement that cause the device to adapt appropriately.

An example will clarify what reinforcement learning in its most elemental form is all about. Suppose a device is to learn from repeated experience the shortest path from point A to point B in a city. The device knows where it is (its current state) and the possible directions it can go in (its space of allowable current actions). After it chooses an action (a direction), it observes the distance to the next intersection (its next decision point). This cost is its immediate reinforcement. It also observes the location of the next intersection (its new situation). The standard AI approach would be to have the device create an internal map of the city based on its experiences and then use that map and some computational algorithm to determine the shortest path. The new approach, like Heideggerian AI, dispenses with models and long-range planning. Instead the device repeatedly takes various paths from A to B, learning in which direction it should go at each intersection to create the shortest path from a given starting intersection to B. It does this not by trying alternative paths and remembering the best but by gradually learning only one piece of information besides its best decision at each intersection, namely the shortest distance from that intersection to B. This is the "value" of the intersection. After each decision and observation of the distance to the next intersection, the reinforcement algorithm evaluates that decision in terms of its current estimates of the value of the intersection it is at and the one to which it is going next. If it looks to be a good decision, it renders that decision more likely to be chosen in the future when the path problem is repeated and it finds itself at the same intersection. It also updates its estimate of the value of the current intersection.[50]

We have so far described a problem in which a given action in a given situation always leads to the same next situation and the same immediate reinforcement, but the approach is equally appropriate to probabilistic environments in which the device seeks actions that minimize or maximize expected long-term reinforcement. Values learned for situations are then minimal or maximal expected values. To cite one example, reinforcement-learning ideas (together with other mechanisms that are less like what brains seem to do but that speed up the learning) have been tried on the stochastic game of backgammon.[51] A program that played hundreds of thousands of games against itself, without expert-specified principles of the game or expert-supplied positional values or correct moves, learned expected values of positions well enough to play at the level of a good human tournament player. It was as proficient as any computer program using more conventional AI or supervised learning methods.[52]

All of this fits well with the phenomena. Most of our skills involve action in evolving situations and are learned from trial-and-error experience with environmental feedback but without teachers (or, sometimes, from experience-based fine-tuning of what we initially learned through instruction). Moreover, while experts generally cannot access any information explaining their ability, they can usually assess the value or desirability of a situation easily and rapidly and recommend an appropriate action.

Assuming that reinforcement-learning ideas correctly capture some of the essence of the human intelligence involved in learning skillful coping, the question naturally arises, Can one build a device that does as well as expert human beings using the phenomenologically plausible minimal essence of reinforcement learning, at least in particular skill domains? At least two improvements on present practice, neither of which appears achievable based on current knowledge, are needed. First, should reinforcement learning be applied to a problem in which the number of situations that might be encountered far exceeds the number that are actually encountered during training, some method of assigning fairly accurate actions and values to the novel situations is needed. Second, if reinforcement learning is to produce something resembling human intelligence, the reinforcement-learning device must exhibit global sensitivity by encountering situations under a perspective and by actively seeking relevant input.

Consider first the problem of behavior in unique situations. This problem has been dealt with by two procedures. The first is an automatic generalization procedure that produces actions or values in previously infrequently encountered situations on the basis of actions or values learned for other situations.[53] The second is to base one's actions on only a relevant subset of the totality of features of a situation and to attach a value to the situation based only on those relevant features; in this way, we lump together experiences with all situations sharing the same relevant features regardless of the nonrelevant ones. Actions are chosen or values learned based on experiences with situations sharing these relevant features. Both of these approaches are unsatisfactory. Concerning an automatic generalization procedure, at the point where generalization is required, the situation is identical with the one faced by supervised learning. No one has any idea how to get a network or any other mechanism to generalize in the way that would be required for human-like intelligence.

The second problem mentioned above—learning what features of a situation should be treated as a relevant subset and used in determining actions and values—is equally difficult. One can find out which features of the current state of affairs are relevant only by determining what sort of situation this state of affairs is. But that requires retrieving relevant past situations. This problem might be called *the circularity of relevance*. To appreciate its implications, imagine that the owner of a baseball team gives the team manager a computer loaded with facts about each player's performance under various conditions. One day, after consulting the computer late in the last inning, the manager decides to replace the current batter, A, with a pinch hitter, B. The pinch hitter hits a home run, and the team wins the game. The owner, however, is upset and accuses the manager of misusing the computer, since it clearly shows that B has a lower batting average than A. But, says the manager, the computer also showed that B has a higher batting average in day games, and this was a day game. Yes, responds the owner, but it also showed that he has a lower average against left-handed pitchers, and there was a leftie on the mound today. And so on. The point is that a manager's expertise, and expertise in general, consists in being able to respond to the relevant facts. A computer can help by supplying more facts than the manager could possibly remember, but only experience enables the manager to see the current state of affairs as a specific situation and so see what is relevant. That expert know-how cannot be put into the computer by adding more facts, since the issue is which is the current correct perspective from which to determine which facts are relevant.

Current procedures attempt to learn about relevance by keeping track of certain statistics during trial-and-error learning. A procedure proposed by Chapman and Kaelbling[54] starts by assuming that no features are relevant to action or value assessment, that is, that the same action should be taken no matter what the situation and that the same value should be attached to all situations. Then, for each possibly relevant feature of a situation, the procedure keeps track of statistics on how things work when that feature takes on each of its possible values (often just "present" or "not present"). If, on the basis of current statistics, the value of the feature seems to affect actions or values significantly, it is declared relevant. The situation receives an ever finer description as the set of features discovered to be relevant grows.

Something vaguely of this sort is probably what the brain does. There are, however, serious problems with the particular procedure described above and variations on it. First, a feature may not be relevant to behavior on its own but may be relevant when combined with one or more other features. To remedy this, we would need to gather statistics on the relevance of combinations of features, leading to an exponential explosion of possibly important statistics.

Second, this approach assumes that the relevance of a feature is a property of the domain; what is measured is the feature's relevance in all situations encountered. But a feature may be relevant in certain situations and not in others. We would therefore need to gather relevance data separately for each situation, again leading to exponential growth in the quantity of statistics gathered. Statistics gathering, therefore, does not seem a practical way for current computer procedures to deal with the relevance-determination aspect of intelligent behavior. As we shall see, given the size and structure of the brain, it may well be no accident that no one currently has any idea how to deal with this problem without gathering an impractical amount of statistical data.

A related third problem is that there is no limit to the number of features that might conceivably be relevant in some situations. We cannot simply start with all features that might possibly be relevant, gather statistics on each, and then leave out those that experience indicates can safely be ignored. But if we start with a finite set of possibly relevant features, there is no known way of adding new features should the current set prove inadequate to account for the learned facts about reinforcement and situation transition.

So how does the brain do it? No one knows. But certain facts seem relevant. First, it appears that experience statistically determines individual neural synaptic connections, so that the brain, with its hundreds of thousands of billions of adjustable synapses, can indeed accumulate statistical information on a scale far beyond current or foreseeable computers. Second, the reinforcement-learning procedures now being studied generally produce simple stimulus-response behavior in the sense that the input, a situation description, maps directly forward into the output, an action or situation value. The brain clearly has internal states that we experience as moods, anticipations, and familiarities that are correlated with the current activity of its hidden neurons when the input arrives. These are determined by its recent inputs as well as by the synaptic connection strengths developed on the basis of long-past experiences, and these as well as the input determine the output. One can in principle include such internal states in reinforcement-learning procedures by adding the current internal state of the device to the situation description, and a few researchers have moved in this direction. In effect, such an extended procedure in which the internal state is viewed as the perspective brought to the problem based on recent events would allow the incorporation of perspective into neural models. But since no one knows how to incorporate internal states appropriately, a breakthrough will be necessary before human behavior can be imitated successfully.

Most important, there is evidence that the internal brain state interacts with an input and then feeds its output to motor-control neurons as well as back into the input pathways, affecting receptors through motor control so that they actively seek information and simultaneously influencing perceived relevance through the feedback into input pathways. This would be the brain basis of the phenomenon of global sensitivity that enables a skilled person to see directly what is relevant in his or her skill domain. This feedback based on the interaction of sensory input and internal brain state would be a powerful mechanism for dealing with information pickup and relevance problems, but currently no details of this mechanism are understood or even hypothesized in a way that could guide AI research. It thus seems reasonable to hold that mechanisms exist in the brain that can in principle be understood and duplicated in hardware so as to produce artificial intelligence in restricted domains and that reinforcement learning is a small step in the right direction, while simultaneously holding that our current ignorance concerning the brain and practical limitations on computer memory size make it highly unlikely that there will be substantial progress toward this kind of brain-inspired AI in the foreseeable future.

One problem would remain even if the above practical problems were solved. In all applications of reinforcement learning the programmer must use his or her knowledge of the problem to formulate a rule that specifies the immediate reinforcement received at each step. For path problems and games the objective nature of the problem dictates the rule. If, however, the problem involves human coping, there is no simple objective answer as to what constitutes immediate reinforcement. Even if we assume the simplistic view that human beings behave so as to maximize their total sense of satisfaction, a reinforcement-learning approach to producing such behavior would require a rule for determining the immediate satisfaction derived from each possible action in each possible situation. But human beings do not have or need any such rule. Our needs, desires, and emotions provide us directly with a sense of the appropriateness of our behavior. If these needs, desires, and emotions in turn depend on the abilities and vulnerabilities of a biological body socialized into a culture, even reinforcement-learning devices still have a very long way to go.

All work in AI, then, seems to face a deep dilemma. If one tries to build a GOFAI system, one finds that one has to represent in a belief system all that a human being understands simply by being a skilled human being. In my preface to the second edition of this book, the extreme unlikelihood of successfully programming the computer to show common sense by making explicit enough of what human beings understand simply by being embodied and skilled led me to skepticism concerning the GOFAI research program. Happily, recent research in machine learning does not require that one represent everything that human beings understand simply by being human. But then, as we have just seen, one encounters the other horn of the dilemma. One needs a learning device that shares enough human concerns and human structure to learn to generalize the way human beings do. And as improbable as it was that one could build a device that could capture our humanity in a physical symbol system, it seems at least as unlikely that one could build a device sufficiently like us to act and learn in our world.

Notes

1 Marvin Minsky, *Computation: Finite and Infinite Machines* (Englewood Cliffs, N.J.: Prentice-Hall, 1967), p. 2.
2 Gina Kolata, "How Can Computers Get Common Sense?," *Science*, Vol. 217, No. 24 (September 1982), p. 1237.

   In their article "Could a Machine Think?" in *Scientific American* (January 1990), Paul and Patricia Churchland give an accurate overview of the role of this book in predicting and reinforcing this change of mood:

> In 1972 Hubert L. Dreyfus published a book that was highly critical of the parade-case simulations of cognitive activity. He argued for their inadequacy as simulations of genuine cognition, and he pointed to a pattern of failure in these attempts. What they were missing, he suggested, was the vast store of inarticulate background knowledge every person possesses and the commonsense capacity for drawing on relevant aspects of that knowledge as changing circumstance demands. Dreyfus did not deny the possibility that an artificial physical system of some kind might think, but he was highly critical of the idea that this could be achieved solely by symbol manipulation . . .
>
> Dreyfus's complaints were broadly perceived within the AI community, and within the discipline of philosophy as well, as shortsighted and unsympathetic, as harping on the inevitable simplifications of a research effort still in its youth. These deficits might be real, but surely they were temporary. Bigger machines and better programs should repair them in due course. Time, it was felt, was on AI's side . . .

> [But] time was on Dreyfus's side as well ... realistic performance required that the computer program have access to an extremely large knowledge base. Constructing the relevant knowledge base was problem enough, and it was compounded by the problem of how to access just the contextually relevant parts of that knowledge base in real time. As the knowledge base got bigger and better, the access problem got worse. Exhaustive search took too much time, and heuristics for relevance did poorly. Worries of the sort Dreyfus had raised finally began to take hold here and there even among AI researchers. [pp. 33–34]

3 For a more detailed account of the stages of skill acquisition, see Hubert Dreyfus and Stuart Dreyfus, *Mind Over Machine: The Power of Human Intuitive Expertise in the Era of the Computer* (New York: Free Press, 1986). The occasion for writing this book was the enthusiasm for expert systems that had replaced the original hope for all-purpose intelligent machines. The idea was that programs that could exhibit intelligence in micro-worlds cut off from common sense, such as SHRDLU, could be adapted to deal with real-world micro-worlds such as blood disease diagnosis or spectrograph analysis. In this first wave of defections from the degenerating GOFAI program, theoretical AI researchers, now renamed knowledge engineers, predicted a race with Japan to develop intelligent machines that would contain all human expertise. *Newsweek* announced in a cover story that "Japan and the United States are rushing to produce a new generation of machines that can very nearly think." Japan's Fifth Generation Project assembled researchers from all of that country's computer companies to produce intelligent machines in ten years or, at least, as more cautious knowledge engineers said, to produce important spin-off results. On the basis of our analysis of expertise, my brother and I predicted defeat.

The ten years are up, and as the *Washington Post* has reported (June 2, 1992, p. Cl), the Japanese government has closed the books on the project, conceding that it has had minimal impact on the global computer market. American designers of expert systems have also faced many disappointments. A typical case is the long-range project at Rockefeller University and Cornell University Medical College to develop computer programs that might help hematologists make diagnostic decisions. The researchers have already conceded defeat:

> Our efforts over many years in trying to develop a suitable diagnostic program for hematologic diseases confirms the great difficulty and even the impossibility of incorporating the complexity of human thought into a system that can be handled by a computer ...
>
> We do not see much promise in the development of computer programs to simulate the decision making of a physician. Well-trained and experienced physicians develop the uniquely human capability of recognizing common patterns from observation of exceedingly large numbers of stimuli. While people perform this intellectual synthesis quite readily, they are unable to spell out in detail how they do it; hence they cannot transfer the ability to a computer. Neither can they develop this ability, except in a very elementary way, by learning from computer-based programs intended to teach decision making.

4 One can, of course, recall the rules one once used and act on them again, but then one's behavior will be as halting and clumsy as it was when one followed the rules as a beginner.

5 Edward Feigenbaum and Pamela McCorduck, *The Fifth Generation: Artificial*

Intelligence and Japan's Computer Challenge to the World (Reading, Mass.: Addison-Wesley, 1983).

6 Allen Newell and Herbert Simon, "Computer Science as Empirical Inquiry: Symbols and Search," in *Mind Design*, ed. John Haugeland (Cambridge, Mass.: MIT Press, 1985), p. 50.

7 D. O. Hebb, *The Organization of Behavior* (New York: Wiley, 1949).

8 The collapse of the GOFAI research program was accelerated by a loss of faith on the part of the U.S. Department of Defense, which had been its longtime supporter. The Defense Department, in what was perhaps a test of GOFAI research, announced in the early 1980s that it would support research aimed at three goals that AI researchers claimed could be reached within ten years, including a project to create a truck that could plot its own course and steer by itself. After five years and $500 million, none of the goals appeared close, and one by one the projects were closed down. Almost all Defense Department support for AI-related research now goes to neural-network projects.

9 Neural nets are being used in many ways other than what are called MLPs, but MLPs are easily the most frequently used procedure for decision-making. For our purposes we take "neural net" to be synonymous with MLP.

10 Paul Smolensky, "Connectionist AI, Symbolic AI, and the Brain," *Artificial Intelligence Review*, Vol. 1 (1987), p. 95.

11 Douglas Lenat, "Computer Software for Intelligent Systems," *Scientific American* (September 1984), p. 204.

12 Douglas Lenat and Edward Feigenbaum, "On the Thresholds of Knowledge," *Artificial Intelligence*, Vol. 47, Nos. 1–3 (January 1991), p. 199.

13 *Ibid.*, p. 216.

14 *Ibid.*, p. 188. Lenat has high hopes: "Our distant descendants may look back on the synergistic man-machine systems that emerge from AI as the natural dividing line between 'real human beings' and 'animals.' We stand, at the end of the 1980s, at the interstice between the first era of intelligent systems and the second era. . . . In that 'second era' of knowledge systems, the 'system' will be reconceptualized as a kind of colleagular relationship between intelligent computer agents and intelligent people" (pp. 224–225).

15 For more on these techniques, see p. 35 of this book.

16 Douglas Lenat and R. V. Guha, *Building Large Knowledge-Based Systems: Representation and Inference in the Cyc Project* (Reading, Mass.: Addison Wesley, 1990), p. 15.

17 Douglas B. Lenat et al., "CYC: Toward Programs with Common Sense," *Communications of the ACM*, Vol. 33, No. 8 (August 1990), p. 33.

18 Lenat and Guha, *Building Large Knowledge-Based Systems*, p. 23.

19 Lenat and Feigenbaum, "On the Thresholds of Knowledge," p. 200.

20 *Ibid.*

21 *Ibid.*, p. 218.

22 Oliver Sacks, *The Man Who Mistook His Wife for a Hat and Other Clinical Tales* (New York: Summit Books, 1986), p. 59.

23 Mark Johnson, *The Body in the Mind: The Bodily Basis of Meaning, Imagination, and Reason* (Chicago: The University of Chicago Press, 1987), p. 168.

24 Lenat and Feigenbaum, "On the Thresholds of Knowledge," p. 187.

25 *Ibid.*, p. 221.

26 Pierre Bourdieu, *Outline of a Theory of Practice* (Cambridge, England: Cambridge University Press, 1977), pp. 5–6.

27 Pierre Bourdieu, *The Logic of Practice* (Stanford: Stanford University Press, 1980), p. 54.

28 Lenat, "Computer Software for Intelligent Systems," p. 209.

29 Douglas Hofstadter, "Metafont, Metamathematics, and Metaphysics," *Visible Language*, Vol. 16 (April 1982). Hofstadter is interested in the various styles of type fonts. This is a case of style of a type of object, like clothing or speech. The pervasive style that interests Bourdieu and Merleau-Ponty, however, opens a disclosive space that allows anything to be encountered *as* something.

30 Lenat and Feigenbaum, "On the Thresholds of Knowledge," p. 201.

31 *Ibid.* (my italics).

32 Lenat and Guha, *Building Large Knowledge-Based Systems*, pp. 11–12.

33 Lenat and Feigenbaum, "On the Thresholds of Knowledge," p. 198.

34 John R. Searle, *Intentionality: An Essay in the Philosophy of Mind* (Cambridge, England: Cambridge University Press, 1983), pp. 95–96.

35 *Ibid.*, p. 149.

36 See, for example, Jerry R. Hobbes et al., *Commonsense Summer: Final Report*, CSLI Report No. 85–35, Center for the Study of Language and Information, Stanford University.

37 Lenat and Feigenbaum, "On the Thresholds of Knowledge," p. 219.

38 Of course, grandmasters do not make that move immediately. They first check out its effects on future events and also, time permitting, examine less plausible alternatives.

39 See Hubert L. Dreyfus, *Being-In-The-World: A Commentary on Heidegger's* Being and Time, *Division I* (Cambridge, Mass.: MIT Press, 1991).

40 Terry Winograd, "Heidegger and the Design of Computer Systems," speech delivered at the Applied Heidegger Conference, Berkeley, California, December 1989.

41 David Chapman, *Vision, Instruction, and Action* (Cambridge, Mass.: MIT Press, 1991), p. 20.

42 *Ibid.*, pp. 20–21.

43 *Ibid.*, p. 30.

44 *Ibid.*, p. 22.

45 When given additional text beyond the training samples, NETtalk's performance degrades noticeably, but it can still be understood by native speakers. Critics have pointed out, however, that this is not so much evidence that the network can generalize what it has learned to new texts as a demonstration of the ability of native speakers to make sense out of a stream of error-corrupted phonemes.

46 Furthermore, no correlations were found between *patterns* of activity over the hidden nodes and the input features. A consistent structure *was* found involving *relations* among patterns of activities among hidden nodes regardless of initial connection strengths. The structure, however, was not determined by the *input* to the net, as would be necessary if this structure were to be taken as a very abstract version of a theory of the domain. Rather, the structure involved not only the input letter to be pronounced but the correct pronunciation as well.

In our article in *Daedalus* (Winter 1988), Stuart and I asserted that the nodes of a particular net that had learned a particular skill could not be interpreted as having picked out stable, reidentifiable features of the skill domain. Our argument was that as soon as the net gave a wrong response and had to be corrected, the weights on its connections and the interpretation of its nodes would change. Thus the features the net picked out would be a function of what it had learned, not of the domain structure alone. But this argument begs the question. If the net *had* abstracted a theory of the domain, it would have converged on the correct features and so would not have had to be further corrected. Paul Churchland's analysis of

NETtalk seems vulnerable to the same objection. See his chapter in Daniel Osherson and Edward E. Smith, eds., *Thinking*, vol. 3 of *An Invitation to Cognitive Science* (Cambridge, Mass.: MIT Press, 1990), p. 217.

47 I found this quoted in Michel Foucault, *The Order of Things* (New York: Vintage Books, 1973), p. xv.

48 For a statistical path to this conclusion, see S. Geman, E. Bienenstock, and R. Doursat, "Neural Networks and the Bias/Variance Dilemma," *Neural Computation*, Vol. 4, No. 1 (1992), pp. 1–58, esp. pp. 46–48. For a discussion of a psychological perspective on this realization, see R. N. Shepard, "Internal Representation of Universal Regularities: A Challenge for Connectionism," in *Neural Connections, Mental Computation*, ed. Lynn Nadel et al. (Cambridge, Mass.: MIT Press, 1989), pp. 104–134.

49 Useful references on this subject are: *Machine Learning*, Vol. 8, Nos. 3/4 (May 1992), and A. G. Barto, "Reinforcement Learning and Adaptive Critic Methods," in *Handbook of Intelligent Control: Neural, Fuzzy and Adaptive Approaches*, ed. D. A. White and D. Sofge (New York: Van Nostrand Reinhold, 1992). In what follows we shall describe what might be called the minimal essence of such reinforcement learning. More complicated schemes using more derived information and optimization over alternatives at each decision point perform better on toy problems than what we shall describe but require much greater memory capacity and, more importantly, deviate from what seems to us to be phenomenologically plausible.

50 The technique can be seen as an asynchronous, successive-approximation version of the dynamic programming optimization procedure; what is being gradually learned, in the terminology of dynamic programming, is the optimal policy and the optimal value functions. In many real-world situations, there are no intermediate payoffs; the reinforcement comes only at the end of a process. In a game of chess, for example, most decisions (move choices) in a situation (board position) produce no reinforcement but only a transition to a new situation. Only a move terminating the game produces a positive, zero, or negative reinforcement. The device would nevertheless attempt to learn from experience a best value for each position (based on whether the position leads to a win, a draw, or a loss with perfect play) and a move that attains that value.

51 Gerald Tesauro, "Practical Issues in Temporal Difference Learning," *Machine Learning*, Vol. 8, Nos. 3/4 (May 1992), pp. 257–277.

52 When eight handcrafted features computed from the board position were added to its board description input features, the device learned to play at very close to grandmaster level and well above the level of any other program known to the net's creator.

53 To implement an automatic generalization procedure, one chooses some parameterized formulas and adjusts their parameters to give what are currently believed to be correct actions and values for situations in which such actions and values have been learned, and then one uses these formulas to produce actions and values in all cases. One often-used formula takes the form of a neural network in which the parameters are the connection strengths.

The backgammon program uses a network to produce its positional values. It avoids directly choosing actions by examining all possible actions in a situation and choosing the one that looks best on the basis of the situational values assigned by the algorithm. This goes beyond what we have called the minimal essence of reinforcement learning and does not fit the phenomenology of human intelligent action. As in the case of supervised-learning networks, there is nothing in the algorithm that guarantees that it will generalize correctly when applied to a new situation. For this very reason, its success surprised its designer. It may well be that, as in the case of NETtalk, this seemingly successful generalization merely shows that in this domain accuracy in generalization is not essential.

54 David Chapman and Leslie Pack Kaelbling, "Input Generalization in Delayed Reinforcement Learning: An Algorithm and Performance Comparisons," *Proceedings of the 1991 International Joint Conference on Artificial Intelligence* (Cambridge, Mass.: AAAI Press/MIT Press, 1991), pp. 726–731.

Section 2.3: The Lighthill Report

62

ARTIFICIAL INTELLIGENCE

A general survey

James Lighthill

Source: *Artificial Intelligence: A Paper Symposium*, Elsevier Science, 1972, pp. 1–21.

1 Introduction

The Science Research Council has been receiving an increasing number of applications for research support in the rather broad field with mathematical, engineering and biological aspects which often goes under the general description Artificial Intelligence (AI). The research support applied for is sufficient in volume, and in variety of discipline involved, to demand that a general view of the field be taken by the Council itself. In forming such a view the Council has available to it a great deal of specialist information through its structure of Boards and Committees; particularly from the Engineering Board and its Computing Science Committee and from the Science Board and its Biological Sciences Committee. These include specialised reports on the contribution of AI to practical aims on the one hand and to basic neurobiology on the other, as well as a large volume of detailed recommendations on grant applications.

To supplement the important mass of specialist and detailed information available to the Science Research Council, its Chairman decided to commission an independent report by someone outside the AI field but with substantial general experience of research work in multidisciplinary fields including fields with mathematical, engineering and biological aspects. I undertook to make such an independent report, on the understanding that it would simply describe how AI appears to a lay person after two months spent looking through the literature of the subject and discussing it orally and by letter with a variety of workers in the field and in closely related areas of research. Such a personal view of the subject might be helpful to other lay persons such as Council members in the process of preparing to study specialist reports and recommendations and working towards detailed policy formation and decision taking.

497

The report which follows must certainly not be viewed as more than such a highly personal view of the AI field. It owes much to the study of published work and of private written communications and spoken comments by numerous individuals, including the following:

J. Annett, H. G. Barrow, S. Brenner, D. E. Broadbent, R. A. Brooker, O. P. Buneman, R. M. Burstall, A. D. B. Clarke, M. B. Clowes, A. H. Cook, D. C. Cooper, J. E. Doran, J. F. Duke, E. W. Elcock, I. J. Good, C. C. Green, R. L. Gregory, P. J. Hayes, A. L. Hodgkin, J. N. Holmes, J. A. M. Howe, D. H. Hubel, S. Isard, H. Kay, T. Kilburn, J. Kulikowski, D. N. L. Levy, H. C. Longuet-Higgins, D. M. MacKay, D. Marr, J. McCarthy, B. Meltzer, D. Michie, M. Minsky, D. Mollison, E. Moore, J. S. Moore, R. M. Needham, N. J. Nilsson, C. Oldfield, J. V. Oldfield, I. Pohl, R. J. Popplestone, B. Raphael, J. A. Robinson, C. Strachey, N. S. Sutherland, M. M. Swann, H. P. F. Swinnerton-Dyer, D. Wilshaw, T. Winograd.

The author is grateful for the large amount of help and advice readily given in reply to his many requests. He must emphasize, however, that none but himself is responsible for the opinions expressed in this report. They represent merely the broad overall view of the subject which he reached after such limited studies as he was able to make in the course of two months.

Readers might possibly have expected that the report would include a summary, but the author decided against this partly because considerable material is summarised already in almost every paragraph. Furthermore, he believes that this kind of report can be valuable only to those who read it all, and for this reason preferred to avoid attempting a condensation.

2 The ABC of the subject

There is a general consensus about which main areas of research are to be grouped within the broad field of AI. This section lists briefly these main areas and divides them further into three categories, A, B and C according to the long-term motivations for the three different types of work.

Here, categories A and C have clearly distinct motivations: each has a well defined general direction of its intended objectives, but the two directions are quite different. In both these categories a certain amount of rather respectable progress has been made during the subject's twenty-five years of life (which may be taken as beginning with Turing's 1947 article "Intelligent Machinery"), although expectations have as we shall see in section 3 been frequently disappointed. During the same period a further category "B" of researches has been pursued: a "bridge" category where aims and objectives are much harder to discern but which leans heavily on ideas from both A and C and conversely seeks to influence them. Research in category B, if acceptable arguments for doing it can be agreed, works by its interdependence with studies in categories A and C to give unity and coherence to the whole field of AI studies. There is, however, a widespread feeling (Section 3) that progress in this bridge category B has been even more disappointing, both as regards the work actually done and as regards the establishment of good reasons for doing such work and thus for creating any unified discipline spanning categories A and C.

Category A

Here, letter A stands for Advanced Automation: the clear objective of this category of work being to replace human beings by machines for specific purposes, which may be industrial or military on the one hand, and mathematical or scientific on the other. The work looks beyond automation of the type that is widely adopted at present in control engineering and data processing, and aims to make a far fuller use of the general-purpose digital computer's logical (as opposed to arithmetical) potentialities. Nevertheless it must be looked at as a natural extension of previous work on the automation of human activities, and be judged by essentially the same criteria.

Industrially important purposes include, for example, machine recognition of printed or typewritten characters (an area where good progress has been made) and of handwritten characters (incomparably more difficult), as well as a much wider range of pattern-recognition activities. The auditory equivalent to this visual area is speech recognition and synthesis. There are great economic incentives for work in machine recognition of speech, as well as in machine translation between languages, although progress in both has so far been very disappointing.

A further industrially important aim is to go beyond the automation of component design and manufacture, towards automation of design and assembly of whole products. It is argued that the complex spatial relationships involved in assembly processes put them far beyond the scope of conventional control engineering and require a much more advanced logical structure in the controlling software. Similar arguments may apply to problems of improving packing ratios in parcel containerisation.

The level of automation that can be called advanced has to be placed higher in the military field with its remarkable achievements both in cryptography and in guided missiles. A modern missile's capability to move in response to its own perception of its target against a noise background is highly reminiscent of the way in which a predator uses its complex central nervous system to home on to its prey. Beyond this the military have an incentive, however, to build less specialised devices that might be programmed to perform in hostile environments a far wider range of actions in response to information from organs of perception. Space exploration and, perhaps, some parts of industry (including firefighting) may look for a similar hostile-environment capability.

In the meantime, the application of digital computers in mathematical work has gone beyond the mere organisation of numerical calculations on a large scale and includes for example some very effective programmes for massive manipulations in algebra and analysis. Category A looks well beyond these, however, to the automation of problems of logical deduction including theorem proving, and still further to the automation of inductive generalisation and "analogy spotting".

In scientific applications, there is a similar look beyond conventional data processing to the problems involved in large-scale data banking and retrieval. The vast field of chemical compounds is one which has lent itself to ingenious and effective programs for data storage and retrieval and for the inference of chemical structure from mass-spectrometry and other data.

Information retrieval is, indeed, one of two dominant themes underlying all work in category A: this work is found to depend essentially on a "knowledge base" which the program causes to be stored in the computer, and the "file structure" of this knowledge base is of crucial importance in determining how data is accessed and used in the machine's operations. The other dominant theme is problem solving. This goes beyond mathematical theorem proving into the solution of numerous "commonsense problems" such as may arise in industrial and other applications. They can often be represented as problems of "transversing a graph", using "graph" in the specialised mathematical sense: an assemblage of points or nodes representing states of the system studied, some but not all pairs of nodes being linked by a line representing a permitted transition between states. Programs may be sought for solving problems in the sense of finding "optimal" (*eg* shortest) paths between remote nodes on such a graph.

Longer-term objectives in category A include that of combining a well structured knowledge base and an advanced problem solving capability to generate improved methods for industrial and economic planning and decision making, although admittedly there will always be serious difficulties in establishing that any particular program must necessarily have an acceptable output of plans and decisions! Another longer-term objective permeating all work in category A, furthermore, is to incorporate into programs an increasingly greater capability of "learning", so as to reach improved levels of performance in response to experience with tasks already undertaken. Efficient modes of learning will, however, be seen in section 3 to remain somewhat elusive.

To sum up, category A is concerned with Advanced Automation aimed at objectives such as written character recognition, pattern recognition, speech recognition and synthesis, machine translation, product design and assembly, container packing, exploration and action in hostile environments, theorem proving, inductive generalisation, analogy spotting, information storage and retrieval, analysis of chemical structures, problem solving, graph traversing, learning and decision making. In marked contrast to the diversity characteristic of all these numerous objectives, whether practical or scientific, is the much more unified fundamental-research aim of category C: computer-based studies related to the Central Nervous System (CNS) in man and animals.

Category C

Thus, letter C stands for Computer-based CNS research. In a lay person's report the extended term central nervous system is used in preference to the term brain which to a lay person may have subjective associations with the more conscious, or more consciously "brainy", parts of the brain activity, as against the emotional parts or those associated with perception and movement. The co-ordination of perception and movement in animals generally is a particularly significant area of research which the lay person (unlike the biologist) might be tempted to forget if the word "brain" conjures up for him the specifically human aspects of brain activity.

Category C is concerned, then, with theoretical investigations related to neurobiology and to psychology. The word "theoretical" is used here to emphasize that we are concerned, not at all with the use of computers merely to process experimental data, but with their use to build models of CNS processes whose performance can in due course be compared with experimental data – a phrase carefully chosen to be uncontroversial as between critics of work in category C who argue that it takes insufficient account of existing data and some of the research workers who feel that the experimentalists will need the stimulus of revolutionary theoretical ideas to produce their best work.

It must be emphasized that the use of computers in building and evaluating theories of neurophysiological and psychological phenomena is a trend in no way out of the ordinary: the great majority of theories in physics and chemistry are built up and evaluated on computers, and similar habits are now increasingly permeating the biological sciences. Biologists generally accept that computer-based theories in their field, far from implying any disrespect to the special characteristics of living matter, may have quite as much value as in physics and chemistry for stimulating understanding and suggesting new kinds of experiment – provided only that the theoretical work takes proper account of available observational data.

Category C is especially concerned with theories to interpret neurobiological data on specific areas of the CNS, using computer-based models of neural nets to test out particular hypotheses on (say) the functioning of the cerebellar cortex. Other theories, of (say) parts of the visual cortex, may seek to relate both to neurobiological and to psycho-physical data. Generally speaking, mathematically educated persons may be most effective in this field after prolonged study of CNS anatomy and physiology. Conversely, experimental psychologists and neurophysiologists may in several cases become expert in the construction of computer models from which new theoretical concepts may develop.

Other important aims in category C include the development of computer models related to observations of a strictly psychological nature, such as data on visual pattern recognition and scene analysis, on visual and auditory memory, on general aspects of associative recall. A further series of aims refer to specifically human types of CNS activity: thus, psycho-linguistic studies are concerned with theories of the psychological processes concerned in the use of language, while other studies probe similarly the processes involved in classification and inductive generalisation. These are areas where the computer-based models of neural activity are inevitably remote from the hard facts of neurobiological observation, but where contact with the data of experimental psychology is of crucial importance.

Some workers in this field identify the essential long-term aim as "understanding the human intellect", but they mean this only in the sense that the aim of cosmology is "understanding the past, present and future of the universe". There is no implication that such generality is apparent in any one group of research lines, merely that a general direction of desired improvement of knowledge is common to many such groups.

One more group of category C researches is concerned with how the human intellect acquires knowledge and skills, and this is related to educational psychology. For example, behavioural data on the order of acquisition of different abstract concepts in childhood may be studied in relation to models for the structuring of such concepts within the CNS.

To sum up, category C is concerned with basic research on Computer-based studies of CNS function, including the function of particular areas like the cerebellar cortex or parts of the visual cortex, and also special functions like visual pattern recognition and scene analysis, visual and auditory memory, associative recall, psycho-linguistics, classification, inductive generalisation and learning. This is work essentially within the life sciences and involving the pursuit, for its own sake, of knowledge which must appear to us as introspective living beings particularly desirable of attainment.

Evidently, there is a vast difference of approach between the practical, technological aims of category A (Advanced Automation of human activities) and the fundamental, biological aims of category C (Computer-based CNS studies). The aims are in each case perfectly clear, and perfectly distinct. The affinities in each case are much stronger with neighbouring fields (category A with general computer science and control engineering; category C with general neurobiology and psychology) than with each other. The appearance of a few common terms among the interests within the two categories (for example: pattern recognition, linguistics, inductive generalisation and learning) does admittedly indicate a degree of overlap, but may exaggerate its extent, as the problems of simulating these functions to achieve practical aims are not necessarily at all like the problems of studying how the CNS achieves them. If categories A and C were the whole body of research with which we had to deal we would recognise a minor extent of overlap of interest but regard the two areas of work as quite sufficiently distinct to warrant completely separate treatment in respect of research support, departmental organisation, etc.

Category B

Thus, the whole case for the existence of a continuous, coherent field of Artificial Intelligence research (AI) depends critically on whether between categories A and C there exists a significant category of research that may be described as a "Bridge" category, B, as well as on the strength of the case for any researches in that category. The existence of research work in this category is hardly in dispute: such work, as stated earlier, has been voluminous for many years, but there are much greater difficulties in any attempt at clear identification of good reasons for putting resources into those researches. The activities and stated aims of work in category B are described in the remainder of section 2.

Here, letter B stands not only for "Bridge activity", but also for the basic component of that activity: Building Robots. The whole concept of Building Robots is, indeed, seen as an essential Bridge Activity justified primarily by what it can feed into the work of categories A and C, and by the links that it creates between them.

Thus, a Robot in the sense used here, and by most workers in the field, is an automatic device that mimics a certain range of human functions without seeking in any useful sphere of human activity to replace human beings. Work in category B (Building Robots) is frequently justified because it simultaneously supports category A (Advanced Automation), in the sense that generalised information on automatic devices may emerge which can be used in practical problems of Automation, and supports category C (Computer-based CNS studies), in the sense that devices that mimic a human function may assist in studying, and in making a theory of, that function.

These are serious arguments, that will need to be considered seriously in sections 3 and 4. On the other hand, they are probably by no means the only reason why Building Robots is a popular activity. At the other extreme of the spectrum of reasons we have to remember the long-standing captivation of the human imagination by the very concept, as shown by its continual prominence in literature, from medieval fantasies of the Homunculus through Mary Shelley's "Frankenstein" to modern science fiction. To what extent may scientists consider themselves in duty bound to minister to the public's general *penchant* for robots by building the best they can?

Incidentally, it has sometimes been argued that part of the stimulus to laborious male activity in "creative" fields of work, including pure science, is the urge to compensate for lack of the female capability of giving birth to children. If this were true, then Building Robots might indeed be seen as the ideal compensation! There is one piece of evidence supporting that highly uncertain hypothesis: most robots are designed from the outset to operate in a world as like as possible to the conventional child's world as seen by a man; they play games, they do puzzles, they build towers of bricks, they recognise pictures in drawing-books ("bear on rug with ball"): although the rich emotional character of the child's world is totally absent. Builders of Robots can justly reply that while robots are still in their infancy they can mimic only pre-adult functions and a limited range of those at most, and that these will lead on to higher things. Nevertheless, the view to which this author has tentatively but perhaps quite wrongly come is that a relationship which may be called pseudomaternal rather than Pygmalion-like comes into play between a Robot and its Builder.

General aspects of work in category B involve work on mimicking some special functions that are particularly highly developed in man: co-ordination of eye and hand; visual scene analysis; use of natural language; "commonsense" problem solving. These areas for work in category B are evidently well chosen for giving good chances of feeding valuable results into the work of categories A and C.

Various reasons including limitations of computer power have restricted the "universe of discourse" in which the functions just mentioned are exercised in existing robots to something like a chessboard, or a simple "table-top world" on which coloured blocks are moved about and stacked on one another. Several workers have argued that games such as chess and draughts are ideal spheres for development of robot potentialities because there is great scope for ingenuity but little waste of programming effort on inessential features resulting from too extensive a universe of discourse.

To sum up, category B is a Bridge Activity concerned with Building Robots for purposes which include the feeding of information into the work of categories A and C; each Robot is designed to mimic some group of human functions, including functions such as eye-hand co-ordination, scene analysis, use of natural language, problem solving, *etc*, within some limited universe of discourse such as we may exemplify by a game (chess, draughts, *etc*), a puzzle, a table top on which blocks are moved about, or a drawing-book. One's views of the fundamental coherence of the whole field of AI spanning categories A, B and C must depend on one's opinion on whether the arguments for this Bridge Activity in category B are sound enough for it to be regarded as a necessary concomitant to, and link between, the rather different and rather easily defensible activities in categories A and C.

3 Past disappointments

Most workers in AI research and in related fields confess to a pronounced feeling of disappointment in what has been achieved in the past twenty-five years. Workers entered the field around 1950, and even around 1960, with high hopes that are very far from having been realised in 1972. In no part of the field have the discoveries made so far produced the major impact that was then promised.

The disappointment felt may be analysed into two kinds: work in the categories A and C of section 2 has some respectable achievements to its credit (and achievement in such categories of work with rather clear aims is clearly discernible), but to a disappointingly smaller extent than had been hoped and expected, while progress in category B has been even slower and more discouraging, tending (as explained in section 2) to sap confidence in whether the field of research called AI has any true coherence. In the meantime, claims and predictions regarding the potential results of AI research had been publicised which went even farther than the expectations of the majority of workers in the field, whose embarrassments have been added to by the lamentable failure of such inflated predictions.

These general statements are expanded in a little more detail in the rest of section 3, which has been influenced by the views of large numbers of people listed in section 1 but which like the whole of this report represents in the last analysis only the personal view of the author. Before going into such detail he is inclined, as a mathematician, to single out one rather general cause for the disappointments that have been experienced: failure to recognise the implications of the "combinatorial explosion". This is a general obstacle to the construction of a self-organising system on a large knowledge base which results from the explosive growth of any combinatorial expression, representing numbers of possible ways of grouping elements of the knowledge base according to particular rules, as the base's size increases.

Category A

Achievements within the sphere of the Advanced Automation (category A) have to be judged in competition with what industry has been able to achieve during the same period by perfectly conventional methods of control engineering and data processing. We may remind ourselves of the toughness of this competition by two examples. The human skills required to land a large aircraft reliably and safely are complex and intricate; yet the Automatic Landing System of Smith's Aviation Ltd., which uses classical control technology, has a better than human performance and has now been certified by the Air Registration Board, which for the purpose had demanded to be convinced of a less than 1 in 10^7 failure rate. Another British firm, Image Analysing Computers Ltd., has had a considerable commercial success using conventional programming methods to analyse images (*eg* microscope slides) as scanned by a television raster and to give numerical data (*eg* on metallographic grain shapes and sizes, or on cell characteristics in blood samples) without human intervention; automatic cervical-smear analysis now seems achievable by these means.

Workers in category A, while recognizing the effectiveness of such conventional control-engineering and data-processing methods applied to particular specialised tasks, have tended to emphasize the likelihood of Advanced Automation techniques of far more *general* applicability emerging from their work. The concept of automatic devices or methods with general capabilities is certainly a most attractive one. It is therefore particularly disappointing that the experience of the last twenty-five years has increasingly forced workers in category A to conclude that Advanced Automation techniques are successful not when they are developed with a high degree of generality of application, but only when a large quantity of detailed knowledge about the problem domain is utilised in the program design.

While this conclusion, which is rapidly gaining acceptance, has been undermining one of the clearest overall justifications for work in category A, performance of Advanced Automation systems developed at great expense in problem domains of particular economic importance has generated a still stronger sense of disappointment. Work in the pattern-recognition field has not yet proved competitive with conventional methods: even the recognition of printed and typewritten characters posed a quite surprising degree of difficulty, while the recognition of handwritten characters appears completely out of reach. Speech recognition has been successful only within the confines of a very limited vocabulary, and large expenditure on schemes to produce machine recognition of ordinary speech has been wholly wasted. Learning techniques, by which a machine's performance at recognising words might improve on receiving identified words from more and more individual speakers, appear feasible only for an exceedingly small vocabulary (such is the power of the combinatorial explosion) like the decimal digits!

The most notorious disappointments, however, have appeared in the area of machine translation, where enormous sums have been spent with very little useful result, as a careful review by the US National Academy of Sciences concluded in 1966; a conclusion not shaken by any subsequent developments. Attempts based on classical grammar and syntax and on the transformational grammar of contemporary general linguistics have been equally unsuccessful in producing acceptable programs. Suggestions from recent research (see below), that analysis and use of natural language by computer succeed only when a very detailed knowledge of the universe of discourse is stored within the machine, augur badly for the future availability of machine-translation programs versatile enough to be commercially valuable.

Mathematical theorem-proving is another area of work in category A that has had its disappointments. Of course, conventional programming is used by many pure mathematicians with great success to generate examples suggesting, or counter-examples disproving, theorems; while conventional proofs that leave a finite residuum of cases unaccounted for may often be completed by a computational survey of those cases. The mathematician is then using the computer as a fast, reliable and "biddable" number-cruncher, the role in which computers generally have been most successful.

In the nineteen-fifties and early nineteen-sixties, however, a great deal of optimism was generated from the concept of realising on a computer the algorithms for theorem proving suggested by the decidability propositions of mathematical logic, starting with the "completeness theorem" of the first-order predicate calculus. Those most involved now emphasize that this is particularly an area where hopes have been disappointed through the power of the combinatorial explosion in rapidly cancelling out any advantages from increase in computer power. The modern trend is to "heuristic" methods, which also are the only methods that have been found effective in the general areas of problem solving and graph traversing.

It is important to understand the meaning attached to this adjective "heuristic" which increasingly permeates the Artificial Intelligence literature: it means that the program stores and utilises a large amount of knowledge derived from human experience in solving the type of problem concerned. Thus, it depends critically on data derived through the use of human intelligence, so that the widespread view that only heuristic methods are effective is a serious setback to more extreme versions of the AI philosophy. For example, a heuristic graph-traversing program requires stored values of a human estimate of the "nearness" of each node to the desired goal.

Some interesting concepts from mathematical logic that have been influential on work in category A are those relating to two or more statements including *variable* elements: namely, their "resolution" or greatest common instantiation, and its "dual" their least common generalisation which represents a sort of "inductive inference" from them. Algorithms exist for obtaining these but limits on their practical use again result from the combinatorial explosion.

There are, in addition, difficulties in using the techniques of mathematical logic in heuristic programs based on stored knowledge, particularly because the type of stored knowledge favoured by logicians, namely a set of axioms, is inconvenient for access by practical programs!

An excellent example of successful work in category A that has resulted from storage of as much detailed information as possible about the problem domain is the "heuristic dendral" program for inference of chemical structure from mass-spectroscope data. Its output is a list of possible molecular "graphs" (*ie* structures) in order of decreasing plausibility that are consistent with the mass spectrum and the empirical formula and in some cases data of certain additional types. It has been the extremely careful study of extensive detailed information affecting the relationship of chemical structures to mass spectra that has brought about the relatively good success in this field.

In just the same way, quite good performance has been achieved in complicated areas of data storage and retrieval where the problems were confined to data of very precisely defined and analysed types. By contrast, generalised information-retrieval systems have been somewhat disappointing, especially when applied to research information involving relatively advanced ideas.

To balance seriously limited successes in achieving the longer-term objectives of work in category A, one must recognize a great deal of "spin-off" from such work, and from associated work in category B, into the "software industry" and into programming technique generally. Certain high-level programming languages developed for this work have proved invaluable in a wide range of programming activity. The list-processing languages have many advantages over conventional programming languages; for example they eliminate the labour of preliminary estimation and organisation of store space. Languages specially suitable for problem solving and for linguistic analysis have also been derived. Their advantages include "automatic backtracking" by which if a particular subroutine fails all activity is "unwound" back to a specific point and then an alternative subroutine is tried. There is a very widespread appreciation of the many merits of this group of programming languages. It must be admitted, on the other hand, that excellent work on developing high-level programming languages has been done also in regular computing laboratories and in research groups devoted to general computational theory.

Category C

The history of work in category C (Computer-based CNS Studies) has been somewhat similar to that in category A: in spite of a respectable volume of achievement resulting from such studies, most workers who entered the field around ten years ago confess that they then felt a degree of "naïve" optimism which they now recognise as having been misplaced. It is, once more, the most generalised types of studies whose end-products have proved most disappointing.

There is a consensus of view that benefits from this work in category C have flowed primarily to the science of psychology: in fact, a new range of attitudes to psychological problems has been generated. Computer models, although yielding no sudden breakthrough, have helped distinguish between theories of psychological phenomena which are possible candidates for consideration and theories that simply cannot be made to work.

As might be expected, some of the best work is by actual experimental psychologists with a good knowledge of a complex mass of data who have acquired the skills needed to build computer models for interpreting it: such work developed, for example, the concept of the visual buffer store. One school of thought emphasizes the value of intimate relation of computer models to detailed CNS data so exclusively as to propose denial of computer capacity to more theoretical groups until the demand for computer capacity from such experimental psychologists and from neurophysiologists is fully met.

Another school of thought sees a real place for the more speculative theorists, however, and points out the potential value of current studies of the types of neural networks that might be effective for functions such as associative recall, classification by attributes and inductive generalisation. It is easy to believe that, as in physics and chemistry, the more speculative theorists do have a real role to play in generating ideas. On the other hand, some of the most significant work in these neural-net theories has been done in close association with local neurobiological data. Furthermore, some of the most remarkable neurobiological discoveries, including many on the structure of the visual cortex, have not required any computer-based modelling at all! A properly balanced view of work in category C may perhaps be that the besetting applied-mathematics sin of taking insufficient trouble to master the experimental facts needs to be carefully guarded against but that, if it is, the work produced can significantly help in the long process of moving towards better understanding of CNS function.

Psycho-linguistics is an area of psychology where this may particularly be the case. The algorithmic approach to the subject apparent already in transformational grammar and its syntactical theories of how sentences are generated is now being extended to involve algorithms taking into account more semantic information; that is, more knowledge about the universe of discourse. This type of algorithm looks much more promising as a model of how the CNS processes language.

The area nearest to an *applied* science which we listed in section 2 as coming within category C was educational psychology. There has recently been speculation on whether the time may be ripe for research aimed at direct application of AI research to educational method through the development of advanced forms of Computer Aided Instruction (CAI).

There is a well established, "classical" approach to CAI that gives quite good results in educational areas that may be described politely as "drill and practice", or less politely as "cramming"! The "teaching machine" is programmed to print out factual information interspersed with multiple-choice questions and to go into various alternative loops, in which it prints out encouraging or corrective comments (with additional questions in the latter case), according as the right answer or one of the wrong answers is chosen.

There are those who hope to go beyond this type of CAI to a type that might be suitable for a wider range of material than mere cramming of facts and might respond more sensitively to the abilities and difficulties of the pupil. It might depend not only on pre-stored material but also on a programmed capability to generate new material, using natural language, from a stored "knowledge base".

These applied-research dreams are in the present author's view singularly untimely and unpromising. Taking into account the very large computer capacity and programming skill needed at present to achieve computer use of natural language on even a very small knowledge base, and adding all the difficulties of structuring and accessing a larger knowledge base and monitoring pupil performance, one can only conclude that the nineteen-seventies are not the right decade in which to begin researches aimed at applying such techniques to the teaching of any body of knowledge big enough to be of practical interest. To avoid misunderstanding however, one should make clear that basic research on developmental psychology by the methods of category C would not on this argument be excluded.

Category B

The balance between numerous disappointments and certain solid achievements from work in categories A and C is, perhaps, typical of scientific research as a whole. It indicates only that these areas of research are not in one of those conditions of exceptional fruitfulness when everything seems to be going right. By contrast, the sense of discouragement about the intended Bridge Activity of category B, centred upon Building Robots, seems altogether more widespread and profound, and this raises doubts about whether the whole concept of AI as an integrated field of research is a valid one.

Quite possibly the sense of discouragement is greater in category B because still greater expectations have been sensed and voiced in this category than in the others. Some workers in the field freely admit that originally they had "very naïve" ideas about the potentialities of intelligent robots, but claim to recognise now what sort of research is realistic. In these circumstances it might be thought appropriate to judge the field by what has actually been achieved than by comparison with early expectations. On the other hand, some such comparison is probably justified by the fact that in some quarters wild predictions regarding the future of robot development are still being made.

When able and respected scientists write in letters to the present author that AI, the major goal of computing science, represents "another step in the general process of evolution"; that possibilities in the nineteen-eighties include an all-purpose intelligence on a human-scale knowledge base; that awe-inspiring possibilities suggest themselves based on machine intelligence exceeding human intelligence by the year 2000; when such predictions are made in 1972 one may be wise to compare the predictions of the past against performance as well as considering prospects for the realisation of today's predictions in the future.

It certainly seems that early enthusiasm for programming and building a robot that would mimic human ability in a combination of eye-hand co-ordination and "commonsense" problem solving has ended up gravely disappointed. The large amount of computer time needed to distinguish between everyday objects of markedly different shapes against a far from noisy background has been most discouraging; the engineering complications required to achieve eye-hand co-ordination (not of human standard but similar to what an octopus can learn) have been repellingly formidable. Reports from the world's different centres for this work are all disenchanting.

Some able research workers, who from their beginning in the field regarded Building Robots as a precarious or even "crazy" enterprise but nevertheless were attracted to participate in such a long-shot or even "shot in the dark" activity, have felt themselves driven now to recognise that the difficulty of achieving good hand-eye co-ordination in quite simple problem situations has proved unexpectedly great, and seems to hold out negligible hope of approaching human levels of achievement. In these circumstances, many good computational theorists are emphasizing that productive research on "robot reasoning" (or, essentially, commonsense problem solving) does *not* necessarily need the physical presence of an eye-hand machine. This line of argument then branches in two directions, one leading to work properly in category A (directed to automating the solution of such problems as may arise in practical fields of application), and the other (which is our concern here) leading to programs for problem solving in an *abstract* "play" situation: for example, in an abstract table-top world with data fed in not as television images but as statements about the positions of blocks on the table-top; or in a similarly defined chessboard or puzzle situation.

The "Category B" research work on problem solving in these abstract play situations has produced many ingenious and interesting programs. A fair description of the success of these programs seems to be that they are effective when and only when the programming has taken into account a really substantial quantity of human knowledge about the particular problem domain. Just as in category A, the pure mathematical-logic methods suffer defeat at the hands of the combinatorial explosion, and have to be replaced by "heuristic" methods. Some very interesting researches have been carried out to develop "general" problem-solving programs, and such work can be of research interest to psychologists, but the performance of these programs on actual problems has always been disappointing. Students of all this work have generally concluded that it is unrealistic to expect highly generalised systems that can handle a large knowledge base effectively in a "learning" or "self-organising" mode to be developed in the 20th century.

Those wishing to decide as between this view and the quite opposite views of the "awe-inspiring" future mentioned earlier can quite helpfully study the state of the art on chess-playing programs. This is partly because chess is a complicated enough game so that in a contest between a computer and a human player the computer's advantages of being able to calculate reliably at a speed several orders of magnitude faster need by no means be decisive (the number of possible positions being incomparably greater) and so there is real interest in whether or not they are outweighed by the human player's pattern-recognition ability, flexibility of approach, learning capacity and emotional drive to win. Another good reason for investigating chess-playing programs is that the long-term interest of the big international computer manufacturers in bringing about some spectacular achievement of "machine intelligence" against such a well developed human intelligence as an able chess player, in order to assist in selling more generally their products' potentiality for superseding human intellectual activity, has been an incentive to the devotion of quite considerable resources to producing an effective program.

It is interesting to consider the results of all this work some twenty-five years after the researches aimed at chess-playing programs began: unfortunately these results are discouraging. The best programs play chess of only "experienced amateur" standard characteristic of county club players in England. Chess masters beat them easily.

More important, progress on constructing chess-playing programs has been made solely by heuristic methods. The programs seek to maximise in what may be called the foreseeable short term a complicated "evaluation function"; this function, constructed entirely from human knowledge and skill, represents an evaluation of a position, depending on large numbers of different measurable features of it with different weights attached to them. What relatively modest success the programs have achieved is a measure primarily of human skill and experience in the concoction of this evaluation function. The computer's contribution is primarily rapidity in looking a few moves ahead and finding a line that produces a position change good on the basis of that evaluation. The intelligence contribution is human; what the computer offers is its speed, reliability and biddability. By contrast, "learning" programs are not considered applicable to computer chess at present.

To sum up, this evidence and all the rest studied by the present author on AI work within category B during the past twenty-five years is to some extent encouraging about programs written to perform in highly specialised problem domains, when the programming takes very full account of the results of human experience and human intelligence within the relevant domain, but is wholly discouraging about general-purpose programs seeking to mimic the problem-solving aspects of human CNS activity over a rather wide field. Such a general-purpose program, the coveted long-term goal of AI activity, seems as remote as ever.

In thus regretfully noting the remoteness of this goal we must not, however, be tempted into overvaluing it because of its inaccessibility. We must remember, rather, that the "intelligent problem solving" and "eye-hand co-ordination" and "scene analysis" capabilities that are much studied in category B represent only a small part of the features of the human CNS that give the human race its uniqueness. It is a truism that human beings who are very strong intellectually but weak in emotional drives and emotional relationships are singularly ineffective in the world at large. Valuable results flow from the integration of intellectual ability with the capacity to feel and to relate to other people; until this integration happens problem solving is no good because there is no way of seeing which are the right problems. These remarks have been included to make clear that the over-optimistic category-B-centred view of AI not only fails to take the first fence but ignores the rest of the steeple-chase altogether. It will suffice, however, to judge the work on its own rules and its own aims in order to conclude that the attempt to construct a true Bridge between categories A and C is not succeeding.

Postscript

It is only fair to add at the end of this section on "Past Disappointments" that some workers in the field would have agreed with the view just expressed until the appearance less than two years ago of an exceptionally good PhD thesis[1] on a computer program for use of natural language, since when they have felt resurgence of optimism about the coherence and viability of the concept of integrated AI researches. It is important to analyse how this reaction has come about and how far such resurgence is justified.

The thesis is exceptional in more than one way. The style in which most papers on AI research are written is depressingly turgid or jargon-dominated and almost makes the authors appear antagonistic to the special human gift for relating to, and communicating with, other people in an imaginative way (as if such authors appreciated *only* those human capabilities which they seek to mimic in robots!). By contrast, the thesis is a pleasure to read, the author's substantial research achievement and attractive personality being communicated infectiously by his style of writing. His gift for language and communication has without doubt contributed to making his researches widely known all over the world, as well as having contributed to the success of the actual linguistic analysis underlying the development of his program.

This analysis is the strongest of those mentioned above under category C as having developed far beyond the transformational-grammar approach of general linguistics into new methods for machine interpretation of natural-language sentences within a limited universe of discourse, that make very substantial use of stored knowledge concerning that universe. Full use of such knowledge is regarded by the author of the thesis as an essential ingredient of the success of his approach, to which however the penetration and originality of the analytical methods he introduced has also made a vital contribution.

Specifically, the universe of discourse is an "abstract table-top world" and in the lengthy, and now rather famous, "conversation" between the author and his program the program accepts, and is deemed to have carried out, certain commands to perform well defined block-stacking operations, while it queries commands that are impossible or ambiguous. The program deals similarly in answer to questions put to it regarding the present and past states of the table-top world. In constructing the program, two of the high-level programming languages referred to under category A above were used: one to program the events in the abstract table-top world and one to perform the linguistic analysis. The thesis well illustrates the value of these high-level languages.

The contribution of brilliant presentation and deep originality has made this thesis deservedly influential on workers in most areas of AI research. The biggest and clearest influence is on psycho-linguistics itself (work in category C), where the studies have been in large part responsible for a movement towards viewing the processes by which the human CNS responds to and uses language as semantics-controlled (or knowledge-controlled) even in their fine structure.

Many workers in category B (the Bridge Activity of Building Robots) have at the same time felt encouraged by this thesis: its program, after all, can properly be described as a Robot "with whom the author converses", and Building this Robot has succeeded in its aim to an extent undreamt-of in the unrewarding world of eye-hand machines. The program seems furthermore to open up more general possibilities of conversing with Robots by means of natural language. There is even a suggestion of an ultimate link through to work in category A if these new studies could revive prospects for achievement of machine translation.

To such somewhat over-generalised euphoria it is necessary to respond, however, with certain cautionary reservations beyond the banal comment that one swallow does not make a summer. Outside the psycho-linguistic area where the thesis has truly helped to establish a new direction of research, suggestions for possible developments in other areas that can properly be inferred from the studies are rather discouraging. Thus, the studies show how the complex problems involved in computer use of natural language are rendered far more complex by the need to interact in detail with systems for structuring and accessing the necessary knowledge base. For an extensive universe of discourse this could put such developments out of practical reach.

In practice, a large computer together with very sophisticated programming using subtle new programming-language developments was found just sufficient to make slow conversation possible on the very limited material represented by the abstract table-top world; material restricted enough, for example, to allow resolution of ambiguities in natural-language sentences by classical theorem-proving techniques. Extension of the methods used to a much wider universe of discourse would be opposed violently by the combinatorial explosion.

Accordingly, the present author's view of the definite (though not over-whelming) promise of work in categories A and C, and of the general failure of work in category B to establish effectively the unity of AI research as a whole, remains unmodified by careful study of one particular piece of work of a very remarkable character. This postscript to the section on "Past Dis-appointments", explaining this, has been included because emotional response to such work is very natural and desirable but needs to be inte-grated properly with an intellectual appraisal of where its significance pri-marily lies. The thesis is, of course, a triumph of human intelligence, and human intelligence can respond to it most correctly by recognising its main contribution as being to aspects of how the use of language by the human race has developed and of what processes within the human CNS that use may involve.

4 Future possibilities

However controversial may be an analysis of the past, a forward look towards the different possibilities that the future may hold in some area must be more controversial still, especially when made in a report to a body whose decisions can have a very substantial influence over a certain part of that area's future (specifically, the British part). Controversy has its unattractive as well as its attractive features, but it cannot be avoided in a period when the abilities of scientists jointly to arrive at wise decisions on research policy is publicly regarded as being on trial.

Research on AI in some other countries may be funded by military agen-cies (ARPA in USA) or by other mission-orientated public bodies. With this type of funding it is common for scientists to "close their ranks" and avoid public disagreement among themselves, in the hope that the total funds available for science may thus be enhanced to an extent that may outweigh any harmful results of a distribution of those funds determined on the basis of insufficient scientific discussion. Such optimism would be unjustified in a poorer country such as Britain, while the alternative approach here advo-cated accords with the desire to "keep our AI research civilian" expressed to the author by various British workers in the field. This suggests that decisions within the UK should be taken only after carefully contrasting and comparing different informed views of the research field's future available to SRC. Thus, due weight should be given to the principle "Heterarchy not Hierarchy" (an AI maxim of considerable soundness concerned with file structures).

To the required debate this report's contribution consists not of any detailed costed recommendations, but of certain general considerations based on the analysis of the past given in section 3 as well as some thoughts about the present and future now to be presented. After omission in this published version of all specific comments on British research work in the field, these consist essentially of an attempt to look to the field's scientific future in the world as a whole, subject to the proviso that any speculations beyond the end of this century are regarded as too uncertain to justify mentioning them or basing on them any present research decisions whatever.

It is assumed that more precise policy formulation and detailed decisions on projects will stem from the normal working of the machinery of the Science Research Council and its Boards and Committees, influenced to some extent by such special reports as may be available, including the 1972 Policy and Programme Review of the SRC Computing Science Committee and also the 1972 report of a joint SRC/MRC panel on Neurobiology, as well as the present "personal view" of AI as a research field.

The next twenty-five years

This "personal view" which saw the past twenty-five years of AI research as having developed a "bimodal" distribution of achievement, with some respectable (though not as yet lofty) peaks of achievement in categories A and C but relatively speaking a valley between them in category B, looks ahead to still greater bimodality, amounting practically to fission, arising during the next 25. Specifically it foresees, whether within category A or category C, certain research areas making very substantial further progress, coupled in each case with the forging of far stronger links to the immediate field of application than to the supposed bridge activity B. Rising confidence about the work's relevance within the associated field of application may add prestige and thence strength to such an area of research, while continued failures to make substantial progress towards stated aims within category B may cause progressive loss of prestige, from which a diminution of funding will ultimately follow even where scientific claims are not always subject to full scientific scrutiny. In due course the overriding significance of the links between each research area and its field of application will rupture the always fragile unity of the general concept of AI research.

For example, in the technological applications within category A the work will become increasingly specialised, in accordance with the common experience that AI researches are successful to a degree closely correlated with the degree of use made of detailed knowledge of the problem domain. Techniques for Advanced Automation can now be expected to move forward fastest where research workers concentrate upon practical problems, acquiring for the purpose good detailed knowledge of the technological and economic contexts of the problems chosen. Benefit to both sides will flow from closer integration with control engineers, who have deep experience not only of the practical but also of the financial and sociological questions arising in automation, and can conversely learn much that is of value to them from experts in advanced computational theory. That theory itself (including the development of new programming languages) can in the meantime forge ahead through a combination of the spin-off from Advanced Automation developments and of the activities (serving far more than AI research) of general computing-science laboratories.

Recently the Japanese government announced a £40M research programme oriented very closely along these lines, aimed at the automation of factory assembly processes, which among the areas within category A mentioned in section 2 may well be one of the most promising. Another clue to how Advanced Automation developments may proceed comes from recent experience in the sister field of Computer Aided Design (CAD): generalised researches dominated early CAD work, but later on several specific industries developed forms of CAD very specialised towards their own problems. This example is mentioned mainly as an analogy to how Advanced Automation may come to experience a similar degree of fragmentation; however, we should also remember from section 2 that CAD is itself an area where advanced computational theory may be found to have a role, especially in the integration of subsystem designs. Close relationships between AI theorists and CAD workers (such as here and there have already come about) are one prerequisite for those developments.

A similar outward-looking trend is expected in the mathematical and scientific applications of researches within category A; in mathematics, for example, from utilisation of far more detailed observation of "how mathematicians actually prove theorems"! The structuring and utilisation of scientific data bases is another area where good results depend on detailed study of the data's special characteristics. The one part of that field with which the present author has been closely involved, as Chairman of the Steering Committee for the Experimental Cartography Unit of NERC since its inception, affords a good example of this: the structuring of geographically located data is found to demand quite specialised techniques, closely related to the cartographic character of the output. Another good example from the scientific sphere is the chemical-structure work described in section 3.

It is not to be expected that, in all the areas within category A listed in section 2, striking successes will be reached during the next twenty-five years. The view here proposed is rather that the chances of success in any one area will be greatly improved through close integration of the researches with the field of application.

Substantial advances are at the same time expected within category C, where success will again be related to how closely the work is linked to the fundamental associated disciplines of psychology and neurobiology. Computer-based CNS studies can from experimental psychology gain greatly through more substantial use of the extensive data available, *eg* on reaction times, on pattern-recognition abilities, and on the types of errors made in different tasks. From modern neurobiology they can derive a valuable appreciation of the detailed evidence to the effect that the CNS uses "specialised hardware" very economically to perform significant and important tasks. Computer-based studies have a role to play in analysing how some of this hardware may function, and conversely can derive a salutary reminder that simulation of the extraordinary self-organising capabilities evolved by the human CNS may actually be unattainable through ingenious software developments.

Conversely, psychology and neurobiology will benefit to an extent closely related to how far Computer-based CNS researches behave as if they felt integrated within one or both of those fields. Psychologists and neurobiologists may especially gain increased appreciation of the value of computers for theorising about complex systems and for making sense of complex masses of data, while integration at a more fundamental level can be expected to follow. With the resulting growth in understanding of the human CNS, respect for it may, perhaps, grow to an extent that will reduce the ebullience characteristic of past predictions of AI possibilities.

In the meantime, the intended Bridge Activities within category B may well have been found increasingly disappointing as achievements from Building Robots of the more generalised types fail to reach their more grandiose aims. On the other hand, some robots designed primarily as computer models for comparison with experiments on how the human CNS performs linguistic or problem-solving tasks will become integrated with work in category C, while others aimed at practical tasks, related *eg* to engineering assembly, will become integrated in category A.

These processes are expected to bring about, at a slow but increasing rate, the fission of the field of AI research predicted at the beginning of this brief attempt at looking into the future. That attempt may now be concluded with the observation that such a broad-brush view, unspecific in matters of detail, is possibly all that can properly be attempted over time-spans as long as twenty-five years.

Note

1 "Understanding Natural Language" by Terry Winograd, MIT. Published in UK by Edinburgh University Press, 1972.

63

REVIEW OF "ARTIFICIAL INTELLIGENCE:

A General Survey"

John McCarthy

Source: *Artificial Intelligence* 5(3), 1974: 317–22.

Professor Lighthill of Cambridge University is a famous hydrodynamicist with a recent interest in applications to biology. His review of artificial intelligence was at the request of Brian Flowers, then head of the Science Research Council of Great Britain, the main funding body for British university scientific research. Its purpose was to help the Science Research Council decide requests for support of work in AI. Lighthill claims no previous acquaintance with the field, but refers to a large number of authors whose works he consulted, though not to any specific papers.

The *Lighthill Report* is organized around a classification of AI research into three categories:

Category A is *advanced automation* or *applications*, and he approves of it in principle. Included in A are some activities that are obviously applied but also activities like computer chess playing that are often done not for themselves but in order to study the structure of intelligent behavior.

Category C comprises studies of the *central nervous system* including computer modeling in support of both neurophysiology and psychology.

Category B is defined as "building robots" and "bridge" between the other categories. Lighthill defines a robot as a program or device built neither to serve a useful purpose nor to study the central nervous system, which obviously would exclude Unimates, etc. which are generally referred to as industrial robots. Emphasizing the bridge aspect of the definition, Lighthill states as obvious that work in category B is worthwhile only in so far as it contributes to the other categories.

If we take this categorization seriously, then most AI researchers lose intellectual contact with Lighthill immediately, because his three categories have no place for what is or should be our main scientific activity – *studying the structure of information and the structure of problem solving processes independently of applications and independently of its realization in animals or humans.* This study is based on the following ideas:

(1) Intellectual activity takes place in a world that has a certain physical and intellectual structure: Physical objects exist, move about, are created and destroyed. Actions that may be performed have effects that are partially known. Entities with goals have available to them certain information about this world. Some of this information may be built in, and some arises from observation, from communication, from reasoning, and by more or less complex processes of retrieval from information bases. Much of this structure is common to the intellectual position of animals, people, and machines which we may design, e.g. the effects of physical actions on material objects and also the information that may be obtained about these objects by vision. The general structure of the intellectual world is far from understood, and it is often quite difficult to decide how to represent effectively the information available about a quite limited domain of action even when we are quite willing to treat a particular problem in an ad hoc way.

(2) The processes of problem solving depend on the class of problems being solved more than on the solver. Thus playing chess seems to require look-ahead whether the apparatus is made of neurons or transistors. Isolation of the information relevant to a problem from the totality of previous experience is required whether the solver is man or machine, and so is the ability to divide a problem into weakly connected subproblems that can be thought about separately before the results are combined.

(3) Experiment is useful in determining what representations of information and what problem solving processes are needed to solve a given class of problems. We can illustrate this point by an example from the *Lighthill Report* which asserts (p. 15) that the heuristics of a chess program are embodied in the evaluation function. This is plausible and was assumed by the first writers of chess programs. Experiment showed, however, that the procedures that select what part of the move tree is examined are even more important, i.e. when the program errs it is usually because it didn't examine a line of play rather than because it mis-evaluated a final position. Modern chess programs concentrate on this and often have simpler evaluators than the earlier programs.

(4) The experimental domain should be chosen to test the adequacy of representations of information and of problem solving mechanisms. Thus chess has contributed much to the study of tree search; one Soviet computer scientist refers to chess as the *Drosophila* of artificial intelligence. I think there is much more to be learned from chess, because master level play will require more than just improving the present methods of searching trees. Namely, it will require the ability to identify, represent, and recognize the patterns of position and play that correspond to "chess ideas", the ability to

solve some abstractions of positions (e.g. how to make use of a passed pawn and a seventh rank rook jointly) and to apply the result to actual positions. It will probably also require the ability to analyze a problem into subproblems and combine the separate results. (This ability is certainly required for a successful *Go* program.)

Having ignored the possibility that AI has goals of its own, Lighthill goes on to document his claim that it has not contributed to applications or to psychology and physiology. He exaggerates a bit here, it seems worthwhile to spend some effort disputing his claims that AI has not contributed to these other subjects.

In my opinion, AI's contribution to practical applications has been significant but so far mostly peripheral to the central ideas and problems of AI. Thus the LISP language for symbolic computing was developed for AI use, but has had applications to symbolic computations in other areas, e.g. physics. Moreover, some ideas from LISP such as conditional expressions and recursive function definitions have been used in other programming languages. However, the ideas that have been applied elsewhere don't have a specifically AI character and might have been but weren't developed without AI in mind. Other examples include time-sharing, the first proposals for which had AI motivations and some techniques of picture processing that were first developed in AI laboratories and have been used elsewhere. Even the current work in automatic assembly using vision might have been developed without AI in mind. However, the Dendral work has always had a specifically AI character, and many of the recent developments in programming such as PLANNER and CONNIVER have an AI motivation.

AI's contributions to neurophysiology have been small and mostly of a negative character, i.e. showing that certain mechanisms that neurophysiologists propose are not well defined or inadequate to carry out the behavior they are supposed to account for. I have in mind Hebb's proposals in his book *The Organization of Behavior*. No-one today would believe that the gaps in those ideas could be filled without adding something much larger than the original work. Moreover, the last 20 years' experience in programming machines to learn and solve problems makes it implausible that cell assemblies *per se* would learn much without putting in some additional organization, and physiologists today would be unlikely to propose such a theory. However, merely showing that some things are unlikely to work is not a *positive* contribution. I think there will be more interaction between AI and neurophysiology as soon as the neurophysiologists are in a position to compare information processing models of higher level functions with physiological data. There is little contact at the nerve cell level, because, as Minsky showed in his PhD dissertation in 1954, almost any of the proposed models of the neuron is a universal computing element, so that there is no connection between the structure of the neuron and what higher level processes are possible.

On the other hand, the effects of artificial intelligence research on psychology have been larger as attested by various psychologists. First of all, psychologists have begun to use models in which complex internal data structures that cannot be observed directly are attributed to animals and people. Psychologists have come to use these models, because they exhibit behavior that cannot be exhibited by models conforming to the tenets of behaviorism which essentially allows only connections between externally observable variables. Information processing models in psychology have also induced dissatisfaction with psychoanalytic and related theories of emotional behavior. Namely, these information processing models of emotional states can yield predictions that can be compared with experiment or experience in a more definite way than can the vague models of psychoanalysis and its offspring.

Contributions of AI to psychology are further discussed in the paper *Some Comments on the Lighthill Report* by N. S. Sutherland which was included in the same book with the Lighthill report itself.

Systematic comment on the main section, entitled *Past Disappointments* is difficult because of the strange way the subject is divided up but here are some remarks:

(1) Automatic landing systems for airplanes are offered as a field in which conventional engineering techniques have been more successful than AI methods. Indeed, no-one would advocate applying the scene analysis or tree search techniques developed in AI research to automatic landing in the context in which automatic landing has been developed. Namely, radio signals are available to determine the precise position of the airplane in relation to a straight runway which is guaranteed clear of interfering objects. AI techniques would be necessary to make a system capable of landing on an unprepared dirt strip with no radio aids which had to be located and distinguished from roads visually and which might have cows or potholes or muddy places on it. The problem of automatically driving an automobile in an uncontrolled environment is even more difficult and will definitely require AI techniques, which, however, are not nearly ready for a full solution of such a difficult problem.

(2) Lighthill is disappointed that detailed knowledge of subject matter has to be put in if programs are to be successful in theorem proving, interpreting mass spectra, and game playing. He uses the word *heuristics* in a non-standard way for this. He misses the fact that there are great difficulties in finding ways of representing knowledge of the world in computer programs and much AI research and internal controversy are directed to this problem. Moreover, most AI researchers feel that more progress on this *representation problem* is essential before substantial progress can be made on the problem of automatic acquisition of knowledge. Of course, missing these particular points is a consequence of missing the existence of the AI problem as distinct from automation and study of the central nervous system.

(3) A further disappointment is that chess playing programs have only reached an "experienced amateur" level of play. Well, if programs can't do better than that by 1978, I shall lose a £250 bet and will be disappointed too though not extremely surprised. The present level of computer chess is based on the incorporation of certain intellectual mechanisms in the programs. Some improvement can be made by further refinement of the heuristics in the programs, but probably master level chess awaits the ability to put general configuration patterns into the programs in an easy and flexible way. I don't see how to set a date by which this problem must be solved in order to avoid disappointment in the field of artificial intelligence as a whole.

(4) Lighthill discusses the *combinatorial explosion* problem as though it were a relatively recent phenomenon that disappointed hopes that unguided theorem provers would be able to start from axioms representing knowledge about the world and solve difficult problems. In fact, the *combinatorial explosion* problem has been recognized in AI from the beginning, and the usual meaning of *heuristic* is a device for reducing this explosion. Regrettably, some people were briefly over-optimistic about what general purpose heuristics for theorem proving could do in problem solving.

Did we deserve it?

Lighthill has his shot at AI and missed, but this doesn't prove that everything in AI is ok. In my opinion, present AI research suffers from some major deficiencies apart from the fact that any scientists would achieve more if they were smarter and worked harder.

(1) Much work in AI has the "look ma, no hands" disease. Someone programs a computer to do something no computer has done before and writes a paper pointing out that the computer did it. The paper is not directed to the identification and study of intellectual mechanisms and often contains no coherent account of how the program works at all. As an example, consider that the SIGART Newsletter prints the scores of the games in the ACM Computer Chess Tournament just as though the programs were human players and their innards were inaccessible. We need to know why one program missed the right move in a position – what was it thinking about all that time? We also need an analysis of what class of positions the particular one belonged to and how a future program might recognize this class and play better.

(2) A second disease is to work only on theories that can be expressed mathematically in the present state of knowledge. Mathematicians are often attracted to the artificial intelligence problem by its intrinsic interest. Unfortunately for the mathematicians, however, many plausible mathematical theories with good theorems such as control theory or statistical decision theory have turned out to have little relevance to AI. Even worse, the applicability of statistical decision theory to discriminating among classes of

signals led to the mistaken identification of perception with discrimination rather than with description which so far has not led to much mathematics. More recently, however, problems of theorem proving and problems of representation have led to interesting mathematical problems in logic and mathematical theory of computation.

(3) Every now and then, some AI scientist gets an idea for a general scheme of intelligent behavior that can be applied to any problem provided the machine is given the specific knowledge that a human has about the domain. Examples of this have included the GPS formalism, a simple predicate calculus formalism, and more recently the PLANNER formalism and perhaps the current Carnegie-Mellon production formalism. In the first and third cases, the belief that any problem solving ability and knowledge could be fitted into the formalisms led to published predictions that computers would achieve certain levels of performance in certain time scales. If the inventors of the formalisms had been right about them, the goals might have been achieved, but regrettably they were mistaken. Such general purpose formalisms will be invented from time to time, and, most likely, one of them will eventually prove adequate. However, it would be a great relief to the rest of the workers in AI if the inventors of new general formalisms would express their hopes in a more guarded form than has sometimes been the case.

(4) At present, there does not exist a comprehensive general review of AI that discusses all the main approaches and achievements and issues. Most likely, this is not merely because the field doesn't have a first rate reviewer at present, but because the field is confused about what these approaches and achievements and issues are. The production of such a review will therefore be a major creative work and not merely a work of scholarship.

While it is far beyond the scope of this review to try to summarize what has been accomplished in AI since Turing's 1950 paper, here is a five sentence try: Many approaches have been explored and tentatively rejected including automaton models, random search, sequence extrapolation, and many others. Many heuristics have been developed for reducing various kinds of tree search; some of these are quite special to particular applications, but others are general. Much progress has been made in discovering how various kinds of information can be represented in the memory of a computer, but a fully general representation is not yet available. The problem of perception of speech and vision has been explored and recognition has been found feasible in many instances. A beginning has been made in understanding the semantics of natural language.

These accomplishments notwithstanding, I think that artificial intelligence research has so far been only moderately successful; its rate of solid progress is perhaps greater than most social sciences and less than many physical sciences. This is perhaps to be expected considering the difficulty of the problem.

Section 2.4: The Frame Problem

64

COGNITIVE WHEELS

The frame problem of AI

Daniel Dennett

Source: C. Hookway (ed.), *Minds, Machines & Evolution: Philosophical Studies*, Cambridge University Press, 1984, pp. 129–51.

Once upon a time there was a robot, named R1 by its creators. Its only task was to fend for itself. One day its designers arranged for it to learn that its spare battery, its precious energy supply, was locked in a room with a time bomb set to go off soon. R1 located the room, and the key to the door, and formulated a plan to rescue its battery. There was a wagon in the room, and the battery was on the wagon, and R1 hypothesized that a certain action which it called PULLOUT (WAGON, ROOM) would result in the battery being removed from the room. Straightway it acted, and did succeed in getting the battery out of the room before the bomb went off. Unfortunately, however, the bomb was also on the wagon. R1 *knew* that the bomb was on the wagon in the room, but didn't realize that pulling the wagon would bring the bomb out along with the battery. Poor R1 had missed that obvious implication of its planned act.

Back to the drawing board. "The solution is obvious", said the designers. "Our next robot must be made to recognize not just the intended implications of its acts, but also the implications about their side effects, by deducing these implications from the descriptions it uses in formulating its plans." They called their next model, the robot-deducer, R1D1. They placed R1D1 in much the same predicament that R1 had succumbed to, and as it too hit upon the idea of PULLOUT (WAGON, ROOM) it began, as designed, to consider the implications of such a course of action. It had just finished deducing that pulling the wagon out of the room would not change the color of the room's walls, and was embarking on a proof of the further implication that pulling the wagon out would cause its wheels to turn more revolutions than there were wheels on the wagon—when the bomb exploded.

Back to the drawing board. "We must teach it the difference between relevant implications and irrelevant implications", said the designers, "and teach it to ignore the irrelevant ones." So they developed a method of tagging implications as either relevant or irrelevant to the project at hand, and installed the method in their next model, the robot-relevant-deducer, or R2D1 for short. When they subjected R2D1 to the test that had so unequivocally selected its ancestors for extinction, they were surprised to see it sitting, Hamlet-like, outside the room containing the ticking bomb, the native hue of its resolution sicklied o'er with the pale cast of thought, as Shakespeare (and more recently Fodor) has aptly put it. "Do something!" they yelled at it. "I am", it retorted. "I'm busily ignoring some thousands of implications I have determined to be irrelevant. Just as soon as I find an irrelevant implication, I put it on the list of those I must ignore, and . . . " the bomb went off.

All these robots suffer from the *frame problem*.[1] If there is ever to be a robot with the fabled perspicacity and real-time adroitness of R2D2, robot-designers must solve the frame problem. It appears at first to be at best an annoying technical embarrassment in robotics, or merely a curious puzzle for the bemusement of people working in Artificial Intelligence (AI). I think, on the contrary, that it is a new, deep epistemological problem—accessible in principle but unnoticed by generations of philosophers—brought to light by the novel methods of AI, and still far from being solved. Many people in AI have come to have a similarly high regard for the seriousness of the frame problem. As one researcher has quipped, "We have given up the goal of designing an intelligent robot, and turned to the task of designing a gun that will destroy any intelligent robot that anyone else designs!"

I will try here to present an elementary, non-technical, philosophical introduction to the frame problem, and show why it is so interesting. I have no solution to offer, or even any original suggestions for where a solution might lie. It is hard enough, I have discovered, just to say clearly what the frame problem is—and is not. In fact, there is less than perfect agreement in usage within the AI research community. McCarthy and Hayes, who coined the term, use it to refer to a particular, narrowly conceived problem about representation that arises only for certain strategies for dealing with a broader problem about real-time planning systems. Others call this broader problem the frame problem—"the whole pudding", as Hayes has called it (personal correspondence)—and this may not be mere terminological sloppiness. If "solutions" to the narrowly conceived problem have the effect of driving a (deeper) difficulty into some other quarter of the broad problem, we might better reserve the title for this hard-to-corner difficulty. With apologies to McCarthy and Hayes for joining those who would appropriate their term, I am going to attempt an introduction to the whole pudding, calling *it* the frame problem. I will try in due course to describe the narrower version of the problem, "the frame problem proper" if you like, and show something of its relation to the broader problem.

Since the frame problem, whatever it is, is certainly not solved yet (and may be, in its current guises, insoluble), the ideological foes of AI such as Hubert Dreyfus and John Searle are tempted to compose obituaries for the field, citing the frame problem as the cause of death. In *What Computers Can't Do* (Dreyfus 1972), Dreyfus sought to show that AI was a fundamentally mistaken method for studying the mind, and in fact many of his somewhat impressionistic complaints about AI models and many of his declared insights into their intrinsic limitations can be seen to hover quite systematically in the neighborhood of the frame problem. Dreyfus never explicitly mentions the frame problem,[2] but is it perhaps the smoking pistol he was looking for but didn't *quite* know how to describe? Yes, I think AI can be seen to be holding a smoking pistol, but at least in its "whole pudding" guise it is everybody's problem, not just a problem for AI, which, like the good guy in many a mystery story, should be credited with a discovery, not accused of a crime.

One does not have to hope for a robot-filled future to be worried by the frame problem. It apparently arises from some very widely held and innocuous-*seeming* assumptions about the nature of intelligence, the truth of the most undoctrinaire brand of physicalism, and the conviction that it must be possible to explain how we think. (The dualist evades the frame problem—but only because dualism draws the veil of mystery and obfuscation over all the tough how-questions; as we shall see, the problem arises when one takes seriously the task of answering certain how-questions. Dualists inexcusably excuse themselves from the frame problem.)

One utterly central—if not defining—feature of an intelligent being is that it can "look before it leaps". Better, it can *think* before it leaps. Intelligence is (at least partly) a matter of using well what you know—but for what? For improving the fidelity of your expectations about what is going to happen next, for planning, for considering courses of action, for framing further hypotheses with the aim of increasing the knowledge you will use in the future, so that you can preserve yourself, by letting your hypotheses die in your stead (as Sir Karl Popper once put it). The stupid—as opposed to ignorant—being is the one who lights the match to peer into the fuel tank,[3] who saws off the limb he is sitting on, who locks his keys in his car and then spends the next hour wondering how on earth to get his family out of the car.

But when we think before we leap, *how do we do it*? The answer seems obvious: an intelligent being learns from experience, and then uses what it has learned to guide expectations in the future. Hume explained this in terms of habits of expectation, in effect. *But how do the habits work*? Hume had a hand-waving answer—associationism—to the effect that certain transition paths between ideas grew more likely-to-be-followed as they became well worn, but since it was not *Hume*'s job, surely, to explain in more detail the mechanics of these links, problems about how such paths could be put to good use—and not just turned into an impenetrable maze of untraversable alternatives—were not discovered.

Hume, like virtually all other philosophers and "mentalistic" psychologists, was unable to see the frame problem because he operated at what I call a purely semantic level, or a *phenomenological* level. At the phenomenological level, all the items in view are *individuated by their meanings*. Their meanings are, if you like, "given"—but this just means that the theorist helps himself to all the meanings he wants. In this way the semantic relation between one item and the next is typically plain to see, and one just assumes that the items behave as items with those meanings *ought* to behave. We can bring this out by concocting a Humean account of a bit of learning.

Suppose there are two children, both of whom initially tend to grab cookies from the jar without asking. One child is allowed to do this unmolested but the other is spanked each time she tries. What is the result? The second child learns not to go for the cookies. Why? Because she has had experience of cookie-reaching followed swiftly by spanking. What good does that do? Well, the *idea* of cookie-reaching becomes connected by a habit path to the idea of spanking, which in turn is connected to the idea of pain . . . *so of course* the child refrains. Why? Well, that's just the effect of that idea on that sort of circumstance. But why? Well, what else ought the idea of pain to do on such an occasion? Well, it might cause the child to pirouette on her left foot, or recite poetry or blink or recall her fifth birthday. But given what the idea of pain *means*, any of those effects would be absurd. True; now *how* can ideas be designed so that their effects are what they ought to be, given what they mean? Designing some internal things—an idea, let's call it—so that it behaves *vis-à-vis* its brethren as if it meant *cookie* or *pain* is the only way of endowing that thing with that meaning; it couldn't mean a thing if it didn't have those internal behavioral dispositions.

That is the mechanical question the philosophers left to some dimly imagined future researcher. Such a division of labor might have been all right, but it is turning out that most of the truly difficult and deep puzzles of learning and intelligence get kicked downstairs by this move. It is rather as if philosophers were to proclaim themselves expert explainers of the methods of a stage magician, and then, when we ask them to explain how the magician does the sawing-the-lady-in-half trick, they explain that it is really quite obvious: the magician doesn't really saw her in half; he simply makes it appear that he does. "But how does he do *that*?" we ask. "Not our department", say the philosophers—and some of them add, sonorously: "Explanation has to stop somewhere."[4]

When one operates at the purely phenomenological or semantic level, where does one get one's data, and how does theorizing proceed? The term "phenomenology" has traditionally been associated with an introspective method—an *examination* of what is presented or given to consciousness. A person's phenomenology just was by definition the contents of his or her consciousness. Although this has been the ideology all along, it has never been the practice. Locke, for instance, may have thought his "historical, plain method" was a method of unbiased self-observation, but in fact it was largely a matter of disguised aprioristic reasoning about what ideas and impressions *had to be* to do the jobs they "obviously" did.[5] The myth that each of us can observe our mental activities has prolonged the illusion that major progress could be made on the theory of thinking by simply reflecting carefully on our own cases. For some time now we have known better: we have conscious access to only the upper surface, as it were, of the multi-level system of information-processing that occurs in us. Nevertheless, the myth still claims its victims.

So the analogy of the stage magician is particularly apt. One is not likely to make much progress in figuring out *how* the tricks are done by simply sitting attentively in the audience and watching like a hawk. Too much is going on out of sight. Better to face the fact that one must either rummage around backstage or in the wings, hoping to disrupt the performance in telling ways; or, from one's armchair, think aprioristically about how the tricks *must* be done, given whatever is manifest about the constraints. The frame problem is then rather like the unsettling but familiar "discovery" that so far as armchair thought can determine, a certain trick we have just observed is flat impossible.

Here is an example of the trick. Making a midnight snack. How is it that I can get myself a midnight snack? What could be simpler? I suspect there is some leftover sliced turkey and mayonnaise in the fridge, and bread in the breadbox—and a bottle of beer in the fridge as well. I realize I can put these elements together, so I concoct a childishly simple plan: I'll just go and check out the fridge, get out the requisite materials, and make myself a sandwich, to be washed down with a beer. I'll need a knife, a plate, and a glass for the beer. I forthwith put the plan into action and it works! Big deal.

Now of course I couldn't do this without knowing a good deal—about bread, spreading mayonnaise, opening the fridge, the friction and inertia that will keep the turkey between the bread slices and the bread on the plate as I carry the plate over to the table beside my easy chair. I also need to know about how to get the beer out of the bottle into the glass.[6] Thanks to my previous accumulation of experience in the world, fortunately, I am equipped with all this worldly knowledge. Of course some of the knowledge I need *might* be innate. For instance, one trivial thing I have to know is that when the beer gets into the glass it is no longer in the bottle, and that if I'm holding the mayonnaise jar in my left hand I cannot also be spreading the mayonnaise with the knife in my left hand. Perhaps these are straightforward implications—instantiations—of some more fundamental things that I was in effect *born knowing* such as, perhaps, the fact that if something is in one location it isn't also in another, different location; or the fact that two things can't be in the same place at the same time; or the fact that situations change as the result of actions. It is hard to imagine just how one could learn these facts from experience.

Such utterly banal facts escape our notice as we act and plan, and it is not surprising that philosophers, thinking phenomenologically *but introspectively*, should have overlooked them. But if one turns one's back on introspection, and just thinks "hetero-phenomenologically"[7] about the purely informational demands of the task—what *must* be known by any entity that can perform this task—these banal bits of knowledge rise to our attention. We can easily satisfy ourselves that no agent that did not *in some sense* have the benefit of the information (that beer in the bottle is not in the glass, etc.) could perform such a simple task. It is one of the chief methodological beauties of AI that it makes one be a phenomenologist in this improved way. As a hetero-phenomenologist, one reasons about what the agent must "know" or figure out *unconsciously or consciously* in order to perform in various ways.

The reason AI forces the banal information to the surface is that the tasks set by AI start at zero: the computer to be programmed to simulate the agent (or the brain of the robot, if we are actually going to operate in the real, non-simulated world), initially knows nothing at all "about the world". The computer is the fabled *tabula rasa* on which every required item must somehow be impressed, either by the programmer at the outset or via subsequent "learning" by the system.

We can all agree, today, that there could be no learning at all by an entity that faced the world at birth as a *tabula rasa*, but the dividing line between what is innate and what develops maturationally and what is actually learned is of less theoretical importance than one might have thought. While some information has to be innate, there is hardly any particular item that must be: an appreciation of *modus ponens*, perhaps, and the law of the excluded middle, and some sense of causality. And while some things we know must be learned—e.g., that Thanksgiving falls on a Thursday, or that refrigerators keep food fresh—many other "very empirical" things could in principle be innately known—e.g., that smiles mean happiness, or that unsuspended, unsupported things fall. (There is some evidence, in fact, that there is an innate bias in favor of perceiving things to fall with gravitational acceleration).[8]

Taking advantage of this advance in theoretical understanding (if that is what it is), people in AI can frankly ignore the problem of learning (it seems) and take the shortcut of *installing* all that an agent has to "know" to solve a problem. After all, if God made Adam as an adult who could presumably solve the midnight snack problem *ab initio*, AI agent-creators can *in principle* make an "adult" agent who is equipped with worldly knowledge *as if* it had laboriously learned all the things it needs to know. This may of course be a dangerous shortcut.

The installation problem is then the problem of installing in one way or another all the information needed by an agent to plan in a changing world. It is a difficult problem because the information must be installed in a usable format. The problem can be broken down initially into the semantic problem and the syntactic problem. The semantic problem—called by Allen Newell the problem at the "knowledge level" (Newell, 1982)—is the problem of just what information (on what topics, to what effect) must be installed. The syntactic problem is what system, format, structure, or mechanism to use to put that information in.[9]

The division is clearly seen in the example of the midnight snack problem. I *listed* a few of the very many humdrum facts one needs to know to solve the snack problem, but I didn't mean to suggest that those facts are stored in me—or in any agent—piecemeal, in the form of a long list of sentences explicitly declaring each of these facts for the benefit of the agent. That is of course one possibility, officially: it is a preposterously extreme version of the "language of thought" theory of mental representation, with each distinguishable "proposition" separately inscribed in the system. No one subscribes to such a view; even an encyclopedia achieves important economies of explicit expression via its organization, and a walking encyclopedia—not a bad caricature of the envisaged AI agent—must use different systemic principles to achieve efficient representation and access. We know trillions of things; we know that mayonnaise doesn't dissolve knives on contact, that a slice of bread is smaller than Mount Everest, that opening the refrigerator doesn't cause a nuclear holocaust in the kitchen.

There must be in us—and in any intelligent agent—some highly efficient, partly generative or productive system of representing—storing for use—all the information needed. Somehow, then, we must store many "facts" at once—where facts are presumed to line up more or less one-to-one with non-synonymous declarative sentences. Moreover, we cannot realistically hope for what one might call a Spinozistic solution—a *small* set of axioms and definitions from which all the rest of our knowledge is deducible on demand—since it is clear that there simply are no entailment relations between vast numbers of these facts. (When we rely, as we must, on experience to tell us how the world is, experience tells us things that do not at all follow from what we have heretofore known.)

The demand for an efficient system of information storage is in part a space limitation, since our brains are not all that large, but more importantly it is a time limitation, for stored information that is not reliably accessible for use in the short real-time spans typically available to agents in the world is of no use at all. A creature that can solve any problem given enough time—say a million years—is not in fact intelligent at all. We live in a time-pressured world and must be able to think quickly before we leap. (One doesn't have to view this as an *a priori* condition on intelligence. One can simply note that we do in fact think quickly, so there is an empirical question about how we manage to do it.)

The task facing the AI researcher appears to be designing a system that can plan by using well-selected elements from its store of knowledge about the world it operates in. "Introspection" on how *we* plan yields the following description of a process: one envisages a certain situation (often very sketchily); one then imagines performing a certain act in that situation; one then "sees" what the likely outcome of that envisaged act in that situation would be, and evaluates it. What happens backstage, as it were, to permit this "seeing" (and render it as reliable as it is) is utterly inaccessible to introspection.

On relatively rare occasions we all experience such bouts of thought, unfolding in consciousness at the deliberate speed of pondering. These are occasions in which we are faced with some novel and relatively difficult problem, such as: How can I get the piano upstairs? or Is there any way to electrify the chandelier without cutting through the plaster ceiling? It would be quite odd to find that one had to think *that* way (consciously and slowly) in order to solve the midnight snack problem. But the suggestion is that even the trivial problems of planning and bodily guidance that are beneath our notice (though in some sense we "face" them) are solved by similar processes. Why? I don't *observe* myself planning in such situations. This fact suffices to convince the traditional, introspective phenomenologist that no such planning is going on.[10] The hetero-phenomenologist, on the other hand, reasons that *one way or another* information about the objects in the situation, and about the intended effects and side effects of the candidate actions, *must* be used (considered, attended to, applied, appreciated). Why? Because otherwise the "smart" behavior would be sheer luck or magic. (Do we have any model for how such unconscious information-appreciation might be accomplished? The only model we have *so far* is *conscious*, deliberate information-appreciation. Perhaps, AI suggests, this is a good model. If it isn't, we are all utterly in the dark for the time being.)

We assure ourselves of the intelligence of an agent by considering counterfactuals: if I had been told that the turkey was poisoned, or the beer explosive, or the plate dirty, or the knife too fragile to spread mayonnaise, would I have acted as I did? If I were a stupid "automaton"—or like the *Sphex* wasp who "mindlessly" repeats her stereotyped burrow-checking routine till she drops[11]—I might infelicitously "go through the motions" of making a midnight snack oblivious to the recalcitrant features of the environment.[12] But in fact, my midnight-snack-making behavior is multifariously sensitive to current and background information about the situation. The only way it could be so sensitive—runs the tacit hetero-phenomenological reasoning—is for it to examine, or test for, the information in question. This information manipulation may be unconscious and swift, and it need not (it *better* not) consist of hundreds or thousands of *seriatim* testing procedures, but it must occur somehow, and its benefits must appear in time to help me as I commit myself to action.

I may of course have a midnight snack routine, developed over the years, in which case I can partly rely on it to pilot my actions. Such a complicated "habit" would have to be under the control of a mechanism of some complexity, since even a rigid sequence of steps would involve periodic testing to ensure that subgoals had been satisfied. And even if I am an infrequent snacker, I no doubt have routines for mayonnaise-spreading, sandwich-making, and getting-something-out-of-the-fridge, from which I could compose my somewhat novel activity. Would such ensembles of routines, nicely integrated, suffice to solve the frame problem for me, at least in my more "mindless" endeavors? That is an open question to which I will return below.

It is important in any case to acknowledge at the outset, and remind oneself frequently, that even very intelligent people do make mistakes; we are not only not infallible planners; we are quite prone to overlooking large and retrospectively obvious flaws in our plans. This foible manifests itself in the familiar case of "force of habit" errors (in which our stereotypical routines reveal themselves to be surprisingly insensitive to some portentous environmental changes while surprisingly sensitive to others). The same weakness also appears on occasion in cases where we have consciously deliberated with some care. How often have you embarked on a project of the piano-moving variety—in which you've thought through or even "walked through" the whole operation in advance—only to discover that you must backtrack or abandon the project when some perfectly foreseeable but unforeseen obstacle or unintended side effect loomed? If we smart folk seldom actually paint ourselves into corners, it may be not because we plan ahead so well as that we supplement our sloppy planning powers with a combination of recollected lore (about fools who paint themselves into corners, for instance) and frequent progress checks as we proceed. Even so, we must know enough to call up the right lore at the right time, and to recognize impending problems as such.

To summarize: we have been led by fairly obvious and compelling considerations to the conclusion that an intelligent agent must engage in swift information-sensitive "planning" which has the effect of producing reliable but not foolproof expectations of the effects of its actions. That these expectations are normally in force in intelligent creatures is testified to by the startled reaction they exhibit when their expectations are thwarted. This suggests a graphic way of characterizing the minimal goal that can spawn the frame problem: we want a midnight-snack-making robot to be "surprised" by the trick plate, the unspreadable concrete mayonnaise, the fact that we've glued the beer glass to the shelf. To be surprised you have to have expected something else, and in order to have expected the right something else, you have to have *and use* a lot of information about the things in the world.[13]

The central role of expectation has led some to conclude that the frame problem is not a new problem at all, and has nothing particularly to do with planning actions. It is, they think, simply the problem of having good expectations about any future events, whether they are one's own actions, the actions of another agent, or the mere happenings of nature. That is the problem of induction—noted by Hume and intensified by Goodman (Goodman 1965), but still not solved to anyone's satisfaction. We know today that the problem of induction is a nasty one indeed. Theories of subjective probability and belief fixation have not stabilized in reflective equilibrium, so it is fair to say that no one has a good, principled answer to the general question: given that I believe all *this* (have all this evidence), what *ought* I to believe as well (about the future, or about unexamined parts of the world)?

The reduction of one unsolved problem to another is some sort of progress, unsatisfying though it may be, but it is not an option in this case. The frame problem is not the problem of induction in disguise. For suppose the problem of induction were solved. Suppose—perhaps miraculously—that our agent has solved all its induction problems or had them solved by fiat; it believes, then, all the right generalizations from its evidence, and associates with all of them the appropriate probabilities and conditional probabilities. This agent, *ex hypothesi*, believes just what it ought to believe about all empirical matters in its ken, including the probabilities of future events. It might still have a bad case of the frame problem, for that problem concerns how to represent (so it can be *used*) all that hard-won empirical information—a problem that arises independently of the truth value, probability, warranted assertability, or subjective certainty of any of it. Even if you have excellent *knowledge* (and not mere belief) about the changing world, how can this knowledge be represented so that it can be efficaciously brought to bear?

Recall poor R1D1, and suppose for the sake of argument that it had perfect empirical knowledge of the probabilities of all the effects of all its actions that would be detectable by it. Thus it believes that with probability 0.7864, executing PULLOUT (WAGON, ROOM) will cause the wagon wheels to make an audible noise; and with probability 0.5, the door to the room will open in rather than out; and with probability 0.999996, there will be no live elephants in the room, and with probability 0.997 the bomb will remain on the wagon when it is moved. How is R1D1 to find this last, relevant needle in its haystack of empirical knowledge? A walking encyclopedia will walk over a cliff, for all its knowledge of cliffs and the effects of gravity, unless it is designed in such a fashion that it can find the right bits of knowledge at the right times, so it can plan its engagements with the real world.

The earliest work on planning systems in AI took a deductive approach. Inspired by the development of Robinson's methods of resolution theorem proving, designers hoped to represent all the system's "world knowledge" explicitly as axioms, and use ordinary logic—the predicate calculus—to deduce the effects of actions. Envisaging a certain situation S was modeled by having the system entertain a set of axioms describing the situation. Added to this were background axioms (the so-called "frame axioms" that give the frame problem its name) which describe general conditions and the general effects of every action type defined for the system. To this set of axioms the system would apply an action—by postulating the occurrence of some action A in situation S—and then deduce the effect of A in S, producing a description of the outcome situation S'. While all this logical deduction looks like nothing at all in our conscious experience, research on the deductive approach could proceed on either or both of two enabling assumptions: the methodological assumption that psychological realism was a gratuitous bonus, not a goal, of "pure" AI, or the substantive (if still vague) assumption that the deductive processes described would somehow model the backstage processes beyond conscious access. In other words, either we don't do our thinking deductively in the predicate calculus but a robot might; or we do (unconsciously) think deductively in the predicate calculus. Quite aside from doubts about its psychological realism, however, the deductive approach has not been made to work—the proof of the pudding for any robot—except for deliberately trivialized cases.

Consider some typical frame axioms associated with the action type: *move x onto y.*

(1) If $z \neq x$ and I move x onto y, then if z was on w before, then z is on w after.
(2) If x is blue before, and I move x onto y, then x is blue after.

Note that (2), about being blue, is just one example of the many boring "no-change" axioms we have to associate with this action type. Worse still, note that a cousin of (2), also about being blue, would have to be associated with every other action-type—with *pick up x* and with *give x to y*, for instance. One cannot save this mindless repetition by postulating once and for all something like

(3) If anything is blue, it stays blue,

for that is false, and in particular we will want to leave room for the introduction of such action types as *paint x red*. Since virtually any aspect of a situation can change under some circumstance, this method requires introducing for each aspect (each predication in the description of S) an axiom to handle whether that aspect changes for each action type.

This representational profligacy quickly gets out of hand, but for some "toy" problems in AI, the frame problem can be overpowered to some extent by a mixture of the toyness of the environment and brute force. The early version of SHAKEY, the robot at S.R.I., operated in such a simplified and sterile world, with so few aspects it could worry about that it could get away with an exhaustive consideration of frame axioms.[14]

Attempts to circumvent this explosion of axioms began with the proposal that the system operate on the tacit assumption that nothing changes in a situation but what is explicitly asserted to change in the definition of the applied action (Fikes & Nilsson 1971). The problem here is that, as Garrett Hardin once noted, you can't do just one thing. This was RI's problem, when it failed to notice that it would pull the bomb out with the wagon. In the explicit representation (a few pages back) of my midnight snack solution, I mentioned carrying the plate over to the table. On this proposal, my model of S' would leave the turkey back in the kitchen, for I didn't explicitly say the turkey would come along with the plate. One can of course patch up the definition of "bring" or "plate" to handle just this problem, but only at the cost of creating others. (Will a few more patches tame the problem? At what point should one abandon patches and seek an altogether new approach? Such are the methodological uncertainties regularly encountered in this field, and of course no one can responsibly claim in advance to have a good rule for dealing with them. Premature counsels of despair or calls for revolution are as clearly to be shunned as the dogged pursuit of hopeless avenues; small wonder the field is contentious.)

While one cannot get away with the tactic of supposing that one can do just one thing, it remains true that very little of what could (logically) happen in any situation does happen. Is there some way of fallibly marking the likely area of important side effects, and assuming the rest of the situation to stay unchanged? Here is where relevance tests seem like a good idea, and they may well be, but not within the deductive approach. As Minsky notes:

> Even if we formulate relevancy restrictions, logistic systems have a problem using them. In any logistic system, all the axioms are necessarily "permissive"—they all help to permit new inferences to be drawn. Each added axiom means more theorems; none can disappear. There simply is no direct way to add information to tell such a system about kinds of conclusions that should *not* be drawn! . . . If we try to change this by adding axioms about relevancy, we still produce all the unwanted theorems, plus annoying statements about their irrelevancy. (Minsky 1981: 125)

What is needed is a system that genuinely *ignores* most of what it knows, and operates with a well-chosen portion of its knowledge at any moment. Well-chosen, but not chosen by exhaustive consideration. How, though, can you give a system *rules* for ignoring—or better, since explicit rule-following is not the problem, how can you design a system that reliably ignores what it ought to ignore under a wide variety of different circumstances in a complex action environment?

John McCarthy calls this the qualification problem, and vividly illustrates it via the famous puzzle of the missionaries and the cannibals.

> Three missionaries and three cannibals come to a river. A rowboat that seats two is available. If the cannibals ever outnumber the missionaries on either bank of the river, the missionaries will be eaten. How shall they cross the river?
>
> Obviously the puzzler is expected to devise a strategy of rowing the boat back and forth that gets them all across and avoids disaster . . .
>
> Imagine giving someone the problem, and after he puzzles for awhile, he suggests going upstream half a mile and crossing on a bridge. "What bridge?" you say. "No bridge is mentioned in the statement of the problem." And this dunce replies, "Well, they don't say there isn't a bridge." You look at the English and even at the translation of the English into first order logic, and you must admit that "they don't say" there is no bridge. So you modify the problem to exclude bridges and pose it again, and the dunce proposes a helicopter, and after you exclude that, he proposes a winged horse or that the others hang onto the outside of the boat while two row.
>
> You now see that while a dunce, he is an inventive dunce. Despairing of getting him to accept the problem in the proper puzzler's spirit, you tell him the solution. To your further annoyance, he attacks your solution on the grounds that the boat might have a leak or lack oars. After you rectify that omission from the statement of the problem, he suggests that a sea monster may swim up the river and may swallow the boat. Again you are frustrated, and you look for a mode of reasoning that will settle his hash once and for all. (McCarthy 1980: 29–30)

What a normal, intelligent human being does in such a situation is to engage in some form of *non-monotonic inference*. In a classical, monotonic logical system, *adding* premises never *diminishes* what can be proved from the premises. As Minsky noted, the axioms are essentially permissive, and once a theorem is permitted, adding more axioms will never invalidate the proofs of earlier theorems. But when we think about a puzzle or a real life problem, we can achieve a solution (and even prove that it is a solution, or even the only solution to *that* problem), and then discover our solution invalidated by the addition of a new element to the posing of the problem; e.g., "I forgot to tell you—there are no oars" or "By the way, there's a perfectly good bridge upstream."

What such late additions show us is that, contrary to our assumption, other things weren't equal. We had been reasoning with the aid of a *ceteris paribus* assumption, and now our reasoning has just been jeopardized by the discovery that something "abnormal" is the case. (Note, by the way, that the abnormality in question is a much subtler notion than anything anyone has yet squeezed out of probability theory. As McCarthy notes, "The whole situation involving cannibals with the postulated properties cannot be regarded as having a probability, so it is hard to take seriously the conditional probability of a bridge given the hypothesis" (*ibid.*).)

The beauty of a *ceteris paribus* clause in a bit of reasoning is that one does not have to say exactly what it means. "What do you mean, 'other things being equal'? Exactly which arrangements of which other things count as being equal?" If one had to answer such a question, invoking the *ceteris paribus* clause would be pointless, for it is precisely in order to evade that task that one uses it. If one could answer that question, one wouldn't need to invoke the clause in the first place. One way of viewing the frame problem, then, is as the attempt to get a computer to avail itself of this distinctively human style of mental operation. There are several quite different approaches to non-monotonic inference being pursued in AI today. They have in common only the goal of capturing the human talent for *ignoring* what should be ignored, while staying alert to relevant recalcitrance when it occurs.

One family of approaches, typified by the work of Marvin Minsky and Roger Schank (Minsky 1981; Schank & Abelson 1977), gets its ignoring-power from the attention-focussing power of stereotypes. The inspiring insight here is the idea that all of life's experiences, for all their variety, boil down to variations on a manageable number of stereotypic themes, paradigmatic scenarios—"frames" in Minsky's terms, "scripts" in Schank's.

An artificial agent with a well-stocked compendium of frames or scripts, appropriately linked to each other and to the impingements of the world via its perceptual organs, would face the world with an elaborate system of what might be called habits of attention and benign tendencies to leap to particular sorts of conclusions in particular sorts of circumstances. It would "automatically" pay attention to certain features in certain environments and assume that certain unexamined normal features of those environments were present. Concomitantly, it would be differentially alert to relevant divergences from the stereotypes it would always begin by "expecting".

Simulations of fragments of such an agent's encounters with its world reveal that in many situations it behaves quite felicitously and apparently naturally, and it is hard to say, of course, what the limits of this approach are. But there are strong grounds for skepticism. Most obviously, while such systems perform creditably when the world co-operates with their stereotypes, and even with *anticipated* variations on them, when their worlds turn perverse, such systems typically cannot recover gracefully from the misanalyses they are led into. In fact, their behavior *in extremis* looks for all the world like the preposterously counterproductive activities of insects betrayed by their rigid tropisms and other genetically hard-wired behavioral routines.

When these embarrassing misadventures occur, the system designer can improve the design by adding provisions to deal with the particular cases. It is important to note that in these cases, the system does not redesign itself (or learn) but rather must wait for an external designer to select an improved design. This process of redesign recapitulates the process of natural selection in some regards; it favors minimal, piecemeal, *ad hoc* redesign which is tantamount to a wager on the likelihood of patterns in future events. So in some regards it is faithful to biological themes.[15] Nevertheless, until such a system is given a considerable capacity to learn from its errors without designer intervention, it will continue to respond in insectlike ways, and such behavior is profoundly unrealistic as a model of human reactivity to daily life. The shortcuts and cheap methods provided by a reliance on stereotypes are evident enough in human ways of thought, but it is also evident that we have a deeper understanding to fall back on when our shortcuts don't avail, and building some measure of this deeper understanding into a system appears to be a necessary condition of getting it to learn swiftly and gracefully.

In effect, the script or frame approach is an attempt to *pre-solve* the frame problems the particular agent is likely to encounter. While insects do seem saddled with such control systems, people, even when they do appear to be relying on stereotypes, have back-up systems of thought that can deal more powerfully with problems that arise. Moreover, when people do avail themselves of stereotypes, they are at least relying on stereotypes of their own devising, and to date no one has been able to present any workable ideas about how a person's frame-making or script-writing machinery might be guided by its previous experience.

Several different sophisticated attempts to provide the representational framework for this deeper understanding have emerged from the deductive tradition in recent years. Drew McDermott and Jon Doyle have developed a "non-monotonic logic" (1980), Ray Reiter has a "logic for default reasoning" (1980), and John McCarthy has developed a system of "circumscription", a formalized "rule of conjecture that can be used by a person or program for 'jumping to conclusions'" (1980). None of these is, or is claimed to be, a complete solution to the problem of *ceteris paribus* reasoning, but they might be components of such a solution. More recently, McDermott has offered a "temporal logic for reasoning about processes and plans" (McDermott 1982). I will not attempt to assay the formal strengths and weaknesses of these approaches. Instead I will concentrate on another worry. From one point of view, non-monotonic or default logic, circumscription, and temporal logic all appear to be radical improvements to the mindless and clanking deductive approach, but from a slightly different perspective they appear to be more of the same, and at least as unrealistic as frameworks for psychological models.

They appear in the former guise to be a step towards greater psychological realism, for they take seriously, and attempt to represent, the phenomenologically salient phenomenon of common sense *ceteris paribus* "jumping to conclusions" reasoning. But do they really succeed in offering any plausible suggestions about how the backstage implementation of that conscious thinking is accomplished *in people*? Even if on some glorious future day a robot with debugged circumscription methods maneuvered well in a non-toy environment, would there be much likelihood that its constituent processes, *described at levels below the phenomenological*, would bear informative relations to the unknown lower-level backstage processes in human beings? To bring out better what my worry is, I want to introduce the concept of a *cognitive wheel*.

We can understand what a cognitive wheel might be by reminding ourselves first about ordinary wheels. Wheels are wonderful, elegant triumphs of technology. The traditional veneration of the mythic inventor of the wheel is entirely justified. But if wheels are so wonderful, why are there no animals with wheels? Why are no wheels to be found (functioning as wheels) in nature? First, the presumption of that question must be qualified. A few years ago the astonishing discovery was made of several microscopic beasties (some bacteria and some unicellular eukaryotes) that have wheels of sorts. Their propulsive tails, long thought to be flexible flagella, turn out to be more or less rigid corkscrews, which rotate continuously, propelled by microscopic motors of sorts, complete with main bearings.[16] Better known, if less interesting for obvious reasons, are the tumbleweeds. So it is not quite true that there are no wheels (or wheeliform designs) in nature.

Still, macroscopic wheels—reptilian or mammalian or avian wheels—are not to be found. Why not? They would seem to be wonderful retractable landing gear for some birds, for instance. Once the question is posed, plausible reasons rush in to explain their absence. Most important, probably, are the considerations about the topological properties of the axle/bearing boundary that make the transmission of material or energy across it particularly difficult. How could the life-support traffic arteries of a living system maintain integrity across this boundary? But once that problem is posed, solutions suggest themselves; suppose the living wheel grows to mature form in a non-rotating, non-functional form, and is then hardened and sloughed off, like antlers or an outgrown shell, but not completely off: it then rotates freely on a lubricated fixed axle. Possible? It's hard to say. Useful? Also hard to say, especially since such a wheel would have to be free-wheeling. This is an interesting speculative exercise, but certainly not one that should inspire us to draw categorical, *a priori* conclusions. It would be foolhardy to declare wheels biologically impossible, but at the same time we can appreciate that they are at least very distant and unlikely solutions to *natural* problems of design.

Now a cognitive wheel is simply any design proposal in cognitive theory (at any level from the purest semantic level to the most concrete level of "wiring diagrams" of the neurons) that is profoundly unbiological, however wizardly and elegant it is as a bit of technology.

Clearly this is a vaguely defined concept, useful only as a rhetorical abbreviation, as a gesture in the direction of real difficulties to be spelled out carefully. "Beware of postulating cognitive wheels" masquerades as good advice to the cognitive scientist, while courting vacuity as a maxim to follow.[17] It occupies the same rhetorical position as the stockbroker's maxim: buy low and sell high. Still, the term is a good theme-fixer for discussion.

Many critics of AI have the conviction that *any* AI system is and must be nothing but a gearbox of cognitive wheels. This could of course turn out to be true, but the usual reason for believing it is based on a misunderstanding of the methodological assumptions of the field. When an AI model of some cognitive phenomenon is proposed, the model is describable at many different levels, from the most global, phenomenological level at which the behavior is described (with some presumptuousness) in ordinary mentalistic terms, down through various levels of implementation all the way to the level of program code—and even further down, to the level of fundamental hardware operations if anyone cares. No one supposes that the model maps onto the processes of psychology and biology *all the way down*. The claim is only that for some high level or levels of description below the phenomenological level (which merely *sets* the problem) there is a mapping of model features onto what is being modeled: the cognitive processes in living creatures, human or otherwise. It is understood that all the implementation details below the level of intended modelling will consist, no doubt, of cognitive wheels—bits of unbiological computer activity mimicking the gross effects of cognitive sub-components by using methods utterly unlike the methods still to be discovered in the brain. Someone who failed to appreciate that a model composed microscopically of cognitive wheels could still achieve a fruitful isomorphism with biological or psychological processes at a higher level of aggregation would suppose there were good *a priori* reasons for generalized skepticism about AI.

But allowing for the possibility of valuable intermediate levels of modelling is not ensuring their existence. In a particular instance a model might descend directly from a phenomenologically recognizable level of psychological description to a cognitive wheels implementation without shedding any light at all on how we human beings manage to enjoy that phenomenology. I *suspect* that all current proposals in the field for dealing with the frame problem have that shortcoming. Perhaps one should dismiss the previous sentence as mere autobiography. I find it hard to imagine (for what that is worth) that any of the *procedural details* of the mechanization of McCarthy's circumscriptions, for instance, would have suitable counterparts in the backstage story yet to be told about how human commonsense reasoning is accomplished. If these procedural details lack "psychological reality" then there is nothing left in the proposal that might model psychological processes except the phenomenological-level description in terms of jumping to conclusions, ignoring and the like—and we already know we do that.

There is an alternative defense of such theoretical explorations, however, and I think it is to be taken seriously. One can claim (and I take McCarthy to claim) that while formalizing commonsense reasoning in his fashion would not tell us anything *directly* about psychological processes of reasoning, it would clarify, sharpen, systematize the purely semantic-level characterization of the demands on any such implementation, biological or not. Once one has taken the giant step forward of taking information-processing seriously as a real process in space and time, one can then take a small step back and explore the implications of that advance at a very abstract level. Even at this very formal level, the power of circumscription and the other versions of non-monotonic reasoning remains an open but eminently explorable question.[18]

Some have thought that the key to a more realistic solution to the frame problem (and indeed, in all likelihood, to any solution at all) must require a complete rethinking of the semantic-level setting, prior to concern with syntactic-level implementation. The more or less standard array of predicates and relations chosen to fill out the predicate-calculus format when representing the "propositions believed" may embody a fundamentally inappropriate parsing of nature for this task. Typically, the interpretation of the formulae in these systems breaks the world down along the familiar lines of objects with properties at times and places. Knowledge of situations and events in the world is represented by what might be called sequences of verbal snapshots. State S, constitutively described by a list of sentences true at time t asserting various n-adic predicates true of various particulars, gives way to state S', a similar list of sentences true at t'. Would it perhaps be better to reconceive of the world of planning in terms of histories and processes?[19] Instead of trying to model the capacity to *keep track of things* in terms of principles for passing through temporal cross-sections of knowledge expressed in terms of terms (*names* for *things*, in essence) and predicates, perhaps we could model keeping track of things more directly, and let all the cross-sectional information about what is deemed true moment by moment be merely implicit (and hard to extract—as it is for us) from the format. These are tempting suggestions, but so far as I know they are still in the realm of handwaving.[20]

Another, perhaps related, handwaving theme is that the current difficulties with the frame problem stem from the conceptual scheme engendered by the serial-processing von Neumann architecture of the computers used to date in AI. As large, fast parallel processors are developed, they will bring in their wake huge conceptual innovations which are now of course only dimly imaginable. Since brains are surely massive parallel processors, it is tempting to suppose that the concepts engendered by such new hardware will be more readily adaptable for realistic psychological modelling. But who can say? For the time being, most of the optimistic claims about the powers of parallel processing belong in the same camp with the facile observations often encountered in the work of neuroscientists, who postulate marvelous cognitive powers for various portions of the nervous system without a clue of how they are realized.[21]

Filling in the details of the gap between the phenomenological magic show and the well-understood powers of small tracts of brain tissue is the immense research task that lies in the future for theorists of every persuasion. But before the problems can be solved they must be encountered, and to encounter the problems one must step resolutely into the gap and ask how-questions. What philosophers (and everyone else) have always known is that people—and no doubt all intelligent agents—can engage in swift, sensitive, risky-but-valuable *ceteris paribus* reasoning. How do we do it? AI may not yet have a good answer, but at least it has encountered the question.[22]

Notes

1 The problem is introduced by John McCarthy and Patrick Hayes in their 1969 paper. The task in which the problem arises was first formulated in McCarthy 1960. I am grateful to John McCarthy, Pat Hayes, Bob Moore, Zenon Pylyshyn, John Haugeland and Bo Dahlbom for the many hours they have spent trying to make me understand the frame problem. It is not their fault that so much of their instruction has still not taken.

  I have also benefited greatly from reading an unpublished paper, "Modelling Change—the Frame Problem", by Lars-Erik Janlert, Institute of Information Processing, University of Umea, Sweden. It is to be hoped that a subsequent version of that paper will soon find its way into print, since it is an invaluable *vademecum* for any neophyte, in addition to advancing several novel themes.

2 Dreyfus mentions McCarthy 1960: 213–14, but the theme of his discussion there is that McCarthy ignores the difference between a *physical state* description and a *situation* description, a theme that might be succinctly summarized: a house is not a home.

  Similarly, he mentions *ceteris paribus* assumptions (in the Introduction to the Revised Edition, pp. 56ff.), but only in announcing his allegiance to Wittgenstein's idea that "whenever human behavior is analyzed in terms of rules, these rules must always contain a *ceteris paribus* condition . . . " But this, even if true, misses the deeper point: the need for something like *ceteris paribus* assumptions confronts Robinson Crusoe just as ineluctably as it confronts any protagonist who finds himself in a situation involving human culture. The point is not, it seems, restricted to *Geisteswissenschaft* (as it is usually conceived); the "intelligent" robot on an (otherwise?) uninhabited but hostile planet faces the frame problem as soon as it commences to plan its days.

3 The example is from an important discussion of rationality by Christopher Cherniak, in "Rationality and the Structure of Memory", forthcoming in *Synthèse*.

4 Note that on this unflattering portrayal, the philosophers might still be doing *some* valuable work; think of the wild goose chases one might avert for some investigator who had rashly concluded that the magician really did saw the lady in half and then miraculously reunite her. People have jumped to such silly conclusions, after all; many philosophers have done so, for instance.

5 See my 1982a, commentary on Goodman 1982.

6 This knowledge of physics is not what one learns in school, but in one's crib. See Hayes 1978, 1979.

7 For elaborations of hetero-phenomenology, see Dennett 1978, chapter 10, "Two Approaches to Mental Images", and Dennett 1982b. See also Dennett 1982c.

8 Gunnar Johannsen has shown that animated films of "falling" objects in which the moving spots drop with the normal acceleration of gravity are unmistakeably distinguished by the casual observer from "artificial" motions. I do not know whether infants have been tested to see if they respond selectively to such displays.

9 McCarthy and Hayes (1969) draw a different distinction between the "epistemological" and the "heuristic". The difference is that they include the question "In what kind of internal notation is the system's knowledge to be expressed?" in the epistemological problem (see p. 466), dividing off *that* syntactic (and hence somewhat mechanical) question from the procedural questions of the design of "the mechanism that on the basis of the information solves the problem and decides what to do".

One of the prime grounds for controversy about just which problem the frame problem is springs from this attempted division of the issue. For the answer to the syntactical aspects of the epistemological question makes a large difference to the nature of the heuristic problem. After all, if the syntax of the expression of the system's knowledge is sufficiently perverse, then in spite of the *accuracy* of the representation of that knowledge, the heuristic problem will be impossible. And some have suggested that the heuristic problem would virtually disappear if the world knowledge were felicitously couched in the first place.

10 Such observations also convinced Gilbert Ryle, who was, in an important sense, an introspective phenomenologist (and not a "behaviorist"). See Ryle 1949.

One can readily imagine Ryle's attack on AI: "And *how many* inferences do I perform in the course of preparing my sandwich? What syllogisms convince me that the beer will stay in the glass?" For a further discussion of Ryle's skeptical arguments and their relation to cognitive science, see my "Styles of Mental Representation", Dennett 1983.

11 "When the time comes for egg laying the wasp *Sphex* builds a burrow for the purpose and seeks out a cricket which she stings in such a way as to paralyze but not kill it. She drags the cricket into her burrow, lays her eggs alongside, closes the burrow, then flies away, never to return. In due course, the eggs hatch and the wasp grubs feed off the paralyzed cricket, which has not decayed, having been kept in the wasp equivalent of deep freeze. To the human mind, such an elaborately organized and seemingly purposeful routine conveys a convincing flavor of logic and thoughtfulness—until more details are examined. For example, the wasp's routine is to bring the paralyzed cricket to the burrow, leave it on the threshold, go inside to see that all is well, emerge, and then drag the cricket in. If, while the wasp is inside making her preliminary inspection the cricket is moved a few inches away, the wasp, on emerging from the burrow, will bring the cricket back to the threshold, but not inside, and will then repeat the preparatory procedure of entering the burrow to see that everything is all right. If again the cricket is removed a few inches while the wasp is inside, once again the wasp will move the cricket up to the threshold and re-enter the burrow for a final check. The wasp never thinks of pulling the cricket straight in. On one occasion, this procedure was repeated forty times, always with the same result" (Dean Wooldridge 1963).

This vivid example of a familiar phenomenon among insects is discussed by me in *Brainstorms*, and in Douglas R. Hofstadter 1982.

12 See my 1982c: 58–9, on "Robot Theater".

13 Hubert Dreyfus has pointed out that *not expecting* x does not imply *expecting y* (where $x \neq y$), so one can be startled by something one didn't expect without its having to be the case that one (unconsciously) expected something else. But this sense of *not expecting* will not suffice to explain startle. What are the odds against your seeing an Alfa Romeo, a Buick, a Chevrolet, and a Dodge parked in alphabetical order some time or other within the next five hours? Very high, no doubt, all things considered, so I would not expect you to expect this; I also would not expect you to be startled by seeing this unexpected sight—except in the sort of special case where you had reason to expect something else at that time and place.

Startle reactions are powerful indicators of cognitive state—a fact long known by the police (and writers of detective novels). *Only* someone who expected the refrigerator to contain Smith's corpse (say) would be *startled* (as opposed to mildly interested) to find it to contain the rather unlikely trio: a bottle of vintage Chablis, a can of cat food, and a dishrag.

14 This early feature of SHAKEY was drawn to my attention by Pat Hayes. See also Dreyfus 1972: 26. SHAKEY is put to quite different use in Dennett 1982b.

15 In one important regard, however, it is dramatically unlike the process of natural selection, since the trial, error and selection of the process is far from blind. But a case can be made that the impatient researcher does nothing more than telescope time by such foresighted interventions in the redesign process.

16 For more details, and further reflections on the issues discussed here, see Diamond 1983.

17 I was interested to discover that at least one researcher in AI mistook the rhetorical intent of my new term on first hearing; he took "cognitive wheels" to be an accolade. If one thinks of AI, as he does, not as a research method in psychology but as a branch of engineering attempting to extend human cognitive powers, then of course cognitive wheels are breakthroughs. The vast and virtually infallible memories of computers would be prime examples; others would be computers' arithmetical virtuosity and invulnerability to boredom and distraction. See Hofstadter (1982) for an insightful discussion of the relation of boredom to the structure of memory and the conditions for creativity.

18 McDermott 1969 ("A Temporal Logic for Reasoning about Processes and Plans", Section 6, "A Sketch of an Implementation",) shows strikingly how many *new* issues are raised once one turns to the question of implementation, and how indirect (but still useful) the purely formal considerations are.

19 Patrick Hayes has been exploring this theme, and a preliminary account can be found in "Naive Physics I: The Ontology of Liquids", (Hayes 1978).

20 Oliver Selfridge's forthcoming monograph, *Tracking and Trailing* (Bradford Books/MIT Press), promises to push back this frontier, I think, but I have not yet been able to assimilate its messages. There are also suggestive passages on this topic in Ruth Garrett Milliken's *Language, Thought, and Other Biological Categories*, also forthcoming from Bradford Books.

21 To balance the "top-down" theorists' foible of postulating cognitive wheels, there is the "bottom-up" theorists' penchant for discovering *wonder tissue*. (Wonder tissue appears in many locales. J.J. Gibson's theory of perception, for instance, seems to treat the whole visual system as a hunk of wonder tissue, for instance, resonating with marvelous sensitivity to a host of sophisticated "affordances". See, e.g., J.J. Gibson 1979.)

22 One of the few philosophical articles I have uncovered that seem to contribute to the thinking about the frame problem—though not in those terms—is Ronald de Sousa's "The Rationality of Emotions" (de Sousa 1979). In the section entitled "What are Emotions For?" de Sousa suggests, with compelling considerations, that:

the function of emotion is to fill gaps left by [mere wanting plus] "pure reason" in the determination of action and belief. Consider how Iago proceeds to make Othello jealous. His task is essentially to direct Othello's attention, to suggest questions to ask . . . Once attention is thus directed, inferences which, before on the same evidence, would not even have been thought of, are experienced as compelling.

In de Sousa's understanding, "emotions are determinate patterns of salience among objects of attention, lines of inquiry, and inferential strategies" (p. 50) and they are not "reducible" in any way to "articulated propositions". Suggestive as this is, it does not, of course, offer any concrete proposals for how to endow an inner (emotional) state with these interesting powers. Another suggestive—and overlooked—paper is Howard Darmstadter's "Consistency of Belief" (Darmstadter, 1971: 301–10). Darmstadter's exploration of *ceteris paribus* clauses and the relations that might exist between beliefs as psychological states and sentences believers may utter (or have uttered about them) contains a number of claims that deserve further scrutiny.

References

Cherniak, C. "Rationality and the Structure of Memory", in *Synthèse* (forthcoming).

Darmstadter, H. 1971. "Consistency of Belief", *Journal of Philosophy* 68, 301–10.

Dennett, D. C. 1978. *Brainstorms*. Hassocks and Cambridge, Mass.

Dennett, D. C. 1982a. "Why do we think what we do about why we think what we do?" in *Cognition* 12, 219–27.

Dennett, D. C. 1982b. "How to Study Consciousness Empirically; or Nothing Comes to Mind", in *Synthèse* 53, 159–80.

Dennett, D. C. 1982c. "Beyond Belief", in *Thought and Object*, ed. A. Woodfield. Oxford.

Dennett, D. C. 1983. "Styles of Mental Representation" in *Proceedings of the Aristotelean Society* 83, 213–26.

Diamond, J. 1983. "The Biology of the Wheel", *Nature* 302, 572–3.

Dreyfus, H. L. 1972. *What Computers Can't Do.* New York.

Fikes, R. and Nilsson, N. 1971. "STRIPS: a New Approach to the Application of Theorem Proving to Problem Solving", *Artificial Intelligence* 2, 189–208.

Gibson, J. J. 1979. *The Ecological Approach to Visual Perception.* New York.

Goodman, N. 1965. *Fact, Fiction and Forecast*, 2nd ed. Indianapolis.

Goodman, N. 1982. "Thoughts without Words", *Cognition* 12, 211–17.

Hayes, P. 1978. "Naive Physics I: The Ontology of Liquids", Working Paper 35, *Institut pour les Etudes Semantiques et Cognitives, Univ. de Génève.*

Hayes, P. 1979. "The Naive Physics Manifesto", in *Expert Systems in the Microelectronic Age*, ed. D. Michie, Edinburgh.

Hofstadter, D. 1982. "Can Inspiration be Mechanized?", *Scientific American* 247, 18–34.

McCarthy, J. 1960. "Programs with Common Sense", *Proceedings of the Teddington Conference on the Mechanization of Thought Processes*, London, a version is reprinted in *Semantic Information Processing*, ed. M. Minsky, Cambridge.

McCarthy, J. 1980. "Circumscription—a Form of Non-Monotonic Reasoning", *Artificial Intelligence* 13, 27–39.

McCarthy, J. and Hayes, P. 1969. "Some Philosophical Problems from the Standpoint of Artificial Intelligence", in *Machine Intelligence* vol. 4, ed. B. Meltzer and D. Michie, 463–502. New York and Edinburgh.

McDermott, D. 1982. "A Temporal Logic for Reasoning about Processes and Plans", *Cognitive Science* 6, 101–55.

McDermott, D. and Doyle, J. 1980. "Non-Monotonic Logic", in *Artificial Intelligence* 13, 41–72.

Millikin, R. G. *Language, Thought and Other Biological Categories*. Cambridge, Mass. (forthcoming).

Minsky, M. 1981. "A Framework for Representing Knowledge", originally published as Memo 3306, AI Lab, MIT. Quotation drawn from excerpts reprinted in *Mind Design*, ed. J. Haugeland. Cambridge, Mass.

Newell, A. 1982. "The Knowledge Level", *Artificial Intelligence* 18, 87–127.

Reiter, R. 1980. "A Logic for Default Reasoning", *Artificial Intelligence* 13, 81–132.

Ryle, G. 1949. *The Concept of Mind*. London.

Schank, R. and Abelson, R. 1977. *Scripts, Plans, Goals and Understanding: An Inquiry into Human Knowledge*, Hillsdale, N.J.

Selfridge, O. *Tracking and Trailing*, Cambridge, Mass. (forthcoming).

de Sousa, R. 1979. "The Rationality of Emotions", *Dialogue* 18, 41–63.

Wooldridge, D. 1963. *The Machinery of the Brain*, New York.

65

MODULES, FRAMES, FRIDGEONS, SLEEPING DOGS, AND THE MUSIC OF THE SPHERES

Jerry A. Fodor

Source: Z. W. Pylyshyn (ed.), *The Robot's Dilemma: The Frame Problem in Artificial Intelligence*, Ablex Publishing, 1987, pp. 139–49.

There are, it seems to me, two interesting ideas about modularity. The first is the idea that some of our cognitive faculties are modular. The second is the idea that some of our cognitive faculties are not.

By a modular cognitive faculty I mean—for present purposes—one that is "informationally encapsulated". By an informationally encapsulated cognitive faculty, I mean one that has access, in the course of its computations, to less than all of the information at the disposal of the organism whose cognitive faculty it is. So, for example, I think that the persistence of the Muller-Lyer illusion in spite of one's knowledge that it *is* an illusion strongly suggests that some of the cognitive mechanisms that mediate visual size perception must be informationally encapsulated. You know perfectly well that the lines are the same length, yet it continues to appear to you that they are not. It would seem to follow that some of what you know perfectly well is inaccessible to the cognitive mechanisms that are determining the appearances. If this is the right diagnosis, then it follows that some of those mechanisms are informationally encapsulated.

It's worth emphasizing a sense in which modular cognitive processing is *ipso facto* irrational. After all, by definition modular processing means arriving at conclusions by attending to less than all of the evidence that is relevant and available. And ignoring relevant and available evidence is, notoriously, a technique of belief fixation that will get you into trouble in the long run. Informational encapsulation is economical; it buys speed and the reduction of computational load by, in effect, drastically delimiting the database that's brought to bear in problem solving. But the price of economy is warrant.

The more encapsulated the cognitive mechanisms that mediate the fixation of your beliefs, the worse is your evidence for the beliefs that you have. And, barring skeptical worries of a boring, philosophical sort, the worse your evidence for your beliefs is, the less the likelihood that your beliefs are true.

Rushing one's hurdles and jumping to conclusions is, then, a characteristic pathology of irrational cognitive strategies; and this disease modular processors have in spades. That is because the evidence they consult is essentially an arbitrary sample of the evidence that is relevant and available. But—and there's the point I want to emphasize for present purposes—rational processes have their debilities too; they have their characteristic hang-ups whose outbreaks are symptoms of their very rationality. If, for example, you undertake to consider a nonarbitrary sample of the available and relevant evidence before you opt for a belief, *you have the problem of when the evidence you have looked at is enough.* You have, that is to say, Hamlet's problem: when to stop thinking.

The frame problem is just Hamlet's problem viewed from an engineer's perspective. You want to make a device that is rational in the sense that its mechanisms of belief fixation are unencapsulated. But you also want the device you make actually to succeed in fixing a belief or two from time to time; you don't want it to hang up the way that Hamlet did. So, on the one hand, you don't want to delimit its evidence searches arbitrarily (as in encapsulated systems); and, on the other hand, you want these searches to come, somehow, to an end. How is this to be arranged? What is a nonarbitrary strategy for delimiting the evidence that should be searched in rational belief fixation? I don't know how to answer this question. If I did, I'd have solved the frame problem and I'd be rich and famous.

Here's what I have argued so far: Rational mechanisms of belief fixation are *ipso facto* unencapsulated. Unencapsulated mechanisms of belief fixation are *ipso facto* nonarbitrary in their selection of the evidence that they consult. Mechanisms of belief fixation that are nonarbitrary in their selection of the evidence that they consult are *ipso facto* confronted with Hamlet's problem. And Hamlet's problem is just the frame problem formulated in blank verse. So, two conclusions:

1. The frame problem goes very deep; it goes as deep as the analysis of rationality.
2. Outbreaks of the frame problem are symptoms of rational processing; if you're looking at a system that has the frame problem, you can assume that it's rational at least to the extent of being unencapsulated.

The second of these conclusions is one that I particularly cherish. I used it, in *The Modularity of Mind*, as an argument against what I take to be modularity theory gone mad: namely, the idea that modularity is the *general* case; that all cognitive processing is informationally encapsulated. Roughly, the argument went like this: When we look at real, honest-to-God *perceptual* processes, we find real honest-to-God informational encapsulation. In parsing, for example, we find computational mechanism with access only to the acoustics of the input and the body of "background information" that can be formulated in a certain kind of grammar. That is why—in my view, and contrary to the received wisdom in psychology—there are no context effects in parsing. AND IT IS ALSO WHY THERE IS NO FRAME PROBLEM IN PARSING. The question what evidence the parser should consult in determining the structural description of an utterance is solved arbitrarily and architecturally: Only the acoustics of the input and the grammar are ever available. Because there is no frame problem in parsing, it is one of the few cognitive processes that we have had any serious success in understanding.

Whereas, by contrast, when we try to build a really SMART machine—not a machine that will parse sentences or play chess, but, say, one that will make the breakfast without burning down the house—we get the frame problem straight off. This, I argued in *MOM*, is precisely BECAUSE smart processes aren't modular. Being smart, being nonmodular, and raising the frame problem all go together. That, in a nutshell, is why, although we have machines that parse sentences and machines that play chess, we have no machines that will make breakfast (excepting stoves).[1] In short, that the frame problem breaks out here and there *but does not break out everywhere* is itself an argument for differences in kind among cognitive mechanisms. We can understand the distribution of outbreaks of the frame problem *on the hypothesis* that it is the chronic infirmity of rational—hence unencapsulated; hence *non*modular—cognitive systems. Or so I argued in *MOM*. And so I am prepared to argue still.

Candor requires, however, that I report to you the following: This understanding of the frame problem is not universally shared. In AI, especially, the frame problem is widely viewed as a sort of a glitch, for which heuristic processing is the appropriate patch. (The technical vocabulary deployed by analysts of the frame problem has become markedly less lovely since Shakespeare discussed it in Hamlet). How could this be so? How could the depth, beauty, and urgency of the frame problem have been so widely misperceived? That, really, is what this paper is about.

What I'm inclined to think is this: The frame problem is so ubiquitous, so polymorphous, and so intimately connected with every aspect of the attempt to understand rational nondemonstrative inference, that it is quite possible for a practitioner to fail to notice when it is indeed the frame problem that he's working on. It's like the ancient doctrine about the music of spheres: If you can't hear it, that's because it's everywhere. Which would be OK except that if you are unable to recognize the frame problem when as a matter of fact you are having it, you may suppose that you have solved the frame problem when as a matter of fact you are begging it. Much of the history of the frame problem in AI strikes me as having that character; the discussion that follows concerns a recent and painful example.

In the paper (this volume) called, "We've Been Framed: Or, Why AI Is Innocent of the Frame Problem," Drew McDermott claims that "there is no one problem here; and hence no solution is possible or necessary." (1) The frame problem, it turns out, is a phantom that philosophers have unwittingly conjured up by making a variety of mistakes that McDermott details and undertakes to rectify.

What philosophers particularly fail to realize, according to McDermott, is that, though no solution of the frame problem is "possible or necessary," nevertheless a solution is up and running in AI. (One wonders how many other impossible and unnecessary problems McDermott and his colleagues have recently solved.) "In all systems since [1969] . . . programs have used the . . . "sleeping dog" strategy. They keep track of each situation as a separate data base. To reason about result (s, e) (i.e., about the result of an event in a situation), they compute all the effects of e in situation s, make those changes, and leave the rest of s (the 'sleeping dogs') alone." In consequence of the discovery of this sleeping dog solution, "since 1970 . . . *no working AI program has ever been bothered at all by the frame problem*" (emphasis McDermott's).

It is, moreover, no accident that the sleeping dog strategy works. For it is supported by a deep metaphysical truth, namely that "most events leave most facts untouched." (2) You can rely on metaphysical inertia to carry most of the facts along from one event to the next; being carried along in this way is, as you might say, the unmarked case for facts. Because this is so, you'll usually do alright if you leave well enough alone when you update your database. Given *metaphysical* inertia, the appropriate *epistemic* strategy is to assume that nothing changes unless you have a special reason for changing it. Sleeping dogs don't scratch where it doesn't itch.

So doesn't the "sleeping dog strategy" solve the frame problem? No. What it does is to convert the frame problem FROM A PROBLEM ABOUT BELIEF FIXATION INTO A PROBLEM ABOUT ONTOLOGY (or, what comes to much the same thing for present purposes, from a problem about belief fixation into a problem about canonical notation). This wants some spelling out.

As we've seen, the sleeping dog strategy depends on assuming that most of the facts don't change from one event to the next. And the trouble with that assumption is that WHETHER IT'S TRUE DEPENDS ON HOW YOU INDIVIDUATE FACTS. Or, to put it a little more in the formal mode, if you want to use a sleeping dog algorithm to update your database, you must first devise a system of canonical representation for the facts; (algorithms— of course—work on facts AS REPRESENTED.) And this system of canonical representation will have to have the following properties:

1. It has to be rich enough to represent all of the facts that you propose to specify in the database;
2. THE CANONICAL REPRESENTATIONS of most of the facts must be unchanged by most events. By definition, a sleeping dog algorithm *won't work* unless the canonical notation does have this second property.

The problem is—indeed, the *frame* problem is—that such notations are a little hard to come by. Oh yes, indeed they are!

Consider, for example, the following outbreak of the frame problem:

It has got to work out on any acceptable model that when I turn the refrigerator on, certain of my beliefs about the refrigerator—and about other things, of course—become candidates for getting updated. So, for example, now that the refrigerator is on, I believe that putting the legumes in the vegetable compartment will keep them cool and crispy. (I did not believe that *before* I turned the refrigerator on because until I turned the refrigerator on I believed that the refrigerator was off. Correctly, as we may assume.) Similarly, now that the refrigerator is on, I believe that when the door is opened the light in the refrigerator will go on too; and I believe that my electricity meter will run slightly faster than it did before . . . And so forth. On the other hand, it should also fall out of a solution of the frame problem that a lot of my beliefs—indeed, MOST of my beliefs—do NOT become candidates for updating (hence don't have to be—as it were—actively reconsidered) in consequence of my plugging in the fridge. As, for example: my belief that cats are animate, my belief that Granny was a Bulgarian, my belief that snow is white . . . and so forth. I want it that most of my beliefs do not become candidates for updating because what I primarily want of my beliefs is that they should *correspond to the facts*; and, as we've seen, metaphysical inertia guarantees me that most of the FACTS are unaffected by my turning on the fridge.

Or does it? Consider a certain relational property that physical particles have from time to time; the property of BEING A FRIDGEON. I define "x is a fridgeon at t" as follows: *x is a fridgeon at t if x is a particle at t and my fridge is on at t.* It is, of course, a consequence of this definition that, when I turn my fridge on, I CHANGE THE STATE OF EVERY PHYSICAL PARTICLE IN THE UNIVERSE; namely, every physical particle becomes a fridgeon. (Turning the fridge off has, of course, the reverse effect.) I take it (as does McDermott, so far as I can tell) that talk about facts is intertranslatable with talk about instantiations of properties, so when I create ever so many new fridgeons, I also create ever so many new facts. The point is, of course, that if you count all these facts about fridgeons, the principle of metaphysical inertia no longer holds even of such homely events as my turning on the fridge. Or, to put the same point less metaphysically and more computationally: If I let the facts about fridgeons into my database (along with the facts about the crisping compartment and the facts about Granny's ethnic affiliations), *pursuing the sleeping dog strategy will no longer solve the frame problem*. Because: The sleeping dog strategy proposes to keep the computational load down by considering as candidates for updating only representations of such facts as an event changes. But now there are BILLIONS of facts that change when I plug in the fridge; one fact for each particle, more or less. And, of course, there's nothing special about the property of being a fridgeon; it's a triviality to think up as many more such kooky properties as you like.

I repeat the moral: Once you let representations of the kooky properties into the database, a strategy which says "look just at the facts that change" will buy you nothing; it will commit you to looking at indefinitely many facts.

The moral was not, please notice, that the sleeping dog strategy is WRONG; it's that the sleeping dog strategy is EMPTY unless we have, together with the strategy, some idea of what is to count as a fact for the purposes at hand. Moreover, this notion—of, as we might call it, a COMPUTATIONALLY RELEVANT fact—will have to be FORMALIZED if we propose to implement the sleeping dog strategy as a computational algorithm. For, algorithms act on facts only as represented, and only in virtue of the form of their representations. So, if we want to keep the kooky facts out of the data base, and keep the computationally relevant facts in, we will have to find a way of distinguishing kooky facts from computationally relevant ones IN VIRTUE OF THE FORM OF THEIR CANONICAL REPRESENTATIONS. The frame problem, in its current guise, is the problem of formalizing this distinction. And, of course, we don't *know* how to formalize it. For that matter,—"formalize" my Bulgarian grandmother—we don't even know how to draw it!

For example, the following ways of drawing it—or of getting out of drawing it—will quite clearly NOT work:

a. Being a fridgeon is a relational property; rule it out on those grounds.

- Answer: Being a father is a relational property too; but we want to be able to come to believe that John is a father when we come to believe that his wife has had a child.

b. "Fridgeon" is a made-up word. There is no such word as "fridgeon" in English.

- Answer: You can't rely on the lexicon of English to solve your metaphysical problems for you. There used to be no such word as "meson" either. Moreover, though there is no such word as "fridgeon", the expression "x is a particle at t and my fridge is on at t" is perfectly well formed. Since this expression is the DEFINITION of "fridgeon", everything that can be said in English by using "fridgeon" can also be said in English without using it.

c. Being a fridgeon isn't a real property.

- Answer: I'll be damned if I see why not, but have it your way. The frame problem is now the problem of saying what a "real property" is.

d. Nobody actually has concepts like "fridgeon"; so you don't have to worry about such concepts when you build your model of the mind.

- Answer: This is another way of begging the frame problem; another way of mistaking a formulation of the problem for its solution.

   Everybody has, of course, an infinity of concepts (corresponding, roughly, to the open sentences of English). According to all known theories, the way a person keeps an infinity of concepts in a finite head is this: He stores a finite primitive basis and a finite compositional mechanism, and the recursive application of the latter to the former specifies the infinite conceptual repertoire. The present problem is that there are arbitrarily many kooky concepts—like fridgeon—which can be defined WITH THE SAME APPARATUS THAT YOU USE TO DEFINE PERFECTLY KOSHER CONCEPTS LIKE, SAY "VEGETABLE CRISPER" OR "BULGARIAN GRANDMOTHER". That is, the same basic concepts that I used to define "fridgeon", and the same logical syntax, are needed to define non-kooky concepts that people actually do entertain. So the problem—viz. the FRAME problem—is to find a RULE that will keep the kooky concepts out while letting the non-kooky concepts in.

   I remind you that, lacking a solution to this problem, YOU CANNOT IMPLEMENT A SLEEPING DOG "SOLUTION" TO THE FRAME PROBLEM; it will not run. It will not run because, at each event, it will be required to update indefinitely many beliefs about the distribution of kooky properties.

e. But McDermott says that solutions to the frame problem have actually been implemented; that nobody in AI has had to worry about the frame problem since way back in '69. So something MUST be wrong with your argument.

- Answer: the programs run because the counterexamples are not allowed to arise. The programmer decides what kinds of properties get specified in the database, but the decision is unsystematic and unprincipled. For example, no database will be allowed to include information about the distribution of fridgeons; but, as we've seen, there appears to be no disciplined way to justify the exclusion and no way to implement it that doesn't involve excluding indefinitely many computationally relevant concepts as well.

There is, of course, a price to be paid for not facing the frame problem. The conceptual repertoires with which AI systems are allowed to operate exclude kooky and kosher concepts indiscriminately. They are therefore grossly impoverished in comparison with the conceptual repertoires of really intelligent systems like you and me. The consequence (one of the worst-kept secrets in the world, I should think) is that these artificially intelligent systems—the ones that have been running since 1970 "without ever being bothered by the frame problem" you know?—are, by any reasonable standards, ludicrously stupid.

You may be beginning to wonder what is actually going on here. Well, because the frame problem is just the problem of nondemonstrative inference, a good way to see what is actually going on is to think about how the "sleeping dog" strategy works when it's applied to confirmation in science; our best case of the systematic pursuit of knowledge through nondemonstrative inference, as I have repeatedly remarked.

Looked at from this perspective, the sleeping dog strategy is precisely analogous to a principle of scientific "conservatism"; that is, to a principle which says "alter the MINIMUM possible amount of prior theory when you go about accommodating new data". Notice, however, that while it is widely agreed that conservatism, in this sense, is constitutive of rational scientific practice, the maxim as I've just stated it doesn't amount to anything like a formal principle for theory choice (just as, of course, the "sleeping dog" strategy as McDermott states it doesn't constitute anything like an algorithm for updating databases). You could, of course, MAKE the principle of conservatism into a formal evaluation metric by specifying (a) a canonical notation for writing scientific theories and (b) a costing system (e.g., the most conservative change in a theory is the one that alters the fewest symbols in its canonical representation). Given (a) and (b), we would have an important fragment of a mechanical evaluation procedure for science. Which would be a NICE thing for us to have. So why doesn't somebody go and build us one?

Well, because not just ANY canonical notation will do the job. To do the job, you have to build a notation such that (relative to the costing system, THE (intuitively) MOST CONSERVATIVE REVISION OF A THEORY DOES INDEED COME OUT TO BE THE SIMPLEST ONE WHEN THE THEORY IS CANONICALLY REPRESENTED. (So, for example, if your accounting system says "choose the alteration that can be specified in the smallest number of canonical symbols", then your notation has to have the property that the intuitively most conservative alteration actually does come out shortest when the theory is in canonical form). And, of course, nobody knows how to construct a notation with that agreeable property. JUST AS NOBODY KNOWS HOW TO CONSTRUCT A NOTATION

FOR FACTS SUCH THAT, UNDER THAT NOTATION, MOST FACTS ARE UNCHANGED BY MOST EVENTS.

It isn't, of course, surprising that such notations don't grow on trees. If somebody developed a vocabulary for writing scientific theories which had the property that the shortest description of the world in that vocabulary was always the best theory of the world available, that would mean that the notation gave FORMAL EXPRESSION to our most favored inductive estimate of the world's taxonomic structure. Well, when we have an inductive estimate of the world's taxonomic structure that's good enough to permit formal expression, and a canonical vocabulary to formulate the taxonomy in, most of science will be finished.

Similarly, *mutatis mutandis*, in cognitive theory. A notation adequate to support an implemented sleeping dog algorithm would be one which represents as facts only what we commonsensically take to really *be* facts: the ethnicity of grandmothers; the situation, temperature-wise, in the vegetable crisper; but not the current distribution of fridgeons. In effect, the notation would give formal expression to our *commonsense* estimate of the world's taxonomic structure. Well, when we have a rigorous account of our commonsense estimate of the world's taxonomic structure, and a notation to express it in, most of *cognitive* science will be finished.

In short, there is no formal conservatism principle for science for much the same sort of reason that there is no workable sleeping dog algorithm. Basically, the solution of both problems requires a notation which formalizes our intuitions about inductive relevance. There is, however, the following asymmetry: We can do science perfectly well without having a formal theory of nondemonstrative inference; which is to say that we can do science perfectly well without solving the frame problem. That's because doing science doesn't require having *mechanical* scientists; we have *us* instead. But we can't do AI perfectly well without having mechanical intelligence; doing AI perfectly well just *is* having mechanical intelligence. So we can't do AI without solving the frame problem. But *we don't know how* to solve the frame problem. That, in a nutshell, is why, though science works, AI doesn't.

I reiterate the main point: The frame problem and the problem of formalizing our intuitions about inductive relevance are, in every important respect, THE SAME THING. It is just as well, perhaps, that people working on the frame problem in AI are unaware that this is so. One imagines the expression of horror that flickers across their CRT-illuminated faces as the awful facts sink in. What could they do but down tools and become *philosophers*? One feels for them. Just *think* of the cut in pay!

God, according to Einstein, does not play dice with the world. Well, maybe; but He sure is into shell games. If you do not understand the logical geography of the frame problem, you will only succeed in pushing it around from one shell to the next, never locating it for long enough to have a chance of solving it. This is, so far as I can see, pretty much the history of the frame problem in AI; which is a main reason why AI work, when viewed as cognitive theory, strikes one as so *thin*. The frame problem—to say it one last time—is just the problem of nondemonstrative inference; and the problem of nondemonstrative inference is—to all intents and purposes—the problem of how the cognitive mind works. I am sorry that McDermott is out of temper with philosophers; but, frankly, the frame problem is too important to leave it to the hackers.

Look guys, we are really going to have to learn to make progress working together; the alternative is to make fools of ourselves working separately.

POSTSCRIPT

Elsewhere in this volume Pat Hayes thrashes about for a reply to this indictment, but as far as I can tell, he gets nowhere beyond insisting upon a terminology that segregates a galaxy of problems which—if my arguments are right—MUST be solved together if they are to be solved at all.

There is, however, one mistake of Hayes' which is central and egregious. He remarks (vis-à-vis the fridgeon problem) that I "seem to believe that a reasoning system is faced with a sort of pressure to create representations of all concepts which are definable in its notation; that because a program COULD, in some sense, define a concept, it therefore MUST define it . . . " and so forth.

Now, the precise sense in which a program with access to the concepts "refrigerator", "particle" . . . etc. and the logical connectives COULD define "fridgeon" is patent; in fact, I gave the definition. So the problem is to say what stops it from doing so? That it isn't forced to create the concept is true but utterly irrelevant; it isn't FORCED to create the concept "chair" either. The point is that it's equipped to do so (in both cases) and that *if* it does so it will thereby be enabled to think true thoughts (again in both cases; for there really are fridgeons, just as there really are chairs).

Strictly speaking, by the way, I don't like this talk of "creating concepts". The point is that the robot's database will specify certain properties of its world and won't specify others. *Ceteris paribus*, we want it to specify the distribution of chairs but not the distribution of fridgeons; and the problem is that we don't know how to bring this about. That problem MUST be solved because, if it's not, sleeping dog algorithms won't work. I agree with Hayes that, if you don't call this the frame problem, that makes what you do call the frame problem easier. What I don't understand is why Hayes finds this banal observation comforting. If you don't call it cancer, then what you do call cancer won't be what you die of. But you end up equally dead either way.

Note

1   Chess playing is not, of course, a perceptual process; so how come it's modular? Some processes are modular by brute force and some are modular in the nature of things. Parsing is a case of the former kind; there IS relevant information in the context, but the architecture of the mind doesn't let the parser use it. Chess playing, by contrast, is modular in the sense that only a very restricted body of background information (call it "chess theory") is relevant to rational play *even in principle*. This second kind of modularity, precisely because it stems from the nature of the task rather than the architecture of the mind, isn't of much *theoretical* interest. It's interesting to the engineer, however, since informational encapsulation makes for feasible simulation regardless of what the source of the encapsulation may be.